AMERICA BUILDS

edited by
LELAND M. ROTH

AMERICA BUILDS

Source Documents in American Architecture and Planning

ICON EDITIONS

HARPER & ROW, PUBLISHERS, New York
Cambridge, Philadelphia, San Francisco, London
Mexico City, São Paulo, Sydney

1817

for Amanda and all those who ask questions;

*for a good question is better than a brilliant answer,
as Louis I. Kahn said*

Grateful acknowledgment is made for permission to reprint:

"The Mies van der Rohe Inaugural Address as Director of Architecture at Armour Institute of Technology," 1938 and "The Mies van der Rohe Address to the Illinois Institute of Technology," 1950 from *Mies van der Rohe* by Philip C. Johnson. Copyright 1947, renewed 1975; 1953, renewed 1981; and 1978 The Museum of Modern Art, New York. All rights reserved. Reprinted by permission.

Program of the Competition and Report of the Jury for the Chicago Tribune Building Competition, 1925. Copyrighted, Chicago Tribune. Reprinted by permission.

"The Trans World Airlines Terminal" from *Eero Saarinen on His Work* edited by Aline Saarinen. "The Shingle Style" from *The Shingle Style* by V. Scully. Reprinted by permission of Yale University Press.

"The Autobiography of an Idea" from *The Autobiography of an Idea* by L. Sullivan. Reprinted by permission of Dover Publications, Inc.

"The Doubles of Post-Modernism" by R. A. M. Stern first appeared in *The Harvard Architecture Review*, Spring 1980, #1. Reprinted by permission of the MIT Press, Cambridge, Massachusetts, and Robert A. M. Stern. Copyright © 1980 by The Harvard Architecture Review, Inc. and The Massachusetts Institute of Technology.

FIRST EDITION

Designer: Ruth Bornschlegel

Library of Congress Cataloging in Publication Data
Main entry under title:

America builds.

(Icon editions)
Includes index.
1. Architecture—United States—Addresses, essays, lectures. 2. Architecture—United States—Designs and plans. I. Roth, Leland M.
NA705.A48   1983   720'.973   82-48151
ISBN 0-06-438489-7   83 84 85 86 87 10 9 8 7 6 5 4 3 2 1
ISBN 0-06-430122-2 (pbk.)   83 84 85 86 87 10 9 8 7 6 5 4 3 2 1

Contents

Illustrations

Preface

Architecture requires a broad definition. It involves more than simply questions of style, esoteric theory, or technical progress; it is the physical record of a culture's relationship to its technology and the land, and, most important, of the system of values concerning men's relationships with one another. Hence this volume, like my *Concise History of American Architecture*, deals with all the spatial and environmental arts. Conceived as a companion volume to the *Concise History*, this similarly surveys architecture, landscape architecture, and planning from the arrival of European settlers up to 1980. The need for this anthology arose from the unavailability of Don Gifford's *The Literature of Architecture* (New York, 1966), a collection most useful but out of print for almost a decade. That anthology, however, covered only architecture in the nineteenth century, and other collections were equally selective in their foci. David R. Weimer, *City and Country in America* (New York, 1962), surveys planning and landscape architecture, while Lewis Mumford, *Roots of Contemporary American Architecture* (New York, 1952), is concerned primarily with the sources of the Modern Movement in the United States. Another collection, William A. Coles and Henry Hope Reed, Jr., *Architecture in America: A Battle of Styles* (New York, 1961), is comprised of many short fragments concerning five subject buildings, and the brevity of its selections is equaled by the clipped fragments in Christopher Tunnard, *The Modern American City* (New York, 1968) which surveys planning. Each of these is good for the limited subject it covers, but architecture in the broad sense outlined here crosses chronological and thematic boundaries. Hence this volume seeks to combine something of the breadth of these previous collections in one anthology. Like the *Concise History*, this sampling of source documents is offered in the hope of spurring the reader to further investigation. For data on the many architects mentioned here, *see* the *Macmillan Encyclopedia of Architects*, 4 vols. (New York, 1982), which appeared as this was going to press.

Grateful thanks are due, as always, to Cass Canfield, Jr., of Harper & Row, who helped this project see the light of day. I must thank, too, the staffs of the University of Oregon Library and the Avery Library, Columbia University, who helped provide material and illustrations, and to David R. Gerhan of the Schaffer Library, Union College, who supplied photocopies of the Hunt-Parmly litigation from the rare *Architects' and Mechanics' Journal*. My sincere thanks are offered to the many living authors who most kindly consented to the reappearance of their words.

I

THE LAND AND FIRST HOMES

1   J. Smith, Of the naturall Inhabitants of Virginia,*   *1624*

Among the earliest observations by an Englishman of native building, those by Captain John Smith (c. 1580–1631) cover the period 1607 through 1609 when he served for a time as the president of the Jamestown colony he had been instrumental in establishing. His account, published later, reveals certain prevalent European prejudices which conditioned Smith's perception. Nonetheless, his observation about the natives placing their villages "not farre distant from some fresh spring" was no doubt prompted by the unfortunate siting of the first Jamestown settlement next to a pitch pine swamp so that the wells repeatedly filled with brackish water, plaguing the first residents with numerous "Fluxes and Agues."

OF THE NATURALL INHABITANTS OF VIRGINIA

The land is not populous, for the men be few; their far greater number is of women and children. Within 60 myles of *Iames* Towne, there are about some 5000 people, but of able men fit for their warres scarce 1500. To nourish so many together they haue yet no means, because they make so small a benefit of their land, be it ever so fertile. Six or seauen hundred haue beene the most hath beene seene together, when they gathered themselues to *haue surprised* mee at *Pamaunkee*, having but fifteene to withstand the worst of their fury. . . .

Their buildings and habitations are for the most part by the rivers, or not farre distant from some fresh spring. Their houses are built like our Arbors, of small young springs bowed and tyed, and so close covered with Matts, or the barkes of trees very handsomely, that notwithstanding either winde, raine, or weather, they are as warm as stooues, but very smoaky, yet at the toppe of the house there is a hole made for the smoake to goe into right over the fire. [Figure 1]

Against the fire they lie on little hurdles of Reeds covered with a Mat, borne from the ground a foote and more by a hurdle of wood. On these round about the house they lie heads and points one by th' other against the fire. some covered with Mats, some with skins, and some stark naked lie on the ground, from 6 to 20 in a house. Their houses are in the midst of their fields or gardens, which are small plots of ground. Some 20 acres. some 40. some 100. some 200. some more. some lesse. In some places from 2 to 50 of those houses together, or but alittle separated by groues of trees. Neare their habitations is little small wood or old trees om the ground by reason of their burning of them for fire. —So that a man may gallop a horse amongst these woods any way, but where the creekes or Rivers shall hinder. . . .

*The Generall Historie of Virginia, New-England, and the Summer Isles, with the Names of the Adventurers, Planters, and Governours, from their First Beginning, an. 1584 to this Present 1624, by Captaine Iohn Smith, Sometymes Governour in those Countryes and Admirall of New-England (London, 1624), pp. 29–31, 32.

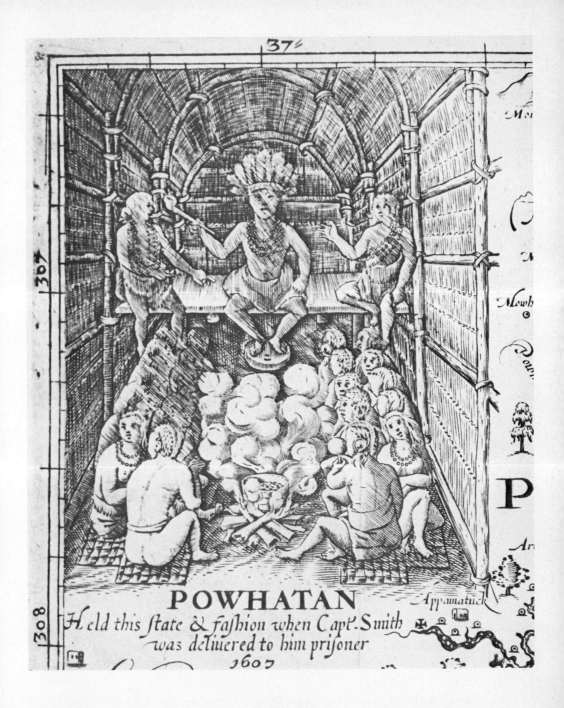

Figure 1. Lodge of Powhatan, Secotan; detail from map of Virginia drawn by Captain John Smith, 1608, engraved by William Hole, published 1624. (Division of Geography and Maps, Library of Congress.) One of the earliest published views of an aboriginal dwelling.

In their hunting and fishing they take extreame paines; yet it being their ordinary exercise from their infancy, they esteeme it a pleasure and are very proud to be expert therein. And by their continuall ranging, and travell, they know all the advantages and places most frequented with Deere, Beasts, Fish, Foule, Roots, and Berries. At their hunting they leaue their habitations, and reduce themselues into companies as the *Tartars* doe, and goe to the most desert places with their families, where they spend their time in hunting and fowling vp towards the mountaines, by the heads of their rivers, where there is plentie of game. For betwixt the rivers the grounds are so narrow, that little cometh here which they devoure not. It is a marvell they can so directly passe these deserts, some 3 or 4 days iourney without habitation. Their hunting houses are like vnto Arbours covered with Mats. These their women beare after them, with corne, Acornes, Morters, and all bag and baggage they vse. When they come to the place of exercise, every man doth his best to shew his desteritie, for by their excelling in those qualities, they get their wiues. Fortie yards will they shoot levell, or very neare the marke, and 120 is their best at Random. At their huntings in the deserts they are commonly two or three hundred together. . . . In one of these huntings they found me in the discovery of the head of the river of *Chickahamania*, where they slew my men, and tooke me prisoner in a Bogmire, where I saw those exercises, and gathered these Observations.

2   Articles of Agreement for Springfield, Massachusetts*   *1636*

The first perceptions of the New World by English colonists to the north were similar to those of Captain John Smith; to them, too, it was at first "a hidious and desolate wilderness, ful of wild beasts and willd men."† The first homes were burrows dug into hillsides; "thus these poore servants of Christ provide shelter for themselves, their Wives and their little ones, keeping off the short showers from their Lodgings, but the long raines penetrate through, to their great disturbance in the night season." Soon, as Edward Johnson relates, the Lord was "pleased to turn all the wigwams, huts, and hovels the English dwelt in at their first coming, in to orderly, fair, and well-built houses, well furnished many of them."‡ But the demand exceeded the

---

New England Historical and Genealogical Register 13 (1859), pp. 295–97.

† William Bradford, *Of Plymouth Plantation*, ed. Harvey Wish (New York, 1962), pp. 59–60.

‡ Edward Johnson, A *History of New England* [*Johnson's Wonder-Working Providence*, 1654], ed. J. Franklin Jameson (New York, 1910), pp. 113–14. A thorough analysis of "fair" framed houses is given in Abbott Lowell Cummings, *The Framed Houses of Massachusetts Bay, 1625–1725* (Cambridge, Mass., 1979).

working capacity of the few carpenters, driving up prices and requiring wage controls; for example: "Carpenters, joyners, bricklayers, sawers, and thatchers shall not take above 2s a day, nor any man shall giue more vnder paine of xs to taker and giver and that sawers shall not take aboue 4s 6d the hundred for boards, att 6 scoote to the hundred, if they have their wood felled and squared for them, and not aboue 5s 6d if they fell and square their wood themselues." §

The "New-England Plantation" in Massachusetts was originally clustered tightly in a small geographical area by necessity for protection and to encourage godly ways. Gradually, however, new settlements were founded to the west, colonized by the established seaboard communities. One was Springfield, founded in 1636 by emigrants from Roxbury led by William Pynchon. To clarify their mutual goals and establish priorities and responsibilities, the founders framed these articles, typical of those written for towns throughout New England.

May the 14th, 1636

We whose names are underwritten, being by God's providence engaged together to make a plantation at and over against Agawam upon Connecticut, do mutually agree to certain articles and orders to be observed and kept by us and by our successors, except we and every [one] of us for ourselves and in our own persons shall think meet upon better reasons to alter our present resolutions.

1ˡʸ. We intend by God's grace, as soon as we can, with all convenient speed, to procure some Godly and faithful minister with whom we purpose to join in church covenant to walk in all the ways of Christ.

2ˡʸ. We intend that our town shall be composed of forty families, or, if we think meet after [ward] to alter our purpose, yet not to exceed the number of fifty families, rich and poor.

3ˡʸ. That every inhabitant shall have a convenient proportion for a house lot, as we shall see meet for everyone's quality and estate.

4ˡʸ. That everyone that hath a house lot shall have a proportion of the cow pasture to the north of End Brook lying northward from the town; and also that everyone shall have a share of the Hassokey Marsh over against his lot, if it be to be had, and everyone to have his proportionable share of all the woodland.

5ˡʸ. That everyone shall have a share of the meadow or planting ground over against them, as nigh as may be on Agawam side.

6ˡʸ. That the long meadow called Masacksick, lying in the way to Dorchester, shall be distributed to every man as we shall think meet, except we shall find other conveniency for some for their milch cattle and other cattle also.

7ˡʸ. That the meadow and pasture called Nayas, toward Patuckett on the side of Agawam lying about four miles above in the river, shall be distributed [erasure of six lines] as above said in the former order—and this was altered with consent before the hands were set to it.

8ˡʸ. That all rates that shall arise upon the town shall be laid upon lands

§ *Records of the Governor and Company of the Massachusetts Bay,* ed. N. B. Shurtleff (Boston, 1853–54), I:74.

according to everyone's proportion, acre for acre of house lots and acre for acre of meadow, both alike on this side and both alike on the other side, and for farms that shall lie further off a less proportion as we shall after agree; except we shall see meet to remit one half of the rate from land to other estate.

9ly. That whereas Mr. William Pynchon, Jeheu Burr, and Henry Smith have constantly continued to prosecute this plantation when others fell off for fear of the difficulties, and [have] continued to prosecute the same at great charges and at great personal adventure: therefore it is mutually agreed that forty acres of meadow lying on the south of End Brook under a hillside shall belong to the said parties free from all charges forever—that is to say, twenty acres to Mr. William Pynchon and his heirs and assigns for ever, and ten acres to Jeheu Burr, and ten acres to Henry Smith, and to their heirs and assigns for ever—which said 40 acres is not disposed to them as any allotments of town lands, but they are to have their accommodations in all other places notwithstanding.

10ly. That whereas a house was built at a common charge which cost 6£, and also the Indians demand a great sum to buy their right in the said lands, and also [considering] two great shallops which was requisite for the first planting: the value of these engagements is to be borne by inhabitants at their first entrance, as they shall be rated by us, till the said disbursements shall be satisfied. Or else in case the said house and boats be not so satisfied for, then so much meadow [is] to be set out about the said house as may countervail the said extraordinary charge.

11ly. It is agreed that no man except Mr. William Pynchon shall have above ten acres for his house lot.

12ly. [Cancelled] It is also agreed that if any man sell any timber out of his lot in any common ground [and] if he let it lie above three months before he work it out, it shall be lawful for any other man to take it that hath present use of it.

13ly. Whereas there are two cow pastures, the one lying toward Dorchester and the other northward from End Brook, it is agreed that both these pastures shall not be fed at once, but that the town shall be ordered by us in the disposing of [them] for times and seasons, till it be lotted out and fenced in severally.

May 16th, 1636

14. It is agreed that after this day we shall observe this rule about [the] dividing of planting ground and meadow: in all planting ground to regard chiefly persons who are most apt to use such ground; and in all meadow and pasture to regard chiefly cattle and estate, because estate is like to be improved in cattle, and such ground is aptest for their use. And yet we agree that no person that is master of a lot, though he have no cattle, shall have less than three acres of mowing ground; and none that have cows, steers, or yearolds shall have under two acres apiece; and [for] all horses not less than four acres. And this order in dividing meadow by cattle [is] is to take place [on] the last of March next; so that all cattle that then appear, and all estate that shall then truly appear at 20£ a cow, shall have this proportion in the meadows on Agawam side, and in the long meadow [called] Masacksick, and in

the other long meadow called Nayas, and in the pasture at the north end of the town called End Brook.

15. It is ordered that for the disposing of the Hassokey Marsh and the granting of home lots these five men undernamed (or their deputies) are appointed to have full power—namely, Mr. Pynchon, Mr. Mitchell, Jeheu Burr, William Blake, Henry Smith. It is ordered that William Blake shall have sixteen poles in breadth for his home lot, and all the marsh in breadth abutting at the end of it to the next high land, and three acres more in some other place.

Next [to] the lot of William Blake [to the] northward lies the lot of Thomas Woodford, being twelve poles broad, and all the marsh before it to the upland.

Next [to] the lot of Thomas Woodford lies the lot of Thomas Ufford, being fourteen rods broad, and all the marsh before it to the upland.

Next [to] the lot of Thomas Ufford lies the lot of Henry Smith, being twenty rods in breadth, and all the marsh before it; and [it is] to run up in the upland on the other side to make up his upland lot [of] ten acres.

Next [to] the lot of Henry Smith lies the lot of Jeheu Burr, being 20 rods in breadth, and all the marsh in breadth abutting at the end of it, and as much upland ground on the other side as shall make up his lot [of] ten acres.

Next [to] the lot of Jeheu Burr lies the lot of Mr. William Pynchon, being thirty rods in breadth, and all the marsh at the east end of it, and an addition at the further end of as much marsh as makes the whole twenty-four acres, and as much upland adjoining as makes the former house lot thirty acres—in all together fifty-four acres.

Next [to] the lot of Mr. Pynchon lies the lot of John Cable, fourteen rods in breadth, and four acres and a half in marsh at the fore end of his home lot.

The lots of Mr. Matthew Mitchell, Samuel Butterfield, Edmond Wood, [and] Jonas Wood are ordered to lie adjoining to Mill Brook—the whole being to the number of twenty-five acres—to begin, three of them, on the great river, and the fourth on the other side of the small river.

It is ordered that for all highways that shall be thought necessary by the five men above named, they shall have liberty and power to lay them out where they shall see meet, though it be at the ends of men's lots, giving them allowance for so much ground.

We testify to the order abovesaid, being all of us first adventurers and undertakers for the said plantation.

William Pynchon
Matthew Mitchell
Henry Smith
the mark L of Jeheu Burr

William Blake
Edmond Wood
the mark T of Thomas Ufford
John Cable

3 Virginia's Cure* *1661*

Virginia had begun with the establishment of Jamestown and the beginnings of a glass works, but the inducement of land grants and the gradual receding of the frontier caused settlers to move farther into the piedmont, away from the fortified towns and churches, inhibiting the growth of towns and repressing manufacturing. It was not only the availability of land but a unique geography that held back the growth of towns; as John Clayton wrote in 1688, "No Country in the World can be more curiously watered. But this Conveniency . . . I look on [as] the greatest Impediment to the Advance of the Country, as it is the greatest Obstacle to Trade and Commerce. For the great Number of Rivers, and the Thinness of the Inhabitants, distract and disperse a Trade. So that all Ships in general gather each their Loading up and down an hundred miles distant. . . . The Number of Rivers, is one of the chief reasons why they have no Towns."† Not only did the expanding estates become self-sufficient, but, wrote Anthony Langston in 1657, "every man builds in the midst of his own land."‡ The lack of strong commercial centers was strongly felt at the end of the century, when it was pointed out that

> for want of towns, markets, and money, there is but little encouragement for tradesmen and artificers. . . . A tradesman having no opportunity of a market, where he can buy meat, milk, corn, and all other things, must either make corn, keep cows, and raise stocks himself; or must ride about the country to buy meat and corn where he can find it . . . which there would be no occasion for if there were towns and markets. . . .
>
> In New-England, they were obliged at their first settlement to settle in towns, and would not permit a single man to take up land, till a certain number of men agreed together, as many as might make a township; then they laid them out a town, with home lots for gardens and orchards, out lots for cornfields, and meadows and country lots for plantations . . . which would have proved an excellent way in such a country as Virginia is. But this opportunity being lost, they seated themselves, without any rule or order, in country plantations.§

In contrast to the focus on towns in the north, and the emphasis on the church, the dispersal in Virginia served to diminish communal spirit and an interest in education and religious life. To correct this, in 1661, a petition signed by "R. G." was

*R. G., *Virginia's Cure: or An Advisive Narrative Concerning Virginia*, September 2, 1661 (London, 1662), reprinted in P. Force, ed., *Tracts and Other Papers Relating Principally to the Origin, Settlement, and Progress of the Colonies in North America*, 4 vols. (Washington, D.C., 1836–46), 3:15.

†John Clayton, "A Letter . . . to the Royal Society," May 12, 1688, reprinted in Peter Force, ed., *Tracts and Other Papers* . . . , 3:11.

‡"Anthony Langston on Towns and Corporation . . . ," *William and Mary Quarterly*, 2nd ser. 1 (1921), pp. 100–102.

§From *Large and True Account of the Present State of Virginia*, 1697, reprinted as "An Account of the Present State and Government of Virginia," *Massachusetts Historical Society, Collections*, 1st ser. 5 (1798), pp. 124–25, 128, 129–30.

addressed to Lord Guilbert, bishop of London (and published the next year), urging increased support for towns and more established parishes.

VIRGINIA'S CURE: OR AN ADVISIVE NARRATIVE CONCERNING VIRGINIA

That part of Virginia which has at present craved Your Lordship's assistance to preserve the Christian religion and to promote the building God's church among them, by supplying them with sufficient ministers of the gospel . . . is divided into several counties. And those counties contain in all about fifty parishes, the families whereof are dispersedly and scatteringly seated upon the sides of rivers, some of which, running very far into the country, bear the English plantations above a hundred miles, and being very broad, cause the inhabitants of either side to be listed in several parishes. . . .

The families of such parishes being seated after this manner, at such distances from each other, many of them are very remote from the house of God, though placed in the midst of them. Many parishes as yet want both churches and glebes; and I think not above a fifth part of them are supplied with ministers. Where there are ministers the people meet together weekly, but once upon the Lord's Day, and sometimes not at all, being hindered by extremities of wind and weather. And diverse of the more remote families being discouraged by the length or tediousness of the way, through extremities of heat in summer, frost and snow in winter, and tempestuous weather in both, do very seldom repair thither.

By which brief description of their manner of seating themselves in that wilderness, Your Lordship may easily apprehend that their very manner of planting themselves has caused hitherto to rob God in a great measure of that public worship and service, which, as a homage due to His great name, He requires to be constantly paid to Him at the times appointed for it in the public congregations of His people in His house of prayer.

This sacrilege I judge to be the prime cause of their long-languishing, improsperous condition. . . . But, though this be the saddest consequence of their dispersed manner of planting themselves (for what misery can be greater than to live under the curse of God?), yet this has a very sad train of attendants which are likewise consequences of their scattered planting. . . .

Their almost general want of schools, for the education of their children, is another consequence of their scattered planting, of most sad consideration, most of all bewailed of parents there, and therefore the arguments drawn from thence most likely to prevail with them cheerfully to embrace the remedy. This want of schools, as it renders a very numerous generation of Christians' children born in Virginia (who naturally are of beautiful and comely persons, and generally of more ingenious spirits then these in England) unserviceable for any great employments either in church or state, so likewise it obstructs the hopefulest way they have for the conversion of the heathen, which is, by winning the heathen to bring in their children to be taught and instructed in our schools, together with the children of the Christians. . . .

The cause of their dispersed seating was at first a privilege indulged by the royal grant of having a right to fifty acres of land for every person they should transport at their own charges; by which means some men transporting many servants thither, and others purchasing the rights of those that did, took possession of great tracts of land at their pleasure; by degrees scattered their plantations through the country after the manner before described, although, therefore, from the premises, it is easy to conclude that the only way of remedy for Virginia's disease (without which all other help will only palliate, not cure) must be by procuring towns to be built and inhabited in their several counties. Yet, lest any man be hereby injured in his just right, even this remedy ought to be procured after such a manner as the present manner of planting themselves, their poverty, and mean condition will permit. According to which, whether the building towns in each county of Virginia will be best promoted by reviving a former act of that county for markets in stated places of each county . . . or whether they may best be promoted by some other way (it being out of my sphere), I dare not presume to determine. . . .

What way soever they determine to be best, I shall humbly, in obedience to Your Lordship's command, endeavor to contribute toward the compassing this remedy by propounding:

1. That Your Lordship would be pleased to acquaint the King with the necessity of promoting the building towns in each county of Virginia, upon the consideration of the forementioned sad consequences of their present manner of living there.

2. That Your Lordship, upon the foregoing consideration, be pleased to move the pitiful and charitable heart of His Gracious Majesty (considering the poverty and needs of Virginia) for a collection to be made in all the churches of his three kingdoms. . . .

3. That the way of dispensing such collections for sending workmen over for the building towns and schools, and the assistance the persons that shall inhabit them shall contribute toward them, may be determined here by the advice of Virginia's present or late honorable governors, if in London; and whom they shall make choice of for their assistants (who have formerly lived in Virginia). And that the King (if he shall approve what is so determined) may be humbly petitioned to authorize it by his special command, lest what is duly ordered here be perverted there.

4. That those planters who have such a considerable number of servants, as may be judged may enable them for it, if they be not willing (for I have heard some express their willingness, and some their averseness) may, by His Majesty's authority, be enjoined to contribute the assistance that shall be thought meet for them, to build themselves houses in the towns nearest to them and to inhabit them; for, they having horses enough in that country, may be convenienced, as their occasions require, to visit their plantations. And the masters who shall inhabit the towns, having families of servants upon remote plantations, may be ordered to take care that upon Saturday afternoons (when, by the custom of Virginia, servants are freed from their ordinary labor), their servants (except one or two, left by turns to secure their plantations) may repair to their houses in the towns, and there remain with their masters until the public worship and service of the Lord's Day be ended.

5. That for a continual supply of able ministers for their churches, after a set term of years, Your Lordship would please to endeavor the procuring an act of Parliament whereby a certain number of fellowships, as they happen to be next proportionably vacant in both the universities, may bear the name of Virginia fellowships, so long as the needs of that church shall require it. And none be admitted to them but such as shall engage by promise to hold them seven years and no longer; and, at the expiration of those seven years, transport themselves to Virginia and serve that church in the office of the ministry seven years more (the church there providing for them), which being expired, they shall be left to their own liberty to return or not. And if they perform not the conditions of their admittance, then to be incapable of any preferment.

These things being procured, I think Virginia will be in the most probable way (that her present condition can admit) of being cured of the forementioned evils of her scattered planting. . . .

Men may wonder why the attempts made by the . . . honorable governors to reduce Virginia's planters into towns did never succeed, and perhaps it may be hard for any that never lived among them rightly to conjecture. But the truth in plain Enrlish is this:

Whatsoever is of public concernment in Virginia is determined by their Grand Assemblies, which are usually held once a year, and consist of governor and Council, which make the Upper House, and the burgesses, which represent the people, and make the Lower House, and are chosen out of every county by the people after the manner that burgesses are chosen for parliaments in England, and are more or fewer according as the people agree, who are to defray their charges.

Whatsoever passes into an act of Assembly must be agreed upon by the major part of burgesses, and these are usually such as went over servants thither; and though, by time and industry, they may have attained competent estates, yet, by reason of their poor and mean education, they are unskillful in judging of a good estate, either of church or commonwealth, or of the means of procuring it. No marvel, therefore, if the best proposals which have been made to such persons for reducing them into towns, offending in the least against their present private, worldly interest (though never so promising for the future), have been from time to time bandied against by such major parts of their burgesses, and the fewer wise heads overvoted by them. . . .

To contemplate the poor church (whose plants now grow wild in that wilderness) become like a garden enclosed, like a vineyard fenced, and watched like a flock of sheep with their lambs safely folded by night and fed by day; all which are the promised fruits of well-ordered towns, under religious pastors and magistrates, with what joy and delight may you likewise think upon their comely and most ingenious children, like hopeful plants growing up in nurseries of learning and piety; and, when their time of fruit is come, transplanted into the enclosed gardens of God, and becoming fruitful and useful trees of righteousness; which is the promised happiness and benefit of well-ordered schools, in well-governed towns. . . .

For encouragement, therefore, of ministers to adventure thither to help them, I humbly propound:

First, that Your Lordship be pleased to procure that the next Grand Assembly in Virginia may enact that what tobacco any parish agrees to pay their minister shall be paid of the best tobacco of every man's own crop, and with cask, otherwise experience has shown that a minister's livelihood there will be very uncertain.

Second, that, at the same Assembly, it be enacted that every parish choose a vestry (in case they have not one already chosen), and the vestry of each parish be enjoined to subscribe what quantity of corn and tobacco of the best of their own crops, with cask, they will allow a sufficient minister yearly.

Third, that, in the next and every Assembly, the act for paying 15 lb. of tobacco per annum for every tithable person in every parish destitute of a minister (which act was made at an Assembly, March 17, 1656) be carefully executed and strict inquiry made whether the tobacco due by that act be duly collected and employed to the ends expressed in that act; viz., building churches, purchasing glebes and stocks of cattle to belong to them. . . .

Fourth, that the act made in the same Assembly concerning disposing intestate estates to public uses, in case no administrator of kin to the deceased proprietor appears, may serve in the first place the needs of the church for furnishing each parish with glebes, and the glebes with stocks of cattle before any part of such estates be employed to any other use.

Fifth, that there being diverse persons already in the colony fit to serve the church in the office of deacon, a bishop be sent over so soon as there shall be a city for his see. As for other needs of that church, so also, that, after due probation and examination, such persons may be ordained deacons, and their duty and service be appointed by the bishop.

Sixth, that the ministers that go thither be not hired by the year, as is now usual, but firmly instituted and induced into livings of stated value. . . .

Seventh, that all ministers desirous to go to Virginia, and not able to transport themselves, be acquainted with an act of Assembly of that country, whereby it is provided that whatsoever sufficient minister shall not be able to pay for his transportation, any merchant that shall defray the charge of it (if such minister agree not with him upon other conditions) shall receive £20 sterling for his passage from the parish that entertains him, or 2,000 lb. of tobacco, who shall also repay any sums of money disbursed for his accommodation, and the minister to be free to choose his parish. . . .

This is all I can think meet to propound at present, only for a conclusion I shall add, for the encouragement both of bishop and ministers that shall adventure thither out of pity and compassion to the souls of so many of their poor brethren, that, as their reward will be great in Heaven, so also they shall (in a very pleasant and fruitful land) meet with a people which generally bear a great love and respect to their ministers. And (if they behave themselves as becomes their high calling) they shall find there ready help and assistance in their needs; and (which should be much more encouraging) they will find a people which generally bear a great love to the stated constitutions of the Church of England, in her government and public worship; which gave us (who went thither under the late persecutions of it) the advantage of liberty to use it constantly among them, after the naval force had reduced that colony under the power (but never to the obedience) of the usurpers; which liberty we could not have enjoyed had not the people generally expressed a great love to it.

And I hope even this will be a consideration (not of least regard) to move Your Lordship to use all possible care and endeavor to supply Virginia's needs with sufficient orthodox ministers, in the first place, and before any other of our foreign plantations which crave your help, because, in the late times of our Church's persecution, her people alone cheerfully and joyfully embraced, encouraged, and maintained the orthodox ministers that went over to them, in their public conformity to the Church of England, in her doctrine and stated manner of public worship.

II

TRANSPLANTATIONS IN THE NEW WORLD

4   J. Gibbs, A Book of Architecture* *1728*

The regional variations of seventeenth-century building along the Atlantic sea-board—the transplanted vernaculars of England, Holland, Flanders, Germany, and perhaps a vague memory of Sweden—gave way to a more canonical and uniform Georgian baroque. Toward the end of the seventeenth century, display of wealth in building was considered an emblem of divine favor, and in the following century this liberated desire for display was manifested in Palladian classicism closely emu-lating high-style English models. It began in newly established Williamsburg, the colonial Virginian capital built to take the place of Jamestown. The present Wil-liamsburg is a painstaking reconstruction of the colonial town whose original build-ings, except for the College of William and Mary, had been repeatedly altered dur-ing the ensuing centuries. Some buildings, such as the Governor's Palace, had burned and been reduced to basement ruins. But contemporary glimpses of the town's origi-nal grandeur survive in the Bodleian Library plate, engraved about 1737 (Figure 2), and in such descriptions as Robert Beverley's of several gentlemen who have "built themselves large Brick Houses of many Rooms on a floor, and several stories high, as also some Stone-Houses. . . . They always contrive to have large Rooms, that they may be cool in summer. Of late they have made their Stories much higher than formerly, and within they adorn their Apartments with rich Furniture." †

By mid-eighteenth century, a few individuals began to advertise themselves as knowledgeable of latest architectural trends. John Ariss, for example, born in Virgin-ia but trained in England, returned and placed this notice in the *Maryland Gazette*, May 22, 1751, which demonstrates the period's lack of concern for consistent spell-ing, even of one's own name:

> John Oriss,—"By the Subscriber (lately from Great Britain) Buildings of all Sorts and Dimensions are undertaken and performed in the neatest Manner, (and at cheaper rates) either of the Ancient or Modern Order of Gibbs' Archi-tect and if any Gentleman should want plans, Bills of Scantling or bill of Charges, for any Fabric, or Public Edeface, may have them by applying to the Subscriber at Major John Bushrods at Westmoreland County, Va., where may be seen a great variety and sundry Draughts of Buildings in Miniature, and some buildings near finished after the Modern Taste." John Orliss ‡

Ariss clearly understood that his familiarity with Gibbs's work bestowed on him greater status as an "architect," but other wealthy gentlemen-amateur designers had the means to acquire for themselves such handsomely produced folios as Gibbs's *Book of Architecture*, the prefatory remarks in which indicate how the architect hoped the plates would serve builders in outlying regions. Ariss apparently owned a

---

*James Gibbs, *A Book of Architecture, containing Designs of Buildings and Orna-ments* (London, 1728).

†Robert Beverley, *The History and Present State of Virginia* (London, 1705, 1722), ed. Louis B. Wright (Chapel Hill, N.C., 1947), pp. 289–90.

‡Thomas T. Waterman, *The Mansions of Virginia, 1706–1776* (Chapel Hill, N.C., 1946), p. 244.

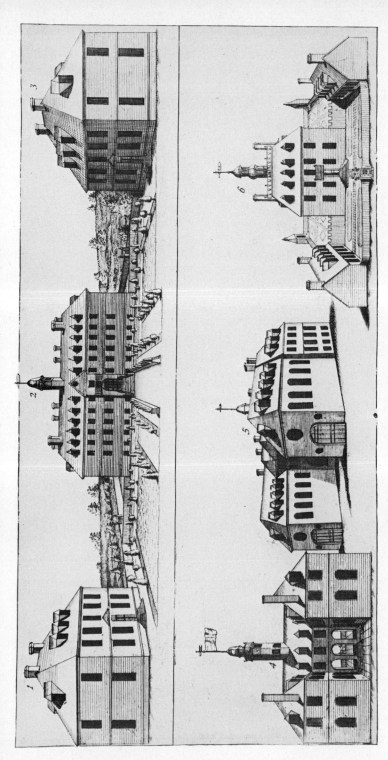

Figure 2. Principal buildings of Williamsburg, Virginia, depicted in the "Bodleian Plate," engraved c. 1737 for a projected publication. (Courtesy, Colonial Williamsburg Foundation.) The buildings, as numbered in the engraving, are: (1) the Brafferton house, 1723; (2) the main building of the College of William and Mary, 1695–1702; (3) President's House, 1732; (4) The Capitol, 1701–05; (5) rear of the College of William and Mary; (6) the Governor's Palace, 1706–20, destroyed but restored on the basis of this view.

A BOOK

OF

ARCHITECTURE,

CONTAINING

DESIGNS

OF

BUILDINGS

AND

ORNAMENTS.

By JAMES GIBBS.

LONDON:

Printed MDCCXXVIII.

copy of this, as well as William Adam's *Vitruvius Scoticus* (Edinburgh, 1750). Another folio used in the colonies was William Kent's *Designs of Inigo Jones*, published by Lord Burlington, 1727; but even more popular were the many carpenter's handbooks such as the following: William Halfpenny, *The Modern Builder's Assistant* (London, 1742); Batty Langley, *The City and Country Builder's and Workman's Treasury of Designs* (London, 1740); Robert Morris, *Rural Architecture* (London, 1750); Robert Morris, *Select Architecture . . .* (London, 1755), much used by Thomas Jefferson; William Salmon, *Palladio Londinensis* (London, 1748); and Abraham Swan, *Britist Architect* (London, 1745), reprinted in Philadelphia, 1775.

TO HIS GRACE JOHN Duke of *Argyll* and *Greenwich*, &c.
One of his Majesty's moft Honourable Privy Council, Colonel of the Queen's own Royal Regiment of Horfe, General of the Foot, Mafter General of the Ordnance, and Knight of the Moft Noble Order of the Garter.

My LORD,
The early Encouragement I received from Your Grace, in my Profeffion, upon my Return from *Italy*, and the Honour of Your Protection ever fince, give Your Name a juft Title to all my Productions in this kind.

AS feveral of the Defigns here exhibited have had Your Grace's Approbation; fo Your Patronage will be a fufficient Recommendation to the whole Work.

IT is a particular Pleafure to me that this Publication gives me an Opportunity to declare the real Sentiments of Gratitude and Refpect with which I am,

My LORD,
Your GRACE's
Moft Dutiful and moft
Obliged humble Servant,
JAMES GIBBS.

Introduction

What is here prefented to the Publick was undertaken at the inftance of feveral Perfons of Quality and others; and fome Plates were added to what was at firft intended, by the particular direction of Perfons of great Diftinction, for whofe Commands I have the higheft regard. They were of opinion, that fuch a Work as this would be of ufe to fuch Gentlemen as might be concerned in building, efpecially in the remote parts of the Country, where little or no affiftance for Defigns can be procured. Such may be here furnifhed with Draughts of ufeful and convenient Buildings and proper Ornaments; which may be executed by any Workman who underftands Lines, either as here Defign'd, or with fome Alteration, which may be eafily made by a perfon of Judgment; without which a Variation in Draughts, once well digefted, frequently proves a Detriment to the Building, as well as a Difparagement to the perfon that gives them. I mention this to caution Gentlemen from fuffering any material Change to be made in their Defigns, by the Forwardnefs of unskilful Workmen, or the Caprice of ignorant affuming Pretenders.

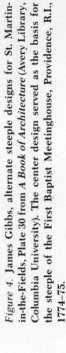

Figure 4. James Gibbs, alternate steeple designs for St. Martin-in-the-Fields, Plate 30 from *A Book of Architecture* (Avery Library, Columbia University). The center design served as the basis for the steeple of the First Baptist Meetinghouse, Providence, R.I., 1774–75.

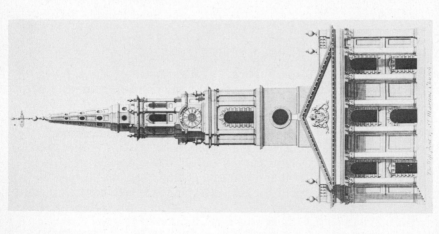

Figure 3. James Gibbs, elevation, St. Martin-in-the-Fields, London, Plate 3 from *A Book of Architecture*, London, 1728 (Avery Library, Columbia University).

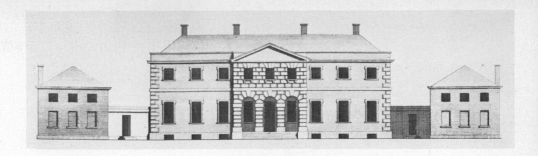

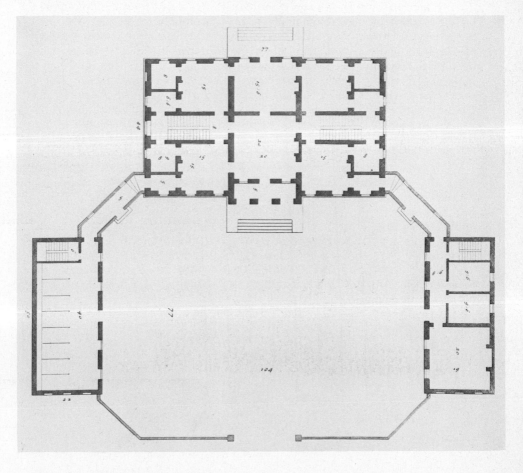

Figure 5. James Gibbs, "A Design made for a Gentlemen in Dorsetshire," Plate 58 from *A Book of Architecture* (Avery Library, Columbia University). This plate served as the basis of the Colonel John Taloe house, "Mount Airy," Richmond County, Virginia.

Some, for want of better Helps, have unfortunately put into the hands of common workmen, the management of Buildings of confiderable expence; which when finifhed, they have had the mortification to find condemned by perfons of Taft, to that degree that fometimes they have been pull'd down, at leaft alter'd at a greater charge than would have procur'd better advice from an able Artift; or if they have ftood, they have remained lafting Monuments of the Ignorance or Parfimonioufnefs of the Owners, or (it may be) of a wrong-judged Profufenefs.

What heaps of Stone, and even Marble, are daily feen in Monuments, Chimneys, and other Ornamental pieces of Architecture, without the leaft Symmetry or Order? When the fame or fewer Materials, under the conduct of a skilful Surveyor, would, in lefs room and with much lefs charge, have been equally (if not more) ufeful, and by Juftnefs of Proportion have had a more grand Appearance, and confequently have better anfwered the Intention of the Expence. For it is not the Bulk of a Fabrick, the Richnefs and Quantity of the Materials, the Multiplicity of Lines, nor the Gaudinefs of the Finifhing, that give the Grace or Beauty and Grandeur to a Building; but the Proportion of the Parts to one another and to the Whole, whether entirely plain, or enriched with a few Ornaments properly difpofed.

In order to prevent the Abufes and Abfurdities above hinted at, I have taken the utmoft care that thefe Defigns fhould be done in the beft Taft I could form upon the inftructions of the greateft Mafters in *Italy*, as well as my own Obfervations upon the antient Buildings there, during many Years application to thefe Studies: For a curfory View of thofe Auguft Remains can no more qualify the Spectator, or Admirer, than the Air of the Country can infpire him with the knowledge of Architecture.

If this Book prove ufeful in fome degree anfwerable to the Zeal of my Friends in encouraging and promoting the Publication of it, I fhall not think my Time mif-fpent, nor my Pains ill beftow'd.

I fhall now proceed to give a fhort Explanation of the Plates as they ftand in the Book.

5   T. Jefferson, Notes on the State of Virginia*   *1782–84*

The *Notes on Virginia*, Jefferson's only full-length book, was written in response to inquiries made by the Marquis de Barbé-Marbois, then secretary of the French legation in Philadelphia. While recovering from a fall from a horse, Jefferson worked over material he had been gathering for some time; this was revised in the years 1782–83, and the first edition printed at Jefferson's expense in Paris, 1784, shortly

The Writings of Thomas Jefferson, ed. Albert E. Bergh and Andrew A. Lipscomb, 20 vols. (Washington, D.C., 1903–05), 2:208, 211–15, 228–30.

after his arrival there to serve as ambassador to the Court of France. Numerous editions in England, Germany, and the United States followed, exerting a particular influence—hence, the significance of Jefferson's views on architecture and on the questionable need for cities.

QUERY XV. THE COLLEGES AND PUBLIC ESTABLISHMENTS, THE ROADS, BUILDINGS, &C.

The college of William and Mary is the only public seminary of learning in this State. It was founded in the time of king William and queen Mary, who granted to it twenty thousand acres of land, and a penny a pound duty on certain tobaccoes exported from Virginia and Maryland, which had been levied by the statute of 25 Car. II. The assembly also gave it, by temporary laws, a duty on liquors imported, and skins and furs exported. From these resources it received upwards of three thousand pounds *communibus annis*. The buildings are of brick, sufficient for an indifferent accommodation of perhaps an hundred students. By its charter it was to be under the government of twenty visitors, who were to be its legislators, and to have a president and six professors, who were incorporated. . . .

The private buildings are very rarely constructed of stone or brick, much the greatest portion being of scantling and boards, plastered with lime. It is impossible to devise things more ugly, uncomfortable, and happily more perishable. There are two or three plans, on one of which, according to its size, most of the houses in the State are built. The poorest people built huts of logs, laid horizontally in pens, stopping the interstices with mud. These are warmer in winter, and cooler in summer, than the more expensive construction of scantling and plank. . . . The only public buildings worthy of mention are the capitol, the palace, the college, and the hospital for lunatics, all of them in Williamsburg, heretofore the seat of our government. The capitol is a light and airy structure, with a portico in front of two orders, the lower of which, being Doric, is tolerably just in its proportions and ornaments, save only that the intercolonations are too large. The upper is Ionic, much too small for that on which it is mounted, its ornaments not proper to the order, nor proportioned within themselves. It is crowned with a pediment, which is too high for its span. Yet, on the whole, it is the most pleasing piece of architecture we have. The palace is not handsome without, but it is spacious and commodious within, is prettily situated, and with the grounds annexed to it, is capable of being made an elegant seat. The college and hospital are rude, mis-shapen piles, which, but that they have roofs, would be taken for brick-kilns. There are no other public buildings but churches and courthouses, in which no attempts are made at elegance. Indeed, it would not be easy to execute such an attempt, as a workman could scarcely be found capable of drawing an order. The genius of architecture seems to have shed its maledictions over this land. Buildings are often erected, by individuals, of considerable expense. To give these symmetry and taste, would not increase their cost. It would only change the arrangement of the materials, the form and combination of the members. This would often cost less than the burthen of barbarous ornaments with which these buildings are sometimes charged. But the first principles of the art are unknown, and there exists scarcely a model among us sufficiently chaste to give an idea of them. Architecture being one of the fine arts, and as such within the department of a professor of the college, according to the new arrangement, perhaps a spark may fall on some young subjects of natural taste, kindle up their genius, and produce a reformation in this elegant and useful art. But all we shall do in this way will produce no permanent improvement to our country, while the unhappy prejudice prevails that houses of brick or stone are less wholesome than those of wood. . . .

A country whose buildings are of wood, can never increase in its improvements to any considerable degree. Their duration is highly estimated at fifty years. Every half century then our country becomes a *tabula rasa*, whereon we have to set out anew, as in the first moment of seating it. Whereas when buildings are of durable materials, every new edifice is an actual and permanent acquisition to the State, adding to its value as well as to its ornament.

QUERY XIX. THE PRESENT STATE OF MANUFACTURES, COMMERCE, INTERIOR AND EXTERIOR TRADE?

We never had an interior trade of any importance. Our exterior commerce has suffered very much from the beginning of the present contest. During this time we have manufactured within our families the most necessary articles of clothing. Those of cotton will bear some comparison with the same kinds of manufacture in Europe; but those of wool, flax and hemp are very coarse, unsightly, and unpleasant; and such is our attachment to agriculture, and such our preference for foreign manufactures, that be it wise or unwise, our people will certainly return as soon as they can, to the raising raw materials, and exchanging them for finer manufactures than they are able to execute themselves.

The political economists of Europe have established it as a principle, that every State should endeavor to manufacture for itself; and this principle, like many others, we transfer to America, without calculating the difference of circumstance which should often produce a difference of result. In Europe the lands are either cultivated, or locked up against the cultivator. Manufacture must therefore be resorted to of necessity not of choice, to support the surplus of their people. But we have an immensity of land courting the industry of the husbandman. Is it best then that all our citizens should be employed in its improvement, or that one half should be called off from that to exercise manufactures and handicraft arts for the other? Those who labor in the earth are the chosen people of God, if ever He had a chosen people, whose breasts He has made His peculiar deposit for substantial and genuine virtue. It is the focus in which he keeps alive that sacred fire, which otherwise might escape from the face of the earth. Corruption of morals in the mass of cultivators is a phenomenon of which no age nor nation has furnished an example. It is the mark set on those, who, not looking up to heaven, to their own soil and industry, as does the husbandman, for their subsistence, depend for it on casualties and caprice of customers. Dependence begets subservience and venality, suffocates the germ of virtue, and prepares fit tools for the designs of ambition. This, the natural progress and consequence of the arts, has sometimes perhaps been retarded by accidental circumstances; but, generally speaking, the proportion which the aggregate of the other classes of citizens bears in any State to that of its husbandmen, is the proportion of its unsound to its healthy parts, and is a good enough barometer whereby to measure its degree of corruption. While we have land to labor then, let us never wish to see our citizens occupied at a workbench, or twirling a distaff. Carpenters, masons, smiths, are wanting in husbandry; but, for the general operations of manufacture, let our workshops remain in Europe. It is better to carry provisions and materials to workmen there, than bring them to the provisions and materials, and with them their manners and principles. The loss by the transportation of commodities across the Atlantic will be made up in happiness and permanence of government. The mobs of great cities add just so much to the support of pure government, as sores do to the strength of the human body. It is the manners and spirit of a people which preserve a republic in vigor. A degeneracy in these is a canker which soon eats to the heart of its laws and constitution.

III

BUILDING A NEW NATION

6   T. Jefferson and the Virginia State Capitol*   1785

Jefferson was well known among his political colleagues in Virginia as an enthusiastic student of architecture. When it was decided by the legislature to vacate the colonial buildings at Williamsburg in favor of a new location, closer to the hinterlands, up river at Richmond, Jefferson, then in Paris, was asked to develop a design. These two letters explain the basis of his design and why he believed it important to adhere to classical models. The fervent urgency of Jefferson's letter to Madison was caused by the start of construction of a locally procured design when it was felt Jefferson's took too long to arrive.

LETTER TO JAMES MADISON, FROM PARIS, SEPTEMBER 20, 1785

Dear Sir,

. . . I received this summer a letter from Messrs. Buchanan and Hay, as Directors of the public buildings, desiring I would have drawn for them, plans of sundry buildings, and, in the first place, of a capitol. They fixed, for their receiving this plan, a day which was within about six weeks of that on which their letter came to my hand. I engaged an architect of capital abilities in this business. Much time was requisite, after the external form was agreed on, to make the internal distribution convenient for the three branches of government. This time was much lengthened by my avocations to other objects, which I had no right to neglect. The plan, however, was settled. The gentlemen had sent me one which they had thought of. The one agreed on here, is more convenient, more beautiful, gives more room, and will not cost more than two-thirds of what that would. We took for our model what is called the *Maison Quarrée* of Nismes, one of the most beautiful, if not the most beautiful and precious morsel of architecture left us by antiquity. It was built by Caius and Lucius Caesar, and repaired by Louis XIV, and has the suffrage of all the judges of architecture who have seen it, as yielding to no one of the beautiful monuments of Greece, Rome, Palmyra, and Balbec, which late travellers have communicated to us. It is very simple, but it is noble beyond expression, and would have done honor to our country, as presenting to travellers a specimen of taste in our infancy, promising much for our maturer age. I have been much mortified with information, which I received two days ago from Virginia, that the first brick of the capitol would be laid within a few days. But surely, the delay of this piece of summer would have been repaired by the savings in the plan preparing here, were we to value its other superiorities as nothing. But how is a taste in this beautiful art to be formed in our countrymen unless we avail ourselves of every occasion when public buildings are to be erected, of presenting to them models for their study and imitation? Pray try if you can effect the

Writings of . . . Jefferson, ed. Bergh and Lipscomb, 5:134–37.

28

stopping of this work. I have written also to E.R. [Edmund Randolph] on the subject. The loss will be only of the laying the bricks already laid, or a part of them. The bricks themselves will do again for the interior walls, and one side wall and one wall may remain, as they will answer equally well for our plan. This loss is not to be weighed against the saving money which will arise, against the comfort of laying out the public money for something honorable, the satisfaction of seeing an object and proof of national good taste, and the regret and mortification of erecting a monument of our barbarism, which will be loaded with execrations as long as it shall endure. The plans are in good forwardness, and I hope will be ready within three or four weeks. They could not be stopped now, but on paying their whole price, which will be considerable. If the undertakers are afraid to undo what they have done, encourage them to it by a recommendation from the Assembly. You see I am an enthusiast on the subject of the arts. But it is an enthusiasm of which I am not ashamed, as its object is to improve the taste of my countrymen, to increase their reputation, to reconcile to them the respect of the world, and procure them its praise.

LETTER TO THE DIRECTORS, FROM PARIS, JANUARY 26, 1786[†]

Gentlemen,

I had the honour of writing to you on the receipt of your orders to procure draughts for the public buildings, and again on the 13th of August. In the execution of those orders two methods of proceeding presented themselves to my mind. The one was to leave to some architect to draw an external according to his fancy, in which way experience shows that about once in a thousand times a pleasing form is hit upon; the other was to take some model already devised and approved by the general suffrage of the world. I had no hesitation in deciding that the latter was best, nor after the decision was there any doubt what model to take. There is at Nismes in the South of France a building, called the *Maison Quarrée*, erected in the time of the Caesars, and which is allowed without contradiction to be the most perfect and precious remain of antiquity in existence. Its superiority over anything at Rome, in Greece, at Balbec or Palmyra is allowed on all hands; and this single object has placed Nismes in the general tour of travellers. Having not yet had leisure to visit it, I could only judge of it from drawings, and from the relation of numbers who had been to see it. I determined therefore to adopt this model, & to have all its proportions justly drewed. As it was impossible for a foreign artist to know what number & sizes of apartments could suit the different corps of our government, nor how they should be

[†]Quoted from Kimball, Fiske, "Thomas Jefferson and the First Monument of the Classical Revival in America," reprinted from the *Journal of the American Institute of Architects* 3 (September 1915), pp. 379–80. Charles-Louis Clérisseau (1721–1820), trained as a painter, and winner of the Prix de Rome, 1746, studied in Rome and was among the first advocates of neoclassicism in France. The plates of the Maison Carrée, Nîmes, in his *Antiquites des la France*, Rome, 1778, were much admired by Jefferson and served as the basis of their collaborative design for the Virginia State Capitol.

connected with one another, I undertook to form that arrangement, & this
being done, I committed them to an Architect (Monsieur Clerisseau) who has
studied this art 20 years in Rome, who had particularly studied and measured the *Maison Quarrée* of Nismes, and had published a book containing 4
most excellent plans, descriptions, & observations on it. He was too well
acquainted with the merit of that building to find himself restrained by my
injunctions not to depart from his model. In one instance only he persuaded
me to admit of this. That was to make the Portico two columns deep only,
instead of three as the original is. His reason was that this latter depth would
too much darken the apartments. Economy might be added as a second
reason. I consented to it to satisfy him, and the plans are so drawn. I knew
that it would still be easy to execute the building with a depth of three
columns, and it is what I would certainly recommend. We know that the
Maison Quarrée has pleased universally for near 2000 years. By leaving out
a column, the proportions will be changed and perhaps the effect may be
injured more than is expected. What is good is often spoiled by trying to
make it better.

The present is the first opportunity which has occurred of sending the
plans. You will accordingly receive herewith the ground plan, the elevation
of the front, and the elevation of the side. The architect having been much
busied, and knowing that this was all which would be necessary in the beginning, has not yet finished the Sections of the building. They must go by some
future occasion as well as the models of the front and side which are making
in plaster of Paris. These were absolutely necessary for the guide of workmen not very expert in their art. It will add considerably to the expence, and
I would not have incurred it but that I was sensible of its necessity. The price
of the model will be 15 guineas. I shall know in a few days the cost of the
drawings which probably will be the triple of the model: however this is but
my conjecture. I will make it as small as possible, pay it, and render you an
account in my next letter. You will find on examination that the body of this
building covers an area but two-fifths of that which is proposed and begun;
of course it will take but about one half the bricks; and of course this circumstance will enlist all the workmen, and people of the art against the plan.
Again the building begun is to have 4 porticos; this but one. It is true that
this will be deeper than those were probably proposed, but even if it be
made three columns deep, it will not take half the number of columns. The
beauty of this is ensured by experience and by the suffrage of the whole
world; the beauty of that is problematical, as is every drawing, however well
it looks on paper, till it be actually executed: and tho I suppose there is more
room in the plan begun, than in that now sent, yet there is enough in this for
all the three branches of government and more than enough is not wanted.
This contains 16. rooms. to wit 4. on the first floor; for the General court,
Delegates, Lobby, & Conference. eight on the 2nd floor for the Executive,
the Senate, & 6 rooms for committees and juries: and over 4. of these smaller
rooms of the 2nd floor are 4. Mezzaninos or Entresoles, serving as offices for
the clerks of the Executive, the Senate, the Delegates & the court in actual
session. It will be an objection that the work is begun on the other plan. But
the whole of this need not be taken to pieces, and of what shall be taken to
pieces the bricks will do for inner work, mortar never becomes so hard &

adhesive to the bricks in a few months but that it may easily be chipped off, and upon the whole the plan now sent will save a great proportion of the expence. In my letter of Aug. 13, I mentioned that I could send workmen from hence as I am in hopes of receiving your orders precisely in answer to that letter I shall defer actually engaging any till I receive them. In like manner I shall defer having plans drawn for a Governor's house until further orders, only assuring you that the receiving and executing these orders will always give me a very great pleasure, and the more should I find that what I have done meets your approbation. I have the honour to be, etc.etc.

7 T. Jefferson, Letter to Trustees of East Tennessee College* *1810*

To Jefferson the philosophical content of public education and the buildings in which that instruction was given were intimately interconnected. He was thinking of such a union of curriculum and architecture when he wrote to the Trustees of a proposed college in Tennessee.

LETTER TO THE TRUSTEES CONCERNING THE LOTTERY OF THE EAST TENNESSEE COLLEGE, MAY 6, 1810

I consider the common plan followed in this country, but not in others, of making one large and expensive building as unfortunately erroneous. It is infinitely better to erect a small and separate lodge for each separate professorship, with only a hall below for his class, and two chambers above for himself; joining these lodges by barracks for a certain portion of the students, opening into a covered way to give a dry communication between all the schools. The whole of these arranged around an open square of grass and trees would make it, what it should be in fact, an academical village, instead of a large and common den of noise, of filth, and of fetid air. It would afford that quiet retirement so friendly to study, and lessen the dangers of fire, infection, and tumult. Every professor would be the police officer of the students adjacent to his own lodge, which should include those of his own class of preference, and might be at the head of their table, if, as I suppose, it can be reconciled with the necessary economy to dine them in smaller and separate parties rather than in a large and common mess. Those separate buildings, too, might be erected successively and occasionally, as the number of professorships and students should be increased or the funds become competent.

*Writings of ... Jefferson, ed. Bergh and Lipscomb, 12:387–88.

I pray you to pardon me if I have stepped aside into the province of counsel; but much observation and reflection on these institutions have long convinced me that the large and crowded buildings in which youths are pent up are equally unfriendly to health, to study, to manners, morals, and order.

8   P. C. L'Enfant's Plan for the Capitol City* *1791*

The establishment of the federal government was both political compromise and symbolic act, and most significant was the decision to build a new federal city on open land, a seat of representative government free of political pressure and commercial influence, or so it was hoped. Eager to participate in this bold enterprise, Pierre Charles L'Enfant, who had served in the Continental army and met Washington, wrote the president on September 11, 1789:

> Your Excellency will not be surprised that my ambition . . . should lead me to wish to share in the undertaking. No nation had ever before the opportunity offered them of deliberately deciding on the spot where their Capitol City should be fixed, or of combining every necessary consideration in the choice of situation, and although the means now within the power of the Country are not such as to pursue the design to any great extent, it will be obvious that the plan should be drawn on such a scale as to leave room for that aggrandizement and embellishment which the increase of the wealth of the nation will permit it to pursue at any period however remote.[†]

L'Enfant's Parisian training as an artist and his experience in the Colonial army engineering corps were well known. Following his appointment to lay out the new city, L'Enfant requested aid from Thomas Jefferson, who replied, April 10, 1791:

> I have examined my papers, and found the plans of Frankfort-on-the-Mayne, Carlsruhe, Amsterdam, Strasburg, Paris, Orleans, Bordeaux, Lyons, Montpelier, Marseilles, Turin, and Milan, which I send in a roll by the post. They are on large and accurate scales, having been procured by me while in those respective cities myself. . . . I will beg your care of them, and to return them when no longer useful to you, leaving you absolutely free to keep them as long as useful. I am happy that the President has left the planning of the town in such good hands, and have no doubt it will be done to general satisfaction. . . . Whenever it is proposed to prepare plans for the Capitol, I should prefer the adoption of some one of the models of antiquity, which have had the approbation of thousands of years; and for the President's house, I should pre-

*Elizabeth S. Kite, ed., *L'Enfant and Washington, 1791–1792* (Baltimore, 1929), pp. 52–58.

[†] Quoted in Kite, *L'Enfant*, p. 34.

fer the celebrated fronts of modern buildings, which have already received the approbation of all good judges. Such are the Galerie du Louire, the Gardes meubles, and the two fronts of the Hotel de Salm. But of this it is yet time enough to consider.‡

In conjunction with his final plan, L'Enfant prepared this written report, presumably addressed to President Washington.

REPORT ON THE PLAN FOR THE INTENDED CITY, JUNE 22, 1791

Sir;

In delineating the plan for the intended city here annexed, I regretted very much being hindered by the shortness of time from making any particular drawing of the several buildings, squares, and other improvements which the smallness of the scale of the general map, together with the hurry with which it had been drawn could not admit of having lain them down, as correct as . . . is necessary to give a perfect idea of the effect when executed. My whole attention was directed to a combination of the general distribution of the several situations, an object which, being of almost immediate moment, and importance, made me sacrifice every other consideration—and here again must I solicit your indulgence, in submitting to your judgment—my ideas, and in presenting to you a first drawing, correct only as it respects the situation and distance of objects, all which were determined and well ascertained having for more accuracy had several lines run upon the ground cleared of the wood, and measured with posts fixed at certain distances to serve as bases from which I might arrange the whole with a certainty of making it fit the various parts of the ground.

Having determined some principal points to which I wished to make the others subordinate, I made the distribution regular with every street at right angles, North and South, east and west, and afterwards opened some in different directions, as avenues to and from every principal place, wishing thereby not merely to contract with the general regularity, nor to afford a greater variety of seats with pleasant prospects, which will be obtained from the advantageous ground over which these avenues are chiefly directed, but principally to connect each part of the city, if I may so express it, by making the real distance less from place to place, by giving to them reciprocity of sight and by making them thus seemingly connected, promote a rapid settlement over the whole extent, rendering those even of the most remote parts an addition to the principal, which without the help of these, were any such settlement attempted, it would be languid, and lost in the extent, and become detrimental to the establishment. Some of these avenues were also necessary to effect the junction of several roads to a central point in the city, by making these roads shorter, which is effected [by directing them] to those

‡*Writings . . . of Jefferson*, ed. Bergh and Lipscomb, 8:162–63. For Jefferson's own proposals for the new city and a thorough treatment of the plan development, see John W. Reps, *Monumental Washington: The Planning and Development of the Capitol Center* (Princeton, 1967).

leading to Bladensburg and the Eastern branch—both of which are made above a little shorter, exclusive of the advantage of their leading immediately to the wharves at Georgetown. The hilly ground which surrounds that place the growth of which it must impede, by inviting settlements on the city side of Rock Creek, which cannot fail soon to spread along all those avenues which will afford a variety of pleasant rides, and become the means for a rapid intercourse with all parts of the city, to which they will serve as does the main artery in the animal body, which diffuses life through the smaller vessels, and inspires vigor, and activity throughout the whole frame.

These avenues I made broad, so as to admit of their being planted with trees leaving 80 feet for a carriage way, 30 feet on each side for a walk under a double row of trees, and allowing ten feet between the trees and the houses. The first of these avenues and the most direct one, begins at the Eastern branch and ends over Rock Creek at the wharves at Georgetown, along the sides of which it is continued to the bridge over to the Virginia shore, and down to the lower canal to the Potomac, along the sides of which it may be of great advantage to have such a road extended to the upper canal to facilitate dragging the boats up and down.

With respect to the point upon which it is expedient first to begin the main establishment, however various the opinions thereon are, I believe the question may be easily solved, not viewing in part but embracing in one view the whole extent from the Eastern branch to Georgetown, and from the banks of the Potomac to the mountains, for in considering impartially the whole extent, viewing it as that of the intended city,. it will appear that to promote a rapid settlement throughout, across the Tiber above tide water is the most eligible one, for an offset of the establishment which . . . should be begun at various points equi-distant as possible from the center; not merely because settlements of this sort are likely to diffuse an equality of advantages over the whole territory allotted, and consequently to reflect benefit from an increase of the value of property, but because each of these settlements by a natural jealousy will most tend to stimulate establishments on each of the opposed extremes, to both of which it will undoubtedly become, as so many points of union, particularly considering that a canal is easily opened from the Eastern branch across those primary settlements of the city to issue at the mouth of the Tiber into the Potomac, giving entrance to the boats from the falls of that river into the Eastern branch harbor, which will undoubtedly facilitate a conveyance, which will be of the utmost convenience to all trading people, and the supplies of the city by markets, as designed in the map, which may be built over ground capable of sheltering any number of boats and to serve as a depository, when the city is grown to its whole extent, from whence all the internal parts may be supplied. At the place first mentioned above, where the tide water comes into Tiber Creek, is the position the most capable of any within the limits of the city, to favor those grand improvements of public magnitude which may serve as a sample for all subsequent undertakings, an edifice erected there such as the peculiarity of the ground may admit, well combined with the various directions of those avenues concentrating there, should stand to future ages a monument of magnificence.

After a minute search for other eligible situations, I may assert without an apprehension of appearing prejudiced in favor of a first opinion, that I could not discover one in all respects so advantageous . . . for erecting the

Federal House . . . [as] the western end of Jenkin's Heights [which] stands really as a pedestal waiting for a superstructure, and I am confident were all the ground cleared of wood, no other situation could bear a competition with this. Some might perhaps require less labor to be made agreeable, but after all none could be made so grand, and all would appear secondary to this.

The other position of a different nature offers a local equality, answerable for a Presidential palace, better calculated for a commodious house and which may be rendered majestic and agreeable. This position which very justly attracted your attention when first viewing the ground which is upon the west side and near the mouth of the Tiber, on that height dividing Burns and Pierces plantations—

The spot I assigned I chose somewhat more in the wood, and off the creek than when you stood in the partition line . . . two considerations determined me; first, to lessen the distance to the Federal House, and secondly to obtain a more extensive view down the Potomac, with a prospect of the whole harbor and town of Alexandria; also to connect with more harmony the public walks and avenue of the Congress House with the garden park and other improvements round the palace, which, standing upon this high ridge, with a garden in a slope towards the canal would overlook the vast esplanade in the center of which, and at the point of intersection of the sight from each of the Houses, would be the most advantageous place for an equestrian statue, which with proper appendages and walks artfully managed, would produce a most grand effect. In the present unimproved state of the ground it will appear that the hight upon which the plan of this monument is marked, will intercept the view of the water from the palace, which in part it would were it not to be observed that to bound the entrance of the Tiber to 200 feet, which is the extreme width of the canal to prevent its being drained at low water, will require a great quantity of ground to fill up, at least as much as will serve to level all the high ground in the way to the edge of the water, especially as there will be a propriety to extend it as far as low water mark upon the Potomac.

Fixed as expressed on the map the distance from the Congressional house will not be too great . . . as . . . no message to nor from the President is to be made without a sort of decorum which will doubtless point out the propriety of Committee waiting on him in carriage should his palace be even contiguous to Congress.

To make however the distance less to other officers I placed the three grand Departments of State contiguous to the principal palace; and on the way leading to the Congressional house, the gardens of the one together with the park and other improvements . . . are connected with the public walk and avenue to the Congress house in a manner as must form a whole as grand as it will be agreeable and convenient to the whole city . . . and all along side of which may be placed play houses, rooms of assembly, academies and all such sort of places as may be attractive to the learned and afford diversion to the idle.

I proposed continuing the canal much farther up, but this not to be effected but with the aid of lock, and from a level obtained from the hight of the spring of the Tiber, the greatest facility being to bring those waters over the flat back of Jenkins. I gave the more readily the preference . . . to supply that part of the city as it will promote the execution of a plan which I propose in this map, of letting the Tiber return to its proper channel by a fall, which issuing from under the base of the Congress building, may there form a cascade of forty feet high, or more than one hundred wide, which would produce the most happy effect in rolling down to fill up the canal and discharge itself in the Potomac, of which it would then appear the main spring when seen through that grand and majestic avenue intersecting with the prospect from the palace, at a point which being seen from both, I have designated as the proper for to erect a grand equestrian statue.

. . . The whole will acquire new sweetness being laid over the green of a field well level and made brilliant by shade of a few trees artfully planted.

I am with respectful submission,

Your most humble and obedient servant,

P. C. L'Enfant.

9   P. C. L'Enfant's Plan for Paterson, New Jersey*   *1792*

Aside from establishing a stable and flexible Federal government, a second important objective of the new union was decreasing dependence of foreign manufactures, for in this respect the new United States was still very much an economic "colony." In January, 1790, Secretary of the Treasury Alexander Hamilton was instructed by Congress to develop a plan "for the encouragement and promotion of such manufactures as will tend to render the United States independent of other nations for essentials." His "Report on Manufactures" presented to the House of Representatives on December 5, 1791, noted that "the expediency of encouraging manufactures . . . which was not long since deemed very questionable, appears at this time to be pretty generally admitted," and he concluded, "there are circumstances which render the present a critical moment for entering, with zeal, upon the important business." † While preparing this report, Hamilton and like-minded associates formed the Society for Establishing Useful Manufactures, purchasing a large tract of land at Paterson, New Jersey, there to lay out the prototype of a new type of American community, devoted to industry. The ambitious scheme was being planned by L'Enfant, and although the plan itself was destroyed in 1840, a description dated August 19, 1792, survives in the proceedings of the Society for Useful Manufactures. Of major concern to L'Enfant was bringing water to Paterson from above the Passaic Falls to power the projected mills, and after he described how this was to be done he turned his attention to street layout:

*Henry James, "A Review of Earlier Planning Efforts," *Regional Plan of New York and Environs,* Regional Survey, Physical Conditions and Public Services (New York, 1929), 8:173.

†Alexander Hamilton, "Report on Manufactures," *American State Papers, Documents, Legislative and Executive, of the Congress of the United States . . .* , ed. Walter Lowrie and Matthew Clarke (Washington, D.C., 1832), 5:123, 144.

The shortness of the time I have had to take a knowledge of the situation, to combine the system of conveying Water as I propose and to satisfy myself of the practicability has left me so little leisure to consider about the plan of Distribution for the Town as induces me to confine to a few general outlines of the manner in which I conceive it is most proper to have it laid out.—Surrounded by high Mountains as is the tract the Society has at disposal, I considered it was not material to observe a regular North and South, and East and West direction for the Streets, a method which I apprehend would farther be improper, because it would end every street against steep Mountain, which would impede a free circulation of air, the better to be secured by determining variously the direction of the principal streets as are marked upon the Map where I have taken advantage of a rising ground to reserve the summit of it for the erection of some Public Building, carrying the streets from thence according as the accidental opening may admit prolonging them at a distance in measure as the town will enlarge, or as arrangement may be made with the owners of the land whose property the prolongation of the streets will increase in value.

Considering also as the opening of proper avenues through the internal part of the country would be of advantage to promote the settlement of the Town, I have caused a line of experiment to be drawn from Newark, parting from the Bull's head Tavern in a particular direction by which the road from Newark to the Town will be made shorter above five Miles. I also propose bringing the Road from above the Mountain along side of the Canal making there by the Aquaduct proposed subservient to the double purpose of facilitating an entrance in the town that way avoiding the inconvenience of passing up and down the Mountain.

A great object also for the Society should be to extend their purchase more downward the River, and up above the fall to become possessed of as much of the Land on the other side of the River as will embrace the whole fall.

10　Report of Commissioners on Plan for New York*　*1811*

To reduce political disputes, the New York State legislature appointed a commission of three in 1807 "to lay out . . . the leading streets and great avenues" for the projected expansion of New York in such a way as to be "final and conclusive" in determining the growth of the city northward on Manhattan Island, particularly in the public lands forfeited to the state by loyalists in the Revolution.[†] The commissioners—Simeon De Witt, Gouverneur Morris, and John Rutherford—took a far more practical view than had L'Enfant, whose geometries they appear to refer to in the opening passages of their manuscript report attached to the plan. The commissioners make it plain:

One of the first objects which claimed their attention was the form and manner in which the business should be conducted; that is to say, whether they should confine themselves to rectilinear and rectangular streets, or whether they should adopt some of those supposed improvements, by circles, ovals, and stars, which certainly embellish a plan, whatever may be their effects as to convenience and utility. In considering that subject, they could not but bear in mind that a city is to be composed principally of the habitations of men, and that strait sided, and right angled houses are the most cheap to build, and the most convenient to live in. The effect of these plain and simple reflections was decisive.

Having determined therefore, that the work should in general be rectangular, a second, and, in their opinion, an important consideration, was so to amalgamate it with the plans already adopted by individuals as not to make any important change in their dispositions. This, if it could have been effected, consistently with the public interest, was desirable, not only as it might render the work more generally acceptable, but also as it might be the means of avoiding the expense. It was therefore a favourite object with the Commissioners, and pursued until after various unfruitful attempts had proved the extreme difficulty; nor was it abandoned at last but from necessity. To show the obstacles which frustrated every effort, can be of no use.

If it should be asked, why was the present plan adopted in preference to any other? the answer is, because, after taking all circumstances into consideration, it appeared to be the best; or, in other and more proper terms, attended with the least inconvenience.

It may, to many, be matter of surprise, that so few vacant spaces have been left, and those so small, for the benefit of fresh air, and consequent

---

*"A Map of the City of New York and Island of Manhattan," manuscript map and report, 1811; published by William Bridges, with plates engraved by Peter Maverick, 1811. "Commissioners Remarks," published by Bridges, reprinted in I. N. Phelps Stokes, *The Iconography of Manhattan Island* (New York, 1913), 1:472.

†Acts of New York, 1807, quoted in John Reps, *The Making of Urban America* (Princeton, 1965), p. 297.

preservation of health. Certainly, if the City of New York were destined to stand on the side of a small stream, such as the Seine or the Thames, a great number of ample places might be needful; but those large arms of the sea which embrace Manhattan Island, render its situation, in regard to health and pleasure, as well as to convenience of commerce, peculiarly felicitous; when, therefore, from the same causes, the price of land is so uncommonly great, it seemed proper to admit the principles of economy to greater influence than might, under circumstances of a different kind, have consisted with the dictates of prudence and the sense of duty. . . .

To some it may be matter of surprise, that the whole Island has not been laid out as a City; to others, it may be a subject of merriment, that the Commissioners have provided space for a greater population than is collected at any spot on this side of China. They have in this respect been governed by the shape of the ground. It is not improbable that considerable numbers may be collected at Haerlem, before the high hills to the southward of it shall be built upon as a City; and it is improbable, that (for centuries to come) the grounds north of Haerlem Flat will be covered with houses. To have come short of the extent laid out, might therefore have defeated just expectation, and to have gone further, might have furnished materials to the pernicious spirit of speculation.

11   A. Benjamin, The American Builder's Companion* *1806*

Throughout the eighteenth century, architectural publication played a crucial role in the development of architecture in the colonies, as the selection from Gibbs's *Book of Architecture* illustrates. So great was the demand for pattern books in the colonies that, in 1775, John Norman of Philadelphia brought out an "American" edition of Swan's *British Architect*, followed in 1786 by his own *Town and Country Builder's Assistant*, largely pirated from English pattern books.† In the same year appeared the *Articles of the Carpenters Company of Philadelphia and Their Rules for Measuring and Valuing House-Carpenters Work*, published in Philadelphia. Although it was the first original work published in the United States, it was loaned only to members under exceedingly strict rules of secrecy; its existence became known to Charles E. Peterson about 1950. John Norman continued to print American editions of British works through 1792, a tradition continued by William Norman into the nineteenth century. The first truly original American pattern book, widely circulat-

---

*Asher Benjamin, *The American Builder's Companion; or, a New System of Architecture Particularly Adapted to the Present Style of Building in the United States of America* (Boston, 1806), pp. iv-vii.

†See Henry-Russell Hitchcock, *American Architectural Books*, rev. ed. with introduction by Adolf Placzek (New York, 1976).

THE

American Builder's Companion ;

OR, A

NEW SYSTEM OF ARCHITECTURE:

PARTICULARLY ADAPTED

TO

THE PRESENT STYLE OF BUILDING

IN

𝔗𝔥𝔢 𝔘𝔫𝔦𝔱𝔢𝔡 𝔖𝔱𝔞𝔱𝔢𝔰 𝔬𝔣 𝔄𝔪𝔢𝔯𝔦𝔠𝔞.

CONTAINING,

FORTY FOUR ENGRAVINGS,

REPRESENTING,

Geometrical Lines.

Twenty different Designs for Mouldings.

The five Orders of Architecture, with great alterations, both in size and expense.

Glueing up and diminishing of Columns.

How to find the different Brackets of a Groind Ceiling.

Base and Surbase Mouldings, Architraves, &c.

Twenty four different Designs for Cornices, both for external and internal finishing.

Stone Window Caps and Sills, showing the manner of setting them in a Brick Wall.

Sash Frames, Sashes, and Shutters.

Straight and Circular Stairs.

Roofs and finding the Length and Backing of Hips, either square or bevel.

Ornamental Capitals, Mouldings, Friezes, Leaves, and Ceilings.

Chimney Pieces.

Frontispieces.

Urns, Banisters, Key Stones, &c.

Plans and Elevations of three Houses for Town, and two for Country.

Plans and Elevations for two Meetinghouses.

Plan and Elevation for a Summerhouse.

Plan and Elevation for a Courthouse.

Plan, Elevation, and Section of the Branch Bank of Boston.

With particular Directions for executing all the above Designs.

BY ASHER BENJAMIN, ARCHITECT AND CARPENTER,

AND

DANIEL RAYNERD, ARCHITECT AND STUCCO WORKER.

𝔅𝔬𝔰𝔱𝔬𝔫:

PUBLISHED BY ETHERIDGE AND BLISS, PROPRIETORS OF THE WORK.

··········

S. ETHERIDGE, PRINTER, CHARLESTOWN

··········

1806.

Plate 42.

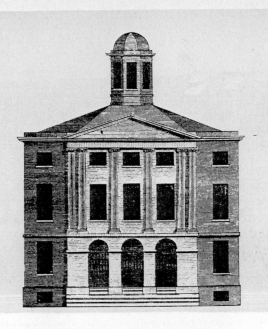

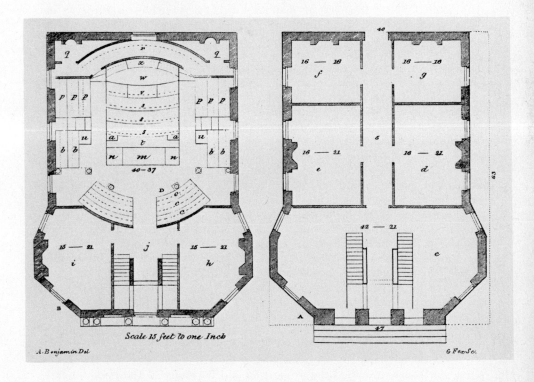

Figure 6. **Asher Benjamin, "Plan and Elevation for a Courthouse," Plate 42 from *The American Builder's Companion*, Boston, 1806 (courtesy, New York Historical Society).**

ed, was Asher Benjamin's *Country Builder's Assistant*, Greensfield, Massachusetts, 1797; the fold-out plate from this, showing a model meeting-house design, is reproduced in the *Concise History*, figure 57. In *The American Builder's Companion*, his second book, Benjamin emphasized the different economic conditions and building materials used in the United States which required now a new set of rules. One might look particularly at figure 6, which presents plans for a courthouse, hundreds of which were now needed in the developing western territories.

Preface

Books on Architecture are already so numerous that adding to their number may be thought to require some apology; but it is well known to any one in the least conversant with the principles of Architecture, that not more than one third of the contents of the European publications on this subject are of any use to the American artist in directing him in the practical part of his business.

The style of building in this country differs very considerably from that of Great Britain, and other countries in Europe, which is partly in consequence of the more liberal appropriations made for building in those countries, and of the difference of materials used, particularly in the external decorations. The American Mechanic is, therefore, in purchasing European publications, under the necessity of paying two thirds the value of his purchase for what is of no real use to him; and as the principal part of our designs have been executed by our own hands, we feel confident that this publication will be found to contain more useful information for the American workman that all the European works which have appeared in this country, and which, for the most part, are mere copies one from the other.

We are well aware that the magnificent temples of ancient times still retain a degree of romantic grandeur, which would do honour to the present age. It will, at the same time, be readily acknowledged, that an exact imitation of those noble productions of former times, on account of the present expense of materials and labour, would require no common degree of opulence for their completion: and, indeed, a strict conformity to the orders of Architecture seems to be demanded in the construction of public buildings only, and others of immense magnitude; in such situations they have a most noble and majestic appearance; but in private buildings, and others of less magnitude, their massy size and the expense attending them, are little suited to our convenience and means of appropriation. A principal part therefore of our design, in this work, is to lighten their heavy parts, and thereby lessen the expense both of labour and materials. This we expect to accomplish so as to effect a saving of one sixth, and, in many cases, one fourth part: the building shall occupy less ground, and, at the same time, be more commodious.

We do not conceive it essentially necessary to adhere exactly to any particular order, provided the proportion and harmony of the parts be carefully preserved. If, for instance, in any of the cornices an ovolo should be changed for an ogee, or for a hollow, so trifling an alteration could not destroy the effect of the whole, provided it were done with any degree of judgment. Attempts which have sometimes been made to compose fancy orders, have only spoiled the work, and no reduction of the expense has been effected. It is, therefore, as necessary that these modern fancies should be reduced to a regular system, as it was in former ages, that the Grecian and Roman orders should assume a fixed character. One important object of improvement, is a method of preserving the apparent size of an object elevated above the eye, while, at the same time, the real size is considerably diminished. It is easy to conceive that the size and effect of a cornice for instance, does not so much depend on its height as it does on its projection; because cornices are always elevated a considerable distance above the eye, and, of course, the apparent size depends principally on the projection. . . . It will at once be perceived, that the diminution in the height of the cornice is not the most considerable advantage to be derived from this construction; but that the same is gained in the height of the wall that is taken from the height of the cornice.

We have ventured to make some alteration in the proportions of the different orders, by lengthening the shafts of the columns two diameters. Their entablatures and pedestals bear nearly the same proportion as formerly, except that the architrave has less height, the frieze more height (except in the Doric) and the cornice less height and more projection.

We have given a great variety of fancy cornices and capitals, both for external and internal finishing; and calculated both for wood and stucco.

Being the first who have for a great length of time, published any New System of Architecture, we do not expect to escape some degree of censure. Old fashioned workmen, who have for many years followed the footsteps of Palladio and Langley, will, no doubt, leave their old path with great reluctance. But impressed, as we are, with a conviction that a reform in some parts of the system of Architecture is loudly demanded, and feeling a confidence from our knowledge of the theory, and from having long been conversant in the practical part of that science, we have ventured, without the aid of subscription, to exhibit our work to public view.

12   B. H. Latrobe on the Responsibilities of an Architect* *1806*

Asher Benjamin's books were aimed at country "mechanics" and housewrights, far from the services of architects. The professional architect—meaning an individual who designs for others and derives his income solely from fees based on construction costs—had only recently appeared in the United States in the person of Benjamin Henry Latrobe, who arrived from England in 1796. Latrobe attempted to inculcate

*Manuscript, Maryland Historical Society; printed in *Annals of America* (Chicago, 1968), 4:204–07.

in his pupils, Robert Mills and William Strickland, high professional standards and responsibilities, although at first there were difficulties with the strongly entrenched conservative builders' companies.† Even his students sometimes regressed under pressure from clients, occasioning this strong but well-intended letter to Mills.

BENJAMIN HENRY LATROBE TO ROBERT MILLS, July 12, 1806

The profession of architecture has been hitherto in the hands of two sorts of men. The first, of those who from traveling or from books have acquired some knowledge of the theory of the art but know nothing of its practice; the second, of those who know nothing but the practice and, whose early life being spent in labor and in the habits of a laborious life, have had no opportunity of acquiring the theory. The complaisance of these two sets of men to each other renders it difficult for the architect to get in between them, for the building mechanic finds his account in the ignorance of the gentleman-architect, as the latter does in the submissive deportment which interest dictates to the former.

It is therefore with sincere regret that I have observed your talents and information thrown into a sort of scramble between the two parties, in the designs of the churches you have given to the congregations at Charleston. You remember the faults I pointed out to you at an early period of your studies in my office, especially in the round church. You corrected them. Your design had, besides, very great and intrinsic merits of its own. What has been the event? Of all those who have contributed their ideas to that church you have been considered as the most ignorant. You have not even been permitted to correct your own errors, and in other points you have been overruled so far as to have been obliged to admit into your plan absolute absurdities, such as, for instance, the gallery within the cupola, which may probably be the cause why, within an interior circle of a certain diameter in the center of the church, the preacher's voice is said to be not perfectly heard.

Such a situation is degrading and would not be submitted to by any other member of a liberal profession, and scarcely by a mechanic whose necessities were not greater than his pride. In our country, indeed, the profession of an architect is in a great measure new. The building artisans, especially the carpenters, have been sufficiently informed to get through the business and supply the orders of a young country. Out of this state of infancy we are now emerging; and it is necessary that those who have devoted their best years and a very considerable expenditure to the attainment of that variety of knowledge which an architect ought to possess should take their legitimate rank themselves or not venture into that ocean of contact with all above and all below them into which a mistaken complaisance will throw them, but adopt some other profession sanctioned by the habits and opinions of the country.

It will be answered, "If you are paid for your designs and directions, he

† See, for instance the difficulties in constructing the Baltimore Cathedral in Talbot Hamlin, *Benjamin Henry Latrobe* (New York, 1955), pp. 238–41.

that expends his money on the building has an undoubted right to build what he pleases." If you are paid! I ask in the first place, are you paid? *No!* The custom of all Europe has decided that 5 percent on the cost of a building, with all personal expenses incurred, shall be the pay of the architect. This is just as much as is charged by a merchant for the transaction of business, expedited often in a few minutes by the labor of a clerk; while the architect must watch the daily progress of the work perhaps for years, pay all his clerk hire, and repay to himself the expense of an education greatly more costly than that of a merchant. But it was not my intention to enter at present into the question of compensation, for in your case, I believe that you have neither asked nor received anything but have given your advice *pour l'amour de dieu.* The question is in how far you ought to permit yourself to be overruled in your opinion by your employers, and in order to answer it, I have neither leisure nor inclination to go into a methodical disquisition but shall in a desultory manner proceed to the end of my letter which, as it is dictated only by friendship, will not be received by you as a regular treatise of the ethics of our profession but as proof of my goodwill. . . .

An architect . . . should be first informed what it is that is wanted; what expense might be contemplated by his design; what are the particular views of the persons who have the management of the money devoted to the work.

There will be on the part of a sensible and good-tempered man no objection to any reasonable extent of revision or rerevision of a first design. Enlargement, contraction, alteration of arrangement, of construction and of decoration may be made by a man of talents in almost infinite variety, and suggestions from unprofessional men politely and kindly made are always acceptable. But no honest man will for a moment listen to the proposal that he shall lend his name to the contrivances of whim or of ignorance, or under the pretense of a cheap, give to the public a bad work. There is, as in most proverbs, a vast deal of good sense in the old Latin proverb . . . *in sua arte credendum* [he should believe in his own work]. We allow full faith to our plainest mechanics in their particular callings. No man thinks himself capable of instructing his shoemaker or his tailor. Indeed, we swallow what the physician orders with our eyes shut, and sign the deed the lawyer lays before us with very little inquiry. But every gentleman can build a house, a prison, or a city. This appears extraordinary, for when a gentleman sets about the work, he has the interests of all those he employs in array against his fortune, without any protection in his own knowledge. The mechanical arts employed in the erection of a capital building are more than twenty. Of these every architect has a competent knowledge, so as to judge of the quality as well as of the value and the amount of the work, but it is at least twenty to one against the gentleman who trusts only himself that he will lose 5 percent, at least.

Then as to the arrangement. Every architect who has been regularly educated knows what has been done before in the same line. This knowledge he necessarily acquires in the office in which he studies, not only from the books and designs which he finds there but in the instructions and actual practice of his principal, provided he be a man of intelligence, candor, and of business.

You are, on the subject of the difference between the professional and regular mode of conducting your works, as well as small buildings, and the desultory guessing manner in which they are otherwise managed, too well informed by experience to render it necessary for me to proceed further on this head. I will now give you with my accustomed frankness my opinion of the conduct you should pursue in respect to the proposed penitentiary house.

1. In the first place, do nothing gratuitously. The state of Carolina is infinitely better able to pay you well than you are to subscribe your time and your talents, which is your subsistence toward the annual revenue of the state—for this is the actual effect of gratuitous professional services. As far as you have hitherto promoted the very laudable design of the government by exhibiting the practicability of such a building as will be necessary, if the penitentiary law be enacted you have done well. For many people despair of the end unless they see the means. But further you ought not to go without a very clear understanding as to what is to be the reward of your labor. You know too well the course of my professional transactions to suppose that this advice is the result of a mercenary disposition. The gratuitous services on a very great scale which I have given to unendowed public institutions for the promotion of religious or literary objects are well known to you, for you have had your share of the labors. But when a rich state is about to execute a project from which great public benefit is expected to result, compensation to those who assist in effecting that object is a thing so much of course that all I have said would appear superfluous, if the example of the donation of time and talent and expense had not in many instances been set by yourself. . . .

You must take it for granted that no liberality, that is, voluntary reward, is ever to be expected from a public body. Individuals, responsible only to themselves in the expenditure of their money, are often generous and reward handsomely, independently of stipulation; but a number of the same individuals, meeting as guardians of the public money, feel in the first place the necessity of pleasing their constituents, and in the second that of involving themselves in no unnecessary responsibility. . . .

To balance this want of liberality in public boards, they have this advantage to offer over individual employment—that when a bargain is made for a salary or a commission, it is always rigidly adhered to, provided it be in writing and clearly expressed, for every ambiguity will always be interpreted for the public and against the individual.

In settling what shall be your compensation, on the presumption of your being employed, I would by all means advise you to prefer a salary to a commission. It will be both more certain to you and more satisfactory to your employers.

2. Take care that before the work begin, the plan is perfectly understood, and stipulate that no alteration but by mutual discussion and agreement shall be made.

3. Stipulate for the following points, all of which are most essential: no workman shall be employed to whom you object; no workman shall be allowed to apply to the board or individual to whom the state may delegate the management of the erection of the work but through you; no account shall be paid, unsanctioned by your signature. . . .

4. I fear you have already committed one blunder—that of leaving your drawings in the hands of the public. Of the honor and the gentlemanly feeling of the governor, far be it from me to suggest the slightest suspicion. But his very admiration of your design will produce its exhibition, and as the principles of the plan are the great merit of it, and these strike at one view, you have armed all those who see it or who hear it described with the weapons of competition against you. But this is not now to be remedied.

My time will not permit me to say more to you at present. In the conduct of the work should my experience be of any service to you, you will know how freely you may use it.

IV

THE LURE OF THE PAST, THE PROMISE OF THE FUTURE

13 R. Upjohn and Rural Gothic* *1852*

There had been sporadic appearances of "Gothick" during the eighteenth century, not very accurate in detail.† Somewhat more informed discussion of the use of Gothic for churches commenced in an article on "The Gothic Style" in a series on "Architecture in the United States," in the *American Journal of Science and Arts*, July 1830, and was continued by Henry Russell Cleveland in the *North American Review* in October 1836. The first American book to direct attention of Episcopal clergy to the appropriateness of Gothic was itself by a minister: Rev. John Henry Hopkins's *Essay on Gothic Architecture* (Burlington, Vermont, 1836), which the author admitted was not the work of a professional architect but was "intended to be of service, where better guides are not yet at hand . . . that it may induce our rising clergy to give attention to a subject which peculiarly concerns themselves."

The church which primarily affected the shift to Gothic was Richard Upjohn's Trinity Church, New York, 1839–46. Indeed, his rise to prominence among church architects was such that by the mid-1840s, he received many requests annually for designs for churches or chapels in regions far from his New York office. To satisfy this demand, he published a pattern book which popularized board-and-batten siding for churches, just as Downing's books would do for houses.

My purpose in publishing this book is simply to supply the want which is often felt, especially in the newly settled parts of our country, of designs for cheap but still substantial buildings for the use of parishes, schools, etc. In the examples given I have kept in view the uses of each building, and endeavored to give it the appropriate character; while, at the same time, care has been taken to make the drawings as plain and practical as possible. A perspective view is given of each design with general plans, and full working drawings and specifications. Bills of timber and lumber are also added for the Church and Chapel. With these, any intelligent mechanic will be able to carry out the design.

The cost of each of the buildings will of course vary with the price of materials and labor, but the following estimate will be found generally correct:

Cost of Church, including furniture,	=	$3,000.
Cost of Chapel including furniture,	=	$900.
Cost of School House,	=	$400 to $500.
Cost of Parsonage,	=	$2,500.

Richard Upjohn

[The twenty-two plates provided designs for: Wooden Church (pls. 1-11); Wooden Chapel (pls. 12-15); Schoolhouse (pls. 16-18); Parsonage (pls. 19-22).]

---

*Richard Upjohn, *Upjohn's Rural Architecture: Designs, Working Drawings and Specifications for a Wooden Church and other rural structures* (New York, 1852), pp. iii–viii.

†See Calder Loth and Julius T. Sadler, Jr., *The Only Proper Style: Gothic Architecture in America* (Boston, 1975).

Figure 7. Richard Upjohn, "Perspective View of Wooden Church," unnumbered plate from *Upjohn's Rural Architecture,* New York, 1852 (Avery Library, Columbia University).

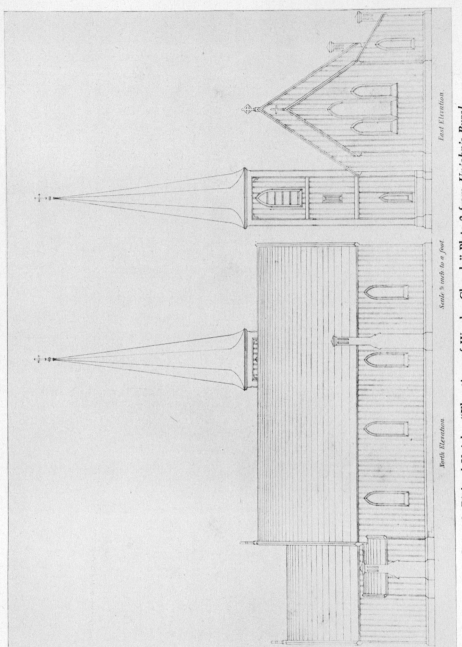

North Elevation. Scale ½ inch to a foot. East Elevation.

Figure 8. Richard Upjohn, "Elevations of Wooden Church," Plate 2 from *Upjohn's Rural Architecture* (Avery Library, Columbia University).

14   G. Wheeler, Cheap Wooden Dwellings* *1855*

It was inevitable, perhaps, that the explosive development of the mid-continent early in the nineteenth century would lead to the development of a quick and inexpensive system of wooden framing for houses and small warehouses, replacing the heavy hewn and joined frame. According to Sigfried Giedion, the first structure built (by Augustine D. Taylor in 1833) solely of "scantling and siding" was Saint Mary's Church, Chicago, although continuing research by Professor Paul E. Sprague now indicates that the critical steps in using small-dimension lumber assembled entirely with nails were taken by George W. Snow in the autumn of 1832 in putting up a warehouse near the mouth of the Chicago River.† Unavailability of skilled joiners and the pressing need for large numbers of inexpensive buildings were the critical factors in the invention of the balloon frame, so-called because such frames seemed to go up with the speed of balloons. The technique was exploited first in Chicago during its phenomenal growth in the 1830s, and then was exported to San Francisco during the California Gold Rush after 1849. At first it utilized mass-produced cut nails and whatever small-size soft wood lumber was at hand; by the end of the Civil War, the technique was perfected with the introduction of standardized lumber (2x4s, etc.) and machine-made iron wire nails. The novel technique, already revolutionizing home building, was first described in Wheeler's *Homes for the People*, quoted below, but clear construction diagrams and structural design tables then appeared in William E. Bell, *Carpentry Made Easy; or, the Science and Art of Framing on a New and Improved System with Specific Instructions for Building Balloon Frames* (Philadelphia, 1858); plate 6 from this is reproduced in the *Concise History*, figure 111. A native of Virginia, but from 1846 until his death around 1890 a resident of Ottawa, Illinois, Bell knew the technique of balloon framing well.

Wheeler's book, while more general in describing how to build a balloon frame, is a thorough investigation of the need for houses for the middle classes, and important for its recognition of the growth of suburbs around major cities. Having begun by discussing the various classes of home builders (the first selection following) and the effectiveness and usefulness of historic styles, Wheeler then examines each of the several house types, starting with small suburban villas costing from $1,800 to $7,000. He then discusses more expansive mansions costing up to $30,000 (a princely sum in 1855), but he also discusses in detail "the cheap home in the city, suburb and country" costing as little as $400. Subsequent chapters deal with farm buildings and "alteration of old buildings." He concludes with the second selection given here.

*Gervase Wheeler, *Homes for the People in Suburb and Country; the Villa, the Mansion, and the Cottage, adapted to American Climate and Wants* (New York, 1855), pp. 1–2, 408–14.

†Sigfried Giedion, *Space, Time and Architecture*, 5th ed. (Cambridge, Mass., 1967), 352–53; Walker Field, Jr., "A Re-examination into the Invention of the Balloon Frame," *Journal, Society of Architectural Historians* 2 (October 1942), 3–29; Paul E. Sprague, "The Origin of Balloon Framing," *Journal, Society of Architectural Historians* 40 (December 1981), 311–19.

The Villa

CHAPTER I

Division of homes sought by the people into three classes—History of architectural styles applicable to modern use.

Three classes of persons seek homes in the country: those who, doing business in the city, make their family home in the suburb, or adjacent rural neighborhood; those who, having retired from town pursuits entirely, or to so great an extent as to make such an arrangement convenient, consider their country retreat the family homestead; and those who select the country from motives of economy. A fourth class may be found in those whose business consists in country pursuits entirely; but the requirements this class would demand in a home, assimilate so closely, in many respects, to those that may be enumerated in describing the wants of the third class, that, for the sake of convenience, the former distribution seems preferable. Thus, we have a classification of houses to suit the wants of each home-seeker thus designated, in the Villa, the Mansion, and the Cottage. Though the peculiarities of each of these are really so distinct as justly to be enumerated under an individual head, they frequently trench so nearly one upon the other, as to render difficult at times, the exact definition of to what class a house in question may belong. The small villa nearly resembles the cottage; the large villa, the mansion; and the cottage, the farm-house, or the country-seat, as the pursuits of the occupants may cause it to assume either character. The villa, mansion, and cottage, however, have, in reality, very strongly marked points of difference, and the attempt to set the laws that regulate their just design at defiance, results in the many architectural incongruities constantly seen.

The object through the following pages will be to supply a popular want, as it appears in each department that has been named, and in classifying examples of homes under each head, to endeavor to explain their excellences and peculiarities. . . .

The *New York Tribune* of January 18th, 1855, reported a meeting of the American Institute Farmers' Club, and contained amongst other items some remarks from one of the members upon a novel mode of constructing cheap wooden dwellings, from which I offer the reader the following extracts. . . .

How to Build Balloon Frames

Mr. Robinson said: "At our last meeting I made some remarks, which were followed by others, upon the subject of 'Balloon Frames' of dwellings and other public buildings, a slight sketch of which I published in *The Tribune*, not deeming it important to enter into the minutiae of hours to make such buildings. I find that I did not appreciate the importance of the subject, for I have received a score of letters and personal inquiries from various parts of the country, showing that a great many farmers would like to know how to build a farm-house for half the present expense. I therefore ask the indulgence of the Club, while I start a balloon from the foundation, and finish it to the roof. I would saw all my timber for a frame-house, or ordinary frame outbuilding, of the following dimensions: Two inches by eight; two by four; two by one. I have, however, built them, when I lived on the Grand Prairie of Indiana, many miles from saw-mills, nearly all of split and hewed stuff, making use of rails or round poles, reduced to straight lines and even thickness on two sides, for studs and rafters. But sawed stuff is much the easiest, though in a timber-country the other is far the cheapest. First, level your foundation, and lay down two of the two-by-eight pieces, flatwise, for side-walls. Upon these set the floor-sleeps, on edge, thirty-two inches apart. Fasten one at each end, and perhaps, one or two in the middle, if the building is large, with a wooden pin. These end-sleepers are the end-sills. Now lay the floor, unless you design to have one that would be likely to be injured by the weather before you get the roof on. It is a great saving, though, of labor, to begin at the bottom of a house and build up. In laying the floor first, you have no studs to cut and fit around, and can let your boards run out over the ends, just as it happens, and afterwards saw them off smooth by the sill. Now set up a corner-post, which is nothing but one of the two-by-four studs, fastening the bottom by four nails; make it plumb, and stay it each way. Set another at the other corner, and then mark off your door and window places, and set up the side-studs and put in the frames. Fill up with studs between, sixteen inches apart, supporting the top by a line or strip of board from corner to corner, or stayed studs between. Now cover that side with rough sheeting boards, unless you intend to side-up with clap-boards on the studs, which I never would do, except for a small, common building. Make no calculation about the top of your studs; wait till you get up that high. You may use them of any length, with broken or stub-shot ends, no matter. When you have got this side boarded as high as you can reach, proceed to set up another. In the meantime, other workmen can be lathing the first side. When you have got the sides all up, fix upon the height of your upper floor, and strike a line upon the studs for the under side of the joist. Cut out a joist four inches wide, half-inch deep, and nail on firmly one of the inch strips. Upon these strips rest the chamber floor joist. Cut out a joist one inch deep, in the lower edge, and lock it on the strip, and nail each joist to each stud. Now lay this floor, and go on to build the upper story, as you did the lower one; splicing on and lengthening out studs wherever needed, until you get high enough for the plate. Splice studs or joist by simply butting the ends together, and nailing strips on each side. Strike a line and saw off the top of the studs even upon each side—not the ends—and nail on one of the inch-strips. That is the plate. Cut the ends of the upper joist the bevel of the pitch of the roof, and nail them fast to the plate, placing the end ones inside the studs, which you will let run promiscuously, to be cut off by the rafter. Now lay the garret-floor by all means before you put on the roof, and you will find that you have saved fifty per cent of hard labor. The rafters, if supported so as not to be over ten feet long, will be strong enough of the two-by-four stuff. Bevel the ends and nail fast to the joist. Then there is no strain upon the sides by the weight of the roof, which may be covered with shingles or other materials—the cheapest being composition or cement roofs. To make one of this kind, take soft, spongy, thick paper, and tack it upon the boards in courses like shingles. Commence at the top with hot tar and saturate the paper, upon which sift evenly fine gravel, pressing it in while hot—that is, while tar and gravel are both hot. One coat will make a tight roof; two coats will make it more durable. Put up your partitions of stuff one by four, unless where you want to support the upper joist—then use stuff two by four, with strips nailed on top, for the joist to rest upon, fastening altogether by nails, wherever timbers touch. Thus you will have a frame without a tenon or mortice, or brace, and yet it is far cheaper, and incalculably stronger when finished, than though it was composed of timbers ten inches square, with a thousand auger holes and a hundred days' work with the chisel and adze, making holes and pins to fill them.

"To lay out and frame a building so that all its parts will come together, requires the skill of a master mechanic, and a host of men and a deal of hard work to lift the great sticks of timber into position. To erect a balloon-building requires about as much mechanical skill as it does to build a board tence. Any farmer who is handy with the saw, iron square and hammer, with one of his boys or a common laborer to assist him, can go to work and put up a frame for an outbuilding, and finish it off with his own labor, just as well as to hire a carpenter to score and hew great oak sticks and fill them full of mortices, all by the science of the 'square rule.' It is a waste of labor that we should all lend our aid to put a stop to. Besides it will enable many a farmer to improve his place with new buildings, who, though he has long needed them, has shuddered at the thought of cutting down half of the best trees in his wood-lot, and then giving half a year's work to hauling it home and paying for what I do know is the wholly useless labor of framing. If it had not been for the knowledge of balloon-frames, Chicago and San Francisco could never have arisen, as they did, from little villages to great cities in a single year. It is not alone city buildings, which are supported by one another, that may be thus erected, but those upon the open prairie, where the wind has a sweep from Mackinaw to the Mississippi, for there they are built, and stand as firm as any of the old frames of New England, with posts and beams sixteen inches square."

These remarks were confirmed by the testimony of other members present, who testified to having adopted the mode of framing referred to with entire success.

15 C. Beecher and H. B. Stowe, The American Woman's Home* *1869*

The reshaping of the American house by Frank Lloyd Wright was based on the less well-known but far more radical proposals advanced a generation earlier by Catharine Beecher (1800–78), daughter of the influential progressive minister, Lyman Beecher. Her architectural analysis of the modern home was radical in that it was rooted in function, not literary stylistic conceits. But her immense influence was socially reactionary, for she conceived of the American woman as a self-sacrificing Christian wife and mother. The ideal home she designed was arranged to reinforce a woman's Christian moral obligation and to enable her to run the household single-handed. While firmly establishing female domesticity for a century to come, she sought nevertheless to decrease demeaning physical labor and to make the American home efficient, healthful, and conducive to Christian family life. The woman was to be both "minister" to the family and a skilled "professional" worker-manager of the household.[†] She proposed these ideals, providing model house designs, in a *Treatise on Domestic Economy* (New York, 1841), with further expansion in an article in *Harper's Monthly Magazine* (31 [1856], page 710). The culmination, enriched by her wide reading in advancing domestic technologies, was *The American Woman's Home*, with its many chapters treating the Christian family, the Christian house (chapter 2, reproduced here), ventilation, stoves and furnaces, interior decoration, food preparation, hygiene, clothing, sewing, manners, charity, infant care, health, yards and gardens, and care of animals.

INTRODUCTION

The authors of this volume, while they sympathize with every honest effort to relieve the disabilities and sufferings of their sex, are confident that the chief cause of these evils is the fact that the honor and duties of the family state are not duly appreciated, that women are not trained for these duties as men are trained for their trades and professions, and that, as the consequence, family labor is poorly done, poorly paid, and regarded as menial and disgraceful.

To be the nurse of young children, a cook, or a housemaid, is regarded as the lowest and last resort of poverty, and one which no woman of culture

*Catharine Beecher and Harriet Beecher Stowe, *The American Woman's Home: or, Principles of Domestic Science, being a Guide to the Formation and Maintenance of Economical, Healthful, Beautiful, and Christian Homes* (New York, 1869), pp. 13–14, 23–42, 424–29.

†See Kathryn K. Sklar, *Catharine Beecher: A Study in American Domesticity* (New Haven, 1973); Dolores Hayden, "Catharine Beecher and the Politics of Housework," in *Women in American Architecture: A Historic and Contemporary Perspective*, ed. Susana Torre (New York, 1977), pp. 40–49; Dolores Hayden, *The Grand Domestic Revolution: A History of Feminist Designs for American Homes, Neighborhoods, and Cities* (Cambridge, Mass., 1981), pp. 54–58.

and position can assume without loss of caste and respectability.

It is the aim of this volume to elevate both the honor and the remuneration of all the employments that sustain the many difficult and sacred duties of the family state, and thus to render each department of woman's true profession as much desired and respected as are the most honored professions of men.

When the other sex are to be instructed in law, medicine, or divinity, they are favored with numerous institutions richly endowed, with teachers of the highest talents and acquirements, with extensive libraries, and abundant and costly apparatus. With such advantages they devote nearly ten of the best years of life to preparing themselves for their profession; and to secure the public from unqualified members of these professions, none can enter them until examined by a competent body, who certify to their due preparation for their duties.

Woman's profession embraces the care and nursing of the body in the critical periods of infancy and sickness, the training of the human mind in the most impressible period of childhood, the instruction and control of servants, and most of the government and economies of the family state. These duties of woman are as sacred and important as any ordained to man; and yet no such advantages for preparation have been accorded to her, nor is there any qualified body to certify the public that a woman is duly prepared to give proper instruction in her profession.

II

A CHRISTIAN HOUSE

In the Divine Word it is written, "The wise woman buildeth her house." To be "wise," is "to choose the best means for accomplishing the best end." It has been shown that the best end for a woman to seek is the training of God's children for their eternal home, by guiding them to intelligence, virtue, and true happiness. When, therefore, the wise woman seeks a home in which to exercise this ministry, she will aim to secure a house so planned that it will provide in the best manner for health, industry, and economy, those cardinal requisites of domestic enjoyment and success. To aid in this, is the object of the following drawings and descriptions, which will illustrate a style of living more conformed to the great design for which the family is instituted than that which ordinarily prevails among those classes which take the lead in forming the customs of society. The aim will be to exhibit modes of economizing labor, time, and expenses, so as to secure health, thrift, and domestic happiness to persons of limited means, in a measure rarely attained even by those who possess wealth.

At the head of this chapter is a sketch of what may be properly called a Christian house; that is, a house contrived for the express purpose of enabling every member of a family to labor with the hands for the common good, and by modes at once healthful, economical, and tasteful.

Of course, much of the instruction conveyed in the following pages is chiefly applicable to the wants and habits of those living either in the country or in such suburban vicinities as give space of ground for healthful outdoor occupation in the family service, although the general principles of house-building and house-keeping are of necessity universal in their application—as true in the busy confines of the city as in the freer and purer quietude of the country. So far as circumstances can be made to yield the opportunity, it will be assumed that the family state demands some outdoor labor for all. The cultivation of flowers to ornament the table and house, of fruits and vegetables for food, of silk and cotton for clothing, and the care of horse, cow, and dairy, can be so divided that each and all of the family, some part of the day, can take exercise in the pure air, under the magnetic and healthful rays of the sun. Every head of a family should seek a soil and climate which will afford such opportunities. Railroads, enabling men toiling in cities to rear families in the country, are on this account a special blessing. So, also, is the opening of the South to free labor, where, in the pure and mild climate of the uplands, open-air labor can proceed most of the year, and women and children labor out of doors as well as within.

In the following drawings are presented modes of economizing time, labor, and expense by the close packing of conveniences. By such methods, small and economical houses can be made to secure most of the comforts and many of the refinements of large and expensive ones. The cottage at the head of this chapter is projected on a plan which can be adapted to a warm or cold climate with little change. By adding another story, it would serve a large family.

Figure 10 shows the ground-plan of the first floor. On the inside it is forty-three feet long and twenty-five wide, excluding conservatories and front and back projections. Its inside height from floor to ceiling is ten feet. The piazzas each side of the front projection have sliding-windows to the floor, and can, by glazed sashes, be made green-houses in winter. In a warm climate, piazzas can be made at the back side also.

In the description and arrangement, the leading aim is to show how time, labor, and expense are saved, not only in the building but in furniture and its arrangement. With this aim, the ground-floor and its furniture will first be shown, then the second story and its furniture, and then the basement and its conveniences. The conservatories are appendages not necessary to housekeeping, but useful in many ways pointed out more at large in other chapters.

The entry has arched recesses behind the front doors, furnished with hooks for over-clothes in both—a box for over-shoes in one, and a stand for umbrellas in the other. The roof of the recess is for statuettes, busts, or flowers. The stairs turn twice with broad steps, making a recess at the lower landing, where a table is set with a vase of flowers. On one side of the recess is a closet, arched to correspond with the arch over the stairs. A bracket over the first broad stair, with flowers or statuettes, is visible from the entrance, and pictures can be hung. . . .

The large room on the left can be made to serve the purpose of several rooms by means of a *movable screen*. By shifting this rolling screen from one part of the room to another, two apartments are always available, of any desired size within the limits of the large room. One side of the screen fronts what may be used as the parlor or sitting-room; the other side is arranged for bedroom conveniences. . . . The front side [is] covered first with strong canvas, stretched and nailed on. Over this is pasted panel-paper, and the upper part is made to resemble an ornamental cornice by fresco-paper. Pictures can be hung in the panels, or be pasted on and varnished with white varnish. . . . The back or inside of the movable screen [is] toward the part of the room used as the bedroom. On one side, and at the top and bottom, it has shelves with *shelf-boxes*, which are cheaper and better than drawers, and much preferred by those using them. . . .

This screen must be so high as nearly to reach the ceiling, in order to prevent it from overturning. It is to fill the width of the room, except two feet on each side. A projecting cleat or strip, reaching nearly to the top of the screen, three inches wide, is to be screwed to the front sides, on which light frame doors are to be hung, covered with canvas and panel-paper like the front of the screen. The inside of these doors is furnished with hooks for clothing, for which the projection makes room. The whole screen is to be eighteen inches deep at the top and two feet deep at the base, giving a solid foundation. It is moved on four wooden rollers, one foot long and four inches in diameter. The pivots of the rollers and the parts where there is friction must be rubbed with hard soap, and then a child can move the whole easily.

A curtain is to be hung across the whole interior of the screen by rings, on a strong wire. The curtain should be in three parts, with lead or large nails in the hems to keep it in place. The wood-work must be put together with screws, as the screen is too large to pass through a door. . . .

The expense of the screen, where lumber averages $4 a hundred, and carpenter labor $3 a day, would be about $30, and the two couches about $6. The material for covering might be cheap and yet pretty. A woman with these directions, and a son or husband who would use plane and saw, could thus secure much additional room, and also what amounts to two bureaus, two large trunks, one large wardrobe, and a wash-stand, for less than $20—the mere cost of materials. The screen and couches can be so arranged as to have one room serve first as a large and airy sleeping-room; then, in the morning, it may be used as sitting-room one side of the screen, and break-fast-room the other; and lastly, through the day it can be made a large parlor on the front side, and a sewing or retiring-room the other side. The needless spaces usually devoted to kitchen, entries, halls, back-stairs, pantries, store-rooms, and closets, by this method would be used in adding to the size of the large room, so variously used by day and by night.

Figure 11 is an enlarged plan of the kitchen and stove-room. The chimney and stove-room are contrived to ventilate the whole house, by a mode exhibited in another chapter.

Between the two rooms glazed sliding-doors, passing each other, serve to shut out heat and smells from the kitchen. The sides of the stove-room must be lined with shelves; those on the side by the cellar stairs, to be one foot wide, and eighteen inches apart; on the other side, shelves may be narrower, eight inches wide and nine inches apart. Boxes with lids, to receive stove utensils, must be placed near the stove.

On these shelves, and in the closet and boxes, can be placed every material used for cooking, all the table and cooking utensils, and all the articles used in house work, and yet much spare room will be left. The cook's galley in a steamship has every article and utensil used in cooking for two hundred persons, in a space not larger than this stove-room, and so arranged

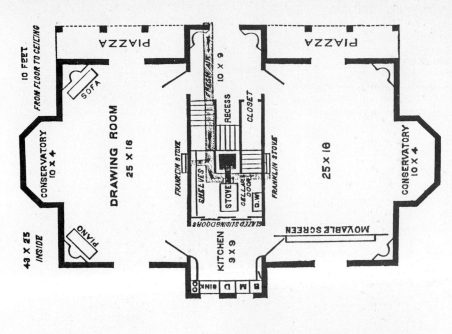

Figure 10. Ground floor plan, figure 1 from Beecher and Stowe, *New American Woman's Home*, p. 26.

Figure 9. "A Christian Home," from Catharine E. Beecher and Harriet Beecher Stowe, *The American Woman's Home*, New York, 1869, p. 23.

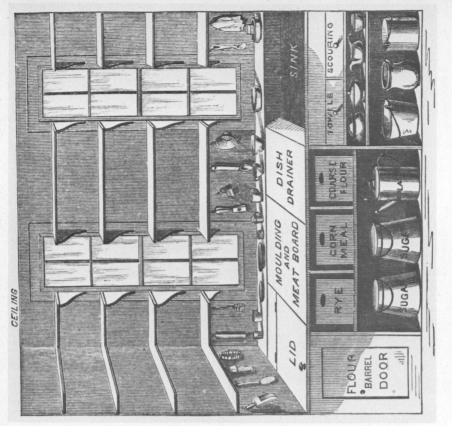

Figure 12. **Kitchen detail, figure 13 from Beecher and Stowe,** *American Woman's Home,* p. 34.

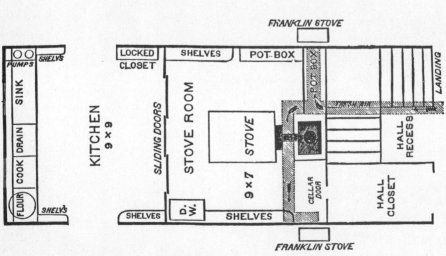

Figure 11. **Enlarged detail of utility kitchen core on ground floor, from Beecher and Stowe,** *American Woman's Home,* p.33.

that with one or two steps the cook can reach all he uses.

In contrast to this, in most large houses, the table furniture, the cooking materials and utensils, the sink, and the eating-room, are at such distances apart, that half the time and strength is employed in walking back and forth to collect and return the articles used.

Figure 12 is an enlarged plan of the sink and cooking form. Two windows make a better circulation of air in warm weather, by having one open at top and the other at the bottom, while the light is better adjusted for working, in case of weak eyes.

The flour-barrel just fills the closet; which has a door for admission, and a lid to raise when used. Beside it, is the form for cooking, with a moulding-board laid on it; one side used for preparing vegetables and meat, and the other for moulding bread. The sink has two pumps for well and for rain-water—one having a forcing power to throw water into the reservoir in the garret, which supplies the water-closet and bath-room. On the other side of the sink is the dish-drainer, with a ledge on the edge next the sink, to hold the dishes, and grooves cut to let the water drain into the sink. It has hinges, so that it can either rest on the cook-form or be turned over and cover the sink. Under the sink are shelf-boxes placed on two shelves run into grooves, with other grooves above and below, so that one may move the shelves and increase or diminish the spaces between. The shelf-boxes can be used for scouring-materials, dish-towels, and dish-cloths; also to hold bowls for bits of butter, fats, etc. Under these two shelves is room for two pails, and a jar for soap-grease.

Under the cook-form are shelves and shelf-boxes for unbolted wheat, corn-meal, rye, etc. Beneath these, for white and brown sugar, are wooden can-pails, which are the best articles in which to keep these constant necessities. Beside them is the tin molasses-can with a tight, movable cover, and a cork in the spout. This is much better than a jug for molasses, and also for vinegar and oil, being easier to clean and to handle. Other articles and implements for cooking can be arranged on or under the shelves at the side and front. . . .

Figure 13 is the second or attic story. The main objection to attic rooms is their warmth in summer, owing to the heated roof. This is prevented by so enlarging the closets each side that their walls meet the ceiling under the garret floor, thus excluding all the roof. In the bed-chambers, corner dressing-tables, instead of projecting bureaus, save much space for use, and give a handsome form and finish to the room. In the bath-room must be the opening to the garret, and a step-ladder to reach it. A reservoir in the garret, supplied by a forcing-pump in the cellar or at the sink, must be well supported by timbers, and the plumbing must be well done, or much annoyance will ensue.

The large chambers are to be lighted by large windows or glazed sliding-doors, opening upon the balcony. A roof can be put over the balcony and its sides inclosed by windows, and the chamber extend into it, and be thus much enlarged.

The water-closets must have the latest improvements for safe discharge, and there will be no trouble. They cost no more than an out-door building, and save from the most disagreeable house-labor.

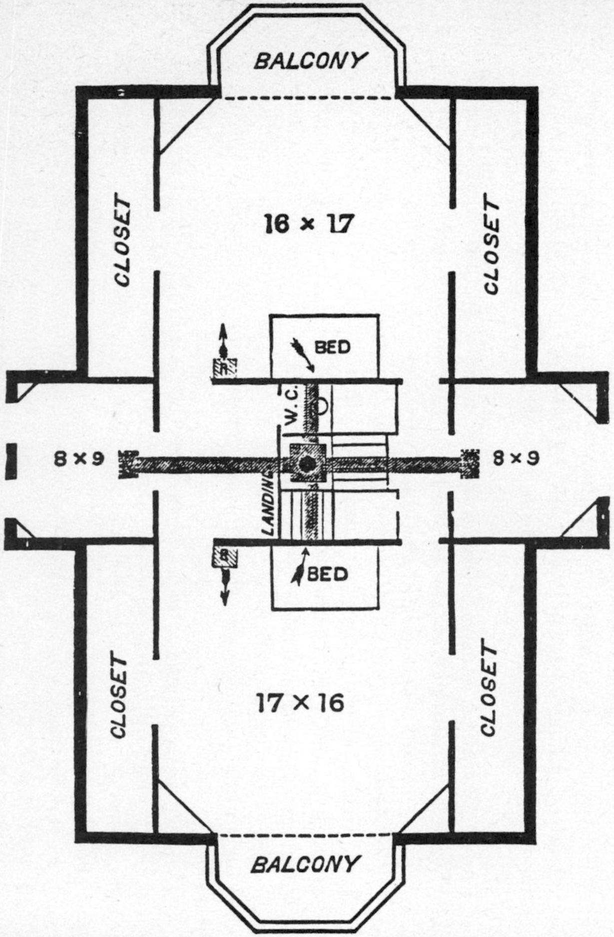

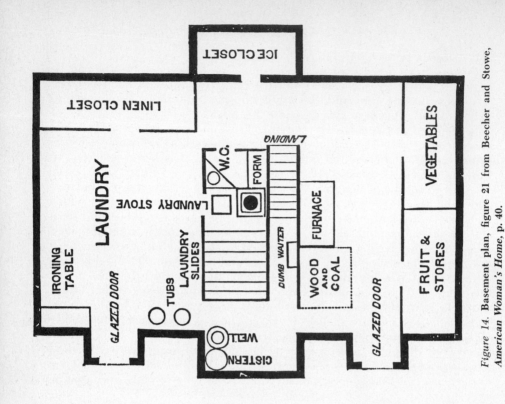

Figure 14. Basement plan, figure 21 from Beecher and Stowe, *American Woman's Home*, p. 40.

Figure 13. Second floor plan, figure 17 from Beecher and Stowe, *American Woman's Home*, p. 37.

A great improvement, called *earth-closets*, will probably take the place of water-closets to some extent; though at present the water is the more convenient. A description of the earth-closet will be given in another chapter relating to tenement-houses for the poor in large cities.

The method of ventilating all the chambers, and also the cellar, will be described in another chapter. . . .

Figure 14 is the basement. It has the floor and sides plastered, and is lighted with glazed doors. A form is raised close by the cellar stairs, for baskets, pails, and tubs. Here, also, the refrigerator can be placed, or, what is better, an ice-closet can be made, as designated in the illustration. The floor of the basement must be an inclined plan toward a drain, and be plastered with water-lime. The wash-tubs have plugs in the bottom to let off water, and cocks and pipes over them bringing cold water from the reservoir in the garret and hot water from the laundry stove. This saves much heavy labor of emptying tubs and carrying water.

The laundry closet has a stove for heating irons and also a kettle on top for heating water. Slides or clothes-frames are made to draw out to receive wet clothes, and then run into the closet to dry. This saves health as well as time and money and the clothes are as white as when dried outdoors.

The wood-work of the house, for doors, windows, etc., should be oiled chestnut, butternut, whitewood, and pine. This is cheaper, handsomer, and more easy to keep clean than painted wood.

In Figure 10 are planned two conservatories, and few understand their value in the training of the young. They provide soil, in which children, through the winter months, can be starting seeds and plants for their gardens and raising valuable, tender plants. Every child should cultivate flowers and fruits to sell and to give away, and thus be taught to learn the value of money and to practice both economy and benevolence.

According to the calculation of a house-carpenter, in a place where the *average* price of lumber is $4 a hundred, and carpenter work $3 a day, such a house can be built for $1600. For those practicing the closest economy, two small families could occupy it, by dividing the kitchen, and yet have room enough. Or one large room and the chamber over it can be left till increase of family and means require enlargement.

A strong horse and carryall, with a cow, garden, vineyard, and orchard, on a few acres, would secure all the substantial comforts found in great establishments, without the trouble of ill-qualified servants.

And if the parents and children were united in the daily labors of the house, garden, and fruit culture, such thrift, health, and happiness would be secured as is but rarely found among the rich.

Let us suppose a colony of cultivated and Christian people, having abundant wealth, who now are living as the wealthy usually do, emigrating to some of the beautiful Southern uplands, where are rocks, hills, valleys, and mountains as picturesque as those of New-England, where the thermometer but rarely reaches 90° in summer, and in winter as rarely sinks below freezing-point, so that outdoor labor goes on all the year, where the fertile soil is easily worked, where rich tropical fruits and flowers abound, where cotton and silk can be raised by children around their home, where the produce of vineyards and orchards finds steady markets by railroads ready made; suppose such a colony, with a central church and school-room, library, hall for sports, and a common laundry, (taking the most trying part of domestic labor from each house,)—suppose each family to train the children to labor with the hands as a healthful and honorable duty; suppose all this, which is perfectly practicable, would not the enjoyment of this life by increased, and also abundant treasures be laid up in heaven, by using the wealth thus economized in diffusing similar enjoyments and culture among the poor, ignorant, and neglected ones in desolated sections where many now are perishing for want of such Christian example and influences?

XXXVI

WARMING AND VENTILATION

. . . The most successful mode before the public, both for warming and ventilation, is that of Lewis Leeds, who was employed by government to ventilate the military hospitals and also the treasury building at Washington. This method has been adopted in various school-houses, and also by A. T. Stewart in his hotel for women in New York City. The Leeds plan embraces the mode of heating both by radiation and convection, very much resembling the open fireplace in operation, and yet securing great economy. It is modeled strictly after the mode adopted by the Creator in warming and ventilating the earth, the home of his great earthly family. It aims to have a passage of pure air through every room, as the breezes pass over the hills, and to have a method of warming chiefly by radiation, as the earth is warmed by the sun. In addition to this, the air is to be provided with moisture, as it is supplied outdoors by exhalations from the earth and its trees and plants.

The mode of accomplishing this is by placing coils of steam, or hot water pipes, under windows, which warm the parlor walls and furniture, partly by radiation, and partly by the air warmed on the heated surfaces of the coils. At the same time, by regulating registers, or by simply opening the lower part of the window, the pure air, guarded from immediate entrance into the room, is admitted directly upon the coils, so that it is partially warmed before it reaches the person: and thus cold drafts are prevented. Then the vitiated air is drawn off through registers both at the top and bottom of the room, opening into a heated exhausting flue, through which the constantly ascending current of warm air carries it off. These heated coils are often used for warming houses without any arrangement for carrying off the vitiated air, when, of course, their peculiar usefulness is gone.

The moisture may be supplied by a broad vessel placed on or close to the heated coils, giving a large surface for evaporation. When rooms are warmed chiefly by radiated heat, the air can be borne much cooler than in rooms warmed by hot-air furnaces, just as a person in the radiating sun can bear much cooler air than in the shade. A time will come when walls and floors will be contrived to radiate heat instead of absorbing it from the occupants of houses, as is generally the case at the present time, and then all can breathe pure and cool air.

We are now prepared to examine more in detail the modes of warming and ventilation employed in the dwellings planned for this work.

In doing this, it should be remembered that the aim is not to give plans of houses to suit the architectural taste or the domestic convenience of persons who intend to keep several servants, and care little whether they breathe pure or bad air, nor of persons who do not wish to educate their children to manual industry or to habits of close economy.

On the contrary, the aim is, first, to secure a house in which every room shall be perfectly ventilated both day and night, and that too without the watchful care and constant attention and intelligence needful in houses not provided with a proper and successful mode of ventilation.

The next aim is, to arrange the conveniences of domestic labor so as to save time, and also to render such work less repulsive than it is made by common methods, so that children can be trained to love house-work. And lastly, economy of expense in house-building is sought. These things should be borne in mind in examining the plans of this work.

In the Cottage plan, (Figure 10) the pure air for rooms on the ground floor is to be introduced by a wooden conductor one foot square, running under the floor from the front door to the stove-room; with cross branches to the two large rooms. The pure air passes through this, protected outside by wire netting, and delivered inside through registers in each room, as indicated in Figure 10.

In case open Franklin stoves are used in the large rooms, the pure air from the conductor should enter behind them, and thus be partially warmed. The vitiated air is carried off at the bottom of the room through the open stoves, and also at the top by a register opening into a conductor to the exhausting warm-air shaft, which, it will be remembered, is the square chimney, containing the iron pipe which receives the kitchen stove-pipe. The stove-room receives pure air from the conductor, and sends off impure air and the smells of cooking by a register opening directly into the exhausting shaft; while its hot air and smoke, passing through the iron pipe, heat the air of the shaft, and produce the exhausting current. . . .

The large chambers on the second floor (Figure 13) have pure air conducted from the stove-room through registers that can be closed if the heat or smells of cooking are unpleasant. The air in the stove-room will always be moist from the water of the stove boiler.

The small chambers have pure air admitted from windows sunk at top half an inch; and the warm, vitiated air is conducted by a register in the ceiling which opens into a conductor to the exhausting warm-air shaft at the centre of the house, as shown in Figure 13.

The basement or cellar is ventilated by an opening into the exhausting air shaft, to remove impure air, and a small opening over each glazed door to admit pure air. The doors open out into a "well," or recess, excavated in the earth before the cellar, for the admission of light and air, neatly bricked up and whitewashed. The doors are to be made entirely of strong, thick glass sashes, and this will give light enough for laundry work; the tubs and ironing-table being placed close to the glazed door. The floor must be plastered with water-lime, and the walls and ceiling be whitewashed, which will add reflected light to the room. There will thus be no need of other windows, and the house need not be raised above the ground. Several cottages have been built thus, so that the ground floors and conservatories are nearly on the same level; and all agree that they are pleasanter than when raised higher.

The preceding remarks illustrate the advantages of the cottage plan in respect to ventilation. The economy of the mode of warming next demands attention. In the first place, it should be noted that the chimney being at the centre of the house, no heat is lost by its radiation through outside walls into open air, as is the case with all fireplaces and grates that have their backs and flues joined to an outside wall.

In this plan, all the radiated heat from the stove serves to warm the walls of adjacent rooms in cold weather; while in the warm season, the non-conducting summer casings of the stove send all the heat not used in cooking either into the exhausting warm-air shaft or into the central cast-iron pipe. In addition to this, the sliding doors of the stove-room (which should be only six feet high, meeting the partition coming from the ceiling) can be opened in cool days, and then the heat from the stove would temper the rooms each side of the kitchen. In hot weather, they could be kept closed except when the stove is used, and then opened only for a short time. The Franklin stoves in the large room would give the radiating warmth and cheerful blaze of an open fire, while radiating heat also from all their surfaces. In cold weather, the air of the large chambers could be tempered by registers admitting warm air from the stove-room, which would always be sufficiently moistened by evaporation from the stationary boiler. The conservatories in winter, protected from frost by double sashes, would contribute agreeable moisture to the larger rooms. In case the size of a family required more rooms, another story could be ventilated and warmed by the same mode, with little additional expense.

16　J. Bogardus, Cast Iron Buildings* *1856*

James Bogardus (1800–1874) was not himself a fabricator of iron, as was his counterpart and neighbor in New York, Daniel Badger, nor was he actually the author of the volume that carries his name on the title page; on the following page he credits John W. Thompson, "in justice to him as the author." Bogardus was an inventor and manufacturer of precision instruments, but about 1840, when he became aware of the potential of cast iron as a building material, he became an avid promoter and entrepreneur. What Bogardus stressed in his pamphlet was the erection of a com-

*Cast Iron Buildings: Their Construction and Advantages, by James Bogardus, C. E., Architect in Iron (New York, 1856), pp. 1–14.

plete iron building frame, its parts tied rigidly together.† Such a system, he correctly foresaw, made possible buildings of ever greater height. Although his own office building (actually constructed in 1850 and *not*, as he asserts, the first iron building ever constructed, may not have had such a frame, Bogardus did use this technique for a fire observation tower, 1851, and the McCullough Shot Tower, 1855, both in New York. His most ambitious project was a gigantic cast iron coliseum, 1,200 feet in diameter, to house the New York World's Fair of 1853. At its center was to be a tower of 300 feet, a mast carrying rods sweeping out in catenary curves supporting a sheet iron roof. It was to be fabricated of standardized parts so as to be dismantled and sold off later.

So much that is erroneous has been said and written concerning Iron Architecture, and so little that is authentic, that but few are yet acquainted with either its merits or its history. To furnish correct information on this important subject is the object of this pamphlet.

The first complete cast-iron edifice ever erected in America, or in the world, was that of the inventor, James Bogardus—being his manufactory on the corner of Centre and Duane streets, New-York. Its foundation was laid in May, 1848: but a cast-iron model of it had been freely exhibited to visitors at his factory, since the summer of 1847. . . . Since that period, he has erected many structures of the same description, not only in New-York, but also in various other cities, such as Philadelphia, Baltimore, Washington, and San Francisco; and persons capable of passing judgment on their merits, have, after a careful investigation, been profoundly convinced of their superiority—that they alone embrace the true principles of safety, durability, and economy. And the inventor himself firmly believes, that, were the public fully aware of its great advantages, cast-iron would be employed, for superior buildings, in every case, in preference to granite, marble, freestone, or brick. . . .

This first cast-iron building, Mr. Bogardus's present factory, is of five stories, and was designed to be a model of its kind. Since its erection, it has not been difficult to convince any one who will take the trouble to examine it, that *such buildings combine unequalled advantages of ornament, strength, durability, and economy; whilst they are, at the same time, absolutely secure against danger from fire, lightning, and an imperfect foundation.*

Whatever be the advantages of cast-iron as a building material, they would be all unavailable, were they not accompanied with stability of structure. But, simple as this problem now appears to be, had it not been hitherto esteemed impracticable, it would not have been left for Mr. Bogardus to solve it. As it is on this point, mainly, that his merit as its inventor depends, a short description is subjoined; and the reader should remember, that the greater the simplicity of an·invention, it is the more meritorious.

The cast-iron frame of the building rests upon sills which are cast in

† See Turpin Bannister, "Bogardus Revisited," *Journal, Society of Architectural Historians* 15 (December 1956), 12–22, and 16 (March 1957), 11–19.

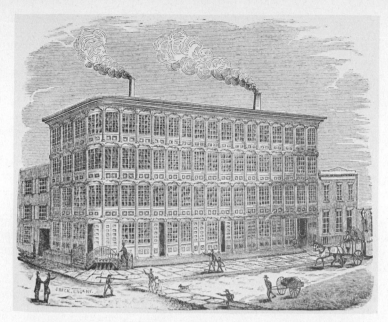

Figure 15. James Bogardus, fabricator, Bogardus Factory Building, Centre and Duane Streets, New York, N.Y., 1848–49, dismantled 1859; from James Bogardus, *Cast Iron Building . . .* , New York, 1856.

Figure 16. The Bogardus Building with elements "removed" to illustrate the strength of the cast iron frame, from Bogardus, *Cast Iron Buildings.*

sections of any required length. These sills, by the aid of the planing machine, are made of equal thickness, so as not to admit of any variation throughout the whole: they are laid upon a stone foundation, and are fastened together with bolts. On the joints of the sills stand the columns or pilasters, all exactly equal in height, and having both their ends faced in a turning lathe so as to make them perfectly plane and parallel; and each column is firmly bolted to the ends of the two adjacent sills on which it rests. These columns support another series of sills, fascias, or cornices, in sections, of the same length as the former, but of greater height according to the design of the architect: they are separately made of equal dimensions by the planing machine, and are bolted to the columns, and to each other, in the same manner as before. On these again stands another row of columns, and on these columns rests another series of fascias or cornices; and so on, continually, for any required number of stories. The spaces between the columns are filled up with windows, doors, and pannels, which may be ornamented to suit any taste.

It may be here remarked that, in certain cases, the first layer of sills may be dispensed with altogether; and also that, immediately before uniting the pieces, it is the practice of Mr. Bogardus to apply a coating of paint to those parts which are designed to be in contract with others; thus rendering the joints absolutely air-tight.

From this description it is plain, that the separate parts are so united as to form one stable whole, equivalent in strength to a single piece of cast-iron. Hence, such a structure must be far more firm and solid than one composed of numerous parts, united only by a feeble bond of mortar. On this account it may be raised to a height vastly greater than by any other known means, without impairing its stability in the least; and, were all the columns of any story removed or destroyed by violence, except the four corner ones, or others equivalent in position, the building would still remain firm as an arch; and the greater its height, the firmer it would be.

It is also plain that such a building may be erected with extraordinary facility, and at all seasons of the year. No plumb is needed; no square, no level. As fast as the pieces can be handled, they may be adjusted and secured by the most ignorant workman: the building cannot fail to be perpendicular and firm. Wedges, mortices, and chairs, are all ignored: they are the subsequent inventions of interested individuals, in order to evade the patent; and to render less dangerous, or less apparent, their imperfect and unstable joints. Strength is secured in the simplest and surest way, and at the least possible expense.

It also follows that, a building once erected, it may be taken to pieces with the same facility and despatch, without injuring or destroying any of its parts, and then re-erected elsewhere with the same perfection as at first. The size and form of the pieces greatly favor their portability, which has enabled Mr. Bogardus to construct them in New-York, and export them to distant cities. This quality is of the greatest importance; for it renders every cast-iron building not only a present, but a permanent addition to our national wealth. Who can estimate the annual saving to the city of New-York alone, were all its buildings of this character? . . .

Cast-iron does not indeed possess the character of wrought iron for resisting tensile strain, but it is far superior to it in resisting a crushing force; and it is vastly superior to granite, marble, freestone, or brick, in resisting any kind of force or strain. It may, however, for building purposes, be considered crushing-proof. According to the tables of our best authorities, which have been often verified, a cubic inch of cast-iron can sustain a weight of eighty tons. Now, since a cubic foot weighs four hundred and fifty-five lbs., it follows, by an easy computation, that a column of cast-iron must be ten miles in height, before it will crush itself by its own weight. It will be readily seen that the joint invented by Mr. Bogardus, effectually secures the whole of this important quality; and that thereby he would be enabled to erect a tower or building many times the height of any other edifice in the world, which would be perfectly safe to visitors, in the face of storm or tempest, though they filled it throughout every story, to its utmost capacity.

The great strength of cast-iron, enables us also to enlarge the interior of a house, by lessening the thickness of its walls; a very important item in this city, where ground is of great value.

Cast-iron also possesses the quality of great durability.—Unlike wrought iron and steel, it is not subject to rapid oxydation and decay, by exposure to the atmosphere. And whatever tendency it may have of slowly imbibing oxygen in a moist atmosphere, can easily be prevented by a proper coating of paint, and thus, at a very small expense, be made to endure a thousand years, unaffected by the winds or the weather. On account of this quality, cast-iron houses do not tax their owners with the cost and the trouble of repairs, which are incident to other buildings, in consequence of their perishable character.

Another recommendation of cast-iron is, "its happy adaptability to ornament and decoration." Were a single ornament only required, it might perhaps be executed as cheaply in marble or freestone: but where a multiplicity of the same is needed, they can be cast in iron at an expense not to be named in comparison, even with that of wood; and with this advantage, that they will retain their original fullness and sharpness of outline long after those in stone have decayed and disappeared. Fluted columns and Corinthian capitals, the most elaborate carvings, and the richest designs, which the architect may have dreamed of, but did not dare represent in his plans, may thus be reproduced for little more than the cost of ordinary castings. Ornamental architecture—which, with our limited means, is apt to be tawdry, because incomplete—thus becomes practicable; and its general introduction would greatly tend to elevate the public taste for the beautiful, and to purify and gratify one of the finest qualities of the human mind. . . .

Some have asserted, and it is generally believed, that, as iron is so good a conductor of heat, it would expand and contract so much by the changes of temperature, as to dislocate its joints in a short time, and render the building unsafe. It has been already mentioned, that the assumed impossibility of forming a safe and economical joint for massive structures of cast-iron, was the probable cause why such buildings had not been earlier introduced. It may now be added, that the supposed necessity of making some provision for the expansion and contraction of the metal, was the probable reason why efforts were not made to overcome this difficulty. . . .

We do not say that cast-iron is without expansibility: we simply assert

Figure 17. **Corinthian capital design from Bogardus,** *Cast Iron Buildings.* **As pointed out in the original caption, such a design would be "far too costly for marble," but "once execut- ed for a pattern, may be rapidly, and cheaply reproduced in iron, with the greatest perfec- tion; and will retain, for ages, its original sharpness of outline."**

that the temperature of our climate, throughout its utmost range, from the greatest cold to the greatest heat, exerts upon it no appreciable effect.

A complete proof of this assertion may be had, by examining any of the numerous cast-iron structures, erected by Mr. Bogardus. His factory building has now, for a number of years, been exposed to every change of atmospheric temperature without, and to the best of steam boilers and the operations of a steam engine and heavy machinery within—and, it should be observed, his engine of twenty-five horse power is placed on the second story, purposely to show the great stability of the building—and yet, so perfect are all its joints, that the blade of a lancet cannot be thrust into one of them; nor can there be discovered, by continual and close observation, where its walls adjoin the neighboring houses, the displacement of a single grain of dust. . . .

It is desirable in most cases, that the floorings and partitions should be . . . fire-proof; so that, should a fire occur, it may be confined to the room in which it originated. This may be accomplished by various well known devices, extensively practiced in Europe, but too much neglected in our country. Mr. Bogardus has also devised for this purpose, and secured by letters patent, a plan of iron flooring, to be supported by Cooper's iron beams, or by his own new sectional truss girders, which he is now taking measures to patent, and which may be seen in use in the buildings of Messrs. Harper & Brothers, the well known publishers. These girders, besides having other advantages, can sustain a heavier load than any others of the same weight yet known, and are therefore more economical. And to those who prefer a wooden floor, Mr. Bogardus offers another plan, in which the flooring rests upon the aforesaid truss girders, in combination with a substratum of solid brick-work, and a net-work of iron wire as a substitute for laths. Of this latter plan a model is now on exhibition at his office. . . .

Every style of architecture, and every design the artist can conceive, however plain or however complicated, can be executed exactly in cast-iron; and, in consequence of its having greater strength than any other known building material, it furnishes us with new ideas of the proportional fitness of parts, and thus opens a wide field for new orders of architecture. Hitherto its use has been confined to factories, stores, lighthouses, and bell towers; but we hope the day is not distant when we shall see it in our city halls, our state houses, our churches, and their spires.

17 S. G. Fisher on Railroads and Suburbs* *1859*

The introduction of iron as a structural building material was exceeded in its impact only by the revolution in transportation caused by the use of iron in railroads. Beginning with the first American rails laid near Baltimore, Maryland, in 1828, a network connecting all major points throughout the eastern states was completed within two decades. Not only were bulky grains, goods, and ores now moved more quickly, masses of people began to enjoy a maneuverability heretofore the privilege of a wealthy few. The move of the middle class to the suburbs, although not yet an exodus, began as soon as railroads made possible easy connections between the city center and outlying districts. The development of the first suburb in which the landscape was specifically enhanced to augment "nature" to contrast with the "artificiality" of city life (Llewellyn Park, West Orange, New Jersey) was dependent on the railroad, in this instance the Erie Railroad.†

The growing interest in "villa and cottage life," already noted by Gervase Wheeler in *Homes for People*, is described in this entry from the diary of Sidney George Fisher, a resident of Philadelphia who greatly desired to move to the country, as had his brother Henry and cousin Joshua Fisher. The latter's country house had grounds landscaped by A. J. Downing, and Henry Fisher engaged Wheeler to design his country place and Downing to landscape his grounds. Sidney Fisher's small legal practice never brought him the means to establish a country seat comparable to the one Henry's thriving business career had made possible, but in 1855, when worsening gout ended his legal practice, through the kindness of Henry and brother-in-law Harry Ingersoll, Sidney Fisher was given the use of the Ingersoll family house, "Forest Hill" in Germantown, where he lived the remainder of his life.‡ References in his diary make it apparent that Fisher had made the acquaintance not only of Downing—because of Downing's landscaping work for his relatives—but also of James Miller McKim, father of future architect Charles Follen McKim. The elder McKim shared Fisher's fondness for country life and had moved his family to Germantown in 1855. A decade later, when a shift in his professional life took Miller McKim to New York, the family resettled in Llewellyn Park, where they moved into the house built by Alexander Jackson Davis for painter Edward W. Nicholls.

FROM THE DIARY OF SIDNEY GEORGE FISHER

July 14, 1859 Delightful weather after the rain last night. Therm. 80 to 85. Geo. Blight stopped here some days ago and asked me to go with him to

---

Pennsylvania Magazine of History 87 (April 1963), 206–07.

†For a historical account of this development, see the *Concise History*, pp. 104–07; Jane B. Davies, "Llewellyn Park in West Orange, New Jersey," *Antiques* 107 (January 1975), 142–58; and Richard Guy Wilson, "Idealism and the Origin of the First American Suburb; Llewellyn Park, New Jersey," *The American Art Journal* 11 (October 1979), 79–90.

‡"The Diary of Sidney George Fisher," *Pennsylvania Magazine of History* 86 (1962), pp. 49, 319–20.

his farm at Chestnut Hill today to look at the cattle he bought from me last year, before they were sold to the butcher, as he thought them very fine. I agreed and so this morning I drove over to his place at 8, taking Daniel & sending my wagon back. We started at 9 in his wagon. He took me thro one or two streets between his place & Germantown, which I had not seen for many years and which are now lined with cottages & villas, surrounded by neat grounds, trees, shrubbery & flowers, many of them costly & handsome, all comfortable and pretty. They are in every variety of taste and size and there are hundreds of them. The same spectacle is to be seen on every lane near Germantown all the way up to Chestnut Hill, and not around German-town only, but at Frankford, West Philada., Chester, along the Delaware, over in Jersey, everywhere, in short, within ten miles of the city where a railroad runs. They are the result of railroads which enable anyone to enjoy the pleasures of country life and at the same time attend to business in town. They are owned by shopkeepers, manufacturers, merchants, &c, and their beauty and general good taste and the care and attention lavished on them show what sources of enjoyment they are and how superior is the life they promote to that of the streets. Fresh air, space, trees, flowers, privacy, a convenient & tasteful house, can now be had for the same expence as a narrow & confined dwelling on a pavement, surrounded by brick walls & all the unpleasant sights & sounds of a crowded town. The advantages are so obvious that this villa & cottage life has become quite a passion and is pro-ducing a complete revolution in our habits. It is dispersing the people of the city over the surrounding country, introducing thus among them, ventila-tion, cleanliness, space, healthful pursuits, and the influences of natural beauty, the want of which are the sources of so much evil, moral & physical, in large towns.

The passenger cars as they are absurdly called, or horse railroads, have given a great impulse to this movement. They are scarcely more than two years old, yet they have become a vast system already. They occupy nearly all the principal streets & traverse the city in every direction and are rapidly extending into the country. They are crowded with passengers & pay large dividends. They operate in two ways to disperse the population over the country, by making the streets inconvenient for all other vehicles and by offering cheap means of reaching the country. It is very unpleasant to drive the streets now because of the rails, so that private carriages have become useless whilst the cars, comfortable & easy, offer to those who live in the country a pleasant way of going to town at all hours & in any weather at trifling expense. One is now constructing on the Germantown road and will be in running order in a few weeks. It spoils the road for driving, but all the people in Germantown can by it go to town for 10 cents every 10 minutes. One consequence of this is the immense improvement of the country & rise in the value of property. In Germantown, they have now gas & water from waterworks in every house. Shops & mechanics follow the rich population of the villas, and soon every luxury of a city can be had in the neighborhood. All the families who own much land here have been enriched, and as the neighborhood was composed of farms only a few years ago, these are very numerous. Some of the estates are immense.

18   H. Greenough on Function in American Architecture* *1843, 1852*

Concurrent with the rise of industry in the United States, critics began to call for clarity of function and truthfulness of expression in American architecture. Ralph Waldo Emerson was among the earliest to make this appeal (see chapter 19), but at almost the same time sculptor Horatio Greenough (1805–52) began to develop a similar argument. The philosophic notion of "organic form" seems to have been passed from Coleridge and Emerson to Greenough via the Romantic painter Washington Allston. Such an expression, however, was seldom evident in Greenough's own literary, anecdotal marble sculpture, best represented by his monumental neoclassical seminude *George Washington*, 1832–41. His writings, on the other hand, developed a more radical aesthetic. The following excerpts from his *Travels . . .* (1852), were published in *The Democratic Review* in 1843. The concept of organic beauty had been discussed earlier with Emerson when the essayist visited Greenough in Florence during 1833, but Emerson had not read the sculptor's development of the idea until contacted by Greenough in December, 1851. In a letter, Greenough wrote: "I broached a theory 10 years since (1843) in the *Democratic Review*—a theory of structure—My occupations since that time have prevented my doing more than to confirm myself in that theory and ripen it. I find this country in such want of an application, practical, immediate and thorough-going of that theory—I find also in the ships—the carriages and engines, a partial illustration of the doctrine and a *glorious* foretaste of what structure can be in this country in 10 years time. . . ." Emerson enthusiastically responded the next month that he had just been reading the work of Edward Lacy Garbett and John Ruskin's *Seven Lamps* and *Stones of Venice*, "and I was proud to find that the doctrine they urge with so much energy, you had been teaching long already. . . . Well, joy & the largest fullest unfolding to your theory!" † Because of his desire for expression of function and use, Greenough criticized the outright replication of Greek temples; those who designed carriages and yachts, he argued, "are nearer to Athens. . . than they who bend the Greek temple to every use. I contend for Greek principles, not Greek things." ‡ These sentiments were paralleled by those of Arthur D. Gilman, who similarly criticized the Greek Revival in the *North American Review*, in April, 1844. Gilman, however, not only proposed turning to the Italian Renaissance, a more flexible idiom, but he also wrote perceptively of Upjohn's rising Trinity Church, for in Gothic architecture, he believed, "the great *aesthetical* principles of building have been fully carried out." §

*Horatio Greenough (pseudonym Horace Bender), *The Travels, Observations, and Experience of a Yankee Stonecutter* (New York, 1852), pp. 131–46, 197–213. "American Architecture," the first section of the two reproduced here, was first published separately in *The United States Magazine, and Democratic Review* 13 (August 1843), pp. 206–10.

†H. Greenough to R. W. Emerson, December 28, 1851, in Nathalia Wright, "Ralph Waldo Emerson and Horatio Greenough," *Harvard Library Bulletin* 12 (Winter 1958), pp. 98–100; Emerson to Greenough, January 7, 1852, in *The Letters of Ralph Waldo Emerson*, ed. Ralph L. Rusk (New York, 1939), 3:121–22.

‡Greenough, *Travels*, p. 33.

§Arthur D. Gilman, "Architecture in the United States," *The North American Review* 58 (April 1844), pp. 436–80.

Chapter IX

AMERICAN ARCHITECTURE

We have heard the learned in matters relating to art express the opinion that these United States are destined to form a new style of architecture. Remembering that a vast population, rich in material and guided by the experience, the precepts, and the models of the Old World, was about to erect durable structures for every function of civilized life, we also cherished the hope that such a combination would speedily be formed.

We forgot that though the country was young, yet the people were old, that as Americans we have no childhood, no half-fabulous, legendary wealth, no misty, cloud-enveloped background. We forgot that we had not unity of religious belief, nor unity of origin; that our territory, extending from the white bear to the alligator, made our occupations dissimilar, our character and tastes various. We forgot that the Republic had leaped full-grown and armed to the teeth from the brain of her parent, and that a hammer had been the instrument of delivery. We forgot that reason had been the dry nurse of the giant offspring, and had fed her from the beginning with the stout bread and meat of fact; that every wry face the bantling ever made had been daguerreotyped, and all her words and deeds printed and labeled away in the pigeonholes of official bureaus.

Reason can dissect, but cannot originate; she can adopt, but cannot create; she can modify, but cannot find. Give her but a cockboat, and she will elaborate a line-of-battle ship; give her but a beam with its wooden tooth, and she turns out the patent plow. She is not young, and when her friends insist upon the phenomena of youth, then is she least attractive. She can initiate the flush of the young cheek, but where is the flash of the young eye? She buys the teeth—alas! she cannot buy the breath of childhood. The puny cathedral of Broadway,[1] like an elephant dwindled to the size of a dog, measures her yearning for Gothic sublimity, while the roar of the Astor House, and the mammoth vase of the great reservoir, shows how she works when she feels at home, and is in earnest.

The mind of this country has never been seriously applied to the subject of building. Intently engaged in matters of more pressing importance, we have been content to receive our notions of architecture as we have received the fashion of our garments, and the form of our entertainments, from Europe. In our eagerness to appropriate we have neglected to adapt, to distinguish—nay, to understand. We have built small Gothic temples of wood, and have omitted all ornaments for economy, unmindful that size, material, and ornament are the elements of effect in that style of building. Captivated by the classic symmetry of the Athenian models, we have sought to bring the Parthenon into our streets, to make the temple of Theseus work in our towns. We have shorn them of their lateral colonnades, let them down from their dignified platform, pierced their walls for light, and, instead of the storied relief and the eloquent statue which enriched the frieze, and

---

[1] Apparently a reference to Richard Upjohn's Trinity Church, New York, N.Y., 1839–46.—Ed.

graced the pediment, we have made our chimney tops to peer over the broken profile, and tell by their rising smoke of the traffic and desecration of the interior. Still the model may be recognized, some of the architectural features are entire; like the captive king stripped alike of arms and purple, and drudging amid the Helots of a capital, the Greek temple as seen among us claims pity for its degraded majesty, and attests the barbarian force which has abused its nature, and been blind to its qualities.

If we trace architecture from its perfection, in the days of Pericles, to its manifest decay in the reign of Constantine, we shall find that one of the surest symptoms of decline was the adoption of admired forms and models for purposes not contemplated in their invention. The forum became a temple, the tribunal became a temple, the theatre was turned into a church; nay, the column, that organized member, that subordinate part, set up for itself, usurped unity, and was a monument! The great principles of architecture being once abandoned, correctness gave way to novelty; economy and vainglory associated produced meanness and pretension. Sculpture, too, had waned. The degenerate workmen could no longer match the fragments they sought to mingle, nor copy the originals they only hoped to repeat. The moldering remains of better days frowned contempt upon such impotent efforts, till, in the gradual coming of darkness, ignorance became content, and insensibility ceased to compare.

We say that the mind of this country has never been seriously applied to architecture. True it is that the commonwealth, with that desire of public magnificence which has ever been a leading feature of democracy, has called from the vasty deep of the past the spirits of the Greek, the Roman, and the Gothic styles; but they would not come when she did call to them! The vast cathedral with its ever open portals, towering high above the courts of kings, inviting all men to its cool and fragrant twilight, where the voice of the organ stirs the blood, and the dim-seen visions of saints and martyrs bleed and die upon the canvas amid the echoes of hymning voices and the clouds of frankincense, this architectural embodying of the divine and blessed words "come to me, ye who labor and are heavy laden, and I will give you rest!" demands a sacrifice of what we hold dearest. Its cornerstone must be laid upon the right to judge the claims of the church. The style of Greek architecture as seen in the Greek temple demands the aid of sculpture, insists upon every feature of its original organization, loses its harmony if a note be dropped in the execution, and when so modified as to serve for a customhouse or a bank departs from its original beauty and propriety as widely as the crippled gelding of a hackney coach differs from the bounding and neighing wild horse of the desert. Even where, in the fervor of our faith in shapes, we have sternly adhered to the dictum of another age, and have actually succeeded in securing the entire exterior which echoes the forms of Athens, the pile stands a stranger among us! and receives a respect akin to what we should feel for a fellow citizen in the garb of Greece. It is a make-believe! It is not the real thing! We see the marble capitals; we trace the acanthus leaves of a celebrated model—incredulous *odi*! It is not a temple.

The number and variety of our experiments in building show the dissatisfaction of the public taste with what has been hitherto achieved; the expense at which they have been made proves how strong is the yearning after excellence; the talents and acquirements of the artists whose services have been engaged in them are such as to convince us that the fault lies in the system, not in the men. Is it possible that out of this chaos order can arise? that of these conflicting dialects and jargons a language can be born? When shall we have done with experiments? What refuge is there from the absurdities that have successively usurped the name and functions of architecture? Is it not better to go on with consistency and uniformity in imitation of an admired model than incur the disgrace of other failures? In answering these questions let us remember with humility that all salutary changes are the work of many and of time; but let us encourage experiment at the risk of license rather than submit to an iron rule that begins by sacrificing reason, dignity, and comfort. Let us consult nature, and in the assurance that she will disclose a mine, richer than was ever dreamed of by the Greeks, in art as well as in philosophy. Let us regard as ingratitude to the author of nature the despondent idleness that sits down while one want is unprovided for, one worthy object unattained.

If, as the first step in our search after the great principles of construction, we but observe the skeletons and skins of animals, through all the varieties of beast and bird, of fish and insect, are we not as forcibly struck by their variety as by their beauty? There is no arbitrary law of proportion, no unbending model of form. There is scarce a part of the animal organization which we do not find elongated or shortened, increased, diminished, or suppressed, as the wants of the genus or species dictate, as their exposure or their work may require. The neck of the swan and that of the eagle, however different in character and proportion, equally charm the eye and satisfy the reason. We approve the length of the same member in grazing animals, its shortness in beasts of prey. The horse's shanks are thin, and we admire them; the greyhound's chest is deep, and we cry, beautiful! It is neither the presence nor the absence of this or that part or shape or color that wins our eye in natural objects; it is the consistency and harmony of the parts juxtaposed, the subordination of details to masses, and of masses to the whole.

The law of adaptation is the fundamental law of nature in all structure. So unflinchingly does she modify a type in accordance with a new position, that some philosophers have declared a variety of appearance to be the object aimed at; so entirely does she limit the modification to the demands of necessity, that adherence to one original plan seems, to limited intelligence, to be carried to the very verge of caprice. The domination of arbitrary rules of taste has produced the very counterpart of the wisdom thus displayed in every object around us; we tie up the camel leopard to the rack; we shave the lion, and call him a dog; we strive to bind the unicorn with his band in the furrow, and to make him harrow the valleys after us!

When the savage of the South Sea islands shapes his war club, his first thought is of its use. His first efforts pare the long shaft, and mold the convenient handle; then the heavier end takes gradually the edge that cuts, while it retains the weight that stuns. His idler hour divides its surface by lines and curves, or embosses it with figures that have pleased his eye or are linked with his superstition. We admire its effective shape, its Etruscan-like quaintness, its graceful form and subtle outline, yet we neglect the lesson it might teach. If we compare the form of a newly invented machine with the perfected type of the same instrument, we observe, as we trace it through the phases of improvement, how weight is shaken off where strength is less needed, how functions are made to approach without impeding each other, how the straight becomes curved, and the curve is straightened, till the straggling and cumbersome machine becomes the compact, effective, and beautiful engine.

So instinctive is the perception of organic beauty in the human eye, that we cannot withhold our admiration even from the organs of destruction. There is majesty in the royal paw of the lion, music in the motion of the brinded tiger; we accord our praise to the sword and the dagger, and shudder our approval of the frightful aptitude of the ghastly guillotine.

Conceiving destruction to be a normal element of the system of nature equally with production, we have used the word "beauty" in connection with it. We have no objection to exchange it for the word "character," as indicating the mere adaptation of forms to functions, and would gladly substitute the actual pretensions of our architecture to the former, could we hope to secure the latter.

Let us now turn to a structure of our own, one which from its nature and uses commands us to reject authority, and we shall find the result of the manly use of plain good sense so like that of taste and genius too, as scarce to require a distinctive title. Observe a ship at sea! Mark the majestic form of her hull as she rushes through the water, observe the graceful bend of her body, the gentle transition from round to flat, the grasp of her keel, the leap of her bows, the symmetry and rich tracery of her spars and rigging, and those grand wind muscles, her sails! Behold an organization second only to that of an animal, obedient as the horse, swift as the stag, and bearing the burden of a thousand camels from pole to pole! What Academy of Design, what research of connoisseurship, what imitation of the Greeks produced this marvel of construction? Here is the result of the study of man upon the great deep, where Nature spake of the laws of building, not in the feather and in the flower, but in winds and waves, and he bent all his mind to hear and to obey. Could we carry into our civil architecture the responsibilities that weigh upon our shipbuilding, we should ere long have edifices as superior to the Parthenon for the purposes that we require, as the *Constitution* or the *Pennsylvania* is to the galley of the Argonauts. Could our blunders on *terra firma* be put to the same dread test that those of shipbuilders are, little would be now left to say on this subject.

Instead of forcing the functions of every sort of building into one general form, adopting an outward shape for the sake of the eye or of association, without reference to the inner distribution, let us begin from the heart as a nucleus and work outward. The most convenient size and arrangement of the rooms that are to constitute the building being fixed, the access of the light that may, of the air that must, be wanted, being provided for, we have the skeleton of our building. Nay, we have all excepting the dress. The connection and order of parts, juxtaposed for convenience, cannot fail to speak of their relation and uses. As a group of idlers on the quay, if they grasp a rope to haul a vessel to the pier, are united in harmonious action by the cord they seize, as the slowly yielding mass forms a thorough bass to their livelier movement, so the unflinching adaptation of a building to its position and use gives, as a sure product of that adaptation, character and expression.

What a field of study would be opened by the adoption in civil architecture of those laws of apportionment, distribution, and connection which we have thus hinted at? No longer could the mere tyro huddle together a crowd of ill-arranged, ill-lighted, and stifled rooms, and masking the chaos with the sneaking copy of a Greek façade, usurp the name of architect. If this anatomic connection and proportion has been attained in ships, in machines, and, in spite of false principles, in such buildings as make a departure from it fatal, as in bridges and in scaffolding, why should we fear its immediate use in all construction! As its first result, the bank would have the physiognomy of a bank, the church would be recognized as such, nor would the billiard room and the chapel wear the same uniform of columns and pediment. The African king standing in mock majesty with his legs and feet bare, and his body clothed in a cast coat of the Prince Regent, is an object whose ridiculous effect defies all power of face. Is not the Greek temple jammed in between the brick shops of Wall Street or Cornhill, covered with lettered signs, and finished by groups of moneychangers and apple women, a parallel even for his African majesty?

We have before us a letter in which Mr. Jefferson recommends the model of the Maison Carrée for the State House at Richmond. Was he aware that the Maison Carrée is but a fragment, and that too, of a Roman temple? He was. It is beautiful! is the answer. An English society erected in Hyde Park a cast in bronze of the colossal Achilles of the Quirinal, and changing the head, transformed it into a monument to Wellington. But where is the distinction between the personal prowess, the invulnerable body, the heaven-shielded safety of the hero of the Iliad, and the complex of qualities which makes the modern general? The statue is beautiful! is the answer. If such reasoning is to hold, why not translate one of Pindar's odes in memory of Washington, or set up in Carolina a colossal Osiris in honor of General Greene?

The monuments of Egypt and of Greece are sublime as expressions of their power and their feeling. The modern nation that appropriates them displays only wealth in so doing. The possession of means, not accompanied by the sense of propriety or feeling for the true, can do no more for a nation than it can for an individual. The want of an illustrious ancestry may be compensated, fully compensated; but the purloining of the coat of arms of a defunct family is intolerable. . . .

The edifices in whose construction the principles of architecture are developed may be classed as organic, formed to meet the wants of their occupants, or monumental, addressed to the sympathies, the faith, or the taste of a people. These two great classes of buildings, embracing almost every variety of structure, though occasionally joined and mixed in the same edifice, have their separate rules, as they have a distinct abstract nature. In the former class, the laws of structure and apportionment, depending on definite wants, obey a demonstrable rule. They may be called machines, each individual of which must be formed with reference to the abstract type of its species. The individuals of the latter class, bound by no other laws than those of the sentiment which inspires them, and the sympathies to which they are addressed, occupy the positions and assume the forms best calculated to render their parent feeling. No limits can be put to their variety; their size and richness have always been proportioned to the means of the people who have erected them.

If from what has been thus far said it shall have appeared that we regard the Greek masters as aught less than the true apostles of correct taste in building, we have been misunderstood. We believe firmly and fully that they can teach us; but let us learn principles, not copy shapes; let us imitate them like men, and not ape them like monkeys. Remembering what a school of art it was that perfected their system of ornament, let us rather adhere to that system in enriching what we invent than substitute novelty for propriety. After observing the innovations of the ancient Romans, and of the modern Italian masters in this department, we cannot but recur to the Horatian precept—

exemplaria Græca
Nocturna versate manu, versate diurna![2]

To conclude. The fundamental laws of building found at the basis of every style of architecture must be the basis of ours. The adaptation of the forms and magnitude of structures to the climate they are exposed to, and the offices for which they are intended, teaches us to study our own varied wants in these respects. The harmony of their ornaments with the nature that they embellished and the institutions from which they sprang calls on us to do the like justice to our country, our government, and our faith. As a Christian preacher may give weight to truth, and add persuasion to proof by studying the models of pagan writers, so the American builder, by a truly philosophic investigation of ancient art, will learn of the Greeks to be American.

The system of building we have hinted at cannot be formed in a day. It requires all the science of any country to ascertain and fix the proportions and arrangement of the members of a great building, to plant it safely on the soil, to defend it from the elements, to add the grace and poetry of ornament to its frame. Each of these requisites to a good building requires a special study and a lifetime. Whether we are destined soon to see so noble a fruit may be doubted; but we can, at least, break the ground and throw in the seed.

We are fully aware that many regard all matters of taste as matters of pure caprice and fashion. We are aware that many think our architecture already perfect; but we have chosen, during this sultry weather, to exercise a truly American right—the right of talking. This privilege, thank God! is unquestioned—from Miller, who, robbing Béranger, translates into fanatical prose, "Finissons en! le monde est assez vieux![3] to Brisbane, who declares that the same world has yet to begin, and waits a subscription of two hundred thousand dollars in order to start. Each man is free to present his notions on any subject. We have also talked, firm in the belief that the development of a nation's taste in art depends on a thousand deep-seated influences

[2] Night and day peruse the Greek models—from Horace, *Ars Poetica, Epistles*, Book III, #3, lines 268–269.

[3] Let us be done with it! the world is old enough!

beyond the ken of the ignorant present; firm in the belief that freedom and knowledge will bear the fruit of refinement and beauty, we have yet dared to utter a few words of discontent, a few crude thoughts of what might be, and we feel the better for it. We promised ourselves nothing more than that satisfaction which Major Downing attributes to every man "who has had his say, and then cleared out," and we already perceive pleasingly what he meant by it.

RELATIVE AND INDEPENDENT BEAUTY

There are threads of relation which lead me from my specialty to the specialties of other men. Following this *commune quoddam vinculum*,[4] I lay my artistic dogma at the feet of science; I test it by the traditional lore of handicraft; I seek a confirmation of these my inductions, or a contradiction and refutation of them; I utter these inductions as they occur to myself; I illustrate them by what they spontaneously suggest; I let them lead me as a child.

Persons whose light I have sought have been worried and fretted at the form, the body of my utterance. Since this soul, if soul it be, took the form of this body, I have received it as it came. If I seek another form, another dress than that with which my thought was born, shall I not disjoin that which is one? Shall I not disguise what I seek to decorate? I have seen that there is in the body and the dress an indication of the quantum and quality of the mind, and therefore doth it seem honest that I seek no other dress than mine own. I also know by heart some lines and proportions of the work of able penmen. The *lucidus ordo*[5] of another mind is not displayed before me as pearls before swine. I love to bear in my bosom a nosegay plucked in classic ground: it sweetens me to myself. I respect too much the glory of Schiller and Winkelmann, of Goethe and Hegel, to dare purloin their vesture for my crudities. The partial development of my mind makes the dress and garb of imperfection proper for me. My notion of art is not a somewhat set forth for sale, that I should show it to advantage, or soldier in uniform anxious to pass muster, but rather a poor babe whom I strip before the faculty, that they may council and advise—peradventure bid me to despair.

Bodies are so varied by climate, and so changed by work, that it is rash to condemn them until impotence is demonstrated. The camelopard was long declared a monster born of fancy, a nightmare of traveler's brain; but when the giraffe stood browsing in the treetops before us, we felt that we had been hasty. God's taste is as far away from our taste as his ways are beyond our ways. I know full well that without dress and ornament, there are places whence one is expelled. I am too proud to seek admittance in disguise. I had rather remain in the street than get in by virtue of borrowed coat. That which is partial and fractional, may yet be sound and good as far as it goes.

In the hope that some persons, studious of art, may be curious to see how I develop the formula I have set up, I proceed. When I defined beauty

[4] "Certain common bond."

[5] "Clear order."

as the promise of function, action as the presence of function, character as the record of function, I arbitrarily divided that which is essentially one. I considered the phases through which organized intention passes to completeness, as if they were distinct entities. Beauty, being the promise of function, must be mainly present before the phase of action; but so long as there is yet a promise of function there is beauty, proportioned to its relation with action or with character. There is somewhat of character at the close of the first epoch of the organic life, as there is somewhat of beauty at the commencement of the last, but they are less apparent and present rather to the reason than to sensuous tests.

If the normal development of organized life be from beauty to action, from action to character, the progress is a progress upward as well as forward; and action will be higher than beauty, even as the summer is higher than the spring; and character will be higher than action, even as autumn is the résumé and result of spring and summer. If this be true, the attempt to prolong the phase of beauty into the epoch of action can only be made through nonperformance; and false beauty or embellishment must be the result.

Why is the promise of function made sensuously pleasing? Because the inchoate organic life needs a care and protection beyond its present means of payment. In order that we may respect instinctive action, which is divine, are our eyes charmed by the aspect of infancy, and our hearts obedient to the command of a visible yet impotent volition.

The sensuous charm of promise is so great that the unripe reason seeks to make life a perennial promise; but promise, in the phase of action, receives a new name—that of nonperformance, and is visited with contempt.

The dignity of character is so great that the unripe reason seeks to mark the phase of action with the sensuous livery of character. The ivy is trained up the green wall, and while the promise is still fresh on every line of the building, its function is invaded by the ambition *to seem* to have lived.

Not to promise for ever or to boast at the outset, not to shine and to seem, but to be and to act, is the glory of any coordination of parts for an object.

I have spoken of embellishment as false beauty. I will briefly develop this view of embellishment. Man is an ideal being; standing, himself inchoate and incomplete, amid the concrete manifestations of nature, his first observation recognizes defect, his first action is an effort to complete his being. Not gifted as the brutes with an instinctive sense of completeness, he stands alone as capable of conative action. He studies himself; he disciplines himself. Heautontimoroumenos![6] Now, his best efforts at organization falling short of the need that is in his heart, and therefore infinite, he has sought to compensate for the defect in his plan by a charm of execution. Tasting sensuously the effect of a rhythm and harmony in God's world, beyond any adaptation of means to ends that his reason could measure and approve, he has sought to perfect his own approximation to the essential by crowning it with a wreath of measured and musical, yet nondemonstrable, adjunct. Now,

[6] Greek, "a man scaring or tormenting himself."

I affirm that, from the ground whereon I stand and whence I think I see him operate, he thus mirrors, but darkly, God's world. By the sense of incompleteness in his plan, he shows the divine yearning that is in him; by the effort to compensate for defect in plan by any makeshift whatever, he forbids, or at least checks, further effort. I understand, therefore, by embellishment, *The instinctive effort of infant civilization to disguise its incompleteness, even as God's completeness is to infant science disguised.* The many-sided and full and rich harmony of nature is a many-sided response to the call for many functions; not an aesthetical utterance of the Godhead. In the tree and in the bird, in the shell and in the insect, we see the utterance of him who sayeth *yea, yea,* and *nay, nay;* and, therefore, whatever is assumed as neutral ground, or margin around the essential, will be found to come of evil, or in other words to be incomplete.

I base my opinion of embellishment upon the hypothesis that there is not one truth in religion, another in the mathematics, and a third in physics and in art; but that there is one truth even as one God, and that organization is his utterance. Now, organization obeys his law. It obeys his law by an approximation to the essential, and then there is what we term life; or it obeys his law by falling short of the essential, and then there is disorganization. I have not seen the inorganic attached to the organized but as a symptom of imperfect plan, or of impeded function, or of extinct action.

The normal development of beauty is through action to completeness. The invariable development of embellishment and decoration is more embellishment and more decoration. The *reductio ad absurdum* is palpable enough at last; but where was the first downward step? I maintain that the first downward step was *the introduction of the first inorganic, nonfunctional element, whether of shape or color.* If I be told that such a system as mine would produce *nakedness,* I accept the omen. In nakedness I behold the majesty of the essential, instead of the trappings of pretension. The agendum is not diminished; it is infinitely extended. We shall have grasped with tiny hands the standard of Christ, and borne it into the academy, when we shall call upon the architect and sculptor and painter, to seek to be perfect even as our Father is perfect. The assertion that the human body is other than a fit exponent and symbol of the human being is a falsehood, I believe. I believe it to be false on account of the numerous palpable falsehoods which have been necessary in order to clinch it.

Beauty is the promise of function. Solomon, in all his glory is, therefore, not arrayed as the lily of the field. Solomon's array is the result of the instinctive effort of incompleteness to pass itself for complete. It is pretension. When Solomon shall have appreciated nature and himself, he will reduce his household and adapt his harness, not for pretension, but for performance. The lily is arrayed in heavenly beauty, because it is organized both in shape and color, to dose the germ of future lilies with atmospheric and solar influence.

We now approach the grand conservative trap, the basis of independent beauty. Finding in God's world a sensuous beauty, not organically demonstrated to us, the hierarchies call on us to shut our eyes and kneel to an aesthetical utterance of the divinity. I refuse. Finding here an apparent embellishment, I consider the appearance of embellishment an accusation of

ignorance and incompleteness in my science. I confirm my refusal after re-
calling the fact that science has thus far done nothing else than resolve the
lovely on the one hand, the hateful on the other, into utterances of the Godhead—the former being yea, the latter nay. As the good citizen obeys the
good law because it is good, and the bad law that its incompleteness be
manifest, so does every wrong result from divine elements, accuse the organization, and by pain and woe represent X, or the desired solution. To assert
that this or that form or color is beautiful per se is to formulate prematurely;
it is to arrogate godship; and once that false step is taken, human-godship or
tyranny is inevitable without a change of creed.

The first lispings of science declared that nature abhors a vacuum;
there we see humanity expressing its ignorance, by transferring a dark passion to the Godhead which is light and love. This formula could not outlive
experiment which has demonstrated that God's care upholds us with so
many pounds to the square inch of pressure on every side, and that the
support is variable.

The ancients knew somewhat of steam. They formulated steam as a
devil. The vessels at Pompeii all speak one language—look out for steam!
The moderns have looked into steam, and by wrestling with him have forced
him to own himself an angel—an utterance of love and care.

We are told that we shall know trees by their fruits; even because of
the fruits of refusing to kneel, and of worshipping with the eyes open, do I
proceed to seek that I may find.

Mr. Garbett, in his learned, amiable treatise on the principles of design
in architecture, has dissected the English house, and found with the light of
two words, fallen from Mr. Emerson, the secret of the inherent ugliness of
that structure. It is the *cruelty* and *selfishness* of a London house, he says
(and I think he proves it, too), which affects us so disagreeably as we look
upon it. Now, these qualities in a house, like the blear-eyed stolidity of the
habitual sot, are symptoms, not diseases. Mr. Garbett should see herein the
marvelous expression of which bricks and mortar can be made the vehicles.
In vain will he attempt to get by embellishment a denial of selfishness, so
long as selfishness reigns. To medicate symptoms will never at best do more
than effect a metastasis—suppress an eruption; let us believe, rather, that the
Englishman's love of home has expelled the selfishness from the boudoir,
the kitchen, and the parlor, nobler organs, and thrown it out on the skin, the
exterior, where it less threatens life and stands only for X, or a desired solution. If I have been clear in what I have said, it will be apparent that the
intention, the soul of an organization, will get utterance in the organization
in proportion to the means at its disposal; in vain shall you drill the most
supple body of him that hates me into a manifestation of love for me; while
my blind and deaf cousin will soon make me feel, and pleasingly feel, that I
was the man in all the world that he wished to meet.

In seeking, through artistic analysis, a confirmation of my belief in one
God, I offend such hierarchies as maintain that there be two Gods, the one
good and *all*-powerful, the other evil and somewhat powerful. It is only
necessary in order to demolish the entire structure I have raised, that some
advocate of independent beauty and believer in the devil—for they go and
come together—demonstrate embellishment for the sake of beauty in a work

of the divine hand. Let me be understood; I cannot accept as a demonstration of embellishment a sensuous beauty not yet organically explained. I throw the *onus probandi*[7] on him who commands me to kneel. I learned this trick in Italy, where the disappointed picture dealer often defied me denying his daub to be a Raphael, to say, then, what it was. No, my friend, I care not whose it is; when I say certainly not a Raphael, I merely mean that I will none of it!

If there be in religion any truth, in morals any beauty, in art any charm, but through fruits, then let them be demonstrated; and the demonstration in regard to morals and faith will work backward and enlighten art.

I have diligently sought, with scalpel and pencil, an embellishment for the sake of beauty, a sacrifice of function to other than destruction. I have not found it. When I, therefore, defy the believer in the devil to show me such an embellishment, I do so humbly. I want help.

It seems to me that a word of caution is necessary before seeking independent beauty. Beauty may be present, yet not be recognized as such. If we lack the sense of the promise of function, beauty for us will not exist. The inhabitants of certain Swiss valleys regard a goiter as ornamental. It is a somewhat superadded to the essential, and they see it under the charm of association. The courtiers of Louis XIV admired the *talon rouge,* and the enormous *perruque.* They were somewhat superadded to the essential, and they saw them under the charm of association; but the educated anatomist in Switzerland sees the goiter as we see it. The educated artist of Louis XIVth's time saw the maiming pretension of his dress as we see it.

The aim of the artist, therefore, should be first to seek the essential; when the essential hath been found, then if ever will be the time to commence embellishment. I will venture to predict that the essential, when found, will be complete. I will venture to predict that completeness will instantly throw off all that is not itself, and will thus command, "Thou shalt have no other Gods beside me." In a word, completeness is the absolute utterance of the Godhead; not the completeness of the Catholic bigot, or of the Quaker, which is a pretended one, gotten by negation of God-given tendencies; but the completeness of the sea, which hath a smile as unspeakable as the darkness of its wrath, the completeness of earth whose every atom is a microcosm, the completeness of the human body, where all relations are resumed at once and dominated. As the monarch rises out of savage manhood a plumed Czar, embellishing his shortcomings with the sensuous livery of promise; yet entering the phase of developed thought and conscious vigor stands the eagle-eyed and gray-coated Bonaparte—so will every development of real humanity pass through the phase of nondemonstrable embellishment, which is a false completeness to the multiform organization which responds to every call.

I hold the human body, therefore, to be a multiform command. Its capacities are the law and gauge of manhood as connected with earth. I hold the blessings attendant upon obedience to this command, to be the YEA, YEA; the woe consequent upon disobedience, NAY, NAY, of the Godhead. These God daily speaketh to him whose eyes and ears are open. Other than these I

[7] "Burden of proof."

have not heard. When, therefore, the life of man shall have been made to respond to the command which is in his being, giving the catholic result of a sound collective mind in a sound aggregate body, he will organize his human instrument or art for its human purpose, even as he shall have adapted his human life to the divine instrument which was given him. I wish to be clear; the instrument or body being of divine origin, we formulate rashly when we forego it before thoroughly responding to its requirement. That it is in itself no final or complete entity is herein manifest, that it changes. The significance of yesterday, today, and tomorrow is this, that we are in a state of development. Now, the idea of development necessarily supposes incompleteness; now, completeness can know no change. The instrument of body is no haphazard datum given as an approximation, whose shortcomings we are to correct by convention, *arbitrium*,[8] and whim, but an absolute requirement, and only then responding to the divine intention when its higher nature shall be unfolded by high function, even as the completeness of the brute responds to the requirement of his lower nature.

Internecine war is the law of brute existence. War! The lion lives not by food alone. Behold how he pines and dwindles as he growls over his butcher's meat? 'Tis in the stealthy march, the ferocious bound and deadly grapple, tearing palpitating flesh from writhing bone—a halo of red rain around his head—that he finds the completion of his being, in obedience to a word that proceeded out of the mouth of God. Now, the law of brute life is the law of human life, in so far as the brute man is undeveloped in his higher tendencies. They therefore, who having formulated a credo for infant intelligence, and finding domination thereby secured, proceed to organize a *perennial infancy*, that they may enjoy an eternal dominion, will sooner or later see their sheep transformed to tigers; for the law of development, being a divine law, can only be withstood by perishing. If what I have said be true, collective manhood will never allow exceptional development to slumber at the helm or to abuse the whip. Collective manhood calls for development. If exceptional development answer—lo! ye are but wolves. Manhood will reply—then have at you! He who cannot guide must come down. We feel that we cannot remain where we are.

I have followed this train of remark whither it led me. Let us resume. Organization being the passage of intention through function to completeness, the expression of its phases are symptoms only. The same philosophy which has cloaked and crippled and smothered the human body as rebelling against its creator, yet always in vain, because the human body, like the Greek hero, says, strike! But learn, that philosophy has set up a theory of beauty by authority, of beauty independent of other things than its own mysterious harmony with the human soul. Thus, we remark that the human soul, so inclined to evil in the moral world, according to the same philosophy, is sovereign arbiter of beauty is the aesthetical world. The creator, who formed man's soul with a thirst for sin, and his body as a temple of shame, has therefore made his taste infallible! Whose taste! Let us seek through the whole history of arbitrary embellishment to find a resting place. We shall look in vain; for the introduction of the inorganic into the organized is de-

---

[8] "Decision of an arbitrator."

struction; its development has ever been a *reductio ad absurdum*.

There is no conceivable function which does not obey an absolute law. The approximation to that law in material, in parts, in their form, color, and relations, is the measure of freedom or obedience to God, in life. The attempt to stamp the green fruit, the dawning science, the inchoate life, as final, by such exceptional minds and social achievements as have produced a wish to remain here, and a call for a tabernacle, THESE ARE ATTEMPTS TO DIVIDE MANHOOD WHICH IS ONE. They are attempts to swim away from brute man sinking in the sea of fate. They will ever be put to shame; for the ignorance of the ignorant confounds the wise; for the filth of the filthy befouls the clean; for the poverty of the poor poisons the quiet of the possessor. The brute man clings to the higher man; he loves him even as himself; he cannot be shaken off; he must be assimilated and absorbed.

I call, therefore, upon science in all its branches to arrest the tide of sensuous and arbitrary embellishment, so far as it can do it, not negatively by criticism thereof alone, but positively, by making the instrument a many-sided response to the multiform demands of life. The craving for completeness will then obtain its normal food in results, not the opiate and deadening stimulus of decoration. Then will structure and its dependent sister arts emerge from the stand-still of *ipse dixit*, and, like the ship, the team, the steam engine, proceed through phases of development toward a response to need.

The truth of such doctrine, if truth be in it, must share the fate of other truth, and offend him whose creed is identified with the false; it must meet the indifference of the many who believe that a new truth is born every week for him who can afford to advertise. But it must earn a place in the heart of him who has sought partial truths with success; for truths are all related.

19   R. W. Emerson,
Thoughts on Art*   *1841*

Ralph Waldo Emerson (1803–82) played a pivotal role, serving as a vehicle of transmission of European aesthetic and philosophical thought to his American countrymen. In literature, his catalytic influence particularly touched Henry David Thoreau and Walt Whitman, themes from whose writing appear in the work of Frederick Law Olmsted and Louis Sullivan. Emerson, like Greenough, developed a positive concept of beauty rooted in function, although Emerson's was more inclusive and less focused on architecture. An early expression of Emerson's concept of beauty appeared in his first major work, *Nature* (Boston, 1836). In 1841, the essay, "Thoughts on Beauty," appeared in *The Dial*, a journal Emerson helped launch the

*"Thoughts on Art," *The Dial* 1 (January 1841), pp. 367–78.

year before, with Margaret Fuller, as an outlet for transcendental ideals. In it appears the injunction that "whatever is beautiful rests on the foundation of the necessary." This notion Emerson further expanded, after Greenough's premature death, in a second essay entitled "Beauty" (1860), in which he wrote: "We ascribe beauty to that which is simple; which has no superfluous parts; which exactly answers its end." Such beauty would tend to hermetic simplicity, for "in the construction of any fabric or organism, any real increase of fitness to its end is an increase of beauty." Most simply stated, then: "all beauty must be organic." † To carry this out would require a bold mind, and in such essays as "Self-Reliance" (1841), Emerson had already voiced his disapproval of houses "garnished with foreign ornaments." "Why need we copy the Doric or the Gothic model," he inquired. "Insist on yourself; never imitate." If the American artist would only "study with hope and love the precise thing to be done by him, considering the climate, the soil, the length of the day, the wants of the people, the habit and form of the government, he will create a house in which all these will find themselves fitted, and taste and sentiment will be satisfied also." ‡

Every department of life at the present day—trade, politics, letters, science, religion—seem to feel, and to labor to express, the identity of their law. They are rays of one sun; they translate each into a new language the sense of the other. They are sublime when seen as emanations of a necessity contradistinguished from the vulgar fate by being instant and alive, and dissolving man, as well as his works, in its flowing beneficence. This influence is conspicuously visible in the principles and history of art.

On one side, in primary communication with absolute truth, through thought and instinct, the human mind tends by an equal necessity, on the other side, to the publication and embodiment of its thought—modified and dwarfed by the impurity and untruth which, in all our experience, injures the wonderful medium through which it passes. The child not only suffers but cries; not only hungers but eats. The man not only thinks but speaks and acts. Every thought that arises in your mind, in its rising, aims to pass out of the mind into act; just as every plant, in the moment of germination, struggles up to light. Thought is the seed of action; but action is as much its second form as thought is its first. It rises in thought to the end that it may be uttered and acted. The more profound the thought, the more burdensome. Always in proportion to the death of its sense does it knock importunately at the gates of the soul, to be spoken, to be done. What is in will out. It struggles to the birth. Speech is a great pleasure, and action a great pleasure; they cannot be forborne.

The utterance of thought and emotion in speech and action may be conscious or unconscious. The sucking child is an unconscious actor. A man in an ecstasy of fear or anger is an unconscious actor. A large part of our habitual actions are unconsciously done, and most of our necessary words are unconsciously said.

The conscious utterance of thought, by speech or action, to any end, is art. From the first imitative babble of a child to the despotism of eloquence,

† "Beauty," from *The Conduct of Life* (Boston, 1860).

‡ "Self-Reliance," from *Essays, First Series* (Boston, 1841).

from his first pile of toys or chip bridge to the masonry of Eddystone Lighthouse or the Erie Canal; from the tattooing of the Owhvhees to the Vatican Gallery; from the simplest expedient of private prudence to the American Constitution; from its first to its last works, art is the spirit's voluntary use and combination of things to serve its end. The will distinguishes it as spiritual action. Relatively to themselves, the bee, the bird, the beaver have no art, for what they do they do instinctively; but relatively to the Supreme Being, they have. And the same is true of all unconscious action; relatively to the doer, it is instinct; relatively to the First Cause, it is art. In this sense, recognizing the Spirit which informs Nature, Plato rightly said, "Those things which are said to be done by Nature are indeed done by divine art." Art, universally, is the spirit creative. It was defined by Aristotle, "The reason of the thing, without the matter," as he defined the art of shipbuilding to be, "All of the ship but the wood."

If we follow the popular distinction of works according to their aim, we should say, the Spirit, in its creation, aims at use or at beauty, and hence art divides itself into the useful and the fine arts.

The useful arts comprehend not only those that lie next to instinct, as agriculture, building, weaving, and so on, but also navigation, practical chemistry, and the construction of all the grand and delicate tools and instruments by which man serves himself; as language; the watch; the ship; the decimal cipher; and also the sciences, so far as they are made serviceable to political economy.

The moment we begin to reflect on the pleasure we receive from a ship, a railroad, a drydock; or from a picture, a dramatic representation, a statue, a poem, we find that they have not a quite simple, but a blended origin. We find that the question What is art? leads us directly to another, Who is the artist? and the solution of this is the key to the history of art.

I hasten to state the principle which prescribes, through different means, its firm law to the useful and the beautiful arts. The law is this. The universal soul is the alone creator of the useful and the beautiful; therefore to make anything useful or beautiful, the individual must be submitted to the universal mind.

In the first place, let us consider this in reference to the useful arts. Here the omnipotent agent is Nature; all human acts are satellites to her orb. Nature is the representative of the universal mind, and the law becomes this—that art must be a complement to nature, strictly subsidiary. It was said, in allusion to the great structures of the ancient Romans, the aqueducts and bridges—that their "Art was a Nature working to municipal ends." That is a true account of all just works of useful art. Smeaton built Eddystone Lighthouse on the model of an oak tree, as being the form in nature best designed to resist a constant assailing force. Dollond formed his achromatic telescope on the model of the human eye. Duhamel built a bridge by letting in a piece of stronger timber for the middle of the under surface, getting his hint from the structure of the shinbone.

The first and last lesson of the useful arts is that Nature tyrannizes over our works. They must be conformed to her law, or they will be ground to powder by her omnipresent activity. Nothing droll, nothing whimsical will endure. Nature is ever interfering with art. You cannot build your house or pagoda as you will, but as you must. There is a quick bound set to our caprice. The leaning tower can only lean so far. The veranda or pagoda roof can curve upward only to a certain point. The slope of your roof is determined by the weight of snow. It is only within narrow limits that the discretion of the architect may range. Gravity, wind, sun, rain, the size of men and animals, and such like, have more to say than he. It is the law of fluids that prescribes the shape of the boat—keel, rudder, and bows—and, in the finer fluid above, the form and tackle of the sails. Man seems to have no option about his tools, but merely the necessity to learn from Nature what will fit best, as if he were fitting a screw or a door. Beneath a necessity thus almighty, what is artificial in man's life seems insignificant. He seems to take his task so minutely from intimations of Nature that his works become as it were hers, and he is no longer free.

But if we work within this limit, she yields us all her strength. All powerful action is performed by bringing the forces of nature to bear upon our objects. We do not grind corn or lift the loom by our own strength, but we build a mill in such a position as to set the north wind to play upon our instrument, or the elastic force of steam, or the ebb and flow of the sea. So in our handiwork we do few things by muscular force, but we place ourselves in such attitudes as to bring the force of gravity, that is, the weight of the planet, to bear upon the spade or the ax we wield. What is it that gives force to the blow of the ax or crowbar? Is it the muscles of the laborer's arm, or is it the attraction of the whole globe below it, on the ax or bar? In short, in all our operations we seek not to use our own, but to bring a quite infinite force to bear.

Let us now consider this law as it affects the works that have beauty for their end, that is, the productions of the fine arts.

Here again the prominent fact is subordination of man. His art is the least part of his work of art. A great deduction is to be made before we can know his proper contribution to it.

Music, eloquence, poetry, painting, sculpture, architecture. This is a rough enumeration of the fine arts. I omit rhetoric, which only respects the form of eloquence and poetry. Architecture and eloquence are mixed arts, whose end is sometimes beauty and sometimes use.

It will be seen that in each of these arts there is much which is not spiritual. Each has a material basis, and in each the creating intellect is crippled in some degree by the stuff on which it works. The basis of poetry is language, which is material only on one side. It is a demigod. But being applied primarily to the common necessities of man, it is not new created by the poet for his own ends.

The basis of music is the qualities of the air and the vibrations of sonorous bodies. The pulsation of a stretched string or wire gives the ear the pleasure of sweet sound before yet the musician has enhanced this pleasure by concords and combinations.

Eloquence, as far as it is a fine art, is modified how much by the material organization of the orator, the tone of the voice, the physical strength, the play of the eye and countenance! All this is so much deduction from the purely spiritual pleasure. All this is so much deduction from the merit of art, and is the attribute of Nature.

In painting, bright colors stimulate the eye before yet they are harmonized into a landscape. In sculpture and in architecture, the material, as marble or granite; and in architecture, the mass—are sources of great pleasure, quite independent of the artificial arrangement. The art resides in the model, in the plan, for it is on that the genius of the artist is expended, not on the statue or the temple. Just as much better as is the polished statue of dazzling marble than the clay model; or as much more impressive as is the granite cathedral or pyramid than the ground plan or profile of them on paper, so much more beauty owe they to Nature than to art.

There is a still larger deduction to be made from the genius of the artist in favor of Nature than I have yet specified.

A jumble of musical sounds on a viol or a flute, in which the rhythm of the tune is played without one of the notes being right, gives pleasure to the unskilled ear. A very coarse imitation of the human form on canvas or in waxwork—a very coarse sketch in colors of a landscape, in which imitation is all that is attempted—these things give to unpracticed eyes, to the uncultured, who do not ask a fine spiritual delight, almost as much pleasure as a statue of Canova or a picture of Titian.

And in the statue of Canova or the picture of Titian, these give the great part of the pleasure; they are the basis of which the fine spirit rears a higher delight, but to which these are indispensable.

Another deduction from the genius of the artist is what is conventional in his art, of which there is much in every work of art. Thus how much is there that is not original in every particular building, in every statue, in every tune, in every painting, in every poem, in every harangue. Whatever is national or usual; as the usage of building all Roman churches in the form of a cross, the prescribed distribution of parts of a theatre, the custom of draping a statue in classical costume. Yet who will deny that the merely conventional part of the performance contributes much to its effect?

One consideration more exhausts, I believe, all the deductions from the genius of the artist in any given work.

This is the adventitious. Thus the pleasure that a noble temple gives us is only in part owing to the temple. It is exalted by the beauty of sunlight, by the play of the clouds, by the landscape around it, by its grouping with the houses and trees and towers in its vicinity. The pleasure of eloquence is in greatest part owing often to the stimulus of the occasion which produces it; to the magic of sympathy, which exhalts the feeling of each, by radiating on him the feeling of all.

The effect of music belongs how much to the place, as the church or the moonlight walk, or to the company, or, if on the stage, to what went before in the play, or to the expectation of what shall come after.

In poetry, "It is tradition more than invention helps the poet to a good fable." The adventitious beauty of poetry may be felt in the greater delight which a verse gives in happy quotation than in the poem.

It is a curious proof of our conviction that the artist does not feel himself to be the parent of his work and is as much surprised at the effect as we, that we are so unwilling to impute our best sense of any work of art to the author. The very highest praise we can attribute to any writer, painter, sculptor, builder, is that he actually possessed the thought or feeling with which he has inspired us. We hesitate at doing Spenser so great an honor as to think that he intended by his allegory the sense we affix to it. We grudge to Homer the wise human circumspection his commentators ascribe to him. Even Shakespeare, of whom we can believe everything, we think indebted to Goethe and to Coleridge for the wisdom they detect in his Hamlet and Antony. Especially have we this infirmity of faith in contemporary genius. We fear that Allston and Greenough did not foresee and design all the effect they produce on us.

Our arts are happy hits. We are like the musician on the lake, whose melody is sweeter than he knows, or like a traveler, surprised by a mountain echo, whose trivial word returns to him in romantic thunders.

In view of these facts, I say that the power of Nature predominates over the human will in all works of even the fine arts, in all that respects their material and external circumstances. Nature paints the best part of the picture; carves the best part of the statue; builds the best part of the house; and speaks the best part of the oration. For all the advantages to which I have adverted are such as the artist did not consciously produce. He relied on their aid, he put himself in the way to receive aid from some of them, but he saw that his planting and his watering waited for the sunlight of nature, or was vain.

Let us proceed to the consideration of the great law stated in the beginning of this essay, as it affects the purely spiritual part of a work of art.

As in useful art, so far as it is useful, the work must be strictly subordinated to the laws of nature, so as to become a sort of continuation, and in no wise a contradiction of nature; so in art that aims at beauty as an end, must the parts be subordinated to ideal nature, and everything individual abstracted, so that it shall be the production of the universal soul.

The artist, who is to produce a work which is to be admired, not by his friends or his townspeople or his contemporaries, but by all men; and which is to be more beautiful to the eye in proportion to its culture, must disindividualize himself, and be a man of no party and no manner and no age, but one through whom the soul of all men circulates, as the common air through his lungs. He must work in the spirit in which we conceive a prophet to speak; or an angel of the Lord to act; that is, he is not to speak his own words or do his own works or think his own thoughts, but he is to be an organ through which the universal mind acts.

In speaking of the useful arts, I pointed to the fact that we do not dig or grind or hew by our muscular strength, but by bringing the weight of the planet to bear on the spade, ax, or bar. Precisely analogous to this, in the fine arts, is the manner of our intellectual work. We aim to hinder our individuality from acting. So much as we can shove aside our egotism, our prejudice, and will, and bring the omniscience of reason upon the subject before us, so perfect is the work. The wonders of Shakespeare are things which he saw whilst he stood aside, and then returned to record them. The poet aims at getting observations without aim; to subject to thought things seen without (voluntary) thought.

In eloquence, the great triumphs of the art are when the orator is lifted above himself; when consciously he makes himself the mere tongue of the occasion and the hour, and says what cannot but be said. Hence the French phrase *l'abandon* to describe the self-surrender of the orator. Not his will, but the principle on which he is horsed, the great connection and crisis of events thunder in the ear of the crowd.

In poetry, where every word is free, every word is necessary. Good poetry could not have been otherwise written than it is. The first time you hear it, it sounds rather as if copied out of some invisible tablet in the eternal mind than as if arbitrarily composed by the poet. The feeling of all great poets has accorded with this. They found the verse, not made it. The muse brought it to them.

In sculpture, did ever anybody call the Apollo a fancy piece? Or say of the Laocoön how it might be made different? A masterpiece of art has in the mind a fixed place in the chain of being, as much as a plant or a crystal.

The whole language of men, especially of artists, in reference to this subject, points at the belief that every work of art, in proportion to its excellence, partakes of the precision of fate; no room was there for choice; no play for fancy; for the moment, or in the successive moments, when that form was seen, the iron lids of Reason were unclosed, which ordinarily are heavy with slumber: that the individual mind became for the moment the vent of the mind of humanity.

There is but one Reason. The mind that made the world is not one mind, but *the* mind. Every man is an inlet to the same, and to all of the same. And every work of art is a more or less pure manifestation of the same. Therefore we arrive at this conclusion, which I offer as a confirmation of the whole view: That the delight which a work of art affords seems to arise from our recognizing in it the mind that formed Nature again in active operation.

It differs from the works of Nature in this, that they are organically reproductive. This is not: but spiritually it is prolific by its powerful action on the intellects of men.

In confirmation of this view, let me refer to the fact that a study of admirable works of art always sharpens the perceptions of the beauty of Nature; that a certain analogy reigns throughout the wonders of both; that the contemplation of a work of great art draws us into a state of mind which may be called religious. It conspires with all exalted sentiments.

Proceeding from absolute mind, whose nature is goodness as much as truth, they are always attuned to moral nature. If the earth and sea conspire with virtue more than vice—so do the masterpieces of art. The galleries of ancient sculpture in Naples and Rome strike no deeper conviction into the mind than the contrast of the purity, the severity, expressed in these fine old heads, with the frivolity and grossness of the mob that exhibits, and the mob that gazes at them. These are the countenances of the firstborn, the face of man in the morning of the world. No mark is on these lofty features of sloth or luxury or meanness, and they surprise you with a moral admonition, as they speak of nothing around you, but remind you of the fragrant thoughts and the purest resolutions of your youth.

Herein is the explanation of the analogies which exist in all the arts. They are the reappearance of one mind, working in many materials to many temporary ends. Raphael paints wisdom; Handel sings it, Phidias carves it, Shakespeare writes it, Wren builds it, Columbus sails it, Luther preaches it,

Washington arms it, Watt mechanizes it. Painting was called "silent poetry"; and poetry "speaking painting." The laws of each art are convertible into the laws of every other.

Herein we have an explanation of the necessity that reigns in all the kingdom of art.

Arising out of eternal reason, one and perfect, whatever is beautiful rests on the foundation of the necessary. Nothing is arbitrary, nothing is insulated in beauty. It depends forever on the necessary and the useful. The plumage of the bird, the mimic plumage of the insect, has a reason for its rich colors in the constitution of the animal. Fitness is so inseparable an accompaniment of beauty that it has been taken for it. The most perfect form to answer an end is so far beautiful. In the mind of the artist, could we enter there, we should see the sufficient reason for the last flourish and tendril of his work, just as every tint and spine in the seashell prexists in the secreting organs of the fish. We feel, in seeing a noble building, which rhymes well, as we do in hearing a perfect song, that it is spiritually organic, that is, had a necessity in nature for being, was one of the possible forms in the Divine mind, and is now only discovered and executed by the artist, not arbitrarily composed by him.

And so every genuine work of art has as much reason for being as the earth and the sun. The gayest charm of beauty has a root in the constitution of things. The Iliad of Homer, the songs of David, the odes of Pindar, the tragedies of Aeschylus, the Doric temples, the Gothic cathedrals, the plays of Shakespeare were all made, not for sport, but in grave earnest, in tears, and smiles of suffering and loving men.

Viewed from this point, the history of art becomes intelligible, and moreover, one of the most agreeable studies in the world. We see how each work of art sprang irresistibly from necessity, and, moreover, took its form from the broad hint of Nature. Beautiful in this wise is the obvious origin of all the known orders of architecture, namely, that they were the idealizing of the primitive abodes of each people. Thus the Doric temple still presents the semblance of the wooden cabin in which the Dorians dwelt. The Chinese pagoda is plainly a Tartar tent. The Indian and Egyptian temples still betray the mounds and subterranean houses of their forefathers. The Gothic church plainly originated in a rude adaptation of forest trees, with their boughs on, to a festal or solemn edifice, as the bands around the cleft pillars still indicate the green withes that tied them. No one can walk in a pine barren, in one of the paths which the woodcutters make for their teams, without being struck with the architectural appearance of the grove, especially in winter, when the bareness of all other trees shows the low arch of the Saxons. In the woods, in a winter afternoon, one will see as readily the origin of the stained-glass window with which the Gothic cathedrals are adorned, in the colors of the western sky, seen through the bare and crossing branches of the forest. Nor, I think, can any lover of nature enter the old piles of Oxford and the English cathedrals without feeling that the forest overpowered the mind of the builder, with its ferns, its spikes of flowers, its locust, its oak, its pine, its fir, its spruce. The cathedral is a blossoming in stone, subdued by the insatiable demand of harmony in man. The mountain of granite blooms into an eternal flower, with the lightness and delicate finish, as well as aerial proportions and perspective of vegetable beauty.

There was no willfulness in the savages in this perpetuating of their first rude abodes. The first form in which they built a house would be the first form of their public and religious edifice also. This form becomes immediately sacred in the eyes of their children, and the more so as more traditions cluster around it, and is, therefore, imitated with more splendor in each succeeding generation.

In like manner, it has been remarked by Goethe that the granite breaks into parallelopipeds, which, broken in two, one part would be an obelisk; that in Upper Egypt the inhabitants would naturally mark a memorable spot by setting u so conspicuous a stone. Again, he suggested we may see in any stone wall, on a fragment of rock, the projecting veins of harder stone which have resisted the action of frost and water, which has decomposed the rest. This appearance certainly gave the hint of the hieroglyphics inscribed on their obelisk. The amphitheatre of the old Romans—anyone may see its origin who looks at the crowd running together to see any fight, sickness, or odd appearance in the street. The first comers gather round in a circle; those behind stand on tiptoe; and further back they climb on fences or window-sills, and so make a cup of which the object of attention occupies the hollow area. The architect put benches in this order, and enclosed the cup with a wall, and behold a coliseum.

It would be easy to show of very many fine things in the world, in the customs of nations, the etiquette of courts, the constitution of governments, the origin in very simple local necessities. Heraldry, for example, and the ceremonies of a coronation are a splendid burlesque of the occurrences that might befall a dragoon and his footboy. The College of Cardinals were originally the parish priests of Rome. The leaning towers originated from the civil discords which induced every lord to build a tower. Then it became a point of family pride—and for pride a leaning tower was built.

This strict dependence of art upon material and ideal nature, this adamantine necessity which it underlies, has made all its past, and may foreshow its future history. It never was in the power of any man, or any community, to call the arts into being. They come to serve his actual wants, never to please his fancy. These arts have their origin always in some enthusiasm, as love, patriotism, or religion. Who carved marble? The believing men, who wished to symbolize their gods to the waiting Greeks.

The Gothic cathedrals were built when the builder and the priest and the people were overpowered by their faith. Love and fear laid every stone. The Madonnas of Raphael and Titian were made to be worshipped. Tragedy was instituted for the like purpose, and the miracles of music—all sprang out of some genuine enthusiasm, and never out of dilettantism and holidays. But now they languish, because their purpose is merely exhibition. Who cares, who knows what works of art our government has ordered to be made for the Capitol? They are a mere flourish to please the eye of persons who have associations with books and galleries. But in Greece, the Demos of Athens divided into political factions upon the merits of Phidias.

In this country, at this time, other interests than religion and patriotism are predominant, and the arts, the daughters of enthusiasm, do not flourish.

The genuine offspring of our ruling passions we behold. Popular institutions, the school, the reading room, the post office, the exchange, the insurance company, and an immense harvest of economical inventions are the fruit of the equality and the boundless liberty of lucrative callings. These are superficial wants; and their fruits are these superficial institutions. But as far as they accelerate the end of political freedom and national education, they are preparing the soil of man for fairer flowers and fruits in another age. For beauty, truth, and goodness are not obsolete; they spring eternal in the breast of man; they are as indigenous in Massachusetts as in Tuscany or the Isles of Greece. And that Eternal Spirit, whose triple face they are, molds from them forever, for this mortal child, images to remind him of the Infinite and Fair.

20   J. Ruskin, The Seven Lamps of Architecture*   *1849*

Jefferson urged the adoption of a classic model for the Virginia Capitol because it would inspire his countrymen; architecture thus was to serve a social purpose. During the nineteenth century this notion was expanded to a moral purpose, as evident in Catharine Beecher's "Christian" domestic architecture. The most important advocate of the social and moral mission of art was the English critic and writer John Ruskin (1819–1900), as he amply demonstrated in "The Poetry of Architecture," a series of essays in *Loudon's Architectural Magazine*, 1837–38, and then in *Modern Painters*, two volumes (London, 1843–46). His single most important critique of architecture was *The Seven Lamps of Architecture* (London, 1849), which ran through even more editions in the United States than in England.[†] Using the metaphor of a "spirit" or lamp which throws its illuminating light into the darkness of ignorance or misconception, Ruskin discussed the seven conditions necessary for good, that is, moral, architecture: Sacrifice (architecture as contrasted to mere building, the necessity of ornament); Truth (no sham materials, machined detail, or disguised structure); Power (expressive and grand massing); Beauty (based on observation of Nature); Life (bold and irregular forms expressive of use and handcraft); Memory (building for posterity and preserving ancient buildings); and Obedience (adherence to traditional Christian architectural forms). Ruskin thus succeeded in elevating the task of building to a sacred vocation with clearly implied moral obligations. He adopted the convention of dividing his long chapters into "paragraphs" or sections (indicated with §); a selection of these are reprinted here.

*John Ruskin, *The Seven Lamps of Architecture* (London, 1849), in *The Works of John Ruskin*, ed. E. T. Cook and Alexander Wedderburn (London, 1903–12), 8:27–39. [Note: the editors' notes are not reprinted here, but those made by Ruskin are.]

†Henry-Russell Hitchcock, "Ruskin and American Architecture, or Regeneration Long Delayed," in *Concerning Architecture*, ed. John Summerson (London, 1968), 166–208.

CHAPTER I. THE LAMP OF SACRIFICE

§1. Architecture is the art which so disposes and adorns the edifices raised by man, for whatsoever uses, that the sight of them may contribute to his mental health, power and pleasure.

APHORISM 4. *All architecture proposes an effect on the human mind, not merely a service to the human frame.*

It is very necessary, in the outset of all inquiry, to distinguish carefully between Architecture and Building.[1]

To build,—literally, to confirm,—is by common understanding to put together and adjust the several pieces of any edifice or receptacle of a considerable size. Thus we have church building, house building, ship building, and coach building. That one edifice stands, another floats, and another is suspended on iron springs, makes no difference in the nature of the art, if so it may be called, of building or edification. The persons who profess that art, are severally builders, ecclesiastical, naval, or of whatever other name their work may justify: but building does not become architecture merely by the stability of what it erects; and it is no more architecture which raises a church, or which fits it to receive and contain with comfort a required number of persons occupied in certain religious offices, than it is architecture which makes a carriage commodious, or a ship swift. I do not, of course, mean that the word is not often, or even may not be legitimately, applied in such a sense (as we speak of naval architecture); but in that sense architecture ceases to be one of the fine arts, and it is therefore better not to run the risk, by loose nomenclature, of the confusion which would arise, and has often arisen, from extending principles which belong altogether to building, into the sphere of architecture proper.

Let us, therefore, at once confine the name to that art which, taking up and admitting, as conditions of its working, the necessities and common uses of the building, impresses on its form certain characters venerable or beautiful, but otherwise unnecessary. Thus, I suppose, no one would call the laws architectural which determine the height of a breastwork or the position of a bastion. But if to the stone facing of that bastion be added an unnecessary feature, as a cable moulding, *that* is Architecture. It would be similarly unreasonable to call battlements or machicolations architectural features, so long as they consist only of an advanced gallery supported on projecting masses, with open intervals beneath for offence. But if these projecting masses be carved beneath into rounded courses, which are useless, and if the headings of the intervals be arched and trefoiled, which is useless, *that* is Architecture. It may not be always easy to draw the line so sharply, because there are few buildings which have not some pretence or colour of being architectural; neither can there be any architecture which is not based on building, nor any good architecture which is not based on good building; but

---

[1] This distinction is a little stiff and awkward in terms, but not in thought. And it is perfectly accurate, though stiff, even in terms. It is the addition of the mental ἀρχή—in the sense in which Plato uses that word in the "Laws"—which separates architecture from a wasp's nest, a rat hole, or a railway station. [1880.]

it is perfectly easy, and very necessary, to keep the ideas distinct, and to understand fully that Architecture concerns itself only with those characters of an edifice which are above and beyond its common use. I say common; because a building raised to the honour of God, or in memory of men, has surely a use to which its architectural adornment fits it; but not a use which limits, by any inevitable necessities, its plan or details.

§2. Architecture proper, then, naturally arranges itself under five heads:—

Devotional; including all buildings raised for God's service or honour.

Memorial; including both monuments and tombs.

Civil; including every edifice raised by nations or societies, for purposes of common business or pleasure.

Military; including all private and public architecture of defence.

Domestic; including every rank and kind of dwelling-place. Now, of the principles which I would endeavour to develope, while all must be, as I have said, applicable to every stage and style of the art, some, and especially those which are exciting rather than directing, have necessarily fuller reference to one kind of building than another; and among these I would place first that spirit which, having influence in all, has nevertheless such especial reference to devotional and memorial architecture—the spirit which offers for such work precious things, simply because they are precious; not as being necessary to the building, but as an offering, surrendering, and sacrifice of what is to ourselves desirable. It seems to me, not only that this feeling is in most cases wholly wanting in those who forward the devotional buildings of the present day;[2] but that it would even be regarded as a dangerous, or perhaps criminal, principle by many among us. I have not space to enter into dispute of all the various objections which may be urged against it—they are many and specious; but I may, perhaps, ask the reader's patience while I set down those simple reasons which cause me to believe it a good and just feeling, and as well-pleasing to God and honourable in men, as it is beyond all dispute necessary to the production of any great work in the kind with which we are at present concerned.

§3. Now, first, to define this Lamp, or Spirit, of Sacrifice, clearly. I have said that it prompts us to the offering of precious things, merely because they are precious, not because they are useful or necessary. It is a spirit, for instance, which of two marbles, equally beautiful, applicable and durable, would choose the more costly, because it was so, and of two kinds of decoration, equally effective, would choose the more elaborate because it was so, in order that it might in the same compass present more cost and more thought. It is therefore most unreasoning and enthusiastic, and perhaps less negatively defined, as the opposite of the prevalent feeling of modern times, which desires to produce the largest results at the least cost.

Of this feeling, then, there are two distinct forms: the first, the wish to exercise self-denial for the sake of self-discipline merely, a wish acted upon

[2]The peculiar manner of selfish and impious ostentation, provoked by the glassmakers, for a stimulus to trade, of putting up painted windows to be records of private affection, instead of universal religion, is one of the worst, because most plausible and proud, hypocrisies of our day. [1880.]

in the abandonment of things loved or desired, there being no direct call or purpose to be answered by so doing; and the second, the desire to honour or please some one else by the costliness of the sacrifice. The practice is, in the first case, either private or public; but most frequently, and perhaps most properly, private; while, in the latter case, the act is commonly, and with greatest advantage, public. Now, it cannot but at first appear futile to assert the expediency of self-denial for its own sake, when, for so many sakes, it is every day necessary to a far greater degree than any of us practise it. But I believe it is just because we do not enough acknowledge or contemplate it as a good in itself, that we are apt to fail in its duties when they become imperative, and to calculate, with some partiality, whether the good proposed to others measures or warrants the amount of grievance to ourselves, instead of accepting with gladness the opportunity of sacrifice as a personal advantage. Be this as it may, it is not necessary to insist upon the matter here; since there are always higher and more useful channels of self-sacrifice, for those who choose to practise it, than any connected with the arts.

While in its second branch, that which is especially concerned with the arts, the justice of the feeling is still more doubtful; it depends on our answer to the broad question, Can the Deity be indeed honoured by the presentation to Him of any material objects of value, or by any direction of zeal or wisdom which is not immediately beneficial to men? . . .

CHAPTER II. THE LAMP OF TRUTH

§5. The violations of truth, which dishonour poetry and painting, are thus for the most part confined to the treatment of their subjects. But in architecture another and a less subtle, more contemptible, violation of truth is possible; a direct falsity of assertion respecting the nature of material, or the quantity of labour. And this is, in the full sense of the word, wrong; it is as truly deserving of reprobation as any other moral delinquency; it is unworthy alike of architects and of nations; and it has been a sign, wherever it has widely and with toleration existed, of a singular debasement of the arts; that it is not a sign of worse than this, of a general want of severe probity, can be accounted for only by our knowledge of the strange separation which has for some centuries existed between the arts and all other subjects of human intellect, as matters of conscience. This withdrawal of conscientiousness from among the faculties concerned with art, while it has destroyed the arts themselves, has also rendered in a measure nugatory the evidence which otherwise they might have presented respecting the character of the respective nations among whom they have been cultivated; otherwise, it might appear more than strange that a nation so distinguished for its general uprightness and faith as the English, should admit in their architecture more of pretence, concealment, and deceit, than any other of this or of past time.

They are admitted in thoughtlessness, but with fatal effect upon the art in which they are practised. If there were no other causes for the failures which of late have marked every great occasion for architectural exertion, these petty dishonesties would be enough to account for all. It is the first step, and not the least, towards greatness, to do away with these; the first, because so evidently and easily in our power. We may not be able to command good, or beautiful, or inventive, architecture; but we *can* command an honest architecture: the meagreness of poverty may be pardoned, the sternness of utility respected; but what is there but scorn for the meanness of deception?

§6. Architectural Deceits are broadly to be considered under three heads:—

1st. The suggestion of a mode of structure or support, other than the true one; as in pendants of late Gothic roofs.

2nd. The painting of surfaces to represent some other material than that of which they actually consist (as in the marbling of wood), or the deceptive representation of sculptured ornament upon them.

3rd. The use of cast or machine-made ornaments of any kind.

Now, it may be broadly stated, that architecture will be noble exactly in the degree in which all these false expedients are avoided. Nevertheless, there are certain degrees of them, which, owing to their frequent usage, or to other causes, have so far lost the nature of deceit as to be admissible; as, for instance, gilding, which is in architecture no deceit, because it is therein not understood for gold; while in jewellery it is a deceit, because it is so understood, and therefore altogether to be reprehended. So that there arise, in the application of the strict rules of right, many exceptions and niceties of conscience; which let us as briefly as possible examine.

§7. 1st. Structural Deceits.[3] I have limited these to the determined and purposed suggestion of a mode of support other than the true one. The architect is not *bound* to exhibit structure; nor are we to complain of him for concealing it, any more than we should regret that the outer surfaces of the human frame conceal much of its anatomy; nevertheless, that building will generally be the noblest, which to an intelligent eye discovers the great secrets of its structure, as an animal form does, although from a careless observer they may be concealed. In the vaulting of a Gothic roof it is no deceit to throw the strength into the ribs of it, and make the intermediate vault a mere shell: Such a structure would be presumed by an intelligent observer, the first time he saw such a roof; and the beauty of its traceries would be enhanced to him if they confessed and followed the lines of its main strength. If, however, the intermediate shell were made of wood instead of stone, and whitewashed to look like the rest,—this would, of course, be direct deceit, and altogether unpardonable. . . .

§8. With deceptive concealments of structure are to be classed, though still more blameable, deceptive assumptions of it,—the introduction of members which should have, or profess to have, a duty, and have none. One of the most general instances of this will be found in the form of the flying buttress in late Gothic. The use of that member is, of course, to convey support from one pier to another when the plan of the building renders it necessary or desirable that the supporting masses should be divided into groups; the most frequent necessity of this kind arising from the intermedi-

---

[3] *Aesthetic* deceits, to the eye and mind, being all that are considered in this chapter— not practical roguery. [1880.]

ate range of chapels or aisles between the nave or choir walls and their supporting piers. The natural, healthy, and beautiful arrangement is that of a steeply sloping bar of stone, sustained by an arch with its spandrel carried farthest down on the lowest side, and dying into the vertical of the outer pier: that pier being, of course, not square, but rather a piece of wall set at right angles to the supported walls, and, if need be, crowned by a pinnacle to give it greater weight. The whole arrangement is exquisitely carried out in the choir of Beauvais. In later Gothic the pinnacle became gradually a decorative member, and was used in all places merely for the sake of its beauty. There is no objection to this; it is just as lawful to build a pinnacle for its beauty as a tower; but also the *buttress* became a decorative member; and was used, first, where it was not wanted, and, secondly, in forms in which it could be of no use, becoming a mere tie, not between the pier and wall, but between the wall and the top of the decorative pinnacle, thus attaching itself to the very point where its thrust, if it made any, could not be resisted. The most flagrant instance of this barbarism that I remember, (though it prevails partially in all the spires of the Netherlands,) is the lantern of St. Ouen at Rouen, where the pierced buttress, having an ogee curve, looks about as much calculated to bear a thrust as a switch of willow; and the pinnacles, huge and richly decorated, have evidently no work to do whatsoever, but stand round the central tower, like four idle servants, as they are——heraldic supporters, that central tower being merely a hollow crown, which needs no more buttressing than a basket does. In fact, I do not know any thing more strange or unwise than the praise lavished upon this lantern; it is one of the basest pieces of Gothic in Europe; its flamboyant traceries being of the last and most degraded forms:[4] and its entire plan and decoration resembling, and deserving little more credit than, the burnt sugar ornaments of elaborate confectionery. There are hardly any of the magnificent and serene methods of construction in the early Gothic, which have not, in the course of time, been gradually thinned and pared away into these skeletons, which sometimes indeed, when their lines truly follow the structure of the original masses, have an interest like that of the fibrous framework of leaves from which the substance has been dissolved, but which are usually distorted as well as emaciated, and remain but the sickly phantoms and mockeries of things that were; they are to true architecture what the Greek

[4] They are noticed by Mr. Whewell as forming the figure of the fleur-de-lys, always a mark, when in tracery bars, of the most debased flamboyant. It occurs in the central tower of Bayeux, very richly in the buttresses of St. Gervais at Falaise, and in the small niches of some of the domestic buildings at Rouen. Nor is it only the tower of St. Ouen which is overrated. Its nave is a base imitation, in the flamboyant period, of an early Gothic arrangement; the niches on its piers are barbarisms; there is a huge square shaft run through the ceiling of the aisles to support the nave piers, the ugliest excrescence I ever saw on a Gothic building; the traceries of the nave are the most insipid and faded flamboyant; those of the transept clerestory present a singularly distorted condition of perpendicular; even the elaborate door of the south transept is, for its fine period, extravagant and almost grotesque in its foliation and pendants. There is nothing truly fine in the church but the choir, the light triforium, and tall clerestory, the circle of Eastern chapels, the details of sculpture, and the general lightness of proportion; these merits being seen to the utmost advantage by the freedom of the body of the church from all incumbrance.

ghost was to the armed and living frame; and the very winds that whistle through the threads of them, are to the diapasoned echoes of the ancient walls, as to the voice of the man was the pining of the spectre.[5]

§9. Perhaps the most fruitful sources of these kinds of corruption which we have to guard against in recent times, is one which, nevertheless, comes in a "questionable shape," and of which it is not easy to determine the proper laws and limits; I mean the use of iron. The definition of the art of architecture, given in the first Chapter, is independent of its materials. Nevertheless, that art having been, up to the beginning of the present century, practised for the most part in clay, stone, or wood, it has resulted that the sense of proportion and the laws of structure have been based, the one altogether, the other in great part, on the necessities consequent on the employment of those materials; and that the entire or principal employment of metallic framework would, therefore, be generally felt as a departure from the first principles of the art. Abstractedly there appears no reason why iron should not be used as well as wood; and the time is probably near when a new system of architectural laws will be developed, adapted entirely to metallic construction. But I believe that the tendency of all present[6] sympathy and association is to limit the idea of architecture to non-metallic work; and that not without reason. For architecture being in its perfection the earliest, as in its elements it is necessarily the first, of arts, will always precede, in any barbarous nation, the possession of the science necessary either for the obtaining or the management of iron. Its first existence and its earliest laws must, therefore, depend upon the use of materials accessible in quantity, and on the surface of the earth; that is to say, clay, wood, or stone: and as I think it cannot but be generally felt that one of the chief dignities of architecture is its historical use, and since the latter is partly dependent on consistency of style, it will be felt right to retain as far as may be, even in periods of more advanced science, the materials and principles of earlier ages.

§10. But whether this be granted me or not, the fact is, that every idea respecting size, proportion, decoration, or construction, on which we are at present in the habit of acting or judging, depends on presupposition of such materials: and as I both feel myself unable to escape the influence of these prejudices, and believe that my readers will be equally so, it may be perhaps permitted to me to assume that true architecture does not admit iron as a constructive material, and that such works as the cast-iron central spire of Rouen Cathedral, or the iron roofs and pillars of our railway stations, and of some of our churches, are not architecture at all. Yet it is evident that metals may, and sometimes must, enter into the construction to a certain extent, as nails in wooden architecture, and therefore, as legitimately, rivets and solderings in stone; neither can we well deny to the Gothic architect the power of supporting statues, pinnacles, or traceries by iron bars; and if we grant this, I do not see how we can help allowing Brunelleschi his iron chain

---

[5] Compare *Iliad,* Σ 219, with *Odyssey,* Ω 5–10.

[6] "Present" (*i.e.* of the day in which I wrote), as opposed to the ferruginous temper which I saw rapidly developing itself, and which, since that day, has changed our merry England into the Man in the Iron Mask. [1880.]

around the dome of Florence, or the builders of Salisbury[7] their elaborate iron binding of the central tower. If, however, we would not fall into the old sophistry of the grains of corn and the heap, we must find a rule which may enable us to stop somewhere. This rule is, I think, that metals may be used as a *cement*, but not as a *support*. For as cements of other kinds are often so strong that the stones may easier be broken than separated, and the wall becomes a solid mass, without for that reason losing the character of architecture, there is no reason why, when a nation has obtained the knowledge and practice of iron work, metal rods or rivets should not be used in the place of cement, and establish the same or a greater strength and adherence, without in any wise inducing departure from the types and system of architecture before established; nor does it make any difference, except as to sightliness, whether the metal bands or rods so employed be in the body of the wall or on its exterior, or set as stays and cross-bands; so only that the use of them be always and distinctly one which might be superseded by mere strength of cement; as for instance if a pinnacle or mullion be propped or tied by an iron band, it is evident that the iron only prevents the separation of the stones by lateral force, which the cement would have done, had it been strong enough. But the moment that the iron in the least degree takes the place of the stone, and acts by its resistance to crushing, and bears super-incumbent weight, or if it acts by its own weight as a counterpoise, and so supersedes the use of pinnacles or buttresses in resisting a lateral thrust, or if, in the form of a rod or girder, it is used to do what wooden beams would have done as well, that instant the building ceases, so far as such application of metal extend, to be true architecture.[8]

§11. The limit, however, thus determined, is an ultimate one, and it is well in all things to be cautious how we approach the utmost limit of lawfulness; so that, although the employment of metal within this limit cannot be considered as destroying the very being and nature of architecture, it will, if extravagant and frequent, derogate from the dignity of the work, as well as (which is especially to our present point) from its honesty. For although the spectator is not informed as to the quantity or strength of the cement employed, he will generally conceive the stones of the building to be separable; and his estimate of the skill of the architect will be based in great measure on the supposition of this condition, and of the difficulties attendant upon it: so that it is always more honourable, and it has a tendency to render the

---

[7]"This way of tying walls together with iron, instead of making them of that substance and form, that they shall naturally poise themselves upon their buttment, is against the rules of good architecture, not only because iron is corruptible by rust, but because it is fallacious, having unequal veins in the metal, some places of the same bar being three times stronger than others, and yet all sound to appearance." (Survey of Salisbury Cathedral in 1668, by Sir C. Wren.) For my own part, I think it better work to bind a tower with iron, than to support a false dome by a brick pyramid.

[8]Again the word "architecture," used as implying perfect ἀρχή or authority over materials. No builder has true command over the changes in the crystalline structure of iron, or over its modes of decay. The definition of iron by the Delphic oracle, "calamity upon calamity" (meaning iron on the anvil), has only been in these last days entirely interpreted: and from the sinking of the *Vanguard* and *London* to the breaking Woolwich Pier into splinters—two days before I write this note,—the "anarchy of iron" is the most notable fact concerning it. [1880.]

style of architecture both more masculine and more scientific, to employ stone and mortar simply as such, and to do as much as possible with their mere weight and strength, and rather sometimes to forego a grace, or to confess a weakness, than attain the one, or conceal the other, by means verging upon dishonesty. . . .

§ 19. The last form of fallacy which it will be remembered we had to deprecate, was the substitution of cast or machine work for that of the hand, generally expressible as Operative Deceit.

There are two reasons, both weighty, against this practice: one, that all cast and machine work is bad, as work; the other, that it is dishonest. Of its badness I shall speak in another place, that being evidently no efficient reason against its use when other cannot be had. Its dishonesty, however, which, to my mind, is of the grossest kind, is, I think, a sufficient reason to determine absolute and unconditional rejection of it.

Ornament, as I have often before observed, has two entirely distinct sources of agreeableness: one, that of the abstract beauty of its forms, which, for the present, we will suppose to be the same whether they come from the hand or the machine; the other, the sense of human labour and care spent upon it. How great this latter influence we may perhaps judge, by considering that there is not a cluster of weeds growing in any cranny of ruin[9] which has not a beauty in all respects *nearly* equal, and, in some, immeasurably superior, to that of the most elaborate sculpture of its stones; and that all our interest in the carved work, our sense of its richness, though it is tenfold less rich than the knots of grass beside it; of its delicacy, though it is a thousand-fold less delicate; of its admirableness, though a millionfold less admirable; results from our consciousness of its being the work of poor, clumsy, toilsome man. Its true delightfulness, depends on our discovering in it the record of thoughts, and intents, and trials, and heart-breakings—of recoveries and joyfulnesses of success: all this *can* be traced by a practised eye; but, granting it even obscure, it is presumed or understood; and in that is the worth[10] of the thing, just as much as the worth of any thing else we call precious. The worth of a diamond is simply the understanding of the time it must take to look for it before it is found; and the worth of an ornament is the time it must take before it can be cut. It has an intrinsic value besides, which the diamond has not; (for a diamond has no more real beauty than a piece of glass;) but I do not speak of that at present; I place the two on the same ground; and I suppose that hand-wrought ornament can no more be generally known from machine work, than a diamond can be known from paste; nay, that the latter may deceive, for a moment, the mason's, as the other the jeweller's, eye; and that it can be detected only by the closest examination. Yet exactly as a woman of feeling would not wear false jewels, so would a

[9] I do not see any reference to the intention of the opposite plate. It is a piece of pencil sketch from an old church at St. Lô (I believe the original drawing is now in America, belonging to my dear friend, Charles Eliot Norton), and it was meant to show the greater beauty of the natural weeds than of the carved crockets, and the tender harmony of both. Some farther notice is taken of this plate in the eighteenth paragraph of Chap. V. [1880.]

[10] Worth is, of course, used here in the vulgar economists sense, "cost of production," intrinsic value being distinguished from it in the next sentence. [1880.]

builder of honour disdain false ornaments. The using of them is just as down-right and inexcusable a lie. You use that which pretends to a worth which it has not; which pretends to have cost, and to be, what it did not, and is not; it is an imposition, a vulgarity, an impertinence, and a sin. Down with it to the ground, grind it to powder, leave its ragged place upon the wall, rather; you have not paid for it, you have no business with it, you do not want it. Nobody wants ornaments in this world, but everybody wants integrity. All the fair devices that ever were fancied, are not worth a lie. Leave your walls as bare as a planed board, or build them of baked mud and chopped straw, if need be; but do not rough-cast them with falsehood. . . .

CHAPTER VI. THE LAMP OF MEMORY

§ 2. . . . We may live without her, [architecture] and worship without her, but we cannot remember without her. How cold is all history, how lifeless all imagery, compared to that which the living nation writes, and the uncorrupted marble bears!—how many pages of doubtful record might we not often spare, for a few stones left one upon another! The ambition of the old Babel builders was well directed for this world: there are but two strong conquerors of the forgetfulness of men, Poetry and Architecture; and the latter in some sort includes the former, and is mightier in its reality: it is well to have, not only what men have thought and felt, but what their hands have handled, and their strength wrought, and their eyes beheld, all the days of their life. The age of Homer is surrounded with darkness, his very personality with doubt. Not so that of Pericles: and the day is coming when we shall confess, that we have learned more of Greece out of the crumbled fragments of her sculpture than even from her sweet singers or soldier historians.[11] And if indeed there be any profit in our knowledge of the past, or any joy in the thought of being remembered hereafter, which can give strength to present exertion, or patience to present endurance, there are two duties respecting national architecture whose importance it is impossible to overrate: the first, to render the architecture of the day, historical; and, the second, to preserve, as the most precious of inheritances, that of past ages.

APHORISM 27. *Architecture is to be made historical and preserved as such.*

§ 3. It is in the first of these two directions that Memory may truly be said to be the Sixth Lamp of Architecture; for it is in becoming memorial or monumental that a true perfection is attained by civil and domestic buildings; and this partly as they are, with such a view, built in a more stable manner, and partly as their decorations are consequently animated by a metaphorical or historical meaning.

As regards domestic buildings, there must always be a certain limitation to views of this kind in the power, as well as in the hearts, of men; still I

[11] [Ruskin rephrased this later in the Preface to *St. Mark's Rest* (London 1877): "Great nations write their autobiographies in three manuscripts;—the book of their deeds, the book of their words, and the book of their art. Not one of these books can be understood unless we read the two others; but of the three, the only quite trustworthy one is the last."]

cannot but think it an evil sign of a people when their houses are built to last for one generation only. There is a sanctity in a good man's house which cannot be renewed in every tenement that rises on its ruins: and I believe that good men would generally feel this; and that having spent their lives happily and honourably, they would be grieved, at the close of them, to think that the place of their earthly abode, which had seen, and seemed almost to sympathise in, all their honour, their gladness, or their suffering,—that this, with all the record it bare of them, and of all material things that they had loved and ruled over, and set the stamp of themselves upon—was to be swept away, as soon as there was room made for them in the grave. . . .

§10. . . . Every human action gains in honour, in grace, in all true magnificence, by its regard to things that are to come. It is the far sight, the quiet and confident patience, that, above all other attributes, separate man from man, and near him to his Maker; and there is no action nor art, whose majesty we may not measure by this test. Therefore, when we build, let us think that we build for ever. Let is not be for present delight, nor for present use alone; let it be such work as our descendants will thank us for, and let us think, as we lay stone on stone, that a time is to come when those stones will be held sacred because our hands have touched them, and that men will say as they look upon the labour and wrought substance of them, "See! this our fathers did for us." For, indeed, the greatest glory of a building is not in its stones, not in its gold. Its glory is in its Age, and in that deep sense of voicefulness, of stern watching, of mysterious sympathy, nay, even of approval or condemnation, which we feel in walls that have long been washed by the passing waves of humanity. It is in their lasting witness against men, in their quiet contrast with the transitional character of all things, in the strength which, through the lapse of seasons and times, and the decline and birth of dynasties, and the changing of the face of the earth, and of the limits of the sea, maintains its sculptured shapeliness for a time insuperable, connects forgotten and following ages with each other, and half constitutes the identity, as it concentrates the sympathy, of nations: it is in that golden stain of time, that we are to look for the real light, and colour, and preciousness of architecture; and it is not until a building has assumed this character, till it has been entrusted with the fame, and hallowed by the deeds of men, till its walls have been witnesses of suffering, and its pillars rise out of the shadows of death, that its existence, more lasting as it is than that of the natural objects of the world around it, can be gifted with even so much as these possess, of language and of life. . . .

§19. Do not let us talk then of restoration. The thing is a Lie from beginning to end. You may make a model of a building as you may of a corpse, and your model may have the shell of the old walls within it as your cast might have the skeleton, with what advantage I neither see nor care: but the old building is destroyed, and that more totally and mercilessly than if it had sunk into a heap of dust, or melted into a mass of clay: more has been gleaned out of desolated Nineveh than ever will be out of re-built Milan. But, it is said, there may come a necessity for restoration! Granted. Look the necessity full in the face, and understand it on its own terms. It is a necessity for destruction. Accept it as such, pull the building down, throw its stones into neglected corners, make ballast of them, or mortar, if you will; but do it honestly, and do not set up a Lie in their place. And look that necessity in the face before it comes, and you may prevent it. The principle of modern times, (a principle which, I believe, at least in France, to be *systematically acted on by the masons*, in order to find themselves work, as the abbey of St. Ouen was pulled down by the magistrates of the town by way of giving work to some vagrants,) is to neglect buildings first, and restore them afterwards. Take proper care of your monuments, and you will not need to restore them. A few sheets of lead put in time upon a roof, a few dead leaves and sticks swept in time out of a water-course, will save both roof and walls from ruin. Watch an old building with an anxious care; guard it as best you may, and at *any* cost, from every influence of dilapidation. Count its stones as you would jewels of a crown; set watches about it as if at the gates of a besieged city; bind it together with iron where it loosens; stay it with timber where it declines; do not care about the unsightliness of the aid: better a crutch than a lost limb; and do this tenderly, and reverently, and continually, and many a generation will still be born and pass away beneath its shadow. Its evil day must come at last; but let it come declaredly and openly, and let no dishonouring and false substitute deprive it of the funeral offices of memory.

§20. Of more wanton or ignorant ravage it is vain to speak; my words will not reach those who commit them,[12] and yet, be it heard or not, I must not leave the truth unstated, that it is again no question of expediency or feeling whether we shall preserve the buildings of past times or not. *We have no right whatever to touch them.* They are not ours. They belong partly to those who built them, and partly to all the generations of mankind who are to follow us. The dead have still their right in them: that which they laboured for, the praise of achievement or the expression of religious feeling, or whatsoever else it might be which in those buildings they intended to be permanent, we have no right to obliterate. What we have ourselves built, we are at liberty to throw down; but what other men gave their strength and wealth and life to accomplish, their right over does not pass away with their death; still less is the right to the use of what they have left vested in us only. It belongs to all their successors. It may hereafter be a subject of sorrow, or a cause of injury, to millions, that we have consulted our present convenience by casting down such buildings as we choose to dispense with. That sorrow, that loss, we have no right to inflict. Did the cathedral of Avranches belong to the mob who destroyed it, any more than it did to us, who walk in sorrow to and fro over its foundation? Neither does any building whatever belong to those mobs who do violence to it. For a mob it is, and must be always; it matters not whether enraged, or in deliberate folly; whether countless, or sitting in committees; the people who destroy anything causelessly are a mob, and Architecture is always destroyed causelessly. A fair building is necessarily worth the ground it stands upon, and will be so until Central Africa and America shall have become as populous as Middlesex: nor is any

---

[12] No, indeed!—any more wasted words than mine throughout life, or bread cast on more bitter waters, I never heard of. This closing paragraph of the sixth chapter is the best, I think, in the book,—and the vainest. [1880.]

cause whatever valid as a ground for its destruction. If ever valid, certainly not now, when the place both of the past and future is too much usurped in our minds by the restless and discontented present. The very quietness of nature is gradually withdrawn from us; thousands who once in their necessarily prolonged travel were subjected to an influence, from the silent sky and slumbering fields, more effectual than known or confessed, now bear with them even there the ceaseless fever of their life; and along the iron veins that traverse the frame of our country, beat and flow the fiery pulses of its exertion, hotter and faster every hour. All vitality is concentrated through those throbbing arteries into the central cities; the country is passed over like a green sea by narrow bridges, and we are thrown back in continually closer crowds upon the city gates. The only influence which can in any wise *there* take the place of that of the woods and fields, is the power of ancient Architecture. Do not part with it for the sake of the formal square, or of the fenced and planted walk, nor of the goodly street nor opened quay. The pride of a city is not in these. Leave them to the crowd; but remember that there will surely be some within the circuit of the disquieted walls who would ask for some other spots than these wherein to walk; for some other forms to meet their sight familiarly: like him who sat so often where the sun struck from the west, to watch the lines of the dome of Florence drawn on the deep sky, or like those, his Hosts, who could bear daily to behold, from their palace chambers, the places where their fathers lay at rest, at the meeting of the dark streets of Verona.

CHAPTER VII. THE LAMP OF OBEDIENCE

§1. It has been my endeavour to show in the preceding pages how every form of noble architecture is in some sort the embodiment of the Polity, Life, History, and Religious Faith of nations. Once or twice in doing this, I have named a principle to which I would now assign a definite place among those which direct that embodiment; the last place, not only as that to which its own humility would incline, but rather as belonging to it in the aspect of the crowning grace of all the rest; that principle, I mean, to which Polity owes its stability, Life its happiness, Faith its acceptance, Creation its continuance,—Obedience. . . .

§2. Obedience is, indeed, founded on a kind of freedom, else it would become mere subjugation, but that freedom is only granted that obedience may be more perfect; and thus, while a measure of license is necessary to exhibit the individual energies of things, the fairness and pleasantness and perfection of them all consist in their Restraint. . . . So also in estimating the dignity of any action or occupation of men, there is perhaps no better test than the question "are its laws strait?" For their severity will probably be commensurate with the greatness of the numbers whose labour it concentrates or whose interest it concerns.

This severity must be singular, therefore, in the case of that art, above all others, whose productions are the most vast and the most common; which requires for its practice the cooperation of bodies of men, and for its perfection the perseverance of successive generations. And, taking into account also

what we have before so often observed of Architecture, her continual influence over the emotions of daily life, and her realism, as opposed to the two
sister arts which are in comparison but the picturing of stories and of
dreams, we might beforehand expect that we should find her healthy state
and action dependent on far more severe laws than theirs: that the license
which they extend to the workings of individual mind would be withdrawn
by her; and that, in assertion of the relations which she holds with all that is
universally important to man, she would set forth, by her own majestic sub-
jection, some likeness of that on which man's social happiness and power
depend. We might, therefore, without the light of experience, conclude, that
Architecture never could flourish except when it was subjected to a national
law as strict and as minutely authoritative as the laws which regulate religion, policy, and social relations; nay, even more authoritative than these,
because both capable of more enforcement, as over more passive matter; and
needing more enforcement, as the purest type not of one law nor of another,
but of the common authority of all. But in this matter experience speaks
more loudly than reason. If there be any one condition which, in watching
the progress of architecture, we see distinct and general; if, amidst the
counter-evidence of success attending opposite accidents of character and
circumstance, any one conclusion may be constantly and indisputably
drawn, it is this; that the architecture of a nation is great only when it is as
universal and as established as its language; and when provincial differences
of style are nothing more than so many dialects. Other necessities are matters of doubt: nations have been alike successful in their architecture in times
of poverty and of wealth; in times of war and of peace; in times of barbarism and of refinement; under governments the most liberal or the most
arbitrary; but this one condition has been constant, this one requirement
clear in all places and at all times, that the work shall be that of a *school*,
that no individual caprice shall dispense with, or materially vary, accepted
types and customary decorations; and that from the cottage to the palace,
and from the chapel to the basilica, and from the garden fence to the fortress wall, every member and feature of the architecture of the nation shall
be as commonly current, as frankly accepted, as its language or its coin.

§4. A day never passes without our hearing our English architects
called upon to be original, and to invent a new style: about as sensible and
necessary an exhortation as to ask of a man who has never had rags enough
on his back to keep out cold, to invent a new mode of cutting a coat. Give
him a whole coat first, and let him concern himself about the fashion of it
afterwards. We want no new style of architecture. Who wants a new style of
painting or sculpture? But we want *some* style. It is of marvellously little
importance, if we have a code of laws and they be good laws, whether they
be new or old, foreign or native, Roman or Saxon, or Norman, or English
laws. But it is of considerable importance that we should have a code of laws
of one kind or another, and that code accepted and enforced from one side
of the island to another, and not one law made ground of judgment at York
and another in Exeter. And in like manner it does not matter one marble
splinter whether we have an old or new architecture, but it matters everything whether we have an architecture truly so called or not; that is, whether
an architecture whose laws might be taught at our schools from Cornwall to

Northumberland, as we teach English spelling and English grammar, or an architecture which is to be invented fresh every time we build a workhouse or a parish school. There seems to me to be a wonderful misunderstanding among the majority of architects of the present day as to the very nature and meaning of Originality, and of all wherein it consists. Originality in expression does not depend on invention of new words; nor originality in poetry on invention of new measures; nor, in painting, on invention of new colours, or new modes of using them. The chords of music, the harmonies of colour, the general principles of the arrangement of sculptural masses, have been determined long ago, and, in all probability, cannot be added to any more than they can be altered. Granting that they may be, such additions or alterations are much more the work of time and of multitudes than of individual inventors. We may have one Van Eyck, who will be known as the introducer of a new style once in ten centuries, but he himself will trace his invention to some accidental by-play or pursuit; and the use of that invention will depend altogether on the popular necessities or instincts of the period. Originality depends on nothing of the kind. A man who has the gift, will take up any style that is going, the style of his day, and will work in that, and be great in that, and make everything that he does in it look as fresh as if every thought of it had just come down from heaven. I do not say that he will not take liberties with his materials, or with his rules: I do not say that strange changes will not sometimes be wrought by his efforts, or his fancies, in both. But those changes will be instructive, natural, facile, though sometimes marvellous; they will never be sought after as things necessary to his dignity or to his independence; and those liberties will be like the liberties that a great speaker takes with the language, not a defiance of its rules for the sake of singularity; but inevitable, uncalculated, and brilliant consequences of an effort to express what the language, without such infraction, could not. There may be times when, as I have above described, the life of an art is manifested in its changes, and in its refusal of ancient limitations: so there are in the life of an insect; and there is great interest in the state of both the art and the insect at those periods when, by their natural progress and constitutional power, such changes are about to be wrought. But as that would be both an uncomfortable and foolish caterpillar which, instead of being contented with a caterpillar's life and feeding on caterpillar's food, was always striving to turn itself into a chrysalis; and as that would be an unhappy chrysalis which should lie awake at night and roll restlessly in its cocoon, in efforts to turn itself prematurely into a moth; so will that art be unhappy and unprosperous which, instead of supporting itself on the food, and contenting itself with the customs, which have been enough for the support and guidance of other arts before it and like it, is struggling and fretting under the natural limitations of its existence, and striving to become something other than it is. And though it is the nobility of the highest creatures to look forward to, and partly to understand the changes which are appointed for them, preparing for them beforehand; and if, as is usual with *appointed* changes, they be into a higher state, even desiring them, and rejoicing in the hope of them, yet it is the strength of every creature, be it changeful or not, to rest, for the time being, contented with the conditions of its existence, and striving only to bring about the changes which it desires, by fulfilling to the uttermost the duties for which its present state is appointed and continued.

§5. Neither originality, therefore, nor change, good though both may be, and this is commonly a most merciful and enthusiastic supposition with respect to either, is ever to be sought in itself, or can ever be healthily obtained by any struggle or rebellion against common laws. We want neither the one nor the other. The forms of architecture already known are good enough for us, and for far better than any of us: and it will be time enough to think of changing them for better when we can use them as they are. But there are some things which we not only want, but cannot do without; and which all the struggling and raving in the world, nay more, which all the real talent and resolution in England, will never enable us to do without: and these are Obedience, Unity, Fellowship, and Order. And all our schools of design, and committees of taste; all our academies and lectures, and journalisms, and essays; all the sacrifices which we are beginning to make, all the truth which there is in our English nature, all the power of our English will, and the life of our English intellect, will in this matter be as useless as efforts and emotions in a dream, unless we are contented to submit architecture and all art, like other things, to English law.

§6. I say architecture and all art; for I believe architecture must be the beginning of arts, and that the others must follow her in their time and order; and I think the prosperity of our schools of painting and sculpture, in which no one will deny the life, though many the health, depends upon that of our architecture. I think that all will languish until that takes the lead, and (this I do not *think*, but I proclaim, as confidently as I would assert the necessity, for the safety of society, of an understood and strongly administered legal government) our architecture *will* languish, and that in the very dust, until the first principle of common sense be manfully obeyed, and an universal system of form and workmanship be everywhere adopted and enforced.

21   J. Ruskin, The Stones of Venice* *1851–53*

Nearly as influential as the *Seven Lamps* was *The Stones of Venice*, published in several sections. It was, in its final form, a massive work—450,000 words—and Ruskin himself produced a condensed version, the "Traveller's Edition" of 1877, deleting, among other parts, all of book two. Chapter four of this second book defined "the nature of gothic" as comprised of various qualities: "savageness," by which Ruskin meant roughness and irregularity of finish; "changefulness," or variation and

* John Ruskin, *The Stones of Venice*, 3 vols. (London, 1851, 1853), *The Works of John Ruskin*, ed. E. T. Cook and Alexander Wedderburn (London, 1903–12); 9:60–73; 10:180–85; 202–04. [Note: the editor's notes are not reprinted here, but those by Ruskin are.]

artistic invention in ornamental detail; "naturalism," or the loving and truthful emulation of foliage; "grotesqueness," or a delight in fantastic and sublime imagery; "rigidity," or elastic tension which communicates the transmission of force from part to part of the structure; and "redundance," or the rich and happy abundance of ornament, for "no architecture is so haughty as that which is simple, . . . which implies, in offering so little to our regard, that all it has offered is perfect."

CHAPTER II. THE VIRTUES OF ARCHITECTURE

§4. We have, then, two qualities of buildings for subjects of separate inquiry: their action, and aspect, and the sources of virtue in both; that is to say, Strength and Beauty, both of these being less admired in themselves, than as testifying the intelligence or imagination of the builder.

For we have a worthier way of looking at human than at divine architecture; much of the value both of construction and decoration, in the edifices of men, depends upon our being led by the thing produced or adorned, to some contemplation of the powers of mind concerned in its creation or adornment. We are not so led by divine work, but are content to rest in the contemplation of the thing created. I wish the reader to note this especially; we take pleasure, or *should* take pleasure, in architectural construction altogether as the manifestation of an admirable human intelligence; it is not the strength, not the size, not the finish of the work which we are to venerate: rocks are always stronger, mountains always larger, all natural objects more finished: but it is the intelligence and resolution of man in overcoming physical difficulty which are to be the source of our pleasure and subject of our praise. And again, in decoration or beauty, it is less the actual loveliness of the thing produced than the choice and invention concerned in the production, which are to delight us; the love and the thoughts of the workman more than his work; his work must always be imperfect, but his thoughts and affections may be true and deep.

§5. This origin of our pleasure in architecture I must insist upon at somewhat greater length, for I would fain do away with some of the ungrateful coldness which we show towards the good builders of old time. In no art is there closer connection between our delight in the work, and our admiration of the workman's mind, than in architecture, and yet we rarely ask for a builder's name. The patron at whose cost, the monk through whose dreaming, the foundation was laid, we remember occasionally; never the man who verily did the work. Did the reader ever hear of William of Sens as having had anything to do with Canterbury Cathedral? or of Pietro Basegio as in anywise connected with the Ducal palace of Venice? There is much ingratitude and injustice in this; and therefore I desire my reader to observe carefully how much of his pleasure in building is derived, or should be derived, from admiration of the intellect of men whose names he knows not.

§6. The two virtues of architecture which we can justly weigh, are, we said, its strength or good construction, and its beauty or good decoration. Consider first, therefore, what you mean when you say a building is well constructed or well built; you do not merely mean that it answers its purpose—this is much, and many modern buildings fail of this much; but if it be verily well built, it must answer this purpose in the simplest way, and with no over-expenditure of means. We require of a lighthouse, for instance, that it shall stand firm and carry a light; if it do not this, assuredly it has been ill built; but it may do it to the end of time, and yet not be well built. It may have hundreds of tons of stone in it more than were needed, and have cost thousands of pounds more than it ought. To pronounce it well or ill built, we must know the utmost forces it can have to resist, and the best arrangements of stone for encountering them, and the quickest ways of effecting such arrangements: then only, so far as such arrangements have been chosen, and such methods used, is it well built. Then the knowledge of all difficulties to be met, and of all means of meeting them, and the quick and true fancy or invention of the modes of applying the means to the end, are what we have to admire in the builder, even as he is seen through this first or inferior part of his work. Mental power, observe; not muscular, nor mechanical, not technical, nor empirical—pure, precious, majestic, massy intellect; not to be had at vulgar price, nor received without thanks, and without asking from whom. . . .

§8. Now, there is in everything properly called art this concernment of the intellect, even in the province of the art which seems merely practical. For observe: in this bridge-building I suppose no reference to architectural principles; all that I suppose we want is to get safely over the river; the man who has taken us over is still a mere bridge-builder,—a *builder*, not an architect; he may be a rough, artless, feelingless man, incapable of doing any one truly fine thing all his days. . . .

§9. You need something more than this, . . . you need that virtue of building through which he may show his affections and delights; you need its beauty or decoration. . . .[1]

§10. Not that, in reality, one division of the man is more human than another. Theologists fall into this error very fatally and continually; and a man from whom I have learned much, Lord Lindsay, has hurt his noble book by it, speaking as if the spirit of the man only were immortal, and were opposed to his intellect, and the latter to the senses; whereas all the divisions of humanity are noble or brutal, immortal or mortal, according to the degree of their sanctification: and there is no part of the man which is not immortal and divine when it is once given to God, and no part of him which is not mortal by the second death, and brutal before the first, when it is withdrawn from God. For to what shall we trust for our distinction from the beasts that perish? To our higher intellect?—yet are we not bidden to be wise as the serpent, and to consider the ways of the ant? Or to our affections? nay; these are more shared by the lower animals than our intelligence:—Hamlet leaps into the grave of his beloved, and leaves it—a dog would have stayed. Humanity and immortality consist neither in reason, nor in love; not in the

[1] In the addenda Ruskin prepared for Lectures 1 and 2 of his *Lectures on Architecture and Painting* (London, 1854), he made his oft-quoted assertion that "*ornamentation is the principal part of architecture,*" meaning specifically painting and sculpture, so that "no person who is not a great sculptor or painter *can* be an architect. If he is not a sculptor or painter, he can only be a *builder.*" See *The Works of John Ruskin*, ed. E. T. Cook and Alexander Wedderburn, 12:83, 85. Ruskin's italics.

body, nor in the animation of the heart of it, nor in the thoughts and stirrings of the brain of it—but in the dedication of them all to Him who will raise them up at the last day.

§11. It is not, therefore, that the signs of his affections, which man leaves upon his work, are indeed more ennobling than the signs of his intelligence; but it is the balance of both whose expression we need, and the signs of the government of them all by Conscience; and Discretion, the Daughter of Conscience. So, then, the intelligent part of man being eminently, if not chiefly, displayed in the structure of his work, his affectionate part is to be shown in its decoration; and, that decoration may be indeed lovely, two things are needed: first, that the affections be vivid, and honestly shown; secondly, that they be fixed on the right things.

§12. You think, perhaps, I have put the requirements in wrong order. Logically I have; practically I have not: for it is necessary first to teach men to speak out, and say what they like, truly; and, in the second place, to teach them which of their likings are ill set, and which justly. If a man is cold in his likings and dislikings, or if he will not tell you what he likes, you can make nothing of him. Only get him to feel quickly and to speak plainly, and you may set him right. And the fact is, that the great evil of all recent architectural effort has not been that men liked wrong things; but that they either cared nothing about any, or pretended to like what they did not. Do you suppose that any modern architect likes what he builds, or enjoys it? Not in the least. He builds it because he has been told that such and such things are fine, and that he *should* like them. He pretends to like them, and gives them a false relish of vanity. Do you seriously imagine, reader, that any living soul in London likes triglyphs?[2]—or gets any hearty enjoyment out of pediments?[3] You are much mistaken. Greeks did: English people never did,—never will. Do you fancy that the architect of old Burlington Mews, in Regent Street, had any particular satisfaction in putting the blank triangle over the archway, instead of a useful garret window? By no manner of means. He had been told it was right to do so, and thought he should be admired for doing it. Very few faults of architecture are mistakes of honest choice: they are almost always hypocrisies.

§13. So, then, the first thing we have to ask of the decoration is that is should indicate strong liking, and that honestly. It matters not so much what the thing is, as that the builder should really love it and enjoy it, and say so plainly. The architect of Bourges Cathedral liked hawthorns; so he has covered his porch with hawthorn,—it is a perfect Niobe of May. Never was such hawthorn; you would try to gather it forthwith, but for fear of being pricked. The old Lombard architects liked hunting; so they covered their work with horses and hounds, and men blowing trumpets two yards long. The base Renaissance architects of Venice liked masquing and fiddling; so

[2] Triglyph. Literally, "Three Cut." The awkward upright ornament with two notches in it, and a cut at each side, to be seen everywhere at the tops of Doric colonnades, ancient and modern.

[3] Pediment. The triangular space above Greek porticoes, as on the Mansion House or Royal Exchange.

they covered their work with comic masks and musical instruments. Even that was better than our English way of liking nothing, and professing to like triglyphs.

§14. But the second requirement in decoration, is that it should show we like the right thing. And the right thing to be liked is God's work, which He made for our delight and contentment in this world. And all noble ornamentation is the expression of man's delight in God's work.

§15. So, then, these are the two virtues of building: first, the signs of man's own good work; secondly, the expression of man's delight in better work than his own. And these are the two virtues of which I desire my reader to be able quickly to judge, at least in some measure; to have a definite opinion up to a certain point. Beyond a certain point he cannot form one. When the science of the building is great, great science is of course required to comprehend it; and, therefore, of difficult bridges, and lighthouses, and harbour walls, and river dykes, and railway tunnels, no judgment may be rapidly formed. But of common buildings, built in common circumstances, it is very possible for every man, or woman, or child, to form judgment both rational and rapid. Their necessary, or even possible, features are but few; the laws of their construction are as simple as they are interesting. The labour of a few hours is enough to render the reader master of their main points; and from that moment he will find in himself a power of judgment which can neither be escaped nor deceived, and discover subjects of interest where everything before had appeared barren. For though the laws are few and simple, the modes of obedience to them are not so. Every building presents its own requirements and difficulties: and every good building has peculiar appliances or contrivances to meet them. Understand the laws of structure, and you will feel the special difficulty in every new building which you approach; and you will know also, or feel instinctively, whether it has been wisely met or otherwise. And an enormous number of buildings, and of styles of building, you will be able to cast aside at once, as at variance with these constant laws of structure, and therefore unnatural and monstrous.

§16. Then, as regards decoration, I want you only to consult your own natural choice and liking. There is a right and wrong in it; but you will assuredly like the right if you suffer your natural instinct to lead you. Half the evil in this world comes from people not knowing what they do like;—not deliberately setting themselves to find out what they really enjoy. All people enjoy giving away money, for instance: they don't know *that*,—they rather think they like keeping it;—and they *do* keep it, under this false impression, often to their great discomfort. Everybody likes to do good; but not one in a hundred finds *this* out. Multitudes think they like to do evil; yet no man ever really enjoyed doing evil since God made the world.

So in this lesser matter of ornament. It needs some little care to try experiments upon yourself; it needs deliberate question and upright answer. But there is no difficulty to be overcome, no abstruse reasoning to be gone into; only a little watchfulness needed, and thoughtfulness, and so much honesty as will enable you to confess to yourself, and to all men, that you enjoy things, though great authorities say you should not.

§17. This looks somewhat like pride; but it is true humility, a trust that you have been so created as to enjoy what is fitting for you, and a willingness to be pleased, as it was intended you should be. It is the child's spirit, which we are most happy when we most recover; remaining wiser than children in our gratitude that we can still be pleased with a fair colour, or a dancing light. And, above all, do not try to make all these pleasures reasonable, nor to connect the delight which you take in ornament with that which you take in construction or usefulness. They have no connection; and every effort that you make to reason from one to the other will blunt your sense of beauty, or confuse it with sensations altogether inferior to it. You were made for enjoyment, and the world was filled with things which you will enjoy, unless you are too proud to be pleased by them, or too grasping to care for what you cannot turn to other account than mere delight. Remember that the most beautiful things in the world are the most useless; peacocks and lilies for instance; at least I suppose this quill I hold in my hand writes better than a peacock's would, and the peasants of Vevay, whose fields in spring time are as white with lilies, as the Dent du Midi is with its snow, told me the hay was none the better for them. . . .

Second, Or Gothic, Period

CHAPTER VI. THE NATURE OF GOTHIC

§1. I shall endeavour . . . to give the reader in this chapter an idea, at once broad and definite, of the true nature of *Gothic* architecture, properly so called; not of that of Venice only, but of universal Gothic; for it will be one of the most interesting parts of our subsequent inquiry to find out how far Venetian architecture reached the universal or perfect type of Gothic, and how far it either fell short of it, or assumed foreign and independent forms.

§2. The principal difficulty in doing this arises from the fact that every building of the Gothic period differs in some important respect from every other; and many include features which, if they occurred in other buildings, would not be considered Gothic at all; so that all we have to reason upon is merely, if I may be allowed so to express it, a greater or less degree of *Gothicness* in each building we examine. And it is this Gothicness,—the character which, according as it is found more or less in a building, makes it more or less Gothic—of which I want to define the nature. . . .

§4. . . . Gothic architecture has external forms and internal elements. Its elements are certain mental tendencies of the builders, legibly expressed in it; as fancifulness, love of variety, love of richness, and such others. Its external forms are pointed arches, vaulted roofs, etc. And unless both the elements and the forms are there we have no right to call the style Gothic. It is not enough that it has the Form, if it have not also the power and life. It is not enough that it has the Power, if it have not the form. We must therefore inquire into each of these characters successively; and determine first, what is the Mental Expression, and secondly what the Material Form of Gothic architecture, properly so called.

1st. Mental Power or Expression. What characters, we have to discover, did the Gothic builders love, or instinctively express in their work, as distinguished from all other builders?

§5. Let us go back for a moment to our chemistry, and note that, in defining a mineral by its constituent parts, it is not one nor another of them, that can make up the mineral, but the union of all; for instance, it is neither in charcoal, nor in oxygen, nor in lime, that there is the making of chalk, but in the combination of all three in certain measures; they are all found in very different things from chalk, and there is nothing like chalk either in charcoal or in oxygen, but they are nevertheless necessary to its existence.

So in the various mental characters which make up the soul of Gothic. It is not one nor another that produces it; but their union in certain measures. Each one of them is found in many other architectures beside Gothic; but Gothic cannot exist where they are not found, or, at least, where their place is not in some way supplied. Only there is this great difference between the composition of the mineral and of the architectural style, that if we withdraw one of its elements from the stone, its form is utterly changed, and its existence as such and such a mineral is destroyed; but if we withdraw one of its mental elements from the Gothic style, it is only a little less Gothic than it was before, and the union of two or three of its elements is enough already to bestow a certain Gothicness of character, which gains in intensity as we add the others, and loses as we again withdraw them.

§6. I believe, then, that the characteristic or moral elements of Gothic are the following, placed in the order of their importance:

1. Savageness.	4. Grotesqueness.
2. Changefulness.	5. Rigidity.
3. Naturalism.	6. Redundance.

These characters are here expressed as belonging to the building; as belonging to the builder, they would be expressed thus:—1. Savageness or Rudeness. 2. Love of Change. 3. Love of Nature. 4. Disturbed Imagination. 5. Obstinacy. 6. Generosity. And I repeat, that the withdrawal of any one, or any two, will not at once destroy the Gothic character of a building, but the removal of a majority of them will. I shall proceed to examine them in their order.

§7. (1.) *Savageness.* I am not sure when the word "Gothic" was first generically applied to the architecture of the North; but I presume that, whatever the date of its original usage, it was intended to imply reproach, and express the barbaric character of the nations among whom that architecture arose. It never implied that they were literally of Gothic lineage, far less that their architecture had been originally invented by the Goths themselves; but it did imply that they and their buildings together exhibited a degree of sternness and rudeness, which, in contradistinction to the character of Southern and Eastern nations, appeared like a perpetual reflection of the contrast between the Goth and the Roman in their first encounter. And when that fallen Roman, in the utmost impotence of his luxury, and insolence of his guilt, became the model for the imitation of civilized Europe, at the close of the so-called Dark ages, the word Gothic became a term of unmitigated contempt, not unmixed with aversion. From that contempt, by the exertion of the antiquaries and architects of this century, Gothic architecture has been sufficiently vindicated; and perhaps some among us, in our admiration of the magnificent science of its structure, and sacredness of its expression, might desire that the term of ancient reproach should be withdrawn, and some other, of more apparent honourableness, adopted in its place. There is no chance, as there is no need, of such a substitution. As far as the epithet was used scornfully, it was used falsely; but there is no reproach in the word, rightly understood; on the contrary, there is a profound truth, which the instinct of mankind almost unconsciously recognizes. It is true, greatly and deeply true, that the architecture of the North is rude and wild; but it is not true, that, for this reason, we are to condemn it, or despise. Far otherwise: I believe it is in this very character that it deserves our profoundest reverence.

§22. . . . Enough, I trust, has been said to show the reader that the rudeness or imperfection which at first rendered the term "Gothic" one of reproach is indeed, when rightly understood, one of the most noble characters of Christian architecture, and not only a noble but an *essential* one. It seems a fantastic paradox, but it is nevertheless a most important truth, that no architecture can be truly noble which is not imperfect. And this is easily demonstrable. For since the architect, whom we will suppose capable of doing all in perfection, cannot execute the whole with his own hands, he must either make slaves of his workmen in the old Greek and present English fashion, and level his work to a slave's capacities, which is to degrade it; or else he must take his workmen as he finds them, and let them show their weaknesses together with their strength, which will involve the Gothic imperfection, but render the whole work as noble as the intellect of the age can make it.

§23. But the principle may be stated more broadly still. I have confined the illustration of it to architecture, but I must not leave it as if true of architecture only. Hitherto I have used the words imperfect and perfect merely to distinguish between work grossly unskilful, and work executed with average precision and science; and I have been pleading that any degree of unskilfulness should be admitted, so only that the labourer's mind had room for expression. But, accurately speaking, no good work whatever can be perfect, and *the demand for perfection is always a sign of a misunderstanding of the ends of art*.

§24. This for two reasons, both based on everlasting laws. The first, that no great man ever stops working till he has reached his point of failure: that is to say, his mind is always far in advance of his powers of execution, and the latter will now and then give way in trying to follow it; besides that he will always give to the inferior portions of his work only such inferior attention as they require; and according to his greatness he becomes so accustomed to the feeling of dissatisfaction with the best he can do, that in moments of lassitude or anger with himself he will not care though the beholder be dissatisfied also. I believe there has only been one man who would not acknowledge this necessity, and strove always to reach perfection, Leonardo; the end of his vain effort being merely that he would take ten years to a picture and leave it unfinished. And therefore, if we are to have great men working at all, or less men doing their best, the work will be imperfect, however beautiful. Of human work none but what is bad can be perfect, in its own bad way.[4]

§25. The second reason is, that imperfection is in some sort essential to all that we know of life. It is the sign of life in a mortal body, that is to say, of a state of progress and change. Nothing that lives is, or can be, rigidly perfect; part of it is decaying, part nascent. The foxglove blossom—a third part bud, a third part past, a third part in full bloom—is a type of the life of this world. And in all things that live there are certain irregularities and deficiencies which are not only signs of life, but sources of beauty. No human face is exactly the same in its lines on each side, no leaf perfect in its lobes, no branch in its symmetry. All admit irregularity as they imply change; and to banish imperfection is to destroy expression, to check exertion, to paralyze vitality. All things are literally better, lovelier, and more beloved for the imperfections which have been divinely appointed, that the law of human life may be Effort, and the law of human judgment, Mercy.

Accept this then for a universal law, that neither architecture nor any other noble work of man can be good unless it be imperfect; and let us be prepared for the otherwise strange fact, which we shall discern clearly as we approach the period of the Renaissance, that the first cause of the fall of the arts of Europe was a relentless requirement of perfection, incapable alike either of being silenced by veneration for greatness, or softened into forgiveness of simplicity. . . .

22   J. J. Jarves, American Architecture*   *1864*

James Jackson Jarves (1818–88), had he written a score of years later, might well have been the first professional American art and architecture critic. Born in Boston, the son of a glassmaker, Jarves traveled extensively, both in the Pacific and in Europe. He spent considerable time in Italy after 1851, acquiring a large collection of late medieval and "proto-Renaissance" paintings which he later sold to Yale University in 1871. His detailed observation of European culture, particularly in the visual arts, persuaded him that his countrymen were ready for instruction in this area; he was convinced significant strides could be taken by Americans if they studied what Europe had to offer. In an early work, *Art-Hints* (New York, 1855), he wrote: "We

---

[4] The Elgin marbles are supposed by many persons to be "perfect." In the most important portions they indeed approach perfection, but only there. The draperies are unfinished, the hair and wool of the animals are unfinished, and the entire bas-reliefs of the frieze are roughly cut.

*James Jackson Jarves, *The Art-Idea: Sculpture, Painting and Architecture in America* (New York, 1864), pp. 286–314.

need art students, men of sincerity and labor, who will not hesitate to go on their backs and knees, if need be in the dust, to read the soul-language of the mightiest minds in Europe." There was much to be learned, for "out of old churches, moldering tombs, time-honored galleries, there go forth eternal principles of truth" (pp. 13–14). In a subsequent book, *The Art Idea*, 1864, he discussed the current state of all arts in the United States, concluding with this analysis of American architecture. Jarves sketched the history of American building from the seventeenth century onward, exemplifying the dislike of colonial architecture prevalent before the centennial in 1876. He then turned to an examination of the current state of affairs.

CHAPTER XVII. REVIEW OF AMERICAN ARCHITECTURE, PAST AND PRESENT—THE PROSPECT BEFORE IT—SUMMARY OF FUNDAMENTAL PRINCIPLES

Our synopsis of the art-idea would be incomplete without referring to the condition of architecture in America. Strictly speaking, we have no architecture. If, as has happened to the Egyptians, Ninevites, Etruscans, Pelasgians, Aztecs, and Central American races, our buildings alone should be left, by some cataclysm of nations, to tell of our existence, what would they directly express of us? Absolutely nothing! Each civilized race, ancient or modern, has incarnated its own aesthetic life and character in definite forms of architecture, which show with great clearness their indigenous ideas and general conditions. A similar result will doubtless in time occur here. Meanwhile we must look at facts as they now exist. And the one intense, barren fact which stares us fixedly in the face is that, were we annihilated tomorrow, nothing could be learned of us, as a distinctive race, from our architecture. It is simply substantial building, with ornamentation, orders, styles, or forms, borrowed or stolen from European races, an incongruous medley as a whole, developing no system or harmonious principle of adaptation, but chaotic, incomplete, and arbitrary, declaring plagiarism and superficiality, and proving beyond all question the absolute poverty of our imaginative faculties, and general absence of right feeling and correct taste. Whether we like it or not, this is the undeniable fact of 1864. And not merely this: an explorer of our ruins would often be at a loss to guess the uses or purposes of many of our public edifices. He could detect bastard Grecian temples in scores, but would never dream they were built for banks, colleges, or customhouses. How could he account for ignoble and impoverished Gothic chapels, converted into libraries, of which there is so bad an example at Cambridge, Massachusetts, or indeed for any of the architectural anomalies which disfigure our soil and impeach our common sense. . . .

If the mechanical features of our civilization were left to tell the national story, our ocean clippers, river steamers, and industrial machines would show a different aspect. They bespeak an enterprise, invention, and development of the practical arts that proclaim the Americans to be a remarkable people. If, therefore, success attend them in whatever they give their hearts and hands to, it is but reasonable to infer that cultivation need but be stimulated in the direction of architecture to produce results commensurate with the advance in mechanical and industrial arts. If one doubt this, let him investigate the progress in shipbuilding from the point of view of beauty alone, and he will discover a success as complete in its way as was that of the builders of Gothic cathedrals and Grecian temples. And why? Simply, that American merchants took pride in naval architecture. Their hearts were in their work; their purses opened without stint; and they built the fastest and handsomest ships.

To excel in architecture we must warm up the blood to the work. The owner, officer, and sailor of a gallant ship love her with sympathy as of a human affinity. A ship is not *it*, but *she* and *her*, one of the family; the marvel of strength and beauty; a thing of life, to be tenderly and lovingly cared for and proudly spoken of. All the romance of the trader's heart—in the West, the steamboat holds a corresponding position in the taste and affections of the public—goes out bountifully toward the symmetrical, stately, graceful object of his adventurous skill and toil. Ocean clippers and river steamers are fast making way for locomotive and propeller, about which human affections scarce can cluster, and which art has yet to learn how to dignify and adorn. But the vital principle, *love of work*, still lives, that gave to the sailing vessel new grace and beauty, combining them with the highest qualities of utility and strength into a happy unity of form. As soon as an equal love is turned toward architecture, we may expect as rapid a development of beauty of material form on land as on the ocean.

Our forefathers built simply for protection and adaptation. Their style of dwelling houses was suited to the climate, materials at hand, and social exigencies. Hence it was true and natural. They could not deal in artifice or plagiarism, because they had no tricks of beauty to display and nothing to copy. Over their simple truth of expression time has thrown the veil of rustic enchantment, so that the farmhouses still standing of the period of the Indian wars are a much more pleasurable feature of the landscape than their pretentious villa-successors of the nineteenth century.

The public buildings of our colonial period are interesting solely from association. Anything of architectural pretense, more destitute of beauty, it would be difficult to originate; and yet as meager a legacy as they are of the native styles of ancestral England and Holland at that date, they avoid the worst faults of ornamentation and plagiarism of later work. . . .

When our people were seized with a mania of fine buildings, one generation ago, their taste turned to classical models. Although the men of Athens to whom Paul spoke might not have viewed the buildings we call Grecian with the same admiration which was bestowed them here, put as they are to uses foreign to their spirit, and debased by utilitarian details and changes which destroy their true character, yet our builders did succeed in erecting tolerable copies of the Parthenon, and temples of the Doric, Ionic, and Corinthian orders, converted into nineteenth-century banks, custom-houses, colleges, and churches. The influence of these examples spread like wildfire over the country. Cottages were hid behind wooden porticoes, while lean or bisected columns, lank pilasters, triangular masses of framework dubbed pediments, rioted everywhere, upheld by a fervor of admiration because of their origin, which now to look back upon borders on the absurd. It was indeed an invasion of Hellenic forms, but distorted into positive ugliness by ignorance of their meaning and want of taste in their application. We do not believe that Grecian architecture, born of a widely different race, country, and religion, can be adapted to America. A literal copying of it only makes it appear still more misplaced; especially, torn as it is from high places to be crowded into narrow streets, overtopped by lofty houses, and confronted with buildings of a wholly opposite character. Indeed, the attempt to reconcile it to our purposes was so manifestly preposterous that it was speedily given up.

Then we had a Gothic flurry, which ended still more absurdly, owing to entire ignorance of the forms and character of Gothic architecture. The Girard College and old United States Bank, at Philadelphia, and the United States Sub-Treasury, Wall Street, New York, could indeed instruct the public eye as to the external anatomy of Grecian temple architecture, but the buildings that were erected as Gothic out-Heroded Herod in their defiance of its instinctive spirit. Anything pointed, having a parapet or towers with obelisk-like blocks perched about them, was palmed off as Gothic. The churches of Boston built a score or more years ago, and the Masonic Temple, are absurd caricatures and wretched parodies of their father style. Peaks and points even invaded our domestic architecture with a wanton enthusiasm, like that which just before multiplied columns and pilasters everywhere. It is only necessary to state the fact, for individuals to select examples of either architectural folly by thousands in every state. We no sooner acquired a dim idea that ornament was needed, than builders turned to their books, and made an indiscriminate raid on whatever was given as Gothic or Grecian, perverted temple and church to false uses, wrenched old forms from their true purposes and positions, and stuck our houses all over with a jumble of ill-applied details, degraded to one low standard of masons' or carpenters' work. . . .

Architecture naturally grows out of the wants and ideas of a people, and its ornamentation should be in harmony with them. Our Grecian and Gothic manias were nothing of this kind. Their forms were simply old fashions, of foreign origin, made ridiculous by ignorant application, just as a savage with new-found trousers is as likely to put his arms through the legs as to wear them properly. We laugh at the mistake of the savage, but tens of thousands of buildings in America betray an ignorance of the elementary principles of architecture quite as great as that of the wild Indian of the uses of a white man's garment. In this relation stands the placing steeples astride of porticoes, or thrusting spires and domes apparently through roofs, and sticking pinnacles and pillars anywhere and everywhere, without regard to their true meaning and uses; the breaking up and confusing Grecian horizontal lines with Gothic angular and pointed, in an attempt to unite two antagonistic styles which can no more mingle than oil and water; and, the climax of solecism, trying to put the new wine of American life into the old bottles of departed civilization. Copying does not necessarily imply falsity. Imitators occasionally gave us clever examples of their originals, like the Doric portico of the Tremont House, Boston, and the circular colonnade of the Exchange, of Philadelphia; but, in general, the whole system of imitation is simply a subterfuge to avoid thought and study. Although it may be carried out at times with good taste, it is essentially extraneous art, like a foreign literature, the delight of a learned few, but having no root in the ideas and affections of the people. The classical and Gothic phases of building of the past generation had no germinating force, because they were not the vernacular speech, but only dead tongues and obsolete characters galvanized into a spasmodic life by transitory fashion. Since then, though there have been no more repetitions of Grecian architecture on a large scale, we have had some better imitations of mediaeval Gothic, especially for ecclesiastical purposes, and with a truer expression of its intention. New York City furnishes conspicuous examples of copies of several of its styles, a well as of early Italian, a mode which has been followed elsewhere, both for civic and commercial purposes, not to enumerate the attempts to adapt it to domestic architecture. . . .

The buildings we fix in our streets are like so many Old-World cousins come over on a visit, not having had time as yet to get other naturalization than Yankee sharpness and awkwardness of outline. We are glad to see them, though they bluntly tell us that we have many masterbuilders but no Giottos. It is encouraging, however, to begin to have a taste for what Giotto loved, though unable to create art in his spirit. In his day men *created* art. That is to say, they invented, designed, and composed with reference to home thoughts and needs. True architecture is not what so many fancy, simply ornamental building, but, as Fergusson emphatically observes, the accumulated creative and constructive powers of several minds harmoniously working out a great central idea. Everything is designed from a penetrative insight into its latent meaning, with reference to a certain position and use. The best men of each craft that enters into its constructive expression, painters, sculptors, carvers, molders, stainers of glass, mosaicists, masons, carpenters, the very hodmen, all labor in unity of feeling for the one great object, which becomes to them the incarnated ambition of their lives, and into which enters a variety of language, fact, and feeling, having a word to all men, and commensurate with the harmonious variety of human capacity when stimulated to its fullest power. Not before we appreciate the possibilities of architecture in a grand combination of the intellectual and spiritual faculties, aroused to action by the deepest emotions, can we expect to create work to rival that of olden time. That was the product of many brains. . . .

Another style of foreign origin is making progress in America, known as the French Renaissance, of which the new City Hall, Boston, is an example. Destitute of the ornate richness of its prototype, it gives no adequate conception of it except in making conspicuous its specific defects, and is stilted and forced compared with the best Italian Renaissance style. Cut up and overladen with alternate courses of tall and stunted pilasters having nothing to do, its ornamentation a meager theft of classical order, or a meaningless exhibition of horizontal or perpendicular lines and the simplest geometrical forms, robbing the building of simplicity without giving it dignity, there is not a single element of original thought in it. Architects who design buildings of this character are mere parasites of art, obstructing natural and tasteful growth, and impeding the right men from being felt and heard. A city given over to their hands so far as indigenous development of art is concerned, becomes a mean sham. If we do not speedily outgrow the present system of erecting public edifices, they will be so many monuments of our moral and intellectual dullness, instead of, as they might be, the incarnation of vivifying thoughts and new shapes of beauty. It is to be conceded that the City Hall is imposing from its height, and attractive from the bright solidity of its material, though the use of granite for the fine and free carving required in the Corinthian order is a waste of money and hard labor not to be commended. But the building cannot be too strongly condemned on account of the entire want of keeping of the conspicuous rear portion with its front and sides. The least that the architect ought to have done was to make that conform to the remainder of the edifice. Instead, it would appear as if, tired of his work by the time he arrived at the farther angles, he gave it to his youngest office boy to finish, who at a loss for what to put in, by a happy thought turned to one of his early copybooks in writing for aid. Opening to the page which precedes the pothook period, he espies a multitude of upright lines. *"Eureka!"* He marks an equal number, divided by window spaces, all over the great wall surface, and at last we have an original American style of architecture. Such work is an insult alike to those who pay for it and those who have to look at it.

But meager imitation does not wholly bear sway. There is, besides, a restless, inquiring, experimentive spirit, approaching the inventive, in our building. At present it is chaotic and capricious, with an imperfect comprehension of beauty. Still, it is an active instinct seeking something new. Evidently the architects are called upon to vary their old hole-in-the-wall styles, a house being a brick box pierced with oblong apertures, or else their patrons are taking the matter in hand, and with a crude, experimentive zeal are striking out new shapes and combinations. Individuality, or the expression of personal taste in architecture, is a spirit to be encouraged; for it is rooted in the freedom of choice which first begat rude Gothic forms, and subsequently developed them into ripe beauty and infinite variety. We could name many buildings for private purposes which manifest this spirit of new life, in some cases almost arriving at the grotesque, and frequently at that climax of bad taste known in Europe as Rococo, but which are refreshing to view because of their departure from old conventionalisms and servile copying. The Boston Organ in its architectural features is a striking example of Rococo. The organ, being essentially a Christian instrument of music, requires a case in harmony with its spirit and purpose, or, if put into any other, the details should be kept strictly in unity with its animating spirit. Instead of this, we have an incongruous, grotesque whole, made up of details partly taken from the Christian art-idea and partly from the pagan, gigantic caryatids and classical masks intermixed with puny cupid-angels, a feeble St. Cecelia, and inane and commonplace ornamentations; fine workmanship throughout substituted for fine art; and the entire mass made the more emphatic in its offensiveness by its want of adaptation to the size and aesthetic character of the hall over which its domineers so unpleasantly.

Though individual taste has not yet accomplished anything worthy of perpetuation or to be an example to other peoples, still recent enterprise is eminently suggestive and hopeful. This new movement springs from a rising passion for something novel and beautiful in the dwellings and places of business of our merchants. They clamor for carving and color, for something that expresses their taste or want of it. Decoration is not wholly left to the architects. People's hearts being with their treasures, it is as natural that they should strive to embody them in appropriate forms as that the medievalist, stimulated by his hopes of heaven and fears of hell, should put his treasure into cathedrals and monasteries. The estimation in which our merchants hold their stores and houses, as compared with their churches and civic edifices, is fairly shown in the relative sums expended on them. Many private buildings cost far more than public. In no respect is the contrast between the spirit of the medievalist and the modernist more striking than in their respective expenditures on their sacred and civic architecture. The one gloried in whatever adorned his city or exalted his religion in the eyes of the world; the other reserves his extravagance for private luxury and the exaltation of the individual in the estimation of the community. Not a few dwelling houses are built on so extravagant a scale, compared with the needs of the proprietor, as to come to be called, in popular talk, such a one's "folly." No public building has ever been made obnoxious to a similar term on account of lavishly exceeding its uses and appropriate ornamentation, though millions of dollars have been profitlessly buried in them by the machinations or peculations of unclean hands.

Without investigating the causes of the differences in the above respects between the merchant of the fourteenth century and his brother of the nineteenth, or enlarging upon their social consequences, we feel justified in stating that our citizens have entered upon a phase of feeling which prompts them to love display in their marts of business and their homes; to feel after beauty, as the untutored mind feels after God, if haply it might find him. We hail this as a fruitful promise of final development of fresh architectural forms, which shall make our century, before its completion, a fit companion in aesthetic progress to any one that has preceded it. True, the motive now is strictly personal, and, therefore, not the highest. But give man liberty, and the good in him is ever striving to assert itself. Already we find solid and handsome blocks of stores, in more or less good taste, appropriate to their purpose, effective as street architecture, and novel in many of their features. This improvement is greatly owing to the infusion of his own individuality, and the greater latitude the merchant gives his architect in designing an edifice which is to distinguish his business than committees do in plans of a public character. So, too, with dwelling houses. Doubtless we have as bad, perhaps the worst, specimens of expensive domestic architecture of any country. Certainly, nothing more mixed, vulgar, overdone with inappropriate ornament, mechanical, presumptuous, and mannered, can be found elsewhere. At the same time, no other country affords more hopeful indications of varied styles for domestic purposes, combining the modern constructive and utilitarian requirements with the privacy, refinement, and luxury that appertain to the Anglo-Saxon ideas of home. Boston, which is so poor in public buildings, is the most advanced in private architecture, both for domestic and commercial uses. If more regard were paid to specific fitness and beauty in details and a better disposition and harmony of masses, Boston might become an elegant as well as picturesque city; all the sooner, too, if her citizens would admit into public edifices, with a view to their own honor and dignity, lavish adornment, and freedom of inventive design similar to that they bestow upon private buildings. In Hammatt Billings they possess an architect capable of fine work. The Methodist Church on Tremont Avenue, a Gothic group, the Bedford Street Church, and the adjoining building for the Mechanics' Association, the finest public architecture Boston has, are but meager examples of what his taste could do if scope were given. One turns instinctively to the Roman Catholics for ecclesiastical architecture commensurate to the aesthetic nature of their ritual. But the Church of the Immaculate Conception is an agglomeration of the worst faults of the most debased types of architecture. Externally, it presents a sort of jumble of the fashions in which we build factories and jails, with much vicious and misplaced ornamentation, or what is meant as such, but, as applied, resulting in absolute ugliness. Internally, it has the air of a bank and café in its staring, hard, common look; no religious repose, abundance of sham decoration, and not one gleam of real spiritual significance. It is inconceivable how a sect with so much feeling in general for religious art, and so liberal in their contributions, should have erected a building for a sacred purpose, which violates so preposterously the aesthetic spirit and aim of their faith. Stranger still is it that a Puritan sect, "Orthodox up to the hub," as we were told by one of its members, should have build the Shawmut Church, on Tremont Avenue. The style is early Lombard, somewhat meagerly carried out, with slight modification for special purposes. But its distinctive features are essentially anti-Puritan and of Roman Catholic origin. These are the detached, massive, lofty clock tower, or campanile, which makes so conspicuous an object in the air line of the city; the superabundance of stained glass, causing the interior to sparkle with brilliant colors, and rendering it fervid with spiritual symbolism; its low-toned frescoed walls and grandly treated roof, its harmonious adaptation of aesthetic taste and design to the requirements of Protestant worship, and chiefly the numerous carved crosses on the outer walls, and *credat Judaeus*, surmounting the very church, astounding innovations, but surpassed by that climax of religious horror to Calvinists, placed over and above the pulpit, the crucified Saviour in stained glass, answering to the crucifix of the Romanists. The persecuting Saul of art among the prophets! Puritanism arraying itself after the fashion of the scarlet lady of the seven-hilled Babylon! Is not this a change of sentiment worthy of historical note? The gentleman who assured us that the church was orthodox up to the hub also added that at first he did not like these innovations on their old system of whitewash and absence of all beauty, but had come to like them. He will find, later, that what he now likes will become indispensable, for it is the unlocking of a divine faculty which has been long closed in his sect through misapprehension of its true nature. And the example of the Shawmut Church is a striking and unlooked-for illustration of the rapid growth, in this instance revolutionary in its abrupt force, of aesthetic taste in America, confirming in a welcome manner our theory of its eventual destiny.

We do not purpose, however, to criticize in detail, but to point out the general grounds of our faith in the aesthetic future of our architecture. Its foundation is the variety of taste and freedom of inventive experiment shown by private enterprise. If a knowledge of the fundamental principles of architecture equaling the zeal displayed in building could be spread among all classes, a better order of things would soon appear. To this end, we condense from the best authorities a number of axioms or truths, which, once comprehended by the public, will go a great way to counteract bad work.

Pugin tells us, "The two great rules for design are: First, that there should be no features about a building which are not necessary for convenience, construction, and propriety; Secondly, that all ornament should consist of enrichment of the essential construction of the building"; and adds that the neglect of these two rules is the cause of all the bad architecture of the present time.

Another English authority who treats architecture comprehensively, J. B. Atkinson,[1] sums up its living principles somewhat as follows:

Construction (or use) is the ground or root out of which decoration (delight) should germinate. It is the bone, marrow, muscle, and nerve of architecture as a decorative art. Architecture is capable of any variety and expression, based on the above principle.

Construction must be decorated; not decoration *constructed*.

Decoration must accord with conditions of situation, fitness, and use.

Each genuine style of architecture demands a corresponding type of ornamentation. Specific types grow out of cognate forms in the outer world, so that decorative art becomes intimately or remotely the offspring of nature.

Decoration is not only the reproduction of external form, but also the representative of inward ideas, the symbol of thought and fancy, and the earnest expression of faith. Consequently, decoration has a distinctive character and is subject to classification, as naturalistic, idealistic, symbolistic, geometric, and descriptive or illustrative.

Naturalistic decoration should accord with natural forms and conform to the principles of organic growth. The flower or leaf should represent its natural qualities or organic structure; so, too, of birds, animals, and so on; of which the public can see some fine examples of carving by workmen after nature in Central Park, New York, a beginning in the right direction, and there to be contrasted with conventional or the architects' work, from similar subjects.

Idealistic ornament is usually natural forms subjected to the control of some governing *idea*. It may be conventional or creative; the one extreme tending to mannerism, the other to extravagance.

Allied in certain points to idealistic is symbolic ornament, or the outward manifestation by form of an inward thought or abstract truth.

Geometric ornament consists only of the symmetric distribution of space and a balanced composition of lines, pointing to a central unity and radiating into erratic variety. The Saracens, whose religion forbade images, were the masters of this style.

Architecture admits also of descriptive, historical, and pictorial painting on wall spaces; also of color, to enhance the effect of light and shade, produce relief, and add emphasis to articulate form, and for purpose of aesthetic delight generally.

The final purpose of decoration being beauty to promote pleasurable delight, it is of paramount importance that every design or detail should conform to aesthetic laws.

Every style must be judged from its peculiar standpoint of principle and aim.

---

[1] *Fine Arts Quarterly Review*, London, No. 2 [Jarves's note].

In fine, architecture is, we emphatically repeat, the materialistic expression of the life, manners, needs, and ideas of a people. It reflects them; expands and develops as they themselves to. Endowed with life of its own, it is *growth*; man's objective creation distinguished from nature's.

23 A. J. Downing, A Treatise on . . . Landscape Gardening* *1841*

The first American to write on landscape and garden design, Andrew Jackson Downing (1815–1852), was the son of a nurseryman and was trained early as a horticulturist. As a youth he saw a need for fusing art and garden design, publishing *A Treatise on the Theory and Practice of Landscape Gardening* when he was but twenty-six. Although diffuse in language and "technical" terminology compared to European treatises which Downing evidently had read, the book was almost instantly popular and eventually went through eight editions up to 1879. What was particularly important was the symbiotic relationship that Downing described between buildings and the landscapes in which they were to be placed, for a significant portion of the book was devoted to "the improvement of country residences," as the subtitle made clear. He proposed, moreover, that different characters of landscape required correspondingly restrained or picturesque buildings, that porches were crucial for embracing the landscape, and that all dwellings were to be fitted to the comfort and convenience of the various members of the family. It was this stress on the union of buildings and landscape that made Downing's *Treatise* so important for later architects such as Frank Lloyd Wright.

ESSAY ON LANDSCAPE GARDENING

Section I

HISTORICAL SKETCHES

Objects of the Art. The ancient and modern styles. Their peculiarities. Sketch of the ancient style, and the rise and progress of the modern style. Influence of the English poets and writers. Examples of the art abroad. Landscape Gardening in North America, and examples now existing.

> L'un à nos yeux présente
> D'un dessein régulier l'ordonnance imposante,
> Prête aux champs des beautés qu'ils ne connaissaient pas,
> D'une pompe étrangère embellit leur appas,

*Andrew Jackson Downing, A Treatise on the Theory and Practice of Landscape Gardening adapted to North America with a view to the Improvement of Country Houses ... with Remarks on Rural Architecture, 2nd. ed. (New York, 1844), pp. 9–12, 52–65, 339–49.

Donne aux arbres des lois, aux ondes des entraves,
Et, despote orgueilleux, brille entouré d'esclaves;
Son air est moins riant et plus majestueux,
L'autre, de la nature amant respectueux,
L'orne sans la farder, traite avec indulgence
Ses caprices charmants, sa noble négligence,
Sa marche irrégulière, et fait naître avec art
Des beautés du désordre, et même du hasard.

Delille.

"Our first, most endearing, and most sacred associations," says the amiable Mrs. Hofland, "are connected with gardens; our most simple and most refined perceptions of beauty are combined with them." And we may add to this, that Landscape Gardening, which is an artistical combination of the beautiful in nature and art—an union of natural expression and harmonious cultivation—is capable of affording us the highest and most intellectual enjoyment to be found in any cares or pleasures belonging to the soil.

The development of the Beautiful is the end and aim of Landscape Gardening, as it is of all other fine arts. The ancients sought to attain this by a studied and elegant regularity of design in their gardens; the moderns, by the creation or improvement of grounds which, though of limited extent, exhibit a highly graceful or picturesque epitome of natural beauty. Landscape Gardening differs from gardening in its common sense, in embracing the whole scene immediately about a country house, which it softens and refines, or renders more spirited and striking by the aid of art. In it we seek to embody our *ideal* of a rural home; not through plots of fruit trees, and beds of choice flowers, though these have their place, but by collecting and combining beautiful forms in trees, surfaces of ground, buildings, and walks, in the landscape surrounding us. It is, in short, the Beautiful, embodied in a home scene. And we attain it by the removal or concealment of every thing uncouth and discordant, and by the introduction and preservation of forms pleasing in their expression, their outlines, and their fitness for the abode of man. In the orchard, we hope to gratify the palate, in the flower garden, the eye and the smell, but in the landscape garden we appeal to that sense of the Beautiful and the Perfect, which is one of the highest attributes of our nature.

This embellishment of nature, which we call Landscape Gardening, springs naturally from a love of country life, an attachment to a certain spot, and a desire to render that place attractive—a feeling which seems more or less strongly fixed in the minds of all men. But we should convey a false impression, were we to state that it may be applied with equal success to residences of every class and size, in the country. Lawn and trees, being its two essential elements, some of the beauties of Landscape Gardening may, indeed, be shown wherever a rood of grass surface, and half a dozen trees are within our reach; we may, even with such scanty space, have tasteful grouping, varied surface, and agreeably curved walks; but our art, to appear to advantage, requires some extent of surface—its lines should lose themselves indefinitely, and unite agreeably and gradually with those of the surrounding country.

In the case of large landed estates, its capabilities may be displayed to their full extent, as from fifty to five hundred acres may be devoted to a park or pleasure grounds. Most of its beauty, and all its charms, may, however, be enjoyed in ten or twenty acres, fortunately situated, and well treated; and Landscape Gardening, in America, combined and working in harmony as it is with our fine scenery, is already beginning to give us results scarcely less beautiful than those produced by its finest efforts abroad. The lovely villa residences of our noble river and lake margins, when well treated—even in a few acres of tasteful fore-ground,—seem so entirely to appropriate the whole adjacent landscape, and to mingle so sweetly in their outlines with the woods, the valleys, and shores around them, that the effects are often truly enchanting.

But if Landscape Gardening, in its proper sense, cannot be applied to the embellishment of the smallest cottage residences in the country, its principles may be studied with advantage, even by him who has only three trees to plant for ornament; and we hope no one will think his grounds too small, to feel willing to add something to the general amount of beauty in the country. . . .

Section II

BEAUTIES AND PRINCIPLES OF THE ART

By Landscape Gardening, we understand not only an imitation, in the grounds of a country residence, of the general forms of nature, but *an expressive, harmonious, and refined imitation.*[1] In Landscape Gardening, we should aim to separate the accidental, and extraneous in nature, and to preserve only the spirit, or essence. This subtle essence lies, we believe, in the expression, more or less pervading every attractive portion of nature. And it is by eliciting, preserving, or heightening this expression, that we may give our landscape gardens a higher charm, than even all the polish of art can bestow.

Now the two expressions in nature most suitable for imitation, lie in Beauty's flowing, graceful outlines; and in the irregular, spirited forms of the Picturesque. The Sublime, and the Grand, characters that abound in nature, scarcely come within the limits of artificial imitation—certainly not in the extent of most places in America.

On the other hand, the *graceful*, and the *picturesque*, are characters abounding even in small portions of nature. In the grounds of a country residence, the force of these expressions may often be greatly increased. Fre-

[1] "Thus, there is a beauty of nature and a beauty of art. To copy the beauty of nature cannot be called being an artist in the highest sense of the word, as a mechanical talent only is requisite for this. The beautiful in art depends on ideas, and the true artist, therefore, must possess, together with the talent for technical execution, that genial power which revels freely in rich forms, and is capable of producing and animating them. It is by this, that the merit of the artist and his production is to be judged; and these cannot be properly estimated among those barren copyists which we find so many of our flower, landscape, and portrait painters to be. But the artist stands much higher in the scale, who, though a copyist of visible nature, is capable of seizing it with poetic feeling, and representing it in its more dignified sense; such for example as Raphael, Poussin, Claude, &c."—Weinbreuner.

quently a group of trees, a rounded, or an abrupt knoll, situated prominently, will give a hint for all future improvement.

If we choose a bit of scenery naturally flowing and beautiful in its
outlines, we heighten that expression by the refinements of care and culture;
by our smoothly mown lawns, curved walks, rich groups of flowering shrubs
and trees. If we fall upon a picturesque locality, we may add to its charm,
both by the removal of every thing inharmonious or out of keeping, and by
winding the walks, selecting and planting the shrubs and trees, adapting the
style of the buildings, and, in short, conducting all our improvements, with
an eye to picturesque expression.

There is no surface of ground, however bare, which has not, naturally,
more or less tendency to one or the other of these expressions. And the improver who detects the true character, and plants, builds, and embellishes, as
he should—constantly aiming to elicit and strengthen it—will soon arrive at
a far higher and more satisfactory result, than one, who, in the common
manner, works at random. The latter may succeed in producing pleasing
grounds—he will undoubtedly add to the general beauty and tasteful appearance of the country, and we gladly accord him our thanks. But the
improver who unites with pleasing forms, an expression of sentiment, will
affect not only the common eye, but, much more powerfully, the imagination, and the refined and delicate taste.

Expression being the master key to the heart, in all landscapes, it follows that the highest imitative sphere of the art of Landscape Gardening,
consists in arranging the materials so as to awaken emotions of grace, elegance, or picturesqueness, joined with unity, harmony, and variety, more
distinct and forcible, than are suggested by natural scenery. This may, at
first sight, seem difficult, to the mere lover of nature; but a moment's
thought will convince him, that the very fact of art and man's habitation
being contrasted, as it is in a Landscape Garden, with a natural expression,
will at once heighten the force of the latter. The sunny, peaceful lake is less
smiling, and the impetuous mountain cascade less stirring, when we cross
them in a wild journey, than when they open upon us, unlooked for, in the
luxuriant grounds of a well kept, rural home.

With these views regarding expression in natural scenery, we shall divide the modern style of Landscape Gardening into two kinds, founded on
the two leading expressions to be imitated, viz: the *graceful* and the *picturesque;* and, these two divisions having each their especial admirers, we shall
distinguish them as the Graceful, and the Picturesque schools of the art.[2] We

[2] Taking Landscape Gardening, as we do in this country, on new starting ground, we
consider ourselves fairly at liberty to define, and clear up, the confused and cloudy views of
the end or aim of imitation, pervading most European authors on this subject. Price, whose
work on the Picturesque (see late edition of Sir T. Lauder,) is most full and complete, we
consider the master, and able exponent of the Picturesque school. Repton, who advocates in his
works a more polished and cultivated style, (see Loudon's edition of Repton,) we hold to be the
first authority in the Graceful School. Mr. Loudon's *Gardenesque* style, is but another word for
what we term the Graceful school; except that we consider the latter exemplified in all flowing, luxuriantly developed forms; while Mr. Loudon, who prefers mere artistical beauty to that
of expression, properly limits the *gardenesque* to artificial planting only. The distinction between the *picturesque,* and the *beautiful,* is perhaps open to some difference of opinion, and

have already suggested that almost all our country places have, naturally, one or the other of these characters; and the unity and harmony—in short, the whole beauty and success of improvements, will depend on our feeling and understanding those characteristics before we commence exercising our taste. The foregoing hints on expression in wild landscape, will perhaps assist our readers in reading nature's physiognomy. Let us now examine, a little, the character of the two schools founded on these expressions.

The Graceful School of Landscape Gardening, Figure 18, aims at the production of outlines whose curves are expressive of grace, surfaces of softness, and growth of richness and luxuriance. In the shape of the ground, it is evinced by easy undulations, melting gradually into each other. In the form of trees, by smooth stems, full, round or symmetrical heads of foliage, and luxuriant branches, often drooping to the ground,—which is chiefly attained by planting and grouping, to allow free development of form; and by selecting trees of suitable character, as the elm, the ash, and the like. In walks and roads, by easy flowing curves, following natural shapes of the surface, with no sharp angles or abrupt turns. In water, by the smooth lake with curved margin, embellished with flowing groups of trees, and full masses of flowering shrubs—or in the easy winding curves of a brook. The keeping of such a scene should be of the most polished kind,—grass mown into a softness like velvet, gravel walks scrupulously firm, dry, and clean, and the most perfect order and neatness should reign throughout. Among the trees and shrubs, should be conspicuous the finest foreign sorts, distinguished by beauty of form, foliage, and blossom; and rich groups of shrubs, and flowering plants, should be arranged in the more dressed portions near the house. And finally, considering the house itself as a feature in the scene, it should, properly, belong to one of the classical modes—the Italian, Tuscan, or Venetian forms are preferable, because these have a domestic air, and readily admit of the graceful accompaniments of vases, urns, and other harmonious accessories. Or, if we are to have a plainer dwelling, it should be simple in its character, and its veranda may be festooned with masses of the finest climbers.

The Picturesque School of Landscape Gardening, Figure 18, aims at the production of outlines of a certain spirited irregularity; surfaces, comparatively abrupt and broken; and growth, of a somewhat wild and bold character. The shape of the ground sought after, has its occasional smoothness varied by sudden variations, and, in parts, runs into dingles, rocky groups, and broken banks. The trees, should, in many places, be old and irregular, with rough stems, and bark; and pines, larches, and other trees of striking, irregular growth, must appear, in numbers sufficient to give character to the woody outlines. As, in the Graceful school the trees are planted singly, in open groups, to allow full expansion, so in the Picturesque school, the grouping takes every variety of form; every object should group with another; trees and shrubs are often planted closely together; and intricacy, and vari-

---

all Landscape Gardening aims at the production of the beautiful. But in the graceful outlines of highly cultivated forms of trees, and beautiful curves of surface and walks, in highly polished scenes, lies so different a kind of beauty from that of the irregular ground, trees, etc., of picturesque landscape, that we conceive the two terms will be found, at least for the moderate scale of the art with us, at once precise and significant.

Fig. 12 Landscape Gardening, in the Graceful School.

Fig 13. Landscape Gardening, in the Picturesque School.

Figure 18. Comparison of the "Graceful School" and the "Picturesque School" of landscape design, figures 12 and 13 from Andrew Jackson Downing, *Treatise on . . . Landscape Gardening,* New York, 1844, p. 54.

ety—thickets—glades—and underwood—as in wild nature, are all indispensable. Walks and roads are more abrupt in their windings, turning off frequently at sudden angles, where the form of the ground, or some inviting object, directs. In water, all the wildness of romantic spots in nature, is to be imitated or preserved; and the lake or stream with bold shore, and rocky, wood-fringed margin, or the cascade in the secluded dell, are the characteristic forms. The keeping of such a landscape will, of course, be less careful than in the graceful school. Firm gravel walks near the house, and a general air of neatness in that quarter, are indispensable to the fitness of the scene in all modes, and, indeed properly evince the recognition of art in all Landscape Gardening. But the lawn may be less frequently mown, the edges of the walks less carefully trimmed, in the picturesque mode. While in portions more removed from the house, the walks may sometimes sink into a mere footpath without gravel, and the lawn change into the forest glade or meadow. The architecture of the Picturesque school, is the Gothic mansion and old English cottage, or the Swiss, or some other bracketted form, with bold projection, deep shadows, and irregular outlines. Rustic baskets, and similar ornaments, may abound near the house, and in the more frequented parts of the place.

The *recognition of art*, as Loudon justly observes, is a first principle in Landscape Gardening, as in all other arts; and those of its professors have erred, who supposed that the object of this art is, merely, to produce a facsimile of nature that could not be distinguished from a wild scene. But we contend that this principle may be equally attained in either school—the picturesque cottage being as much a work of art, as the classic villa; its baskets, and seats of rustic work, indicating the hand of man, as well as the marble vase, and balustrade; and a walk, sometimes narrow and crooked, is quickly recognized as man's work, as one always regular and flowing. Foreign trees, of picturesque growth, are as readily obtained, as those of graceful forms. The recognition of art is, therefore, always apparent in both modes. The evidences are indeed stronger, and more multiplied, in the careful polish of the Graceful school; and looking at the effects, with this principle mainly in view, as many persons will, whose only standard is cost and expense, this school must be acknowledged the most beautiful and perfect.[3] But, assuming the principle of *beauty of expression* to be the higher, many imaginative persons will prefer the picturesque school, as affecting the mind with much of the peculiar beauty of wild nature, combined with the advantages of a suitable convenience for habitation. A certain artist-like feeling is necessary, to enable one to relish the picturesque. For this reason, the many, see and feel the power of beauty in her graceful, flowing forms; but it is only the imaginative few, who appreciate her more free and spirited charms.

[3] The *beau ideal* in Landscape Gardening, as a fine art, appears to us, to be embraced in the creation of scenery expressive of a peculiar kind of beauty, as the graceful, or picturesque, the materials of which are, to a certain extent, different from those in wild nature, being composed of the floral and arboricultural riches of *all climates*, as far as possible; uniting, in the same scene, a richness and a variety never to be found in any one portion of nature;—a scene characterized as a work of art, by the variety of the materials, as foreign trees, plants, &c., and by the polish and keeping of the grounds in the natural style, as distinctly as by the uniform and symmetrical arrangement, in the ancient style.

There are perhaps a thousand, who admire the smoothness, softness, and flowing outlines, that predominate in the lawn and pleasure grounds, as we usually see them, where there is one who would prefer a cottage in a highly irregular and picturesque valley, or a castle on a rocky crag; though the latter, may, to certain minds, be incomparably more enchanting.

We shall, therefore, keep distinctly in view the two schools, in treating of the practice of the art. There are always, circumstances which must exert a controlling influence over amateurs, in this country, in choosing between the two. These are, fixed locality, expense, individual preference in style of building, and many others which readily occur to all. The great variety of attractive sites, in the older parts of the country, afford an abundance of indications for either taste. Within the last five years, we think the picturesque is beginning to be preferred. It has, when a suitable locality offers, great advantages for us. The raw materials of wood, water, and surface, by the margin of many of our rivers and brooks, are at once appropriated with so much effect, and so little art, in the picturesque mode; the annual tax on the purse too, is so comparatively little, and the charm so great!

On the other hand, the residences of a country of level plains, usually allow only, the beauty of simple, and graceful forms; and the larger demesne, with its swelling hills and noble masses of wood, (may we not, prospectively, say the prairie too,) should always, in the hands of the man of wealth, be made to display all the freeness and beauty of the Graceful school.

But there are many persons with small, cottage places, of little decided character, who have neither room, time, nor income, to attempt the improvement of their grounds fully, after either of those two schools. How shall they render their places tasteful and agreeable, in the easiest manner? We answer, *by attempting only the simple and the natural;* and the unfailing way to secure this, is by employing only trees and grass. A soft verdant lawn, and a few forest or ornamental trees, well grouped, give universal pleasure— they contain in themselves, in fact, the basis of all our agreeable sensations in a landscape garden—(natural beauty, and the recognition of art,) and they are the most enduring sources of enjoyment in any place. There are no country seats, in the United States, so unsatisfactory and tasteless as those in which, without any definite aim, every thing is attempted; and a mixed jumble of discordant forms, materials, ornaments, and decorations, is assembled—a part in one style and a bit from another, without the least feeling of unity, or congruity. These rural bedlams, full of all kinds of absurdities, without a leading character or expression of any sort, cost their owners a vast deal of trouble, and money, without giving a tasteful mind, a shadow of the beauty which it feels, at the first glimpse of a neat cottage residence, with its simple, sylvan character of well kept lawn and trees. If the latter does not rank high in the scale of Landscape Gardening, as an art, it embodies much of its essence, as a source of enjoyment—the production of the beautiful in country residences.

Besides the beauties of form and expression in the different modes of laying out grounds, there are certain universal and inherent beauties, common to all styles, and, indeed, to every composition in the fine arts. Of these, we shall especially point out those growing out of the principles of *unity, harmony,* and *variety.*

Unity, or the *production of a whole*, is a leading principle of the highest importance, in every art of taste or design, without which, no satisfactory result can be realized. This arises from the fact, that the mind can only attend, with pleasure and satisfaction, to one object, or one composite sensation, at the same time. If two distinct objects, or class of objects present themselves at once to us, we can only attend satisfactorily to one, by withdrawing our attention, for the time, from the other. Hence the necessity of a reference to this leading principle of unity.

To illustrate the subject, let us suppose a building, partially built of wood, with square windows, and the remainder of brick or stone, with long and narrow windows. However well such a building may be constructed, or however nicely the different proportions of the edifice may be adjusted, it is evident, it can never form a satisfactory whole. The mind can only account for such an absurdity, by supposing it to have been built by two individuals, or at two different times, as there is nothing indicating an unity of mind in its composition.

In Landscape Gardening, violations of the principle of unity are often to be met with, and they are always indicative of the absence of correct taste in art. Looking upon a landscape from the windows of a villa residence, we sometimes see a considerable portion of the view embraced by the eye, laid out in natural groups of trees and shrubs, and upon one side, or, perhaps, in the middle of the same scene, a formal avenue leading directly up to the house. Such a view can never appear a satisfactory whole, because we experience a confusion of sensations in contemplating it. There is an evident incongruity in bringing two modes of arranging plantations so totally different under the eye at one moment, which distracts, rather than pleases the mind. In this example, the avenue, taken by itself, may be a beautiful object, and the groups and connected masses may, in themselves, be elegant, yet if the two portions are seen together, they will not form a whole, because they cannot make a composite idea. For the same reason, there is something unpleasing in the introduction of fruit trees among elegant ornamental trees on a lawn, or even in assembling together, in the same beds, flowering plants, and culinary vegetables—one class of vegetation suggesting the useful, and homely, alone to the mind, and the other, avowedly, only the ornamental.

In the arrangement of a large extent of surface, where a great many objects are necessarily presented to the eye at once, the principle of unity will suggest that there should be some grand or leading features to which the others should be merely subordinate. Thus, in grouping trees, there should be some large and striking masses to which the others appear to belong, however distant, instead of scattered groups, all of the same size. Even in arranging walks, a whole will more readily be recognized, if there are one or two, of large size, with which the others appear connected as branches, than if all are equal in breadth, and present the same appearance to the eye in passing.

In all works of art which command universal admiration, we discover an unity of conception and composition, an unity of taste and execution. To assemble in a single composition, forms which are discordant, and portions dissimilar in plan, can only afford pleasure for a short time, to tasteless minds, or those fond of trifling and puerile conceits. The production of an accordant whole, is, on the contrary, capable of affording the most permanent enjoyment to educated minds, every where and at all periods of time.

After unity, the principle of *variety* is worthy of consideration, as a fertile source of beauty in Landscape Gardening. Variety must be considered as belonging more to the details, than to the production of a whole; and it may be attained by disposing trees and shrubs in numerous different ways; and by the introduction of a great number of different species of vegetation, or kinds of walks, ornamental objects, buildings and seats. By producing intricacy, it creates in scenery a thousand points of interest, and elicits new beauties, through different arrangements and combinations of forms and colours, light and shades. In pleasure-grounds, while the whole should exhibit a general plan, the different scenes presented to the eye, one after the other, should possess sufficient variety in the detail, to keep alive the interest of the spectator, and awaken further curiosity.

Harmony may be considered the principle presiding over variety, and preventing it from becoming discordant. It, indeed, always supposes *contrasts*, but neither so strong, nor so frequent, as to produce discord; and *variety*, but not so great, as to destroy a leading expression. In plantations, we seek it in a combination of qualities, opposite in some respects, as in the colour of the foliage, and similar in others, as the form. In embellishments, by a great variety of objects of interest, as sculptured vases, sun dials, or rustic seats, baskets, and arbors, of different forms, but all in accordance, or keeping, with the spirit of the scene.

To illustrate the three principles, with reference to Landscape Gardening, we may remark, that, if unity, only, were consulted, a scene might be planted with but one kind of tree, the effect of which would be sameness; on the other hand, variety might be carried so far as to have every tree of a different kind, which would produce a confused effect. Harmony, however, introduces contrast, and variety, but keeps them subordinate to unity, and to the leading expression, and is, thus, the highest principle of the three.

In this brief abstract of the nature of imitation in Landscape Gardening, and the kinds of beauty which it is possible to produce by means of the art, we have endeavoured to elucidate its leading principles, clearly, to the reader. These grand principles we shall here succinctly recapitulate, premising, that a familiarity with them is of the very first importance in the successful practice of this elegant art, viz.

The Imitation of the Beauty of Expression, derived from a refined perception of the sentiment of nature: *The Recognition of Art,* founded on the immutability of the true, as well as the beautiful: *And the Production of Unity, Harmony, and Variety,* in order to render complete, and continuous, our enjoyment of any artistical work.

Neither the professional Landscape Gardener, nor the amateur, can hope for much success in realizing the nobler effects of the art, unless he first make himself master of the natural character, or prevailing expression, of the place to be improved. In this nice perception, at a glance, of the natural expression, as well as the capabilities of a residence, lies the secret of the superior results produced even by the improver, who, to use the words of Horace Walpole, "is proud of no other art than that of softening nature's harshness, and copying her graceful touch." When we discover the *picturesque,* indicated in the grounds of the residence to be treated, let us take advantage of it; and while all harshness incompatible with scenery near the house is removed, the original expression may in most cases be heightened, in all, rendered more elegant and appropriate, without lowering it in force or spirit. In like manner good taste will direct us to embellish scenery expressive of *graceful* beauty, by the addition of forms, whether in trees, buildings, or other objects, harmonious in character, as well as in colour and outline.

Section IX

LANDSCAPE OR RURAL ARCHITECTURE

Difference between a city and a country house. The characteristic features of a country house. Examination of the leading principles in Rural Architecture. The different styles. The Grecian style, its merits and defects, and its associations. The Roman and Italian styles. The Pointed or Gothic style. The Tudor Mansion. The English Cottage, or Rural Gothic style. These styles considered in relation to situation or scenery. Individual tastes. Entrance Lodges.

> A house amid the quiet country's shades,
> With length'ning vistas, ever sunny glades;
> Beauty and fragrance clustering o'er the wall,
> A porch inviting, and an ample hall.

Architecture, either practically considered, or viewed as an art of taste, is a subject so important and comprehensive in itself, that volumes would be requisite to do it justice. Buildings of every description, from the humble cottage to the lofty temple, are objects of such constant recurrence in every habitable part of the globe, and are so strikingly indicative of the intelligence, character, and taste of the inhabitants, that they possess in themselves a great and peculiar interest for the mind. To have a "local habitation,"—a permanent dwelling, that we can give the impress of our own mind, and identify with our own existence—appears to be the ardent wish, sooner or later felt, of every man. . . .

What then are the proper characteristics of a rural residence? The answer to this, in a few words, is, such a dwelling, as from its various accommodations, not only gives ample space for all the comforts and conveniences of a country life, but by its varied and picturesque form and outline, its porches, verandas, etc., also appears to have some reasonable connection, or be in perfect keeping, with surrounding nature. *Architectural beauty* must be considered conjointly with the *beauty of the landscape* or situation. Buildings of almost every description, and particularly those for the habitation of man, will be considered by the mind of taste, not only as architectural objects of greater or less merit, but as component parts of the general scene; united with the surrounding lawn, embosomed in tufts of trees and shrubs, if properly designed and constructed, they will even serve to impress a character upon the surrounding landscape. Their effect will frequently be good or bad, not merely as they are excellent or indifferent examples of a certain style of building, but as they are happily or unhappily combined with the adjacent scenery. The intelligent observer will readily appreciate the truth of this, and acknowledge the value, as well as necessity, of something besides architectural knowledge. And he will perceive how much more likely to be successful, are the efforts of him, who in composing and constructing a rural residence, calls in to the aid of architecture, the genius of the landscape;—whose mind is imbued with a taste for beautiful scenery, and who so elegantly and ingeniously engrafts art upon nature, as to heighten her beauties; while by the harmonious union he throws a borrowed charm around his own creation.

The English, above all other people, are celebrated for their skill in what we consider *rural adaptation.* Their residences seem to be a part of the scenes where they are situated; for their exquisite taste and nice perception of the beauties of Landscape Gardening and rural scenery, lead them to erect those picturesque edifices, which by their varied outlines, seem in exquisite keeping with nature; while by the numberless climbing plants, shrubs, and fine ornamental trees with which they surround them, they form beautiful pictures of rural beauty. Even the various offices connected with the dwelling, partially concealed by groups of foliage, and contributing to the expression of domestic comfort, while they extend out, and give importance to the main edifice, also serve to connect it, in a less abrupt manner, with the grounds. . . .

There are two features, which it is now generally admitted, contribute strongly to the expression of purpose in a dwelling-house, and especially in a country residence. These are the chimney-tops and the entrance porch. . . .

A *Porch* strengthens or conveys expression of purpose, because, instead of leaving the entrance door bare, as in manufactories and buildings of an inferior description, it serves both as a note of preparation, and an effectual shelter and protection to the entrance. Besides this, it gives a dignity and importance to that entrance, pointing it out to the stranger as the place of approach. A fine country house, without a porch or covered shelter to the doorway of some description, is therefore, as incomplete, to the correct eye, as a well-printed book without a title page, leaving the stranger to plunge at once in *media res,* without the friendly preparation of a single word of introduction. Porches are susceptible of every variety of form and decoration, from the embattled and buttressed portal of the Gothic castle, to the latticed arbor-porch of the cottage, around which the festoons of luxuriant climbing plants cluster, giving an effect not less beautiful than the richly carved capitals of the classic portico.

In this country, no architectural feature is more plainly expressive of purpose in our dwelling-houses than the *veranda,* or piazza. The unclouded splendor and fierce heat of our summer sun, render this very general appendage a source of real comfort and enjoyment; and the long veranda round many of our country residences stand in stead of the paved terraces of the English mansions as the place for promenade; while during the warmer portions of the season, half of the days or evenings are there passed in the enjoyment of the cool breezes, secure under low roofs supported by the open colonnade, from the solar rays, or the dews of night. The obvious utility of the veranda in this climate, (especially in the middle and southern states,) will, therefore, excuse its adoption into any style of architecture that may be selected for our domestic uses, although abroad, buildings in the style in question, as the Gothic, for example, are not usually accompanied by such an appendage. An artist of the least taste or invention, will easily compose an addition, of this kind, that will be in good keeping with the rest of the edifice. . . .

24   A. J. Downing, The Horticulturist* *1846–52*

Before his *Treatise* appeared, and increasingly thereafter, Downing was engaged to design country estate landscapes, first along the Hudson highlands near his home in Newburgh and then further afield. In his diary, Sidney G. Fisher had noted Downing's work for both his brother and cousin, observing with particular interest that Downing was paid a fee for his services.[†] To reach an even larger audience, Downing established *The Horticulturist*, in which he published a series of articles covering a broad range of practical and theoretical interests in gardening and horticulture, including such topics as shade and fruit trees, agriculture, landscape gardening (that is, landscape architecture), the design of country houses, and rural architecture. He was especially adamant in support of urban parks, joining with Willaim Cullen Bryant in pressing for the creation of a public landscaped park in New York. Following his drowning in a steamboat accident near Yonkers in 1852, these articles from *The Horticulturist* were collected, edited, and published as *Rural Essays;* two of these are reprinted here with the dates of their original publication.

PUBLIC CEMETERIES AND PUBLIC GARDENS

July, 1849

One of the most remarkable illustrations of the popular taste, in this country, is to be found in the rise and progress of our rural cemeteries.

Twenty years ago, nothing better than a common grave-yard, filled with high grass, and a chance sprinkling of weeds and thistles, was to be found in the Union. If there were one or two exceptions, like the burial ground at New Haven, where a few willow trees broke the monotony of the scene, they existed only to prove the rule more completely.

Eighteen years ago, Mount Auburn, about six miles from Boston, was made a rural cemetery. It was then a charming natural site, finely varied in surface, containing about 80 acres of land, and admirably clothed by groups and masses of native forest trees. It was tastefully laid out, monuments were built, and the whole highly embellished. No sooner was attention generally roused to the charms of this first American cemetery, than the idea took the

*Andrew Jackson Downing, *Rural Essays*, edited, with a "Memoir of the Author" by George William Curtis; and a "Letter to his Friends" by Frederika Bremer, (New York, 1853), 139–42, 147–59, 209–13.

[†] See the publication of Fisher's diary noted in Chapter 17.

public mind by storm. Travellers made pilgrimages to the Athens of New England, solely to see the realization of their long cherished dream of a resting-place for the dead, at once sacred from profanation, dear to the memory, and captivating to the imagination.

Not twenty years have passed since that time; and, at the present moment, there is scarcely a city of note in the whole country that has not its rural cemetery. The three leading cities of the north, New-York, Philadelphia, Boston, have, each of them besides their great cemeteries,—Greenwood, Laurel Hill, Mount Auburn—many others of less note; but any of which would have astonished and delighted their inhabitants twenty years ago. Philadelphia has, we learn, nearly twenty rural cemeteries at the present moment,—several of them belonging to distinct societies, sects or associations, while others are open to all.[1]

The great attraction of these cemeteries, to the mass of the community, is not in the fact that they are burial-places, or solemn places of meditation for the friends of the deceased, or striking exhibitions of monumental sculpture, though all these have their influence. All these might be realized in a burial-ground, planted with straight lines of willows, and sombre avenues of evergreens. The true secret of the attraction lies in the natural beauty of the sites, and in the tasteful and harmonious embellishment of these sites by art. Nearly all these cemeteries were rich portions of forest land, broken by hill and dale, and varied by copses and glades, like Mount Auburn and Greenwood, or old country-seats, richly wooded with fine planted trees, like Laurel Hill. Hence, to an inhabitant of the town, a visit to one of these spots has the united charm of nature and art,—the double wealth of rural and moral associations. It awakens at the same moment, the feeling of human sympathy and the love of natural beauty, implanted in every heart. His must be a dull or a trifling soul that neither swells with emotion, or rises with admiration, at the varied beauty of these lovely and hallowed spots.

Indeed, in the absence of great public gardens, such as we must surely one day have in America, our rural cemeteries are doing a great deal to enlarge and educate the popular taste in rural embellishment. They are for the most part laid out with admirable taste; they contain the greatest variety of trees and shrubs to be found in the country, and several of them are kept in a manner seldom equalled in private places.[2]

The character of each of the three great cemeteries is essentially distinct. *Greenwood*, the largest, and unquestionably the finest, is grand, dignified, and park-like. It is laid out in a broad and simple style, commands noble ocean views, and is admirably kept. *Mount Auburn* is richly pictur-

---

[1] We made a rough calculation from some data obtained at Philadelphia lately, by which we find that, including the cost of the lots, more than a million and a half of dollars have been expended in the purchase and decoration of cemeteries in that neighborhood alone.

[2] Laurel Hill is especially rich in rare trees. We saw, last month, almost every procurable species of hardy tree and shrub growing there,—among others, the Cedar of Lebanon, the Deodar Cedar, the Paulownia, the Araucaria, etc. Rhododendrons and Azaleas were in full bloom; and the purple Beeches, the weeping Ash, rare Junipers, Pines, and deciduous trees were abundant in many parts of the grounds. Twenty acres of new ground have just been added to this cemetery. It is a better *arboretum* than can easily be found elsewhere in the country.

esque, in its varied hill and dale, and owes its charm mainly to this variety and intricacy of sylvan features. *Laurel Hill* is a charming *pleasure-ground*, filled with beautiful and rare shrubs and flowers; at this season, a wilderness of roses, as well as fine trees and monuments.[3]

To enable the reader to form a correct idea of the influence which these beautiful cemeteries constantly exercise on the public mind, it is only necessary to refer to the rapidity with which they have increased in fifteen years, as we have just remarked. To enable them to judge how largely they arouse public curiosity, we may mention that at Laurel Hill, four miles from Philadelphia, an account was kept of the number of visitor during last season; and the sum total, as we were told by one of the directors, was nearly 30,000 persons, who entered the gates between April and December, 1848. Judging only from occasional observations, we should imagine that double that number visit Greenwood, and certainly an equal number, Mount Auburn, in a season.

We have already remarked, that, in the absence of public gardens, rural cemeteries, in a certain degree, supplied their place. But does not this general interest, manifested in these cemeteries, prove that public gardens, established in a liberal and suitable manner, near our large cities, would be equally successful? If 30,000 persons visit a cemetery in a single season, would not a large public garden be equally a matter of curious investigation? Would not such gardens educate the public taste more rapidly than anything else? And would not the progress of horticulture, as a science and an art, be equally benefited by such establishments? The passion for rural pleasures is destined to be the predominant passion of all the more thoughtful and educated portion of our people; and any means of gratifying their love for ornamental or useful gardening, will be eagerly seized by hundreds of thousands of our countrymen.

Let us suppose a joint-stock company, formed in any of our cities, for the purpose of providing its inhabitants with the luxury of a public garden. A site should be selected with the same judgment which has already been

---

[3] Few things are perfect; and beautiful and interesting as our rural cemeteries now are,—more beautiful and interesting than any thing of the same kind abroad, we cannot pass by one feature in all, marked by the most violent bad taste; we mean the hideous *ironmongery*, which they all more or less display. Why, if the separate lots *must* be inclosed with iron railings, the railings should not be of simple and unobtrusive patterns, we are wholly unable to conceive. As we now see them, by far the greater part are so ugly as to be positive blots on the beauty of the scene. Fantastic conceits and gimcracks in iron might be pardonable as adornments of the balustrade of a circus or a temple of Comus; but how reasonable beings can tolerate them as inclosures to the quiet grave of a family, and in such scenes of sylvan beauty, is mountain high above our comprehension.

But this is not all; as if to show how far human infirmity can go, we noticed lately several lots in one of these cemeteries, not only inclosed with a most barbarous piece of *irony*, but the gate of which was positively ornamented with the coat of arms of the owner, accompanied by a brass doorplate, on which was engraved the owner's name, and city residence! All the world has amused itself with the epitaph on a tombstone in Père la Chaise, erected by a wife to her husband's memory; in which, after recapitulating the many virtues of the departed, the bereaved one concludes—"his disconsolate widow still continues the business, No.—, Rose-street, Paris." We really have some doubts if the disconsolate widow's epitaph advertisement is not in better taste than the cemetery brass doorplate immortality of our friends at home.

shown by the cemetery companies. It should have a varied surface, a good position, sufficient natural wood, with open space and good soil enough for the arrangement of all those portions which require to be newly planted.

Such a garden might, in the space of fifty to one hundred acres afford an example of the principal modes of laying out grounds,—thus teaching practical landscape-gardening. It might contain a collection of all the hardy trees and shrubs that grow in this climate, each distinctly labelled,—so that the most ignorant visitor could not fail to learn something of trees. It might have a botanical arrangement of plants, and a lecture-room where, at the proper season, lectures on botany could be delivered, and the classes which should resort there could study with the growing plants under their eyes. It might be laid out so as, in its wooded position, to afford a magnificent drive for those who chose so to enjoy it; and it might be furnished with suitable ices and other refreshments, so that, like the German gardens, it would be the great promenade of all strangers and citizens, visitors, or inhabitants of the city of whose suburbs it would form a part. But how shall such an establishment be supported? Cemeteries are sustained by the prices paid for lots, which, though costing not a large sum each, make an enormous sum in the aggregate.

We answer, by a small admission fee. Only those who are share-holders would (like those owning lots in a cemetery) have entrance for their horses and carriages. This privilege alone would tempt hundreds to subscribe, thus adding to the capital, while the daily resort of citizens and strangers would give the necessary income; for no traveller would leave a city, possessing such a public garden as we have described, without seeing that, its most interesting feature. The finest band of music, the most rigid police, the certainty of an agreeable promenade and excellent refreshments, would, we think, as surely tempt a large part of the better class of the inhabitants of our cities to such a resort here as in Germany. If the road to Mount Auburn is now lined with coaches, continually carrying the inhabitants of Boston by thousands and tens of thousands, is it not likely that such a garden, full of the most varied instruction, amusement, and recreation, would be ten times more visited? Fêtes might be held there, horticultural societies would make annual exhibitions there, and it would be the general holiday-ground of all who love to escape from the brick walls, paved streets, and stifling atmosphere of towns.

Would such a project pay? This is the home question of all the calculating part of the community, who must open their purse strings to make it a substantial reality.

We can only judge by analogy. The mere yearly rent of Barnum's Museum in Broadway is, we believe, about $10,000 (a sum more than sufficient to meet all the annual expenses of such a garden); and it is not only paid, but very large profits have been made there. Now, if hundreds of thousands of the inhabitants of cities, like New-York, will pay to see stuffed boa-constrictors and *un*-human Belgian giants, or incur the expense and trouble of going five or six miles to visit Greenwood, we think it may safely be estimated that a much larger number would resort to a public garden, at once the finest park, the most charming drive, the most inviting pleasure-ground, and the most agreeable promenade within their reach. That such a project, carefully planned, and liberally and judiciously carried out, would not only *pay*, in money, but largely civilize and refine the national character, foster the love of rural beauty, and increase the knowledge of and taste for rare and beautiful trees and plants, we cannot entertain a reasonable doubt.

It is only necessary for one of the three cities which first opened cemeteries, to set the example, and the thing once fairly seen, it becomes universal. The true policy of republics, is to foster the taste for great public libraries, sculpture and picture galleries, parks and gardens, which *all* may enjoy, since our institutions wisely forbid the growth of private fortunes sufficient to achieve these desirable results in any other way.

THE NEW-YORK PARK

August, 1851

The leading topic of town gossip and newspaper paragraphs just now, in New-York, is the new park proposed by Mayor Kingsland. Deluded New-York has, until lately, contented itself with the little door-yards of space—mere grass-plats of verdure, which form the squares of the city, in the mistaken idea that they are parks. The fourth city in the world (with a growth that will soon make it the second), the commercial metropolis of a continent spacious enough to border both oceans, has not hitherto been able to afford sufficient land to give its citizens (the majority of whom live there the whole year round) any breathing space for pure air, any recreation ground for healthful exercise, any pleasant roads for riding or driving, or any enjoyment of that lovely and refreshing natural beauty from which they have, in leaving the country, reluctantly expatriated themselves for so many years—perhaps for ever. Some few thousands, more fortunate than the rest, are able to escape for a couple of months, into the country, to find repose for body and soul, in its leafy groves and pleasant pastures, or to inhale new life on the refreshing seashore. But in the mean time the city is always full. Its steady population of five hundred thousand souls is always there; always on the increase. Every ship brings a live cargo from over-peopled Europe, to fill up its over-crowded lodging-houses; every steamer brings hundreds of strangers to fill its thronged thoroughfares. Crowded hotels, crowded streets, hot summers, business pursued till it becomes a game of excitement, pleasure followed till its votaries are exhausted, where is the quiet reverse side of this picture of town life, intensified almost to distraction?

Mayor Kingsland spreads it out to the vision of the dwellers in this arid desert of business and dissipation—a green oasis for the refreshment of the city's soul and body. He tells the citizens of that feverish metropolis, as every intelligent man will tell them who knows the cities of the old world, that New-York, and American cities generally, are voluntarily and ignorantly living in a state of complete forgetfulness of nature, and her innocent recreations. That because it is needful in civilized life for men to live in cities,—yes, and unfortunately too, for children to be born and educated without a daily sight of the blessed horizon,—it is not, therefore, needful for them to be so miserly as to live utterly divorced from all pleasant and healthful intercourse with gardens and green fields. He informs them that cool umbrageous groves have not forsworn themselves within town limits, and that half a million of people have a *right* to ask for the "greatest happiness" of parks and pleasure-grounds, as well as for paving stones and gas-lights.

Now that public opinion has fairly settled that a park is necessary, the parsimonious declare that the plot of one hundred and sixty acres proposed by Mayor Kingsland is extravagantly large. Short-sighted economists! If the future growth of the city were confined to the boundaries their narrow vision would fix, it would soon cease to be the commercial emporium of the country. If they were the purveyors of the young giant, he would soon present the sorry spectacle of a robust youth magnificently developed, but whose extremities had outgrown every garment that they had provided to cover his nakedness.

These timid tax-payers, and men nervous in their private pockets of the municipal expenditures, should take a lesson from some of their number to whose admirable foresight we owe the unity of materials displayed in the New-York City-Hall. Every one familiar with New-York, has wondered or smiled at the apparent perversity of taste which gave us a building—in the most conspicuous part of the city, and devoted to the highest municipal uses, three sides of which are pure white marble, and the fourth of coarse, brown stone. But few of those who see that incongruity, know that it was dictated by the narrow-sighted frugality of the common council who were its building committee, and who determined that it would be useless to waste marble on the rear of the City-Hall, *"since that side would only be seen by persons living in the suburbs."*

Thanking Mayor Kingsland most heartily for his proposed new park, the only objection we make to it is that it is *too small.* One hundred and sixty acres of park for a city that will soon contain three-quarters of a million of people! It is only a child's play-ground. Why London has over six thousand acres either within its own limits, or in the accessible suburbs, open to the enjoyment of its population—and six thousand acres composed too, either of the grandest and most lovely park scenery, like Kensington and Richmond, or of luxuriant gardens, filled with rare plants, hot-houses, and hardy shrubs and trees, like the National Garden at Kew. Paris has its Garden of the Tuileries, whose alleys are lined with orange-trees two hundred years old, whose parterres are gay with the brightest flowers, whose cool groves of horse-chestnuts, stretching out to the Elysian Fields, are in the very midst of the city. Yes, and on its outskirts are Versailles (three thousand acres of imperial groves and gardens there also), and Fontainbleau, and St. Cloud, with all the rural, scenic, and palatial beauty that the opulence of the most profuse of French monarchs could create, all open to the *people* of Paris. Vienna has its great *Prater,* to make which, would swallow up most of the "unimproved" part of New-York city. Munich has a superb pleasure-ground of five hundred acres, which makes the Arcadia of her citizens. Even the smaller towns are provided with public grounds to an extent that would beggar the imagination of our short-sighted economists, who would deny "a greenery" to New-York; Frankfort, for example, is skirted by the most beautiful gardens, formed upon the platform which made the old ramparts of the city— gardens filled with the loveliest plants and shrubs, tastefully grouped along walks over *two miles* in extent.

Looking at the present government of the city as about to provide, in the People's Park, a breathing zone, and healthful place for exercise for a city of half a million of souls, we trust they will not be content with the limited number of acres already proposed. *Five hundred acres* is the smallest area that should be reserved for the future wants of such a city, *now*, while it may be obtained. Five hundred acres may be selected between Thirty-ninth-street and the Harlem River, including a varied surface of land, a good deal of which is yet waste area, so that the whole may be purchased at something like a million of dollars. In that area there would be space enough to have broad reaches of park and pleasure-grounds, with a real feeling of the breadth and beauty of green fields, the perfume and freshness of nature. In its midst would be located the great distributing reservoirs of the Croton aqueduct, formed into lovely lakes of limpid water, covering many acres, and heightening the charm of the sylvan accessories by the finest natural contrast. In such a park, the citizens who would take excursions in carriages or on horseback, could have the substantial delights of country roads and country scenery, and forget, for a time the rattle of the pavements and the glare of brick walls. Pedestrians would find quiet and secluded walks when they wished to be solitary, and broad alleys filled with thousands of happy faces, when they would be gay. The thoughtful denizen of the town would go out there in the morning, to hold converse with the whispering trees, and the weary tradesmen in the evening, to enjoy an hour of happiness by mingling in the open space with "all the world."

The many beauties and utilities that would gradually grow out of a great park like this, in a great city like New-York, suggest themselves immediately and forcibly. Where would be found so fitting a position for noble works of art, the statues, monuments, and buildings commemorative at once of the great men of the nation, of the history of the age and country, and the genius of our highest artists? In the broad area of such a verdant zone would gradually grow up, as the wealth of the city increases, winter gardens of glass, like the great Crystal Palace, where the whole people could luxuriate in groves of the palms and spice trees of the tropics, at the same moment that sleighing parties glided swiftly and noiselessly over the snow-covered surface of the country-like avenues of the wintry park without. Zoological Gardens, like those of London and Paris, would gradually be formed by private subscription or public funds, where thousands of old and young would find daily pleasure in studying natural history, illustrated by all the wildest and strangest animals of the globe, almost as much at home in their paddocks and jungles, as if in their native forests; and Horticultural and Industrial Societies would hold their annual shows there, and great expositions of the arts would take place in spacious buildings within the park, far more fittingly than in the noise and din of the crowded streets of the city.

We have said nothing of the *social* influence of such a great park in New-York. But this is really the most interesting phase of the whole matter. It is a fact not a little remarkable, that, ultra democratic as are the political tendencies of America, its most intelligent social tendencies are almost wholly in a contrary direction. And among the topics discussed by the advocates and opponents of the new park, none seem so poorly understood as the social aspect of the thing. It is, indeed, both curious and amusing to see the stand taken on the one hand by the million, that the park is made for the "upper ten," who ride in fine carriages, and, on the other hand, by the wealthy and refined, that a park in this country will be "usurped by rowdies and low people." Shame upon our republican compatriots who so little understand the elevating influences of the beautiful in nature and in art, when enjoyed in common by thousands and hundreds of thousands of all classes without distinction! They can never have seen, how all over France and Germany, the whole population of the cities pass their afternoons and evenings together, in the beautiful public parks and gardens. How they enjoy together the same music, breathe the same atmosphere of art, enjoy the same scenery, and grow into social freedom by the very influences of easy intercourse, space and beauty that surround them. In Germany, especially, they have never seen how the highest and the lowest partake alike of the common enjoyment—the prince seated beneath the trees on a rush-bottomed chair, before a little wooden table, supping his coffee or his ice, with the same freedom from state and pretension as the simplest subject. Drawing-room conventionalities are too narrow for a mile or two of spacious garden landscape, and one can be happy with ten thousand in the social freedom of a community of genial influences, without the unutterable pang of not having been *introduced* to the company present.

These social doubters who thus intrench themselves in the sole citadel of *exclusiveness* in republican America, mistake our people and their destiny. If we would but have listened to them, our magnificent river and lake steamers, those real palaces of the million, would have had no velvet couches, no splendid mirrors, no luxurious carpets. Such costly and rare appliances of civilization, they would have told us, could only be rightly used by the privileged families of wealth, and would be trampled upon and utterly ruined by the democracy of the country, who travel one hundred miles for half a dollar. And yet these, our floating palaces and our monster hotels, with their purple and fine linen, are they not respected by the majority who use them, as truly as other palaces by their rightful sovereigns? Alas, for the faithlessness of the few, who possess, regarding the capacity for culture of the many, who are wanting. Even upon the lower platform of liberty and education that the masses stand in Europe, we see the elevating influences of a wide popular enjoyment of galleries of art, public libraries, parks and gardens, which have raised the people in *social* civilization and social culture to a far higher level than we have yet attained in republican America. And yet this broad ground of popular refinement *must* be taken in republican America, for it belongs of right more truly here, than elsewhere. It is republican in its very idea and tendency. It takes up popular education where the common school and ballot-box leave it, and raises up the working-man to the same level of enjoyment with the man of leisure and accomplishment. The higher social and artistic elements of every man's nature lie dormant within him, and every laborer is a possible gentleman, not by the possession of money or fine clothes—but through the refining influence of intellectual and moral culture. Open wide, therefore, the doors of your libraries and picture galleries, all ye true republicans! Build halls where knowledge shall be freely diffused among men, and not shut up within the narrow walls of narrower institutions. Plant spacious parks in your cities, and unloose their gates as wide as the gate of morning to the whole people. As there are no dark places at noon day, so education and culture—the true sunshine of the soul—will banish the plague spots of democracy; and the dread of the ignorant exclusive who has no faith in the refinement of a republic, will stand abashed in the next century, before a whole people whose system of voluntary education embraces (combined with perfect individual freedom), not only common schools of rudimentary knowledge, but common enjoyments for all classes in the higher realms of art, letters, science, social recreations, and enjoyments. Were our legislators but wise enough to understand, to-day, the destinies of the New World, the gentility of Sir Philip Sidney, made universal, would be not half so much a miracle fifty years hence in America, as the idea of a whole nation of laboring-men reading and writing, was, in his day, in England.

25   A. J. Downing, Cottage Residences* *1842*

Downing's influence on architecture surpassed his considerable impact on landscape gardening. This architectural impact was due largely to two books. In *Cottage Residences*, illustrated with the work of such architects as A. J. Davis and John Notman, Downing gave fuller expression to his earlier discussion of "rural architecture"; in the selection reprinted here, although stating his preference for masonry, he provides an alternative frame design, utilizing the board-and-batten siding, that soon became popular across the country and was used for houses from Maine to Oregon. In all his work, Downing relied on professional architects (he readily acknowledged Davis and Notman in the preface to *Cottage Residences*), but, in view of his growing landscape practice, a partnership was in order. In 1850, while in England, Downing met the young architect Calvert Vaux (1824–95) whom he encouraged to come to the United States; Vaux became Downing's draftsman and then partner. Meanwhile, so voluminous were the inquiries coming to Downing after publication of *Cottage Residences* that he published a second work with more examples: *The Architecture of Country Houses* (New York, 1850). After Downing's death, Vaux produced his own volume, *Villas and Cottages* (New York, 1857), written along the same lines.

PREFACE

A hearty desire to contribute something to the improvement of the domestic architecture and the rural taste of our country, has been the motive which has influenced me in preparing this little volume. With us, almost

*Andrew Jackson Downing, *Cottage Residences, or, A Series of Designs for Rural Cottages and Cottage Villas and their Gardens and Grounds, adapted to North America* (New York, 1842), v–viii, 1–5, 8–16, 17–26, 92–98, 102–06.

every man either builds, or looks forward to building, a home for himself, at some period of his life; it may be only a log hut, or a most rustic cottage, but perhaps also, a villa, or a mansion. As yet, however, our houses are mostly either of the plainest and most meagre description, or, if of a more ambitious, they are frequently of a more objectionable character—shingle palaces, of very questionable convenience, and not in the least adapted, by their domestic and rural beauty, to harmonize with our lovely natural landscapes.

Now I am desirous that every one who lives in the country, and in a country-house, should be in some degree conversant with domestic architecture, not only because it will be likely to improve the comfort of his own house, and hence all the houses in the country, but that it will enlarge his mind, and give him new sources of enjoyment.

It is not my especial object at this moment, to dwell upon the superior convenience which may be realized in our houses, by a more familiar acquaintance with architecture. The advantages of an ingeniously arranged and nicely adapted plan, over one carelessly and ill-contrived, are so obvious to every one, that they are self-evident. This is the ground-work of domestic architecture, the great importance of which is recognized by all mankind, and some ingenuity and familiarity with practical details are only necessary to give us compact, convenient, and comfortable houses, with the same means and in the same space as the most awkward and unpleasing forms.

But I am still more anxious to inspire in the minds of my readers and countrymen livelier perceptions of the *beautiful*, in everything that relates to our houses and grounds. I wish to awaken a quicker sense of the grace, the elegance, or the picturesqueness of fine forms that are capable of being produced in these, by Rural Architecture and Landscape Gardening—a sense which will not only refine and elevate the mind, but open to it new and infinite resources of delight. There are perhaps a few upon whose souls nearly all emanations of beauty fall impressionless; but there are also many who see the Beautiful, in nature and art, only feebly and dimly, either from the want of proper media through which to view her, or a little direction as to where she is found. How many, too, are there, who even discover the Beautiful, in a picture, or a statue, who yet fail to admire her, rounding with lines of grace, and touching with shades of harmony all common nature, and pervading silently all material forms! "Men," says Goethe, "are so inclined to content themselves with what is commonest, so easily do the spirit and the sense grow dead to the impression of the Beautiful and the Perfect, that every person should strive to nourish in his mind the faculty of feeling these things, by everything in his power, for no man can bear to be wholly deprived of such enjoyment; it is only because they are not used to taste of what is excellent, that the generality of people take delight in silly and insipid things, provided they be new. For this reason, every day one ought to see a fine picture, read a good poem, hear a little song, and if it were possible, to speak a few reasonable words."

It is in this regard, that I wish to inspire all persons with a love of beautiful forms, and a desire to assemble them around their daily walks of life. I wish them to appreciate how superior is the charm of that home where we discover the tasteful cottage or villa, and the well designed and neatly kept garden or grounds, full of beauty and harmony,—not the less beautiful and harmonious, because simple and limited; and to become aware that these superior forms, and the higher and more refined enjoyment derived from them, may be had at the same cost and with the same labor as a clumsy dwelling, and its uncouth and ill designed accessories.

More than all, I desire to see these sentiments cherished for their pure moral tendency. "All *beauty* is an outward expression of inward good," and so closely are the Beautiful and the True allied, that we shall find, if we become sincere lovers of the grace, the harmony, and the loveliness with which rural homes and rural life are capable of being invested, that we are silently opening our hearts to an influence which is higher and deeper than the mere *symbol;* and that if we thus worship in the true spirit, we shall attain a nearer view of the Great Master, whose words, in all his material universe, are written in lines of Beauty.

And how much happiness, how much pure pleasure, that strengthens and invigorates our best and holiest affections, is there not experienced, in bestowing upon our homes something of grace and loveliness—in making the place dearest to our hearts a sunny spot, where the social sympathies take shelter securely under the shadowy eaves, or grow and entwine trustfully with the tall trees or wreathed vines that cluster around as if striving to shut out whatever of bitterness or strife may be found in the open highways of the world. What an unfailing barrier against vice, immorality, and bad habits, are those tastes which led us to embellish a home to which at all times and in all places we turn with delight as being the object and the scene of our fondest cares, labors, and enjoyments; whose humble roof, whose shady porch, whose verdant lawn and smiling flowers, all breathe forth to us, in true, earnest tones, a domestic feeling, that at once purifies the heart, and binds us more closely to our fellow beings.

In this volume, the first yet published in this country devoted to Rural Architecture, I am conscious of offering but a slight and imperfect contribution to this important subject, which I trust will be the precursor of more varied and complete works from others, adapted to our peculiar wants and climate. The very great interest now beginning to manifest itself in rural improvements of every kind, leads us to believe and to hope, that at no very distant day our country residences may rival the "cottage homes of England," so universally and so justly admired.

The relation between a country-house and its "surroundings," has led me to consider, under the term Residences, both the architectural and the gardening designs. To constitute an agreeable whole, these should indeed have a harmonious correspondence, one with the other; and although most of the following designs have not actually been carried into execution, yet it is believed that they will, either entirely or in part, be found adapted to many cases of every day occurrence, or at least furnish hints for variations suitable for peculiar circumstances and situations.

My acknowledgments are due to J. Notman, Esq., Architect, of Philadelphia, for the architectural portion of Design IX.; and to Alexander J. Davis., Esq., Architect, of New York, for that of Design X., and for a revision of some of the architectural drawings and details.

A. J. D.

Highland Gardens
Newburgh, N.Y., June, 1842

COTTAGE RESIDENCES

Architectural Suggestions

True Taste is an excellent economist. She confines her choice to few objects, and delights to produce great effects by small means; while False Taste is for ever sighing after the new and rare; and reminds us, in her works, of the scholar of Apelles, who, not being able to paint his Helen beautiful, determined to make her fine.

There are certain leading principles connected with architecture, which earnestly demand our attention on the very threshold of the subject. In an indefinite manner they are, perhaps, acknowledged by all intelligent minds, but they are only distinctly and clearly understood by those, who, having analysed the expressions or characters inherent in various forms and modes of buildi z, have traced the impressions derived, whether of utility or beauty, to their proper origin. When the mind has arrived at this point, the satisfaction it enjoys in an admirable work, is proportionably greater; in the same manner (though in less degree) as the "devout astronomer" enjoys, with a far more intelligent and fervent rapture, his starry gaze, than the ignorant eye that sees only a myriad of lights hung above to dispel the gloom of midnight.

As the first object of a dwelling is to afford a shelter to man, the first principle belonging to architecture grows out of this primary necessity, and it is called the principle of Fitness or *usefulness*. After this, man naturally desires to give some distinctive character to his own habitation, to mark its superiority to those devoted to animals. This gives rise to the principle of *Expression of* Purpose. Finally, the love of the beautiful, inherent in all finer natures, and its exhibition in certain acknowledged forms, has created the principle of the *Expression of* Style. In other words, all these principles may be regarded as sources of beauty in domestic architecture; Fitness being the *beauty of utility;* Expression of Purpose, the *beauty of propriety;* and Expression of Style, the *beauty of form and sentiment*, which is the highest in the scale. We shall say a few words in illustration of our ideas on each particular division.

Fitness, or use, is the first principle to be considered in all buildings. Those indeed who care little for any other character in a dwelling, generally pride themselves upon the amount of convenience they have been able to realize in it; and nothing could be in worse taste than to embellish or decorate a dwelling-house which is wanting in comfort, as the beautiful is never satisfactory when not allied to the true.

In a dwelling-house, our every day comfort is so entirely dependent on a convenient arrangement of the rooms, or plan of the interior, that this is universally acknowledged to be the most important consideration. To have the principal rooms or apartments situated on the most favorable side of the house with regard to aspect, in order that they may be light, warm, or airy, and, in respect to view, that they may command the finest prospects, are desiderata in every kind of dwelling. In all climates the stormy quarters are the worst aspects, and the fair weather quarters the best ones. Thus, in the middle states, a south-west aspect (all other things being equal) is the best for the finer rooms, and a north-east the most disagreeable. In hot climates, a north exposure may be agreeable on account of its coolness, but in all temperate latitudes, a southern one is more desirable for the entire year.

In arranging the different apartments of a cottage or villa, great variations will naturally arise out of the peculiar circumstances, mode of living, or individual wants of the family by whom it is to be inhabited. Thus, a small family living a secluded life, or one composed of infirm persons, would prefer to have their sleeping apartments, their kitchen, and other conveniences, on the same floor with the parlor or living room, even at the expense of one or two handsome rooms, for the sake of the greater convenience in conducting domestic affairs, and the greater ease and comfort thereby realized. On the other hand, a family fond of social intercourse, and accustomed to entertain, would greatly prefer, in a cottage or villa of moderate size, to have several handsome apartments, as a drawing-room, library, dining-room, etc., occupying almost exclusively the principal floor, placing the kitchen and its offices in the basement, and the bedrooms in the second story. This arrangement would perhaps be less convenient in a few respects for the family, but it would be more elegant and more satisfactory for the kind of residence intended—each department of the house being complete in itself, and intruding itself but little on the attention of the family or guests when not required to be visible, which is the *ideal* of domestic accommodation. A kitchen on the first floor has the advantage of being more accessible, and more completely under the *surveillance* of the mistress of the house, but, on the other hand, it is open to the objection of being occasionally offensive in the matter of sound, sight, and smells; unless, in the case of large houses, where these may be excluded by long passages and double doors. Some families have a literary taste, and to them a library would be an indispensable apartment, while others, caring less for books, would in the same space prefer a bedroom. We mention these circumstances to show in what a relative sense the term fitness, as regards accommodation, must be used, and how many peculiar circumstances must be considered before we can pronounce decidedly upon the merits or demerits of a plan. What may be entirely fit and convenient for one, would be considered quite unsuitable for another. Hence the great difficulty of arranging plans exactly to suit all wants. And hence the importance to all persons, and especially ladies, who understand best the principle of convenience, of acquiring some architectural knowledge. There are doubtless many desiring to build a cottage, who will find no one of the plans hereafter submitted precisely what they want, and this will be found to arise mainly from their having certain peculiar wants growing out of their habits or position, for which no artist, not familiar with these, could possibly provide.

There are some rules of fitness of nearly universal application. Thus a dining-room should obviously have connected with it, either a pantry or a large closet, or both; and it should be so placed as to afford easy ingress and egress to, and from the kitchen. The drawing-room, parlor, or finest apartment, should look out on the most beautiful view, either over a distant prospect, if there be such, or, if not, upon the fine home landscape of trees, lawn, or flower-garden. A library may occupy a more secluded position, and requires less attention to outward circumstances, as the *matériel* from whence it dispenses enjoyment is within itself. Again, there are other minor points more generally understood, which may be considered under this principle, and to which we need scarcely allude. Among these are the construction of proper drains to the kitchen and basement, the introduction of water pipes, cisterns, etc. A bathing room requires little space, and may be easily constructed in any cottage, and its great importance to health renders it a most desirable feature in all our houses. No dwelling can be considered complete which has not a water-closet under its roof, though the expense may yet for some time prevent their general introduction in small cottages.

In a country like ours, where the population is comparatively sparse, civil rights equal, and wages high, good servants or domestics are comparatively rare, and not likely to retain their places for a long time. The maximum of comfort, therefore, is found to consist in employing the smallest number of servants actually necessary. This may be greatly facilitated by having all the apartments conveniently arranged with reference to their various uses, and still further by introducing certain kinds of domestic labor-saving apparatus to lessen the amount of service required, or to render its performance easy. . . .

The mode of construction, and the materials employed, are also comprised under the head of fitness. In this country, from the great abundance and cheapness of wood, it has, until within a few years, been almost the only material employed in constructing country houses; but as timber has grown scarcer in the forest, it has become dearer, until, in many parts of the Atlantic States, stone or brick is equally economical. Wood is acknowledged by all architects to be the worst material for building, and should never be employed when it is in the power of the builder to use any other. Its want of durability, the expense of painting it and keeping it in repair, and its frailness and liability to decay by the action of the weather, are all very serious objections to it as a material for dwelling-houses. A cottage of wood is, from the thinness of the exterior, necessarily warmer in summer, and colder in winter, than one built of more solid materials. Filling-in with brick decreases this objection, but does not entirely remove it. In point of taste, a house built of wood strikes us the least agreeably, as our pleasure in beholding a beautiful form is marred by the idea of the frailness of the material composing that form. We are aware that the almost universal prevalence of wooden country houses in the United States has weakened this impression, but the strength with which it strikes an European, accustomed to solidity and permanence in a dwelling, is the best proof of the truth of our remark. And even in this country, the change of feeling which is daily taking place on this subject, shows very plainly in how little estimation wood will be held as a building material, compared with brick or stone, by the next generation.

Brick is the next best material to wood, and is every day coming into more general use. The walls formed of it, if well constructed, have a solidity and permanence appropriate for a dwelling, and requiring little cost to keep it in repair. The offensive hue of red brick walls in the country, is easily removed by coloring them any agreeable tint, which will also render them dryer and more permanent. Brick and stucco (that is, a wall built of rough brick, and coated exteriorly with a cement) is, when well executed, one of the best materials for cottages or villas. It is much warmer and dryer than wood, or even stone, and is equal to the latter in external effect, when marked off and colored to resemble it. We have no doubt that in a short time it will have a very general preference in most sections of the country.[1]

Stone is generally conceded to be superior, on the whole, to any other material for building. This is owing to its great durability and solidity, both in expression and in reality; and to its requiring no trouble to keep it in repair, as it suffers little or no injury from the action of the elements.

When houses are built of brick or stone, the interior plastering should never be put directly upon the inner face of the wall, as is sometimes done by careless or ignorant mechanics: but the lathing upon which it is formed should always be separated from the solid wall by what is technically called "furring off," which leaves a space of two or more inches between the solid wall, and that of plaster. This vacuity is, of course, occupied by air, which is a better non-conductor than any wall, prevents effectually the penetration of all dampness, and renders the wall warmer than would three times the same thickness of solid material.

When we are necessarily restricted to the employment of a certain material, both fitness and good taste require that there should be a correspondence between the material used and the style adopted for the building. Heavy and massive architecture, a temple, a castle, or a mansion, should be built of stone only, or some solid enduring substance, but cottages in some light and fanciful styles may with more propriety be erected in wood, that material being in harmony with the expression of the form and outlines. There cannot well be a greater violation of correct taste, than to build a Gothic castellated villa with thin wooden boards. It is a species of counterfeit coin which will never pass current with cultivated minds. De Tocqueville, in his remarks on the spirit in which the Americans cultivate the art, says, "When I arrived for the first time at New York, by that part of the Atlantic ocean which is called the Narrows, I was surprised to perceive along the shore, at some distance from the city, a considerable number of palaces of white marble, several of which were built after the models of ancient architecture." His surprise was still greater, however, when he went the next day to inspect the temple that had particularly attracted his notice, to find that its imposing portico was supported by huge *columns of painted wood*.

Something might be said on the subject of fitness, with regard to the furniture and interior decoration of our dwelling-houses. There is a great charm about a country house, fitted up or furnished simply, appropriately, and comfortably. A profusion of mirrors, of gilding, or of chairs or sofas, too magnificent except for show, strikes us disagreeably amid the freshness, the silence, and simplicity of nature, which quietly looks us in the face at every window of a house in the country.

---

[1] The common hydraulic cements of New York are unfit for plastering the exterior of houses, and many persons who have only seen these employed (mixed perhaps with dirty, instead of sharp, clean sand), suppose that all cements are equally liable to crumble by exposure to damp and frost. The cement (or hydraulic limes) of Connecticut and Pennsylvania are greatly superior for stucco or external plaster, becoming, when well applied, nearly as firm and durable as stone.

The *expression of purpose* in architecture is conveyed by features in a building, or by its whole appearance, suggesting the end in view, or the purpose for which it is intended. A church, for example, is easily known by its spire, or a barn by its plain large doors, and the absence of chimneys, and the reason acknowledges a satisfaction in finding them to be what they appear, or, in other words, with the *truthfulness* of their expression. Whatever, therefore, tends to heighten expression of purpose, must grow out of some quality which connects itself in the mind with the use for which it is designed, and a genuine mode of increasing our admiration of any building, is to render it expressive of the purpose for which it is built.

Although, at first thought, it would appear that persons would be little likely to fall into error in violating the truthfulness of a building, yet examples do not unfrequently occur. Some of our dwelling-houses are so meagre and comfortless in their exteriors, that one might be fairly pardoned for supposing them barns, and, on the other hand, we have seen stables so decorated with green shutters and pilasters, that they have actually been mistaken for dwelling-houses. A blind passion for a particular style of building may also tend to destroy expression of purpose. It would certainly be difficult for a stranger in some of our towns, where the taste for Grecian temples prevails, to distinguish with accuracy between a church, a bank, and a hall of justice.

Not only should the whole house have a general character denoting the end in view, but every portion of it should be made, as far as possible, to convey the same impression. The various useful features entering into its composition, should all be expressive of the end for which they are intended, and should appear to answer their purpose. Thus large windows indicate spacious and well ventilated apartments, and although propriety requires the windows of the principal rooms to be made larger than those of the chamber story, yet the latter should not be shorn of their due proportions so as to be expressive of imperfect accommodation. One of the most common errors, which of late has crept into our suburban builders' heads, is the introduction of short attic windows into the second or third story of their houses. However satisfactory such dwellings may otherwise be, the expression of low and confined chambers, conveyed by these cramped windows, destroys all pleasure in contemplating their exteriors.

The prominent features, conveying expression of purpose in dwelling-houses, are, the chimneys, the windows, and the porch, veranda, or piazza; and for this reason, whenever it is desired to raise the character of a cottage or villa above mediocrity, attention should first be bestowed on those portions of the building.

The chimney tops, in all countries where fires are used, are decidedly expressive of purpose, as they are associated with all our ideas of warmth, the cheerful fire-side, and the social winter circle. The learned Bishop Hall says,

> Look to the tower'd chimnies, which should be
> The wind-pipes of good hospitalitie.

"In every human habitation," says Loudon, "these chimney tops ought to be conspicuous objects, because they are its essential characteristics. They distinguish apartments destined for human beings from those designed for lodging cattle. They also distinguish a dwelling-house from a manufactory or workshop, by their size, number, form, or disposition." As chimney tops are thus so essential a part of dwelling-houses, we should endeavor to render them pleasing objects, and increase their importance by making them ornamental. The clumsy mass of bricks should be enlivened and rendered elegant by varying its form, ornamenting its sides and summit, or separating the whole into distinct flues, forming a cluster, in modes of which there are a multitude of suitable examples in the various styles of architecture. The chimney tops generally occupy the highest portions of the roof, breaking against the sky boldly, and, if enriched, will not only increase the expression of purpose, but add also to the picturesque beauty of the composition.

The porch, the veranda, or the piazza, are highly characteristic features, and no dwelling-house can be considered complete without one or more of them. The entrance door, even in the humblest cottage, should always be a conspicuous feature in its front, and it may be rendered so, by a porch or veranda of some kind, which will serve to keep the entrance dry and warm in inclement weather. In all countries like ours, where there are hot summers, a veranda, piazza, or colonnade, is a necessary and delightful appendage to a dwelling-house, and in fact during a considerable part of the year, frequently becomes the lounging apartment of the family. Hence a broad shady veranda suggests ideas of comfort, and is highly expressive of purpose. For the same reason bay or oriel windows, balconies, and terraces, added to villas, increase their interest, not only by their beauty of form, but by their denoting more forcibly those elegant enjoyments which belong to the habitation of man in a cultivated and refined state of society.

The *color* of buildings may very properly be made to increase their expression of truthfulness. Thus a barn or stable being regarded entirely in a useful point of view, may have a quiet, unobtrusive tone of color, while a cottage or villa should be of a cheerful mellow hue harmonizing with the verdure of the country. A mansion may very properly have a graver color than a cottage, to be in unison with its greater dignity and extent. There is one color, however, frequently employed by house painters, which we feel bound to protest against most heartily, as entirely unsuitable, and in bad taste. This is *white*, which is so universally applied to our wooden houses of every size and description. The glaring nature of this color, when seen in contrast with the soft green of foliage, renders it extremely unpleasant to an eye attuned to harmony of coloring, and nothing but its very great prevalence in the United States could render even men of some taste so heedless of its bad effect. No painter of landscapes, that has possessed a name, was ever guilty of displaying in his pictures a glaring white house, but, on the contrary, the buildings introduced by the great masters have uniformly a mellow softened shade of color, in exquisite keeping with the surrounding objects.[2]

[2] To render the effect still worse, our modern builders paint their venetian window shutters a bright green! A cool dark green would be in better taste, and more agreeable to the eye, both from the exterior and the interior.

[There follows a discussion of the proper colors to use on the exterior, including six hand-tinted samples, running from yellow ochre through olive green to slate gray.]

Aside from certain styles of architecture, which have received the approbation of all men for their acknowledged beauty, and which are generally followed by architects, there are also some leading rules which should govern us in the composition of buildings in any style, however simple, because they are inherent sources of beauty, common to all styles.

The first of these is the principle of Unity, a principle of the highest importance in all works of art. There should be an unity of design in all portions of the same building, showing, by a correspondence of its various parts, that they all originated in the same mind; an unity of style, avoiding the introduction, in an established mode, of any portions or members not in keeping with that mode; and an unity of decoration, evinced in the appropriate application of enrichment to the whole, rather than to a single part, of an edifice. These rules of Unity are not unfrequently violated by architects, but always at the expense of the beauty and perfection of their works, as no artist is superior to principles.[3] The production of a *whole* follows as the result of attention to the principles of Unity, and our pleasure in every work of art is enduring, precisely in proportion as it forms a perfect whole. Unity is the principle of *Oneness*, and its violation always shocks a tasteful and consistent mind. As an example of the violation of unity of style, we might refer to a number of country chapels or churches, within our knowledge, where a Grecian portico and Gothic or pointed windows occur in the same composition! Or to illustrate the like in unity of decoration or of design, how many country dwellings have we all seen, with a highly elegant colonnade in front, accompanying bare sides, without the least corresponding enrichment in the windows!

The next principles of composition are those of *Uniformity* and of *Symmetry;* two words which frequently pass as synonymous in common language.

Uniformity in building is the repetition of the same forms in the different portions or sides of a building. "A hut may be recognised as a work of art, however rude or anomalous its form; because, according to human experience, its sides, its roof, and its door, could never have been arranged so as to form a hut by chance. Such a hut is satisfactory as a work of art, but nothing more; but a hut in a square form, gives additional satisfaction by the regularity of its figure; which gives an idea not only of art, but of cultivated or improved art. There can be no doubt, therefore, that the love of regularity is strongly implanted in the human mind; since regularity is the first principle which displays itself in the works of man, composed with a view to beauty."[4] Hence, those persons who have the least taste or imagination, will be found to prefer a plain square or cube, above all others, for a house, as

[3] "Every opportunity should be taken to discountenance that false and vulgar opinion, that rules are the fetters of genius; they are fetters only to men of no genius."—Sir Joshua Reynolds.

[4] "Architectural Magazine," i., 221.

being the first principle of beauty which they are able to discover in architecture.[5]

As Uniformity is the balance of two regular parts, so the principle of Symmetry may be defined the balance of two irregular parts; in other words, Uniformity in works of art is *artistical regularity*, Symmetry, *artistical irregularity*. There are irregular buildings without symmetry, but in all irregular compositions entirely satisfactory, it will generally be found that there is a kind of hidden proportion which one half of the whole bears to the other, and it is this balance which constitutes symmetry.

A building may be highly irregular, it may abound in variety and picturesqueness, and yet be perfectly symmetrical. A pile of building, which is full of irregularity, is also symmetrical, for if we divide it by the imaginary line *a*, the portion on the right balances that on the left; that is, though not in shape, yet in bulk and in the mass of composition; while in a uniform or regular building, the portion to the right balances that on the left both in form and bulk. Now almost all persons, who have not cultivated a taste for architecture, or whose organizations are deficient in this faculty, would prefer a regular house to a symmetrically irregular one, because with them the reason only demands to be satisfied, but with more cultivated minds the taste and imagination are active, and call for a more lively and varied kind of beauty, and the irregular building would be chosen, as affording more intense and enduring pleasure.

As the principles of *Harmony, Variety, &c.*, are intimately connected with, and may be said to grow out of, Unity, Uniformity, and Symmetry, we shall not in our present limits offer any remarks upon them.

The different styles in architecture are certain modes of building, which have had their origin in different countries, and may be considered as standard forms of architectural beauty. They have, almost without exception, had their origin in some lofty enthusiasm of the age, which was embodied by the master artists of the time, generally in the enthusiasm of religion. To the pagan gods were reared the beautiful temples of the Greeks, and, under the more spiritual influence of Christianity, arose those Gothic cathedrals, in which the ponderous stone was wrought in the most exquisite modifications of intricacy and beauty—those cathedrals which, says an eloquent writer, are "a blossoming in stone, subdued by the insatiable demand of harmony in man." In like manner the oriental style, distinguished by its mosques and minarets, and the Egyptian, by its pyramids and cavernous temples, have all had their origin in the same lofty aspirations of the artist.

All domestic architecture, in a given style, should be a subdued expression or manifestation of that style adjusted to the humbler requirements of the building and the more quiet purposes of domestic life. Hence it would evidently be absurd to copy a cathedral, in building a dwelling in the Gothic

---

[5] As, besides this, a square or parallelogram is the most economical form in which a house can be built, and as a small house does not easily permit irregularity, we have adopted it in designing the greater number of cottages which follow, but we have endeavored to raise them above mere uniformity, by adding such characteristic ornaments as give also some *variety* to the compositions.

style, or a temple in a cottage after the Grecian mode.

Nearly all the modes of building in modern use may be referred to two original styles, of which they are only modifications or varieties, viz. to the Grecian, in which horizontal lines prevail, and to the Gothic, in which vertical lines prevail; and there have not been wanting artists who have caught something of the spirit and beauty of the original masterpieces of art, and transfused them into the more domestic styles which have grown out of these to suit the wants of civilized life. Thus, although the pure Grecian style (the temple) was not intended, and is not suitable for domestic purposes, the Roman and the Italian styles, which are modified forms of it, are elegant adaptations of its characteristic forms to this purpose. The Italian style, by its verandas and balconies, its projecting roofs, and the capacity and variety of its form, is especially suited to a warm climate.

In the same manner the Swiss, the Flemish, and other continental modes of building, with exterior galleries, and wide horizontal cornices, are all variations of this mode, only differing in some peculiar adaptations to the climate of the country, or the customs of the people.

Neither has the Gothic been confined to the cathedral, where, as the noblest form, it exists in its grandeur and purity, but its beauty and picturesqueness have reappeared in the old English styles of domestic architecture. The most perfect examples are those of the castles and mansions of England of the time of the Tudors, but the whole of the cottage architecture of England is imbued with its spirit, and the manifestations are everywhere visible, in quaintly carved gables or verge boards, wreathed and clustered chimneys, beautiful windows ornamented with tracery, and numberless other details, highly expressive and characteristic.

In adopting any style for imitation, our preference should be guided not only by the intrinsic beauty which we see in a particular style, but by its appropriateness to our uses. This will generally be indicated by the climate, the site, or situation, and the wants of the family who are to inhabit it. In a high northern latitude, where it is evident colonnades and verandas would be unsuitable for most of the year, the Italian or Grecian styles should not be chosen, and in a tropical one, the warm, solid, comfortable features of the old English architecture would not be necessary or appropriate. In a country like the middle portions of the United States, where the summers are hot and the winters cold, there is sufficient latitude for the adoption of various styles of building, and therefore more judgment or taste is requisite in the selection.

The different styles of architecture have been very aptly compared to different languages, employed by various architects to express their ideas, and which, when perfect, always remain nearly fixed, and best express the wants of a particular age or country. We may safely carry out this illustration, and say that the temples and cathedrals are the orations and epic poems, the dwelling-houses the familiar epistles or conversations of the particular styles.

In expressing our architectural ideas by the medium of a certain style or language, we shall succeed best, and our efforts will afford most delight, the more nearly we approach to the nature of the circumstances under which the style or language originated. Thus, if we talk pure Greek, and build a Grecian temple for a dwelling, we shall be little understood, or perhaps only laughed at by our neighbors. It is not much better in the present day to recite an epic poem by building a cathedral, or a heroic one by constructing a castle for our habitation. Let us rather be more sensible, though not less graceful in our architectural utterance, and express a pleasant, every-day language, in an old English mansion, a Rural Gothic cottage, or an Italian villa.

For domestic architecture, we would strongly recommend those simple modifications of architectural styles, where the beauty grows out of the enrichment of some useful or elegant features of the house, as the windows or verandas, rather than those where some strongly marked features, of little domestic beauty, overpower the rest of the building. The Rural Gothic style, characterized mainly by pointed gables, and the Italian, by projecting roofs, balconies, and terraces, are much the most beautiful modes for our country residences. Their outlines are highly picturesque and harmonious with nature. Their forms are convenient, their accessories elegant, and they are highly expressive of the refined and unostentatious enjoyments of the country. We have pointed out in another work the objections that may fairly be urged against the false taste lately so prevalent among us, in building our country houses in the form of Greek temples, sacrificing thereby the beauty of variety, much convenience, and all the comfort of low and shady verandas, to the ambitious display of a portico of stately columns; and we are happy to see that the fashion is on the decline. Let us hope speedily to see in its place a correct taste springing up in every part of the country, which shall render our cottage homes beautiful, not by borrowing the features or enrichments of a temple or palace, but by seeking beautiful and appropriate forms, characteristic of domestic life, and indicative of home comforts.

Not a little of the delight of beautiful buildings to a cultivated mind grows out of the *sentiment* of architecture, or the associations connected with certain styles. Thus the sight of an old English villa will call up in the mind of one familiar with the history of architecture, the times of the Tudors, or of "Merry England," in the days of Elizabeth. The mingled quaintness, beauty, and picturesqueness of the exterior, no less than the oaken wainscot, curiously carved furniture, and fixtures of the interior of such a dwelling, when harmoniously complete, seem to transport one back to a past age, the domestic habits, the hearty hospitality, the joyous old sports, and the romance and chivalry of which, invest it, in the dim retrospect, with a kind of golden glow, in which the shadowy lines of poetry and reality seem strangely interwoven and blended.

So too an Italian villa may recall, to one familiar with Italy and art, by its bold roof lines, its campanile and its shady balconies, the classic beauty of that fair and smiling land, where pictures, sculptured figures, vases, and urns, in all exquisite forms, make part of the decorations and "surroundings" of domestic and public edifices. A residence in the Roman style (more suitable than the Grecian) may, by its dignified elegance of arrangement and decoration, recall to the classic mind the famed Tusculum retreat of Pliny. And one fond of the wild and picturesque, whose home chances to be in some one of our rich mountain valleys, may give it a peculiar charm to some minds by imitating the Swiss cottage, or at least its expressive and striking

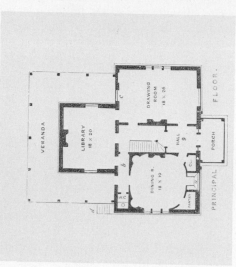

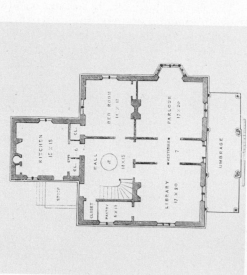

Figure 20. "A Cottage Villa in the Bracketed Mode," Design V, figure 37 from Downing, *Cottage Residences.*

Figure 19. "A Cottage in the English of Rural Gothic Style," Design II, figure 10 from Andrew Jackson Downing, *Cottage Residences,* New York, 1842.

features. A great deal of the charm of architectural style, in all cases, will arise from the happy union between the locality or site, and the style chosen, and from the entireness with which the architect or amateur enters into the spirit and character of the style, and carries it through his whole work. This may be done in a small cottage, and at little cost, as well as in a mansion, at great expense; but it requires more taste and skill to achieve the former admirably, although the latter may involve ten times the magnitude.

Design V

A COTTAGE-VILLA IN THE BRACKETTED MODE

We trust that the exterior of this villa will generally please, as although it is simple in form, we have endeavored to add to its domestic, comfortable air, a more forcible and elegant expression than rectangular buildings generally possess. The strongly marked character which it has, is derived mainly from the bold projection of the roof supported by ornamental brackets, and from the employment of brackets for supports, in various other parts of the building.

This bracketted mode of building, so simple in construction, and so striking in effect, will be found highly suitable to North America, and especially to the southern states. The coolness and dryness of the upper story, afforded by the almost veranda-like roof, will render this a delightful feature in all parts of our country, where the summers are hot, and the sun very bright during the long days of that season. Indeed, we think a very ingenious architect might produce an *American cottage style*, by carefully studying the capabilities of this mode, so abounding in picturesqueness, and so easily executed.

In actual fitness for domestic purposes, in this country, we think this bracketted mode has much to recommend it. It is admirably adapted to the two kinds of construction which must, for some time, be the most prevalent in the United States—wood, and brick covered by cement. Its comparative lightness of character renders it well suited for wood, and the protection afforded by the projection of the roof, will give complete security and dryness to the walls, rendering good stucco or cement in such a situation as durable as stone. The facility of its construction is an additional circumstance in its favor, as the details are extremely simple—the ornamental brackets, which are the principal features of decoration, being cut out of pine or oak plank, two inches thick, and one or two patterns serving for the whole exterior.

Extending the roof in the manner shown in this design, gives expression and character at once to the exterior, and the broad and deep shadows thrown by the projection are not only effective and pleasing to the artistical eye, but they increase the actual comfort of the chamber apartments; a projection of from 20 inches to three feet, serving as a hood to shelter the windows from the summer sun during all the sultry portion of the day; while in winter, the sun being low in position, this effect will not be felt, when it is not desirable.

On entering the hall (see plan of principal floor, Figure 20), we find on the left an oval dining, or living room, lighted by a large and handsome window on the side, and another in front: the latter finished with a window-seat. There are two pantries, or closets, in this room, in the spaces formed by the ovals in front, and the opposite end of the room may be finished with shallow closets for plate, glass, or valuable china. At the opposite end of this room, is a door opening into the passage *b*, which communicates with the stairs to the kitchen (under the main stairs), and also with the open air, by the door on the veranda. At the left of this passage is the water-closet (W. C.).

On the opposite side is the parlor or drawing-room, occupying the whole space, 18 by 26 feet. This room is of very handsome size, and if well finished would make a splendid apartment. The ceiling should be 13 or 14 feet high, and might be supported by a bracketted cornice, tastefully executed in plaster, to harmonize with the character of the exterior. Our own taste would lead us to prefer greatly, in all cases, the simplicity and dignity of a single large apartment of this kind in the country, to two apartments connected by folding or sliding doors. In the later, the single room, considered by itself, is comparatively of no importance, because it is evidently only one half of the architect's idea, and the *coup d'œil* of the whole is greatly injured, by the partition still remaining, after the doors are open. A large room like this drawing-room, will, on the contrary, be a complete whole in itself, and regarding its effect either with or without company, it will be found much more satisfactory than that of the two smaller ones connected. Access to the veranda from this room, is afforded by the window at its further end, *c*, which is a casement-window opening to the floor, and may therefore be used as a door.

At the end of the hall a door opens into the library, 18 by 20 feet, which is a cool airy apartment, shaded by the veranda that surrounds it on three sides. It communicates directly with the drawing-room by one door, and with the passage *b*, leading to the veranda, by another.

On the second floor are five bedrooms, Figure 21. The two bedrooms on the right being connected by a door, one of them may be used as a nursery, and the other as a family bedroom. Three bedrooms for servants may be finished in the attic story, which will be lighted by the windows in the gable. There is a handsome balcony, which is entered upon from the casement-window, at the end of the hall in this story, shaded by the broad overhanging roof, and two other balconies which accompany, in a similar manner, the large windows in the two principal bedrooms on either side of this hall. These two large windows are each composed of three compartments, and the middle compartment of that on the right, against which the partition of the nursery abuts, is made solid on the inside, which still gives one window, or compartment of moderate size, for each room. The basement accommodation, Figure 21, consists of a kitchen, laundry, store-room, and cellar. The basement story is raised about three and a half feet above ground, with areas built around the windows, to admit an abundance of light. The outer entrance to this story is by the steps descending under the veranda, indicated on the left of this plan.

The chimneys in this elevation are bold and striking, and show what would be in good keeping with the style of the house. Their construction is simple. They are each covered on the top by two flat coping stones, of bold

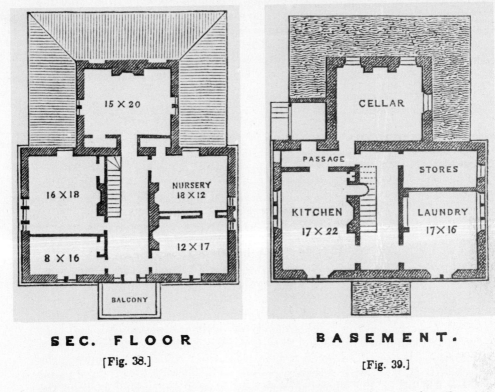

SEC. FLOOR

[Fig. 38.]

BASEMENT.

[Fig. 39.]

Figure 21. Basement and second floor plans of Design V, figures 38 and 39, from Downing, *Cottage Residences*, p. 95.

projection, the smoke escaping on two sides. Chimneys built in this manner are much more likely to draw well than those with an open top, in the common mode. This form, however, is not by any means essential, and square flues in a body, with a bold cornice supported on bricks projecting as brackets, or separate detached flues carried up in clusters, with heavy tops, would also be suitable for a building in this style.

Variation of this design, as constructed in wood. The foregoing engravings being in illustration of this design, as built of solid materials, we introduce another elevation, Figure 22, to show its appearance constructed of wood. The common mode of *siding* is sufficiently well understood by every one, but in this elevation a less general mode is shown, which consists in tongue and grooving the boards, nailing them vertically on the frame, and covering the joint by a strip one to two inches wide. We suggest this mode as a variation, as it makes a very warm and dry house, and the effect is good. A section to the scale of half an inch to a foot shows this kind of siding.

There are, perhaps, some families who would much prefer a bedroom, to the library in our previous plan of the principal floor. We have, in the annexed Figure 22, shown how this wing, originally intended for a library, may, by a little variation in the plan, be made to afford a pleasant bedroom, with a closet adjoining, and a pretty little boudoir opening either into the bedroom or the drawing-room, as may be thought best. If this variation should be preferred to the original plan of this floor, it will only be necessary to carry though the partitions introduced in this wing, which will make a similar alteration in the plan of the second and basement stories so easily understood, that it will not require any further plans in illustration. . . .

[The following paragraphs deal with types of ornament, porch supports, water-closets, and a cost estimate of $5,500, in either brick or wood.]

LAYING OUT THE GROUND

The situation for which this cottage is designed borders the public road, and contains about two acres, which are nearly level. At the back of the garden, Figure 23, is a steep hill *a*, the side covered with trees, which is ascended by a walk *b*, leading to a rustic summer-house on the top at *c*, from whence a prospect of the surrounding country is obtained.

The house is at *d*, and the objects in laying out the ground were to create an airy, cheerful aspect around the house, especially in front; to pre-serve a view of the steep picturesque hill from the veranda in the rear, and with the appearance of a good deal of ornamental effect to retain about one acre, or nearly half the level ground, for a kitchen garden *e*, and a fruit garden *f*.

In order to give an air of some extent and elegance about the house, the whole surface in this neighborhood, not devoted to the kitchen and fruit gardens, is laid down in lawn *g*, to be kept neatly mown; with the exception of the long borders *h*, devoted to a miscellaneous collection of flowers; the circular beds, filled with verbenas, petunias, and monthly roses, three plants which will bloom the whole summer, and have a brilliant effect from the drawing-room windows; and the two beds *j* filled with choice double Dahl-ias. In the turf is planted a number of the finest species of ornamental trees and shrubs, some being allowed to grow alone and assume all their beauty of development, and others planted in groups, or thickets, for effect or shelter. The novice will be assisted in making a selection of these trees and shrubs, by referring to the list given earlier. Some of the less hardy and robust of these trees and shrubs, being planted in groups in this way, will require that the surface around each tree for a small area of about two feet in diameter be kept loose by culture to promote their growth, until they attain consider-able size.

The entrance gate is shown at *k*, and there is a large oval of turf, around which to turn carriages immediately before the door. The carriage road *l*, after approaching the entrance to the kitchen for the convenience of delivering heavy articles, leads to the carriage-house *m*, adjoining which are the barn and stable *n*, and the stable yard *o*, the latter communicating di-rectly with the public road by the lane *p*.

The kitchen and fruit gardens are enclosed on three sides by hedges of the *privet* or *prim*, a rapid growing plant which forms a thick hedge in three years, has neat foliage and flowers, and is easily cultivated from slips or cuttings planted in March or April. These verdant fences will scarcely ap-pear barriers, and a spectator standing on the veranda in the rear of the

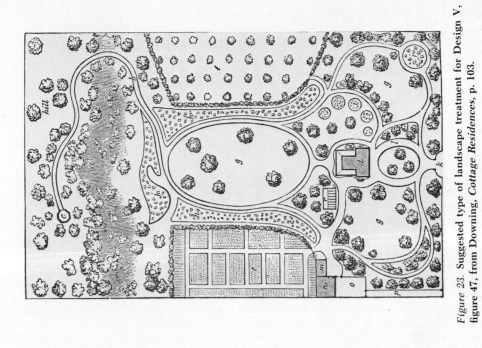

Figure 23. Suggested type of landscape treatment for Design V, figure 47, from Downing, *Cottage Residences,* p. 103.

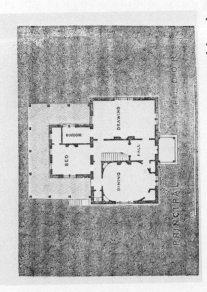

Figure 22. Variation on Design V showing vertical board and batten siding, figures 40 and 41, from Downing, *Cottage Residences,* p. 97.

house, and looking over the open, oval lawn g, bordered by the flower borders, and these backed by the deep green hedges, would scarcely be impressed with that idea of confinement which this moderate space would otherwise convey.

A detached green-house is shown at r, which, like the dwelling-house, fronts due south. This green-house is 14 feet wide by 40 feet long, and has a lean-to, or shed, at the rear, which affords a cover for the furnace, with a place for fuel, and a long narrow apartment for a gardener's seed room, tool room, or work room, the latter being a place absolutely necessary in every residence of the size of half an acre, if appropriated to ornamental purposes. Not only the front, but also both ends of this green-house should be glazed, as the sun will then, in the course of the day, shine on all sides. In the middle or eastern states, where the winters are severe, it will be found a great economy of both fuel and labor, to have light shutters made for all the sashes in a green-house detached like this one. When the sun is shining the shutters can be speedily removed, and in cold dull days, and at night, the glass may be kept covered, which will prevent the house from losing its heat rapidly. No green-house in this country, where even the wintry sun is brilliant, will require a particle of fire while the sun shines, and by the aid of shutters we may preserve the warmth of the green-house, collected during the afternoon, through a considerable portion, and often the whole of the night.

The hill side a, in its original state, was sprinkled over with trees, tufts of grass, ferns, etc., and was disfigured by the presence of a number of rough piles of rock. In order to render them ornamental, a quantity of hardy climbers, as the Trumpet vine (Bignonia), the coral or trumpet Honeysuckles, the double flowering Bramble, and the Virginia creeper, may be planted at the foot and among these rocks, and they will in two or three season render them highly picturesque by enwreathing them with beautiful garlands of foliage and flowers.

As the lawn will be a great source of beauty in all places of this kind, it is important that attention should be paid to this feature early in the preparation of the grounds. No lawn will retain its freshness and verdure throughout our hot summers, unless particular attention is paid to two circumstances. The first of these is the preparation of a *deep* soil before it is sown, or laid down in grass—the second consists in frequent mowings. When there is a large surface to be kept in lawn, the soil may be rendered suitable by manuring and ploughing thoroughly beforehand with the sub-soil plough, or by going through the same furrow three times in ploughing the soil. When the area is small, it may be trenched with the spade. The roots of the grasses strike much deeper in a mellow prepared soil, than persons are generally aware, and are thereby enabled to withstand a severe drought, when, if sown in the ordinary mode, they would have dried up and the foliage become brown in a short time. A rich soil for a lawn is not desirable, but rather a deep one capable of retaining moisture for a long time. Wood ashes will be found an excellent top-dressing for invigorating a worn-out lawn.

Frequent mowing is necessary to insure that velvet-like appearance, so much admired in English lawns. To perform this operation neatly, the mower must be provided with a scythe, the blade of which is very broad, and hung nearly parallel to the surface of the lawn; and the mowing should always be performed if possible, after a shower, or a heavy dew, while the grass is yet damp. The best mixture of grass seeds in use among us, and to be had at our seed shops, is the same as composes the natural growth of our commons and the turf by the road sides, viz. Red top and white Clover (*Agreslis vulgaris* and *Trifolium repens*). They should be sown thickly for a lawn, at the rate of four bushels to the acre.[6]

[6]Mr. Loudon recommends the following mixture of grasses for a lawn; viz. *Agreslis vulgaris var. tenuifolia, Festuca duriuscula, F. ovina, Cynosurus cristatus, Poa pratensis, Avena flavescens,* and *Trifolium minus.*

V

AGE OF ENTERPRISE

26 F. L. Olmsted and C. Vaux, A Description of Central Park* *1858*

As a result of Downing's and Bryant's continued pressure, the New York State Legislature passed enabling legislation in 1851 so that a large parcel could be purchased by the city in mid-Manhattan. After amendment in 1853, purchases commenced and continued until 1856, by which time the entire area between Fifth and Eighth Avenues (Central Park West now), from 59th Street to 106th Street, was acquired (the additional sixty-five acres up to 110th Street were added in 1863). A year passed before state legislation set up a board of commissioners to undertake development of the park. At the urging of one of the commissioners, Frederick Law Olmsted agreed to apply for the position of superintendent. In the autumn, while he was working as superintendent, the commissioners announced the competition for design of the entire park grounds. Of the thirty-three entries, that code-named "Greensward" was adjudged the winner and was then revealed to have been submitted by Olmsted and Calvert Vaux in collaboration.

Up to this point, Frederick Law Olmsted (1822–1903) had little practical planning experience, though he had studied scientific farming, had operated a model farm on Staten Island, and had traveled widely. Visiting English parks, he had been particularly impressed with Joseph Paxton's Birkenhead Park, Liverpool, which he described in *Walks and Talks of an American Farmer in England* (New York, 1852). Yet in his manifold and diverse enterprises he had prepared himself perfectly for the career of landscape architect that he took up at the age of thirty-five. He understood plants and land forms, and he was convinced, like Downing, that planned landscapes should serve a social and democratic purpose. His vision was ably supported by the professional training of Vaux. Their relationship with the political machine in New York City was difficult, the partners insisting on professional labor, the latter granting jobs in the park as political rewards. In 1872, Olmsted and Vaux parted quite amicably to pursue their diverging careers, and in 1878 Olmsted resigned his post as landscape architect of Central Park, having battled to the end with the Tweed Ring.

The description of the park was prepared in 1858 and amended with progress report footnotes by the partners in 1868. The notes are omitted here.†

---

*Frederick Law Olmsted and Calvert Vaux, *Description of a Plan for the Improvement of the Central Park: "Greensward"* (New York, 1858).

†See Albert Fein, *Landscape into Cityscape: Frederick Law Olmsted's Plans for a Greater New York City* (Ithaca, N.Y., 1967), pp. 63–88. The best introduction to Olmsted's work and philosophy is Fein's *Frederick Law Olmsted and the American Environmental Tradition* (New York, 1972).

DESCRIPTION OF A PLAN FOR THE IMPROVEMENT OF THE CENTRAL PARK: "GREENSWARD," NEW YORK, 1858.

Report

TOPOGRAPHICAL SUGGESTIONS

A general survey of the ground allotted to the park, taken with a view to arrive at the leading characteristics which present themselves as all-important to be considered in adapting the actual situation to its purposes, shows us, in the first place, that it is very distinctly divided into two tolerably equal portions, which, for convenience sake, may be called the upper and lower parks.

The Upper Park   The horizon lines of the upper park are bold and sweeping and the slopes have great breadth in almost every aspect in which they may be contemplated. As this character is the highest ideal that can be aimed at for a park under any circumstances, and as it is in most decided contrast to the confined and formal lines of the city, it is desirable to inter-fere with it, by cross-roads and other constructions, as little as possible. For-mal planting and architectural effects, unless on a very grand scale, must be avoided; and as nearly all the ground between the Reservoir and 106th Street (west of the Boston road) is seen in connection, from any point within itself, a unity of character should be studiously preserved in all the garden-ing details.

The Lower Park   The lower park is far more heterogencous in its character and will require a much more varied treatment. The most impor-tant feature in its landscape is the long rocky and wooded hill-side lying immediately south of the Reservoir. Inasmuch as beyond this point there do not appear to be any leading natural characteristics of similar consequence in the scenery, it will be important to draw as much attention as possible to this hill-side, to afford facilities for rest and leisurely contemplation upon the rising ground opposite, and to render the lateral boundaries of the park in its vicinity as inconspicuous as possible. The central and western portion of the lower park is an irregular table-land; the eastern is composed of a series of graceful undulations, suggesting lawn or gardenesque treatment. In the ex-treme south we find some flat alluvial meadow; but the general character of the ground is rugged and there are several bold, rocky bluffs, that help to give individuality to this part of the composition.

Such being the general suggestions that our survey has afforded, it be-comes necessary to consider how the requirements of the Commissioners, as given in their instructions, may be met with the least sacrifice of the charac-teristic excellencies of the ground.

PRELIMINARY CONSIDERATIONS

Up to this time, in planning public works for the city of New York, in no instance has adequate allowance been made for its increasing population and business; not even in the case of the Croton Aqueduct, otherwise so well considered. The City-Hall, the best architectural work in the State, and built to last for centuries, does not at this time afford facilities for one-third the business for which it was intended. The present Post-Office, expensively fitted up some ten years ago, no longer answers its purpose, and a new one of twice its capacity is imperatively demanded. The Custom-House, expressly designed for permanence and constructed to that end at enormous expense less than twenty years ago, is not half large enough to accommodate the present commerce of the city.

The explanation of this apparently bad calculation is mainly given with the fact that, at every census since that of 1800, the city's rate of increase has been found to be overrunning the rate previously established.

A wise forecast of the future gave the proposed park the name of Central. Our present chief magistrate, who can himself remember market-gardens below Canal street, and a post-and-rail fence on the north side of City-Hall park, warned his coadjutors, in his inaugural message, to expect a great and rapid movement of population toward the parts of the island adjoining the Central Park. A year hence, five city railroads will bring passengers as far up as the park, if not beyond it. Recent movements to transfer the steamboat-landings and railroad stations, although as yet unsuccessful, indicate changes we are soon to expect.

The 17,000 lots withdrawn from use for building purposes in the park itself, will greatly accelerate the occupation of the adjoining land. Only twenty years ago Union Square was "out of town;" twenty years hence, the town will have enclosed the Central Park. Let us consider, therefore, what will at that time be satisfactory, for it is then that the design will have to be really judged.

No longer an open suburb, our ground will have around it a continuous high wall of brick, stone, and marble. The adjoining shores will be lined with commerical docks and warehouses; steamboat and ferry landings, railroad stations, hotels, theatres, factories, will be on all sides of it and above it; all which our park must be made to fit.

The demolition of Columbia College, and the removal of the cloistral elms which so long enshadowed it; the pertinacious demand for a division of Trinity churchyard; the numerous instances in which our old graveyards have actually been broken up; the indirect concession of the most important space in the City-Hall park for the purposes of a thoroughfare and the further contraction it is now likely to suffer; together with the constant enormous expenditure of the city and sacrifices of the citizens, in the straightening and widening of streets, are all familiar facts, that teach us a lesson of the most pressing importance in our present duty. To its application we give the first place in our planning.

THE TRANSVERSE ROADS

Our instructions call for four transverse roads. Each of these will be the sole line of communication between one side of the town and the other, for a distance equal to that between Chambers street and Canal street. If we suppose but one crossing of Broadway to be possible in this interval, we shall realize what these transverse roads are destined to become. Inevitably they will be crowded thoroughfares, having nothing in common with the park proper, but every thing at variance with those agreeable sentiments which we should wish the park to inspire. It will not be possible to enforce the ordinary police regulations of public parks upon them. They must be constantly open to all the legitimate traffic of the city, to coal carts and butchers' carts, dust carts and dung carts; engine companies will use them, those on one side the park rushing their machines across it with frantic zeal at every alarm from the other; ladies and invalids will need special police escort for crossing them, as they do in lower Broadway: eight times in a single circuit of the park will they oblige a pleasure drive or stroll to encounter a turbid stream of coarse traffic, constantly moving at right angles to the line of the park movement.

The transverse roads will also have to be kept open, while the park proper will be useless for any good purpose, after dusk, for experience has shown that even in London, with its admirable police arrangements, the public cannot be secured safe transit through large open spaces of ground after nightfall.

Foreign Examples These public thoroughfares will then require to be well lighted at the sides and, to restrain marauders pursued by the police from escaping into the obscurity of the park, strong fences or walls, six or eight feet high, will be necessary. A public road thus guarded passes through the Regent's Park of London, at the Zoological Gardens. It has the objection that the fence, with its necessary gates at every crossing of the park drives, roads or paths, is not only a great inconvenience but a disagreeable object in the landscape.

To avoid a similar disfigurement an important passage across the garden of the Tuileries is closed by gates at night, forcing all who would otherwise use it to go a long distance to the right or left.

The form and position of the Central Park are peculiar in respect to this difficulty, and such that precedent in dealing with it is rather to be sought in the long and narrow Boulevards of some of the old Continental cities of Europe, than in the broad parks with which, from its area in acres, we are most naturally led to compare it. The Boulevards referred to are, however, generally used only as walks, not as drives or places of ceremony. In frequent instances, in order not to interrupt their alleys, the streets crossing them are made in the form of causeways and carried over on high arches. This, of course, destroys all landscape effect, since it puts an abrupt limit to the view. Some expedient is needed for the Central Park by which the convenience of the arrangement may be retained, while the objection is as far as possible avoided.

The Present Design In the plan herewith offered to the Commission, each of the transverse roads is intended to be sunk so far below the general surface that the park drives may, at every necessary point of intersection, be carried entirely over it, without any obvious elevation or divergence from their most attractive routes. The banks on each side will be walled up to the height of about seven feet, thus forming the protective barrier required by police considerations, and a little judicious planting on the tops or slopes of the banks above these walls will, in most cases, entirely conceal both the roads and the vehicles moving in them, from the view of those walking or driving in the park.

If the position which has just been taken with regard to the necessity for permanently open transverse thoroughfares is found to be correct, it follows necessarily that the 700 acres allowed to the new park must, in the first instance, be subdivided definitely, although it is to be hoped to some extent invisibly, into five separate and distinct sections, only connected here and there by roads crossing them; and if the plan of making these thoroughfares by sunken roads is approved, they will, as it appears to us, from the nature of the ground, have to be laid down somewhat on the lines indicated on the plan. If so, the problem to be solved is narrowed in its dimensions, and the efforts of the designer can be no longer directed to an arrangement that shall agreeably use up the space of 700 acres allotted, but to making some plan that shall have unity of effect as a whole, and yet avoid collision in its detailed features with the intersecting lines thus suggested. It is on this basis that the present plan has, in the first instance, been founded. If the sunken transverse roads were omitted, the design would not be less complete in character; but it is, on the other hand, so laid out that the transverse thoroughfares do not interfere materially with its general or detailed effect.

Surface Transverse Roads   After having planned the park drives agreeably to these views, we observed that three additional moderately direct, transverse roads had occurred. These will afford facilities for crossing the park to all vehicles of classes which it will be proper to admit upon them, such as hackney coaches and all private carriages; and thus seven transverse roads will be really provided to be used during daylight. Four roads will probably be amply adequate for the night traffic needing to cross the park; but it might be questioned if this number would be sufficient during the day. . . .

FIFTH AVENUE ENTRANCE

The finest approach from the city is certain to be along the Fifth avenue, and it has been thought necessary to view with special care the angle of the park first reached from this direction, because it will be generally felt that immediate entrance should be had at this point.

The grade of the avenue has been established so high that considerable filling-in would be required to avoid a rapid descent, but directly this single difficulty is overcome, the ground beyond has great advantages for the purpose of a dignified entrance to the park. A massive rock that will be found in connection with this requisite made-ground, offers a sufficiently large natural object to occupy the attention, and will at once reduce the artificial feature to a position of minor importance. If, next, we stand upon that portion of the rock which (a little north of the large cherry-tree) is at grade-height, we find that there is another rocky hillock within a short distance, in the direction a visitor to the park would most naturally pursue—that is to say, towards the centre of the park. This can be easily reached by slightly raising the intermediate ground; by then sweeping to the right, the natural conformation of the surface offers an easy ascent (by the existing cart-way over

Sixty-Third street) to a plateau (two rods west of the powder-house), directly connected with the extensive table-land which occupies the centre of the lower half of the park.

From this plateau (now occupied mainly by the nursery) a view is had of nearly all the park up to the Reservoir, in a northerly direction; and on looking to the south and west, we perceive that there are natural approaches from these directions, which suggest that we have arrived at a suitable point of concentration for all approaches which may be made from the lower part of the city to the interior of the park.

THE AVENUE

Vista Rock, the most prominent point in the landscape of the lower park, here first comes distinctly into view, and fortunately in a direction diagonal to the boundary lines, from which it is desirable to withdraw attention in every possible way. We therefore accept this line of view as affording an all-sufficient motive to our further procedure. Although averse on general principles to a symmetrical arrangement of trees, we consider it an essential feature of a metropolitan park, that it should contain a grand promenade, level, spacious, and thoroughly shaded. This result can in no other way be so completely arrived at, as by an avenue, which in itself even, exclusive of its adaptability for this purpose, contains so many elements of grandeur and magnificence, that it should be recognized as an essential feature in the arrangement of any large park. The objection to which it is liable is that it divides the landscape into two parts, and it is therefore desirable to decide at what point this necessity can be submitted to with the least sacrifice to the general effect. The whole topographical character of the park is so varied, so suggestive of natural treatment, so picturesque, so individual in its characteristics, that it would be contrary to common sense to make the avenue its leading feature, or to occupy any great extent of ground for this special purpose. It must be subservient to the general design, if that general design is to be in accordance with the present configuration of the ground, and we have therefore thought that it should, so far as possible, be complete in itself, and not become a portion of any of the leading drives. There is no dignity of effect to be produced by driving through an avenue a quarter of a mile long, unless it leads to, and becomes an accessory of, some grand architectural structure, which itself, and not the avenue, is the ultimatum of interest. An avenue for driving should be two or three miles long, or it will be petite and disappointing. We have therefore thought it most desirable to identify the idea of the avenue with the promenade, for which purpose a quarter of a mile is not insufficient, and we can find no better place for such a grand mall, or open air hall of reception, as we desire to have, than the ground before us.

The Promenade In giving it this prominent position, we look at it in the light of an artificial structure on a scale of magnitude commensurate with the size of the park, and intend in our design that it should occupy the same position of relative importance in the general arrangement of the plan that a mansion should occupy in a park prepared for private occupation. The importance that is justly connected with the idea of the residence of the owner in even the most extensive private grounds, finds no parallel in a public park, however small, and we feel that the interest of the visitor, who, in the best sense is the true owner in the latter case, should concentrate on features of natural, in preference to artificial, beauty. Many elegant buildings may be appropriately erected for desirable purposes in a public park, but we conceive that all such architectural structures should be confessedly subservient to the main idea, and that nothing artificial should be obtruded on the view as an ultimatum of interest. The idea of the park itself should always be uppermost in the mind of the beholder. Holding this general principle to be of considerable importance, we have preferred to place the avenue where it can be terminated appropriately at one end with a landscape attraction of considerable extent, and to relieve the south entrance with only so much architectural treatment as may give the idea that due regard has been paid to the adornment of this principal promenade, without interfering with its real character.

This avenue may be considered the central feature in our plan for laying out the lower park, and the other details of arrangement are more or less designed in connection with it.

PARADE GROUND

To the west is the parade ground, containing about 25 acres, that may, at a moderate expense, be levelled and made suitable for its purpose;[1] and also some eight or ten acres of broken ground, that will be more or less available for military exercises. Such a broad open plane of well-kept grass would be a refreshing and agreeable feature in the general design, and would bear to be of much greater extent than is here shown, if the lot were of a different shape; but under the circumstances, 25 acres seems as much as can well be spared for the purpose. A military entrance from Eighth avenue is proposed to be made at Sixty-Ninth street, which has been already, at considerable expense, cut through the rock at this point, and offers a suggestion for a picturesque approach, with a portcullis gate, and with the main park drive carried over it at a higher level. . . .

THE LOWER LAKE

To the south-east of the promenade, and between the Fifth and Sixth avenue entrances, it is proposed to form a lake of irregular shape, and with an area of 8 or 9 acres. This arrangement has been suggested by the present nature of the ground, which is low and somewhat swampy. It is conceived that, by introducing such an ornamental sheet of water into the composition at this point, the picturesque effect of the bold bluffs that will run down to its edge and overhang it, must be much increased; and that by means of such a natural boundary, this rocky section of the park will be rendered more retired and attractive as a pleasant walk or lounge. The proposed effect of this part of the design, as it will appear from the Fifth avenue entrance, is indicated on study No. 1. . . .

[1] Note, 1868—A Parade ground was demanded by the schedule of instructions furnished to competitors. In execution this open space under the name of "The Green" has been retained as a prominent feature of the design, but has not been and is not intended to be used for military exercises.

THE ARBORETUM

The north-east section of the upper park is shown as an arboretum of American trees, so that every one who wishes to do so may become acquainted with the trees and shrubs that will flourish in the open air in the northern and middle sections of our country.

This arboretum is not intended to be formally arranged, but to be so planned that it may present all the most beautiful features of lawn and wood-land landscape, and at the same time preserve the natural order of families, so far as may be practicable. The botanical student will thus be able to find any tree or shrub without difficulty. We have selected this tract, of about 40 acres, in the upper angle of the site, so as to interfere with the more special requirements of the park as little as possible. The spot chosen is in some measure separated from the rest of the grounds, by a ridge of land between Fifth and Sixth avenues, and includes the buildings on Mount St. Vincent. The wooden structures would be removed, and the brick chapel converted into a museum and library of botany, similar to that at Kew, but with more specific regard to landscape and decorative gardening. In the park itself there will be numerous specimens of all the trees, native or foreign, that are likely to thrive; but it is proposed to limit this particular collection to American trees, because the space necessary for a complete arboretum would occupy several hundred acres, and also because it will afford an opportunity to show the great advantage that America possesses in this respect. No other extra-tropical country could furnish one quarter the material for such a collection. In the whole of Great Britain, for example, there are less than twenty trees, native to the island, that grow to be over 30 feet in height; while in America we have from five to six times that number. There are, indeed, already over forty species of the largest native trees standing in the park, which is nearly equivalent to the number to be found in all Europe.

It is proposed to plant from one to three examples of each species of tree on open lawn, and with sufficient space about each to allow it to attain its fullest size with unrestricted expanse of branches; the effect of each tree is also to be exhibited in masses, so as to illustrate its qualities for grouping. Space is provided to admit of at least three specimens of every native which is known to flourish in the United States north of North Carolina; also for several specimens of every shrub; these latter, however, except in particular instances, are not expected to be planted singly, but in thickets, and as underwood to the coppice masses; as may best accord with their natural habits, and be most agreeable to the eye. Further details of this part of the design will be found in the explanatory guide to the arboretum, submitted with the plan, in which the proposed arrangement of all the trees is set forth in order.

The leading features of the plan have now, it is thought, been referred to. It has now been considered necessary to especially particularize the different trees proposed to be used in the various parts of the park. For the purposes of the avenue, the American elm naturally suggests itself at once as the tree to be used; and it is to be hoped that the fine effect this produces, when planted in regular lines, may in a few years be realized in Central Park.

There is no other part of the plan in which the planting calls for particular mention, except to the south of the skating pond; an opportunity is there offered for an exhibition of semi-tropical trees, and it is intended to treat that portion of the park in the manner suggested in the study. A list of the trees to be used is appended to the explanation of the arboretum.

The plan does not show any brooks, except a small one in connection with the pool at the foot of Bogardus Hill, which can always be kept full by the waste of water from the New Reservoir. Mere rivulets are uninteresting, and we have preferred to collect the ornamental water in large sheets, and to carry off through underground drains the water that at present runs through the park in shallow brooks.

As a general rule, we propose to run footpaths close to the carriage roads, which are intended to be 60 feet wide, allowing a space of four feet of turf as a barrier between the drive and the path. Other more private footpaths are introduced, but it is hardly thought that any plan would be popular in New York, that did not allow of a continuous promenade along the line of the drives, so that pedestrians may have ample opportunity to look at the equipages and their inmates.

It will be perceived that no long straight drive has been provided on the plan; this feature has been studiously avoided, because it would offer opportunities for trotting matches. The popular idea of the park is a beautiful open space, in which quiet drives, rides, and strolls may be had. This cannot be preserved if a race-course, or a road that can readily be used as a race-course, is made one of its leading attractions.

27   F. L. Olmsted, Public Parks and the Enlargement of Towns*   1870

Perhaps Olmsted's most thorough if discursive statement of the relationship between the growth of cities and the need for and the purposes of parks is this address prepared for presentation at the Lowell Institute in February 1870. The paper, prepared at the request of the American Social Science Association, was intended to spur interest in public parks in Boston; it is reproduced only in part here.†

There can be no doubt . . . that, in all our modern civilization, as in that of the ancients, there is a strong drift townward. . . . It should be observed

---

*Frederick Law Olmsted, "Public Parks and the Enlargement of Towns" (Cambridge, Mass., 1870).

†For a more complete reprinting see S. B. Sutton, *Civilizing American Cities: A Selection of Frederick Law Olmsted's Writings on City Landscapes* (Cambridge, Mass.), 1971, 52–99.

that possession of all the various advantages of the town to which we have referred, while it very certainly cannot be acquired by people living in houses a quarter or a half mile apart, does not, on the other hand, by any means involve an unhealthy density of population. Probably the advantages of civilization can be found illustrated and demonstrated under no other circumstances so completely as in some suburban neighborhoods where each family abode stands fifty or a hundred feet or more apart from all others, and at some distance from the public road. And it must be remembered, also, that man's enjoyment of rural beauty has clearly increased rather than diminished with his advance in civilization. There is no reason, except in the loss of time, the inconvenience, discomfort, and expense of our present arrangements for short travel, why suburban advantages should not be almost indefinitely extended. Let us have a cheap and enjoyable method of conveyance, and a building law like that of old Rome, and they surely will be.

As railroads are improved, all the important stations will become centres or sub-centres of towns, and all the minor stations suburbs. For most ordinary every-day purposes, especially house-keepers' purposes, these will need no very large population before they can obtain urban advantages. I have seen a settlement, the resident population of which was under three hundred, in which there was a public laundry, bath-house, barber's shop, billiard-room, beer-garden, and bakery. Fresh rolls and fresh milk were supplied to families before breakfast time every morning; fair fruit and succulent vegetables were delivered at house doors not half an hour after picking; and newspapers and magazines were distributed by a carrier. I have seen a town of not more than twelve hundred inhabitants, the streets and the yards, alleys, and places of which were swept every day as regularly as the house floors, and all dust removed by a public dustman.

The construction of good roads and walks, the laying of sewer, water, and gas pipes, and the supplying of sufficiently cheap, rapid, and comfortable conveyances to town centres, is all that is necessary to give any farming land in a healthy and attractive situation the value of town lots. And whoever has observed in the French agricultural colonies how much more readily and cheaply railroads, telegraph, gas, water, sewer, and nearly all other advantages of towns may be made available to the whole population than under our present helter-skelter methods of settlement, will not believe that even the occupation of a farm laborer must necessarily and finally exclude his family from a very large share of urban conveniences.

But this opens a subject of speculation, which I am not now free to pursue It is hardly a matter of speculation, I am disposed to think, but almost of demonstration, that the larger a town becomes simply because of its advantages for commercial purposes, the greater will be the convenience available to those who live in and near it for cooperation, as well with reference to the accumulation of wealth in the higher forms,—as in seats of learning, of science, and of art,—as with reference to merely domestic economy and the emancipation of both men and women from petty, confining, and narrowing cares.

It also appears to be nearly certain that the recent rapid enlargement of towns and withdrawal of people from rural conditions of living is the result mainly of circumstances of a permanent character.

We have reason to believe, then, that towns which of late have been increasing rapidly on account of their commercial advantages, are likely to be still more attractive to population in the future; that there will in consequence soon be larger towns than any the world has yet known, and that the further progress of civilization is to depend mainly upon the influences by which men's minds and characters will be affected while living in large towns.

Now, knowing that the average length of the life of mankind in towns has been much less than in the country, and that the average amount of disease and misery and of vice and crime has been much greater in towns, this would be a very dark prospect for civilization, if it were not that modern science has beyond all question determined many of the causes of the special evils by which men are afflicted in towns, and placed means in our hands for guarding against them. It has shown, for example, that under ordinary circumstances, in the interior parts of large and closely built towns, a given quantity of air contains considerably less of the elements which we require to receive through the lungs than the air of the country or even of the outer and more open parts of a town, and that instead of them it carries into the lungs highly corrupt and irritating matters, the action of which tends strongly to vitiate all our sources of vigor. . . .

It is evident that if we go on in this way, the progress of civilized mankind in health, virtue, and happiness will be seriously endangered.

It is practically certain that the Boston of today is the mere nucleus of the Boston that is to be. It is practically certain that it is to extend over many miles of country now thoroughly rural in character, in parts of which farmers are now laying out roads with a view to shortening the teaming distance between their wood-lots and a railway station, being governed in their courses by old property lines, which were first run simply with reference to the equitable division of heritages, and in other parts of which, perhaps, some wild speculators are having streets staked off from plans which they have formed with a rule and pencil in a broker's office, with a view chiefly to the impressions they would make when seen by other speculators on a lithographed map. And by this manner of planning, unless views of duty or of interest prevail that are not yet common, if Boston continues to grow at its present rate even for but a few generations longer, and then simply holds it own until it shall be as old as the Boston in Lincolnshire now is, more men, women, and children are to be seriously affected in health and morals than are now living on this continent.

Is this a small matter—a mere matter of taste; a sentimental speculation?

It must be within the observation of most of us that where, in the city, wheel-ways originally twenty feet wide were with great difficulty and cost enlarged to thirty, the present width is already less nearly adequate to the present business than the former was to the former business; obstructions are more frequent, movements are slower and oftener arrested, and the liability to collision is greater. The same is true of sidewalks. Trees thus have been cut down, porches, bow-windows, and other encroachments removed, but every year the walk is less sufficient for the comfortable passing of those who wish to use it.

It is certain that as the distance from the interior to the circumference of towns shall increase with the enlargement of their population, the less sufficient relatively to the service to be performed will be any given space between buildings.

In like manner every evil to which men are specially liable when living in towns, is likely to be aggravated in the future, unless means are devised and adapted in advance to prevent it.

Let us proceed, then, to the question of means, and with a seriousness in some degree befitting a question, upon our dealing with which we know the misery or happiness of many millions of our fellow-beings will depend.

We will for the present set before our minds the two sources of wear and corruption which we have seen to be remediable and therefore preventible. We may admit that commerce requires that in some parts of a town there shall be an arrangement of buildings, and a character of streets and of traffic in them which will establish conditions of corruption and of irritation, physical and mental. But commerce does not require the same conditions to be maintained in all parts of a town.

Air is disinfected by sunlight and foliage. Foliage also acts mechanically to purify the air by screening it. Opportunity and inducement to escape at frequent intervals from the confined and vitiated air of the commercial quarter, and to supply the lungs with air screened and purified by trees, and recently acted upon by sunlight, together with opportunity and inducement to escape from conditions requiring vigilance, wariness, and activity toward other men,—if these could be supplied economically, our problem would be solved.

In the old days of walled towns all tradesmen lived under the roof of their shops, and their children and apprentices and servants sat together with them in the evening about the kitchen fire. But now that the dwelling is built by itself and there is greater room, the inmates have a parlor to spend their evenings in; they spread carpets on the floor to gain in quiet, and hang drapery in their windows and papers on their walls to gain in seclusion and beauty. Now that our towns are built without walls, and we can have all the room that we like, is there any good reason why we should not make some similar difference between parts which are likely to be dwelt in, and those which will be required exclusively for commerce?

Would trees, for seclusion and shade and beauty, be out of place, for instance, by the side of certain of our streets? It will, perhaps, appear to you that it is hardly necessary to ask such a question, as throughout the United States trees are commonly planted at the sides of streets. Unfortunately they are seldom so planted as to have fairly settled the question of the desirableness of systematically maintaining trees under these circumstances. In the first place, the streets are planned, wherever they are, especially alike. Trees are planted in the space assigned for sidewalks, where at first, while they are saplings, and the vicinity is rural or suburban, they are not much in the way, but where, as they grow larger, and the vicinity becomes urban, they take up more and more space, while space is more and more required for passage. That is not all. Thousands and tens of thousands are planted every year in a manner and under conditions as nearly certain as possible either to kill them outright, or to so lessen their vitality as to prevent their natural and beautiful development, and to cause premature decrepitude. Often, too, as their lower limbs are found inconvenient, no space having been provided for trees in laying out the street, they are deformed by butcherly amputations. If by rare good fortune they are suffered to become beautiful, they still stand subject to be condemned to death at any time, as obstructions in the highway.[1]

What I would ask is, whether we might not with economy make special provision in some of our streets—in a twentieth or a fiftieth part, if you please, of all—for trees to remain as a permanent furniture of the city? I mean, to make a place for them in which they would have room to grow naturally and gracefully. Even if the distance between the houses should have to be made half as much again as it is required to be in our commercial streets, could not the space be afforded? Out of town space is not costly when measures to secure it are taken early. The assessments for benefit where such streets were provided for, would, in nearly all cases, defray the cost of the land required. The strips of ground reserved for the trees, six, twelve, twenty feet wide, would cost nothing for paving or flagging.

The change both of scene and of air which would be obtained by people engaged for the most part in the necessarily confined interior commercial parts of the town, on passing into a street of this character after the trees had become stately and graceful, would be worth a good deal. If such streets were made still broader in some parts, with spacious malls, the advantage would be increased. If each of them were given the proper capacity, and laid out with laterals and connections in suitable directions to serve as a convenient trunk line of communication between two large districts of the town or the business centre and the suburbs, a very great number of people might thus be placed every day under influences counteracting those with which we desire to contend.

These, however, would be merely very simple improvements upon arrangements which are in common use in every considerable town. Their advantages would be incidental to the general uses of streets as they are. But people are willing very often to seek recreations as well as receive it by the way. Provisions may indeed be made expressly for public recreations, with certainty that if convenient they will be resorted to.

We come then to the question: what accommodations for recreation can we provide which shall be so agreeable and so accessible as to be efficiently attractive to the great body of citizens, and which, while giving de-

[1] On the border of the first street laid out in the oldest town in New England, there yet stands what has long been known as "the Town Tree," its trunk having served for generations as a publication post for official notices. "The selectmen," having last year removed the lower branches of all the younger roadside trees of the town, and thereby its chief beauty, have this year deliberately resolved that they would have this tree cut down, for no other reason, so far as appears in their official record, than that if two persons came carelessly together on the roadway side of it, one of them might chance to put his foot in the adjoining shallow street-gutter. It might cost ten dollars to deepen and bridge this gutter substantially. The call to arms for the Old French War, for the War of the Revolution, the war for the freedom of the seas, the Mexican War, and the War of the Rebellion, was first made in this town under the shade of this tree, which is an American elm, and, notwithstanding its great age, is perfectly healthy and almost as beautiful as it is venerable.

cided gratification, shall also cause those who resort to them for pleasure to subject themselves, for the time being, to conditions strongly counteractive to the special enervating conditions of the town?

In the study of this question all forms of recreation may, in the first place, be conveniently arranged under two general heads. One will include all of which the predominating influence is to stimulate exertion of any part or parts needing it; the other, all which cause us to receive pleasure without conscious exertion. Games chiefly of mental skill, as chess, or athletic sports, as baseball, are examples of means of recreation of the first class, which may be termed that of *exertive* recreation; music and the fine arts generally of the second or *receptive* division.

Considering the first by itself, much consideration will be needed in determining what classes of exercises may be advantageously provided for. In the Bois de Boulogne there is a race course; in the Bois de Vincennes a ground for artillery target-practice. Military parades are held in Hyde Park. A few cricket clubs are accommodated in most of the London parks, and swimming is permitted in the lakes at certain hours. In the New York Park, on the other hand, none of these exercises are provided for or permitted, except that the boys of the public schools are given the use on holidays of certain large spaces for ball playing. It is considered that the advantage to individuals which would be gained in providing for them would not compensate for the general inconvenience and expense they would cause.

I do not propose to discuss this part of the subject at present, as it is only necessary to my immediate purpose to point out that if recreations requiring spaces to be given up to the use of comparatively small number, are not considered essential, numerous small grounds so distributed through a large town that some one of them could be easily reached by a short walk from every house, would be more desirable than a single area of great extent, however rich in landscape attractions it might be. Especially would this be the case if the numerous local grounds were connected and supplemented by a series of trunk roads or boulevards such as has already been suggested.

Proceeding to the consideration of receptive recreations, it is necessary to ask you to adopt and bear in mind a further subdivision, under two heads, according to the degree in which the average enjoyment is greater when a large congregation assembles for a purpose of receptive recreation, or when the number coming together is small and the circumstances are favorable to the exercise of personal friendliness.

The first I shall term *gregarious;* the second, *neighborly*. Remembering that the immediate matter in hand is a study of fitting accommodations, you will, I trust, see the practical necessity of this classification.

Purely gregarious recreation seems to be generally looked upon in New England society as childish and savage, because, I suppose, there is so little of what we call intellectual gratification in it. We are inclined to engage in it indirectly, furtively, and with complication. Yet there are certain forms of recreation, a large share of attraction of which must, I think, lie in the gratification of the gregarious inclination, and which, with those who can afford to indulge in them, are so popular as to establish the importance of the requirement.

If I ask myself where I have experienced the most complete gratification of this instinct in public and out of doors, among trees, I find that it has been in the promenade of the Champs Elysées. As closely following it I should name other promenades of Europe, and our own upon the New York parks. I have studiously watched the latter for several years. I have several times seen fifty thousand people participating in them; and the more I have seen of them, the more highly have I been led to estimate their value as means of counteracting the evils of town life.

Consider that the New York Park and the Brooklyn Park are the only places in those associated cities where, in this eighteen hundred and seventieth year after Christ, you will find a body of Christians coming together, and with an evident glee in the prospect of coming together, all classes largely represented, with a common purpose, not at all intellectual, competitive with none, disposing to jealousy and spiritual or intellectual pride toward none, each individual adding by his mere presence to the pleasure of all others, all helping to the greater happiness of each. You may thus often see vast numbers of persons brought closely together, poor and rich, young and old, Jew and Gentile. I have seen a hundred thousand thus congregated, and I assure you that though there have been not a few that seemed a little dazed, as if they did not quite understand it, and were, perhaps, a little ashamed of it, I have looked studiously but vainly among them for a single face completely unsympathetic with the prevailing expression of good nature and light-heartedness.

Is it doubtful that it does men good to come together in this way in pure air and under the light of heaven, or that it must have an influence directly counteractive to that of the ordinary hard, hustling working hours of town life?

You will agree with me, I am sure, that it is not, and that opportunity, convenient, attractive opportunity, for such congregation, is a very good thing to provide for, in planning the extension of a town. . . .

If the great city to arise here is to be laid out little by little, and chiefly to suit the views of land-owners, acting only individually, and thinking only of how what they do is to affect the value in the next week or the next year of the few lots that each may hold at the time, the opportunities of so obeying this inclination as at the same time to give the lungs a bath of pure sunny air, to give the mind a suggestion of rest from the devouring eagerness and intellectual strife of town life, will always be few to any, to many will amount to nothing.

But is it possible to make public provision for recreation of this class, essentially domestic and secluded as it is?

It is a question which can, of course, be conclusively answered only from experience. And from experience in some slight degree I shall answer it. There is one large American town, in which it may happen that a man of any class shall say to his wife, when he is going out in the morning: "My dear, when the children come home from school, put some bread and butter and salad in a basket, and go to the spring under the chestnut-tree where we found the Johnsons last week. I will join you there as soon as I can get away from the office. We will walk to the dairy-man's cottage and get some tea, and some fresh milk for the children, and take our supper by the brookside;" and this shall be no joke, but the most refreshing earnestness.

There will be room enough in the Brooklyn Park, when it is finished, for several thousand little family and neighborly parties to bivouac at frequent intervals through the summer, without discommoding one another, or interfering with any other purpose, to say nothing of those who can be drawn out to make a day of it, as many thousand were last year. And although the arrangements for the purpose were yet very incomplete, and but little ground was at *all* prepared for such use, besides these small parties, consisting of one or two families, there came also, in companies of from thirty to a hundred and fifty, somewhere near twenty thousand children with their parents, Sunday-school teachers, or other guides and friends, who spent the best part of a day under the trees and on the turf, in recreations of which the predominating element was of this neighborly receptive class. Often they would bring a fiddle, flute, and harp, or other music. Tables, seats, shade, turf, swings, cool spring-water, and a pleasing rural prospect, stretching off half a mile or more each way, unbroken by a carriage road or the slightest evidence of the vicinity of the town, were supplied them without charge, and bread and milk and ice-cream at moderate fixed charges. In all my life I have never seen such joyous collections of people. I have, in fact, more than once observed tears of gratitude in the eyes of poor women, as they watched their children thus enjoying themselves.

The whole cost of such neighborly festivals, even when they include excursions by rail from the distant parts of town, does not exceed for each person, on an average, a quarter of a dollar; and when the arrangements are complete, I see no reason why thousands should not come every day where hundreds come now to use them; and if so, who can measure the value, generation after generation, of such provisions for recreation to the overwrought, much confined people of the great town that is to be?

For this purpose neither of the forms of ground we have heretofore considered are at all suitable. We want a ground to which people may easily go after their day's work is done, and where they may stroll for an hour, seeing, hearing, and feeling nothing of the bustle and jar of the streets, where they shall, in effect, find the city put far away from them. We want the greatest possible contrast with the streets and the shops and the rooms of the town which will be consistent with convenience and the preservation of good order and neatness. We want, especially, the greatest possible contrast with the restraining and confining conditions of the town, those conditions which compel us to walk circumspectly, watchfully, jealously, which compel us to look closely upon others without sympathy. Practically, what we most want is a simple, broad, open space of clean greensward, with sufficient play of surface and a sufficient number of trees about it to supply a variety of light and shade. This we want as a central feature. We want depth of wood enough about it not only for comfort in hot weather, but to completely shut out the city from our landscapes.

The word *park*, in town nomenclature, should, I think be reserved for grounds of the character and purpose thus described.

Not only as being the most valuable of all possible forms of public places, but regarded simply as a large space which will seriously interrupt cross-town communication wherever it occurs, the question of the site and bounds of the park requires to be determined with much more deliberation and art than is often secured for any problem of distant and extended municipal interests.

A Promenade may, with great advantage, be carried along the outer part of the surrounding groves of a park; and it will do no harm if here and there a broad opening among the trees discloses its open landscapes to those upon the promenade. But recollect that the object of the latter for the time being should be to see *congregated human life* under glorious and necessarily artificial conditions, and the natural landscape is not essential to them; though there is no more beautiful picture, and none can be more pleasing incidentally to the gregarious purpose, than that of beautiful meadows, over which clusters of level-armed sheltering trees cast broad shadows, and upon which are scattered dainty cows and flocks of black-faced sheep, while men, women, and children are seen sitting here and there, forming groups in the shade, or moving in and out among the woody points and bays.

It may be inferred from what I have said, that very rugged ground, abrupt eminences, and what is technically called picturesque in distinction from merely beautiful or simply pleasing scenery, is not the most desirable for a town park. Decidedly not in my opinion. The park should, as far as possible, complement the town. Openness is the one thing you cannot get in buildings. Picturesqueness you can get. Let your buildings be as picturesque as your artists can make them. This is the beauty of a town. Consequently, the beauty of the park should be the other. It should be the beauty of the fields, the meadow, the prairie, of the green pastures, and the still waters. What we want to gain is tranquillity and rest to the mind. Mountains suggest effort. But besides this objection there are others of what I may indicate as the housekeeping class. It is impossible to give the public range over a large extent of ground of a highly picturesque character, unless under very exceptional circumstances, and sufficiently guard against the occurrence of opportunities and temptations to shabbiness, disorder, indecorum, and indecency, that will be subversive of every good purpose the park should be designed to fulfill.

Nor can I think that *in the park proper*, what is called gardenesque beauty is to be courted; still less that highly artificial and exotic form of it, which, under the name of subtropical planting, the French have lately introduced, and in suitable positions with interesting and charming results, but in following which indiscretely, the English are sacrificing the simple beauty of their simple and useful parks of the old time. Both these may have places, and very important places, but they do not belong within a park, unless as side scenes and incidents. Twenty years ago Hyde Park had a most pleasing, open, free, and inviting expression, though certainly it was too rude, too much wanting in art; but now art is vexed with long black lines of repellent iron-work, and here and there behind it bouquets of hot-house plants, between which the public pass like hospital convalescents, who have been turned into the yard to walk about while their beds are making. We should undertake nothing in a park which involves the treating of the public as prisoners or wild beasts. A great object of all that is done in a park, of *all* the art of a park, is to influence the mind of men through their imagination, and the influence of iron hurdles can never be good.

We have, perhaps, sufficiently defined the ideal of a park for a large town. It will seldom happen that this ideal can be realized fully. The next thing is to select the situation in which it can be most nearly approached without great cost; and by cost I do not mean simply cost of land or of construction, but cost of inconvenience and cost of keeping in order, which is a very much more serious matter, and should have a great deal more study.

A park fairly well managed near a large town will surely become a new centre of that town. With the determination of location, size, and boundaries should therefore be associated the duty of arranging new trunk routes of communication between it and the distant parts of the town existing and forecasted.

These may be either narrow informal elongations of the park, varying say from two to five hundred feet in width, and radiating irregularly from it, or if, unfortunately, the town is already laid out in the unhappy way that New York and Brooklyn, San Francisco and Chicago, are, and, I am glad to say, Boston is not, on a plan made long years ago by a man who never saw a spring carriage, and who had a conscientious dread of the Graces, then we must probably adopt formal parkways. They should be so planned and constructed as never to be noisy and seldom crowded, and so also that the straightforward movement of pleasure carriages need never be obstructed, unless at absolutely necessary crossings, by slow-going heavy vehicles used for commercial purposes. If possible, also, they should be branched or reticulated with other ways of a similar class, so that no part of the town should finally be many minutes' walk from some one of them; and they should be made interesting by a process of planting and decoration, so that in necessarily passing through them, whether in going to or from the park, or to and from business, some substantial recreative advantage may be incidentally gained. It is a common error to regard a park as something to be produced complete in itself, as a picture to be painted on canvas. It should rather be planned as one to be done in fresco, with constant consideration of exterior objects, some of them quite at a distance and even existing as yet only in the imagination of the painter.

I have thus barely indicated a few of the points for which we may perceive our duty to apply the means in our hands to ends far distant, with reference to this problem of public recreations. Large operations of construction may not soon be desirable, but I hope you will agree with me that there is little room for question, that reserves of ground for the purposes I have referred to should be fixed upon as soon as possible, before the difficulty of arranging them, which arises from private building, shall be greatly more formidable than now. . . .

28 F. L. Olmsted and C. Vaux, Plan for Riverside, Illinois* *1868*

Olmsted recognized that, although American cities were attracting greater numbers, certain portions of the middle class were moving to the semirural suburbs. Following the general principles sketched out in Llewellyn Park, West Orange, New Jersey, Olmsted and Vaux in 1868 laid out Riverside, Illinois, for the Riverside Improvement Company headed by Emery E. Childs. The planners' aims were clearly outlined in their report reprinted in part here. Of its several innovative provisions, two warrant special notice—the reservation of a significant portion of the most desirable property along the Des Plaines River as public land, and the proposed carriage parkway connecting Riverside with Chicago. Although never built, the carriage drive was nonetheless the ancestor of such landscaped motor ways as the Merritt Parkway and the Hutchinson River Parkway, extending to the northeast from New York City, or the Baltimore-Washington Parkway. The actual construction of the streets, walks, drains, and sewers of Riverside and the initial planting were supervised by civil engineer L. Y. Schermerhorn, of Jenney, Schermerhorn and Bogart. William Le Baron Jenny, moreover, designed many of the first homes and resided in Riverside himself. A number of these homes, together with the John C. Dore house by Olmsted and Vaux, still stand. The Gothic Riverside Church and the Riverside Stores, a high Victorian Gothic block of shops and offices, were designed by Frederick Withers, whom Vaux was to join later after leaving Olmsted.[†] Development of the community was slowed somewhat due to the Chicago fire in 1871, but the success of the venture was such that, in 1891, Olmsted's firm was engaged to lay out Roland Park, then four miles north of the edge of Baltimore.

PRELIMINARY REPORT UPON THE PROPOSED SUBURBAN VILLAGE AT RIVERSIDE, NEAR CHICAGO

To The Riverside Improvement Company.
Gentlemen:
    You have requested a report from us, upon an enterprise which you desire to bring before the public, and which appears to rest on the following grounds:
    First.—Owing partly to the low, flat, miry, and forlorn character of the greater part of the country immediately about Chicago, and the bleak surface, arid soil, and exposure of the remainder to occasional harsh and frigid gusts of wind off the lake, and partly to the fact that the rapidity with which the town is being enlarged, causes all the available environs to be laid

---

*Reprinted in Theodora Kimball Hubbard, "Riverside, Illinois," *Landscape Architecture* 21 (July 1931), 257–91.

    †See the pamphlet by Riverside Improvement Company, *Riverside in 1871 with a Description of Its Improvements* (Chicago, 1871).

out with a view to a future demand solely for town purposes, and with no regard to the satisfaction of rural tastes, the city, as yet, has no true suburbs or quarters in which urban and rural advantages are agreeably combined with any prospect of long continuance.

Second.—If, under these circumstances, sites offering any very decided and permanent advantages for suburban residences could be put in the market, there would at once be a demand for them, which would continue and increase with the enlargement and progress in wealth and taste of the population of the city.

Third.—You have secured a large body of land, which, much beyond any other, has natural advantages for this purpose.

Fourth.—If, by a large outlay, these advantages could be developed to the utmost, and could be supplemented by abundant artificial conveniences of a high order, and the locality could thus be rendered not only very greatly superior to any other near Chicago, but could be made to compare satisfactorily, on the whole, with the most favored suburbs to be found anywhere else, a good return for such outlay might reasonably be expected.

We propose to review these grounds so far as they are not matters of fact easily put to the test of observation by those interested.

To understand the character of the probable demand for semi-rural residences near Chicago, it must be considered that the most prominent characteristic of the present period of civilization has been the strong tendency of people to flock together in great towns. This tendency unquestionably is concurrent, and probably identical, with an equally unprecedented movement of invention, energy, and skill, toward the production of certain classes of conveniences and luxuries, which, even yet, can generally be fully enjoyed by great numbers of people only in large towns. Arrangements for the easy gratification of certain tastes, which, until recently, were possessed by but a very few, even of the most wealthy class of any country, have consequently, of late, become common to thousands in every civilized land, while numerous luxuries, that the largest fortunes in the old world could not have commanded even half a century since, are enjoyed by families of comparatively moderate means, in towns which have sprung up from the wilderness, within the memory of some still living in them.

Progress in this way was never more rapid than at the present moment, yet in respect to the corresponding movement of populations there are symptoms of a change; a counter-tide of migration, especially affecting the more intelligent and more fortunate classes, although as yet of but moderate strength, is clearly perceptible, and almost equally so, in Paris, London, Vienna, Berlin, New York, Boston and Philadelphia. The most substantial manifestation of it perhaps, is to be found in the vast increase in value of eligible sites for dwellings near public parks, and in all localities of much natural beauty within several hours' journey of every great town. Another evidence of the same tendency, not less conclusive because it indicates an impulse as yet undecided and incomplete, is found in the constant modification which has occurred in the manner of laying out all growing towns, and which is invariably in the direction of a separation of business and dwelling streets, and toward rural spaciousness in the latter. The broader the streets are made, provided they are well prepared in respect to what are significantly designated "the modern conveniences," and especially if some slight rural element is connected with them, as by rows of trees or little enclosures of turf and foliage, the greater is the demand for dwelling-places upon them.

There is no evidence that the large class of conveniences, comforts and luxuries, which have been heretofore gained by close congregation, is beginning to have less positive attractiveness or commercial value, but it is very clear that the conviction is becoming established in the minds of great numbers of people that the advance in this respect, which has occurred in towns, has been made at too great a sacrifice of certain advantages which can at present be only enjoyed by going out of them. That this is a sound conviction, and not a mere whim, caprice, or reaction of fancy, temporarily affecting the rich, fashionable and frivolous, appears from the fact that it is universally held as the result of careful study by philanthropists, physicians and men of science. . . .

It thus becomes evident that the present outward tendency of town populations is not so much an ebb as a higher rise of the same flood, the end of which must be, not a sacrifice of urban conveniences, but their combination with the special charms and substantial advantages of rural conditions of life. Hence a series of neighborhoods of a peculiar character is already growing up in close relation with all large towns, and though many of these are as yet little better than rude over-dressed villages, or fragmentary half-made towns, it can hardly be questioned that, already, there are to be found among them the most attractive, the most refined and the most soundly wholesome forms of domestic life, and the best application of the arts of civilization to which mankind has yet attained.

It would appear then, that the demands of suburban life, with reference to civilized refinement, are not to be a retrogression from, but an advance upon, those which are characteristic of town life, and that no great town can long exist without great suburbs. It would also appear that whatever element of convenient residence is demanded in a town will soon be demanded in a suburb, so far as is possible for it to be associated with the conditions which are the peculiar advantage of the country, such as purity of air, umbrageousness, facilities for quiet out-of-door recreation and distance from the jar, noise, confusion, and bustle of commercial thoroughfares.

There need then be no fear that a happy combination of these conditions would ever fail to be exceedingly attractive to the people of Chicago, or that a demand for residences where it is found, would be liable to decline; on the contrary, it would be as sure to increase, as the city is sure to increase in population and in wealth, and for the same reason.

We proceed to consider the intrinsic value of your property for the purpose in view.

The question of access first demands attention. The centre of the proposed suburb is nine miles from the business centre of Chicago, the nearer points being about six miles apart. There is a double-track railroad from Chicago of remarkably good construction, with its first out-of-town station, at which every train is required to stop in the midst of your property. The advantages of the locality, in this respect, are already superior to those of many thriving suburbs.

A railroad, however, at the best affords a very inadequate and unsatis-factory means of communication between a rural habitation and a town, either for a family or for a man of business: as, moreover, one of the chief advantages of a suburban home, is the opportunity which it gives of taking air and exercise in driving, riding, and walking, it is a great desideratum, especially where time is so valuable as it is generally in Chicago, that a business man should be able to enjoy such an opportunity incidentally to his necessary communication with his store or office. . . .

How can the present difficulties of carriage access be overcome?

We find that drainage, not only for a road, but for the whole district through which it would pass, can be obtained by forming a series of large conduits a few miles in length, and that the neighboring landowners are fully prepared to co-operate with you in thus removing the chief obstacle to a good road.

We find, that in such small small portions of the land, through which a direct road would pass, as have already been artificially drained, trees, sever-al years planted, of the most valuable species for suburban purposes, are growing with great vigor and beauty.

We also find that upon the property which you have already secured at the end of the route, there are ledges of rock which will afford the means of forming a substantial foundation for frost-proof and water-proof wheel-ways, and beds of gravel for their superstructure.

On reviewing these conditions we conclude that the formation of an approach road, much better adapted to the requirements of pleasure-driving than any other leading out of Chicago, and with varied and agreeable acces-sories and appurtenances, is perfectly practicable.

We should advise you, in the first place, to obtain possession, if possi-ble, of a strip of ground from two hundred to six hundred feet wide, extend-ing from the city to the nearest border of your property, to secure its thor-ough drainage, to plant it with trees, and to carry through it a series of separate, but adjoining ways, especially adapted in construction—first for walking, second for riding, third for pleasure-driving, and fourth to give convenient access to houses to be built on the route and accommodate heavy freighting, without inconvenience to the through pleasure travel.

The main drive should be constructed in a very thorough and finished manner, so that, without perfect rigidity of surface, it will be storm- and frost-proof.

The ride should adjoin the drive, so that equestrians can at pleasure turn from it to converse with friends in carriages; it should have a soft and slightly yielding surface, that the great jar and danger of slipping, which occurs in a paved road, may be avoided.

The grateful influences of the grove extending through the prairie, with the amelioration of climate and soil which would result from thorough drainage and wind-breaks, and the advantages which would be found in the several proposed means of communication at all seasons of the year, would be such that continuous lines of villas and gardens would undoubtedly soon be established adjoining it, and the hour's drive through it, necessary to reach your property, would be neither tedious nor fatiguing.

At certain intervals upon the route, it would be desirable to provide openings with some special decorations, and here should be sheltered seats and watering places.

We see no reason why, if this suggestion is carried out liberally, it should not provide, or, at least, begin to provide, another pressing desideratum of the city of Chicago, namely, a general promenade ground. The promenade is a social custom of great importance in all the large towns of Europe. It is an open-air gathering for the purpose of easy, friendly, unceremonious greetings, for the enjoyment of change of scene, of cheerful and exhilarating sights and sounds, and of various good cheer, to which the people of a town, of all classes, harmoniously resort on equal terms, as to a common property. There is probably no custom which so manifestly displays the advantages of a Christian, civilized and democratic community, in contra-distinction from an aggregation of families, clans, sects, or castes. There is none more favorable to a healthy civic pride, civic virtue, and civic prosperity. As yet, the promenade has hardly begun to be recognised as an institution in Chicago, but there is no doubt that it soon must be, and it is evident from the present habits and manners of the people, that when once established, the custom will nowhere else be more popular or beneficent in its influence. Even now, with no tolerable accommodations for a general out-of-door pleasure gathering, nor any drives adapted for pleasure vehicles, which are not crowded when a few hundred carriages come together, there are probably more horses, in proportion to the population, kept for pleasure use, than in any city of the old, if not of the new world. There is understood to be no ground about the city possessing natural advantages for the formation of a public pleasure-ground of the character of the great parks in which the promenades of other metropolitan cities are generally held. By making the accommodations of your approach sufficiently large and sufficiently attractive, by associating with it several turning-points and resting-places in the midst of pleasure-grounds of moderate extent, your enterprise would, therefore, not merely supply Chicago, as you propose that it shall do, with a suburb, as well adapted as any of the suburbs of other cities, both for permanent habitations and country seats, and for occasional rural fetes and holiday recreations of families living in the town, but, in all probability, would provide it also with a permanent promenade-ground, having a character peculiar to itself, and not without special advantages. This result would be greatly enhanced if, as would probably be the case, certain entirely practicable improvements of the plan of the city should be made in connection with the construction of your approach.

The benefit which would result from this to your original enterprise is evident. Having means of communication with the city through the midst of such a ground, made gay and interesting by the movement of fine horses and carriages, and of numbers of well-dressed people, mainly cheerful with the enjoyment of recreation and the common entertainment, the distance would not be too great for the interchange of friendly visits, for the exercise of hospitality to a large circle of acquaintance, or for the enjoyment of the essential, intellectual, artistic, and social privileges which specially pertain to a metropolitan condition of society; and yet it would be sufficient to justify a neglect, on the part of a suburban resident, of most of those ceremonial social duties which custom seems to require, and in which so much time is necessarily spent in all great towns.

Turning next to your present property, we find that it extends for a distance of two miles upon the banks of the Aux [Des] Plaines River. Upon the river side, the land has a somewhat higher elevation than at any point nearer Chicago; the unctuous character of the prairie soil is also somewhat modified, and for considerable spaces wholly disappears. Sandy ridges extend along the river border. . . .

The more elevated parts of the ground, and the banks of the river everywhere, are occupied by groves of trees consisting of oaks, elms, hickories, walnuts, limes and ashes, with a scattered undergrowth of hazels, and various shrubs; most of the trees are young, but there are many specimens of large size and umbrageous form. In a private garden, planted apparently eight or ten years since, there are a number of transplanted shrubs, evergreens, and choice herbaceous plants in perfect health, and growing with such luxuriance as to indicate satisfactory conditions of soil and climate.

The water of the river is said to be ordinarily very clear, and we found it tolerably so after a heavy rain, which is remarkable in a prairie stream. It abounds with fish and wild fowl, is adapted to pleasure-boating, and can be improved in this respect. In parts, it already presents much beauty, and is everywhere susceptible of being refined and enriched by art to a degree which will render it altogether charming.

It appears to us, on the whole, as the result of our survey, that no essential natural requirement of an attractive and healthful suburb is here wanting.

We proceed to consider the artificial requirements.

The chief advantages which a suburb can possess over a town on the one hand, and over a wilderness on the other, will consist in those which favor open-air recreation beyond the limits which economy and convenience prescribe for private grounds and gardens. The main artificial requirements of a suburb then, are good roads and walks, pleasant to the eye within themselves, and having at intervals pleasant openings and outlooks, with suggestions of refined domestic life, secluded, but not far removed from the life of the community.

The misfortune of most existing suburbs is, that in such parts of them as have been built up little by little, without any general plan, the highways are usually adapted only to serve the bare irresistible requirements of agriculture, and that in such other parts as have been laid out more methodically, no intelligent design has been pursued to secure any distinctly rural attractiveness, the only aim apparently being to have a plan, which, seen on paper, shall suggest the possibility of an extension of the town-streets over the suburb, and of thus giving a town value to the lots upon them.

Exactly the opposite of this should be aimed at in your case, and, in regard to those special features whereby the town is distinguished from the country, there should be the greatest possible contrast which is compatible with the convenient communication and pleasant abode of a community; economy of room, and facilities for business, being minor considerations.

In the highways, celerity will be of less importance than comfort and convenience of movement, and as the ordinary directness of line in town-streets, with its resultant regularity of plan would suggest eagerness to press forward, without looking to the right hand or the left, we should recommend the general adoption, in the design of your roads, of gracefully-curved lines, generous spaces, and the absence of sharp corners, the idea being to suggest and imply leisure, contemplativeness and happy tranquility.

Without turf, and foliage, and birds, the character of the highways, whatever their ground plan, would differ from those of the town chiefly in the quality of desolation and dreariness. Turf and trees should abound then, and this implies much space in the highways, besides that which is requisite for the passage of vehicles and people on foot.

The first requirement of convenience in a wheelway or footway is the absence from it of whatever would serve no clearly good purpose in it, because whatever serves no good purpose will obviously interfere with its primary object of offering a route of easy locomotion. In other words, the first requirement is cleanliness and smoothness of surface. The fact that this primary requirement is found in American suburban highways, much less frequently, even, than in towns, notwithstanding the apparent disadvantages of towns growing out of the greater amount of travel which their highways have to sustain, shows how difficult it must be to secure, and makes it our business to enquire in what the difficulty consists.

The chief essential difference between town and suburban highway arrangements comes from the fact that in the suburb there is much greater space on an average between the houses fronting upon the roadways than in the town. This condition involves that of a larger frontage for each lot, and this again the condition that the cost of making a given length of the highways, and keeping them in order, must be distributed among a smaller number of persons; consequently, the assessments upon each lot owner must either be much heavier, or the highways must be of less expensive character, than those of the town. Invariably, the latter alternative is taken, not merely because a complete town-street arrangement would be to each man enormously expensive, but because it seems apparent that it would be unnecessarily expensive. A suburban village road, bordered by villas and cottages and their appropriate grounds, and not a thoroughfare of general commerce, is required to sustain not a tenth part of the wear and tear from travel of an ordinary town street. This being obvious to every one, a proposition that each house should pay more than one-tenth as much for street expenses as is paid by each house for good town streets, would be generally thought preposterous. It might be so but for the fact that the chief wear and tear to be provided against in the construction of a good wheel-way is not that of travel, either light or heavy, pleasure or commercial, but that of water and frost, the amount of which to be resisted in a suburb is not materially less than in the densest part of a town. If sufficient arrangements are not made to guard against the action of these destructive agencies, country roads and village streets become sometimes quite impassable and useless, sometimes merely very inconvenient and uncomfortable to use, and most of them are, in fact, throughout the whole of the year, untidy, shabby, uninviting, and completely contradictory to the ideal which most townspeople have in view when they seek to find a pleasant site for a suburban home.

Worse than this, they not only go far to destroy the charm of the country to the eye, but they really nullify that which is its greatest value to people seeking to escape the confinement of the town. Our country-women and girls, instead of taking more exercise in the open air, educating their perceptive faculties by a variety of observation of natural objects, and cultivating a true taste for the beautiful by familiar converse with the greatest and best of masters, are far more confined in their habits by the walls of their dwelling, than their town sisters, and mainly because they have been obliged to train and adapt themselves during a large part of the year to an avoidance of the annoyances and fatigue of going out.

These facts are perfectly familiar to every intelligent man, and yet, as we have already intimated, it is extremely rare to find an American village or suburb in which the highways can be driven through in the spring or early summer with light-pleasure vehicles, or walked through by women and children at any time, without absolute discomfort.

We find, then, that frost-proof, rain-proof wheelways and footways let them cost what they will, should, in selecting the site of a suburban residence, be the first consideration; in planning a suburb, the first requirement to provide for. The important question then is—What is the least expensive way of providing for it? . . .

However expensive it is, in nearly all cases an arrangement of this kind must be considered absolutely indispensable to the maintenance of a decent and convenient country road. It must simply be a chief object, if we desire it to have a quiet rural character, to avoid anything like the ordinary high curb of the town streets, and to make the gutter as shallow and inconspicuous as, with frequent gratings, it can be, and yet be safe to accomplish the required duty.

The turf of the road-side will be cut up and destroyed if driven over when water-soaked by loaded wagons, and this it certainly will be if the proper wheelway is allowed to become miry or excessively rough. It is sure to be so when the frost comes out in the spring, if at no other time, if it is either an ordinary earth road, or a road formed by a deposit of six or eight inches in depth of gravel, or of Macadam metal, upon a substratum of earth liable to be surcharged with water. Frost, in fact, is the chief enemy of convenience and of comfort, as well as of neatness and rural prettiness in all our high roads, and the only way by which, after ceaseless experiments, it has been found possible to offer any effectual resistance to its attack, is by means of a firm, deep, solid pavement, placed upon a thoroughly-drained foundation.

A structure of this kind, as ordinarily seen, however, encounters two very strong objections. First, it is decidedly expensive, second, it is rigid, hard, jarring, noisy, hot, and fatiguing to man and horse, and discordant with the rural sentiment which should rule in a suburb. The latter class of objections can be in a great degree overcome by placing the pavement itself at a sufficient depth, and forming a surface wheelway of several layers of finely broken stone, or what amounts to the same thing, of good gravel made so compact by heavy pressure as to be essentially waterproof. The first objection cannot be removed. A road suitable for pleasure-driving is one of the greatest common luxuries a civilized community can possess, but it is, when compared with our common, pioneer, earth teaming-ways, unavoidably an expensive luxury.

Reviewing what we have said of suburban roads, it will be evident that the two following conditions, among others, are required in their surface plan: first, they must have considerably greater breadth than is necessary merely for wheeling and walking-ways; second, wheels must be kept to the wheelways. It follows that the front line of lots, and consequently that the roadside houses, must be placed at much greater distance from the wheelways than is usual or necessary in our city streets. This, as far both as general rural effect and domestic seclusion is concerned, gives a clear advantage, against which, experience will simply place the greater inconvenience of communication between the carriage-way and the house-door.

There is but one remedy for this inconvenience which will not be destructive of neatness and good order in the road, and that is the adoption of private roads leading into the house lots.

It should here be considered that there is nothing in all the expensive constructions which have been prescribed as the necessary foundation work of a satisfactory suburban highway, that would attract as much attention as the rude and inefficient appointments ordinarily seen. There is nothing town-like about them, narrow strips of clean gravel, with other strips of undulating turf from the higher parts of which trees would spring, are all that would appear of them above ground. But all that can be said of this arrangement is that it is inoffensive; it is convenient and tidy, nothing more. Line a highway, so formed, with coal-yards, breweries, forges, warehouses, soap-works, shambles, and shanties, and there certainly would be nothing charming about it. Line it with ill-proportioned, vilely-colored, shabby-genteel dwelling-houses, pushing their gables or eaveboards impertinently over the sidewalk as if for the advertising of domestic infelicity and eagerness for public sympathy, and it would be anything but attractive to people of taste and refinement. Line it again with high dead-walls, as of a series of private mad houses, as is done in some English suburbs, and it will be more repulsive to many than the window-lighted walls of the town blocks. Nothing of this kind is wanted in a suburb or a rural village. Nothing of this kind must be permitted if we would have it wholly satisfactory. On the contrary, we must secure something very different.

We cannot judiciously attempt to control the form of the houses which men shall build, we can only, at most, take care that if they build very ugly and inappropriate houses, they shall not be allowed to force them disagreeably upon our attention when we desire to pass along the road upon which they stand. We can require that no house shall be built within a certain number of feet of the highway, and we can insist that each house-holder shall maintain one or two living trees between his house and his highway-line.

A few simple precautions of this kind, added to a tasteful and convenient disposition of shade trees, and other planting along the roadsides and public places, will, in a few years, cause the whole locality, no matter how far the plan may be extended, to possess, not only the attraction of neatness and convenience, and the charm of refined sylvan beauty and grateful umbrageousness, but an aspect of secluded peacefulness and tranquility more general and pervading than can possibly be found in suburbs which have grown up in a desultory hap-hazard way. If the general plan of such a suburb is properly designed on the principles which have been suggested, its character will inevitably also, notwithstanding its tidiness, be not only informal, but, in a moderate way, positively picturesque, and when contrasted with the constantly repeated right angles, straight lines, and flat surfaces which characterize our large modern towns, thoroughly refreshing.

We have thus far addressed ourselves mainly to questions of construction, because in them the difficulties of your undertaking will be chiefly found. If you can afford to construct wheelways and drainageways, such as we have described, there is but little more difficulty or expense in laying them out, and decorating them in such a manner as will increase the more important natural attractions which we have shown the site to possess, than in making straight streets in the ordinary way without the slightest respect for nature.

The suggestion that your property might be formed into a "park," most of the land within which might be divided by lines, mainly imaginary, into building lots, and sold as demand should require, has been publicly made with apparent confidence in its feasibility and advantage, and as it seems to have attractions, we shall endeavor to show why we cannot advise you to adopt it.

The landscape character of a park, or of any ground to which that term is applied with strict propriety, is that of an idealized, broad stretch of pasture, offering in its fair, sloping surfaces, dressed with fine, close herbage, its ready alternatives of shade with sunny spaces, and its still waters of easy approach, attractive promises in every direction, and, consequently, invitations to movement on all sides, go through it where one may. Thus the essential qualification of a park is *range*, and to the emphasizing of the idea of range in a park, buildings and all artificial constructions should be subordinated. . . .

We should recommend the appropriation of some of the best of your property for public grounds, and that most of these should have the character of informal village-greens, commons and play-grounds, rather than of enclosed and defended parks or gardens. We would have, indeed, at frequent intervals in every road, an opening large enough for a natural group of trees, and often provide at such points croquet or ball grounds, sheltered seats and drinking fountains, or some other objects which would be of general interest or convenience to passers-by.

It will probably be best to increase the height of the mill-dam so as to enlarge the area of the public water suitable for boating and skating, and so as to completely cover some low, flat ground now exposed in low stages of the river. At the same time, a larger outlet should be provided to prevent floods above the dam from injuring the shore. A public drive and walk should be carried near the edge of the bank in such a way as to avoid destroying the more valuable trees growing upon it, and there should be pretty boat-landings, terraces, balconies overhanging the water, and pavilions at points desirable for observing regattas, mainly of rustic character, and to be half overgrown with vines.

All desirable improvements of this character, more and better than can be found in any existing suburb in the United States, can be easily supplied at comparatively small cost. That which it is of far more consequence to secure at the outset, and which cannot be obtained at small cost, unfortunately, is a system of public ways of thoroughly good construction.

As we have already shown, in speaking upon the question of approach, your property is not without special advantages for this purpose, and, on the whole, we feel warranted in expressing the opinion that your scheme, though it will necessarily require a large outlay of capital, is a perfectly practicable one, and if carried out would give Chicago a suburb of highly attractive and substantially excellent character.

It should be well understood that this is a preliminary report, and that our observations have been necessarily of a somewhat superficial character. A complete topographical survey, and a much more deliberate study of the conditions to be dealt with, must precede the preparation of a definite plan, if it is to have any assured value.

Respectfully,

OLMSTED, VAUX & CO.,

Landscape Architects.

110 Broadway, New York, Sept 1, 1868.

29   R. T. Ely, Pullman: A Social Study* *1885*

The twenty years following the Civil War witnessed the beginning of a massive shift of population toward the cities. This, coupled with the arrival of ever greater numbers of immigrants, put incredible pressure on the available housing in the eastern seaboard cities, often resulting in overcrowding. Following the models established by English philanthropists, several organizations were set up to build model apartments, available at low rents to wage earners yet paying modest returns on the investment. It was hoped such model apartment blocks would encourage speculative builders to erect more such units, gradually eliminating the densely overcrowded slum tenements for which New York, in particular, was becoming notorious. One of the most energetic advocates was Alfred Tredway White (1846–1921) who had been influenced specifically by Sir Sidney Waterlow's Industrial Dwellings Company, London. He founded the Improved Dwellings Company in Brooklyn, and from 1877 to 1890 built there several model apartment blocks which proved both popular with tenants and reasonably profitable, earning a steady five to seven percent.† As successful as this demonstration was, White's model buildings unfortunately had little effect in reforming the thousands of tenements built over the next twenty years.

What Alfred Tredway White endeavored to provide for urban wage earners, many enlightened employers and corporate directors provided for those who worked

---

* *Harper's Monthly* 70 (February 1885), pp. 452–66.

† See Alfred T. White, *Better Homes for Workingmen* (Washington, D.C., 1885), which outlines his objections and methods. His Home, Tower and Riverside apartments, Brooklyn, New York, are discussed in the *Concise History*, pp. 141–42.

Figure 24. "The Arcade and Public Square," from Richard T. Ely, "Pullman: A Social Study," *Harper's Monthly* 70 (February 1885), p. 452.

and lived in company towns. Many who invested extensively in such planned communities viewed it as one of the costs of business and were content to realize modest returns of 2½ to 3½ percent.‡ One of the most ambitiously planned and constructed of these company towns was Pullman, south of Chicago. George Mortimer Pullman viewed the town as a branch of his business and expected a more substantial return of nearly six percent. The town was operated not for the inhabitants but solely with a view to the profits of the parent company. Consequently, when wages were reduced due to the business recession in 1893–94, rents were kept at the high level, precipitating a workers' strike and the resulting riot when federal troops were sent in to break it. Because of the clash, Pullman brought discredit to company towns as a class. Prior to 1893, however, Pullman was considered by many to be a model community, architecturally as well as socially. Yet to a perceptive social critic and economist such as Richard Theodore Ely (1854–1943), the conditions which eventually were to lead to the riot were evident even as early as 1885. To Ely, the basis of Pullman was un-American: "it is benevolent, well-wishing feudalism, which desires the happiness of the people, but in such a way as shall please the authorities." Ely, the son of a self-

‡ See my "Three Industrial Towns by McKim, Mead & White," *Journal, Society of Architectural Historians* 38 (December 1979), pp. 317–47, which includes data on other contemporary planned communities.

educated civil engineer, was raised in upstate New York, graduated from Columbia University in 1876, and pursued graduate study in economics in Germany, at Halle and at Heidelberg, where he received his Ph.D. in 1879. After post-doctoral study in Europe, he returned to the United States, where he joined the faculty of Johns Hopkins University in Baltimore in 1881. In 1885, the year this essay appeared in *Harper's Monthly*, Ely was instrumental in founding the American Economic Association, serving as its secretary and later its president. He was appointed director of the new school of economics, political science, and history at the University of Wisconsin in 1892, where he remained for nearly a third of a century.

Pullman, a town of eight thousand inhabitants, some ten miles from Chicago, on the Illinois Central Railroad, was founded less than four years ago by the Pullman Palace Car Company, whose president and leading spirit is Mr. George M. Pullman. Its purpose was to provide both a centre of industry and homes for the employés of the company and such additional laborers as might be attracted to the place by other opportunities to labor. Simply as a town, Pullman has not sufficient interest to justify a description of it in a great magazine. Its natural beauties are not remarkable, situated as it is on the low prairie land surrounding Chicago, and its newness makes such romances impossible as one can associate with villages like Lenox, and Stockbridge, and other ancient towns in New England. Like many other Western cities, its growth has been rapid, its population having increased from four souls in January, 1881, to 2084 in February, 1882, and to 8203 in September, 1884. A manufacturing town, it embraces the principal works of the Pullman Palace Car Company, in addition to the Allen Paper Car-wheel Company, the Union Foundry and Pullman Car-wheel Company, the Chicago Steelworks, the Steel-forging Company, and numerous less important enterprises. Many of the last-mentioned are connected with building operations in the town of Pullman, or furnish commodities to its residents, and in many cases they also supply customers elsewhere, such as the gas-works, the ice-houses, the brick-yards, the carpenter shops, and the large farm which receives the sewage of Pullman. The number of men employed in the place is at present about four thousand, of whom over three thousand are employed by the Palace Car Company. The products of the various establishments are valued at many millions of dollars. As all the Pullman enterprises are conducted with what seems to the writer a needless air of secrecy, reliable statistics are obtained with difficulty. However, the car-works claims a capacity to turn out $8,000,000 worth of passenger and freight cars per annum, and it is expected that they will be able to manufacture forty of the latter per day hereafter. On August 18, 1884, one hundred freight cars were built in ten hours. The Allen Paper Car-wheel Company claims a capacity of fifteen thousand paper car-wheels a year. The brick-yards are large, and two hundred and twenty thousand bricks is one days work. Many of the men who work in the brick-yard in summer harvest ice in winter, and it is expected to store about twenty-five thousand tons this winter. The carpenter shops, which do considerable work in Chicago, have employed at times as many as five hundred men. These are some of the principal material facts of interest to the general reader. Much could be said of Pullman as a manufacturing

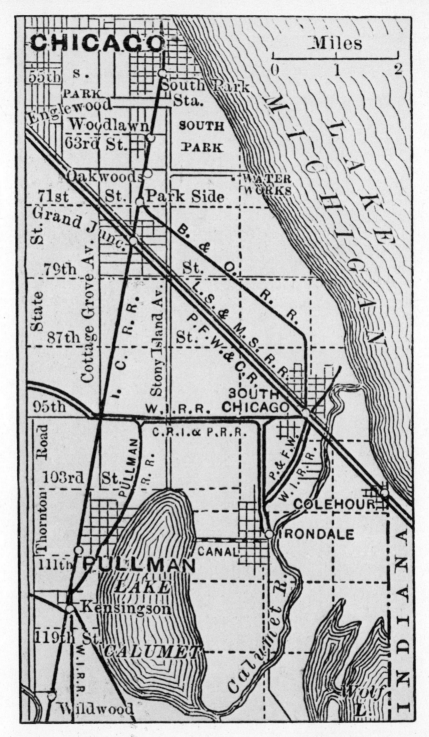

Figure 25. "Suburbs of Chicago," from *Harper's Monthly* 70 (February 1885), p. 453.

Hotel.

Palace Car Works.

Figure 26. View of hotel and Pullman Palace Car Works, with a plan of Pullman, from *Harper's Monthly* 70 (February 1885), p. 454.

centre, but the purpose of this article is to treat it as an attempt to furnish laborers with the best homes under the most healthful conditions and with the most favorable surroundings in every respect, for Pullman aims to be a forerunner of better things for the laboring classes.

The questions to be answered are these: Is Pullman a success from a social standpoint? Is it worthy of imitation? Is it likely to inaugurate a new era in society? If only a partial success, what are its bright features and what its dark features?

Pullman as an attempt to realize an ideal must be judged by an ideal standard. The measure to be applied is the reasonable ideal of the social reformer. What is this ideal? Is it not that each individual be so situated as to participate, as fully as his nature will allow, in the advantages of the existing civilization? This is a high standard, but not so high as might at first appear. All those who have more than this measure calls for are by no means included in the class of *nouveaux riches*. The writer well remembers a visit to some brassworks in Baltimore, where rude, uneducated Welshmen were earning eighteen dollars a week. Society was doing well by these men, and in their case there could be no serious social question as far as wages were concerned. One needed to be with the men but a short time to be convinced that their income enabled them to participate in all the benefits of this nineteenth-century civilization which they were capable of enjoying. Now what the student of society wants to know is the nearness with which Pullman approaches the social ideal.

Very gratifying is the impression of the visitor who passes hurriedly through Pullman and observes only the splendid provision for the present material comforts of its residents. What is seen in a walk or drive through the streets is so pleasing to the eye that a woman's first exclamation is certain to be, "Perfectly lovely!" It is indeed a sight as rare as it is delightful. What might have been taken for a wealthy suburban town is given up to busy workers, who literally earn their bread in the sweat of their brow. No favorable sites are set apart for drones living on past accumulations, and if a few short stretches are reserved for residences which can be rented only by those whose earnings are large, this is an exception; and it is not necessary to remain long in the place to notice that clergymen, officers of the company, and mechanics live in adjoining dwellings.

One of the most striking peculiarities of this place is the all-pervading air of thrift and providence. The most pleasing impression of general well-being is at once produced. Contrary to what is seen ordinarily in laborers' quarters, not a dilapidated door-step nor a broken window, stuffed perhaps with old clothing, is to be found in the city. The streets of Pullman, always kept in perfect condition, are wide and finely macadamized, and young shade trees on each side now ornament the town, and will in a few years afford refreshing protection from the rays of the summer sun.

Unity of design and an unexpected variety charm us as we saunter through the town. Lawns always of the same width separate the houses from the street, but they are so green and neatly trimmed that one can overlook this regularity of form. Although the houses are built in groups of two or more, and even in blocks, with the exception of a few large buildings of cheap flats, they bear no resemblance to barracks; and one is not likely to make the mistake, so frequent in New York blocks of "brown-stone fronts," of getting into the wrong house by mistake. Simple but ingenious designs secure variety, of which the most skillful is probably the treatment of the sky line. Naturally, without an appearance of effort, it assumes an immense diversity. French roofs, square roofs, dormer-windows, turrets, sharp points, blunt points, triangles, irregular quadrangles, are devices resorted to in the upper stories to avoid the appearance of unbroken uniformity. A slight knowledge of mathematics shows how infinite the variety of possible combinations of a few elements, and a better appreciation of this fact than that exhibited by the architecture of Pullman it would be difficult to find. The streets cross each other at right angles, yet here again skill has avoided the frightful monotony of New York, which must sometimes tempt a nervous person to scream for relief. A public square, arcade, hotel, market, or some large building is often set across a street so ingeniously as to break the regular line, yet without inconvenience to traffic. Then at the termination of long streets a pleasing view greets and relieves the eye—a bit of water, a stretch of meadow, a clump of trees, or even one of the large but neat workshops. All this grows upon the visitor day by day. No other feature of Pullman can receive praise needing so little qualification as its architecture. Desirable houses have been provided for a large laboring population at so

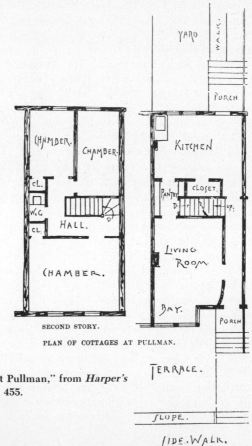

Figure 27. "**Plan of Cottages at Pullman,**" from *Harper's Monthly* 70 (February 1885), p. 455.

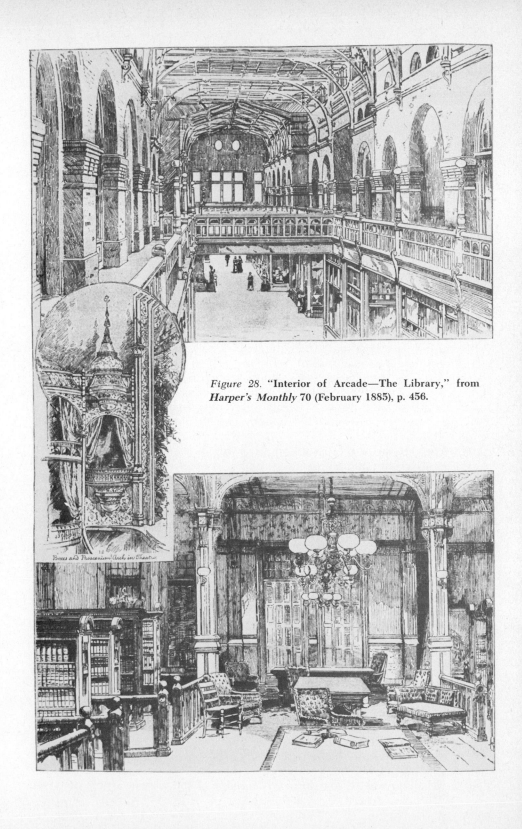

Figure 28. "Interior of Arcade—The Library," from *Harper's Monthly* 70 (February 1885), p. 456.

small a cost that they can be rented at rates within their means and yet yield a handsome return on the capital invested. Rents are probably about three-fifths what they are in Chicago, and, all things considered, this seems not to be an unfair standard of comparison. It is a mere matter of course that there are architectural defects even in Pullman. The diversity is not quite all that could be desired. What may be called the public buildings, that is to say, the hotel, school-house, arcade, etc., are detached, but no private house stands by itself, though there are quite a number of detached double houses. Spaces have, however, been reserved for a few detached private residences, which will improve the appearance of the town. With the exception of the church and parsonage, built of green serpentine stone from Philadelphia, all the buildings are of brick. This is monotonous, and rather wearying to the eye, but the slate roofs, and a large use of light stone trimmings, and stripes of black across the houses, help matters somewhat. The general character of the architecture is what has been called advanced secular Gothic. This is skillfully varied, and in the hotel particularly there is a feeling of the Queen Anne style. But there ought to be some bold break in the general design. The newness of things, which time will remedy, is a little distressing, as is also the mechanical regularity of the town, and it is this, perhaps, which suggests the epithet "machine-made." The growth of shade trees will break into the sameness, and the magnificent boulevard which divides the shops on the north from the residences on the south, stretching from east to west across the town, and bordered with double rows of elms, will, twenty years from now, be a vast improvement. Great overarching trees will hide one part of the town from another, and give opportunity for pleasant surprises in nature and art.

The interior of the houses affords scarcely less gratification than their exterior. Even the humblest suite of rooms in the flats is provided with water, gas, and closets, and no requisite of cleanliness is omitted. Most of the cottages are two stories in height, and contain five rooms, besides a cellar, closets, and pantry, as seen in Figure 27. Quite a large number of houses contain seven rooms, and in these larger dwellings there is also a bath-room.

Outside of the home one finds other noteworthy provisions for the comfort, convenience, and well-being of the residents in Pullman. There is a large Market-house, 100 by 110 feet in size, through which a wide passage extends from east to west. This building contains a basement and two stories, the first divided into sixteen stalls, the second a public hall. The dealers in meat and vegetables are concentrated in the Market-house. The finest building in Pullman is the Arcade, a structure 256 feet in length, 146 feet in width, and 90 feet in height. It is built of red pressed brick, with stone foundations and light stone trimmings, and a glass roof extends over the entire wide central passage. In the Arcade one finds offices, shops, the bank, theatre, library, etc. As no shops or stores are allowed in the town outside of the Arcade and Market-house, all shopping in Pullman is done under roof— a great convenience in wet weather, and a saving of time and strength.

The theatre, situated in the Arcade as just mentioned, seats eight hundred people, and is elegantly and tastefully furnished. The illustration (Figure 28) of the Arcade includes a view of the boxes, which are Moorish in design. It was intended to embrace in this theatre many of the best features of the Madison Square Theatre, but the scope of the present article does not admit of a detailed description of them, exquisite and perfectly appointed as they are. Representations are given by various troupes about once in two weeks. There is nothing peculiar in the management. The company rents it to applicants, but attempts to exclude immoral pieces, and admit only such as shall afford innocent amusement and instruction. The prices for tickets are thirty-five, fifty, and seventy-five cents, which have been found to be the most profitable in Pullman, higher prices keeping the people away, and lower ones not attracting enough more to compensate for the diminished return on each ticket.

In the interior of the Arcade a balcony extends around the passage in front of the rooms and offices of the second story, which it thus conveniently connects. It produces a pleasing effect, and affords a favorable position from which to view the busy throng below. The library, which opens on this balcony, contains six thousand volumes, the gift of Mr. Pullman, and numerous periodicals, among which were noticed several likely to be of special importance to mechanics, such as the *Railway Age, the Iron Age, Scientific American,* and *Popular Science Monthly.* The library rooms are elegantly furnished with Wilton carpets and plush-covered chairs, and the walls are beautifully painted. Objection has been raised to this luxuriousness by those who think it repels the ordinary artisan, unaccustomed in his own home to such extravagance; but it must be remembered that it is avowedly part of the design of Pullman to surround laborers as far as possible with all the privileges of large wealth. The annual charge for the use of the Public Library, for nothing in Pullman is free, is three dollars—rather high for workmen in these days of free libraries. The management of the librarian is most commendable, and every aid is given to those who patronize it to render it as instructive and elevating as possible. A special effort has been made to induce the subscribers to choose a superior class of literature, but the record shows that seventy-five per centum of the books drawn are still works of fiction, which is about the usual percentage in public libraries.

The educational facilities of Pullman are those generally afforded in larger American villages by the public-school system. The school trustees are elected by the citizens, and rent of the Pullman Company a handsome building, which harmonizes in architecture and situation with the remainder of the town.

There are no barns in the place, but a large building provides accommodation for livery-stables, and a fire department sustained by the Pullman Company. The hotel, the property of the company, and managed by one of its officers, is a large structure, surrounded on three sides by beautiful public squares covered with flowers and shrubbery. It is luxuriously furnished, admirably kept, and contains the only barroom allowed in Pullman, though there are thirty on the outskirts of the place in Kensington. However, the temptation "to drink" does not constantly stare one in the face, and this restriction has not entirely failed to accomplish its end, the promotion of temperance.

There is nothing so peculiar in these features of Pullman as to require further description. It was necessary to make brief mention of them to help the reader to understand the nature and extent of the experiment called Pullman.

The whole is the work of the Pullman Palace Car Company and the

Pullman Land Association, which are both under one management, and, to a considerable extent, the same practically, although two separate legal persons. Colonel James Bowen, who appears to have been one of the interesting characters in the early history of Chicago, had long prophesied that the true site for a great city was upon the shores of Lake Calumet—an expanse of water some six feet deep, about three miles long, and a mile and a half wide, and connected with Lake Michigan by the Calumet River. Having found a believer in Mr. Pullman, he was commissioned by that gentleman to purchase quietly four thousand acres in the neighborhood, and this has become the site of Pullman. The entire town was built under the direction of a single architect, Mr. S. S. Beman, an ambitious young man whose frequently expressed desire for an opportunity to do a "big thing" was here gratified. This is probably the first time a single architect has ever constructed a whole town systematically upon scientific principles, and the success of the work entitles him to personal mention. The plans were drawn for a large city at the start, and these have been followed without break in the unity of design. Pullman illustrates and proves in many ways both the advantages of enterprises on a vast scale and the benefits of unified and intelligent municipal administration. All articles employed in the construction of the town were purchased at the lowest figures, as orders were given for unusually large quantities, and thus the outlay was far less than it would have been had each building, or even each block, been built by a separate individual. It is manifest, for example, that a man will obtain hinges at the most favorable rates who orders twenty-five thousand pairs at one time. An additional saving was effected by the establishment of the carpenter shops and brick-yards, which enabled the company to avoid the payment of profits on the wood-work and on the bricks. The bricks were manufactured of clay from the bottom of Lake Calumet, and thus the construction of the town helped to deepen its harbor and prepare it for the large shipping which is one day expected there, for its proprietors prophesy that vessels will yet sail from Pullman to London. Then, as there is no competition at Pullman, and no conflicting municipal boards, gas, water, and sewerage pipes were laid once for all, and the pavement, when completed, not again disturbed. The money saved by this wise, unified, and consequently harmonious action must be reckoned by the hundred thousand.

There are over fifteen hundred buildings at Pullman, and the entire cost of the town, including all the manufacturing establishments, is estimated at eight millions of dollars. The rents of the dwellings vary from $4.50 per month for the cheapest flats of two rooms to $100 a month for the largest private house in the place. The rent usually paid varies from $14 to $25 a month, exclusive of the water charge, which is generally not far from eighty cents. A five-roomed cottage . . . rents for $17 a month, and its cost is estimated at $1700, including a charge of $300 for the lot. But it must be understood that the estimated value of $1700 includes profits on brick and carpenter work and everything furnished by the company, for each industry at Pullman stands on its own feet, and keeps its own separate account. The company's brick-yards charge the company a profit on the brick the latter buys, and the other establishments do the same; consequently the estimated cost of the buildings includes profits which flowed after all into the company's coffers.

The Pullman companies retain everything. No private individual owns to-day a square rod of ground or a single structure in the entire town. No organization, not even a church, can occupy any other than rented quarters. With the exception of the management of the public school, every municipal act is here the act of a private corporation. What this means will be perceived when it is remembered that it incudes such matters as the location, repairs, and cleaning of streets and sidewalks, the maintenance of the fire department, and the taking of the local census whenever desired. When the writer was in Pullman a census was taken. A superior officer of the company said to an inferior, "I want a census," and told what kind of a census was desired. That was the whole matter. The people of the place had no more to say about it then a resident of Kamtchatka. All this applies only to what is generally known as Pullman, which is in reality no political organization, and is called a town or city simply in a popular sense for the sake of convenience. Pullman is only a part of the large village and town of Hyde Park, but the latter appears to have relinquished the government of this portion of its territory bearing the name of Pullman to private corporations, and the writer was not able to find that a single resident of Pullman, not an officer of the Pullman companies, was either in the board of trustees of Hyde Park or in the staff of officers. The town clerk and treasurer are both officers of the Pullman Palace Car Company, and the directory of Hyde Park reveals the fact that with one exception every member of the board of education of the Pullman school district is an officer of the Palace Car Company or some concern which bears the name of Pullman.

One of Mr. Pullman's fundamental ideas is the *commercial value of beauty*, and this he has endeavored to carry out as faithfully in the town which bears his name as in the Pullman drawing-room and sleeping cars. He is one of the few men who have thought it a paying investment to expend millions for the purpose of surrounding laborers with objects of beauty and comfort. In a hundred ways one sees in Pullman to-day evidences of its founder's sagacious foresight. One of the most interesting is the fact that the company finds it pays them in dollars and cents to keep the streets sprinkled with water and the lawns well trimmed, the saving in paint and kalsomine more than repaying the outlay. Less dust and dirt are carried and blown into houses, and the injury done to walls and wood-work is diminished. For the rest, the neat exterior is a constant example, which is sure sooner or later to exert its proper effect on housewives, stimulating them to exertion in behalf of cleanliness and order.

It should be constantly borne in mind that all investments and outlays in Pullman are intended to yield financial returns satisfactory from a purely business point of view. The minimum return expected is six per centum on expenditure, and the town appears to have yielded a far higher percentage on cost up to the present time. Much of the land was bought at less than $200 per acre, and it is likely that the average price paid did not exceed that. A large part of this now yields rent on a valuation of $5000 per acre, and certain sections in the heart of Pullman are to-day more valuable, and will continue to increase in value in the future, if the town grows as is expected. The extreme reluctance of the officers of the company to make precise statements of any kind renders it impossible to obtain the accurate information desired. Yet there seems to be no reason to doubt the emphatic assertion that the whole establishment pays handsomely. A large part of Pullman belongs to the Palace Car Company, which claims to have paid nine and one-half per centum on its entire stock for the last three years, and to have averaged about ten per centum since its organization in 1867. As far as the Land Association is concerned, it is sufficient to know that all its houses are rented at a high valuation, and the land put in at twenty-five times its cost.

It pays also in another way. The wholesome, cheerful surroundings enable the men to work more constantly and more efficiently. . . .

The wages paid at Pullman are equal to those paid for similar services elsewhere in the vicinity. In a visit of ten days at Pullman no complaint was heard on this score which appeared to be well founded. . . .

The great majority at Pullman are skilled artisans, and nearly all with whom the writer conversed expressed themselves as fairly well satisfied with their earnings, and many of them took pains to point out the advantages of the steady employment and prompt pay they always found there. The authorities even go out of their way to "make work" for one who has proved himself efficient and faithful.

There are many other pleasant and interesting features of Pullman, to which it is possible only to allude here. One is the perfect system of sewerage, similar to that which has been found so successful in Berlin, Germany. The sewerage is all collected in a great tank under the "water tower," and then pumped on to a large garden farm of one hundred and seventy acres, called the "Pullman Farm." This is already profitable, and it is hoped that in time it will pay interest on the cost of the entire sewerage system of the town, which was $300,000. It is worthy the careful study of municipal authorities.

There are a thousand and one little ways in which the residents of Pullman are benefited, and in many cases without cost to the company. . . .

But admirable as are the peculiarities of Pullman which have been described, certain unpleasant features of social life in that place are soon noticed by the careful observer, which moderate the enthusiasm one is at first inclined to feel upon an inspection of the external, plainly visible facts, and the picture must be completed before judgment can be pronounced upon it.

One just cause of complaint is what in government affairs would be called a bad civil service, that is a bad administration in respect to the employment, retention, and promotion of employés. Change is constant in men and officers, and each new superior appears to have his own friends, whom he appoints to desirable positions. Favoritism and nepotism, out of place as they are in an ideal society, are oft-repeated and apparently well-substantiated charges.

The resulting evil is very naturally dissatisfaction, a painful prevalence of petty jealousies, a discouragement of superior excellence, frequent change in the residents, and an all-pervading feeling of insecurity. Nobody regards Pullman as a real home, and, in fact, it can scarcely be said that there are more than temporary residents at Pullman. One woman told the writer she had been in Pullman two years, and that there were only three families among her acquaintances who were there when she came. Her reply to the question, "It is like living in a great hotel, is it not? was, "We call it camping out."...

The desire of the American to acquire a home is justly considered most commendable and hopeful. It promotes thrift and economy, and the habits acquired in the effort to pay for it are often the foundation of a future prosperous career. It is a beginning in the right direction. Again, a large number of house owners is a safeguard against violent movements of social discontent. Heretofore laborers at Pullman have not been allowed to acquire any real property in the place. There is a repression here as elsewhere of any marked individuality. Everything tends to stamp upon residents, as upon the town, the character expressed in "machine-made." Not only are strikes regarded as the chief of social sins, a view too widely disseminated by works like Charles Reade's *Put Yourself in His Place*, but individual initiative, even in affairs which concern the residents alone, is repressed. Once several of the men wanted to form a kind of mutual insurance association to insure themselves against loss of time in case of accident, but it was frowned down by the authorities, and nothing further has been heard of the matter. A lady attempted to found a permanent charitable organization to look after the poor and needy, but this likewise was discouraged, because it was feared that the impression might get abroad that there was pauperism in Pullman.

In looking over all the facts of the case the conclusion is unavoidable that the idea of Pullman is un-American. It is a nearer approach than anything the writer has seen to what appears to be the ideal of the great German Chancellor. It is not the American ideal. It is benevolent, well-wishing feudalism, which desires the happiness of the people, but in such way as shall please the authorities. One can not avoid thinking of the late Czar of Russia, Alexander II., to whom the welfare of his subjects was truly a matter of concern. He wanted them to be happy, but desired their happiness to proceed from him, in whom everything should centre. Serfs were freed, the knout abolished, and no insuperable objection raised to reforms, until his people showed a decided determination to take matters in their own hands, to govern themselves, and to seek their own happiness in their own way. Then he stopped the work of reform, and considered himself deeply aggrieved. The loss of authority and distrust of the people is the fatal weakness of many systems of reform and well-intentioned projects of benevolence.

Pullman ought to be appreciated, and high honor is due Mr. George M. Pullman. He has at least attempted to do something lasting and far-reaching, and the benefits he has actually conferred upon a laboring population of eight thousand souls testify that his heart must be warm toward his poorer brother. Mr. Pullman has partially solved one of the great problems of the immediate present, which is a diffusion of the benefits of concentrated wealth among wealth-creators....

Not a few have ventured to express the hope that Pullman might be widely imitated, and thus inaugurate a new era in the history of labor. But if this signifies approval of a scheme which would immesh our laborers in a net-work of communities owned and managed by industrial superiors, then let every patriotic American cry, God forbid! What would this mean? The establishment of the most absolute power of capital, and the repression of all freedom. It matters not that they are well-meaning capitalists; all capitalists are not devoted heart and soul to the interests of their employés, and the history of the world has long ago demonstrated that no class of men are fit to be intrusted with unlimited power. In the hour of temptation and pressure it is abused, and the real nature of the abuse may for a time be concealed even from him guilty of it; but it degrades the dependent, corrupts the morals of the superior, and finally that is done unblushingly in the light which was once scarcely allowed in a dark corner. This is the history of a large share of the degeneracy of manners and morals in public and private life. . . .

30   The Architect's Fee: R. M. Hunt versus E. Parmly*   1861

By about 1900 American architects had achieved a professional stature which has remained essentially unchanged since that time. Of particular importance in this was the establishment of the first collegiate programs in architectural education during 1868–74.[†] The right to specify and supervise all construction and to retain ownership of all drawings had been won by Latrobe in 1804–18.[‡] The right of an architect to receive a percentage payment on the basis of his conceptual scheme, his preliminary drawings, even when the structure remained unbuilt, was established by Richard Upjohn in his successful suit against the town of Taunton, Massachusetts, in 1850.[§] That an architect was entitled to a percentage fee based on the cost of building construction, even when the drawings had somehow been turned over to another, was successfully contested by Richard Morris Hunt in his suit brought against Dr. Eleazer Parmly in 1861. In 1855, while still in Paris, Hunt was asked by his friend Thomas P. Rossiter, then in Paris studying painting, to sketch out a plan for a house which his father-in-law had agreed to build in New York. Rossiter had married the daughter of Parmly, a successful dentist and real estate speculator; although father and daughter wished to be closer once again, Mrs. Rossiter wanted her own house, which Dr. Parmly then agreed to build. Rossiter devised a scheme for a house combining separate but connected studio, exhibition, and residential sections which Hunt then drew up and took to New York to show Dr. Parmly. On seeing the ambitious

*Architects' and Mechanics' Journal 3 (March 9 through 30, 1861), pp. 222–224, 231–34, 242–45, 252–55; 4 (April 6, 1861), pp. 4, 9.

[†] For the history of architectural education in the United States, see T. C. Bannister, The Architect at Mid-Century, vol 1 (New York, 1954); Arthur C. Weatherhead, The History of Collegiate Education in Architecture in the United States (Los Angeles, 1941); and Spiro Kostof, ed., The Architect (New York, 1977), pp. 209–37, 280–344.

[‡] See Selection 12, The Virginia Journals of Benjamin Henry Latrobe, 1795–1798, ed. Edward C. Carter II (New Haven, 1977), pp. xxxii–xxxiv.

[§] See Everard M. Upjohn, Richard Upjohn, Architect and Churchman (New York, 1939), p. 145.

plans, Parmly insisted the house was far too expensive and instructed Hunt to reduce the size. This Hunt did, preparing a full set of working drawings. However, he then went to Washington, D.C., to assist Thomas U. Walter in the additions to the Capitol, and he turned over supervision of construction to a colleague, architect Joseph C. Wells. Inexperienced with building practice in the United States, Hunt had failed to ask Parmly for a contract specifying his authorship of the design and outlining his duties during construction. Meanwhile Mrs. Rossiter had become ill and died in Paris, and when Mr. Rossiter then brought the children home to New York, Dr. Parmly decided he would occupy the house with his son-in-law and grandchildren, and instructed Hunt to add a fourth story to the house plans, leaving negotiation of the details to Hunt and Rossiter. Nonetheless, later, when Hunt sued for his fee, Parmly denied ever hiring Hunt "to make a line of architecture for me in my life, in any way, shape, or manner." The misunderstanding arose because Parmly had acted as his own general contractor, hiring John Thomson, a carpenter-builder, and others whom he had employed several times before, to carry out construction. Hunt, however, visited the building site frequently, providing Thomson with detailed drawings. When the house was completed in November 1857, Hunt presented Parmly with a bill for his fee, computed at 5 percent of $35,000, a figure considerably lower than what the building had actually cost. Parmly, unaccustomed to dealing with professional architects, utterly refused to pay, thus forcing Hunt to bring suit.

For his part, Hunt had make several strategic errors, not the least of which were mistakes he made in changing the design to accommodate the added fourth floor. He had let Parmly act as his own hiring agent and construction supervisor, and, most serious, he had not obtained a contract specifying what his charges were to be. The charge to the jury by Judge Hoffman (reprinted below) laid out the options open to them. Their decision, although in favor of Hunt (in that they based their decision on the higher figure of $46,000, much nearer the true cost of the house), was also somewhat against him since they concluded he had not been the legal construction superintendent—hence the fee awarded of only 2½ percent. Nevertheless, while only a partial victory for Hunt, the trial established a legal precedent for architects' fees. Its importance was immediately evident to the editors of the *Architects' and Mechanics' Journal*, who ran a near-verbatim court record in five weekly installments, March 9 through April 6, 1861; the most important portions of this are reprinted here.

IMPORTANT TRIAL: COMPENSATION OF ARCHITECTS

Hunt *versus* Parmly

BEFORE JUDGE HOFFMAN, IN THE SUPERIOR COURT, NEW YORK FEBRUARY 21, 22, 25, 26, 1861.

Mr. Sedwick opened the case to the jury on behalf of the plaintiff.

Richard M. Hunt, sworn executor, by counsel for plaintiff:

I am the plaintiff in this action; I am by profession an architect, I have been so between sixteen and seventeen years; I know the house in question; I designed and superintended its erection from the foundation to the coping

Figure 29. Richard Morris Hunt, E. K. Rossiter house, New York, N.Y., 1855–57, from *American Architect and Building News* 3 (June 22, 1878), no. 130.

stone—throughout—front and rear—everything that is usually done; I designed as architect everything that went into the house, masonry, wood
work, plaster work, and chose the marble mantels; I made one original
sketch in Paris, for a house to be built for Mr. Rossiter, 50 feet by 100; I
brought that to this country; I made several sketches, some four, five or half
a dozen to begin with, until one was approved of, and then made the plans,
elevations, and sections, and working drawings to the amount of perhaps,
two or three hundred; I have, I suppose, over two hundred drawings with
me in court. I rendered these services for Dr. Parmly, the defendant; the
usual compensation, five per cent, on the amount expended on the cost of
the work, is the value of my services; that is the usual compensation, not only
in this city, but in every country that I know of in Europe; I have received, I
think, $300 for my services, $200 I am sure. . . . The plan made by me in
Paris was drawn as near as I can recollect, in the month of July or August,
1855; I then worked on the Louvre and was so occupied that I could only
work on this drawing during evenings and such times as I could get; I exhibited that plan at the request of Mr. Rossiter to the defendant; Mr. Rossiter
who was then in Paris, desired me to show it to Dr. Parmly, who was to put
a building up for him, he not having the means to do it. I came to this
country in the month of August, 1855; I was taken sick immediately on my
return and was sick for a week. . . . I called on the defendant immediately on
my return in Sept., 1855, and showed him the plan which I had drawn for
Mr. Rossiter in Paris; the Dr. stated that it would be too expensive a house,
that he did not wish to put up so expensive a house for Mr. Rossiter. I told
him then that I thought the house would cost 40 or $45,000, but as I had
been absent in France for twelve years studying my profession, Mr. Rossiter
told me I could form no just idea of what the cost would be; the Dr. said that
he would have the plans estimated however, and I left them with him at his
office in Bond street, to be estimated; a day or two after, I called on him and
the estimates he had had made came to about 40 or $45,000, rough; the
result was, the Dr. objected to building anything so expensive and refused to
build that; he then handed me a plan of Mr. Rossiter, the same motive, idea
or general distribution in the house, but cut down to 37½ instead of 50 feet
front; by motive I mean theory, design or general distribution; this was materially the same plan which I had made for Mr. Rossiter, which had been
cut down—the staircase diminished and other things of that sort; the Dr.
gave me that plan to study up and make an architectural drawing of; I took
it to my office and made a plan of a house 37½ feet front, keeping as near as
I could the idea given in this plan of Mr. Rossiter, but being obliged to
change here and there, the walls, in order to get vistas in the house; the plans
of the different stories, the elevations front and rear and the sections I
showed to Dr. Parmly, which he approved of. I was working upon those
plans during January and February, and till about the sixth or seventh of
March, 1856, when I went to Washington; before leaving the city I told Dr.
Parmly I would remain here if necessary, but having a place offered me at
Washington I wished to see how public buildings were constructed in this
country; and I told him if I left town it would be with the condition that I
could return at any moment, but I would give the plans and superintendence
of the building to a first-rate architect here, in order that they might be

thoroughly carried out, and I named Joseph C. Wells, an architect who had been practicing in the city twelve or fourteen years. I went to the Dr.'s office with Mr. Wells, with the plans and elevations, and asked him in the presence of Mr. Wells, "Is this the house you wish to build? Shall I give these plans to Mr. Wells to carry out?" Dr. Parmly said yes, and I gave them in a roll to Mr. Wells in the Dr.'s office, and then went on to Washington; that was about the 6th of March, 1856; I returned from Washington sometime in May, 1856. . . . After my return from Washington in May, I used at first to go to the house in 38th street every day, sometimes twice a day, and for over a year I went there at least three times a week as the work progressed. I went to Duncan's stone-yard to guide them in cutting the stone; alterations were made in the original plan in two or three cases; the original plan was to have been three stories in front; about June or July, 1856, it was decided to enlarge the house and put in another suit of rooms in front, in order to accommodate Dr. Parmly's family, as well as Mr. Rossiter's, Mrs. Rossiter had then died and that led to the change; I made several sketches of an elevation to accompany this change introducing another story; two of those sketches I handed to Mr. Rossiter; he brought them back to me, and the alterations were carried out according to that plan precisely; with that exception, the whole plan was carried out as I had made it; some slight alterations may have been made; of course increasing the number of stories in front increased also the amount of stone-work, and an entire estimate was made for the additional story; and in the original design the bands on the columns were to have been of vermiculated work, for which carving was substituted by Mr. Duncan; he charged an extra bill for cutting the bands and I would not sign the bill. I told Dr. Parmly there had been a misunderstanding between Mr. Duncan and myself, and rather than have a bill of extras come into him I would deduct a reasonable amount for the carving on those columns from my commission, because I did not want to have extra bills handed in to a person who employed me; the Dr. acquiesced; this was Feb. 19, 1857; this house was peculiar in construction; there was a marked difference from any house I have seen in this city, both in its general plan and its elevation; the object to be attained was to have with one entrance door two entrances in fact—one to the public and the other to the private part, that is to say, after entering the vestibule there were two doors, one leading to the house and the other to a public exhibition-room, portrait studio and also to a large atelier, where Mr. Rossiter was to have his scholars; the whole house was distributed in such a way that in every story a person having a certain pass-key could get into the private house, but strangers could only go into the exhibition room, portrait studio and up to the top, without being able to see the private part of the house at all; it was a thing that necessitated a good deal of study and trouble; there is also another feature in the house which is peculiar, the center room is two stories high with a gallery around it on the second story; the front of the house is also different from any in the city, in its way. . . . I sent in my bill November 22d, 1857; I received an answer to my letter about the bill, written, I should think not in the handwriting of the defendant, but signed Eleazer Parmly, dated Dec. 5, 1857; I employed two draftsmen in this work—Wightman and Bradbury— both in my office; most of the work I did myself; Wightman was employed nearly three weeks. . . .

[Under cross-examination Hunt reiterated:] The building on 38th street was started during my absence, under the direction of Mr. Wells, who took my place; Dr. Parmly consulted him during my absence and I paid him for his services. . . . The house has not been occupied by Dr. Parmly; I do not know that any one occupies it now; I do not know that it is vacant; Rossiter, Stirling and Sherwood last occupied it to my knowledge, I think they left last summer or fall; I do not know when; I do not know what the house cost; the Dr. said he would employ his own men—that he had built a good deal in the city and would employ his own mechanics; I said I wished he would if he knew good ones; he said this when he requested me to make a plan for a 37½ foot house, before I introduced Wells to him—in the latter part of 1855.

Re-direct.

When I first went to him on my return from Europe to show him this design of the house, and during the conversation about making the 37½ feet front, he stated that I had been out of the country a long time, and probably did not know who the good mechanics in the city were; that he had built a good deal and would employ certain men; towards the end of the work I designated the painters. . . . Dr. Parmly made all the payments to the mechanics as far as I know; on one occasion I was present when he stated he had difficulty in making some payment already due. The doctor introduced me to some of the mechanics, also to the Rev. Dr. Spring—he went with me to his house and introduced me as the architect he was employing in putting up a house for his son-in-law, Rossiter, on Murray Hill, and said he thought I would be a good person to make designs for the brick church—which designs I made, but they were not sent in. There was nothing said about the cost of the reduced plan at the interview in January or February, 1856, when the plan for a 37½ feet front was talked of. I was boss or superintendent—whatever you may call it; I gave orders in every department; there was no other superintendent who gave orders in all the departments. . . .

Thomas P. Rossiter sworn, examined by counsel for plaintiff:

I am a painter by profession, and have been for many years; I was the son-in-law of Dr. Parmly; Mrs. Rossiter died on the 30th of April, 1856, in Paris. . . . I knew Mr. Hunt in Paris; I had known him some years before I spoke to him about the house in question, which was, I think, in March or April, 1855; Mr. Hunt took a motive or idea or drawing that I had, and worked upon it at my suggestion, which ultimated in a design which he brought to this country—a finished plan with details for a house 50 feet front and some 60 or 70 feet deep, for myself and Dr. Parmly. . . . I conversed with the Dr. in reference to Mr. Hunt's charges at the time of one of the payments made to Mr. Hunt; he asked me what his charges were, and I told him the usual rate of architects' fees were 5 per cent. on the cost of the building; he said he had never paid such a fee, and had never heard of it before; he objected to the price. . . .

George Bradbury sworn, examined by counsel for plaintiff:—

I have been called an architect; I have studied architecture professionally for seven years; I went into the employment of the plaintiff in the Spring of 1857 as draughtman, and left one week after the day the banks suspended in the fall; I was employed as assistant, on a salary; he was then employed upon a dwelling-house in Thirty-eight street, of very peculiar construction, adapted to several very unusual uses; it was Dr. Parmly's house; I visited it frequently; I was employed upon the drawings; made some of the original details, and some I copied from Mr. Hunt's drawings. . . . I saw all the drawings that were used in building; I saw Mr. Hunt make a great many of them, and being a pupil of his I knew his characteristics and I feel less hesitation in swearing to the drawings which I did not see him make than I should in swearing to his hand-writing; I think that any architect that is acquainted with him could identify his drawings. Mr. Hunt used frequently to receive notes from some quarter; I told the counsel for the plaintiff that I thought I never saw Dr. Parmly, but since I have seen him in Court I am sure I have seen him before, though I could not swear where; I was in the habit of taking notes to Dr. Parmly's house, but not from there that I remember; I went to the building in Thirty-eight street, the first part of the time I was with him every day; the latter part of time, two or three times a week; I used generally to spend the morning there, although sometimes when a friend came in I would take him up in the afternoon; I heard Mr. Hunt give orders to the workmen continually. . . .

I know of Mr. Hunt's going to the house two or three times a day and afterwards two or three times a week by the conversation of the workmen and contractors who came into the office and whom I saw there; and I met him there several times—three times I went with him, I think, and once I met him there accidentally. . . .

James S. Wightman, sworn, examined by counsel for plaintiff:—

I am an architect, practicing in this city, at 195 Broadway; I entered the office and employment of the plaintiff on the 23d of March, 1857, as I find by a memorandum which I kept at that time; I was there certainly two weeks—I believe three; I was engaged most of the time upon the drawings for Dr. Parmly's house—with the exception of three or six hours; I made several detailed drawings; drew the plan of the hall on a scale of 1½ inches to the foot; drew the section lines showing the projections according to a scale of my own dimensions; made detailed drawings of the architraves, moldings and bases; for trimmings of the doors showing the panels and moldings; also for the cornices in the hall; I went up there three times, I think—once with Mr. Hunt who showed me the building; the second time I went he told me he wanted me to take measurements for detailed drawings for the several rooms. . . . I think I saw the carpenter at the office; he brought the base moldings for the rooms previous to putting it in and inquired of Mr. Hunt how he liked it; Mr. Hunt told him to alter one of the faciae and make it narrower. . . .

Richard Upjohn, sworn, examined by counsel for plaintiff:—

I am an architect. I have been engaged in the profession nearly twenty-two years; I have known Mr. Hunt since 1836.

Q.—What is the customary charge of an architect for his services in making the drawings, plans, working drawings, and superintending the erection of a building in the city of New York?

A.—Five per cent. on the cost of the house; that has been the customary charge for ten or twelve years, if not longer; I think it is eleven years ago that I knew it was the charge carried out; I am acquainted with Mr. Hunt's professional capacity and skill; it is good; I have seen this house two or three times, and examined it with reference to Mr. Hunt's plans, it is constructed in conformity with them in every respect, to my knowledge; the house is peculiar in this: first, it is made expressly for an artist, and second, it is made expressly for a family that shall not interfere with the professional or business part of an artist's life; that is carried out fully and very well—very much to the purpose; so that the persons coming to see the artist on business sees nothing of the family, nor is seen by them unless they wish it; I have seen two plans drawn by Mr. Thomas; I do not think the building is constructed according to that plan in any respect. No plan can be departed from at any point or stage of work without great care on the part of the architect; I do not think that house could be built with the interior brick walls as they exist according to Mr. Thomas's plan; some men will take a set of plans and carry them out with much less trouble than others; some are not able to understand plans and do not know what they are about. I think 5 per cent. on the cost of this building would be a very reasonable and proper charge for the architect's work.

Cross-examined.

The first I knew of 5 per cent. being paid was to Mr. Diaper for alterations of the New York Hotel and additions thereto, in 1848 or '49; the charge before that, so far as I am concerned, was 5 per cent.; in one case previous to that time I made some plans for a town hall in Taunton, Mass., and I sent in my bill for 2½ per cent. on the plans so far as they were then executed, and they paid me 2½ per cent.—merely for plans, without any specifications, writings, or anything else—simply line drawings; I calculated the 2½ per cent. on the estimated cost of the building, which was $10,000; they made strong objections; they said it was an outrageous charge and they would not pay it; I carried it into court in Taunton, but they were still very averse to paying it; it was then taken to Boston and they paid it.

Q.—Did you prove that it was a customary charge?

[Objected to—objection overruled]

A.—As far as that goes I know nothing about it; I told a lawyer there to get the money and he got it; he got the testimony too; I told him that was his business and not mine; they sent for me but I was too busy to go, and I wrote to him, saying it was his business to attend to it—I put it into his hands and I expected him to do it—and he did it; the building was not erected; it was ordered by a committee, and by a change in politics another committee was appointed. In the case of the New York Hotel the plans were carried out; the evidence of architects at that time showed that 5 per cent. was the charge; it was resisted; I was an arbitrator with Judge Ruggles; I decided in favor of Diaper. At this present moment I do not recollect any other case where I knew that charge to be made; I am now building two large buildings, one a dwelling-house and the other a church, at 5 per cent.; I have contracted for the 5 per cent.; I have made some plans within three months, for which 10 per cent. was my charge, and not a word was said—I got it; I cannot specify the number of times that I have got 5 per cent. without contracting for it;

there was no contract in the case in which I got 10 per cent.; it is the custom of many architects in this city to make a bargain before they begin; they will do it for anything; if they can't get $10 they will take $5; they are men who are half way between builders and architects; they are not architects.

Q.—Do you recollect a single instance in which you have been allowed 5 per cent. commission without having stipulated for it in your contract?

A.—I cannot recollect any specific instance, but that is the general charge; I think it is not usual in the contracts with the architect to stipulate what he shall be paid; the design, working plans and superintendence were included in the work for which I received 10 per cent.; it was an altar screen for a church in the West . . . ; the services included in the charge of 5 per cent. are, the design, the drawings, the working drawings and general supervision; in my own work, if I go and see the building, perhaps once a month, or in six weeks, that is general supervision; there is a great difference between the office of superintendent and of supervisor; I supervise the plan, I do not superintend; the superintendent is the man who is on the ground most of the time; the 5 per cent. is for making the drawings and going once a month or six weeks to the house—and very well earned at that . . . ; where I merely draw plans and do not superintend I charge sometimes 3 and sometimes 3½ per cent.; never as low as 2½ per cent.; the altar screen for which I received 10 per cent. commission cost $200; I received $20; it was a decorated, Gothic screen. Specifications can be drawn by any man that is able to count; it is more the business of a clerk than an architect; when plans are simply referred to, a very elaborate specification accompanies them, for the reason that the plans are not half delineated or carried out; but where the plans are carried out and developed very fully the specifications are not of so much consequence. When I made the drawings for the townhall I charged 2½ per cent. for mere drawing; that was my charge twenty years ago; I think I got for [work?] on church more than 5 per cent.

Q.—You say you charge 3½, 5, and sometimes 10 per cent., and in no case 2½; now is it not your practice to charge just such a per-centage as in your own consideration the value of your services as architect is worth?

A.—Yes, I charge such a per-centage according to the value of the work.

Q.—Without regard to your services?

A.—Of course I include the value of my services; I include both; I think a young man, just established in business, would be entitled to charge the same rate, if he is capable of carrying on his work.

Q.—There is no guide among architects—they are all, you think, on a dead level? Is that your view?

A.—That is my view.

Q.—Would one who is half-way between a contractor and an architect be entitled to charge the same as an architect?

A.—That is his business—not mine; I have nothing to do with such persons. There is a case in which I charge[d] one per cent.; a gentleman requested me to give him some sketches for a library, and asked me what the charge would be; he said it was possible that he could not go on with the building but probably he should; the building he said would cost $60,000; he asked what I would charge for my sketches; I told him one per cent., he to return the sketches if he did not use them.

Q.—And return the sketches?

A.—Yes, sir; he to pay me $600 for it. You will understand—the idea.

Q.—One per cent. for the idea?

A.—You as a lawyer, when you give your opinion, do not charge for pen, ink and paper, but for your opinion.

[Speaking next on behalf of Hunt was architect Frederick A. Peterson, who had designed and built the Polytechnic Institute in Brooklyn and the Cooper Institute; he stipulated the same breakdown of charges for services described by Upjohn.]

Jacob Wrey Mould, sworn, examined by counsel for the plaintiff:—

I have followed the profession of architecture since 1838; I learned it in London; I have practiced it here since the fall of 1852; I have made designs, drawings and plans of public and private buildings in New York, and super-intended their erection—Church of All Souls, Parish School for Trinity Corporation, now erecting in 25th street, the banking house for Matthew Morgan, in William street, and sundry other buildings; also private buildings in this city, and in Lenox, Mass., and Meriden, Conn.; the customary charge for designing, drawing working plans and superintending the erection of a building in this city is 5 per cent. on the cost of the work; that has been the custom since I have been in the city. I knew the plaintiff well; I have known him four years; his standing as an architect is the very highest in my opinion.

Q.—Would 5 per cent. on the cost of the building be a reasonable and just compensation for the services of an architect?

A.—For what Mr. Hunt has done in this case it would not; I consider him entitled to ten, on account of the enormous amount of drawing he has done. I have been through the building in question.

Cross-examined:

There is no custom for charging ten per cent.; there is for 5; there is a difference in the charges of architects according to their grade and standing; I concur in the distinction and the rates of charge and compensation for the designing, drawing and superintending; one per cent. is for the mere idea or design, estimated on the approximate value of the building; a building is always designed with reference to an estimated value.

Q.—Suppose the calculation is for a building worth $10,000 and you make it $40,000, do you charge commission on $40,000?

A.—You would not design one for $40,000 if the owner tells you to design one for $10,000; I would make a specific arrangement with him unless he told me what the cost was to be; I would say, "Within what limits am I to design it?" The charge of 2½ per cent. includes a set of plans to an eighth or a quarter scale, and a certain amount of working drawings—enough to give an intelligent mechanic a clue whereby to finish the building; that is within the custom; there are very different grades of mechanics; if you are familiar with them you give them a certain amount; if not, you give them more; that would be 2½ or 3½ per cent., the 5 per cent. includes designing, making the working drawings, details in full, and general superintendence of the erection of the building; also the specifications and auditing the bills, if the work is done by contract; otherwise not—merely seeing that the charges are not exorbitant, without any check upon the exact amount of the builders; that is, if the work is done by day-work.

[Other New York architects who then testified on behalf of Hunt and who supported the 5 per cent standard commission were Samuel Curtis, Isaac G. Pearson, Detlef Lienau, and Henry Dudley.

The trial continues with the defendant's case, with testimony first by John Thomson the carpenter and builder who built the house in question; he had regularly worked for Dr. Parmly, building a number of houses during the previous twenty years. He indicated that Hunt had indeed prepared a great number of drawings for the house, although he often did not choose to follow them to the extent Hunt specified. Hunt, he said, was at the building site nearly every day and sometimes twice or three times a day. Subsequently the sub-contractors testified—William Lambier, mason; Francis Duncan, stone-cutter; Joseph Lynch, excavator—but their remarks were not conclusive as to who the primary designing architect was. Dr. Eleazer Parmly then was called to the stand.]

Eleazer Parmly, sworn, examined by counsel for defendant:—

I am the defendant in this suit; Mr. Rossiter was my son-in-law; I bought the lots for the house in question in Oct. 1855; I had previously conversed with Mr. Rossiter about a house for him to live in; the first conversation I had with him was in Paris; he had written to me before; he submitted a plan; I did not accept it; it was too expensive; it was drawn by himself; I saw it first in Paris; at the time I bought the lot, I had no plan for a building; Mr. Hunt had submitted a plan for my inspection within a few days after his arrival, which was I think in the month of August; he submitted the plan to me in Sept., for a house 50 feet by nearly 100, I think; I rejected it at once after I had had the estimates made upon it, on account of the magnitude both in size and price . . . ; I told Mr. Hunt it was entirely out of the question to build such a house as that; my son then wrote to Rossiter that it would not answer at all to build such a house . . . ; the idea of building was for a time entirely suspended, but inasmuch as the return of my daughter and her little children depended on having a house (for that was the main thing) built for them, I devised a plan of a house 37½ feet front and submitted it to Mr. Thomson, who threw it into architectural proportions for me; from that plan I made a small plan with dividers and rule in the same proportion, and enclosed it to Mr. Rossiter about the 1st of December, 1855; he received it . . . and after elaborating the plan sent me back that elaborated plan, with which I was exceedingly well pleased and wrote to him so; I immediately sent for Thomson to come and have the plans drawn by an architect . . . ; he took the tissue paper plan to Mr. Thomas, the architect, and in the course of two weeks he brought me a set of plans drawn accordingly; those are the plans produced here; I submitted them at once to builders who made estimates under cover, and when I received eleven estimates I opened them . . . ; I found Mr. Lambier's estimate was the lowest and gave him the job; I did not see Mr. Hunt to my recollection from the 10th of November till after the 1st of March; the specification and plans were put into the hands of all the builders.

Q.—Had you any thought or intention, or did you in any way, either by letter or otherwise, engage Mr. Hunt at that time to do any part of the work, or anything connected with the house.?

A.—No, sir; I have never engaged Mr. Hunt to make a line of architecture for me in my life, in any way, shape or manner, and never authorized any one else to do so . . . ; I gave him no authority to superintend, nor any reason to suppose he was engaged in any way in connection which [*sic*, with] that building . . . ; a day or two before he left for Washington, he came in with a letter from Rossiter and told me that Rossiter required him to make a facade of a peculiar character, but, said he, "I cannot make it; I am going to Washington; but I will employ my friend Wells to make it, and I will pay him for it;" I made no sort of objection to it, because I had been requested by Rossiter to employ Hunt to make a facade and was perfectly willing that he should make it; not a word was said on that occasion by Mr. Hunt on the subject of his employment by me as architect. . . .

The Judge's Charge.
Gentlemen of the Jury:—
This is a case peculiarly, I apprehend, for your own consideration. The wisdom of our law has left these questions of fact, and the weighing of the evidence as to the facts entirely and exclusively to the jury; and I have no doubt, from the patient attention you have given during the progress of the trial to the great mass of testimony, that the evidence will be duly weighed by you, and that your conclusion will be dictated by your sound appreciation of the credibility of the witnesses and the force of the statements they have given; I shall, therefore, only attempt to assist you by giving to you a few leading points which have struck my mind, and with regard to which it will, perhaps, be well to direct your examination as you proceed in canvassing the testimony.

This case appears to me to divide itself into three branches:—
1.—Was there a contract between the plaintiff and the defendant by which the plaintiff was employed in manner and to the extent alleged, and for the compensation claimed?
2.—If that is not proven, or still stronger, if it is disproven, was there any other contract between the parties for the rendition of services by the plaintiff in his capacity of architect in and about this building in question; and if so, what was the extent of such service?
3.—What is the fair compensation to be awarded to the plaintiff in case you find that there was a contract entered into to the extent claimed, or that there was some contract to a less extent, or to any extent?

The plaintiff sets forth in his complaint that there was a contract by which he was employed to design for the defendant the house in question, and to superintend the building thereof, and that his compensation was to be at the usual rate of commission; and he puts the value of his services at that rate at $1,750, from which he deducts for payments already made, $300, leaving a balance of $1,450. The first question therefore for you to consider is, has the plaintiff proven that allegation? The defendant explicitly denies it.

And here, let me explain to you what I understand to be the scope and extent of the plaintiff's assertion of his employment. I cannot do it better, it appears to me, than by quoting the statements of the witness Pearson, an architect of very large experience. Corroborated as his testimony is by so many other witnesses, I feel myself warranted in submitting it to you as a clear and comprehensive statement of the duties of an architect and the customary charges of compensation in this city.

1.—He says that, generally speaking, for a new sketch or plan of an intended building, the compensation is usually one per cent. upon the estimated cost of the edifice, unless a contract is made otherwise.

2.—If that plan is accompanied with all the details which would enable the owner to have the work done by putting those detailed plans and specifications into the hands of proper workmen or builders, then the compensation is 2½ per cent.

3.—If, in addition to such services, there is an employment of the architect for the purpose of superintending the conduct of the work, examining into the contracts or preparing them, the discharging of the bills or seeing to the payments, relieving the owner from any care and trouble about the business, then the customary commission is 5 per cent.

I understand the plaintiff's claim to be of the latter character—that he was not only employed to prepare the plans and specifications, but that he superintended the entire conduct of the work.

The first question then is, has he made out that contract? Upon this point I shall call your attention to the evidence which appears to bear upon it. I am now speaking in reference to an express contract between the parties. You have the plaintiff's positive and explicit statement of an engagement made with the defendant to that extent; you have that contradicted in equally explicit and positive terms by the defendant. It is unfortunate that such a contradiction exists between persons apparently entirely and equally entitled to credit. It is for you to say that you believe the one or the other, or to see if there is not some escape for the unhappy result of finding one or the other of them utterly wrong in his statement of the alleged contract. If you can find any mode of reconciling these opposite statements, so much the better; and you will be happy, I am sure, to do so. And for that purpose, let me call your attention to the history of the transaction.

As I gather from the testimony, without going back to the origin of the idea of building a house for the use of the defendant's son-in-law, it appears that sometime in the year 1855, a scheme or plan of a house was started between Mr. Rossiter and Mr. Hunt, the plaintiff, in Paris, attended by a sketch of a plan for a very extensive house, 50 feet by nearly 100. That plan, more or less matured, was brought by Mr. Hunt from Paris to this country. Letters, in the meantime, had passed between Dr. Parmly and Mr. Rossiter, connected with the subject; among the rest, one which has just been read to you, in which the defendant writes that he cannot make up his mind what to do definitely until he sees Mr. Hunt, whose arrival he anxiously waits for. Mr. Hunt, therefore, at this early period, was connected in Dr. Parmly's mind with this plan of a house. Mr. Hunt arrives with these plans in the fall of 1855; he sees Dr. Parmly speedily after his arrival—sometime in September, 1855; he submits the plans to Dr. Parmly for consideration; after obtaining some estimates from certain persons whom Dr. Parmly was in the habit of employing, they were rejected as entirely too costly. And there, so far as the erection of that building and the employment of Mr. Hunt for it on that basis or plan, the scheme was dropped.

There is then some further negotiation. A sketch is made or suggested and procured, as I understand, first by Dr. Parmly himself, roughly drawn, of a house 37½ feet front, preserving as nearly as possible the main features upon which this house was subsequently built. That sketch was sent out to Mr. Rossiter in Paris, and returned with his elaboration upon it to a greater or less extent. When Dr. Parmly receives it, he writes that it meets his entire approbation. That letter was written some time in January, 1856.

Down to this time you will probably conclude that there was no evidence of an express contract between the parties, because there had been no avowed decision on the part of Dr. Parmly to build a house at all.

This plan was received January, 1856, and speedily thereafter a conversation took place between the plaintiff and defendant, and Mr. Hunt states that other conversations took place. These conversations led to nothing definite till the end of February or beginning of March, 1856. It is to the transaction about that time that I want to call your particular attention. If there was an express contract—and I wish you to mark that I am looking now solely to the point of an express contract—it took place on or about that time. It is at that interview, or those interviews, towards the end of February or beginning of March, that an express contract is insisted upon by the plaintiff to have been proven, to the extent claimed. Upon that point you have nothing but the positive statement of the plaintiff before adverted to, and the no less positive denial of the defendant, together with the testimony of Mr. Wells, deceased. The testimony of Mr. Wells may be of some moment on this branch of the case. Shortly before the departure of Mr. Hunt for Washington—and the witnesses seem to fix that towards the end of February or beginning of March—Mr. Wells says he went with Mr. Hunt and called on Dr. Parmly; that the purport of that meeting was that they received directions from the defendant; that the defendant consented to his proceeding during Mr. Hunt's absence; that he went for the express purpose of being introduced to the defendant, and after that interview Mr. Hunt handed one of the plans over to the defendant.

That, together with the testimony of the plaintiff and defendant, is all the direct testimony with regard to an express contract entered into at that time.

Another point to which I call your attention is this: It is not necessary in order to sustain the plaintiff's claim that you should be satisfied that there was an express agreement and contract between these parties, in writing or words, of the nature and the extent that the plaintiff insists. An agreement may be deduced from facts and circumstances which may speak as loudly and as clearly as if a written instrument, disclosing its terms, had been produced; or as if many witnesses had sworn to it in clear and decided language. I therefore instruct you that you have a right to deduce the existence of this contract to the extent claimed, from the acts of the defendant himself, and further from his acquiescence and silence in regard to Mr. Hunt's proceeding, for a reasonable length of time, with the work; provided you are satisfied that the defendant was aware of the plaintiff's claiming to be in the position of architect and superintendent on the defendant's behalf, and was doing the work for which he claims compensation. If, in this mass of testimony, you find that the defendant, knowing of Mr. Hunt's claim to be the architect and superintendent in that sense and to that extent, for a reasonable length of time, was silent or acquiesced in it, and then if you find that the plaintiff did render all the services or the bulk of the services which, according to Mr. Pearson's testimony, an architect is accustomed to render, who is employed as architect and superintendent also, then there will be ground for your finding a verdict for the plaintiff.

But supposing that you are not satisfied that there was any express contract to the extent claimed, then there is another question for your consideration, to wit, whether there was not an employment by the defendant to a more limited extent, deduced from his acquiescence and knowledge of what the plaintiff was doing, and what that extent was.

Now, I am not sure—I speak with great hesitation—but I suggest to you whether you may not trace throughout this whole maze of evidence, through all its obscurity, ambiguity, and, in some respects, of its contradictions, something of this description: that the acts of the defendant in February or March, 1856, and subsequent thereto, are all reconcilable, or better reconcilable with this view of the case than with any other, namely, that there was an understanding that the plaintiff should go on to the extent of giving all the details of the plans for a 37½ feet house, such as would come under the head of that portion of an architect's work described by Mr. Pearson and others, for which the usual compensation is 2½ per cent. I say you may possibly be able to reach that conclusion as the safest one to be drawn from all this mass of testimony. I submit it entirely for your consideration. You may find it more reconcilable with that which is indisputable and which does not admit of contradiction in the case. You may find it reconcilable with a great deal of testimony which has not been contradicted, namely, for instance, that Dr. Parmly did employ on his own account men whom he had been previously in the habit of employing in erecting other building (and Mr. Hunt says that he stated to him—Hunt—that he knew a number of mechanics and builders in the city that he had employed); and that he made verbal contracts with the carpenter, mason, stone-cutter, and others, for the building of this house. It is clear that the original agreement or contract with Lambier and Thomson were made directly by Dr. Parmly.

And you may find this view reconcilable with the testimony of Mr. Bradbury, which does not seem to admit of a doubt, corroborated as it is with other testimony, that Mr. Hunt did render most important and most extensive services in and about the building. The enormous mass of plans spread before you shows you the great extent of the labor that the plaintiff performed, and those plans are explained by those who understand the subject far better than I do. The plaintiff has sworn that he was at the house at the beginning of his employment, almost every day, and subsequently that he was there frequently in the course of a week. It is also clear that he would be there naturally from the ambition of seeing his own artistic work carried out fully, as well as his desire to do justice to his friend Rossiter, with whom he had formed an intimate acquaintance. I say this view of the case may present itself to your mind as a mode of reconciling the great mass of ambiguous and conflicting testimony, better than any other that may occur to you. Then the question for your consideration will be, in those instances as well as in the first instance, the compensation to be allowed, which is the third branch of the case to which I will now call your attention.

In case you find that there was an express contract between the parties to the extent claimed by the plaintiff; or in case you find that there was such a knowledge, recognition and acquiescence (on the part of the defendant) of the plaintiff's work as is tantamount to an express contract; then in either case, the rule of damages can hardly be less than five per cent., which such an abundance of witnesses have proved to be the usual rate when there is no specified contract. That five per cent. will be estimated upon one of two sums—either the absolute cost of the building, as computed by Dr. Parmly, namely, $56,000 (adding everything that he has done), or about $46,000; with this qualification, however, that in no event can you go beyond the amount demanded in the complaint, which is $1,750, less $300 received, or $1,450. The cost of the building undoubtedly is more then $46,000, but you are limited on that basis to $1,450.

Should you come to the conclusion, however, that there was a contract to the limited extent to which I have adverted—that is to say, furnishing the plans, elevations, and all the details for carrying on the work, which services, in point of fact, do appear to have been rendered—then the amount of compensation will be graduated upon one of two sums, to wit: either the amount of $25,000, the sum which the defendant originally contemplated and apprised Mr. Rossiter that he intended the building should cost, and no more; or with the additional cost, which I think, was fixed at $7,000 or $8,000, in consequence of the change of plan assented to by the defendant—either $25,000, or, with the addition of $7,000 or $8,000, about $33,000. Or perhaps you may extend that amount to the actual cost of the building. Your estimate would, therefore, be on the basis I have mentioned—the rate of compensation sworn to by Mr. Pearson, and corroborated by the other witnesses—2½ per cent. on one of those sums. According to my recollection there is evidence of the assent of the defendant to the additional cost of $7,000 or $8,000. If, therefore, you come to the conclusion that a contract existed or was recognized to the limited extent I have mentioned, you will graduate the compensation on the basis of 2½ per cent. on $25,000, or $32,000 or thereabouts; or, perchance—and I leave that to your consideration—upon the actual cost of the building.

[Counsel for defendant excepted to the refusal of the court to charge the points handed up in writing.]

VERDICT

Two-and-one-half per cent. on $46,000 = ($1,150) deducting therefrom $450, with interest from November 22, 1857.

31   C. F. McKim (?), on Colonial Architecture* *1874*

For more than half a century before the nation's Centennial celebration, the architecture of the seventeenth and eighteenth centuries was regarded as ill-designed and wholly unsuitable for modern use. Hundreds of older buildings were pulled down to make way for the new. Yet during the decade before 1876 an appreciation of colonial architecture began to grow, becoming fervent as the centenary of independence was celebrated.† The young architect Charles Follen McKim, having only recently left H. H. Richardson's office, was among the first to direct his colleagues' attention to preserving some visual record of the nation's fast disappearing architectural tradition. Given the responsibility of editing the newly established *New-York Sketch Book of Architecture* by Richardson in 1874, McKim placed this invitation for drawings in the premier issue.

New York, Dec. 22, 1873

 The New-York Sketch Book of Architecture has been projected in the hope that it may be made useful and interesting not only to Architects, by supplying them with the means of keeping themselves and each other informed in regard to what is going on in their special world, but to the public, by giving them an opportunity of comparing the work of different members of the profession, by reproductions not only of drawings, but so far as possible of executed works.

 That its usefulness and interest may be more widely diffused, the Editors hope to receive drawings from all parts of the country; with the only restriction, that, in case more material shall come in than can be used, the gentlemen who act as Editors will exercise their judgement in choosing for publication what seems to them most original in design, or best adapted to the process of reproduction.

 Any of our brother professionals who [would] like to take advantage of this invitation should accompany their drawings with a description, sufficient for explanation only, but as short as may be.

 The Editors also hope to be able to do a little toward the much-needed task of preserving some record of the early architecture of our country, now fast disappearing. For this purpose they would most gratefully welcome any sketches, however slight, of the beautiful, quaint, and picturesque features which belong to so many buildings, now almost disregarded, or our Colonial and Revolutionary period.

---

* *New-York Sketch Book of Architecture* 1 (January 1874), p. v. McKim's editorial authority is attested by Montgomery Schuyler, then on the staff, in "Charles Follen McKim," *Architectural Record* 26 (November 1909), pp. 381–82.

 † At first there was little distinction between late Gothic seventeenth-century vernacular and eighteenth-century Palladian classicism. See Vincent Scully, *The Shingle Style* (New Haven, 1955), pp. 19–33; and William Rhoads, *The Colonial Revival*, 2 vols. (New York, 1977).

All drawings or sketches for publication, and communications relating to the editorial conduct of the "New-York Sketch Book," must be addressed to Mr. H. H. Richardson, 57 Broadway, New York. Subscriptions, or letters relating to advertisements or money affairs, must be sent to Messrs. James R. Osgood & Co., Boston, or E. P. Dutton & Co., New York.

[The young McKim made clear his admiration of Colonial architecture in this caption for a view of the rear of the Bishop Berkeley house, Middletown, Rhode Island, which appeared in the *Sketch Book* at the end of 1874—the first photograph published in an American architectural journal (Figure 30).]‡

We offer this time one of a number of old Newport houses, recently photographed by private subscription.

The collection referred to contains not only early public building, but a number of the better class of dwelling-houses; amongst which may be mentioned the "Bull Fortification" (1639), the Overing house (known as "Prescott's headquarters"), the Berkeley house, the Vernon house, Coe, Hunter, Wanton, and other houses, whose names and records form a part of the distinction of Newport.

Besides the above, many buildings of lesser note, but equally deserving of photography, were pried out, and negatives of them made. Along Broad Street, and in the neighborhood known as the "Point," the old gables and chimneys of fishermen's houses offer an abundance of material not heretofore taken advantage of by either the local photographers or outsiders, so far as we have been able to learn.

The picturesque surroundings and architectural merit of many of these old buildings are not to be disputed; nor are they the less deserving of recognition because some people call them "ugly," and others build shingle-palaces alongside. If they *must* be ugly, it is of an ugliness not belonging to our time; and, if they *are* ugly, at least they are never aggressively so, like too many of their more modern neighbors. To our mind there is greater charm to be found about the front-door step of one of these old houses, more homeliness and promise of comfort within, even more interest about its wrought scraper, than in most of the ambitious dwellings of the present day. They are always reasonable, simple in outline, and frequently show great beauty of detail. Nor is it a small merit that many of them have stood up for a hundred and fifty years, while a few of the survivors can count over two hundred.

Just now, while streets are widening, and committees have full swing, is the time to make amends.

We submit, that if it is worth while to write the genealogies of generations of men, the roofs that have faithfully sheltered them come in for a greater tribute of respect than mere occasional magazine or newspaper articles can furnish, since these must be necessarily imperfect and incomplete.

Hitherto they have been brought before the public either as curious objects, or as haunted houses, or as the scene of some story or other, mentioned as shadows, and admired for their ivy.

Now let somebody write about them as *Architecture*. The architects are their true historians.

‡ *New-York Sketch Book of Architecture* 1 (December 1874), pl. 45.

Figure 30. "Old House at Newport, R.I.," Bishop Berkeley house, Middletown, 1728. Plate 45 from *New York Sketch Book of Architecture* 1 (December 1874).

The present plate is interesting mainly from a historical point of view. The house was built by Bishop Berkeley in 1729, and with a large estate sold for the benefit of Yale College on his return to England. The Bishop lived here while in America, and used frequently to preach before large crowds here assembled from the town three miles distant. The house stands in the very midst of an ancient apple-orchard. He named it "White-Hall."

32   R. S. Peabody, Georgian Houses
of New England*   *1877–78*

In the summer of 1877, after the Centennial, Charles McKim, with William Mead, William Bigelow, and Stanford White, made a sketching tour of the Massachusetts and New Hampshire coast in search of colonial buildings. A similar excursion was made simultaneously by Robert Swain Peabody, an architect of Boston, the result of which was not only sketches but this two-part article that appeared during the winter of 1877–78. Peabody, like so many others, had been struck by the way vernacular Elizabethan and Jacobean domestic architecture had been drawn upon by Thomas Harris for the British pavilions at the Centennial. As Peabody suggested in this article, Americans had their own tradition which could be studied with equal success. Robert Swain Peabody (1845–1917) was educated at Harvard, worked briefly in the office of Gridley J. F. Bryant in Boston, studied at the École des Beaux-Arts in Paris, from 1867–70, and then established a practice in Boston with John Goddard Stearns, Jr. His firm remained one of the most important in that city until 1917.[†] Following Peabody's article, the *American Architect* began running views and short entries on selected eighteenth-century buildings. In particular, the sketches of the Fairbanks house, Dedham, Massachusetts, 1633, published in volume 10 (November 26, 1881), included a floor plan with scale, the first such measured plan to be reproduced (Figure 32).

The *American Architect and Building News*, the first of the successful long-running architectural periodicals, published four or more views of contemporary work in each weekly issue (interspersed with a few historical examples such as the Fairbanks house view and plan) with articles on various topics including metal framing, new developments in plumbing, building legislation, as well as papers and addresses by prominent architects. Examples might include the essays by Peter Bonnet Wight, published in 1876 through 1878, on concrete, brick, and their use in fireproof construction, and the serialization of E. E. Viollet-le-Duc's *Habitations of Man in All Ages*, during 1876.[‡]

PART I

The English Queen Anne designers have a way of justifying their many vagaries as follows. They say: In the seventeenth century men had rather ceased to think of style. Classical detail as introduced in Renaissance days had become completely naturalized, and gradually it had ceased to be used

* "Georgian" (pseudonym for R. S. Peabody), "The Georgian Houses of New England," *American Architect and Building News* 2 (October 20, 1877), pp. 338–39; 3 (February 16, 1878), pp. 54–55.

† See Wheaton A. Holden, "The Peabody Touch: Peabody & Stearns of Boston, 1870–1917," *Journal, Society of Architectural Historians* 32 (May 1973), 114–31.

‡ See Sarah Bradford Landau, *P. B. Wight, Architect, Contractor, and Critic, 1838–1925* (Chicago, 1981); and H.-R. Hitchcock, "Ruskin and American Architecture . . . ," in *Concerning Architecture*, John Summerson, ed. (London, 1968), pp. 188–96.

Figure 31. "The Fairbanks House, Dedham, Mass.," gelatine print from *American Architect and Building News* 10 (November 26, 1881), no. 309.

in a servile way, or with great regard for precedent; but it simply made things seem attractive without much thought for purity of style, or style at all. Following this came the successive revivals,—of Palladian art, then of Grecian work, then of all the phases of Gothic,—all these lifeless imitations of the antique. From this study of archaeology the Queen Anne men profess to rebell, and to turn to the point where our art was before all this direct imitation of obsolete forms began. They find more of the spirit of independence and carelessness for precedent which they seek for in the work of the seventeenth century than elsewhere; so they study and work on that basis, but are ready to combine any thing with it which is attractive. They say they have red brick and white mortar for their walls, tiles for their roofs, and white sash frames for their windows; and of these the house shall be made.

All this sounds like good reasoning, although in practice the antiquarian spirit makes the movement seem much like other revivals. In fact, we really know that reasoning is not at the bottom of it at all, but that Mr. Norman Shaw and others like him admired and studied and sketched all the quaint old work they could find, and that this work enlivened by their talent has set a quietly imitated example to other designers. If we follow their lead without any native Jacobean or Queen Anne models of importance to inspire

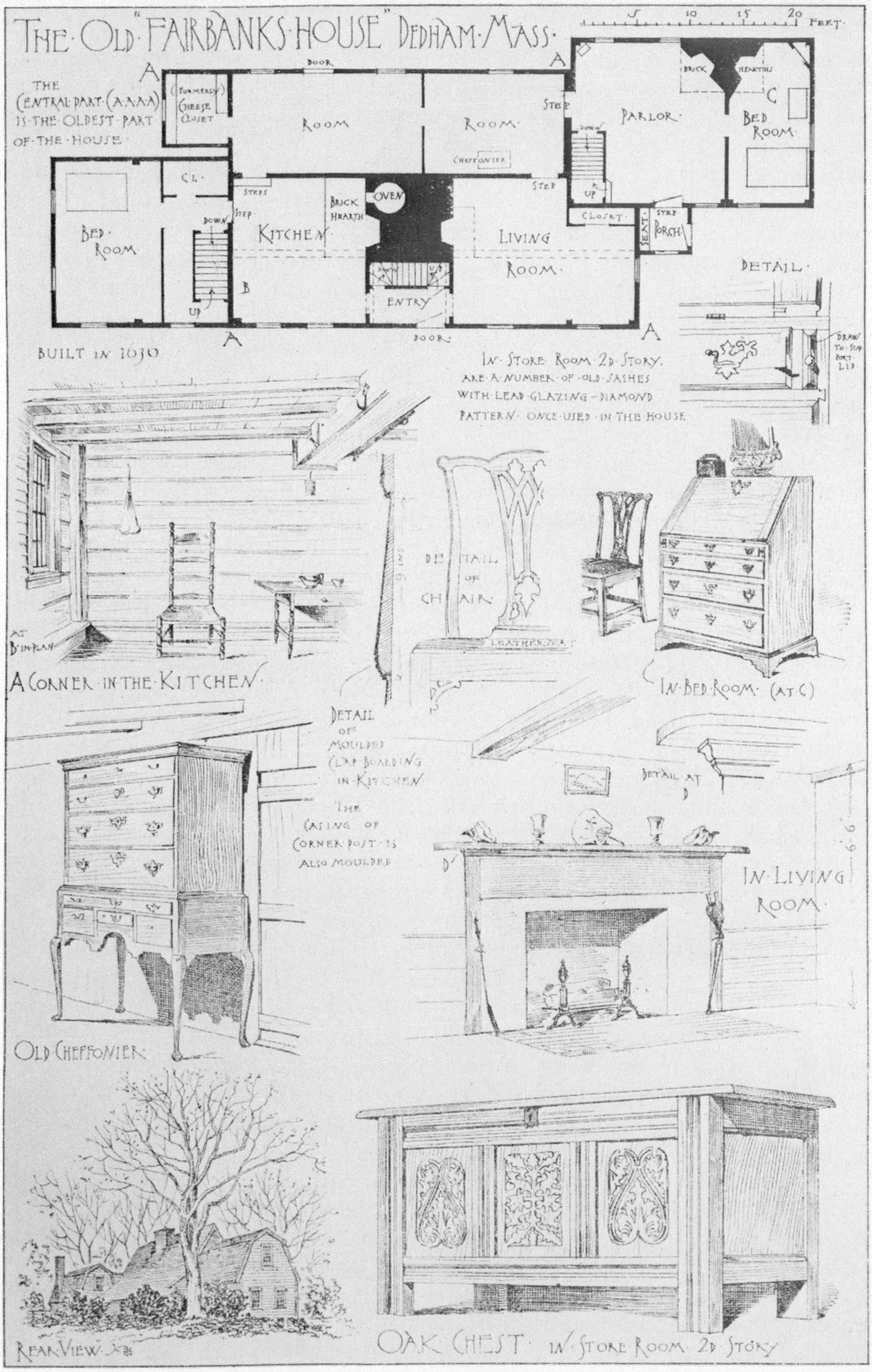
THE OLD "FAIRBANKS HOUSE" DEDHAM MASS.
THE CENTRAL PART (A A A A) IS THE OLDEST PART OF THE HOUSE
BUILT IN 1636
ROOM
ROOM
PARLOR
BED ROOM
BED ROOM
KITCHEN
LIVING ROOM
ENTRY
OVEN
PORCH
CLOSET
IN STORE ROOM 2D STORY ARE A NUMBER OF OLD SASHES WITH LEAD GLAZING - DIAMOND PATTERN ONCE USED IN THE HOUSE
DETAIL
A CORNER IN THE KITCHEN
DETAIL OF CHAIR
IN BED ROOM (AT C)
DETAIL OF MOULDED CLAP BOARDING IN KITCHEN
THE CASING OF CORNER POST IS ALSO MOULDED
IN LIVING ROOM
OLD CHEFFONIER
REAR VIEW
OAK CHEST IN STORE ROOM 2D STORY

Figure 32. **"Details of the Fairbanks House, Dedham, Mass.," from *American Architect and Building News* 10 (November 26, 1881), no. 309.**

us, we shall but be adding one more fashion to our already rather long list. A neo-Jacobean table can join the Eastlake chairs, the American Rococo mantel, and the Puginesque sideboard in our dining-rooms; but there is nothing in this but an additional fashion. Now, however, that this wave is felt along our shores, can it not be directed into more fitting channels here even than it has worn for itself in England? We too have had our revivals; and if we go behind them we find in the Georgian days men working without thought of style, simply, delicately, beautifully. Many a choice wooden cornice, many a stiff mantel in our farmhouses attest this. Plancia, fascia, and soffit still are Yankee words in spite of our mediaeval period. With our Centennial year have we not discovered that we too have a past worthy of study?—a study, too, which we can subsequently explain and defend by all the ingenious Queen Anne arguments, strengthened by the fact that our colonial work is our only native source of antiquarian study and inspiration.

Put our heirlooms—any old material we have—into a Gothic room, it is more or less out of keeping. In fact, with these successive fashions, we have to build not new houses alone, but all their furnishings to match. Our heirlooms are tall clocks, Copley or Stuart portraits, convex mirrors, ancient chests and drawers, bits of carving perhaps by Gibbons, Paul Revere tankards or andirons, brass candlesticks, and chairs that came over in the Mayflower. We think with interest of the parish glebes of Cambridge and Portsmouth, of the old Tories' Row in Cambridge; while many are the old wainscoted rooms for which we have an affectionate remembrance; the staircases with boxed steps with a rich scroll under each box, and the varied balusters carved into a twist by hand; the great brick chimney-corners with Dutch tile borders, and crane, pot-hooks and trammels, and hanging kettles, and the yawning flues resting on oak mantel bars and opening a clear road to the stars above. With all this in the old houses, we find a classical detail universally used, the common language of every carpenter, and treated freely with regard only to comfort, cosiness, or stateliness, and with no superstitious reverence for Palladio or Scamozzi, those bugbears of later years. In studying this colonial work, we find all the delicacy, grace, and picturesqueness, that any model can suggest to us; and combined with it a familiar aspect and a fitness to harmonize with all those heirlooms and old possessions, that might be put to shame by other fashions. In short, we like it all; and if we want to excuse it we can with the Queen Anne men say we are returning for models to the time when men worked naturally and without regard to style, and that on that stock we propose to graft whatever else now attracts us.

I have said that our sources and the period that interests us, varied from that which the Queen Anne men affect. True, we have our Charles River, our Cape Ann, our Queen Anne's Corner, and we have many houses of early date. The Craddock mansion was built in the days of Charles the First; the Fairbanks house in Dedham, and the Curtis in Jamaica Plain, during the Commonwealth; and these are still occupied by the families of their builders. The Province House is of the time of Charles II.; the Sudbury Inn of James II.; the Batchelder House in Cambridge dates from William and Mary; the old Corner Bookstore from Queen Anne; while the President's House and Massachusetts Hall at Cambridge, and the Adams (once Vassal) house at Quincy, all date from the reign of George the First. These are but represen-tative houses, yet the richest and finest models we have date from between 1727 and 1760, when George II. reigned: Pepperell House in Ki-tery, 1730; Hancock House, 1737; Royall House, Medford, 1738; Holden Chapel, Cambridge, 1745; Wells mansion, Cambridge, 1745; Wentworth House, Little Harbor, 1750; Longfellow (Vassal) House, 1759; Ladd House, Portsmouth, 1760.

If we study these colonial buildings, we see nearly all the early work in this neighborhood roofed with steep-pitched gable roofs. Rare instances oc-cur like the stone Craddock House at Medford, when the gambrel roof ap-pears earlier; but from 1686, the date of the Sudbury Inn, to 1737, the date of the Hancock House, the gambrel roof is common. Later it became fre-quent to pitch the roof in from all sides to a ridge or to a second pitch surrounded by a balustrade, and it is under such roofs that the richest interi-ors of our neighborhood still are found; such as the Longfellow and Wells and Riedesel houses in Cambridge, the Ladd and Langdon at Portsmouth, the Winslow at Plymouth, the Lee at Marblehead (?)

Thus we see that the gambrel roof is typical of but one period of colo-nial work. Where it comes from, I cannot imagine. I recall no English type of the sort, and I should be glad if somebody can explain it. It is said that the bricks of Peter Sergeant's house, afterwards the Province House, were brought from Holland; and is it at about that date that the gambrel roof became prevalent. Is it a reminiscence of Holland? It could hardly be a fashion adopted from New York.

The later and richer mansions were large and square, and with so little detail outside, that one built now would, without the glamour of age, seem unpleasantly angular and box-like. But this is by no means a characteristic of all colonial work. The old Fairbanks house at Dedham, partly early with high-pitched roof and partly later with gambrel roof, forms a most pictur-esque pile; and so does the scattered house at Little Harbor, with gables at different heights, and floors at different levels; while the council-chamber wing runs off at an uncalled-for angle with the main building, that would delight Mr. Norman Shaw. Again, among the gambrel roofs, the great lum-bering Sudbury Inn forms a most hospitable group, with its wide-spread barns and outhouses; while the Goodman cottage at Lenox smiles through its shrubbery, and winks its many-eyed sashes at the wayfarer. This pictur-esqueness I have endeavored to illustrate in the sketches with this paper, and we see that a picturesque group of any sort is thus not incongruous with our purpose; while of the interiors there is no need of words. We all know and like them; and it is because we too want to live amid wainscoting, nestle in elliptical arched nooks, warm ourselves beneath the high mantels at blazing wood-fires, and go to bed over boxed stairs with ramped rails and twisted balusters, and see our old chairs and pictures thus appropriately envi-roned,—it is because we like and want all this, that we seek for an excuse to do it all again. But isn't our liking reason enough?

In all this I have dwelt on the colonial mansions, not because we have no public buildings. The Old North Church, the Old State House, the New-port State House, the "Old Ship Meeting-House" at Hingham,—all are ex-cellent buildings. But except in peculiar spots, there is less to suggest such

PALLISER'S
NEW COTTAGE HOMES

AND

DETAILS,

CONTAINING

Nearly Two Hundred & Fifty New & Original Designs in all the Modern Popular Styles,

SHOWING

Plans, Elevations, Perspective Views and Details of low-priced, medium and first-class

Cottages, Villas, Farm Houses, Town and Country Places, Houses for the Seashore, the South, and for Summer and Winter Resorts, etc., etc.

CITY BRICK BLOCK HOUSES,

Farm Barn, Stables and Carriage Houses.

AND

1500 DETAIL DRAWINGS,

Descriptive and Instructive Letter Press, also Specifications and Form of Contract.

Elevations and Plans to Scale of 1-16 inch to the Foot.

Details to Scale of 3-8 inch to the Foot.

Making in all a most practical book for Architects, Builders, Carpenters, and all who are interested in the subject of Building, and those who contemplate building, or the improvement of Wood, Stone or Brick Buildings.

NEW YORK:

PALLISER, PALLISER & CO.,

24 East Forty-Second Street.

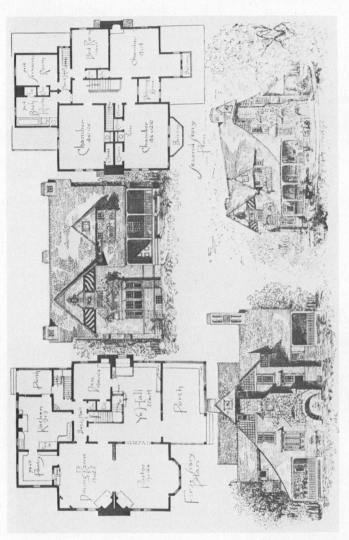

Figure 33. "Design 122, Plate 39," from *Palliser's New Cottage Homes*, New York, 1887, illustrating the popularization of "Colonial" architecture. Accompanying the design was this caption: "Design 122 brings us very forcibly back to the days of our great grandfathers and at once puts us in mind of the times of the revolution. The plan is very conveniently arranged and is a very desirable layout, and would provide ample room for a large family. The style of architecture here illustrated is termed by many, 'Old Colonial', with the large stone chimneys built on the exterior walls, up which the ivy vine could be trained to good advantage; and the other quaint features here shown we think the aesthetically inclined will in this design find something worth studying. Such a house as this will harmonize finely with nature and properly placed on a suitable site with rocks, trees, and perhaps a running brook to blend in with it, and about two or three acres of nice ground of an uneven nature, nicely undulating, is a home fit for a prince to live in, and the cost is $5,000."

work in public buildings than there is in the home. A schoolhouse soon to be built in Deerfield, near the site of the Indian massacre, not unfitly recalls colonial architecture; but for a Western State House there would seem to be no more reason for this spirit than for a Gothic of Italian one. This lays bare at once the thinness of argument in the matter; and we come back to that always satisfying reason, that in one case it is eminently appropriate, because we like it; and in the other, eminently inappropriate, because we don't like it. For once, at least, let us reason like our clients.

But this, after all, is not a very bad reason, if, as I think, we are past the battle of styles, and the fancies of the artist are become of proportionally greater importance. As soon as we begin to design detail, we must, as it were, talk some intelligible language, or in a *patois* formed from several. Many influences may guide us to different sources of inspiration. I think we, most of us, admit the good in most of these sources, and feel that as any designing worthy the name will hereafter be done by men who are more artists than their predecessors, so what we shall care for in the design is not its historical accuracy, but the artist's clever art in harmonizing whatever his fancy leads him to, with itself and its surroundings. From this point of view, whatever the attractions of other sources, from no field can suggestions be drawn by an artist more charming and more fitted to our usages, than from the Georgian mansions of New England.

33   M. G. Van Rensselaer, American Country Dwellings*   *1886*

The decade of the 1880s witnessed the emergence of professional art and architectural criticism in the United States; chief among the architectural critics were architect Henry Van Brunt, former architect Russell Sturgis, and Mariana Griswold Van Rensselaer (1851–1934).† Mariana Griswold, born in New York, was educated by tutors at home and traveled in Europe where she met her husband, American mining engineer Schuyler Van Rensselaer.‡ Four years before his death, Mrs. Van Rensselaer had begun to publish articles on painting and architecture in the *American Architect* and the *Century*, but afterward she devoted particular energy to her writing. By 1886 she began to collect various of her essays, publishing them in book form, in-

*Mariana Griswold Van Rensselaer, "Recent Architecture in America: American Country Houses I, II, III," *Century* Magazine 32 (May, June, and July, 1886), pp. 3–5, 19–20, 206–08, 214–20, 421–24, 426–34.

† For Van Brunt's writing see *Architecture and Society: Selected Essays of Henry Van Brunt*, ed. William A. Coles (Cambridge, Mass., 1969). Neither the writing of Sturgis nor that of Mrs. Van Rensselaer has been collected and annotated.

‡ See "Mariana Griswold Van Rensselaer," by Talbot F. Hamlin, *Dictionary of American Biography* 19:207–08.

cluding *American Etchers* (New York, 1886), *English Cathedrals* (New York, 1892), and *Six Portraits* (Boston, 1889). She was a friend of Henry Hobson Richardson, whose architecture she greatly admired, and upon his early death she began a biography, one of the monuments of American architectural historiography, *Henry Hobson Richardson and His Works* (Boston, 1888). Her most extensive historical study was the *History of the City of New York in the Seventeenth Century* (two volumes, New York, 1909), but aside from the study of Richardson, her most important contribution to the critical study of American architecture was a series of articles she published in the *Century*, May 1884 through July 1886. Her remarks, more penetrating than those of Montgomery Schuyler at this time, were aimed at the general public, especially potential patrons. While she acknowledges that "there is much good building going on at the present moment," the even more prevalent bad architecture demonstrates "a widespread deficiency of knowledge" among clients, for as she clearly understood, "architecture always comes in answer to a distinct call of patronage." § The series opened by examining current public and commercial buildings, churches and urban houses; the concluding three installments dealt with country houses, in which Mrs. Van Rensselaer recognized that American architects were grappling with completely new problems. Portions of the last three installments, surveying her discussion of country houses, are reprinted here with selected line cuts from the *Century*.

AMERICAN COUNTRY DWELLINGS. I

Passing from one branch of our architecture to another, we realize how many are the dangers which beset its path. Much of our ecclesiastical work, as we have seen, has been fettered by the wish to follow inappropriate precedents; very many of our buildings for commercial use have been pauperized by complete indifference; and for long our city dwellings were stereotyped and stunted in dull reiteration of some unintelligent design. And now, in considering the domestic architecture of our smaller towns and our country places, we shall see still another tendency at work for evil—the tendency toward ignorant, reckless "originality." But the same fundamental sin has underlaid all these various superficial sins, and the reformation which now begins to show in each and every branch is due in each and all to the fact that we are repenting of this fundamental sin—are beginning to feel the necessity for basing all our work on *rational* foundations, for taking as our guide intelligent, cultivated thought, not apathy or impulse, not mere vague artistic aspirations nor a merely formal adherence to the examples of some other age.

It is not strange that in building our country homes we should have shown ourselves more original, more "American" than elsewhere. Here most of all have we been forced to meet—or at least to deal with—new and diverse requirements. Our climate and the habits of life it engenders, our social conditions and the variety of needs they create, our sites and surroundings, as well as our main material, wood—all have been most unlike those of other nations. In no other architectural branch have we been thrown so

§ *Century* 28 (May 1884), pp. 48–49.

largely upon our own resources; therefore in none was the development of some kind of originality so probable. And thus that native character which gives more general signs of its existence than are commonly perceived— which somewhat tinges all our work, however featureless or however imitative—nowhere else reveals itself so clearly as in our country homes. Nowhere has its accent been so pronounced, and nowhere has its voice been broken by so few wholly alien notes. An inquiry into its various manifestations must begin with our very earliest products.

Every one knows what were the first of all our country dwellings— those old farm-houses, built by Dutch or English settlers, which still survive in many a quiet spot. Nothing could be more simple, more utilitarian, more without thought of architectural effectiveness. And yet such a farm-house is often extremely good in its own humble way—good in is general proportions, and especially in the agreeable and sometimes picturesque, yet simple and sensible, outlines of its roof.

More decided in character, of course, are those colonial dwellings which soon were built for a higher than the farming class. Whether of Dutch or of English origin, a family likeness marks them all, for the English model itself had been influenced by Dutch ideas. Everywhere the details are "classic," but in their choice and application many variations showed themselves as the years went on. Sometimes a very plain pattern has been followed, sometimes columns and pilasters give a more ambitious air. The openings are now rectangular and now round-arched, with fan-lights in their heads. The porches, and especially the doorways, are often charmingly designed and delicately carved. But here again, as with the farm-house, the roof is apt to be the best and most attractive feature. Truly good and very charming is the "gambrel roof" with its quaint and useful dormers, and the hipped roof, which does not run to a peak but is stopped at a broad balustraded central platform—as, for example, in the oft-illustrated Longfellow house at Cambridge.

Hundreds of these colonial dwellings still stand all through New England and New York State and all along the Atlantic seaboard; and even when they are built of wood their charm is incontestable. Of course we know that many of their features are not intrinsically appropriate to this material. Yet how much of the original excellence survives the unlawful translation from one material into another—how much solidity and simplicity of effect, how much of the truly architectural merit of good outlines and beautiful proportions, how much of that expression of mingled dignity and refinement, which is surely a pleasant expression for any dwelling to put on. In his sparse but intelligently applied detail, moreover, the colonial architect showed a truly artistic perception of the way in which the ornamentation appropriate to stone should be altered when it came to be wrought in wood. And inside his structures he built such spacious, well-proportioned rooms, such comfortable or such stately stairways, and, once more, such simple yet pure and artistic decoration, that we cannot but respect his memory, cannot but rejoice in the legacy he has left us. . . .

We need not quarrel over the question whether the colonial house is "American" or not. In any strict sense, of course, it does not deserve the name; nothing does save the wigwam of the North and the pueblo of the

South. Of course its patterns were all imported, and sometimes their treatment was very strictly imitative—more strictly imitative, I should say, than the treatment of any of our later products whatsoever. But certain frequent features—as, for instance, one or two sensible and charming modes of roofing—may fairly be called original; and when the translation into wood occurred, that was certainly American enough. Then our colonial work has stood longer than any other, and is identified with whatever historic associations we can call our own; and it is all so analogous as to offer an instance of the flourishing on our soil of something that may be called a coherent, comprehensible, all-pervading "style." All these facts, together with its undeniable charm, certainly give it a strong hold upon our affections, and a priority of claim among the proper objects of our study. But the main question is not as to its Americanism, and is not as to its charm; the main question is, does it indeed wholly meet the needs of to-day, practically, expressionally, and artistically?

Practically it does not. Its air is indeed as of a delightfully complete domesticity, but it by no means fulfills to the modern American mind the promise it holds out to the eye. In relation to the habits we have acquired during more than a century of rapidly changing existence, it is not one-half so "livable" as it looks. It provides only for the simplest, most unvaried and homogeneous domestic and social customs, and only for housekeeping of what now seems a very primitive pattern. Whatever the *paterfamilias* might feel about it, neither the *mater* nor her executives could live at their ease to-day or work at their best in an unmodified colonial interior. If they happen to dwell in an old one, there are sentimental compensations which perhaps suffice. But when a new home is in question the case seems wholly different. And the alterations in plan and arrangement which are necessary to meet the change in main requirements, and to provide for a hundred subordinate new requirements, must be of such a character that the old exterior pattern cannot often be retained. For this is certainly not flexible, elastic, given to indefinite extension and the indefinite multiplication of minor constructive features. The effect of quiet dignity which is its greatest charm depends very largely just upon its simple, unbroken outlines, and its broad, unbroken masses.

And in thus deciding with regard to its practical sufficiency, have we not also decided with regard to the expressional and artistic sufficiency of the colonial home? Our more freely social, more lavish, more varied and complex ways of living cannot find full and truthful expression in any colonial pattern, nor our growing love of art full and lawful satisfaction. We still want to be dignified in our architectural voice, still to be refined, still to be quiet; but the dignity, the refinement, and the repose must be of a different character from those which appropriately marked the dwellings of our ancestors. The simpler types among these are extremely puritanical; and I do not think the adjective fits ourselves, And the ornater types, even if they had not also much of the same accent, are the least well fitted for reproduction in our most usual material; for, excusable though the practice was a hundred years ago, it would be inexcusable to-day to build Doric porticoes or to frame Ionic pilasters out of pine boards painted.

In short, we may say of our colonial homes what we may say of the contemporary homes of England: our architects should study them, but cannot copy them. When to a certain degree their features and their general effect have been reproduced, the result seems peculiarly pleasing and most appropriately "American." (At least this is true of the Eastern States. It would not be so true, I think, of the Western—which may be taken as proof in passing of how desirabilities vary in this department of our art.) But many extraneous features and many variations of old features and old modes of working must be introduced if the result is to be sensible and satisfactory. And for some of these the point of departure must be found in the "vernacular." Incapable of self-development into anything good, it yet cannot be cut down root and branch; it must yield us certain buds of excellence for development along with other grafts. Its piazza, for example, absolutely imposes itself upon the conscience of every American architect. To develop it into a beautiful and constructive instead of an ugly, make-shift, superadded feature, and to bring it into perfect harmony with all his other features, many of which will have come from very different sources—this is one of the most vital problems with which he has to deal; and also one of the most difficult, and the one of all others which most emphatically forbids him to imitate any previous product, most emphatically prescribes that if he builds good country houses for the Americans of to-day, they will be essentially unlike all others. . . .

AMERICAN COUNTRY DWELLINGS. II

Our best new country homes are still the most "American" of any of our products; good or bad, I say, they hardly could be otherwise. But their individuality is now a thing we can contemplate with satisfaction, and in which we can read the signs of a greater satisfaction yet to come.

We must not look to them for examples of that almost palatial dignity and richness which we conceive, for instance, when we speak of the best country homes of England. We are not essentially a country-loving but a city-loving people; and our country homes are thus allotted, in the great majority of cases, but a secondary station. Our most frequent, most characteristic, most typical product is not the country residence in the old world acceptation of the term, but the mere *summer residence* built for those whose longer days are passed in a city home. Moreover, our gregarious tendencies are so strong that most (of course not by any means all) of our summer homes are more or less closely grouped together in colonies which have no exact parallel abroad. There is nothing abroad which really represents such a place as Newport, for example, or as Mt. Desert or Lenox, or any of those resorts which line the northern Massachusetts shore. The most "select" of English watering-places is a mere congeries of lodging-houses, intermixed with villas whose indwellers' thought is but for repose or recuperation. In the most modest of American watering-places, on the other hand, social ends have largely been considered.

The fact may seem unimportant, but it is vital enough to decree a wholly different architectural problem. Though in the majority of cases the owner's chief home is not his summer "cottage" (the term has survived its literal truth), yet this is none the less a *true* home, wherein he wishes not only to gain new life but to *live*—wishes to have his most private and personal needs as completely provided for as in town, and often to have his social needs quite as completely met. And this last point is not unapt to mean that his "cottage" must be big enough to house many guests as well as to provide for those transient demands which occur in cities.

Does not all this indeed imply that for other reasons, as well as for those which lie in difference of climate, our most frequent and most characteristic summer homes cannot be patterned on any foreign scheme? And does it not also imply that the task of building them is extremely difficult? . . .

As we might expect, the best among the recent Newport houses do not stand on quite such exacting sites or deal with problems quite so ambitious. Some of the smaller homes built by Mr. Luce, by Mr. Emerson, by Messrs. Rotch & Tilden, and by Messrs. McKim, Mead & White are extremely sensible, attractive, and appropriate in design. The one which the last-named artists have built for Mr. Samuel Coleman, on Red Cross Lane, seems to me particularly happy in expression—dignified yet rural, simple yet refined, almost picturesque yet quiet, and wholly devoid of that affectation, that attitudinizing (so to say) which too often accompanies picturesqueness. The

HOUSE OF MRS. MARY HEMENWAY, MANCHESTER, MASS.

Figure 34. **William Ralph Emerson, Mrs. Mary Hemenway house, Manchester-by-the-Sea, Mass., c. 1883, from** *Century* **10 (May 1886), p. 9.**

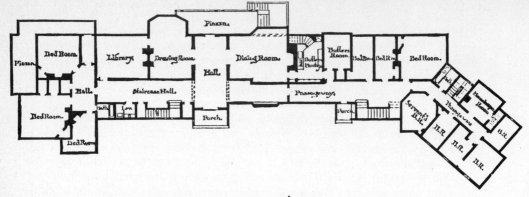

PLAN OF MR. WARD'S HOUSE.

Figure 35. McKim, Mead & Bigelow, plan of Samuel Gray Ward house, "Oakswood," Lenox, Mass., 1877–78, from *Century* (June 1886), p. 219.

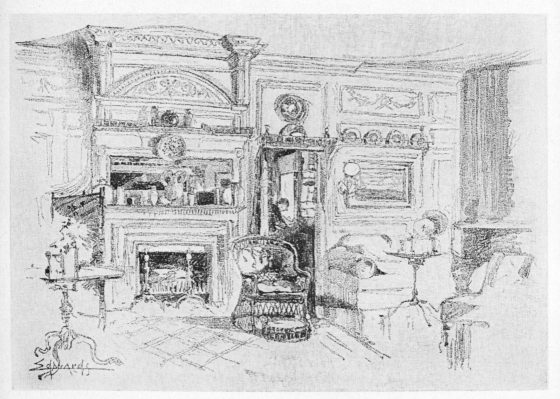

DRAWING-ROOM IN MR. WARD'S HOUSE.

Figure 36. McKim, Mead & Bigelow, drawing room of the Ward house, from *Century* 10 (June 1886), p. 208.

colonial roof has been cleverly adapted on the one hand and the "vernacular" piazza on the other. These points may be guessed from our illustration; but I am sorry to say it does not reveal the best qualities of the design, its pleasing outlines, its harmonious general effect, or the way in which a commonplace situation has been given individuality and dignity by a terrace which unites the house with the lawn below. It fails to show that it is a *good house,* and not merely a house with certain good features. But it is, I think, one of the very best in Newport, in spite of the fact that we can take exception to a few minor features here and there—as to the details of the piazza in the foreground of our print; and it is also one of those which are most distinctly "American" in effect.

It is time, however, that I should speak a little of the interior of our country homes. As a rule they are more entirely satisfactory than the exterior. Even some of those houses which most painfully affect the eye as features in the Newport landscape, are models within of the intelligent design and artistic decoration. In truth, the interiors of our country homes are getting to be so good, not only in exceptional but also in average examples, that I think I should point to them first of all, were I asked by the "intelligent foreigner" of fiction to show what art can do in the New World to-day.

It is impossible for me to dwell at length upon the great, the vitally important matter of planning. I should have to use far too many words and far too many large-scale plans in illustration. Be it only said that that peculiar kind of ingenuity which in directions other than artistic has long been recognized as a distinctively American gift, now at last shows very clearly in our architectural planning too—that ingenuity which combines practical good sense with quick imagination, and is heedless of conventions while not in love with needless novelty. . . .

The chief point to be noted is the great importance now given to the hall. Colonial architects made it very important and very charming, though not often in just the way which would be most desirable now. But in our transition period it fell into a condition which was not more deplorable than it was utterly inexcusable outside of city limitations. Even in the country, as I have just remarked, it was most often nothing more than a narrow "entry," an ugly, contracted passageway, which occupied valuable space and gave us nothing in return but the mere means of access to the various apartments. Mr. Hunt, so far as I know, was the first to make this innovation. But now in homes of every size the tendency is to make the hall at once beautiful and useful, the most conspicuous feature in the architectural effect and the most delightful living-room of all; not a living-room like the others, but one with a distinct purpose and therefore a distinct expression of its own. In our climate and with our social ways of summer-living, we absolutely require just what it can give us—a room which in its uses shall stand midway between the piazzas on the one hand and the drawing-rooms and libraries on the other; perfectly comfortable to live in when the hour means idleness, easy of access from all points outside and in, largely open to breeze and view, yet with a generous hearthstone where we may find a rallying-point in days of cold and rain; in short, a spacious yet cozy and informal lounging-place for times when we cannot lounge on our beloved piazzas. Try living in a house with a hall of new yet already customary kind, and then remember how you used

to live in a house which had nothing but an "entry," and do not forget that
the space once wasted on that "entry" is now utilized in every inch; and you
will see that the change in our methods of planning has not been prompted
by caprice or even by the desire for beauty. Yet, as we might feel sure, a
great gain in beauty has come hand in hand with the great gain in practical
fitness. Not only the hall itself but the whole house profits by its alteration. It
supplies what was lacking before, a logical center to the most extended and
complicated design. It makes grouping possible; it divides and yet connects
the various apartments; it unifies the plan while permitting it a far greater
degree of variety than was possible with the old box-like scheme.

And with the rehabilitation of the hall has come the rehabilitation of
that staircase which also our forefathers once treated so charmingly, and
which also we long maltreated so abominably and inexcusably. Even in the
tiniest cottage the staircase must now be seductive to the foot and pleasing to
the eye; and in some of our larger homes it is a very splendid feature.

Of course the possibilities of treatment offered by hall and staircase are
infinite in variety. In a hundred different ways the staircase may be made
the chief feature, or a more subordinate feature, of the hall itself; in a hundred different ways it may be set a little apart from this and yet be sufficiently connected with it for architectural coherence and for perfect comfort. And the expression secured may be merely snug and cheerful, or be of
any degree of stateliness leading up to the very highest, and yet the effect as
of a true hall and not a mere room still be preserved. If I could describe, for
instance, those halls which may be seen in the houses which Messrs. McKim,
Mead & White have built for Mr. Tilton and for Mr. Bell at Newport; in
their Francklyn cottage and their Newcomb house at Elberon; in General
Loring's smaller home, built by Mr. Emerson, at Pride's Crossing, and in a
larger one built for Mrs. Bowler at Mt. Desert by Messrs. Rotch & Tilden (I
cite but a few examples out of many just as worthy of citation), I should
describe designs utterly different each from the other in conception and
effect, each perfectly in keeping with the general character of the structure,
each a delightful and most comfortable living-room, yet each very plainly to
the eye a hall and *not* a room, its own due and proper purpose well preserved in plan, in features, and in decoration.

One of the finest halls we have yet to show is in the large house Messrs.
McKim, Mead & White have built for Mr. Robert Goelet on the Cliff at
Newport. It runs the whole depth of the house, with the entrance door at
one end and wide windows looking on the ocean at the other, yet is wide in
due proportion; and runs up to the roof as well, and the beautiful curved
staircase near the entrance leads to encircling galleries. Above the great fireplace rises a carved chimney-piece of oak which once held its place in a
French château. But its origin is not unduly apparent; it has not been left as
an isolated, alien trophy, but is used as the key-note for the whole decorative
scheme, the entire hall being paneled with oak to match and roofed with
oaken beams. When I say *to match*, moreover, I am quite conscious of the
force of the term; for the new carving strikes no note of discord with the old
either in motive or in execution.

The decoration all through this house is very charming; and it is all
conceived architecturally and carried out in harmony of design. And some-

MAIN HALL IN MR. NEWCOMB'S HOUSE.

Figure 37. McKim, Mead & White, plan of H. Victor Newcomb house, "Sunny Sands," Elberon, N.J., 1880, from *Century* 10 (June 1886), p. 217.

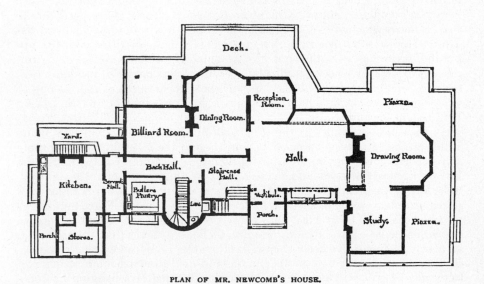

PLAN OF MR. NEWCOMB'S HOUSE.

Figure 38. McKim, Mead & White, hall of Newcomb house, from *Century* 10 (June 1886), p. 211.

thing similar may be said (although, of course, with very different degrees of emphasis and very different grades of praise) with regard to our new houses as a rule. The architect is now called upon to finish his task of house-building, not merely to begin it; to complete his interior, not merely to block it out. There is a change, indeed, since the days when we tried for no interior beauty whatsoever; as great a change since the days when we left the carpenter to work his will in machine-cut black-walnut monstrosities; and almost as great since those when we tried very hard for something better, but tried in the wrong way; when instead of a beautiful room we got merely a room full of pretty furnishings and ornaments and hangings. Then our one thought was to cover up the interior of our home as completely as we could; then all its charm would vanish with the exit of its owner. Now this charm *is built in*, is integrally part and parcel of the fabric. It is the architect's hand which has fashioned the richly screened or balustraded staircase; which has placed the cozy window-seats with an artist's eye for every item of loveliness the landscape offers; which has built the great hospitable fire-places and the graceful mantels—now part of the wall itself and not mere excrescences; which has designed every portion of the wood-work from kitchen up to attic; which has colored the walls and ceilings, and often has prescribed the colors and the forms and the materials of the furnishings which are to complete his scheme.

Nor when our new interiors are most simple are they by any means least interesting, least excellent. Indeed, there is no task more imperative, and none which some of our architects have taken up more intelligently and enthusiastically, than the task of showing that almost utter simplicity need not mean barrenness, that economy need not be synonymous with poverty of effect or artistic dearth. . . . Unfortunately it must be noted that not every owner *is* intelligent; not every one who is given a simply charming home to live in is wise enough to let it retain the accent a wise architect's hand has given. Too often its modest architectural charm is covered up with the upholsterer's devices, or with the motley trophies of foreign travel, or the plunderings of some antiquary-shop at home; with things beautiful in themselves, perhaps, but inartistic in effect, as any beauty must be which is out of place—and, especially, which hides and kills some other beauty that has a better right to show itself. . . .

Look, for example, at the great oak-lined hall in Mr. Goelet's house which has already been referred to, and then at the exquisite drawing-room in ivory and gold. The same beautiful Renaissance style prevails throughout, but the contrast in color and material and in application of forms and details, and consequently in general effect, is as entire as it is harmonious. Nor need we fear to place in such an interior any *good* object of any period. All we need fear is so to crowd it with many objects—good or bad—that its own expression will be lost, or to intrude into its beauty things that are not things of art at all, but are merely showy, fashionable, costly, new. Shall I be believed when I say that in another white-and-gold drawing-room of a modified colonial pattern I once saw a chandelier formed of a hanging basket— gilded straw and artificial roses? For *such* things there is certainly no home nor haven in our new architectural creations. Blessed be the fact, and soon may it impress itself more clearly than it does to-day upon that somewhat

HOUSE OF H. A. C. TAYLOR, ESQ., NEWPORT, R. I.

Figure 39. McKim, Mead & White, Henry Augustus Coit Taylor house, Newport, R.I., 1882–86, from *Century* 10 (July 1886), p. 427. The correct proportions and details of this house inaugurated a true "Colonial Revival."

CHATWOLD.—HOUSE OF MRS. BOWLER, MT. DESERT.

Figure 40. Rotch & Tilden, Mrs. Bowler house, Mt. Desert Island, Me., c. 1884–85, from *Century* 10 (July 1886), p. 431.

ungrateful beneficiary whom we call the client. Soon may he learn more thoroughly than he yet has learned that when a work of art is given into his keeping he has no right to ruin it—no, not even when it is the interior of his own home.

I have not half said all I wished to say and began to say about the exteriors of our newest houses, but the rest must now stand over to a final chapter.

AMERICAN COUNTRY DWELLINGS. III

The exteriors of our new country homes are so various that it is easier to characterize their general virtues by negative than by positive description. We may most clearly note their divergence from "vernacular" results by noting what "vernacular" expedients and features have been abandoned or greatly modified in their creating. The "French roof," for example, has disappeared. I do not mean altogether: there is still no quarter of the land where it does not often recur in work produced by the rural builder. But this builder and his devices are no longer typical of our best temper, and doubtless will gradually die out before the spreading of that new influence which naturally shows as yet most strongly in the neighborhood of our larger towns. When an *architect*, as we may fairly interpret the name to-day, has been set to work, then it is certain the French roof will not show itself. Truly it is, as the children say, a very "good riddance."

We may rejoice almost as heartily that our adherence to the clapboard is no longer so single-minded as it was. The old-time shingle, long despised as the humble expedient of unskilled, primitive hands, has very generally been adopted in its stead, and is a better thing, its small size and irregular shape being far more helpful as regards possibilities of good tone and color. In place of a succession of straight, close-drawn, mathematically parallel long lines it supplies an infinitude of short, broken, varied lines, which of themselves give tone to the surface. And this surface is no longer mechanically smoothed, but is pleasantly roughish to the eye, and may be stained instead of painted, or left to the "weathering" of its natural hue. Thus its color may have gradation and vitality, and the resultant tone may be as soft and broken as we will. We have already experimented widely in this direction; indeed, a little too widely. We have sometimes tried for too much variety of color, and have lost simplicity, even temperance and unity, in the result. We have sometimes tried for too much mellowness, and ended by being weak and vague and over-subtile in our tone. And we have often shown a desire, which cannot but savor of affectation, to antedate those effects which only the hand of time can legitimately give. But all this has been, perhaps, a not unnatural reaction from the old hardness and monotony of our clapboard days. Doubtless we shall soon see and respect the limits of the really good possibilities in the way of tone and color which the shingle offers.

Except in very small houses, we ought not, I think, to use it quite alone; for it is palpably a mere sheath and covering, expresses nothing of the true structure, and if used by itself in a large building can hardly give sufficient evidence of solidity. But we do not very often thus employ it. Much more often there is at least a visible foundation of more solid aspect—another improvement on our "vernacular" practices; and the best effect results, solidity is still more apparent, and the design gains in both coherence and variety, when the stone or brick is not strictly confined to the foundations or to a low basement-story, but is carried up in certain places, as in outside chimneys or possibly in the staircase wall. A very good example of such treatment may be seen in the illustration, given with my last chapter, of Messrs. McKim, Mead & White's house for Mr. Newcomb at Elberon, and in a Newport house built by Messrs. Rotch & Tilden for Mr. Augustus Jay. Here bricks were the most natural and therefore the best resource; but in many places, especially in those New England regions where half the surface of mother-earth is not soil but rocks, a stone substructure, not too carefully "finished," commends itself alike to common sense and to the eye. . . .

Neither clapboard nor shingle is always, I repeat, a very good resource. Yet it is not true to say—as so often has been said—that wood is in itself a poor resource, is essentially but a primitive, makeshift material; that our work must suffer, must be condemned to pettiness in treatment and to poverty or at least rusticity in effect, just in so far as we insist upon its use. We should rather rejoice that we have it to use, since it gives us one more factor than is possessed by any other civilized land toward the production of variety in effect, which means toward the true expression of varied needs and purposes. . . .

Unaccustomed as we are to the thought, plaster is yet a very admirable material for many of our purposes. Not in the shape of thin coats of stucco, painted in futile imitation of some other substance, but solid and straightforward, frankly confessing itself for what it is, plaster may be given qualities unattainable in any other material; a surface, for example, that is neither too rough nor too smooth, but exactly suited to the production of those effects of *tone* which we have learned to recognize as most desirable. And for color, especially for color at once light and strong,—which is to say, for color peculiarly well in keeping with our atmospheric conditions,—there is nothing like it. What pinks and yellows, what golden browns and lovely grays and tender greens one sees in the plastered walls of Italy and South Germany, and even of the southern English counties; and what dullards we shall show ourselves if we fail to take the hints they offer! Moreover, there is nothing but plaster (save only that marble which is all but out of the question as concerns summer houses) with which we can well get *white*.

The way in which we used white in our clapboard days—in unbroken stretches of oil-paint applied to a hard, smooth, mechanically ruled-off surface, and contrasted with grass-green blinds—was certainly not an artistic way. But when we became convinced of this fact, we were rather stupid to fall into the opposite extreme—to condemn white as such, *in toto*, without appeal. Surely it is not a bad color for our use. Who can say so if he knows its·effect in those southern lands abroad the physical condition of which resembles ours, and where the use of white has been constant in every age? Who can say so if with an unprejudiced eye he judges its effects even from one of our old-fashioned home-examples, when this is seen at such a distance that only the white and not its quality is perceptible? As yet, I think, we use our eyes too little in such matters—depend too much upon theories and sentiments drawn from that north of Europe whence we came, which from an intellectual point of view may be our proper teacher, but which from an artistic point of view has much less than we have fancied in common with ourselves and our environment. When we *do* learn to use our eyes, then I believe we shall often ask for white again, and for other light and bright and cheerful hues; and perhaps decide that in wood and plaster we have one of the very best ways—if not *the* very best way—of getting them.

A word now as to the development of that piazza which was the one good feature of the "vernacular" period. Two tasks were laid upon us with regard to it. On the one hand, we had to make it more architectural in itself—less fragile and shed-like and trumpery-looking; and on the other, we had to bring it into more vital architectural relation with the main body of the structure. From the illustrations in this and the two foregoing chapters some idea may be gained of a few of the fashions in which we have tried to deal with it; but it would take a far longer list of pictures to typify our general advance or to suggest all our best experiments.

Fortunate is it, indeed, that we *have* advanced in our efforts to bring it within the domain of art; for, as I said long ago, it is the one thing which no one who builds a country house in America can escape from,—the one thing more essential than all others to the comfort, dearer than all others to the affection, of every American client. Better do without even that "livable" hall which we now enjoy so greatly than without that piazza which went far to compensate us for the lack of so much else in our "vernacular" homes. It is more necessary to our well-being than is his *loggia* to the Italian, or his paved terrace to the Frenchman, or his vine-clad arbor to the German. As far as comfort and variety of service go, it is a better thing than any of them; and it remains for us to prove that it may be made, from the point of view of art, as good a thing as even the first named of the three. . . .

I know the danger of letting one's self be tempted into prophecy about a matter one has near at heart, but it is a danger I cannot quite escape from here. In fact, if from the first I had not meant to incur it,—if from the first I had not meant to express the strong hope I feel in the future of our art,—these pages would not have been written at all. For, good and interesting as are, intrinsically considered, many of our new results, I hardly think I should have been justified in speaking of them at such length and to so large and so mixed an audience if they had seemed to me to have intrinsic worth and interest *only;* if I had looked upon them as casual, sporadic, merely individual examples of success—uncharacteristic of any growing, widening, spreading stream of effort, unprophetic of any broad and common excellence to follow. No; the chief importance of our best results seems to me to lie in the fact that they are but the most successful outcome of aims which have much more often been followed; their chief value to consist in their hopefully prophetic character.

This character I identify with the fact—I think it *is* a fact—that in them all, beneath their manifold degrees of excellence and diversities of aspect, we can discern as a common foundation *the desire to do rational work and to prepare for it in a rational way.* We can discern that their creators have felt that the main question was the manner in which their own particular problems might best be resolved, not the manner in which some other problem had been resolved by some other hand; and that, while feeling this, they have felt none the less that they could not approach the main question intelligently or answer it artistically unless they had made a preparatory study of the history which tells and the monuments which show how an infinite number of other problems had been resolved by a long line of other hands. In short, I think we are getting to desire, not that we should be independent merely, and not that we should be scholarly and nothing else, but that we should be *independent in a scholarly way,*—unconventional, yet law-abiding; spontaneous, yet cultivated; free to do new things, yet bound not to do them in crude and blundering and illiterate fashions. I am sure this is the right, the only right, ideal. But I know, of course, how lofty an ideal it is—so lofty that no modern people can dare to boast of its full realization. Far be it from me to boast thus of ourselves, even in remote anticipation! I only think that we are beginning to *perceive* the right ideal, and to strive toward its realization in a vigorous and not unintelligent or inartistic manner. Yet this belief is surely enough to warrant the cherishing of a hope that there may be a future in store for American architecture,—not a future of immediate general excellence, certainly not a future of quick-coming perfection, very likely not of perfection at all as we use the word when thinking of the great old times of art; but still a future of growing, spreading, developing excellence, and perchance even of an ultimate degree of accomplishment which will be an expression of national characteristics through a truly national and artistic form of speech.

If a foreign critic should read these words and test them only by the evidence of the illustrations it has been possible to print with nine brief chapters, he might perhaps think them too confident. Even if he should come here and look about for himself, he might still not see the full grounds of my faith. He would view as an undecipherable, undated mass the whole of the work we have so rapidly built during our century of national life, and would see the bad results outnumbering the good, the senseless results the sensible, the ugly results the beautiful, in the proportion of hundreds to one. But I can see what he could not—the date when each was built, the circumstances under which each arose. I can see, as in a panorama by themselves, the products of the last ten or fifteen years, and can contrast them with the aggregate of those of earlier days. I can see how young our art is in its best estate, and how young are many of the artists who have wrought it; and thus can speak with confidence of advance and promise.

Moreover, I could cite for his convincing many items of evidence besides those which stand revealed in our new work itself. For example, there has lately been an immense improvement in the equipment, the standards, and the frequentation of our architectural schools. There is a strong and waxing belief in the desirableness of foreign study, the necessity of foreign travel. We have recently seen established such student-clubs as the "Architectural League" of New York, which prove the serious and enthusiastic way in which the young profession now approaches its life's work. And such facts encourage us to believe that the days are fairly over when a man could open an office and call himself an architect, pretty much as he might open a shop and call himself a grocer,—indeed, with far less sense of responsibility, and with far less time and thought and money spent in the laying-in of a stock-in-trade.

We have more than one architectural journal, unborn ten years ago, which is now well established and well entitled to respect. And another good sign, another good influence, deserves citation,—and, be it said, should excite to imitation on a generous scale. Those who founded the "Rotch Traveling Scholarship" for architectural students of the State of Massachusetts have done much more than the mere good work of promising to send every year for a two-years' stay in Europe a properly prepared and capable young artist. They have offered an incentive to earnest study which will yearly profit many more than the one who wins the prize; and they have proclaimed, distinctly enough to impress the most indifferent ear, that our architecture should be fostered, and that private generosity must play the part which our governments are not yet in a mental condition to assume.

And now, in conclusion, there are certain interesting questions we may ask ourselves. If there is indeed a possible future for our art, what is likely to be the character of its development? Will it have a very marked or only a very slight degree of originality? Shall we have a new style, an "American style"? If so, what is it likely to be? If not, what historic style are we likely to embrace? Or shall we embrace no one more closely than another, but always have, as we have had thus far, many men of many minds, only each one touched to a finer issue? Or these questionings may take a different turn: instead of asking what we are likely to have, we may ask what we *ought* to have. Indeed, we not only may but must ask ourselves all these questions in both these ways, if we really take an interest in the matter. But to answer them—even to think of answering them—is quite another thing!

As regards, for instance, what we *ought* to have, certain of our architects are convinced in theory and pretty consistent in practice. But they are not in agreement among themselves, while many of their brethren seem to have no very marked convictions—try one road with one kind of problem and another road with another kind; often, indeed, now one road and now a different, although the problems are analogous. When the doctors thus not only disagree but fail to arrive at individual conclusions, how shall a layman hold even the shyest theory?

Yet there is just one oft-propounded query which I think even a layman is justified in answering with decision. If our art is to be good—practically, expressionally, and aesthetically—must it be radically *novel*? Must we pray, as for our sole salvation, for the dawning of an "American style"? Its advent, its perfectioning would be agreeable, of course: it is always pleasant to create, to originate, to found, and not to follow. But a *necessary* advent it is not. We want an American architecture which shall be perfectly fitted to our needs, perfectly expressive of ourselves, and perfectly satisfying to our eyes. But we might have it, I am sure, with but few new forms or features or details of decoration. The general effect would at times be new—as we see in our country homes which are as "American" in their late and good as they were in their old and evil state. But this is not all that is meant by those who have raised the foolish clamor for an "American style"; and it is no more imperative that we should have such a novel architectural language as they desire, than that we should write something else than English ere we can have a literature essentially our own.

And it is idle even to discuss the question; for even if both the possibility and the desirability of a "new style" could be clearly proved, such proof would not help us toward it. It could not be formulated in advance. It ought never to be held up as a definite goal. The mere effort to foretell it and work up to it would be a negation of the true principles of progress. For that intimate coherence of forms and features and details which constitutes a *style* has never been, can never be, the starting-point even in idea. It always has been and always must be the final flowering of a long and gradual development. If an "American style" is to come, it will come step by step and inevitably—not suddenly and by an effort of will.

But we have no more need, I say, to pin our hopes upon its advent than has any other people. In truth, we have less need than any other, for we are peculiarly entitled to make free with all earlier inventions of every age and clime. We are more at liberty than is any other civilized nation to choose what and how and where we will from the world's great museum of precedents and ideas. No style, no scheme, no motive, feature, or manner of expression has with us an ancient local root. No venerable monuments excite a fear lest what is erected now shall strike a clashing discord. No existing or once existing form of architectural speech can show a really valid title to our allegiance. The little parallel I just drew with regard to literature was not quite correctly drawn, for in architecture we have a score of languages to choose among for the expression of our ideas, and are not bound to the artistic tongue of England only. Not the north more than the south, not the west of Europe more than farthest Asia, need be accepted as our magazine of forms and details; and not any one alone, but all together, may be drawn upon for the notes of a possible future harmony. To some this limitless freedom of choice seems but an added difficulty in our path. To my mind, on the contrary, it seems a vast advantage, of which the good results may already be traced with much distinctness, while the current efforts of most European countries do not seem to force an envy of the conditions amid which *they* work. But from either point of view that logic is equally at fault which would deduce from our condition an especial need for some absolute novelty of our own invention.

I might easily let myself be tempted quite beyond the bounds of discretion, and try a little definite prophesying with regard to what the future holds in store for us. But the attempt would be as profitless as indiscreet unless I could put my readers actually in face of all the evidence which has worked on my own mind.

So I will only say that it seems as though the architecture of the South (broadly speaking), and not the architecture of the North, would furnish us with our main devices. Theoretical examination—based not on mere facts of descent in blood, but on climate and atmosphere, and on our actual tastes and habits and minds and tempers—would lead us to such a belief, and the aspect of the majority of our best results seems to confirm it. I think that of all the constructive and decorative schemes which have been born in elder times, and are now struggling together for readoption in the Europe of to-day, the ones least likely to be acclimatized in America are those Gothic schemes which are most characteristic of the spirit of the North. But to say this is not to say much in the way of prophecy. How wide is still the range of possibilities with the round arch and the lintel of the South as our resources!

The round arch, we know, has been very conspicuously used of late. Alike in its Romanesque and in its Renaissance phases (both essentially creations of the South) it has many devoted adherents and many skillful adapters. Mr. Richardson has been perhaps its most energetic champion, and has preferred not only its Romanesque development, but the most pronouncedly Southern type of this. His work is always seductive and impressive; and if sometimes it seems exotic in its charm,—individual, willful, rather than purely natural and exactly *right*,—very often it has an accent which could hardly be imagined more appropriate, truthful, sensible. In marking this difference I do not mean that he sometimes seeks charm at the expense of usefulness; that his wish to reproduce the beauty of ancient examples sometimes works to the detriment of practical fitness. I only mean that sometimes, in the features and the decorations of those buildings which he plans so wisely, he reproduces the almost barbaric strength and exuberance of Romanesque days without due remembrance that those days were unlike our own, and that the unlikeness springs from our greater intellectual refinement, and from the greater feeling this gives us for *artistic* refinement as distinguished from artistic vigor and luxuriance. We, who know so well the art as well as the thought of classic Greece, cannot but exact from modern art a fuller measure of repose and reticence and balance and grace and purity than satisfied the mediaeval nations.

It is not to be wondered at that many of those who recognize this fact should have but small faith in the wisdom of attempting to draw at all from mediaeval precedents; should say that a better quarry is to be found in that Renaissance art wherein mediaeval ideas have already been modified by the reborn influence of Greece; wherein we have the language of a time whose civilization is the true parent of our own. Yet there are arguments which plead the other way, or, at least, which plead that we need not base our efforts wholly on Renaissance suggestions.

All the various Renaissance schemes save one or two of the very earliest came, alike in construction and in decoration, to be pretty definitely and completely worked out. It is hard, therefore, to treat them now with freedom without incurring the reproach of unscholarliness. Nay, it is hard to treat them with freedom even if we are content to incur such reproach; for there seems to be a singular analogy between architectural and human life. When a style has really run its course, has developed gradually and naturally up to the highest imaginable perfection, and then gradually and naturally fallen into decay, it seems impossible that it should be resuscitated and made the basis of new developments. For example, we have seen the experiment tried in England with that Pointed art which there lived a long life of many phases and died at last of inanition. We have seen it tried very faithfully and earnestly and cleverly, but are growing every year more conscious that the trial has been a failure.

Of course the styles we call by the general name of Later Renaissance have not died out in the same hopeless way. They are certainly vital still in France, which is the only modern land that can boast of a living and national form of architectural speech. But it would be useless for us to try to take them up as employed by France to-day. For they are *fully developed*, and French wants, French tastes, French ideas, are so singularly unlike our own that French expedients would but poorly serve our turn even if we could make ourselves content to copy them.

What we need is some scheme or schemes able to meet all demands, however lofty, however modest; fitted for use with many different materials; possible of modification into new expressions; and (should we ever work these out) capable of receiving new decorative motives. That is to say, we want some scheme or schemes more susceptible of *fresh development* than is any which has already once run a complete and perfect course. Those are undoubtedly right who think that such a scheme is offered to us by the earlier Renaissance fashions of the northern parts of Italy—by those which used the round arch and the lintel very straightforwardly without much reliance upon the column; for in the first place they are very sensible and very flexible, and in the second place they never lived out their life and came to a death of natural exhaustion: they were replaced, while they seem to us to have been still instinct with latent capabilities, by those columnar fashions known as "Roman" or "Later Renaissance."

But these early Renaissance styles are close akin in spirit, though not always in superficial effect, to the Romanesque fashions of a still earlier day. Both sprang from the same primal root; both incorporated the same general ideas and used the same main features. See, for example, how hard it is for an unskilled eye to tell in Venice which are the true "Byzantine" house-fronts, and which are those that were built in the first flush of the classic revival—although the long interval that lay between included all the Pointed work that Venice ever wrought. And the Romanesque of the South is another scheme which never lived out its life to natural expiration. The true Byzantine style of the East flowered very early into the most splendid blossoms, but then ceased from effort and neither developed nor declined. And its foster-children in the West—alike in Auvergne, in Tuscany, in Lombardy, and in the upper Rhine lands—were superseded, while still very vital, by Pointed fashions imported bodily from those more northern countries where they had had their birth. It is important to note that their typical ecclesiastical structures offer us, in the rectangular ground-plan, something far more appropriate to our modern needs than do the Gothic churches of the North; and quite as important to remember that in every other class of buildings we may take up their somewhat primitive elements and develop them as we will without any very stringent fetters in the way of precedents which it would be "unscholarly" to ignore. Their decoration, as I have said, if literally reproduced from western prototypes, seems too emphatic, too luxuriant, too barbaric for the expression of modern sentiment; yet it offers us—and especially in its eastern, Byzantine examples—types and motives and manifold lovely suggestions capable of development into a most appropriate form of artistic speech.

Nothing, for example, could be fresher, more unhackneyed, newer to modern western eyes, than the decoration based on Byzantine motives which Mr. Richardson has wrought in many of his interiors—as, for instance, in the exquisite wood carvings which line the Quincy Library; yet nothing could be

more refined, more modern in feeling, more entirely appropriate and satisfactory.

Of course it will be understood that I have not said all this with the
foolish idea of "giving advice," with the least wish to point out any road
which our art "ought" to follow. I have only been trying to explain that the
impulses which already have so strongly led our artists in these two directions are both sensible, both promising; and that they are *kindred* impulses,
and therefore perhaps prophetic of some still closer accord to follow in the
future.

Mr. Richardson's example seems already to have had a very strong
influence upon the younger rank of the profession. But if it proves to be a
lasting influence, the reason will be found, not in his mere personal force
and accomplishment, but in the fact that through these he gave the first
outspoken voice to tastes and sympathies latent in his countrymen at large. If
our architecture ever really develops upon the basis of the round arch into
anything that may be called a *style* proper to ourselves, it will be because
such a style is really what would suit us best, and because our artists will
have felt the fact in their own souls and not believed it upon the mere
evidence of one single man among them.

But (I must remind myself, I see, as well as you) speculation is quite
idle. We cannot even pretend to guess whether we shall grow into architectural concord of any sort whatever. But here, you may protest, we can surely
say what *ought* to be our course. Yes, surely, if this is a point where the
course of past developments must be accepted as illustrating a natural, unescapable law. Success in the past has certainly meant concord in style. But
can we be sure that success in the future *must* come in the same manner?
Can we be quite sure that individuality, personality, which today in so many
directions is so much more potent a force than it ever was in days gone by,
may not be destined to play a greater rôle in architecture than it has ever
played before? Of course I am not desirous of predicting that such will be
the case; I only think that no one should too dogmatically say that the case is
in itself impossible.

Time alone can give the answer to this as to all questions of the sort.
Our task is not to theorize or prophesy, certainly not to guide, dictate, or
dogmatize; but first *to help in the education of the artist and then to give
him liberty to work in his own way and opportunity to work his best.*

And if almost always we yet find something in our architects' results to
criticise, and sometimes much to condemn, much to deplore, let us remember how difficult are many of their tasks, and how often we make their
difficulty greater. Let us remember how ignorant we are ourselves, and how
our ignorance reacts on them. Let us remember what our condition was but
a few short years ago—how young, as I have said, is our good work, how
young are most of our good workers. Let us remember all this, and then, not
their sins and stumbles, but their virtues and successes will seem to us remarkable. We shall then pause from condemnation, hesitate to criticise, and
cultivate a grateful mood;—at the same time frankly confessing with the
French philosopher that the liveliest source of gratitude is the expectation of
greater benefits to come.

34 M. G. Van Rensselaer, Henry Hobson Richardson . . .* *1888*

Mrs. Van Rensselaer's penetrating biography of H. H. Richardson, a major work of American architectural historiography superseded only by Henry-Russell Hitchcock's *The Architecture of H. H. Richardson and His Times* (New York, 1936), was sumptuously illustrated with gravure plates (a number of which are reproduced in the *Concise History*). Reprinted here are portions of the three concluding chapters which summarize Richardson's contribution to American architecture.

CHAPTER XVII. CHARACTERISTICS AS AN ARTIST [I]

The more we study Richardson's works the more we feel that something deeper than style constitutes their individuality—that we must look behind his round arches and square-sectioned openings, his stone mullions, his arcades and loggias, and his Byzantinesque decoration to find the fundamental qualities which really reveal him.

These qualities are: Strength in conception; clearness in expression; breadth in treatment; imagination; and a love for repose and massive dignity of aspect, and often for an effect which in the widest meaning of the word we may call "romantic." The first is the most fundamental and important quality, and upon it depends to a very large degree the presence of the others.

The chief thing which made Richardson's works alike among themselves and unlike the works of almost all his contemporaries was his power to conceive a building as a whole, and to preserve the integrity of his conception no matter how various might be the features or how profuse the decoration he employed. Each of his best buildings is an organism, an entity, a coherent vital whole. Reduce it by distance to a mere silhouette against the sky, or draw it down to a thumb-nail sketch, and it will still be the same, still be itself; yet the nearer we approach it the more its individuality will be emphasized. This is because its character depends upon no one feature, no one line, but upon the concord of all and the vigor of the impression which all together give. No feature is of dominant importance, but each is of the right relative importance from any given point of view, and all are vitally fused together;—the building seems to have grown, developed, expanded like a plant. We cannot dismember it in thought without hurting both what we leave and what we take away; and whether we study it up or down— from particulars to generals or from generals to particulars—there is no point where conception seems to end and mere treatment to begin. It would be as impossible, without injuring the conception, to change the surface

---

*Mariana Griswold Van Rensselaer, *Henry Hobson Richardson and His Works* (Boston, 1888), pp. 111–16, 118–22, 136–38.

character of the walls or the distribution of the ornament, as to alter the relative proportions of walls and roof or the size and position of the chief constructional features. When these facts are perceived together with the great difference in general aim which exists between Richardson's best buildings, his versatility is by implication confessed. It matters nothing that he drew from the same historic source most of the elements with which he built church and warehouse, civic palace and country cottage. In each case a radically different idea was needed and in each case it came to him.

In each case, too, it came as a strikingly appropriate idea. While conceiving and developing a structure as a whole, he worked from the inside out, not from the outside in. The nature of the service it should render was his first thought, its plan his next; and these rule his exterior in its major and its minor features. We do not find him taking schemes or features which were beautiful because appropriate in one building and trying to make them beautiful in another at the expense of fitness; and there is no favorite feature he does not sacrifice if fitness demands—not the last trace of decorating, not the visible roof which he loved to make so prominent, nor the round arch itself. Of course he sometimes sinned against perfect appropriateness of expression, but his slips were few, and the longer he lived the rarer they became. Here lies the true greatness of Richardson's works—in the fact that they are true conceptions, clearly expressing an idea as appropriate as vigorous. The great value of the Quincy Library, for instance, or of the Pittsburgh Court-house, or—at the other end of the scale—of the Marion cottage, lies in the fact that it is a coherent vital entity and at the same time a speaking entity—unmistakably a library, a municipal palace, a gentleman's seaside home.

Another fundamental quality in Richardson's work is breadth of treatment. It is this which gives his results their air of "bigness"—not the actual size which in many of them chances to be great. Artistically speaking, his smallest structures are as big as his largest, and they are so because they are as largely treated. Whatever his faults he never worked in a small, hesitating, feeble way. Clearness in aim and strength in rendering were the gods of his idolatry in art. If combined with refinement, so much the better; if not, they were still to be preferred to refinement without them. We are sure that he excused the faults of a Rubens on canvas, of a Michael Angelo in architecture, but never those of a painter who had microscopically elaborated a weak conception, of an architect who had delicately adorned a fabric that was not in the true sense a building. In his own work he was over-exuberant at times, but, so to say, with a broad brush and a vigorous touch, and with that truly architectural instinct which makes ornament accentuate the meaning of constructional lines. Of course it was the strength of his basic conception which encouraged him to be thus broad and definite in treatment. There was no temptation to fritter away his effect when he felt that his fundamental idea would impress the imagination and charm the eye. There was every reason why he should present this idea as frankly as possible, either in bold simplicity or with lavish decoration which emphasized leading lines and important features. I have said that the greatness of his work rests first of all upon the strength and the appropriateness of his conceptions; but perhaps the breadth of treatment through which they were expressed is as important a quality. Certainly it is as rare a quality in modern art.

The strong imaginative power which Richardson's works reveal should perhaps not be called a separate characteristic, being implied in the existence of those just named. Yet we realize it most fully when we understand not only how strong and vital his conceptions are and how unlike each other, but how unlike they most often are to the conceptions of any earlier day or of modern men in any other land. He took the elements of the language with which he voiced his thoughts from other thinkers, but his thoughts were his own. Whenever fitness demanded—and with our novel needs this was very often the case—he took counsel of his own imagination, began at the bottom of the problem, and produced a result which differed essentially from all others. Yet he was too true an artist to prize novelties as such, and he had too strong a faith in the individuality of his talent to fear that if he were not "original" he would not seem himself. He never needlessly sought for a new conception. It could never have occurred to him to wish merely to do something unlike what his predecessors had done or what he himself had already done. When a problem presented itself which was similar to some preceding problem, he frankly re-adapted the same idea which had already served. His versatility developed in the only way that it could have developed hand-in-hand with excellence—through the effort to fulfill the given task in the best possible manner, to find clear and full expression for the appropriate idea.

When such qualities as these are found conspicuous and persistent in an artist's work, his choice of style seems a matter of secondary importance. His thoughts have made his work great and individual, not the language in which he has expressed them. Yet Richardson's choice of language was by no means fortuitous or without deep and interesting significance. It is true that working in some other style he might as clearly have shown us the value of definiteness in conception and breadth in treatment, of harmonious effects of color and strong effects of light and shade; the beauty of a roof, the meaning of a wall; the nature of good surface treatment and of decoration which explains construction. But his chosen style was essentially favorable to the teaching of such lessons, as well as to the display of that romantic kind of beauty for which he had so strong a liking. And better than any other style it could meet his fundamental love for massiveness and repose.[1]

[1] By repose is not here implied quietness in the sense of simplicity of surface and a moderate number of features, but structural repose—repose of line and mass, repose in the form of features; and it is not too much to say that Richardson could best secure this quality by developing the suggestions of Romanesque art. Greek art, making all its lines straight and its horizontal accentuations preponderant, does not express repose so much as great strength gracefully bearing a downward pressing load. We realize the fact when we study Egyptian art, which is similar in essence to Greek, minus the grace. Gothic art, accenting vertical lines, actually expresses motion—an upward lifting as of a growing tree; so much so that when, as in its Venetian forms, it strives to be more restful, we feel that it is not really itself, that it is trying to achieve a result which could have been more perfectly secured with round arches. Roman art, when it passed from the engineer's into the artist's hand, was not a simple concrete

When he recognized the serviceableness of its forms he instinctively preferred to study them in their southern developments. His temperament was essentially a southern one—loving breadth and light and color, variety and luxuriance, not cold grandeur, solemnity, and mystery. Refinement was not one of his most fundamental qualities as an artist. Yet his steady development towards a refined simplicity could not have had its starting-point in a paraphrase of Norman work. It could only have begun with such a paraphrase of southern Romanesque as we see in the Woburn Library.

In matters of treatment Richardson's attitude towards the precedents of ancient art was the same as in matters of conception. He studied them with love and care but in no slavish, idolatrous mood, and from a practical or purely aesthetic, not from an antiquarian standpoint. He viewed them as the work of men of like nature with himself, not of demi-gods inspired to a quality of performance which modern men need not try to improve upon. They were helps for him not fetishes, starting-points not patterns. What he wanted was their aid in building a good structure, not their prescriptions how to build a "scholarly" one. He looked upon them as a dictionary not as a grammar, and still less as a collection of attractive features which might be stowed away in the mind like quotations isolated from their context. None of his pupils ever heard him say, "This is a charming thing—some day we must manage to use it." The context, he knew, was what made the worth of an architectural phrase. Only when a man is sure of the general meaning he wants to express, the general effect he wants to produce, can he turn to his predecessors for assistance.

In minor as in major matters Richardson invented when he was obliged to and borrowed when he could. He took the Romanesque art of the south of France as his chief but not as his only quarry. He was ready to draw from other sources any special features which a special need required;—later mediæval fashions furnished him with much material at the outset of his life, and towards its end he was more and more attracted by Byzantine forms and decorations. Whatever he took he remodeled as freely as he saw fit, and there was no more effort to conceal his alterings than his borrowings. What he wished was simply that to an intelligent eye his work should look right in the outcome; and if it did, then he knew it was right, though to a dull eye it might seem a copy or though to an antiquarian eye all the precedents of all the ages might seem to protest against it. Sometimes, of course, he was not entirely successful in his adaptations. But often he was, as in that tower of Trinity, the genesis of which has been described at length because it so clearly typifies his constant way of working. No one could mistake this tower for an ancient one, wherever it might chance to stand. Yet the impression it

scheme, but a splendid bastard mingling of two alien schemes. Only when it was again stripped of its Greek overlay did it clearly reveal its intrinsic qualities. It is in Romanesque art only, and in those early Renaissance modes which were directly based upon it, that we find that balance between vertical and horizontal accentuations which means perfect repose. The semicircle demands neither that ascending lines nor that retreating lines shall preponderate; and in itself it is neither passive like the lintel nor soaring like the pointed arch. It seems to have grown to its due bearing power and thus to remain, vital yet restful, making no effort either to resist downward pressure or to press upward itself.

produces is similar to that which good ancient works produce—an impression as of a vital, homogeneous entity. And, it cannot be too often said, this is the impression made by all of Richardson's best structures. Therefore, the more eclecticism appears when they are analyzed, the more cheering is their evidence with regard to the future of our art. In nothing did Richardson do us better service than in proving that the modern artist need not be cowed into a purist, straightened into an archæologist, cramped and confined within the limits of a single narrow stretch of by-gone years—or, on the other hand, thrown wholly on his own inventive powers—if he would do work to satisfy and delight us as the men of early years satisfied and delighted themselves. The tendencies of American art have been chiefly towards a reckless inventiveness. Those of foreign art are too strongly towards mere scholasticism. But Richardson, keeping to a middle path, worked as those whom we call the demi-gods had worked. Eclecticism is more patent in his results than in theirs, for the store of precedents which lay open to him was vastly wider than that upon which any of them could draw. But in spirit his process was the same as theirs. Many other modern artists have shared this spirit theoretically but very few have had the power to express it in work which can be compared with his for excellence. Few, indeed, have had the boldness to attempt the task as frankly. It is hard to say which fact proves Richardson's independence of mind and self-trust more—the fact that he dared so visibly to borrow the general scheme of so famous a piece of work as the Salamanca tower, or the fact that having borrowed it he dared to remould it with so radical a hand. One success of this kind is a better lesson for after-comers than a hundred correct and scholarly plagiarisms. Nor need we ask the antiquary whether or no it is a success. Perhaps he might say that the builders of Salamanca would not have approved of the tower of Trinity. But very likely the builders of the Parthenon or even of the Pantheon would not have approved of Salamanca. The world has had too much—infinitely too much—of such appeals to the artistic conscience of the past. It is time to remember that the past itself never had any artistic conscience except that of the current age, and that we in our turn should make the present our judge—or that if we look outside the present it should be forward and not back. The true question to be asked with regard to work like Richardson's is whether it has those fundamental qualities of harmony, vitality, appropriateness, meaning, and beauty which will make it seem good in the eyes of men born seven hundred years from now. How it would have looked in the eyes of men born seven hundred years ago—incapable of understanding our conditions, of sympathizing with our tastes, of seeing the currents which have been all this time at work in science and in art—is indeed a matter of small concern.

Yet, as has been hinted, there is another danger besides that which lies in an overweening respect for the past. We Americans are more ready than the rest of the world to acknowledge that adaptation, not imitation, should be the artist's formula. But we do not realize all that is meant by our own words when we add that of course adaptation must be sensible and skillful. We do not realize that it needs not only more power but more knowledge and labor to adapt well than to copy well. Here again Richardson's example is infinitely instructive. He adapted well—so well that the process was a creative one in the truest sense of the word—because he had thoroughly studied the principles of his art, and because he practiced it with an exceptional degree of love and patience.

CHAPTER XVIII. CHARACTERISTICS AS AN ARTIST [II]

"About a fortnight before Richardson's death," writes Mr. Frederick Law Olmsted, "I was with him in Washington, and it is remarkable that he was led to speak in this last interview that I had with him of a point of professional economy of which he had been led to speak (by seeing a lot of rough tracings on a drawing-board) the first time he came to my house fifteen years before. . . . Richardson repeated what he had first said to me at Staten Island. This was, in effect, that the most beguiling and dangerous of all an architect's appliances was the T-square, and the most valuable were tracing-paper and india-rubber. Nothing like tracing over tracing, a hundred times. There was no virtue in an architect more to be cultivated and cherished than a willing spirit to waste drawings. Never, never, till the thing was in stone beyond recovery, should the slightest indisposition be indulged to review, reconsider, and revise every particle of his work, to throw away his most enjoyed drawing the moment he felt it in him to better its design.

"From something like this he went on discussing for the better part of an hour, growing to sit up erect, his voice becoming clear, his utterance emphatic, his eyes flashing, smiling, laughing like a boy, really hilarious, much as in some of our all-night debates years ago in Albany when he was yet a lithe, active, healthy fellow. I was afraid it would be too much for him, and, rising to go, said, 'Eidlitz asked me to let him know how I found you: I shall have to tell him, never better in your life;' and he laughingly assented."

One phrase of Richardson's repeated here, hints at something which it is important to make plain. An architect's revisings, he believed, should never end until his building is "in stone, beyond recovery;" and he exemplified this belief by altering much and often after construction had been actually begun. No one could have used preparatory pencil and paper more conscientiously, yet it was one of his firmest dogmas that they could not be implicitly trusted. If his scorn was great for the recklessness which says, No matter about the drawings—we can set things right as we build, it would have been just as great for the closet-spirit which should say, No matter how the work is looking as it grows—it was all right on paper. "The architect," he often explained, "acts on his building, but his building reacts on him—helps to build itself. His work is plastic work, and, like the sculptor's, cannot be finished in a drawing. It cannot be fully judged except in concrete shape and color, amid actual lights and shadows and its own particular surroundings; and if when it is begun it fails to look as it should, it is not only the architect's privilege but his duty to alter it in any way he can." Therefore he kept his judgment awake until his last stone was set and his last touch of decoration had been given. Therefore, too, he thought needful those long frequent hurried journeys which must have done so much to sap his strength. His representatives on the ground were capable and conscientious. He knew that he could trust them to carry out a design quite faithfully. But he could trust only his own eye to see whether the design was carrying itself out well or not, and so would leave the sick-room to find how some far-off building looked which he had seen but a few weeks before. As long as he possibly could he kept up his custom of making monthly tours through all the distant towns where he had work under way; and when journeys were at last forbidden he sent one of his chief assistants to bring him back verbal reports, and exacted daily detailed letters by means of which he could follow the placing of every stone.

There are many architects, I believe, who hold a different creed from the one which Richardson exemplified. They point with pride to the exact correspondence between their studies and their completed buildings while Richardson delighted to explain the disparities in his. It would be idle to try to lay down rules of right and wrong as decisive between such opposite ways of thinking; yet the paramount success of Richardson's results should at least be taken into account by those whose own theories and methods are not yet established.

The chief faults which have been charged against Richardson as an artist are: Extravagance; a willingness to secure a striking effect at the cost of conscientious care for all parts of a building; a neglect for the expression of construction; and a lack of refinement.

In one sense Richardson was certainly extravagant—or, to speak more exactly, lavish. He always wished to spend enough money on a building to make it perfect, and his ideas of perfection were high. In consequence, he often persuaded his clients into a larger outlay than they had anticipated. . . .

We have very good reason, therefore, to rejoice that Richardson often secured the chance to make his buildings as sumptuous as appropriateness allowed. Our public needed to be taught two complementary truths—that architectural excellence need not always be costly, and that some kinds of architectural excellence cannot be cheap. It needed a sight of beautiful simplicity to convince it that neither nakedness nor cheap elaboration should ever be allowed; but it also needed a sight of really rich monumental beauty to convince it that niggardly attempts at grandeur are absurd.

The charge that Richardson was apt to neglect some parts of his buildings in order to secure the effectiveness of other parts seems merely to mean a belief that his exteriors are more complete and beautiful than his interiors. No belief could be more mistaken;—as a rule they are quite as carefully conceived and quite as carefully completed. They show the same harmony between part and part and the same uniting of all parts to produce a single impression. . . .

CHAPTER XX. INFLUENCE UPON PROFESSION AND PUBLIC.

It is difficult to explain why Richardson's work appealed so immediately and so strongly to the public. But the question is of such importance that his biographer cannot escape from the attempt to give at least a partial explanation.

The mere originality of any of his buildings can have had little to do with the matter. Originality of one sort or another has so long been the rule in American architecture that the most striking novelty, if it is nothing more, can hardly excite even a passing curiosity. The solid popular success of Richardson's work—great at once and growing greater year by year—has certainly been due in large degree to those qualities which have already been described as setting it conspicuously apart from modern architectural work in general—to the clearness and vigor of the primary conceptions which it embodies, and to the consistency yet flexibility in matters of treatment which it displays. The strength and clearness of each of Richardson's conceptions attracted the eyes of men whom more scholarly arrangements of beautiful features or elaborate schemes of decoration left unmoved—putting before them a body which they could not help noticing as a whole and which plainly showed what the aim of the artist had been and what was the nature of his aesthetic ideal. And then his steady yet pliant and sensible adherence to the same ideal in the fulfillment of many different aims impressed its character upon the observer's mind, made him think not of each work by itself but of all together, and thus caused him to realize the difference between an architectural creed and a mere succession of architectural recipes. It was Richardson who first proved to the American public that the speech of a modern architect may be something wholly different from a series of varying quotations or of ever-new inventions—that it may be a consistent yet plastic language, one which inspires the artist yet is ductile in his hands, one which borrows its terms from ancient tongues yet has a thoroughly modern accent and can express a fresh and powerful individuality. It was Richardson who first proved this, and it is not strange, therefore, that he should first have excited a genuine interest in the art he practiced.

A part of the popularity of his works may in this way be explained. But only a part—interest is not necessarily admiration, and they have excited an admiration which seems doubly strong in contrast with the cool indifference that had greeted the best works of his forerunners. This fact is best accounted for, perhaps, by regarding him as the unconscious exponent of an unconscious, latent, yet distinctly marked national taste in architecture. An artist so strong as he would in any case have impressed his generation deeply; but to have made the extraordinary mark he did seems to imply a peculiar concord in feeling between himself and his public.

Upon the question whether this concord was a fact turns the interesting question whether Richardson will be recognized by later generations as the founder and inspirer of a national architectural development. It does not involve the future of his fame as a great artist, or the vitality of his fostering influence upon our love for art in general and our understanding of architectural excellence. These in any case are well assured. And so, we cannot doubt, is the permanence in certain respects of his influence upon the actual character of American architecture. If the collective work of the American architects of to-day is compared with that of fifteen or twenty years ago, the effect of Richardson's example clearly appears;—it would be hard to overstate the degree to which he should receive credit for the growth of this work in vigor, breadth, and simplicity, in coherence and clearness of expression. As far as such qualities as these are concerned his influence must endure. But they are not the only ones in which, at the moment, it is conspicuously embodied. His special schemes and features and types of decoration—

his actual creed and style—have found so many adherents that they are fast setting a distinct impress upon the aspect of our towns. We have had many architectural fashions in America but nothing to compare with the vogue of that neo-Romanesque work which often seems to reproduce the true spirit of Richardson's art if at other times it seems merely to imitate or caricature it. And it is the permanence, the spread, the vital development, the eventual triumph in quality and in quantity of this special form of art which are involved in the question whether, in using it, Richardson merely expressed his personal taste or unconsciously expressed the taste of the American people too.

It is not important that we should discuss this question in advance, but it is imperative that we should recognize its exact form and bearing. It cannot be too often repeated that if the renewed Romanesque art which Richardson gave us does in truth continue to grow and flourish, it will not be because he taught us to like it but because when he produced it we liked it by native instinct. This cannot be too often repeated, especially by the young architect for his own guidance. If he clearly understands it he will know that, however great his admiration for Richardson's success, the main thing he has to do is to seek within himself the direction which his work should take. From the beginning to the end of his career Richardson frankly and emphatically expressed himself, and thus he did the very best that it was possible to do for the great talent which had been given him. It remains for the future to prove whether in expressing himself he really voiced a broad national instinct and thus was fortunate enough to do the best that could possibly be achieved for the art of his country. But no man can help this art or can assist Richardson's influence upon it by trying to work in Richardson's manner unless he feels as clearly as Richardson felt that it is the best manner.

To say this—to say that we should not blindly accept even Richardson as a guide in finding out things which suit us best in art—is not to impugn his talent or his force. It needed immense talent and force to do what many cannot help believing that he did—clearly to reveal the fact that we had innate artistic tastes. To do more than this—to create tastes—is not within the compass of human power. A man may teach art in one way—by demonstrating its broad principles and by exciting a spirit which shall intelligently appreciate good results of every kind; and in this way Richardson was a very great teacher. But no man ever taught an art, in the sense of prescribing a special manner of practice, except to a people for whom he was the sympathetic spokesman. In fact, the highest praise we can give to an artist is to say that he was his public's spokesman. All narrowly individual merits pale before the great merit of being the one who says first what his fellow-countrymen are eager to hear and thus opens other mouths to give full expression to a national instinct. Not to be isolated but to be representative is to be a true leader, a true creator in art.

Richardson's right to this high title cannot now be decided. But the spirit in which he labored and the work which he produced have already done so much for us, and in the coming years will assuredly do so much more, that we may call him with confidence not only the greatest American artist but the greatest benefactor of American art who has yet been born.

VI

THE SEARCH FOR ORDER

35 L. Eidlitz, Form and Function in Architecture* *1881*

Richardson's functional and expressive work, so highly respected by his fellows, seems to have served as a catalyst, for increasingly after 1880 architects began to examine their role in society and to seek a clearer expression of building function and structure. Louis Sullivan was far from alone in this, and there follow a selection of essays by his contemporaries which take up this concern. One individual frequently overlooked in focusing on the "Chicago School" is Leopold Eidlitz (1823–1908), active during the third quarter of the century. However, nearly all of his High Victorian Gothic buildings have now been demolished. Born in Prague, Bohemia (now Czechoslovakia), Eidlitz studied at the Vienna Polytechnical School and then emigrated to New York; there he worked for Richard Upjohn, whose Gothic work strongly appealed to his own interests. Eidlitz hoped to reunite engineering and building design as he had seen them fused in European Gothic cathedrals. His most important buildings were in New York City, but the work for which he may be best known today is the upper exterior of the New York State Capitol, 1875–83.[†]

Eidlitz's book, *The Nature and Function of Art* (1881), attempted this reconciliation between structure and design. As he examined work around him, he eventually came to the conclusion that "American architecture is the art of covering one thing with another thing to imitate a third thing which, if genuine, would not be desirable." The theme of the book he outlined in the introduction: "If architecture is to be a living and creative art, the study of styles must be directed at the art principles manifested in the relation of their forms to contemporary ideas, and knowledge of construction, to the end that new forms, based upon modern ideas and the present development of construction, may supersede the forms of the past" (p. xxi). There was, as he suggested in the heading to chapter 28, a specific "relation of form to function." All this appeared in print almost a decade before Adler & Sullivan's pivotal Wainwright Building in St. Louis.

CHAPTER II. THE AIM OF ARCHITECTURE

Science, common sense, and taste supply the world with knowledge. Let us see how art, and more especially architecture, are thriving with the help of this knowledge. In order to form a correct view of the condition of architecture, it will be well to examine its great aim at the present day, to create a new style.

The present condition of architecture may be inferred from the question constantly asked, "Will the civilized world, England, America, France,

---

*Leopold Eidlitz, *The Nature and Function of Art, More Especially of Architecture* (London, 1881), pp. 33–36, 42–43, 251–53, 269–91, 481–89.

[†] The most extended account of Eidlitz is a three-part article by Montgomery Schuyler in *Architectural Record* 24 (September through November, 1908), reprinted in M. Schuyler, *American Architecture* . . . , ed. Jordy and Coe, 1:136–87.

or any other civilized country, ever have a new style of architecture?" There
is no indication that this question was ever asked by the Egyptians, Greeks,
and Romans, or by the nations of Europe during the Middle Ages; nor are
the Chinese, Japanese, and Persians interested in it at the present day; it is
eminently the concern of the so-called civilized world and of the nineteenth
century.

If architecture as an art were complete, or if it ever had been perfect
at any one time, that is to say, if all the demands now made upon it could be
fully supplied by past experience, or if we could find in any one period of its
history an answer to every current aesthetic question, there would be no
need of progress in architecture; new styles would arise from time to time as
society changed its needs and nature, and as human ingenuity multiplied its
material; we should then see springing up around us buildings of a character
entirely new in expression, representing the many new ideas and wants of
civilized society made possible by modern science, and called forth by political, social, and religious changes, and by a vast increase in the best building
material. We should be overwhelmed with new architectural forms and
combinations, and have not only a new style of architecture, but a constantly
growing and changing style. Indeed the *various* styles of the present century
would be spoken of with confidence and approval. The present activity in
building has no parallel in the history of the world. The complexity of modern society demands more various buildings than are furnished by any past
period of architecture, or by all past periods put together, and the conditions
which govern erections vary constantly from those which preceded them.
What state of things ever seemed more forcibly to compel a new style in
architecture than that in which we live?

And yet, though monuments are built of new materials, in new places,
to answer new and heretofore unknown purposes, they merely repeat, when
they do not caricature, past architecture, and we call in vain for a new style.
A new style, it is evident, will not come simply because it is called for, or
hoped for. Architects think of it and dream of it; attempt it and fail; and
finally, in despair, change their designs from one style to another, vaguely
hoping to stumble upon one that contains all the elements they need, in the
combination in which they need them.

As we know of no such struggles in the past, we come to the conclusion
that architecture is dead, and that we can do no more than to dig up its
varied forms from the past and apply them to the need of the present. The
question then becomes, What forms are we to take, Egyptian, or Greek, or
Roman, or medieval: The current answer to this question is, Take them all,
familiarize yourself with them all; but when you reproduce them, be careful
to keep them separate, and to use only such as were originally used together,
lest by mixing forms of different periods you produce discord.

And thus the student reads the history of architecture, and if he is very
clever and industrious he dives deep into archaeology. Give him a section of
a label molding, or of an abacus, and he will reconstruct the building for you
from which it is taken. His mind is a museum of architectural history, and
architecture becomes to him a knowledge of forms, connected with dates
and places, but not quite clearly with the ideas which have given them

existence. He finds that these forms harmonize best in the relation in which they are placed by their authors; and in order to preserve the harmony and unity of works of architectural art as they appear in the past, he copies them in the exact relation in which he finds them. Hence mere division into styles no longer affords a well-arranged index of art. It becomes necessary to divide and subdivide styles, until there are as many types almost as there are individual monuments, and when the problem of designing a new structure is met face to face, and it is found that its requirements do not agree with those of any monument erected at least five hundred years ago, the architect becomes indignant at modern wants, and declares them to be outside the pale of architectural art.

It would be unjust to the profession not to remember some good results of this lamentable condition of things, viz., the archaeological work in the excavations of antique, and the active and successful restoration and completion of medieval monuments.

Nevertheless architecture today is practically nothing more than a collection of assorted forms, the elements of which are but little considered, and the origin of which is hardly known. When architects speak of progress in architecture, they mean possible new forms which must be *invented* with great labor of the imagination. When old forms are applied, it is done without reference to construction and material. A cornice is supposed to be a sort of architectural decoration, and not a stone covering a wall, hence wooden and zinc cornices, cast-iron capitals, gargoyles in places where no water runs, and buttresses where there is no lateral pressure, arches of lath and plaster where there is no abutment, columns which support nothing; balustrades in places where no one can possibly walk, and battlements upon peaceful libraries and schoolhouses. It is true that a very respectable number of modern architects are never guilty of these gross errors, but how many are there who are willing to forego a tower simply because it is not needed either physically or aesthetically, or a flying buttress, if by an ingenious argument it may be justified?

Architectural forms, like musical compositions, contain but few elements, but these are capable of a great number of combinations. Nor is it necessary that these combinations should be laboriously sought for; they arise naturally out of the conditions of the structure, out of the idea which has given rise to it, and out of the material used in its construction. They are of value only in expressing all these conditions, and of no art value whatever if brought about in any other way.

The modern architect, for reasons which will hereafter be discussed, but rarely refers an architectural composition to the idea which has given rise to it. He often ignores or neglects the construction and the possibilities of the material employed, as technical matters beneath his notice, but imagines that after a structure has been technically designed, so far as it is necessary to answer its practical purposes, either by some engineer or by himself, *then* the labor of the architect begins by enclosing the structure on the outside and lining it on the inside with a skin of architectural forms gathered from his general fund, in accordance with the dictates of his *taste*.

CHAPTER XIX. FORM AND CONSTRUCTION

Architectural construction teaches the application of well-known mathematical reasoning to questions arising in statical mechanics. It deals primarily with the laws which determine the just proportions of matter under a given relation, and with the use of certain given materials; and, secondly, it investigates possible forms or possible relations of material, as also the application of mechanical laws to all available materials for all possible purposes. In this manner methods of construction are multiplied, and new materials are brought into use. Methods of construction are geometrical demonstrations in matter of mechanical ideas, and are for that reason not works of fine art. Fine art means representation and not demonstration. The author of a demonstration of an idea is, therefore, not an artist—but inasmuch as the work produced by him is to the uninformed mind often a satisfactory representation of an idea, without becoming absolutely a demonstration (which can be the case only when the construction is mathematically understood), the effect upon the subject is very much akin to that of a work of fine art in this, that it produces surprise, or, as it is commonly called, a pleasurable emotion.

Surprise is enhanced in the degree in which the construction excels as a scientific achievement, and also in the degree in which the essence of the argument involved is sufficiently revealed to betray, not the scheme itself, but its fitness for the purpose.

Methods of construction also appeal to the imagination, and compel admiration for boldness of conception, daring, and enterprise. Hence it follows that superior or inferior methods are applied to monumental structures in the degree in which these monuments rank in the scale of ideas represented by them.

It needs no special argument to show that form is the result of construction, and that construction determines the elements of form. Form and construction are indeed so intimately related that they may be advantageously connected in the same chapter, that we may, as it were, step from one to the other, and gain thereby in the understanding of both.

It is rarely the case that one and the same structure represents more than one idea; but inasmuch as fine art deals with acts and emotions (phases of an idea), we can point to but few modern monuments which do not involve the consideration of a number of acts and emotions; and it needs to be considered what elements of form and construction may be used to serve the architect in expressing them. To illustrate: the Greek temple contemplates the idea *religion*, also a *habitation* for its services, a receptacle of the god, accessible only to a priest, whose act, whatever it may be, forms no element in the structure, as this act is not observed by anyone. No congregation is admitted inside the temple. So far as the people are concerned this temple is the habitation of a statue without function or motion; and it follows that this purpose may be represented by a single cell which needs expression only on the outside. A Christian church, on the other hand, admits into its interior the whole congregation, and accommodates various groups as they range themselves for prayer, private and congregational, music, confession, baptism, the communion, processions, and sermons. The service and government of the church also demand vestry rooms, a chapter house, corridors, and cloisters; and thus a church structure may be termed a group of cells. In this case, as in many others, cells need not be separated from each other by walls, but may be indicated by colonnades, screens, or archways, for the reason that the separation does not arise from a physical necessity but from an aesthetic necessity which demands a representation of the separate acts which illustrate the idea in the organism of the group; and also for the purpose of distinguishing special acts by giving greater height to the cells devoted to them, and a more refined treatment in modeling and decoration.

It frequently occurs that the architect is called upon to join two or more groups, as is the case, for instance, in parliamentary structures. Such a combination of groups becomes a pile, wherein the groups are separated sufficiently to prevent practical inconvenience, and mainly to give an expression to the whole, which will tell the story of the functions of each group, and hence of the whole pile.

A series of single cells, coordinate in their import and use, may be treated as divisions of one great single cell, as, for instance, the rooms of a hospital, prison cells, warehouse divisions, clerks' rooms attached to one and the same department, committee rooms, and so on. If in such a hive it becomes necessary to distinguish one or more special cells, it may be done by simply accentuating and grouping their openings as well as by distinguishing them from others in magnitude, special modeling, and decoration. This may be done, say, in a warehouse where the proprietor's office occupies an appreciable part of the building; or in the case of a physician's room in a hospital, and so on. But in structures of a monumental character it should be the care of the architect to see that the representation of no separate purpose of the structure be omitted, for all features of it, if justly treated, contribute to its expression.

It is the function of the architect, in the first place, to master the idea to be expressed, to understand the various methods used to illustrate it by acts, and to appreciate the import of the resulting emotions, that they may be able to designate the various human groups which form the basis of his design.

It is often the case that the proprietors of buildings, or managers of building enterprises, commissioners, committees, or other persons do not understand the relation between the idea and the structure, or the meaning of the structure as a work of fine art. In that case the architect must supply the defect and point out these relationships; he must, if need be, awaken a sufficient interest to supplant the prevailing prejudice that a structure is merely intended as a convenient shelter for its occupants.

The next step is to determine the magnitude and form of the single cells and their relative positions, the modeling, as it were, of the group. This process is impossible either as a problem for the imagination, or as a fact to be reduced to drawing, without a thorough knowledge of methods of construction and of the principles which govern these methods. We cannot think of spaces merely; we must think of them as surrounded by matter. This matter is called into use, and its mass is determined by laws of mechanical construction. Now, it is not true that a structure (a monumental structure) is, first of all, a shelter, a place for human convenience, and afterward an object of fine art—that the domain of architecture begins when the engineer and builder have done their work of planning. It will be too late then. Architectural art must, as we have seen, initiate the work and take hold of it at the very beginning.

Why is it, then, that a different view of the functions of construction and architectural art is entertained by a large majority of modern architects? An examination of this may help us to a better understanding of the true relations of construction to architecture as a fine art. Many architects believe that every structure is a single cell, the outer form of which has no special relation to its interior. Architects love to modify this single cell in its outline, especially if it be of a respectable magnitude; but these very modifications amount only to arbitrary projections which are not the result of a relation of parts. In addition to this they view a structure as consisting of three parts—an exterior and an interior (which need artistic consideration), and the construction proper, which is placed between the two, and which needs no artistic treatment. This construction is to be overlaid on both sides with forms which please the fancy of their author. These forms do not involve mechanical ideas, inasmuch as they may be affixed to, or supported by, the real construction. Can this be architecture? No. If construction were the vulgar thing it is said to be, the work of the mere builder or engineer; if this construction were not an integral part or motive in the aesthetic development of a monument, and if it were not possible so to modify this vulgar thing as to make it an artwork, why then, surely, it would be well to conceal it from sight with something that is recognized as a work of fine art, say with hangings, screens, and paintings, with anything that is capable of expressing an idea in matter, and which is not itself a mechanical construction. But what is really done is this: the real construction is covered with a false construction which is not applicable here, or with an impossible construction not borrowed from anything real, but purely the result of architectural aberration, a thing which, if really built of stone or wood or any material capable of doing mechanical work, would fall to pieces by reason of its own weight, but which the ingenious artist persuades to stay in its place by making it of plaster, zinc, cast iron, or something else in imitation of stone, or wood, and sustaining it by means of nails and bolts.

Now, why do architects do this? Obviously because they prefer this sham construction to the real construction; they like its form better. Then the question arises, Why not use the construction they prefer, and discard the one really employed? The reason why this is not done is that they have lost the art of architecture, the art of building. The forms they affect are not regarded by them as constructions at all, but as an aggregation of pretty things derived from interesting antique and medieval monuments, where they have a charming effect. . . .

At the bottom of all this we may see a misconception of the laws of construction. All matter is subject to gravitation, and every organism in consequence deteriorates with time. Whether this time shall be short or long depends not upon the magnitude of the masses employed so much as upon their relation. It depends upon this: whether the relation is in accordance with the principles involved in the construction adopted or not.

To say that the Egyptians and Greeks knew the arch system of vaulting as we find it in medieval cathedrals, or as the arching of spaces may be done in the light of modern mechanics, is probably not what the author of the *History of Architecture in All Countries* intended to convey. He probably refers merely to the arch over an opening in the field of a wall. That the arch never sleeps means only that all matter is possessed of the property of gravitation, the law of which is not as universally understood in the case of the resultant lateral pressure of the arch and its order of equilibrium as the more simple law of the pressure of the lintel. We cannot advance the process of expressing an idea in a monument, either by resorting exclusively to primitive methods of construction or by ignoring its laws in trifling with structural masses to suit our fancy. All known constructions, from the simplest to the most refined or complicated, should be brought into requisition by the architect as a means to express corresponding ideas, simple or complicated, materialistic or refined. It is perfectly consistent with the stability of a monument to employ a system of vaulting, provided its lines and abutments are mechanically considered and arranged. Such a structure can be made fully as stable as a mere pile of stones in a pyramid.

When a group of cells is projected in a ground plan, and the altitude of the cells determined with due regard to their individual importance, the various roofs outlined, and the openings for light are arranged, as to size and position, with reference to practically lighting and aesthetically illuminating the interior; if the structure is composed in accordance with mechanical principle, and a perspective view of such a composition painted on canvas in black against a light background, it will fairly represent the masses in the rough, and will effectually express the nature of the structure, and the accruing forms will be aesthetically correct. Such a picture is, as far as a drawing on a reduced scale can be made to be, a representation of the phonetic expression of the contemplated monument. No additional expression can be attained by modeling, by carved and color decoration, or the introduction of statuary. All these serve only to accentuate or to heighten the expression inherent in the structural masses, but not to add to it. If this picture seems still lacking in expression the artist must look for the probable defects, first, in a misapprehension of the idea; second, of the acts illustrating the idea; and, third, of the groups prompted by the emotions arising from the acts; fourth, in the absence of a just arrangement of the cells in relation to each other; and, finally, in bad or feeble construction. The latter may be bad because, first, the author of the design does not understand the principles involved; or, second, he may understand those principles, and fail to apply them; or, third, he may not be familiar with known methods of construction, or capable of devising methods to suit the case; or, fourth, because the order of elegance of constructive methods does not correspond with the importance of the individual cells.

It would be of no use to retouch an unsuccessful group of this kind without due reasoning, merely in accordance with personal feeling, or in accordance with forms which at some time have made a favorable impression upon us; nor to pile on additional features that have no foundation in fact; nor to strike out those that have this foundation in fact; nor to make the whole larger or smaller. It will not help us to add favorable surroundings which do not exist; nor to fret and fume over it and wipe it all out, in order to substitute something else which foggily exists in our brain; nor to rush to a collection of books and photographs to look for better things, unless it be for the purpose of examining them critically in their individual relation, and to find by that means where, in our composition, we have failed either to do that which is true and just, or to achieve an expression as truthful and brilliant as may seem desirable under the circumstances.

If you find that your dining hall bears no proper relation to your library, and upon examination you are convinced that it is not your fault, but that your client either studies or eats too much, let it be so. The structure must express the *morale* of your client, not yours.

But above all things do not search for special effects. Do not expand a plain country house into a palace, nor squeeze it into a cottage, nor into any known or given shape, because you admire that shape more than others. Do not add battlements when there is no opportunity to walk behind them, because you think this a fine medieval feature. Do not build a buttress because you think you would like to have a mass in this place and a shadow next to it. Do not sketch balconies where the orientation of the structure or the surrounding landscape does not warrant such a feature; nor bay windows, nor porticoes, nor any other appendage of this nature, unless they are needed, not merely physically but aesthetically; that is, unless the going out upon such balconies, or the entering into bay windows affords a mental entertainment which cannot otherwise be reached, or at least so fully enjoyed.

But if, after close scrutiny and correction for good aesthetic reasons, the groups or the pile fail to please you, what then? Consider that this may be owing to the fact that you are not familiar with the forms which result from your idea and its phases. The forms you know and love represent other ideas than those you are endeavoring to treat; and you may be sure if you have otherwise committed no error of judgment, you are on the road to a good architectural result. Proceed with your work, model the parts, decorate them in accordance with their functions, and before long the thing will speak to you in a new language expressing new thoughts; it will speak to you intelligibly, and with surprising force, and you will admit that this is by far the best arrangement of forms, *better* than you could have imagined them in your most enthusiastic moods.

The question may now be asked, Which of the many scientific constructions is the architect to select for use in his monuments? All of them. None must be rejected; none can be rejected; our *repertoire* is small enough as it is. But the Egyptians and the Greeks did not make use of the arch, and the Normans did not use the pointed arch. The Egyptians, the Greeks, and the Normans did perfectly right in not doing what they did not know of. You can have no such motive. You know the arch in all the forms in which it has been used, and in forms in which it has not been used, as yet, to any extent; you know a catenary arch, an arch which is purely a curve of pressures; use it, use them all, not indiscriminately, not unwisely, but, as they are all at your command, use each of them whenever it is the best thing to be used.

What is sad is to see a flat ceiling divided into impossible panels, supported by impossible girders which are not the result of any construction whatever—a ceiling which, if it were attempted to be built in stone or wood, would drop down by its own weight, but which is worked in plaster upon a framework of wood and tied to the floor beams above.

Look at the constructions that have resulted from the modern invention of the rolled iron beam. All of these are mere attempts to cover this unfortunate beam (one of the cleverest expedients of the age), and none to make the beam itself presentable, to arrange the arches between the beams in a logical manner that they may be sightly, and an aesthetical element.

Look at the treatment of cast-iron columns and other structural parts made possible by modern use of metals. They are more or less imitations of stone and wood constructions; but few of them devised by architects are modelings which can possibly result from the nature of the metal, yet the engineer has developed pure metallic forms unknown before, simply because he derives his wisdom from the laws of mechanics. But how can we preserve purity of style in architecture if we are to use and to exhibit constructions which find no place in the style we are working in. This subject of style we must reserve for a separate chapter, of which it is well worthy. But we may ask here, Did the architects of the Norman or Gothic school neglect constructive elements because they interfered with the style of the day or of their past? If this had been so, we should be still engaged in building pyramids. The elements of the architectural result of any time are construction (in its methods and perfection), materials, fundamental ideas, mechanical and artistic skill in their development. Of all these the progress of construction has exercised the most potent influence upon past development of architecture. This is true of the state of architecture in Europe up to the fourteenth century, but not since.

A post, column, or strut of stone or wood, meaning a part of a structure which is subject to a negative strain (compression), is strongest (the transverse area being the same) if it is circular in ground plan. Although this fact is not generally known to laymen, or thought of much by architects, it happens that when we see a post or pier which has a circular or octagon ground plan, it seems to us stronger than a square pier containing the same area and length.[1]

From this there is but a short step to the impression that round piers or columns look strong. Hence it is that the jamb of an opening seems more rigid if we chamfer its corners. This is actually done, not only in the case of door and window jambs and posts, but also at the intrados of arches and ribs, in fact, in all parts of structure which are subject to compression. More frequently the reduction is accomplished by modeling the corners in a manner which still more heightens this effect by imparting to it an expression of strength and elegance as well as of rigidity. The transition of piers to their bases and capitals, the underside of projecting corbels, sill courses, and cornices are all treated in a similar manner. The Greeks were familiar with this process, and practiced it in modeling their columns and cornices, but did not extend it to the jambs of their doorways.

[1] The experiment is easily tried by comparing a square and round post of equal length and area; the diameter of the square post will be proportional to the diameter of the round post as 1.7 is to 2.

The purpose of modeling masses in architectural work is to make the functions performed more apparent, and to heighten the expression of rigidity in the direction in which the forces are acting; also, in some cases, to multiply the apparent surface of the matter treated. When surfaces are molded, light and shade are the natural result; but light and shade are not the object of the process, they are merely an incident.

When two or three modeled groups of a structure succeed each other perpendicularly, the organization of the lower part must be more simple than the one immediately above it, and there should be a relation of mass between the parts whereby they continue each other. The lower pier, may, however, be a simple shaft, unless the organism immediately above it is so highly organized as to produce a contrast which would make the inferior organism rude, or the superior one weak or meager. This process of subdividing masses by modeling was undoubtedly carried to excess in late medieval work. This is evidently owing to an erroneous tendency to attentuate matter for the purpose of giving a sublime spiritual expression to the work, which well accords with the ideas of Christianity of the times, as well as to express function minutely. The times have changed, and with the times our ideas have changed; we do not now look upon matter as the despicable thing it was then held to be. This is no reason, however, why we should reject the scheme of Gothic architecture, as it is vulgarly termed, or Christian architecture, as Kugler properly calls it. The architecture of the medieval cathedrals, considered as a system, especially when we contemplate it in its principles rather than in its completed forms, may, without fear, be accepted as the most perfect development of architectural art known to us, and may well serve as a proper starting point for future efforts—always provided that we confine ourselves to the principles manifested in it, and not to its forms; and that we apply these principles to create such forms as will express our own ideas, and not those of the Middle Ages.

The analysis of the human body is the work of the anatomist, but to depict human emotions in stone or on canvas is the work of the artist. He deals with the material motions of the human figure, and must, therefore, understand its anatomy. More than this, the human frame is created to the artist's hands, and we may presume that nature has adopted the most brilliant construction which could be devised to combine expression with function. It is the problem of the architect to depict the emotions of the structure he deals with; to depict, as it were, the soul of that structure. But the emotions of this soul, like the emotions of any soul, can be depicted only by representing modifications of the body under the influence of emotions; and for that purpose the architect must understand the anatomy of his structure, which amounts to an analytical knowledge of its construction. More than this, the architect's structure, unlike the painter's or the sculptor's is, in the first place, necessarily a human creation; not a natural organism which contains within itself a perfect system of mechanical construction, not only the best to perform the functions assigned to it, but also the best to give expression to those functions, to the end that man may, if not understand, at least know them without a scientific analysis. Thus the architect must create his structure (while the sculptor and painter only re-create) upon principles supplied him by nature, which are the principles of mechanics. It is necessary, moreover, that his construction should perform not only certain physical functions, but also others superadded to these, which may be termed ideal functions, and which pertain solely to the ideas which have called together the persons occupying the structure; and, finally, this construction must be capable of an expression which conveys the idea of the motive for the existence of the monument.

This knowledge of mechanical construction should be also sufficiently positive to furnish the architect, at every stage of the composition, with a clear view of the mechanical relation of the parts of the structure as he develops them, that he may at all times in the production of an organism, and afterward, in the external modeling of its parts, justly express its functions.

Carved ornament and color decoration have no other purpose than to heighten the expression of mechanical resistance to load and pressure in architectural organisms. They do this (as will be hereafter more minutely shown) by their density, magnitude, projection, form, and the direction in which they are placed, which direction must coincide with the direction of resistance to load and pressure. They do it also by the peculiar treatment known as conventionalizing ornament, by which natural forms of animals and vegetables are so modified as to conform to the nature of the material in which they are wrought, and to the mechanical work which they perform.

The motives which influence modern architects in composing a design, and the quality of mind which enables them to compose, may be summed up as personal notions of the proper character of the structure, and of the effect which it may produce upon themselves and others; all of which is matter of *taste*. This taste some admit to need cultivation, and this cultivation is exclusively sought in the contemplation of the architectural work of the past, which is not applicable to the needs of the present, and which tends to fill the imagination of the zealous student with pictures which it would be better he should not know, if he is not to analyze them intelligently; for the greatest and first lesson which they teach is how not to do it.

The motive which governs the modern architect in composing a monument may be stated as a desire to please the public, or, as he says, produce a favorable effect. The education of the architect consists in looking at architectural forms which have produced favorable effects upon others. Such a course of education cannot certainly be productive of new forms or of a proper use of old forms. In truth a proper art use of old forms under new conditions is a practical impossibility. To illustrate: a painter who depicts the warriors paints him in medieval armor; he thinks a knight in armor exceedingly picturesque. The word "picturesque" with him embodies all that is good and proper in the way of dress, accoutrement, and physical development responding to a system of attack and defense carried on with certain given weapons and with an armor devised to resist these weapons. If you visit the studio of this artist you will find there swords, foils, breastplates, helmets, spears, and chain armor—in fine, every contrivance of offense and defense known in the Middle Ages. The artist has lived among these objects so long that he is able to draw them on paper or paint them on canvas in every conceivable combination consistent with their use. What is more, he has acquired a love for these forms, and he deems them eminently beautiful. Now let us imagine that a patron of this painter demands a picture of a warrior which shall not be a medieval knight, nor a Roman, or Greek, or modern soldier, but purely an ideal invention. Could the artist invent the figure of a warrior by merely trying to sketch and paint one? Certainly not. He could produce nothing but Greek, Roman, medieval, and modern warriors, or imperfect and incongruous combinations of all of these. Is the thing impossible? No, it is not impossible; but the process demands a species of skill not possessed by the artist. In the first place, a series of weapons would have to be devised upon principles heretofore not applied, and then an armor to resist these weapons. All this may be theoretically executed by a skillful armorer, and then the painter could paint a picture of an ideal warrior which would rank in beauty with pictures of the warriors of the past. If architecture is to be equally successful, the architect must combine with his art other technical skill corresponding to that of the general, the military engineer, and the armorer, and which in his case amounts simply to a thorough knowledge of the theory and practice of mechanical construction.

Relations of matter cannot be clearly understood nor successfully reasoned upon unless they are numerically considered. To say that the earth moves around the sun, conveys an idea; but it is a very confused idea, which cannot be made positive until we know that it completes a revolution around the sun in one year, and that the mean radius of its orbit is ninety-two millions of miles long. Now, when we say that this latter statement gives us a positive idea of the motion of the earth in its orbit, it is not meant to be an assertion that we can form in our minds a picture of that orbit or of the velocity of the motion of the earth; but that we can proceed to reason from these data with certainty, and arrive at the final conclusion that the earth moves in its orbit around the sun during a second of time over a space nearly 18.5 miles in length. It is true that a velocity of 18.5 miles per second is as much an enigma to the human mind as ninety-two millions of miles measured out in space; but with the help of the figures presented to us we can proceed to reason from one step to another without fear of error; in fact, with the certainty that every conclusion arrived at will be numerically correct.

Now, architecture is the art of representing ideas by masses of matter. We can gauge these masses, we can mathematically determine their dimensions under certain conditions of work to be performed by them, and also under certain conditions of apparent energy in resisting a given load.

Shall we abandon this opportunity to reason numerically? If we do so, we relinquish the only method of reasoning which never fails, and we must drift into a shoreless sea of architectural aberration.

CHAPTER XXVII. CULTIVATION OF ARCHITECTURE

This is not the place to enter into the detail of instruction, but it is desirable to make it perfectly clear that the architect, to compose well, must compose a monument which he may jot down as he proceeds in the form of a drawing, and he must not compose a drawing, which, when executed, may be a monument.

Only those who are capable of analyzing the relation of the various external elevations of modern monuments to each other, and to their internal sections, and who perceive the existing discords, can realize the pernicious influence of the modern system of doing architecture purely through drawings.

How shall I build this thing? should be the constant question of the architect while composing, instead of What form shall I give to it? If the former question is responded to in our composition; if this question is intelligently answered at every step of progress, forms will grow out of it; but if we design monuments in response to the latter question, the monument is never contemplated seriously, scientifically, or artistically as a whole, but as an aggregation of disjointed parts; hence the other question, How can I join this and that together with architectural propriety? is the question which most frequently occurs in modern architectural composition. The moment the architect finds it necessary to ask or answer this fatal question, he may be sure that he is pursuing the wrong course. He has started his work with completed forms, and is not developing them.

All parts of structure perform mechanical functions; hence their form must be primarily determined by mechanical laws. The modern architect ignores this fundamental law. He believes that there is a relation of a mechanical nature between superincumbent mass and the area of the supporting pier, between the lateral thrust of an arch and the resistance of its abutment, but he deems it an intrustion to remind him that no part of structure can be determined in its mass or outline without due mathematical consideration. . . .

36   J. W. Root, A Great Architectural Problem*   *1890*

A younger architect who, like Eidlitz, endeavored to combine engineering and design was John Wellborn Root (1850–91). Born in Georgia, Root early studied music and drawing, and was sent to England during the Civil War where he studied for a time at Oxford. After the war he joined his family in New York where he pursued a degree in civil engineering at New York University, an early indication of his desire to combine the science and art of building. Perhaps he hoped to attend the École des Beaux-Arts in Paris, but instead he first entered the office of James Renwick and then of J. B. Snook in New York. Eventually he moved to Chicago to the office of Carter, Drake and Peter B. Wight, whom he had met in New York. There he encountered Daniel H. Burnham, and, in 1873, they formed their own partnership. In the flourishing practice they enjoyed in the 1880s, Root not only devised new footing and foundation types, he also began to formulate a comprehensive theory of design and ornamental embellishment, independent of, but certainly touched by, that of

*John Wellborn Root, "A Great Architectural Problem." *Inland Architect and News Record* 15 (June 1890), pp. 66–71.

Louis Sullivan. His ideas were shaped by extensive reading, evident in the translation he made with Fritz Wagner of Gottfried Semper's "Development of Architectural Style," published in the *Inland Architect* in four installments from December 1889 through March 1890. Apparently Root had had this in mind when writing his own essay, "Style," published in the *Inland Architect* three years earlier, in January 1887.[†] The following essay was presented first as a lecture before the architecture class of the Art Institute of Chicago in June 1890.

Like all forms of civilization, architectural development has for centuries moved from homogeneity to heterogeneity. As human needs become more complex, and as human industries multiply, human habitations take upon themselves forms continually more intricate. But at no time has this development been so rapid as during the latter part of this century. The age of steam has witnessed a material revolution a thousand times more significant and radical than had occurred during all the preceding centuries. In essence, the requirements of men, as expressed in their architecture, had remained comparatively simple up to the end of the eighteenth century, and even to the middle of this. The fourteenth-century dwelling and shop combined was, in its essential arrangement, a very simple and obvious affair, whose type had existed in substance for centuries; and the combined shop and dwelling of the last century was scarcely more complex. In the great monuments of early Egypt, of Greece and even of medieval Europe, as well as in such smaller buildings as have survived to this day, very few and very simple ideas dominated the whole structure as well as its art expression. The architect was not distracted, therefore, by antagonistic elements in his problem, but moved straight forward toward a simple and definite result. If called upon to design a temple he aimed only to produce an edifice which should be a unit within itself, and at the same time expressive of that religious sentiment which was predominant at the time, and whose characteristics were for this reason instinctively grasped by him. If the problem was of some other character it was nearly always marked by equal simplicity of purpose. Even the greatest of castles and palaces in their most complex conditions rarely became more than well-regulated assemblies of simple structures, each one maintaining its own individuality.

Not only were early buildings comparatively simple because of the simple needs of the inhabitants, but also because of the fact that early architecture was created in climates where an outdoor life was so largely possible and even desirable that the dwelling, shop or temple itself, being to a large degree unnecessary from a material point of view, took upon itself a much less complex condition than if the climate had been more austere. Thus, being from one point of view unnecessary, or the necessity demanding such structures being comparatively slight, they became in their more enduring forms monumental in the expression of simple ideas, as places for worship and for defense.

Another cause for this obvious and simple expression lay in the fact

[†] A cross section of Root's writing is reprinted in *The Meanings of Architecture: Buildings and Writings of John Wellborn Root*, ed. Donald Hoffmann (New York, 1967). The Semper translation, however, is not included.

that the architect was then further than now removed from the mass of people, who, indeed, were ignorant of many of their own physical necessities, as well as of their moral aspirations. He was, therefore, left free to work out his problem undiverted by the thousand considerations begotten of individual caprice.

It was the Renaissance, with its wonderfully vital and complex thought, which first began in a marked way to impress upon architecture the stamp of individual whim or desire; and it is the earlier monuments of the Renaissance, built by men who were still imbued with something of the more primitive and simpler spirit, that remain to us most significant and interesting. For so rapid was the growth of ideas in the Renaissance that even the greatest among the architects of later periods were able only partially to give these ideas adequate realization in architectural form.

In the expression of this straightforwardness of intention, this unity of idea, characteristic of earlier architecture, the Parthenon, the Erectheum, even the great medieval cathedrals like Chartres and Amiens, are the embodiment of ideas in their essence as direct as any picture or statue can be.

But with the enormous growth in wealth and civilization of the Northern nations, as well as those in the South, since the Renaissance, especially since the beginning of this century, the change has been beyond the wildest flight of the imagination. The luxuries most rare to even great kings like Louis XIV are now the necessities of life to the day-laborer; and following every modern necessity is a vast nebulous train of luxuries, whose end may not be seen, all in their turn to become fixed and solid as necessities. These all demand accommodation and expression in modern architecture, and architecture must meet the demand.

As yet, sufficient time has not passed for this expression to be fully wrought out. The age of steam, of electricity, of gas, of plumbing and sanitation, is new. What its impress will be upon man himself no one will venture to prophesy, and this being true no man may foresee how architecture will adjust itself to these changed conditions. Especially is the forecast difficult when we reflect that not only preëxisting types of buildings have been revolutionized by modern needs, but new types have been created adapted solely to the present, and of which twenty years ago no man could have dreamed. Among these I mention the vast edifices which have lifted themselves in New York, Boston, Chicago and other cities, until they tower heavenward nine, ten, twelve and sixteen stories, containing sometimes three or four thousand people upon whom depend the support of eight or ten thousand souls. These buildings, the result of commercial conditions without precedent, are new in every essential element.

Looking at the problems presented by these buildings, as well as by many others of a different type in a lesser degree, we may certainly guess that all preëxisting architectural forms are inadequate for their solution, and that no logical combination of those forms can be made efficient without changes so great as to be practically destructive.

We must grant that, to be true, architecture must normally express the conditions of life about and within it, not in a fragmentary and spasmodic way, but in the mass and structure; the life of the building, in large and comprehensive type. As yet, the search after a national or new architectural style is absolutely useless for this purpose. Architectural styles, national or new, were never discovered by human prospectors, however eagerly they have searched. Styles are found truly at the appointed time, but solely by those who, with intelligence and soberness, are working out their ends by the best means at hand, and with scarce a thought of the coming new or national style.

Architecture is, like all other art, born of its age and environment. So the new type will be found by us, if we do find it, through the frankest possible acceptance of every requirement of modern life in all of its conditions, without regret for the past or idle longing for a future and more fortunate day, this acceptance being accompanied by the intelligent and sympathetic study of the past in the spirit of aspiring emulation, not servile imitation. If the new art is to come, I believe it will be a rational and steady growth from practical conditions outward and upward toward a more or less spiritual expression, and that no man has the right to borrow from another age an architectural idea evolved from the life of that age, unless it fits our life as normally and fully as it fitted the other. I say practical conditions, and this is fully meant—practical conditions without qualification or abridgment.

Whenever in the past such a full acceptance occurred, and a building was erected in the effort frankly to express the conditions thus accepted, art has been willing and ready to consecrate the effort. But, on the contrary, whenever art has been invoked to abridge in architecture one of those normal conditions, she has been distant and cold.

The ethical proposition is true that the presence of art may be most accurately known in the attitude of the workman as well as in the nobleness of his aim. And yet philosophers and critics have striven to find the path by which artists reached the exalted heights of inspiration, by which genius conceived the immortal monuments of antiquity. The path has not been found by them. But in studying our own age, I believe some guess may be made as to the road by which our own highest level may be reached.

We live in an age beyond all others reasonable. The ethical and art status apparently reached by the Greeks and Venetians through processes almost intuitive must be reached by us, if at all, by processes entirely rational.

If the problem before us were the design of a temple to Jupiter, with its simple portico and cella, the whole attitude of the mind would be different from that which is demanded in the effort to design in homogeneous and expressive form a great and complex office building of twelve stories, constructed of steel and terra-cotta. Here the pure art expression can, perhaps, never be so high as in the simpler problem, for reasons inherent in the problem; but if it is to be truly an art expression worth considering, it will be reached at the point where intellectual action, intensely concentrated upon vital conditions about and within us, passes into an unconscious spiritual clairvoyance. Here is the path, the end of which, indeed, may not be reached by us, but the effort to reach which will be to move in the right direction.

Criticisms upon art are apt to be unsatisfactory and are often unfruitful, and such I do not propose to essay. It is rather my purpose to enumerate some of the structural and commercial conditions which lie at the beginning of a typical architectural problem of the present, and to indicate something of the methods by which they are met and are given characteristic architectural expression.

The subject, then, of this paper, to which the foregoing is a preface, is some of the processes by which a large office building in Chicago is evolved, from the time when the site is determined to the time of its occupancy. The subject is chosen because no class of buildings is more expressive of modern life in its complexity, its luxury, its intense vitality. The purely artistic side of the question will not be enlarged upon, because, as I have said, it is the practical and even commercial sides which at this moment need special attention, not so much for themselves, but as factors, and most important factors, in the evolution of every aspect of a great problem; and which occupy a much greater and more significant relation to the ultimate art expression than has generally been conceded to them.

How much "per cent" has always been considered foreign to art, and generally it is. Yet, curiously enough, it may sometimes guide art, if not positively foster it. Art has never grown vitally without some sort of check, whether in the limitation of the age, the narrow yet intense idea which was the inspiration of the epoch, the specialized occupations of the moment, or some other equally valid cause. And in this age the question, purely commercial, of "per cent" often intrudes itself at a time when thoughtfulness is about to give way to mere lavishness, and asks of the mind the pertinent question "why?" and in the answer, art, if enriched by the splendor of material, is not concluded by it alone, but by the more valuable thing, expenditure of thought.

At the moment when an architect is entrusted with work to be executed by him "regardless of expense," let him beware that he lose not the thoughtful temperateness which should underlie even the most splendid effort. But when a certain income must be derived by revenue from the building designed, every question must be carefully weighed, investigated in every possible light; and the result is apt to be interesting, at least as expressive of thought, and will, if solved with truth and imagination, be also interesting from an art standpoint, as art in architecture is merely the expression in solid material that someone has thought for our comfort and delight.

Let us begin, then, at the moment when the questions involved in such a building arise and are propounded to the architect for solution.

Let us suppose that in the business center of this city a piece of ground has been purchased, lying upon the corner of two prominent streets, the dimensions of the ground being 150 feet north and south, 100 feet east and west, with a 16-foot alley on the south. It is surrounded by buildings averaging in height nine stories, and the average width of the streets on which it fronts is 70 feet, being in one case 66 and in the other 80. Of course, the first radical question to suggest itself is that of light. And this will at once dictate certain general and entirely preliminary conditions of the plan upon the ground. Experience has demonstrated that all spaces within the enclosure of four walls which are not well lighted by sunshine, or at least direct daylight, are in office buildings non-productive. The elementary question, therefore, is how to so arrange the building upon its lot that every foot within it shall be perfectly lighted, and all spaces which would be dark thrown out. To ascertain this it is necessary to know by experiment to what depth from the front wall daylight will reach, upon the average, in a story of convenient height, and giving to the space to be lighted the largest possible windows. This has been found to be in Chicago not more than twenty-four feet, assuming the height of the story to be about eleven, and the window to be placed close to the ceiling, the average street width being assumed. This fact will, of course, dictate in general our depth of offices.

Taking the lot of 150 by 100 feet, as given us, the first method or general disposition or plan which suggests itself will perhaps be a central court. It is found at once that this plan is not feasible, for there is not sufficient width in the lot to give light to the interior tier of offices opening upon this court.

A second plan would be an open court facing the east. This has manifest advantages. . . . A large amount of office space is here obtained, all of which would seem to be well lighted, and all of which would have open aspects to the street. An objection, however, to this plan, consists of the fact that the south wing of the building would constantly throw its shadow across the narrow court whose smallest dimension is north and south, whereas the distance north and south should be its greatest dimension to fully admit sunshine. Another criticism is that at a time when light is most valuable and most difficult to obtain—late in the afternoon—the court is thrown into shadow by the main portion of the building. Still another objection would lie in the fact that the court being so essentially a part of the street facades, it would scarcely be possible to face its walls with a material which would brilliantly reflect the light, as such a treatment would cut the main facade into three pieces and destroy all architectural unity of expression.

The next idea would be to place the court within the building and to the west of it, as illustrated in Figure 41. Here only one tier of offices is placed to the north and south of the court, and the plan seems to present many advantages. It is necessary, however, in order to get even moderately good light in the south tier of offices, that the width of the alley should be considerably increased. Let us do this by ten feet, using the widened alley for light. The court in the center, of a very good size, with its longer axis running north and south, thus freely admits sunshine; it is, moreover, in such position that it may be readily faced with glazed and light colored material, and generally presents a very convenient and serviceable arrangement.

The criticism upon this plan would be that if tall buildings exist on the south of it, the alley, even when widened, will not be wide enough to give perfect light to the south offices in the first five or six stories. This is a very grave objection, which would also be accented by the fact that so large a per cent of the offices have an alley frontage, which is nearly always objectionable.

Suppose, therefore, we take the offices which lie immediately south of the court and remove them to the north of the court, thus making the plan C (Figure 42). Here as you see, the court is open to the south toward the alley, and has the great advantage of the long north and south axis, which is 26 feet longer than the length of the court in plan B. In this case scarcely an office is solely dependent upon the alley for light; nearly everyone faces the principal streets, or, what has proven to be in Chicago quite as desirable, the

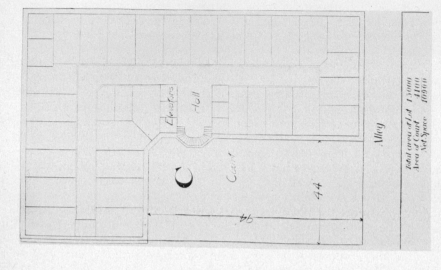

Figure 42. Plan of hypothetical commercial building, C, from *In-land Architect* 15 (June 1890), p. 68 (courtesy, Burnham Library, Art Institute of Chicago).

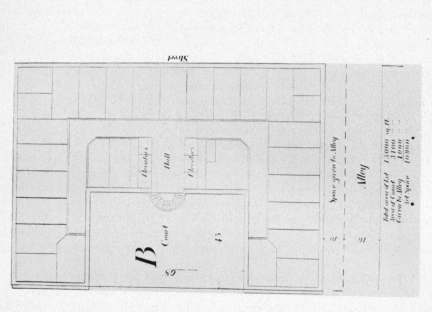

Figure 41. Plan of hypothetical commercial building, B, from *In-land Architect* 15 (June 1890), p. 67 (courtesy, Burnham Library, Art Institute of Chicago).

open court. This court may be constructed as lightly as is consistent with strength; it may be faced with any brilliant reflecting material; possesses all the attractions of the enclosed court of plan B, and is superior for service. And although the net space included within the building seems somewhat less than in B it is considerably more available and therefore would produce considerably more revenue. Remember also that this slight percentage of net space in favor of B is apparent only, for in B there is a somewhat larger proportion of walls which will more than counterbalance this difference. The general plan marked C is therefore taken.

The next general question is the number of stories. And in Chicago, at present, the difficulty is not to determine how few, but how many. Nothing to a stranger seems more irrational than the present rage in Chicago for high buildings; but the reasons for it are obvious and the fact apparently fairly well established, so that we must accept it. Let us assume that twelve stories are determined upon.

The next step to take is to approximate the cost of the building; a question of decidedly keen interest, and one in which it would not be generally conceded that the architect puts his best foot forward. Here experience has shown that the cost may be obtained within a very small fraction by ascertaining the gross cubic contents of the building from the bottom of the foundations to the top of the roof and inclusive, also, of all the space enclosed within walls in the shape of areas, etc. Dependent upon the elaborateness of finish, the cost per cubic foot of such a building will vary from 25 to 40 cents, although in Eastern cities the latter figure is often greatly exceeded. Thus, a building of this sort, containing 2,500,000 cubic feet, will cost, according to its elaboration, from $625,000 to $1,000,000, the average being about $750,000.

The general plan being now determined, and the question of cost discussed, we proceed to other points relating more in detail to the arrangement of the building, and which still have especially to do with the question of revenue.

The following is a partial statement of these points:

1. *Height of stories*—Ideally, the stories of such a building should be highest at the bottom, for here the light is least adequate. A system of graded heights, greatest at the ground and diminishing toward the top would be best. Motives of economy, however, tend to prevent this and the arrangement generally found most satisfactory is to have at the bottom a story level with the street and as high as consistent with easy access by stairs to a higher story immediately above it, thus obtaining revenue practically from two "first" stories. The third story is somewhat higher than those above, because it is apt, like the second, to be occupied by large corporations, or other tenants requiring considerable space in one room. Above this there is generally no cause for stories over eleven feet high.

2. *Main entrance*—This is to be as wide and convenient as possible, leading in the most obvious way to the elevators and provided in a building of this size with at least four pairs of easily moving doors. A very important feature of the entrance is the storm vestibule, which is always necessary and rarely adequately provided. These vestibules should be sufficiently deep to allow the two sets of storm doors to move freely past each other, with consid-

erable space between. Immediately inside of this vestibule one or more wide flights of stairs lead to the second or banking story.

3. *Elevators*—The number of elevators is very important, as are their size and shape. The number is proportionate to the cubic contents of the building, with an added percentage if the building be tall; for the length of time consumed by an elevator car in making a "round trip" depends as much on the number of stoppages for receiving and discharging passengers as on the speed with which it runs. In size the elevator car may not be much greater than 40 square feet in any event, two smaller cars being better than one of larger size than this. The shape should be wide and shallow, with the door as wide as possible.

4. Ample space must be left for all forms of supply and waste pipes to run up through the building, as well as for the elevator cylinders, and for ventilation ducts. These shafts can scarcely be too large.

5. On each story convenient and accessible toilet rooms must be provided, and in two stories these rooms should have large anterooms with barber shops and attendants.

6. Heavy burglar and fireproof vaults will be needed in a few places, especially in the first and second stories, though, generally speaking, the building being non-combustible, vaults of hollow tile may be placed anywhere tenants may wish.

7. The utmost space possible must be obtained in the basement, not only for renting but for boilers and all forms of machinery.

8. All plumbing and steam fixtures must be so placed that they are easily accessible, and at the same time do not deface the building. The same is true of all telephone and electric wires, all tubes for pneumatic service and discharge of letters.

9. The spacing of windows, and their size and height from the floor, are indicated to us with almost unavoidable exactness.

Think of the feelings of an Athenian architect of the time of Pericles to whom the problem should have been presented to design a building of fourteen stories, imposing upon him the following conditions: all of the stories except two to be 10 feet 6 inches high, all window sills to be exactly 2 feet from the floor, all lintels to be 6 inches from ceilings, and all windows to be in width not less than 4 and not more than 6 feet, and to be situated at distances apart of not more than 6 feet. If these conditions did not paralyze the architect, give him a few more: that all windows should have flat lintels, and that he must avoid as much as possible all projecting members on the façade, since these catch dirt and soot; and give him instructions to put on a few ten-story bay windows.

Yet these conditions are common enough now, if not in their entire number, certainly in the majority.

The next group of questions of vital importance relates to structure.

The building must be fireproof. Formerly a fireproof building meant one which was constructed with iron columns and beams, the beam spaces being filled with brick arches. The defect of this system lies in the fact that iron is not reliable in case of fire. At comparatively a low temperature it loses its carrying capacity and gives way; or else when very hot and suddenly chilled by water it is apt to break. The present fireproof structure is provided with metal columns and beams, all of which are enclosed in an envelope of hollow terra-cotta, which is securely fastened to the supporting metal. By this device heat is kept away from all metal work, and absolute safety secured (Figure 43).

Steel columns are rapidly coming into use instead of cast iron, for the reason that iron presents many unreliable features in the difficulty of obtaining perfect castings, and of ascertaining whether the casting is perfect or not. The steel columns are made of rolled plates of steel which are bent into proper form and riveted together. Thus they may be perfectly inspected and are absolutely trustworthy.

In the enormously tall buildings now erecting, scarcely any form of masonry is strong enough to use alone in the construction of the fronts; when, as noted above, windows must be placed at distances not much more than 12 feet apart, and should be at least 4 feet wide. This leaves a pier of not more than 8 feet at best, and this is often not strong enough to carry its loads without making it very thick, or by strengthening it with metal.

The first is costly, both in itself and because of the renting space it consumes. The second is entirely practicable and satisfactory. An iron or steel column is placed within the masonry pier, attached to it by anchors which do not interfere with any difference of expansion of the metal and masonry, and this column carries the loads of the various floors, the masonry being a mere fire and weather proof protection.

Another and still simpler method is to enclose the metal column in an envelope of hollow terra-cotta supported at each story on the column itself by brackets. In this case the column does all of the work. And any portion of the terra-cotta covering may be removed without injuring the structure.

Beneath all of these various supporting members foundations lie, which present some of the most interesting features of Chicago architecture or engineering.

The greater portion of the center of the city is built upon a bed of clay, more or less soft, the firmest part of which lies at an average depth of 12½ feet from the grades of streets. This clay, firmest at the top, is of varying depths, the upper part, called "hard pan," varying from 3½ to 7 feet thick; and borings through it to a depth of 75 feet often show no very great variation in the texture of clay beneath, although at greater depth there is more water, and therefore softer clay.

By tests made by the government, and also by individuals, this clay is found to be capable of carrying loads of not more than three and a half tons to each square foot. Practically this is greater than is safe, and the load generally assumed as conservative varies from one and a half to two tons, as greater loads per square foot create settlements so large as to be embarrassing.

Into this clay, every building built upon it settles to a greater or less degree. In several cases this settlement is considerably over a foot.

The general theory of foundation plan is to exactly proportion the area of each foundation pier to the amount resting upon it, keeping it free from every other foundation pier, so that the whole settlement will be equal, each pier being entirely independent. Thus a pier weighing, with the floors supported by it, 150 tons, should have a footing of 100 square feet, and one of

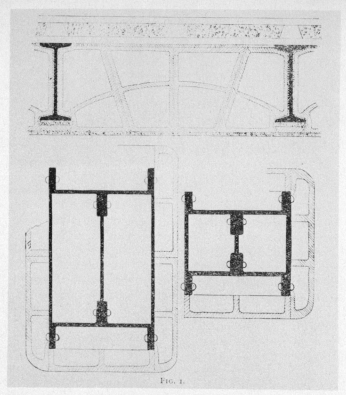

FIG. 1.

Figure 43. **Fireproofing of metal columns and floor joists, figure 1 from** *Inland Architect* **15 (June 1890), p. 69 (courtesy, Burnham Library, Art Institute of Chicago).**

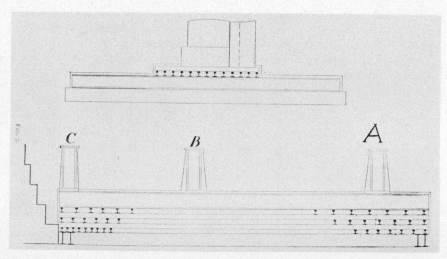

Figure 44. **Construction of "floating raft" foundation, figure 3 from** *Inland Architect* **15 (June 1890), p. 70 (courtesy, Burnham Library, Art Institute of Chicago).**

75 tons, footings of 50 square feet. Several very nice variations must be made from this general law, but this is the rule.

How best to construct this floating raft is the vital question. Formerly it was made in the shape of a pyramid of stone laid in cement, but this is costly, filling up the basement with its bulk and adding often twenty per cent to the gross weight of the whole pier.

The present method is to lay down upon the level clay a thin bed of cement upon which are placed steel rails or beams, spaced at closer or wider intervals according to the weights to be carried and the length of the beams. The rails are then filled between and covered by cement, thus excluding air and water; another set of beams is laid upon them, somewhat less in area, and so on, the whole forming a solid mass of cement webbed with a mesh or grill of steel, giving it very great transverse as well as crushing strength (Figure 44).

Such a foundation is made covering areas of 20 feet square or more, the total height of which is not over 3 feet 6 inches, thus leaving the basement unobstructed. Under the old system of construction a stone pyramid 12 or 14 feet high would have been necessary properly to do the same work, and entirely filling not only the basement, but some of the first story also.

I have said that whatever construction of foundations be employed, some settlement of the building takes place. This creates several very delicate and interesting problems. It frequently happens that a very heavy building is to be erected by the side of another already completed. The new building will, of course, settle, and in doing so will work injury to the old one, cracking its walls, destroying the level of its floors, etc. Besides this, the old foundations are not large enough for the new and larger weights.

To overcome this difficulty, arrangements are made to underpin the old wall, and support it temporarily with heavy timbers extending far enough east and west to span the width of the proposed new foundations. While the wall is thus supported the new foundations are put in place, and that portion of the new wall begun which is needed to make, with the old, a composite wall strong enough for all of the work. The old wall, up to this time carried on timbers, is not reconstructed for some time, but instead of the timbers originally used jack screws are substituted (Figure 45).

As the new construction proceeds, the new wall, with its foundations, slowly settles, and to hold the old wall and the building to which it belongs in place, the jack screws supporting it are turned from time to time, becoming slightly lengthened, and thus keeping the former levels undisturbed. This will probably be necessary to continue for a year or more, as the new building will continue to settle for that time. When all settlement has ceased the jack screws are one by one removed, and the space occupied by them filled with brick.

This is simple enough; but sometimes it happens—in this case let us suppose—that the old building adjacent to us is so occupied in the basement that we may not go into it without underpinning, and are thus prevented from using the above device. We cannot rebuild the foundations, yet we must not add to the load they carry. Here comes in one of the architect's best friends, the "cantilever."

Some distance from the old wall, columns are placed which are used as

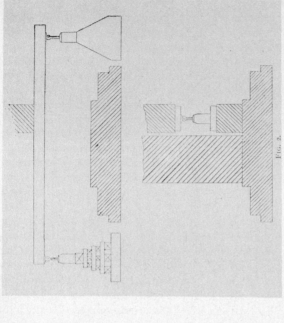

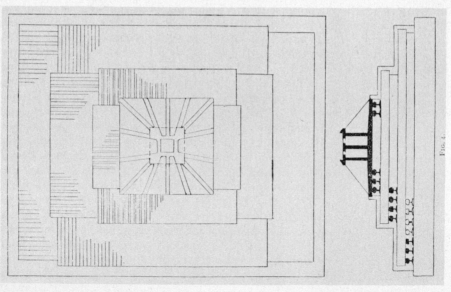

Figure 45. Method of laying new foundations under existing walls, figure 2 from *Inland Architect* 15 (June 1890), p. 69 (courtesy, Burnham Library, Art Institute of Chicago).

Figure 46. Foundation with cast iron "shoe" for columns, figure 4 from *Inland Architect* 15 (June 1890), p. 71 (courtesy, Burnham Library, Art Institute of Chicago).

fulcrums of a lever. Farther away, on the long arm of the lever, another line of columns is placed, and against the old wall still another. Beneath these a foundation has been built, widest next the columns next the wall, and narrowest beneath the columns farthest from it. The columns next to the old wall will carry, on beams connecting them, whatever height of new wall we may require to be added to the old for the completion of our building. A very heavy girder runs beneath these three columns, and you will see by this diagram (Figure 44) that if our calculations be correct, the column A will tend to settle most, the column C least, and the intermediate column B should settle exactly like all columns carrying simple and direct weights. Thus we carry our own new wall from within, and in no way disturb the neighboring building.

When the foundations are completely built, as I have indicated, large cast-iron shoes are put upon them to receive the base of the steel columns and distribute the loads carried by them over a larger area upon the footings (Figure 46). When the steel columns have been placed upon these shoes, and the structure has reached the first floor, the steel or iron beams are all bolted to the columns through wrought-iron brackets, and each beam is bolted to the next, forming a perfectly rigid skeleton of metal.

To guard against all lateral movement from wind pressure or other causes, diagonal braces are carried along the tops of the beams between extreme points of the building, so as to tie the whole structure together like a truss. So strongly may this be done that a section of floor framing might almost be turned on edge and hold itself intact like a bridge truss.

Thus, this great iron skeleton is slowly articulated from story to story, and during this process the flesh and skin begin to grow upon it.

It will not do to wait till the roof framing is done before covering the anatomy of the building with its fire-clay, for here a nice point peculiar to our soil comes in.

The plans of our foundations have necessarily been made for the completed building, and at each stage of the construction the same relationship between the weights of each pier must be as nearly as possible maintained as will ultimately exist in the completed building; otherwise one part will settle lower than another, and needless strain be imposed upon the building. If the soft clay kept its original condition after the building were complete as it had before, the whole structure might resume its levels with completion, though, as just remarked, with considerable strain; but the clay is compressed by the loads placed upon it, and is drained of its water to some extent, thus becoming harder and capable of resisting greater pressure.

Those weights which are last placed upon it do not settle as much as those placed upon it in the beginning. The whole construction of the building should, therefore, develop together.

All that has been written relates to those portions of the building with which the public at large can have but little interest, but which are the inner and significant principle about which every external aspect must arrange itself.

The truest and best forms which this external aspect is to present will be found by a reasonable appreciation of conditions of our civilization, of our social and business life and of our climatic conditions.

And even a slight appreciation of these would seem to make it evident to every thoughtful man in Chicago that all conditions, climatic, atmospheric, commercial and social, demand for this external aspect the simplest and most straightforward expression. Bearing in mind that our building is a business building, we must fully realize what this means. Bearing also in mind—though this, like the other conditions, is not likely to escape us—that dust and soot are the main ingredients of our native air, we must realize what this means. Both point the same way. Every material used to enclose the structure we have seen raised must be, first, of the most enduring kind, and, second, it must be wrought into the simplest forms.

These buildings, standing in the midst of hurrying, busy thousands of men, may not appeal to them through the more subtle means of architectural expression, for such an appeal would be unheeded; and the appeal which is constantly made to unheeding eyes loses in time its power to attract.

They inevitably become an integral part of the machinery of business, and may scarcely ever be fortunate enough to be thoughtfully and leisurely studied by the contemplative mind.

In them there should be carried out the ideas of modern business life: simplicity, stability, breadth, dignity. To lavish upon them a profusion of delicate ornament is worse than useless, for this had better be preserved for the place and hour of contemplation and repose. Rather should they by their mass and proportion convey in some large elemental sense an idea of the great, stable, conserving forces of modern civilization.

Enough has been said to suggest how radically new in type such edifices are, and to cause us to note how essential is the difference between the modern and any of the preceding recognized architectural types.

The cathedral of Cologne, in its structural development, is complete in itself. Its structure and art expression are one. So of the dome of St. Peter's or of any one of the great monuments of the world, except those of the Roman period. With the Romans, constructive methods as related to the ultimate completed building are suggested by those mentioned in this paper, for the Romans built of cheap material the framework of their temples, palaces and bridges, which was afterward covered and decorated with costly marbles and bronzes. Employing unskilled labor in the erection of the structure, and skilled labor only in its decoration, they were compelled to use vast masses of material—much more, generally, than would have been necessary for the same work if scientifically employed.

But in modern instances, such as we have mentioned, the reverse is the case. The utmost economy of material is employed, not a useless pound being admissible.

In the Roman régime, one mind, the architect, must have foreseen the completed building and provided for all of its final adornment in each part of the structure. So with us. But it does not follow that in the most rigid adherence to scientific law we need to lose sight of the broad and artistic features through which our buildings may express themselves.

One result of methods such as I have indicated will be the resolution of our architectural designs into their essential elements. So vital has the underlying structure of these buildings become that it must absolutely dictate the general departure of external forms; and so imperative are all the commercial and constructive demands that all architectural detail employed in expressing them must become modified by them.

Under these conditions we are compelled to work definitely with definite aims, permeating ourselves with the full spirit of the age, that we may give its architecture true art forms.

To other and older types of architecture these new problems are related as the poetry of Darwin's evolution is to other poetry.

They destroy indeed much of the most admirable and inspiring of architectural forms, but they create forms adapted to the expression of new ideas and new aspects of life. Here, vagaries of fashion and temporary fancies should have no influence; here the arbitrary dicta of self-constituted architectural prophets should have no voice. Every one of these problems should be rationally worked out alone, and each should express the character and aims of the people about it.

I do not believe it is possible to exaggerate the importance of the influence which may be exerted for good or evil by these distinctively modern buildings. Hedged about as they are by so many unavoidable conditions, they become either gross and self-asserting shams, untrue both in the material realization of their aims and in their art function as expressions of the deeper spirit of the age; or they are sincere, noble and enduring monuments to the broad and beneficent commerce of the age.

37 J. W. Root, A Few Practical Hints on Design* *c. 1889?*

In this unpublished essay, Root sketches out a more general theory of architecture, less strictly based on the requirements of office blocks. The original manuscript was once in the possession of his sister-in-law, Harriet Monroe, and is now lost.

The art of architecture, moreover, is different from other arts in the largeness of this purely reasonable and (if the word be allowed) explainable side. Not to avail himself of this fact is for the architect a great mistake, for when the client has fully grasped the reasons for that part of a design which can be explained, he is inspired to completer trust for those parts which lie in the realm of the imagination and fancy. Often by such an interview floods of light will be shed upon questions otherwise vague and indeterminate and methods of solving them will be indicated which will have a pertinence and beauty not otherwise attainable. It is not uncommon that an intelligent layman will have a breadth of view in architectural matters which will

*From Harriet Monroe, *John Wellborn Root, A Study of His Life and Work* (Boston and New York, 1896), pp. 64–75.

not be suspected if he be held rigidly to professional interviews. He lacks technical vocabulary; he fears perhaps to express an opinion which from a professional point of view will seem ridiculous; he hesitates to commit himself to what may be out of style. All this is wrong and should be discouraged. His opinions and tastes may be the result of careful study and close observation by a mind at once acute, discriminating and retentive; and, moreover, may have for the architect an especial value because they have been formed without professional prepossessions. The technical and professional point of view in art is not always the truest. Artists are often victims to artificially acquired judgment, when unaided vision in dry light should be the only communication with the mind. How great would be the value to an architect of being able at will to free himself from all the prejudices and theories which in his practice have grown about him, and for an occasional hour see as an intelligent layman may see! This is possible, unfortunately, only at second-hand, but at second-hand it is possible. If, however, it is to be done, care must be taken that for the time being the mind is not swayed by the very professional habit that prevents its own clear sight. Statements will be made, opinions expressed which will be shocking enough to archaeologists and art critics; questions will be asked impossible to answer; the profound student and brilliant designer of the moment before may find himself dangerously near a most unpleasant un-masking. This is as it should be and should not be shirked.

The temptation is almost irresistible often to take refuge in the books, among the Greeks, among the French; to seek cover in the darkness of the middle ages, or concealment in the glitter of the seventeenth century; to quote precedents, and turn to buildings erected by great men. All this is nonsense. Be assured that no reason is good, no answer worth giving that does not spring from the present question and is not inherently connected with it. It is of course very easy to say what men of other times did, but it is not easy to tell whether our conceptions of those men and their surroundings are true to the life, or are pictures painted by ourselves and without models. No building nor architect of this or any other time can be a conclusive precedent until we get a stenographic report of the interviews which were held between the architect and his client, and even this is incomplete without a photograph of both.

It will be seen that this tends directly against the literal use of historic styles. True. But so much the better for the styles as we understand them. A style has never been made by copying, with the loving care of a dry-as-dust, some preceding style. Styles grow by the careful study of all the conditions which lie about each architectural problem, and thus while each will have its distinct differentiation from all others, broad influences of climate, of national habits and institutions will in time create the type, and this is the only style worth considering. This position is reasonable and is susceptible of rational statement. It does not mean the monstrous method, sometimes advocated, which would gather fragments from all ages and build them into one hideous whole. It does not mean the reconciliation in one design of the "chaste beauty of the Greek with the rugged strength of the Egyptian," which is as if nature should essay a combination of the chaste beauty of the gazelle with the rugged strength of the rhinoceros. It means rather to use all that men have done, to use it all intelligently and consistently, with study and the nicest discrimination, and to make sure that the particular thing chosen for the given purpose shall be the best fitted for that purpose—shall in short grow out of it. This is as obvious as to say that a man's exterior form shall be the result of his interior structure, that his skin and hair shall be colored by the climate where he lives; and being thus obvious it becomes the true position to assume in relation to the client. Answers to his questions, corrections of his false, and approval of his right, tastes, estimating the value of his suggestions and the possibility of their realization—all these are possible upon this plane.

Having thus mastered the outer conditions of the problem—its theorem—we pass to its solution. We sit down with the conditions before us. What next? The mind wanders; the question seems barren of interest. How shall we quicken and concentrate the mind—how give interest to the problem? First, saturate ourselves with it; fully realize all of its essential conditions. This may take time, which seems wasted, for meanwhile the design does not seem to grow. But wait: what sort of a town is the house to be in? How wide are the streets it faces? Where do the prevalent winds blow from? How much hot and cold weather has the town? How much rain? Which way is south? How far from the street is the house to stand? Has the town smoky or clear air? What are the native building materials? What is the character of the workmen likely to be employed? Is the occupant of the house a student? a family man? a public man with many friends? one who has many guests? who gives many entertainments? Is he a man fond of display, or one who shirks it and rather prefers the simplicity of "solid comfort"? These and many other questions will suggest themselves, and being answered will, when added to suggestions obtained directly from the client, point out very plainly the general solution of the problem. This assumes that the architect will frankly accept the consequences involved in each answer, and also that he is not burdened by prepossessions so strong as to prevent his acting dispassionately.

Before proceeding with our design, one other point must be carefully weighed, as it will exercise upon the character of the building a very strong influence: what sort of houses is the new house to have for its neighbors? Probably in no country in the world are architects so indifferent to this as in America. Here, if any attention is given to the matter, it is for the purpose of avoiding deference to the neighbors, of making the house as emphatic a contrast as possible. The existing houses are old and quiet? Then the new house must be as spick-and-span and as noisy and offensive as we can make it. The old houses are broad and low? The new house must stand tip-toe to the clouds. The old houses are of stone? The new house must be of brick, and as red as possible. Thus we succeed in compelling every passerby to stop and gaze upon our new house, but this gaze is too often that of baleful fascination, as one finds his eyes riveted by the antics of a drunken man. Any new design should be carefully adjusted to its neighbors. If out of key with them, it becomes invariably impertinent and offensive, be the design as clever as you please.

Assuming now that the architect has been brought into entire sympathy with his client, that he has fully mastered the environments and conditions of his problem, he is prepared for its actual solution. The stage of mental preparation, based as it is upon the previous exchange of ideas between client and adviser, has undoubtedly brought about a tolerably trustworthy scheme of general procedure. We have now to determine more accurately what form our design shall take. It is not probable that any first study will be best, and for this reason it seems a waste of time even to consider the first study until several other sketches of plans and designs shall have been made, differing from each other as widely or as slightly as may be. Then an intelligent comparison becomes possible. To make this first comparison as little prejudiced as possible, it is wise to make each rough study independently, if possible with scarcely the memory of the others, and also (so far as the design is concerned) to make it as rapidly as possible. Thus the impression left upon the mind at the moment of production is less lasting, and the sketches come back to us from their temporary seclusion as if they were the work of another man. They can be criticised therefore without bias, and from among them can be determined more accurately the true path. From this test-sketching come new light and more accurate direction, and the design is ready to take on a growth more nearly like its full development.

Further study will probably bring us to our libraries. Books are dangerous things and need most careful handling. Reference to them will often tend to confuse ideas which before were well defined, and inject others totally irrelevant to the case in hand. In this hour with books, however freely they may have been used at other hours, reject as unworthy of consideration everything, however fascinating, which conflicts with the predetermined plan of procedure, and beware of a single detail which suggests itself as perfectly appropriate for our purpose. Nothing found in a book will add a feather's weight to a really good design if it be bodily transferred, or indeed transferred with anything of literal translation. For this reason the study of the hour should be close and sympathetic, continued until the mind is fully refreshed and inspired by a process precisely similar to that by which it became saturated with preliminary conditions. Then shut the book and do not go back to your design; do something else. After a day or two, find what impressions remain with you and work them out of yourself without reference to the originals. Any impression which remains so vague that reference must be made to the original source before it can be made to assume coherent and approximately satisfactory shape should be thrown aside as worthless. It is undigested food from which no muscle or vitality can be expected, and in the varied constitutions of men some mental foods as often disagree with individuals as physical foods. This fact is so palpable that it often becomes a question not of accident, but of constitution. Some architects can no more digest a bit of thirteenth-century detail than they can digest a nail. The only difference is that they readily learn whether the nail has been digested, while they may not know if the detail has been.

During this time the critical study of the house plans will have been going on; each minutest point will have been discussed, and this not only in relation to the convenience and beauty of the interior, but also in its capabilities of artistic external treatment. The development of the design and of the plan should in all cases go on together; one should never get away from the other. No feature should ever be allowed to form into a plan, about the external treatment of which the architect has not a well defined idea.

By study and sketching, we are now prepared to make a somewhat carefully rendered design of the building as we intend it to be. At this stage of the design we are open to dangers which arise from several causes, different in architecture from other arts, but still dangerous. Several of these are loss of scale; over-application or wrong application of detail, and hence a loss of simplicity; loss of homogeneity. To avoid the loss of scale, it is of course necessary to realize through every means in our power the exact meaning of each part sketched in terms of the executed work; ... and therefore not a single drawing should be made to a scale which has not been mastered.

Over-application of detail will be avoided by similar means as loss of scale; but beyond what may be taught by observation is the simple law that beautiful detail is a precious commodity, not to be prodigally flung away, but to be used with wise discrimination. A broad wall surface should fairly cry out for an ornament before it gets one, and also a moulding or a column. In a drawing every plain surface or moulding seems of much less interest than when built or cut. Nature steps in here, and nature's decorations of sunshine and shadow, her warm glow of ever beautiful colors, varied and enriched by rain and wind, are always lovely, while our decorations often fall short of loveliness. . . . If, however, the mind is surcharged with brilliant inspirations—consistent, truthful, poetic—free rein may be given to it. But do not confuse the operation of the imagination with the operation of the pencil. Loss of simplicity does not necessarily follow when a design is enriched; it follows only when the design is falsely enriched, as when adventitious and impertinent products of ungoverned fancy interfere with the effect of some great and essential part. Adventitious features in a building should, like children, be seen and not heard.

Homogeneity is in these days more difficult to maintain because the prevailing habits of the time have prevented architects from closely following traditions which would compel homogeneity, while no new habits dependent upon the nature of the case have taken their places. Every structure has some few conditions so are beyond all others in importance that in expression all others should be subordinated to them and influenced by them. These conditions may seem at first contradictory, but they can always be reconciled, and rightly considered will impress upon each detail of the design an effect distinct and unavoidable. The whole matter is summed up, as in painting, in the necessity of keeping a true perspective, giving prominence to objects in proportion to their importance. Yet nothing about a house is too small for close attention—for frequent revision and re-study.

[Such points are] sometimes forgotten, not because they are unfamiliar, but because they are so well known.

They are important, but beyond all questions of method in importance lies the inherent character of the architect. Architecture is so noble a profession that to allow its influence to be swayed by ephemeral fashions, to make its creations things lightly considered and cheaply wrought, is the basest of crimes.

38   M. Schuyler, Architecture in Chicago* *1895*

Montgomery Schuyler (1843–1914) was perhaps the major architectural critic of the turn of the twentieth century. Descended from Dutch settlers in the area of Albany, New York, he had studied briefly at Hobart College before writing literary reviews for the New York *World* and then joining the small staff of the *New York Sketch Book of Architecture* during its short life from 1874 through 1876. He served two years as the managing editor of *Harper's Weekly*, 1885–87, where some of his early columns had appeared. In 1891 he began his long association with the *Architectural Record*, which by the time of the First World War became the pre-eminent architectural journal. At first his critical comments focused largely on external features, but his view steadily broadened, being greatly influenced by the writing of Leopold Eidlitz, whom Schuyler admired. In 1892 Schuyler published a collection of his essays, *American Architecture—Studies*, but it was not until 1961 that his impact was properly credited and a more thorough and annotated edition of his essays appeared.[†]

Like Eidlitz, Schuyler believed that good architecture would bring about a fusion of science and art, and hence he was intensely interested in the development of the high-rise office block, particularly its expression as a coherent tall building. Whether or not it had an internal metal frame was not, for Schuyler, a determining factor. He was also keenly aware of the rapid changes taking place in this field of design, as this and the following essay attest. In making a critical assessment of the work of Adler and Sullivan, Schuyler felt it was first necessary to sketch out the background of commercial architecture in Chicago. In this excerpt from that essay, in the *Architectural Record*'s Great American Architects Series, Schuyler quotes a telling passage by Paul Bourget, *Outre-Mer: Notes sur l'Amérique* (Paris, 1894; translation *Outre-Mer: Impressions of America*, New York, 1895), in which the French essayist and journalist is similarly awed by the raw energy of Chicago.

It is impossible fairly to estimate the work of the leading architects of Chicago without some preliminary reference to the conditions of their work. In part, perhaps in the main, these are the same conditions that preside over the evolution of American architecture in general, but some of them are really local, and those of them that are general are applied in Chicago with a peculiar strictness and intensity. It is from this stringency of application that the characteristics of Chicago building come, and that it comes that the individuality of that building is so much more local than it is general that from the first sight in a photograph of a new Chicago building one can "place" it so much more readily than one can assign it to its particular au-

*Montgomery Schuyler, "Architecture in Chicago" (introduction to essay on the work of Adler and Sullivan), *Architectural Record*, Great American Architects Series, number 2 (December 1895), pp. 3–14.

[†]Montgomery Schuyler, *American Architecture and Other Writings*, 2 vols., Eds. W. H. Jordy and R. Coe (Cambridge, Mass., 1961).

thor. Here, more than elsewhere, "the individual withers, and the world is more and more."

Of course, what I have in mind in saying this is "the heart of Chicago," the business quarter, for it is by that that Chicago is characterized, especially in its architecture. Its architectural expressions are twofold only, places of business and places of residence. It would be impossible to mention another great city of which this is so strictly true. It is indeed curious how the composite image of Chicago that remains in one's memory as the sum of his innumerable individual impressions is made up exclusively of the sky-scraper of the city and the dwellings of the suburbs. Not a church enters into it, so as to count, as churches count for so much elsewhere. Scarcely a public building enters into it. . . . Even before the introduction of the "Chicago construction," which first appeared in the Home Insurance building some six years ago, the sky-scrapers were noticeable for two Chicagoan characteristics, their extreme altitude and their strictly utilitarian treatment. Now that the Chicago construction has come to prevail, they are still noteworthy in comparison with the sky-scraper of other towns for these same qualities. And this brings me to remark upon the very great share which the Chicago "business man" has had in the evolution of commercial architecture in Chicago, a share not less important than that of the architects, and not less important for being in the main negative. We all like to hear the intelligent foreigner upon the characteristic manifestations of our national spirit, if he be candid as well as intelligent, to see ourselves as others see us, and it gives me pleasure to quote a very intelligent and a very candid foreigner, M. Paul Bourget, in "Outre Mer," upon the commercial architecture of Chicago, what he says is so true and so well put:

> At one moment you have around you only "buildings." They scale the sky with their eighteen, with their twenty stories. The architect who has built, or rather who has plotted them, has renounced colonnades, mouldings, classical embellishments. He has frankly accepted the condition imposed by the speculator; multiplying as many times as possible the value of the bit of ground at the base in multiplying the supposed offices. It is a problem capable of interesting only an engineer, one would suppose. Nothing of the kind. The simple force of need is such a principle of beauty, and these buildings so conspicuously manifest that need that in contemplating them you experience a singular emotion. The sketch appears here of a new kind of art, an art of democracy, made by the crowd and for the crowd, an art of science in which the certainty of natural laws gives to audacities in appearance the most unbridled the tranquillity of geometrical figures.

It is noteworthy that the observer had seen and described New York before he saw Chicago. The circumstance makes more striking his recognition that it is in Chicago that the type of office building has been most clearly detached and elucidated. One is arrested by the averment that this art, so evidently made "for the crowd," is also made "by the crowd," since a crowd cannot be an artist, one is inclined to say. But there is not only the general consideration that in architecture an artist cannot even produce without the co-operation of his public, and cannot go on producing without being popular. There is the particular consideration that in this strictly utilitarian building the requirements are imposed with a stringency elsewhere unknown in the same degree, and very greatly to the advantage of the architecture. Elsewhere the designer of a business building commonly attempts to persuade or to hoodwink his client into sacrificing something of utility to "art," and when he succeeds, it is commonly perceptible that the sacrifice has been in vain, and that the building would have been better for its artistic purpose if it had been better for its practical purpose. There used to be an absurd story current in New York of how that the owner of two examples of florid classic in cast-iron (the Gilsey Building in lower Broadway and the Gilsey House in upper Broadway they were), exclaimed, when the second was finished, that now he had done enough for art, and henceforth he meant to build as a matter of business. Commercial architecture in Chicago is long past that stage, and that it is so is due rather to the business man than to the architect. In this way and to this extent the architecture is made "by the crowd," is an architecture of the people and by the people as well as for the people. I asked one of the successful architects of Chicago what would happen if the designer of a commercial building sacrificed the practical availableness of one or more of its stories to the assumed exigencies of architecture, as has often been done in New York, and as has been done in several aggravated and conspicuous instances that will readily occur to the reader familiar with recent building there. His answer was suggestive: "Why, the word would be passed and he would never get another to do. No, we never try those tricks on our business men. They are too wide-awake." Another successful architect explained to me his procedure in designing a sky-scraper. "I get from my engineer a statement of the minimum thickness of the steel post and its enclosure of terra cotta. Then I establish the minimum depth of floor beam and the minimum height of the sill from the floor to accommodate what must go between them. These are the data of my design." It is not the question whether the piers would not look better for somewhat more of massiveness, whether the skeleton could not be more "padded round with flesh and fat" to its aesthetic advantage, without too serious an infringement upon its suitableness for its purpose, whether the designer could not make a workable compromise between what it might please him to call his artistic conscience and the duty he owes as the agent and adviser of the owner in directing an investment for the largest possible return. Modern commercial architecture in general, when it is done by artistic designers, is such a compromise. It bears the scars of a conflict, if not between the architect and the client, between the claims of utility and of art, or I should prefer to say between the facts of the case and the notions of the architect. It is only the work of the "architect," the work that nobody looks at twice or thinks of once, or cares to talk about, that evinces a purpose, not indeed to fulfill perfectly the real requirements of the building, but to carry out the "architect's" confused notion of the owner's confused notion of the manner of satisfying those requirements. That is as different a matter as possible from putting the resources of a trained and artistic intelligence absolutely at the service of an employer, and the results are as different as possible. The architects of Chicago are not so radically different as all this from architects elsewhere. They are different on compulsion. They have "frankly accepted the conditions imposed by the speculator," (the word I translate "frankly" is *brutalement,* and I wish that M. Bourget had chosen to say "loyally" instead), because they are really imposed, and there is no getting away from them, if one would win and keep the reputation of a "practical" architect. And mark that the business men who impose these conditions are not the most private-spirited; they are the most public-spirited body of business men of any commercial city in the world. They are willing to make the most generous sacrifices for their city to provide it with ornaments and trophies which shall make it something more than a centre of pig-sticking and grain-handling. They are willing to play the part of Mæcenas to the fine arts, only they insist that they will not play it "during business hours." They are too clear-headed to allow themselves or their architects to confuse their several and distinct capacities of money-makers and Mæcenases. If they allow themselves to be confused upon this point, in the first place they would not have so much money to do their public benefactions withal, and in the second place their commercial architecture would not have the character that in fact it has, and that comes from their insistence upon a rigid adherence to the real requirements of their commercial undertakings. Into that architecture, then, their influence enters as a very potent factor, and, whatever the architect beginning his practice in Chicago with his head full of "classical embellishments" may have thought or said, it enters, as every discerning beholder must now perceive, as a very beneficent factor.

In one respect, and this a respect that more or less affects commercial architecture everywhere, the influence is not beneficial. The architect is too much pressed for time. His client is aware that parsimony is not economy, and is willing to give him all the money that he really needs. He is aware also that mere greediness defeats its own purpose, that to erect a very lofty building on a very restricted site is to increase the comparative cost both of building and of maintenance, and that to occupy with rentable apartments space that is needed for light and air is a very costly proceeding. In all such things he shows a spirit of large and intelligent liberality. But it is especially true of him, what our French critic has noted as a national characteristic, that he cannot spare time. From the hour that the ground for a new building is put at his disposal the work of construction must go on at the highest rate of speed. If the plans are not matured at that moment, they must be executed in their immaturity, or with such ripening only as can be allowed while the work is actually going forward. There is after that no time left for the leisurely correction and completion upon which artistic perfection depends. There is no atmosphere in the world that less resembles "the still air of delightful studies" than that of the heart of Chicago. And so the successful practitioner of architecture in Chicago is primarily an administrator. He absolutely must be that. If he be secondarily an artist, all the better; but in that case he is an artist working under pressure, a condition which is peculiarly abhorrent to the "artistic temperament." All the questions of arrangement of construction and of design which enter into the design of that very complicated organism, the modern office building, are presented at once, with a peremptory demand for an immediate answer. In the answer to them must concur the constructor, the designer and the "practical man." Whether these three are united in one person or distributed among three, the primary and co-ordinating qualification is that of an administrator. "The readiness is all."

A busy practitioner must have his professional apparatus, including his professional library, at his fingers' ends. The irrefutable criticism in the Vicar of Wakefield that "the picture would have been better if the artist had taken more pains," is irrelevant. It is not a question whether the study of another month might not invigorate the masses and chasten the detail. The foundation-plans must be ready as soon as the ground is cleared, and the building must not at any stage wait a day for drawings. Here, it is true, the general uniformity of the problem is a great resource to the designer. An architect who lives by and upon office buildings has always, it is to be presumed, designs adumbrated in his mind—alternative designs, very possibly, for past buildings, rejected as less eligible for the past purpose than the design executed, but more eligible for the future purpose, or designs entirely ideal, drawn from a consideration of the abstract skyscraper. Much of the preliminary and general work of design may thus be done before the commission arrives, much more than if the practice were more varied. But with whatever mitigations there may be of the conditions, the conditions are so especially stringent in Chicago as to make the successes all the more remarkable. And, indeed, it would be worse than idle to find fault with the conditions because, as we have seen, the successes have been won by an absolute loyalty to the conditions, and by the frank abandonment of every architectural convention that comes in conflict with them.

39   M. Schuyler, The Evolution of the Sky-Scraper* *1909*

By the time Schuyler published this piece, the Chicago skyscrapers were far over-reached by New York examples. Indeed, some of the earliest framed buildings in the city already were being demolished to make way for larger towers as urban lots became ever more valuable; the demolition of New York's first metal-framed "sky-scraper" prompted this retrospective.† Several years before, Schuyler had written "The Sky-Scraper Up to Date," for the *Architectural Record* (January–March 1899), but much had happened in the meantime. Schuyler questions what limit, if any, should be placed on the height of the new commercial "Babels." Soon, as he foresaw with the erection of the Singer and Metropolitan towers, the public welfare would be significantly diminished through the creation of the dark befouled street-canyons. In fact, in 1916, in response to a detailed study into building height, the city passed set-

*Montgomery Schuyler, "The Evolution of the Sky-Scraper," *Scribner's Magazine* 46 (September 1909), pp. 257–71. Reprinted in M. Schuyler, *American Architecture . . .* , ed. Jordy and Coe, pp. 419–36.

†The Tower Building, New York City, by Bradford Lee Gilbert, was designed in 1887 and was built in 1888–89 after protracted analysis of the drawings by the New York City building department because of its novel construction.

back legislation requiring the diminution of the upper stages of new office towers. Reproduced here are a selection of the half-tone views by E. C. Peixotto which accompanied the article in *Scribner's Magazine*.

Schuyler asserts that Jenney's Home Insurance Building, Chicago, was of "cage" construction (the outer masonry walls bearing their own weight but no floor loads); he should not be faulted for this, for it was only when the building was demolished in 1931 that it was discovered that the upper wall loads were in fact carried entirely by the internal metal skeleton.[‡]

The occasion of these ensuing remarks is the demolition,—no doubt, when they come to publication, accomplished or plainly impending, already, even while they are making, irrevocably determined,—of "the earliest example of the skeleton construction, in which the entire weight of the walls and floors is borne, and transmitted to the foundations, by a framework of metallic posts and beams." Such is the proclamation which the doomed front of the "Tower Building" at No. 50 Broadway has for some years made, from a bronze tablet, to the passer-by. Whereas in "1888–9," to repeat the date of the inscription, an altitude of eleven stories to a latitude of twenty-one feet and six inches was plainly out of the question, except through the mediation of some unfamiliar and unprecedented mode of construction, twenty years later it is found that the ground of lower Broadway has grown too valuable for so humble an erection. The erection which is projected to occupy the site is of thirty-eight stories. And this later altitude is by no means a "record."

Is there any parallel, in the history of human building, to the rapid and revolutionary process which has raised the building of American towns, within the memory of men who need not be so very old, from a "norm" of five stories to an uncertain and unpredictable height; so high that forty stories are already realized, and fifty are projected by a "conservative" corporation, not as a monument as of Babel, but as a "practical business proposition"? Probably none. Certainly none. No parallel, but a striking prototype. The prototype is to be found in the building of northern France in the early part of the thirteenth century. A Frenchman born in 1175 and surviving in 1250 might have boasted that he had "rocked the cradle" of Gothic architecture, if not quite that he had "followed its hearse." For he had at least lived to see it radically differentiated from the Romanesque which had proceeded it, and, in one or another of its phases, had held sway for near a thousand years. Such a Frenchman might have seen "the Gothic principle" both virtually germinate and variously effloresce, in the great cathedrals of Paris, Chartres, Rheims, and Amiens. If of a critical turn, he might have noted that this wonderful and fruitful development had all come from the application of a single mechanical expedient. "It is this necessity for a stone roof," says Fergusson, "that was the problem to be solved by the architects, and to accomplish which the style took almost all those forms which are so much admired in it." If of a hypercritical turn, our supposititious mediaeval friend might even have noted that the development, wonderful as it was, after all failed really to attain this object. The inwardly ostensible "stone roof" con-

[‡] For the Home Insurance Building see Carl W. Condit, *The Chicago School of Architecture* (Chicago, 1964), 79–87.

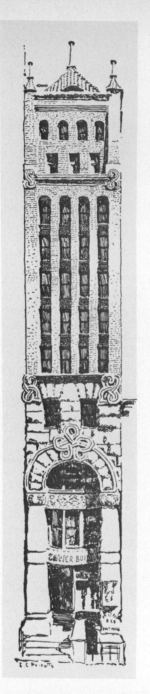

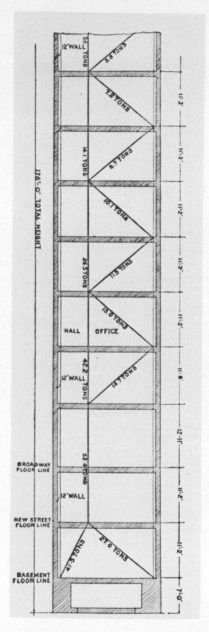

Figure 47. (*left*) Bradford Lee Gilbert, Tower Building, New York, N.Y., 1888–89, from *Scribner's* 46 (September 1909), p. 258. Although neither large nor tall, this was the first metal-framed "skyscraper" in New York City.

Figure 48. Bradford Lee Gilbert, diagram of wind-bracing of Tower Building, from *Scribner's* 46 (September 1909), p. 258.

tinued to be covered with an outwardly ostensible wooden roof. Only such sporadic and unfruitful experiments as the roofs of Seville Cathedral and Roslyn Chapel remain to show that the necessity for a stone roof was felt, as well as the necessity for a stone "ceiling," which was what the historian of architecture really "wished to say."

The even more rapid and bewildering development, under his own eyes, of the even more insistent and conspicuous "sky-scraper" may well strike an elderly American who has turned the first corner of the twentieth century, as the earlier development might have struck the Frenchman who had turned the first corner of the thirteenth. Not at all that the sky-scraper has given evidence of architectural achievements comparable, in their probable interest for posterity, with those of the builders of the mighty minsters. But the beginnings of the later development are no humbler and no less respectable than the beginnings of the earlier. To superpose stories so as to make two tiers of tenants "grow" where only one grew before is as respectable and dignified a motive for architecture as to cover a church with a stone ceiling which, after all, is not a roof. The American observer, if at all of a cynical turn, might say that the ultimate motive of the modern structure was as symptomatic of the period as that of the mediaeval, that these "skeletons" of our building, after the veneer of masonry had fallen from them, and they were left to assert themselves in their original crudity and starkness, before returning altogether to oxide of iron, might still be, in the majestic Ruskinian phrase, "the only witnesses that remained to us of the faith and fear of nations," the faith in the dollar toward which they so plainly aspired, the fear of "the hell of not making money." "Commodity," in the crowded centres of great cities, is as strikingly subserved by these towering structures as comity is defied. And the wonder why they were not devised and built before only grows on study. Paxton's Crystal Palace of 1851, only fill some of its panels with baked clay instead of glass, was already an example of the "skeleton construction." The Tour Eiffel of 1887, only close it in with opaque panelling and increase its provision of "ascenseurs," would be a negotiable "sky-scraper," and even the Saul among the actual, though not among the projected, sky-scrapers. At least, there existed at the date of its erection no structure which so completely fulfilled the current American definition. Nay, there stood in "The Swamp," on Manhattan Island, from 1856 to 1907, a "shot-tower" which was essentially an example of the skeleton construction, that is to say, a building of many stages in which a structural skeleton of metal sustained panels of brickwork which concealed and sheltered its inmates and their operations.

Be that as it may, it is certain that the earliest and the most indispensable of the factors which have enabled the construction of these mighty monsters was the "passenger elevator," and that this was brought into use during the sixties, its first appearance in New York being in the Fifth Avenue Hotel, just lately demolished after a life of close upon half a century. It was at about the same time introduced into the Astor House, then already a generation old. So obvious was the utility of this device that the wonder again is that it had not been brought into practice long before. "Hoists" are, of course, as old as the Dutch warehouses, of which the picturesqueness is enhanced by the projecting cranes that worked the hoists, doubtless as old as

Archimedes. But hotels, even when the Fifth Avenue was built, were conditioned in altitude as were all other buildings not exclusively monumental, by the powers of ascension of the unassisted human leg. Five stories was the maximum for commercial buildings, except that an attical sixth might be added for the discommodation of the janitor, whose name was Hobson, and who had to go where he was sent, which, naturally, was where no "paying guest" could be induced to go. He and his may have taken their outlook on life from slits or bull's-eyes just under the roof. In the cases of hotels, the sixth story was assigned to servants and store-rooms. Tenants or inmates could not be induced to climb more than four flights of stairs, and grumbled grievously, in the case of inmates of hotels, and accused the hotel clerk of perfidy, when they had to climb so many. A device which would make all the floors, even of a five-story hotel, equally accessible, and so equally desirable, was a device very sure of immediate adoption, so sure that the only wonder was that the supply of it should so have lagged behind the demand. The beginnings of the elevator were, it is quite true, the beginnings also of what, in their earlier stages, were known as the "elevator buildings." But this development was hidden alike from the owners and keepers of hotels, from their architects, and from the mechanics who set themselves to supply the obvious and clamant demand. It was not expedition, but only relief, that the hotel guests, relegated to the fifth floor, demanded, and that the progress of invention supplied. And, "because of their importunity," the hotel keeper and his visible vice-gerent, the hotel clerk, entertained the proposals of the mechanic who undertook to make the fifth story as desirable as the second. The transit of the "plunger" elevator which met the prayer was by no means rapid. Ascending on a slow artesian screw, the thread of which fitted a groove embedded in the car, the aged or infirm or fatigued, or even only lazy occupants of the cage were easily distanced by the circumambient athletes who continued to prefer the enclosing staircase. The present reminiscent remembers the pace of his ascent in his first ascenseur, that of the Revere House in Boston, in the early seventies. As Stevenson says about the progress of his donkey in the Cevennes, "What that pace was, there is no word mean enough to describe." But the artesian, aspiring, spiralizing thing was at least safe, being painfully hoisted by means of a solid metallic post which sank underground as far as the car ascended above. How singular to learn that the "plunger type" is not only still in use, but, in some of the latest sky-scrapers where "time is of the essence," has been chosen in place of the arrangement of ropes and pulleys which seem to promise so much more speed at the price of so much more danger!

To equalize the desirableness of rooms on the fifth floor with that of rooms on the second remained the humble office of the elevator for nearly or quite a decade. Such a creature of habit is man, and perhaps particularly mechanical man, that, throughout that decade, it did not occur to anybody that the new appliance might enable the construction of taller buildings. The first building in which this discovery was utilized in design was the Equitable Building on Broadway, since remodelled, it is true, and now threatened with demolition in favor of a more aspiring successor, but even in its first estate, as projected in 1869, attaining seven stories of offices for rental instead of the theretofore Procrustean five. The addition of two stories now

Figure 49. Richard Morris Hunt, *Tribune* Building, New York, N.Y., 1873–76, enlarged with additional upper floors, 1905; in the background, left, is the *World* Building, 1889–90, by George B. Post; from *Scribner's* 46 (September 1909), p. 259.

seems timid and tentative enough; then doubtless it seemed audaciously venturesome. The controlling spirit of the corporation, Henry B. Hyde, was not the man to be deterred from what to him promised profit by lack of precedent. From the first he foresaw the prospects of the higher vertical extension of his building. Mr. George B. Post, though not the designer of the original as he was of the reconstructed Equitable, yet sustained some consultative relation to its construction. Before it was completed he made, for one of the suites in the additional stories, an offer based on and equalling the highest rents then paid on Broadway for the like accommodations. Mr. Hyde tranquilly doubled the amount of the offer, and the tenant acquiesced, retaining the offices until he sold out his lease for a substantial advance even upon the unprecedented rental he had agreed to pay. Of course, such an object-lesson as this in the advantages of elevator buildings was not thrown away upon the commercial community. Before the Equitable was completed, the Tribune Building and the Western Union Building were projected and under way; much more visibly than the Equitable the products of the elevator. For, in the older building, the stories were so grouped in pairs as to increase the "scale" and to diminish their apparent number, whereas in each of the later two its nine or ten stories stood confessed. Each, by the way, has since been reconstructed by vertical extension; the Tribune Building by a superstructure merely repeating the substructure; the Western Union by a superaddition paying scant respect to the beginnings. Yet it was in their original estate, and with the altitude since so far outgrown, that Professor Huxley found them the most conspicuous objects on Manhattan Island, as he neared it in 1875, and congratulated his hosts that these monuments of mere utility should be thus distinguished, instead of the castle or the cathedral which he would have been apt to find dominating a European town.[1]

A certain timidity accompanied these tentatives, bold as they looked to the wayfaring man, who saw the commercial sky-line suddenly lifted to nearly twice its previous and normal height. The real-estate speculator who puts his speculations into practice is slow to push his "premises" to their logical conclusions. When all the cells of the new honeycomb were found to be tenantable and rentable, the successors naturally bettered the instruction of the pioneer, and "built to the limit."

The limit, the limit of altitude, was none the less fixed, though the level of the fixity was still subject to some dispute, and was admitted to vary with circumstances. "It is looked out for," says the German proverb, "that the trees shall not grow into the sky." It was looked out for that the tall buildings of the seventies and the early eighties should not scrape the sky. The restraining condition, before the introduction of the passenger elevator, had been, as we have pointed out, the powers of ascension of the human leg. Five stories had been found to be the maximum beyond which no tenant would pay rent, and even to which no "paying guest" would ascend without grumblings and reluctations. After the introduction of the passenger elevator the restraining condition was as real, though not, perhaps, so definite. It was the necessity of thickening the walls as they arose, and of occupying more of

[1] Leonard Huxley, *Life and Letters of Thomas Henry Huxley* (New York, 1900), 1:494.—ED.

the total area with the points of support. With the points of support, and with the increasing spaces that must, with an increase of altitude, be reserved for the elevators themselves. But the necessity of thickening the walls and the partitions was the main limiting condition. And also, it is to be borne in mind, while the interior horizontal divisions, the floors, might be of brick arches, turned between beams of rolled iron, yet it was assumed that, for the vertical divisions, the partitions, actual masonry was required. The necessity of making these new and towering structures more securely fireproof was, of course, recognized as an indispensable condition. And the chief lesson of the great fires of Chicago, in 1871, and of Boston, in 1872, was held to be that exposed metal uprights were not to be trusted in a great conflagration.

You see how the thickening of outer and inner walls made necessary by this enormous burden of interior construction operated as an automatic restriction upon altitude, how it provided that the sky-scrapers should not grow into the sky. For more than a decade Necessity directed the efforts of her offspring, Invention, to lightening the load. The rolled iron beams continued to be the framing of the floors. But the brick arches that had been turned between them were replaced by hollow blocks of terra-cotta. Already, in that pioneer, the Tribune Building, "terra-cotta arches" were specified, and constituted one of the novelties of the construction. But even from these it was a long stride to the present accepted construction of arches of hollow tile, with horizontal surfaces above for the reception of the floors, and below for the reception of the ceilings. Other inventors were meanwhile laboring diligently at "fireproofing" the iron columns with envelopes of baked clay, so that their lesser bulk and weight might be substituted for the cumbrous, costly, and slowly constructible piers in brickwork. The result of these labors was that the limit of practicable altitude in commercial buildings rose, within a decade, from the nine stories of the Tribune Building, of which one or two, by the way, were added during the construction, and the ten and a half of the Western Union, of which, however, the upper three were contained in the sharply diminishing wedge roof which originally crowned the edifice—to twelve stories, to thirteen, to fourteen, in such cases as that of the Monadnock, in Chicago, to sixteen; from once and a half the level of the ancient sky-line of lower New York to more than twice, to almost three times, that height.

But, in the matter of sky-scrapers, it was not the first but the last step which has brought with it the most perplexing civic problems to which the new building has given rise. Looking back, it seems only strange, not that the step should have been taken, but that it should so long have been delayed. The gestation of Necessity seems to have been singularly protracted. For, logically, if you can protect an interior framework of metal against the elements—the elements being in this case Air, in the form of wind, and Fire—so can you the outer framework. There is no more compulsion to build a real wall of costly, and still more of space-consuming, masonry in the one case than in the other. Yet our constructors were quite a decade in taking that final and obvious step. It was at last the legitimate offspring of necessity. Early in the eighties, to be sure, Mr. Post, in the interior court of the Produce Exchange, had produced an example not only of the "cage" construction, but of the "skeleton" construction, which is not quite the same thing,

Figure 50. Burnham & Root, Monadnock Building, Chicago, Ill., 1884–85, 1889–92, from *Scribner's* 46 (September 1909), p. 260.

though the terms are often used interchangeably by architects and engineers. In the cage construction the walls still carry themselves, though they carry nothing else, a metallic frame alongside of them, or embedded in them, taking from them the burden of the interior construction. It is this latter construction, a core of metal embedded in the masonry of the outer piers, which was first fully exemplified in Mr. Jenney's design for the Home Fire Insurance Company, erected in Chicago in 1884, while in the earlier court of the Produce Exchange, considered as a separate building, the "skeleton" construction had already arrived. Not long after the Chicago example, if, indeed, not rather before, Mr. Buffington, of Minneapolis, had produced a "project" which startled the members of his profession, for a building of twenty-eight stories, under a patent of his own for an "Iron Building Construction," which "consists of a continuous skeleton of iron, commencing on the iron footings and continuing of iron and steel to the full height." This project, however, remains on paper. But there never was a more legitimate birth of "Necessity" than the Tower Building, now doomed. The architect, Mr. Bradford L. Gilbert, found himself confronted with the imperious necessity, in 1888, of erecting a building as high as would be constructible and rentable, on a Broadway frontage of twenty-one feet and a half, by a depth of over a hundred feet, giving access to a considerably wider building at the rear. According to the regulations of the Building Department, such a building, erected with self-sustaining outer walls of masonry, even if the whole weight of floors and partitions had been assigned to an auxiliary construction of metal, would have been narrowed to a mere corridor and unavailable for rental. It was a Gordian knot that simply had to be cut, and the cutting was the proposal to abolish the walls altogether. Naturally, so drastic a solution was looked upon askance by the authorities, but the permit was at last issued. Columbus had shown how the egg could be stood on end.

Of course the Columbuli rushed in at that demonstration conspicuously made in the outer front of a building on Broadway. It ought to be explained that the demonstration nearly coincided with a still further lightening of the interior construction by reason of the popularization of the Bessemer process. It was, in truth, this change in the interior fireproof construction, rather a cheapening than a lightening. The most recent form of floor, with flat arches of hollow tile turned between steel beams, has, it seems, no very marked advantage in weight over the older brick arch turned between beams of wrought iron. Its advantages are that it "dries out" far quicker, that it presents a flat under surface to the plasterer, and particularly that it is far cheaper. The steel beams can now be furnished cheaper than in the early days [when] iron could be had cast, not to say wrought. Already, in the Home Life Building in Chicago, there was an additional record to that of the scheme of construction, being the incorporation into the structure, by Mr. Carnegie's concern, of a specimen steel beam or two, though rather as a trophy of what had been accomplished than as a "practical business proposition." But it was not long before the proposition became grimly practical. The new and cheapened alembication of iron saved a considerable fraction of the cost of fireproof building. Put that saving into terms of altitude, and you will see what a vertical extension it invited and made possible.

With these advances and object-lessons the limit was, in truth, re-

Figure 51. (*left*) Louis H. Sullivan, Condict-Bayard Building, New York, N.Y., 1897–98, from *Scribner's* 46 (September 1909), p. 264.

Figure 52. Ernest Flagg, Singer Building (561 Broadway), New York, N.Y., 1902–04, with a metal and glass front, from *Scribner's* 46 (September 1909), p. 268. Two years later Flagg began work on the far larger Beaux-Arts baroque Singer Tower Building, 1906–08.

moved. One no longer perceives how "es ist dafür gesorgt"[2] that the sky-scrapers should not scrape the sky. What, if any, is the limit of the new commercial Babels? As many architects engineers, "promoters," as you may consult to-day, "tot sententiae." It is true that, as thirty years ago the proportion of total area to be taken up with your enclosing and subdividing walls seemed to form a limit, so you will now find those who place the limit in the proportion of area necessary to be reserved for the elevators themselves which primarily enable the lofty construction. But those who compare the area and the altitude of the Singer Tower, or the Metropolitan Life Tower, those strictly utilitarian erections which tower so far above all the erections of man that have a monumental purpose, the Eiffel alone excepted, and who consider the "practical" projects that threaten to overtop even that, will hesitate to find any effective limitation in this indefinite ratio. The well-meant efforts to fix a limit by legislation to the altitudes which are converting the slits of street between them into Cimmerian and wind-swept ravines have thus far turned out to be either chimerical or futile and ridiculous. They have also the misfortune of being plausibly, however invidiously, regarded as urged in the interest of those who have already "improved" their landholdings in the commercial quarters of the great cities by building sky-scrapers, and whose pretence of being "affected by a public interest" in opposing the building of other sky-scrapers, is ridiculed by those who have not yet "improved," and who desire to substitute competition for monopoly. Their attitude has already been likened, in print, to the attitude of the British rector, according to *Punch's* British agriculturist: "Pa'sson, 'e gets in 'is own hay, then 'e claps on the prayer for rain." Apparently it must be left to that future, not so far off, in which the multiplication and magnification of the sky-scrapers will become plainly incompatible with the well-being of the communities in which individual interest is permitted to override public interest, to devise some effectual limitation or restriction.

Meanwhile, it is to be noted that, architecturally, the skeleton construction has by no means "found itself." It was not to be expected that a new architectural type should be soon evolved from the exposition of a construction of which, as we have seen, concealment, by means of a "protective envelope," is of the essence. That the sky-scraper is essentially a frame building, not an agglutination of masonry, is, I was about to say, a manifest truth. But it is only during construction that it is manifest. When the building is "closed in," when the panels of masonry that fill up the frames of metal are in place, it is manifest no longer. Efforts toward manifesting it have indeed been made, in such hopeful experiments as the Guaranty Building in New York, and the Singer Building, by no means to be confounded with that one of the same name and in the same city which wears the "record" tower. But upon the whole it is not an encouraging reflection how much less the skeleton construction has done toward the establishment of an architectural type, toward the creation of an architectural organism, than was done in the transitional tall buildings, when, of the coefficients that have gone to produce the extreme sky-scraper, the passenger elevator was the only one in full force and effect. In those transitional buildings, when walls were still walls, the

[2] "It is arranged."

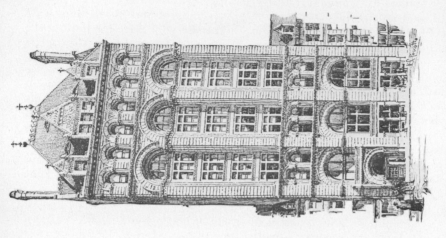

Figure 54. George Browne Post, Union Trust Building, New York, N.Y., 1889–90, from *Scribner's* 46 (September 1909), p. 262.

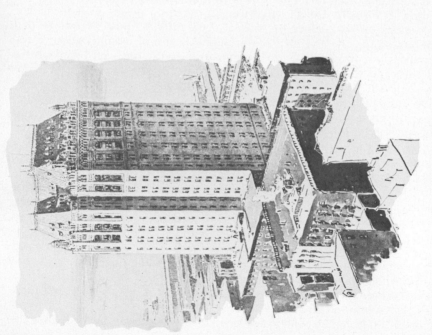

Figure 53. Cass Gilbert, West Street Building, New York, N.Y., 1905, from *Scribner's* 46 (September 1909), p. 265.

effect of depth and mass inhered in the thickness of the wall, requiring only artistic modelling and modification to elicit and emphasize its impressiveness. In the later development, the smooth expanse of wall, broken only by shallow openings, with a mimimum of what is technically and happily called "reveal," is expressionless, the more that the frame is hidden that would give it the beginning of expressiveness. The architect who would give his wall surface expression comparable to that of his prototypes of real masonry is driven to project his wall for the very purpose of withdrawing it again. True, he may crown it with a factitious and more or less fictitious feature, like the beetling tower of the Times Building, or the pinnacled diadem of the West Street building, which the uninteresting building beneath lifts into the empyrean to become the cynosure of a justified admiration. But it were too much to say that he has succeeded in realizing in his skeletons such an impressiveness of expressiveness as belongs to the best of the transitional buildings, to the front of the Union Trust in Broadway, to the corniced tower of the Ames Building in Boston, to the towering pylons of the Monadnock in Chicago.

40   J.-A. Guadet, Elements and Theories of Architecture* *1901*

In addition to the moralizations of Ruskin and the rationalist theories of E. E. Viollet-le-Duc, the third major European influence on American architects at the turn of the nineteenth century was the teaching of the École des Beaux-Arts, in Paris. Many aspiring American architects went to Paris after Richard Morris Hunt, and scores more who studied at home were taught by French graduates of the École brought over to head design studios in American architectural schools. The École method of design was pervasive, influencing even the work of Louis Sullivan.[†] Design at the École was taught in the individual ateliers, while theory was propounded in the classroom; eventually, at the end of the century, this body of theory was codified by Julien-Azaïs Guadet (1834–1908) in four massive volumes, which, in their chatty style, presented his actual lectures. Guadet's work supplanted the six volumes of Jacques-François Blondel's *Cour d'architecture* . . . (Paris, 1771–77). Although Gua-

*Julien Guadet, *Éléments et théories de l'architecture*, 4 vols. (Paris, 1901–04), pp. 95–103; 117–36. Trans. L. M. Roth and Jean-François Blassel. The reason Guadet's expansive treatise has not been fully translated has been due partly to its size and also to the appearance of several similar works: John V. Van Pelt, *A Discussion of Composition* (New York, 1902); John F. Harbeson, *The Study of Architectural Design* (New York, 1926); and Nathaniel C. Curtis, *Architectural Composition* (Cleveland, 1923).

†See John Burchard and Albert Bush-Brown, *The Architecture of America: A Social and Cultural History* (Boston, 1961), p. 276; and Turpin Bannister, *The Architect at Mid-Century* (New York, 1954), 93–104 ff.

det's teaching came at the end of the century, from 1894 until his death, what he presented summed up the principles as they had been taught him during the 1860s and so epitomized design theory at the École that his work became a veritable bible at the École itself and at schools worldwide.

Guadet had been a student in the atelier of Henri Labrouste and then Louis-Jules André; he won the *Premier Grand Prix de Rome* in 1864, subsequently working in Rome on a detailed restoration of the axially planned Forum of Trajan. He conducted a series of ateliers upon his return to Paris in 1868, being appointed to teach theory in 1894. Among his most important pupils was Auguste Perret. Guadet adhered to the traditional view of the school that "in architecture the first studies ought to be essentially classic," although neither he nor the school taught one style (*Elements* 1:82). Vitally important was the axis, "the key of a design and . . . the key to the composition," so that "in an architectural design it is necessary to proceed before all by means of axes" (*Elements* 1:40—41). Nevertheless, he believed symmetry had to be tempered with variety (*Elements* 1:28).

These short passages can only suggest the scope of Guadet's extensive treatise; École instruction in design was far more complex and subtle than can be sketched here.‡ Yet some of the basic concepts bear discussion since the terms used at the École require explanation when translated into English. At the very outset of a design problem, students were expected to develop a *parti* (from *prendre parti*, "to make a decision")—to seize upon a basic conceptual idea out of which the building and all its constituent elements could be developed. Usually designs were for public buildings, thus forcing students to learn how to analyze utilitarian functions and, even more, how to organize circulation. Good plans were those with *point*, or focus on a dominant central volume around which ancillary spaces were disposed hierarchically. The *marche* of such plans was thus clear, with carefully organized—one might say orchestrated—sequences of space, a *promenade architecturale*, leading one through the building with logical inevitability.

CHAPTER II. GUIDING PRINCIPLES

Summary—Emancipation from numerical formulae; beauty in architecture and its identification with truth; method of architectural composition, from the ensemble to details, the architectural program; siting, the building site, position, climate; truth of construction expressed by architecture; artistic lies; physical stability and the appearance of stability.

I will now summarize in a word my opening lecture; I have endeavored to show you the full and grand extent of your studies. If you came away from that session with lifted spirit, ambitious thought, I will not have wasted my time.

Today I propose to present to you—as far as possible—the general principles which should always guide your studies. I wish you to see for yourselves the unity of your studies otherwise so diverse in appearance. To-

‡See Donald D. Egbert, *The Beaux-Arts Tradition in French Architecture* (Princeton, 1980); and David Van Zanten, "Architectural Composition at the École des Beaux-Arts," in *The Architecture of the École des Beaux-Arts*, ed. Arthur Drexler (New York, 1977), pp. 111–324.

day you work on sketches for a church, tomorrow a theater; your programs are sometimes rigorous, sometimes mundane; your building sites tightly restricted in a city or open and airy in the country. This diversity is necessary to develop in you suppleness and ingenuity, but beyond the studies of the present hour or day, there are higher and more permanent studies; study your art, by means of all these opportunities; study yourselves. This is the true end and culmination of your work; it is the realm of the principles of which I was speaking; these will be your guide, your safeguard, your light.

To begin with, so as to prepare our path, let us start with some background.

To be sure—and I need not tell you this—I am not an enemy of the ancient orders, whether they be three, four, or even five. But I am always shocked at putting these ancient orders at the starting point of the course of study, when the student is as yet incapable of comprehending them, above all by those who seek in them a form. A form, that is an expression, is not a conception. I will show you, I hope, that the orders are better than their annotators, and—if you will permit me to say so—they are better than the recipes into which they have been turned. I cannot see in the orders a pivotal importance for architecture nor a basis of design.

For more than two centuries, the study of architecture has been subjected to a particular tyranny. While the Renaissance, in its great elevation of the human spirit, renewed philosophy, literature, science, the arts, and generated admiration and enthusiasm for the great monuments of antiquity, it admired them uncritically and absolutely. Still it did not renounce itself; it drew its inspiration from antiquity, but it remained the Renaissance nonetheless, the springtime of history, full of vigor and so untrammeled that even in attempting to copy there was imprinted in its masterworks the spirit of its own time and a hardy independence. But it had its pedants who wished to rediscover the theory underlying the wonders they admired; they examined the ruins, but unfortunately—and I say this quite frankly—they relied too much on the baneful Vitruvius.

Vitruvius, who wrote with decided mediocrity, and was probably a mediocre architect (if indeed he was one at all), collected more or less approximately the rules of Greek architecture in a very disputable book. Having lived at the virtual beginning of this art, he is to the origin of architecture what the early rhetoriticians are to the great orators, or the Sophists to the great philosophers. But, among ancient architectural writers only his work survives, and critical writing had not yet then developed. The sixteenth century took his word, as they believed then everything that had been written in Latin; and the authors of the Renaissance—Alberti, Vignola, Palladio, Philibert Delorme, all great artists—followed him in taking a mathematical view of architecture; nevertheless the *spirit* of the Renaissance remained free despite everything, and the art of the period was superior to the theory being taught.

But much later, under the aged Louis XIV, when the great thinkers of the first half of the seventeenth century had disappeared, the French spirit was transformed, a proud independence gave way to superstition in authority, narrow devotion to rules, and the cult of despotism. And in architecture, too, it was more desired to obey than to comprehend. There arose a curious deliberation within the Royal Academy of Architecture (only just barely founded) which proclaimed the magistracy of Vitruvius, and made him something of a father of the Church-artistic. Consequently, his theories became quasi-royal, and the triumph of the Module was nearly an article of faith. The Module, or controversies concerning the Module, took precedence in teaching, and, improbably, Number became sovereign in the realm of art. Despite the inextinguishable independence of true artists of all time, despite the temporary renaissance and brilliance of [Jacques Ange] Gabriel and his imitators, the rule of Number became ever more tyrannical until very recent times. Even today there are those who believe architecture is a mathematical art, a codex of rigid mathematical formulae.

Enough. Architecture is not a numerical science, and if it were necessary to prove it, I would do so with a single word: art. Otherwise it should not be taught here! On the contrary, I am going to demonstrate that a subtle understanding of proportions is simply the power to perceive their countless nuances. This power not only frees the artist, it can bring distinction or become a pitfall, but it is the pre-requisite glorious triumph.

I will speak about the ancient orders, and with respect and admiration, but I will do so at the right time and in the right place. The architects who built the first colonnades—undoubtedly a bold move—had built walls before, with doors and windows. Even if these elements were later influenced by the study of orders, it nevertheless remains true that this study could only have followed their existence. Here is the logical way: to teach the orders, first one teaches images; to teach the wall, first one teaches reality.

Let me return to principles.

Science has axioms; art has principles. Both are the basis of study. Architecture has the most rigorous principles of all art, but principles, like axioms, are proven only by the enduring superiority of the works which have most faithfully abided by them. Great artistic periods have been created by the invariable compliance of their works to principles. Those periods deserve the noble name of classical; their works are worthy of meditation and study, and their eloquent examples convey to us the very consciousness of art through time.

Principles are not restrictions, they are a light; they also enoble art; they give sustenance and encouragement to artists. Although it is always true, the more you study, the more you are convinced of it. It is doubly true because you are presently studying. Later your own personality or impinging necessities may lead you to yield, to compromise, but during your studies and in your projects these principles are inviolable.

Let us examine together the principles that shall guide you, both in your first attempts and in your advanced studies.

Beauty, said Plato in his magnificent definition, is the splendor of truth. Art is the means given to man to create beauty; thus, art is the pursuit of beauty in and through truth.

For the arts of imitation, truth lies in nature; for the arts of creation, architecture especially, truth is harder to define; yet personally I will do it in one word—conscience. For the painter or sculptor, truth lies in the external world; in our case it dwells within ourselves.

It is within ourselves, but we must learn to question ourselves fairly. Seek this inner and deep truth, this truth of conscience. You will thus protect yourselves from the contagion of fleeting successes, from the tyranny of fashions, from the constraints of pastiche, from the mirage of irrational whims.

Moreover, you will have secure guides, provided that you have the will to follow them. I will attempt to demonstrate them to you.

The writers of antiquity identified three divisions in the work of an architect:

Disposition—or what we call composition.

Proportion—that is to say, study.

Construction—the scientific control of studies and, ultimately, realization of the building.

Composition cannot be taught; one learns it through multiple trials, by example, through advice, and by one's own experience building on that of others.

Moreover, although an eminent artist can be more or less confident of his ability to make studies, daily luck still plays an important part in composition. He who discovered something today might not have found anything yesterday on the same subject, nor will he necessarily find anything tomorrow.

But remember this well, for it is the very reward of study: this bold and fleeting idea offers itself only to strong people; and if it comes to you, once you have prepared yourself by good and earnest studying, you will know how to welcome it and take advantage of it; you will be able to compose. If it miraculously presents itself to an unlearned person, he will let it escape or torture it without result.

Thus, to compose one needs the idea (which may be luck); one needs the confidence gained by making studies, by putting the idea to work.

Rarely will this idea result from a deliberate piling-up of logically derived elements; more often it will be a synthesis, springing suddenly complete in your mind. This mode of creation, contradicting the methods and theories of traditional logic, denying Bacon and Descartes, is intuition—the very genesis of artistic ideas. This phenomenon will remain the same whether the subjects are limited or immense in scope.

Indeed, in the more general program you will first leave out details to outline two, three, four, or maybe five main categories of varying importance; you will understand the proportional relationships. Which element will occupy the preponderant position, to which one will the largest or smallest area be devoted? These questions require considering the program and understanding its requirements and purpose. Then, moving from the whole to the parts, from the building to its details, you will progress easily, provided that your main starting point [the *parti*] is a sensible one, especially if it was *found*. If necessary you will set aside for later study many details belonging to the composition, as long as it is consistent and provides a favorable framework.

I do not mean at all to leave out reasoning and criticism; they will come in their turn, when later you examine your design. After imagining, you have to learn how to judge your imagination.

In your compositions you will be guided initially by accurate fidelity to the program. The program ought not to be the architect's task; the roles should already be clearly allotted. The architect is an artist able to translate a program into form, but it is not up to him to decide whether the client wants one or several bedrooms, or whether he needs stables and storage, etc. (I am choosing from well-known examples.) In reality the architect often does not get any program, and many of our most extensive buildings have been built without any program at all. This is very unfortunate, and do you know the reason why? Three times out of four, clients and managers do not know what they want. However, it should be them who know, not us.

At least this does not happen here. You will be given programs. I suppose they are well made; I should believe so. It is up to you to learn to read them well.

In a program you are given a list of functions; their relationships are sketched, but neither their combination nor their relative importance are suggested. These are part of your task. The program should not impose solutions. I have never understood that kind of specificity. One might as well be holding your hand. The program leaves you free to choose your way, but you should understand clearly what is expected of you; you will have to attain a proper understanding of the relative importance of the different parts. It may happen that in essence a single word will define the crux of the scheme, whereas it will take a whole paragraph to detail trifling outbuildings. Read the program with intelligence and common sense.

But there is more to it. There is also the relationship between the specific immediate program and all such programs—to the type. You easily tend to exaggerate, and one sees among your competition projects law-courts designed at the scale of Saint Peter's, Rome—a mistake in proportion and in taste. There are large programs, medium ones, and small ones; choose the appropriate measure, for it is the only way you will get appropriate variety, that is, character.

The program also indicates elements essential to the composition—location and site. Architecture has many domains: cities with a whole range of sites; the country side with its broad horizon and surroundings; the seaside; the mountains—a variety of latitudes even within France itself.

In a city, Paris for example, although it is not always true, monuments are generally located on monumental sites. It is common sense that a program for a Maritime Ministry, for instance, will remain the same wherever it is in the city. Yet a Maritime Ministry will differ depending on whether it is designed for a Place de la Concorde or for a common street. The Panthéon would probably have been completely different had it not been put atop Ste.-Genevieve hill; nobody would ever design a Cour des Comptes in conjunction with the old Palais d'Orsay if the views of the Seine and the Tuileries were not there. Yet Paris is level. If you were living in a city built in a natural amphitheater, such as Genoa, you would be able to see exactly what you see in the work of Gautier; every program receiving in its turn an original solution based on its particular situation in its city.

One should sense in your compositions for the country the exploitation of views and natural ventilation. One side is always more attractive than the others, and it should be evident that the plan of any rural abode is composed with careful attention to the preferred horizon as a priority.

If the site is steeply sloping, this attention to the view, combined with construction requirements, dictates the composition. Indeed, if you need extensive outbuildings in symmetrical arrangements, you will be able to realize them only in the direction of the horizontals of the plan, that is in the direction of the site contours, unless you resort to using enormous bases or formidable excavations or embankments. . . .

CHAPTER III. THE MAJOR RULES OF COMPOSITION

Summary—Areas of utility and circulation; economy in composition; lighting and ventilation; easy drainage of water, determination of the importance of the parts of a building program in regards to the plan as a whole; sacrifices; utilitarian plans, beautiful plans; symmetry; what is meant by a beautiful plan; the picturesque; variety; character; character and diversity; tradition; the action of society and the state on the architecture of every period.

Let us come somewhat closer to the necessities of composition. In each building program, if it is complex, there are two distinct parts—first of all what we call utilitarian areas, then those necessary for circulation or communication. In order to make this a little less abstract, let us take a familiar example, the house; let us take, if you wish, the plan of a great *hôtel* of the 18th century [he illustrates this with the plan of the Hôtel de Salm, Paris, 1782–86, by Pierre Rousseau].

The utilitarian areas are all those parts in which we live, that we enjoy, or are otherwise required. We build to have living rooms, salons, dining rooms, bed chambers, offices, kitchens, etc.

But to unite all this, to provide access, it is necessary to have circulation areas—horizontal circulation by means of galleries, corridors, antechambers, and exits; vertical circulation by means of large and small stairs! These are inevitable as are courtyards for lighting and ventilating the house; we cannot call these areas useless, since they are necessary, yet we do not actively use them; without being the purpose of construction, they are absolutely required. I can compare them appropriately to overhead expenses in industry.

Just as in industry we must seek to limit as much as possible this overhead, so in architecture we must limit as much as possible the areas devoted to circulation. This is intelligent economy, the economy of the artist. But understand me well:

I do not wish to say, nor did I say, that vestibules or stairs should be paltry, nor galleries or particoes; far from it. Rather, do not multiply them without reason. Every non-functional circulation area becomes an obstruction and contributes to congestion.

In general, the principal difficulty in composition is to obtain easy movement throughout so that all parts are commodiously united; the simpler the means used for this the clearer the plan will be and more reliably grasped. Ensure circulation, but do not abuse porticoes, galleries, etc. And it is in this, especially, that you will recognize simplicity as an exquisite quality in composition.

From this point of view, look at these magnificent plans: the Baths of Caracalla; the Invalides; the Palais de Justice, Paris; and the Hôtel de Ville, Paris. You will be struck at the simplicity of means by which the architects have assured circulation without being at all niggardly. In the contrary, the simpler the basic concept [i.e.*parti*], the more you are allowed to make more magnificent the circulation, although not to abusive excess.

Another considerable difficulty is illumination of all parts of the composition. It is necessary to react, or rather continue to react against the too-convenient habit, started at the beginning of this century, of providing overhead illumination. In this connection, consult the rather curious first volume of collected grand prix designs—curious, that is, as an example of what not to practice. You will see invariably what we call "compact plans," with at least three and often five or seven thicknesses of contiguous buildings, all unilluminable, except by skylights. No ventilation is possible, suffocation assured; and, strange to say, a desperate struggle of conscience and the passing of that generation was required so that a window—a pleasure to open—could be tolerated in designs long enough to be recognized as necessary. How did this aberration come about? It would take too long to explain if I were to go into it. It is for you to guard against it happening again; even today, you plan court rooms lit from above—a pure monstrosity.

Remember, we must have light and air. Horizontal [i.e., overhead] lighting is appropriate for specific cases—museum rooms, for example. It can be tolerated only under some circumstances, but those are exceptions; other than these exceptions we want windows, only windows!

Besides, this consideration is related to another, just as essential—the easy discharge of rain water. A good composition necessarily lends itself to a rational roof plan; organize your design so that water can be shed easily; avoid the combination of internal gutters, or of long water paths. Certainly, you will not always study your roof plan, but your floor plan prefigures it and may augur its complications or even its impossibility. Consider the plan of the Invalides; this floor plan is sufficient and you will not need a roof plan to realize that water will easily flow away. This roof plan will not be ingenious and, even better, it will not have to be ingenious. Also, see how it reveals a clear and simple composition of the roofs.

Simplicity, always simplicity!

Moreover, how will you order the different parts of a composition? One cannot rely on rules, but follow common sense, a comprehension of the program, and, as much as possible, a thorough understanding of its needs. Composition is nothing but a series of sacrifices. In every plan there is one part more exposed, more central, in a word, prime. This prime space might be chosen from many; which one do you choose? It depends on many things.

Look at the plan of Versailles; the prime location, the place of honor is clearly marked in the center of the Cour de Marbre, in the center of the main building, overlooking the flower beds of the gardens. Mansart placed there the royal bedroom and the main reception gallery; the chapel was set aside in a wing. It is magnificent but finally sacrificed to royal majesty. Louis XIV was certainly a Christian, but above all he was king.

On the other hand, look at the Escorial. There the chapel is the center and the heart; the whole composition converges towards it. Phillip II was the king of an empire on which the sun never set, but above all he was the *catholic* king.

Here and there architects understood, through hints dropped by the patron maybe, what had to be centermost and what had to be sacrificed.

One must learn to proportion or grade these sacrifices in every composition. One must sensibly place, in the lesser parts of floors, everything that has to give way to the main parts. By the way, this is the reason why architects receive so much criticism. The architect can hardly not displease people who carefully conceal their private displeasure. Oh, no! they are speaking of the common interest—and are only slightly irritated, perhaps, at being housed on the fifth floor overlooking a service court!

All of what I have just said was related to sensible, economical, useful composition.

But that is not enough. We are not utilitarian. A nation which would look only for usefulness in architecture, without looking for beauty as well, would relinquish its whole civilization. In an odd study Beule demonstrated that Spartans—the men with the black gruel—wished to have an art that surpassed that of the Athenians. I believe it, readily, for otherwise they would have been nothing but savages.

Thus your compositions shall be determined by another concern——beauty. It is the eternal adage: *utile dulci.*[1]

Do I need to define a beautiful composition? First of all, it will be *good*, but it must also possess beauty of appearance. Your rooms will be made mutually complete by the effect of the whole if you have been able to create axially-arranged suites of rooms [*enfilades*]; your courtyards, if they are extended visually one to another by skillfully arranged perspective views; your facades, if you have arranged good projecting and recessed elements, accented pavilions, emphatic or elegant silhouettes; if all is varied, if you have opposites in contrast—in a word, if you know how to be artists in your composition. I could cite for you a great number of compositions which show well this attention to beauty; actually, everything demonstrates this. I will point out only a few examples: The House of Pansa, Pompeii; the Barberini Palace, Rome; the Abbey of Monte Cassino, Italy. I have difficulty in making a choice from so many. These examples will suffice to show you composition which is concerned with beauty of appearance and the skillful succession of perspectives.

Symmetry, with variety at the same time, generally should be sought after. But symmetry should be defined.

Symmetry is the regularity of everything you would see in a single glance.

[1] "The useful with the agreeable." Horace, *Ars Poetica*, 343.—Ed.

Symmetry is intelligent regularity.

I spoke to you just now of the first volume of the grand prix. You will find there a great number of plans conceived thusly: a longitudinal axis and a transverse axis dividing the plan into four quarters completely interchangeable; not one pilaster more or less. That is not symmetry; it is nonsense.

The Hôtel de Ville, Paris, for example, in each of its symmetrical facades, is beautiful, but the facade on the quai is not a duplicate of that on the Rue de Rivoli; this is not a negation of symmetry, only the difference between the principal and the rear facade. On the contrary, this variety only intensifies beauty. Versailles is symmetrical within the radius of a glance, but not beyond that, and so too many other monuments.

Symmetry is without question beautiful and it is rare that a monumental composition can give it up with detriment. And it is still the basis of composition today. Take care, indeed, that you do not focus solely on one facade of a project, for even the facades which you do not study are made implicit in the plan; the lateral facades, the rear facade, the court facades —all should be studied. In composing your plans you must arrange everything.

This leads me to explain the term "a good plan." This expression is concise; we mean by it a plan which allows and promises good things, good interiors and good facades. For about forty years we spoke with pleasure of plans beautiful in themselves, abstractions in every detail. We spoke of the "silhouette of plans," meaning the symbolism of a horizontal projection. An example of this kind of affectation is the plan of the Palace of the Legion of Honor, with five elements forming a star with a round chamber at the center; with just as much reason this same plan was used some years later for the Mazas prison.

Yes, there are beautiful plans and I find this a legitimate expression —but in the sense that good books are good because we read them or a musical score is good because of its content and not because of the arabesque look of the calligraphy with which is is written.

The picturesque is readily contrasted with the discipline of general composition, especially its symmetry. Thus the Palais de Justice, for good reason, is considered one of the picturesque elements of the capital, with its Palais de Saint-Louis, its clock tower, its great hall, the Sainte-Chapelle in the middle of an ensemble three or four centuries in construction.

I adore the picturesque, and most certainly for the visitor to a city it is the picturesque which catches his interest.

But we do not set out to compose something to be picturesque; it shapes itself solely through the agency of the greatest of all artists—time. On the Palais de Justice seven centuries have left their imprint; who would dare, therefore, to flatter himself by setting out to do this in one day? One may plan out—provided one is an artist of genius—the Place de la Concorde; one does not design the Piazza di San Marco in Venice, nor the Piazza della Signoria in Florence, nor that in Siena, nor the Campidoglio in Rome.

I will go a step further; if you want picturesqueness, do not seek it. That is the only way you will succeed perhaps. During the past centuries, in adding to older buildings no one felt impelled to use outdated styles; one would go on building the Palais de Justice without perpetuating the 13th century style—yet the Palais de Justice is picturesque. In Notre Dame, Paris, and in many churches one may find successive styles, ranging from the 12th to the 15th centuries—yet Notre Dame is picturesque. Nothing is more picturesque than the interior of the cathedral of Toulouse and the incoherence of its two parts built at two different times. Archaeological anachronism kills picturesqueness.

What is the picturesque then?

It is variety. Isn't there a variety belonging particularly to us, architects, that we could, and should, be taking care of?

This legitimate variety is nothing but *character*, the identity between the architectural impressions and the moral impressions of the program.

No doubt, there is an intrinsic beauty of architecture; we admire superb remains of buildings, the use of which is otherwise unknown to us. But beauty is not a commonplace quality, and while seeking it one must not forsake character. If the magnificent forms of a palace were put to use for a prison, they would be ridiculous; in a school or an industrial building they would seem out of place.

Thus the character of buildings is a condition of their diversity, and protects a city or an era from monotony. The architect should, if necessary, use self-denial and resist temptation.

Moreover, this quest for character is a relatively modern idea. During antiquity buildings were clearly characterized; however, character apparently was not valued as having outstanding merit then. The Parthenon, a temple dedicated to the goddess of Athens, and the Propylaea, a military portal to a citadel, display similar elements; so too do Roman baths and Constantine's Basilica. In medieval architecture (as in modern architecture) character was emphasized in churches, cloisters, monasteries, where architecture was special; also in city halls, palaces, and later in administrative, judicial, and educational buildings.

This is not surprising, for it confirms an often-verified historical law. Since Christianity, mankind has become more varied and complex. Let us not complain, for variety of character in our buildings makes them attractive and increases the richness of our language.

Finally, tradition will also support and guide you. I know it is considered backward to speak of tradition; there is a trend to disregard tradition now. Well, it comes from despising the work of centuries of hard-working generations who came before us. Generally it is an attempt to deceive people as to one's ignorance; by pretending to disdain what he does not know, one avoids the effort of learning about it. Keep yourselves free of such self-delusions. Progress is slow and must be sure. "He who travels slowly travels surely; he who travels surely travels far."

Do you want to know something really clever and really new? It is to do *very* well what others have done only well.

The finest artistic periods occurred when tradition was most respected, when progress was a continuous improvement, an evolution not a revolution. In art there is not, and there never has been, a spontaneous generation; the Parthenon differs from earlier temples only by nuances.

Moreover tradition is particularly valuable for studying. In order to forsake it, one has to be able to judge it, and in order to judge it, one has to know. Tradition is a patrimony; if one throws it away imprudently, one risks wandering randomly.

This is what may be said in general of composition. Let us sum it up:

(1.) You must follow accurately the building program—fathom it, and understand fully the relative importance of the building's elements, the moderation to be observed.

(2.) The environment and building site will modify the entire expression of a program, as does climate.

(3.) Every architectural composition must be buildable; any unbuildable project is utterly worthless. Any project requiring a means of construction more difficult or complicated than necessary is poor or mediocre.

(4.) Truth is required in architecture; any architectural lie is vicious. Even when one of these lies is redeemed by virtue of talent and ingenuity, there remains the impression of inferior art.

(5.) Effective strength is not enough; it must be obvious.

(6.) In your compositions take care of necessary circulation, but do it as simply as possible and without excess. Make certain all parts are well illuminated, that air penetrates everywhere, that rain water can be easily drained away.

(7.) Composition proceeds by necessary sacrifices. Composition must be good first, but it must be beautiful as well. You must therefore compose a building with a view towards its usefulness and its beauty. You will seek character, which contributes to beauty by creating variety.

Thus you will have taken care of that part of architecture which is shaped by architects, but the greatest "architects" of a period are society and the state. Individual architects translate but do not create or direct the aspiration of their times; they can only adapt to them for the best of their art. Beyond individual words, beyond specific programs, there is the program of programs, civilization itself, faith or unbelief, aristocracy or democracy, severity or loosening of morality. It is commonplace to point to the identity between art and civilization in Greece; in Rome, increasing exaggeration of pomp and scale distinguishes the architecture of the emperors which differs from that of the Republic more in its compositions and programs than in its style or profiles. At home, do not the Sainte-Chapelle or Notre Dame evoke Louis IX [Saint Louis] who so personified medieval piety? Could the architecture of Renaissance palaces be conceived out of its historical sphere? Versailles and the Place Vendome are Louis XIV himself. Later, Rousseau was the great architect of the contemporary reaction of David's school, as Chateaubriand was the architect of the subsequent counter-reaction. We ourselves are swept up in the general and complex movement resulting from our ideas, habits, our present civilization. Today our social state is both democratic and refined, its instincts are both utilitarian and luxurious. You yourselves are too much a part of it to be able to escape from it—and besides, why would you withdraw into an anachronism. Be the artists of your own times—that is always a noble mission.

41 L. Sullivan, Characteristics and Tendencies of American Architecture* 1885

Louis Henri Sullivan (1856–1924) was one of the most keenly perceptive American architects since Latrobe. Yet the history of his career after 1900 is tragic. In those later years, deprived of the mitigating influence of his former partner, Dankmar Adler, and receiving fewer commissions, he turned his attention to exploring a question he had broached at the very outset of his career—what is the architecture of America to be and what role is the American architect to play? Julien Guadet, in the preceding selection, took the view that the architect can only reflect the prevalent culture which calls buildings into being; the architect does not redirect culture or the art of a period. To a certain extent Sullivan would have agreed, but as he first took up this question in 1885, when this paper was presented before a meeting of the Western Association of Architects in St. Louis, Sullivan was optimistically confident that a new spontaneous expression of American needs was arising. But he was critical, nonetheless, of those architects who "as a professional class have held it more expedient to maintain the traditions of their culture than to promulgate vitalizing thought." Still, he believed the progressive American spirit would encourage and support a new national architecture; it was, he thought, inevitable, for "no architectural style can become a finality that runs counter to popular feeling." Unfortunately for Sullivan, he would misread what that popular feeling was.

In this, the first of his many publications, Sullivan already employs the poetically rich and effusive language he was to develop further.[†] He also introduces the concept of the organic development of ideas, although the sense here is closer to the École's *parti* than to the purely biological metaphor he was to favor later.

Many who have commented upon the practice of architecture in this country have regarded the absence of a style, distinctively American, as both strange and deplorable; and with a view to betterment they have advanced theories as to the nature, and immediate realization, of such a style that evidence a lack of insight equally strange and deplorable. These theories have been for the greater part suggested by the feelings awakened in contemplating the matured beauty of Old World art, and imply a grafting or transplanting process. They have been proved empirical by the sufficient logic of time; their advocates having ignored the complex fact, that, like a

* Louis H. Sullivan, "Characteristics and Tendencies of American Architecture," *Inland Architect and Builder* 6 (November 1885), pp. 58–59, reprinted in *Builder's Weekly Reporter* (London), 1885.

† For bibliographies of Sullivan's writing see: Hugh Morrison, *Louis Sullivan: Prophet of Modern Architecture* (New York, 1935), pp. 306–09; Louis Sullivan, *Kindergarten Chats and Other Writings*, ed. I. Athey (New York, 1947), pp. 8–10. One important article by Sullivan, which is cited in neither of these, concerns the pressing need for setbacks on tall skyscrapers: "The High-Building Question," *The Graphic* 5 (December 19, 1891), p. 405; see Donald Hoffman, *Journal, Society of Architectural Historians* 29 (May 1970), pp. 181–87, in which the article is reprinted.

new species of any class, a national style must be a growth, that slow and gradual assimilation of nutriment and a struggle against obstacles are necessary adjuncts to the purblind processes of growth, and that the resultant structure can bear only a chemical or metaphysical resemblance to the materials on which it has been nurtured.

We will, therefore, for the purposes of this paper disregard these dreams of a Minerva-like architectural splendor springing full-formed into being, and look rather for the early signs of a spontaneous architectural feeling arising in sympathy with the emotions latent or conspicuous in our people.

It is reasonable to believe that an unconquered country, peopled by colonization and natural increase, may bear in its younger and its coming generations a race whose birthright, implying freedom to receive and assimilate impressions, shall nurture emotions of rare quality and of a fruitfulness commensurate with the energy in an unexhausted soil.

It would be erroneous to assume that there will be no evidence of the activity of such emotions until as a large accumulation they break all bonds asunder. The individual is from day to day seeking expedients by means of which to shape his immediate surroundings into a realization of his desires, and we may assume it to be quite probable that the initial impelling force, operating through the individual, has already in many cases produced significant and valuable results. These results, if not thoroughly typical, must have in them much that is eminently characteristic, and that bear the stamp of internal origin.

To test this hypothesis we have therefore but to look into the daily life of our architecture, and, in the complexion of its many fleeting phases, seek here and there for instances, some perhaps almost trivial, in which the existence of spontaneous and characteristic emotional feeling may be detected. Sometimes we shall find this impulse appearing as an element of warmth tingeing scholastic formalism; sometimes as a seemingly paradoxical inspiration in the works of the uncultivated. We may certainly expect to meet with it in the efforts of those upon whose imagination the chromatic eloquence of words and of music have taken strong hold; and above all, we are to look for it in the creations of the gifted ones whose souls are finely attuned to the touching beauty of nature and of humanity. To an apprehension of this subtle element, we may be happily guided by the suggestions of analogy. Our recent American literature comes aptly to this use. Glancing through its focusing substance, as through the lens of a camera, we may perceive an image of the abstraction we seek, and, by an extension of the process, we may fix an impression of its form and texture, to be developed at will.

Our literature is the only phase of our national art that has been accorded serious recognition, at home and abroad. The noticeable qualities of its present phases seem to be: excessive regard for minute detail, painful self-consciousness of finish, timidity and embarrassment in the delineation of all but the well-behaved and docile emotions, and a tacit fiction as to the passions: all beautifully executed with much patient, earnest labor, and diplomatically tempered to the understanding.

Exquisite, but not virile, our latter-day literature illustrates quite emphatically the quality of our tentative and provisional culture, which must ere long throw off these seedling leaves, when a higher temperature shall infuse glowing vitality into root and stem, and exuberant foliation give more certain assurance of the coming flower of our soil. Our literature, and in fact all that which we Americans complacently call our art, is too much a matter of heart and fingers, and too little an offspring of brain and soul. One must indeed have faith in the processes of nature to prophesy order eventuating upon so strange a chaos of luxuries. But to this end, transmitted knowledge must gradually be supplemented by the fresh impressions of the senses and the sensibilities, the fund so accumulated yielding richly of its own increase. This supplemental acquisition must of necessity be of slow growth, for we have all been educated to a dependence upon our artistic inheritance.

Our art is for the day, is suited to the day, and will also change as the day changes. The law of variation is an ever present force, and coordination is its goal. The first step toward a new order of things is accomplished when there appear minds receiving and assimilating fresh impressions, reaching new conclusions, and acting upon them. By this sign, we may know that such a movement is already upon us, and by the aid of the indicated literary analogy we may follow its erratic tendencies, and note its increase in strength and individuality: we may see the germ of poetry which each man has within him, slowly awakening into life, and may feel the presence of an American romanticism.

This romanticism is, in the main, also exquisite but not virile. It seeks to touch all things with softened hand. Under the influence of its warmth of feeling, hard lines flow into graceful curves, angularities disappear in a mystical blending of surfaces.

One by one the completed styles of foreign climes are passing under this hand, each in turn being quietly divested of its local charm, and clothed in a sentiment and mannerism unmistakably our own. Power laments, meanwhile, at the feet of a modern Omphale, his voice attuned to the domestic hum of the times.

Appreciation of the beauties of this romanticism is to some extent dependent upon the verbal explanation and comment of its exponents. A knowledge of their vocabulary is often of assistance in disclosing softness and refinement in many primitive expedients, and revealing beauty in barren places. Familiarity with the current phraseology of the allied arts is also useful in assisting the student to a comprehension of many things apparently incomprehensible. Metaphor and simile are rampant in this connection, a well-chosen word often serving to justify an architectural absurdity.

But overloaded as is this fabric of impulse with florid and complicated intertwinings of affection, when we examine the material thereof, we find it excellent and valuable.

Searching critically among the works executed in this feeling, we note in the varying examples, and indeed in parts of the same structure, a curious *mélange* of supersentimentalisms. Conspicuous at first glance, in some an offensive simplicity, in others a highly wrought charlatanism; further, we perceive ingenuity in device, or superb flow of spirits—all more or less leavened with stubborn common sense. After such an investigation, we may gladly become convinced that behind a somewhat uncertain vision resides a marvelous instinct.

National sensitiveness and pride, conjoined with fertility of resource, will aid as active stimuli in the development of this instinct toward a more rational and organic mode of expression, leading through many reactions to a higher sphere of artistic development.

We are now in the primary department, vaguely endeavoring to form a plastic alphabet by means of which to identify our beliefs. Progress in this respect has been very slow and results meagre: for our beliefs have still within them too much of uncertainty and diffidence to take rank as convictions. Without these latter a sufficient creating power is lacking. The formation of an alphabet, and the simplest combinations of its terms, are matters of much importance; and easy progress in this respect is seriously impeded by complications of thought. To look at things simply and clearly is quite easy, until counter influences are set at work; then comes a struggle for survival, which now and then is successful—the result being an addition, however small, to our stock of elementary forms.

The ability to develop elementary ideas organically is not conspicuous in our profession. In this respect, the architect is inferior to the business man and financier, whose capacity to expand a simple congenial idea, once fixed, into subtle, manifold and consistent ramifications is admirable, and a shining example which we have often ignored, creating thereby an undesirable impression.

This view leads us on to a consideration of the element of power. Until this element is widely introduced into our work, giving it the impress of brilliancy, intuition and great depth of feeling, that work, exhaustively considered, will remain but little more than a temporary expedient.

The presence of power, as a mental characteristic in one class of our people, augurs well for the belief that it may pervade our ranks. The beginnings of power are usually so crude and harsh as to be revolting to a refined taste, and hence it is instinctively shunned; but once subtilized, flushed with emotion and guided by clear insight, it is a worker of miracles; responsive to its ardent wooings, nature yields up her poetic secrets.

We surely have in us the germ of artistic greatness—no people on earth possessing more of innate poetic feeling, more of ideality, greater capacity to adore the beautiful, than our own people; but architects as a professional class have held it more expedient to maintain the traditions of their culture than to promulgate vitalizing thought. Here then we are weak, and should sentiment gain a pronounced ascendency, we may remain weak.

On us rests partially the responsibility, and partially on the public. We have at times individually sought to lead the public, when we more wisely should have followed it; and have, as a body, often followed, when, with beneficent results we could have led. While we may compromise for a time, through a process of local adaptation, no architectural style can become a finality, that runs counter to popular feeling. The desire at once to follow and to lead the public should be the initial attitude of our profession toward the formation of a national style. For while we conduct the technical operations, the shaping and controlling process is mainly in the hands of the public who are constantly keeping us within bounds. We cannot wholly escape this control, while we are without a national architecture fully representing the wishes of the public, and ministering to its conceptions of the beautiful and the useful. This can evidently not come to pass forthwith, for the public itself can only partially and imperfectly state its wants. Responding readily, however, to the intuition of those who anticipate its desires, it accepts provisionally year by year all the satisfaction it can get; so that while one recognized style after another shall pass through our hands to be tried and finally rejected in the search for permanent satisfaction, a modified residuum from each will doubtless be added to a fund representing our growth in emotional and spiritual wealth. The progress of this growth toward consummation in a national style, involves the lives of many generations, and need be of but little practical concern to us of today. We work at short range and for immediate results. Perhaps, however, there would be infused into our profession an abiding *esprit de corps*, should consideration of this subject and its associated themes lead to a substantial agreement upon our status, our tendencies and our policy.

If the conclusions set forth in this paper be accepted as correct, it becomes clearly evident, however, that the formative beginnings of this national style, now in progress, are of the utmost immediate interest to us, in part through feelings of patriotism, in part because of a surmise that those who approach most nearly in the substance of their work and administration to the qualities inherent to [in] our race and potential to [of] a national style, will come nearest to the hearts of our people.

Harassed though the architect may be, by the cares and responsibilities of his daily life, there exists nevertheless within him, in the midst of this turmoil, an insuppressible yearning toward ideals. These delicate promptings should be both protected and nourished, that, like the flowering plants springing by the sun's gentle persuasion from little seeds buried in the coarser elements of the soil, they also, because of the warmth of human feeling, may bloom at times by the wayside, yielding refreshing odors and the joy of color to the plodding wayfarer.

The soft beams of the full-orbed moon fall with pathetic caress upon the slumbering life of the world; paling with the dawn, her tender vigil ended, she melts into the infinite depths when the ruddy herald of day proudly summons the workers. So does the soul watch over its greater ideals until the thrilling radiance of power shall awaken them to action.

Ideal thought and effective action should so compose the vital substance of our works that they may live, with us and after us, as a record of our fitness, and a memorial of the good we may have done. Then, in the affluence of time, when a rich burden of aspiring verdure may flourish in the undulating fields of thought, wrought into fertility through the bounty of nature and the energy of the race, the mellowed spontaneity of a national style reaching its full and perfect fruition shall have come from out the very treasury of nature.

42   L. Sullivan, The Tall Office
Building Artistically Considered* *1896*

This is perhaps Louis H. Sullivan's most detailed and specific analysis of the building type on which he focused his creative energy. It is a summation, in fact, of what he and Adler had already done in the Wainwright Building, St. Louis, in 1890–91, and the Guaranty Building, Buffalo, 1894–95. Practicing alone, Sullivan applied this analysis in a more subtly proportioned way in the Bayard-Condict Building, New York, in 1897–98. Sullivan had come to grips in those office blocks, as he also did in this essay, with the fundamentally new character of these office buildings—they were far loftier than business buildings had ever been before. He recognized that the tall block should exploit its height, that "it must be every inch a proud and soaring thing, rising in sheer exultation." It was now time for architects to express that spirit, and to give to the tall office block a form that would express the inner life of the building, for "form ever follows function." When this was done, he believed, the office tower would take its place with all other great architectural types.

The architects of this land and generation are now brought face to face with something new under the sun—namely, that evolution and integration of social conditions, that special grouping of them, that results in a demand for the erection of tall office buildings.

It is not my purpose to discuss the social conditions; I accept them as the fact, and say at once that the design of the tall office building must be recognized and confronted at the outset as a problem to be solved—a vital problem, pressing for a true solution.

Let us state the conditions in the plainest manner. Briefly, they are these: offices are necessary for the transaction of business; the invention and perfection of the high-speed elevators make vertical travel, that was once tedious and painful, now easy and comfortable; development of steel manufacture has shown the way to safe, rigid, economical constructions rising to a great height; continued growth of population in the great cities, consequent congestion of centers and rise in value of ground, stimulate an increase in number of stories; these successfully piled one upon another, react on ground values—and so on, by action and reaction, interaction and inter-reaction. Thus has come about that form of lofty construction called the "modern office building." It has come in answer to a call, for in it a new grouping of social conditions has found a habitation and a name.

Up to this point all in evidence is materialistic, an exhibition of force, of resolution, of brains in the keen sense of the word. It is the joint product of the speculator, the engineer, the builder.

Problem: How shall we impart to this sterile pile, this crude, harsh,

*Louis H. Sullivan, "The Tall Office Building Artistically Considered," *Lippincott's Magazine* 57 (March 1896), pp. 403–09, reprinted in *Inland Architect and News Record* 27 (May 1896), pp. 32–34; *Western Architect* 31 (January 1922), pp. 3–11; published as "Form and Function Artistically Considered," *The Craftsman* 8 (July 1905), pp. 453–58.

brutal agglomeration, this stark, staring exclamation of eternal strife, the graciousness of those higher forms of sensibility and culture that rest on the lower and fiercer passions? How shall we proclaim from the dizzy height of this strange, weird, modern housetop the peaceful evangel of sentiment, of beauty, the cult of a higher life?

This is the problem; and we must seek the solution of it in a process analogous to its own evolution—indeed, a continuation of it—namely, by proceeding step by step from general to special aspects, from coarser to finer considerations.

It is my belief that it is of the very essence of every problem that it contains and suggests its own solution. This I believe to be natural law. Let us examine, then, carefully the elements, let us search out this contained suggestion, this essence of the problem.

The practical conditions are, broadly speaking, these:

Wanted—1st, a story below-ground, containing boilers, engines of various sorts, etc.—in short, the plant for power, heating, lighting, etc. 2nd, a ground floor, so called, devoted to stores, banks, or other establishments requiring large area, ample spacing, ample light, and great freedom of access. 3rd, a second story readily accessible by stairways—this space usually in large subdivisions, with corresponding liberality in structural spacing and expanse of glass and breadth of external openings. 4th, above this an indefinite number of stories of offices piled tier upon tier, one tier just like another tier, one office just like all the other offices—an office being similar to a cell in a honey-comb, merely a compartment, nothing more. 5th, and last, at the top of this pile is placed a space or story that, as related to the life and usefulness of the structure, is purely physiological in its nature—namely, the attic. In this the circulatory system completes itself and makes its grand turn, ascending and descending. The space is filled with tanks, pipes, valves, sheaves, and mechanical etcetera that supplement and complement the force-originating plant hidden below-ground in the cellar. Finally, or at the beginning rather, there must be on the ground floor a main aperture or entrance common to all the occupants or patrons of the building.

This tabulation is, in the main, characteristic of every tall office building in the country. As to the necessary arrangements for light courts, these are not germane to the problem, and as will become soon evident, I trust need not be considered here. These things, and such others as the arrangement of elevators, for example, have to do strictly with the economics of the building, and I assume them to have been fully considered and disposed of to the satisfaction of purely utilitarian and pecuniary demands. Only in rare instances does the plan or floor arrangement of the tall office building take on an æsthetic value, and this usually when the lighting court is external or becomes an internal feature of great importance.

As I am here seeking not for an individual or special solution, but for a true normal type, the attention must be confined to those conditions that, in the main, are constant in all tall office buildings, and every mere incidental and accidental variation eliminated from the consideration, as harmful to the clearness of the main inquiry.

The practical horizontal and vertical division or office unit is naturally based on a room of comfortable area and height, and the size of this standard office room as naturally predetermines the standard structural unit, and, approximately, the size of window openings. In turn, these purely arbitrary units of structure form in an equally natural way the true basis of the artistic development of the exterior. Of course the structural spacings and openings in the first or mercantile story are required to be the largest of all; those in the second or quasi-mercantile story are of a somewhat similar nature. The spacings and openings in the attic are of no importance whatsoever (the windows have no actual value), for light may be taken from the top, and no recognition of a cellular division is necessary in the structural spacing.

Hence it follows inevitably, and in the simplest possible way, that if we follow our natural instincts without thought of books, rules, precedents, or any such educational impedimenta to a spontaneous and "sensible" result, we will in the following manner design the exterior of our tall office building—to wit:

Beginning with the first story, we give this a main entrance that attracts the eye to its location, and the remainder of the story we treat in a more or less liberal, expansive, sumptuous way—a way based exactly on the practical necessities, but expressed with a sentiment of largeness and freedom. The second story we treat in a similar way, but usually with milder pretension. Above this, throughout the indefinite number of typical office tiers, we take our cue from the individual cell, which requires a window with its separating pier, its sill and lintel, and we, without more ado, make them look all alike because they are all alike. This brings us to the attic, which, having no division into office-cells, and no special requirement for lighting, gives us the power to show by means of its broad expanse of wall, and its dominating weight and character, that which is the fact—namely, that the series of office tiers has come definitely to an end.

This may perhaps seem a bald result and a heartless, pessimistic way of stating it, but even so we certainly have advanced a most characteristic stage beyond the imagined sinister building of the speculator-engineer-builder combination. For the hand of the architect is now definitely felt in the decisive position at once taken, and the suggestion of a thoroughly sound, logical, coherent expression of the conditions is becoming apparent.

When I say the hand of the architect, I do not mean necessarily the accomplished and trained architect. I mean only a man with a strong, natural liking for buildings, and a disposition to shape them in what seems to his unaffected nature a direct and simple way. He will probably tread an innocent path from his problem to its solution, and therein he will show an enviable gift of logic. If he have some gift for form in detail, some feeling for form purely and simply as form, some love for that, his result in addition to its simple straightforward naturalness and completeness in general statement, will have something of the charm of sentiment.

However, thus far the results are only partial and tentative at best; relatively true, they are but superficial. We are doubtless right in our instinct but we must seek a fuller justification, a finer sanction, for it.

I assume now that in the study of our problem we have passed through the various stages of inquiry, as follows: 1st, the social basis of the demand for tall office buildings; 2nd, its literal material satisfaction; 3rd, the elevation of the question from considerations of literal planning, construction, and equipment, to the plane of elementary architecture as a direct outgrowth of sound, sensible building; 4th, the question again elevated from an elementary architecture to the beginnings of true architectural expression, through the addition of a certain quality and quantity of sentiment.

But our building may have all these in a considerable degree and yet be far from that adequate solution of the problem I am attempting to define. We must now heed the imperative voice of emotion.

It demands of us, what is the chief characteristic of the tall office building? And at once we answer, it is lofty. This loftiness is to the artist-nature its thrilling aspect. It is the very open organ-tone in its appeal. It must be in turn the dominant chord in his expression of it, the true excitant of his imagination. It must be tall, every inch of it tall. The force and power of altitude must be in it, the glory and pride of exaltation must be in it. It must be every inch a proud and soaring thing, rising in sheer exultation that from bottom to top it is a unit without a single dissenting line—that it is the new, the unexpected, the eloquent peroration of most bald, most sinister, most forbidding conditions.

The man who designs in the spirit and with the sense of responsibility to the generation he lives in must be no coward, no denier, no bookworm, no dilettante. He must live of his life and for his life in the fullest, most consummate sense. He must realize at once and with the grasp of inspiration that the problem of the tall office building is one of the most stupendous, one of the most magnificent opportunities that the Lord of Nature in His beneficence has ever offered to the proud spirit of man.

That this has not been perceived—indeed, has been flatly denied—is an exhibition of human perversity that must give us pause.

One more consideration. Let us now lift this question into the region of calm, philosophic observation. Let us seek a comprehensive, a final solution: let the problem indeed dissolve.

Certain critics, and very thoughtful ones, have advanced the theory that the true prototype of the tall office building is the classical column, consisting of base, shaft and capital—the moulded base of the column typical of the lower stories of our building, the plain or fluted shaft suggesting the monotonous, uninterrupted series of office-tiers, and the capital the completing power and luxuriance of the attic.

Other theorizers, assuming a mystical symbolism as a guide, quote the many trinities in nature and art, and the beauty and conclusiveness of such trinity in unity. They aver the beauty of prime numbers, the mysticism of the number three, the beauty of all things that are in three parts—to wit, the day, subdividing into morning, noon, and night; the limbs, the thorax, and the head, constituting the body. So they say, should the building be in three parts vertically, substantially as before, but for different motives.

Others, of purely intellectual temperament, hold that such a design should be in the nature of a logical statement; it should have a beginning, a middle, and an ending, each clearly defined—therefore again a building, as above, in three parts vertically.

Others, seeking their examples and justification in the vegetable kingdom, urge that such a design shall above all things be organic. They quote the suitable flower with its bunch of leaves at the earth, its long graceful stem, carrying the gorgeous single flower. They point to the pine-tree, its massy roots, its lithe, uninterrupted trunk, its tuft of green high in the air. Thus, they say, should be the design of the tall office building: again in three parts vertically.

Others still, more susceptible to the power of a unit than to the grace of a trinity, say that such a design should be struck out at a blow, as though by a blacksmith or by mighty Jove, or should be thought-born, as was Minerva, full grown. They accept the notion of a triple division as permissible and welcome, but non-essential. With them it is a subdivision of their unit: the unit does not come from the alliance of the three; they accept it without murmur, provided the subdivision does not disturb the sense of singleness and repose.

All of these critics and theorists agree, however, positively, unequivocally, in this, that the tall office building should not, must not, be made a field for the display of architectural knowledge in the encyclopædic sense; that too much learning in this instance is fully as dangerous, as obnoxious, as too little learning; that miscellany is abhorrent to their sense; that the sixteen-story building must not consist of sixteen separate, distinct and unrelated buildings piled one upon the other until the top of the pile is reached.

To this latter folly I would not refer were it not the fact that nine out of every ten tall office buildings are designed in precisely this way in effect, not by the ignorant, but by the educated. It would seem indeed, as though the "trained" architect, when facing this problem, were beset at every story, or at most, every third or fourth story, by the hysterical dread lest he be in "bad form"; lest he be not bedecking his building with sufficiency of quotation from this, that, or the other "correct" building in some other land and some other time; lest he be not copious enough in the display of his wares; lest he betray, in short, a lack of resource. To loosen up the touch of this cramped and fidgety hand, to allow the nerves to calm, the brain to cool, to reflect equably, to reason naturally, seems beyond him; he lives, as it were, in a waking nightmare filled with the disjecta membra of architecture. The spectacle is not inspiriting.

As to the former and serious views held by discerning and thoughtful critics, I shall, with however much of regret, dissent from them for the purpose of this demonstration, for I regard them as secondary only, non-essential, and as touching not at all upon the vital spot, upon the quick of the entire matter, upon the true, the immovable philosophy of the architectural art.

This view let me now state, for it brings to the solution of the problem a final, comprehensive formula.

All things in nature have a shape, that is to say, a form, an outward semblance, that tells us what they are, that distinguishes them from ourselves and from each other.

Unfailingly in nature these shapes express the inner life, the native quality of the animal, tree, bird, fish, that they present to us; they are so characteristic, so recognizable, that we say, simply, it is "natural" it should be so. Yet the moment we peer beneath this surface of things, the moment we look through the tranquil reflection of ourselves and the clouds above us, down into the clear, fluent, unfathomable depth of nature, how startling is the silence of it, how amazing the flow of life, how absorbing the mystery. Unceasingly the essence of things is taking shape in the matter of things, and this unspeakable process we call birth and growth. Awhile the spirit and the matter fade away together, and it is this that we call decadence, death. These two happenings seem jointed and interdependent, blended into one like a bubble and its iridescence, and they seem borne along upon a slowly moving air. This air is wonderful past all understanding.

Yet to the steadfast eye of one standing upon the shore of things, look-ing chiefly and most lovingly upon that side on which the sun shines and that we feel joyously to be life, the heart is ever gladdened by the beauty, the exquisite spontaneity, with which life seeks and takes on its forms in an accord perfectly responsive to its needs. It seems ever as though the life and the form were absolutely one and inseparable so adequate is the sense of fulfillment.

Whether it be the sweeping eagle in his flight or the open apple-blos-som, the toiling work-horse, the blithe swan, the branching oak, the winding stream at its base, the drifting clouds, over all the coursing sun, form ever follows function, and this is the law. Where function does not change form does not change. The granite rocks, the ever-brooding hills, remain for ages; the lightning lives, comes into shape, and dies in a twinkling.

It is the pervading law of all things organic, and inorganic, of all things physical and metaphysical, of all things human and all things superhuman, of all true manifestations of the head, of the heart, of the soul, that the life is recognizable in its expression, that form ever follows function. This is the law.

Shall we, then, daily violate this law in our art? Are we so decadent, so imbecile, so utterly weak of eyesight, that we cannot perceive this truth so simple, so very simple? Is it indeed a truth so transparent that we see through it but do not see it? Is it really then, a very marvelous thing, or is it rather so commonplace, so everyday, so near a thing to us, that we cannot perceive that the shape, form, outward expression, design or whatever we may choose, of the tall office building should in the very nature of things follow the functions of the building, and that where the function does not change, the form is not to change?

Does this not readily, clearly, and conclusively show that the lower one or two stories will take on a special character suited to the special needs, that the tiers of typical offices, having the same unchanging function, shall con-tinue in the same unchanging form, and that as to the attic, specific and conclusive as it is in its very nature, its function shall equally be so in force, in significance, in continuity, in conclusiveness of outward expression? From this results, naturally, spontaneously, unwittingly, a three-part division, not from any theory, symbol, or fancied logic.

And thus the design of the tall office building takes its place with all other architectural types made when architecture, as has happened once in many years, was a living art. Witness the Greek temple, the Gothic cathe-dral, the medieval fortress.

And thus, when native instinct and sensibility shall govern the exercise of our beloved art; when the known law, the respected law, shall be that form ever follows function; when our architects shall cease struggling and prattling handcuffed and vainglorious in the asylum of a foreign school; when it is truly felt, cheerfully accepted, that this law opens up the airy sunshine of green fields, and gives to us a freedom that the very beauty and sumptuousness of the outworking of the law itself as exhibited in nature will deter any sane, any sensitive man from changing into license, when it becomes evident that we are merely speaking a foreign language with a noticeable American accent, whereas each and every architect in the land might, under the benign influence of this law, express in the simplest, most modest, most natural way that which it is in him to say; that he might really and would surely develop his own characteristic individuality, and that the architectural art with him would certainly become a living form of speech, a natural form of utterance, giving surcease to him and adding treasures small and great to the growing art of his land; when we know and feel that Nature is our friend, not our implacable enemy—that an afternoon in the country, an hour by the sea, a full open view of one single day, through dawn, high noon, and twilight, will suggest to us so much that is rhythmical, deep, and eternal in the vast art of architecture, something so deep, so true, that all the narrow formalities, hard-and-fast rules, and strangling bonds of the schools cannot stifle it in us—then it may be proclaimed that we are on the highroad to a natural and satisfying art, an architecture that will soon become a fine art in the true, the best sense of the word, an art that will live because it will be of the people, for the people, and by the people.

43   L. Sullivan, Kindergarten Chats*
1901–02, 1918

As Hugh Morrison points out in his biography, Sullivan was forced, in spite of himself, to become not an architect but a teacher in his later years. His first extended literary venture was "Kindergarten Chats," each no more than two pages, published in the weekly issues of *The Interstate Architect and Builder* of Cleveland, running an entire year, February, 1901, through February, 1902. In these, Sullivan created a dialogue between an experienced master (himself) and an imaginary pupil, "young, well-educated, self-confident and unsuspecting hopeful." He purposely avoided technical language, keeping the character simple and elementary, hence the title he selected. Some of the chats are bitter scathing sarcasm and strident criticism, others are patient analyses of form and function and still others are epigrammatic prose poems. They were eagerly awaited by younger readers such as Claude Bragdon, and

* *The Interstate Architect and Builder* 2 and 3 (February 16, 1901 through February 8, 1902) reprinted in *Kindergarten Chats and Other Writings*, ed. I. Athey (New York, 1947).

Sullivan hoped they would reach "the laity," for he was certain "the architects will not understand much of what is in them." "I am writing for the people," he explained to Lyndon Smith, "not for architects."[†] Although issued in fragments, the chats were part of a preconceived whole, gradually unfolded. Sullivan revised the entire collection in 1918 with a view to republication in book form, but no publishers were forthcoming. Eventually Bragdon prepared a new manuscript from back issues of *Interstate Architect*, and this was published in 1934.[‡] Reprinted here is the second half of a two-part discussion of form and function and a discussion of the role of the architect, both extending ideas Sullivan had introduced before.

XIII. FUNCTION AND FORM

It seems to me that I could have gotten a clearer idea of your recent harangue on function and form, if you had used half as many words. Still, I think I catch your meaning after a fashion. The gist of it is, I take it, behind every form we see there is a vital something or other which we do not see, yet which makes itself visible to us in that very form. In other words, in a state of nature the form exists *because* of the function, and this something behind the form is neither more nor less than a manifestation of what you call the infinite creative spirit, and what I call God. And, allowing for our differences in education, training, and life associations, so that we may try to see the same thing in the same way, what you want me to understand and hold to is, that, just as every form contains its function, and exists by virtue of it, so every function finds or is engaged in finding its form. And, furthermore, while this is true of the every-day things we see about us in nature and in the reflection of nature we call human life, it is just as true, because it is a universal law, of everything that the mind can take hold of.

You are "arriving," as we say.

Well, I suppose of course there is some application of this to architecture?

Well rather. It applies to everything else, why not to architecture?

But there must be a definite application of the theory. What is the application?

Can't you figure it out?

I suppose if we call every building a form—

You strain my nerves—but go on.

I suppose if we call a building a form, then there should be a function, a purpose, a reason for each building, a definite explainable relation between the form, the development of each building, and the causes that bring it into that particular shape; and that the building, to be good architecture, must, first of all, clearly correspond with its function, must be its image, as you would say.

[†] Louis Sullivan to Lyndon P. Smith, February 18 and 22, 1901, reprinted in *Kindergarten Chats . . .* , ed. I. Athey, p. 243.

[‡] For the various stages in the preparation of the manuscript and a schedule of publications of *Kindergarten Chats* see *Kindergarten Chats . . .* , ed. I. Athey, Editor's Note and Appendices A and E, pp. 5–6, 243–45, 251.

Don't say good architecture, say, merely, architecture; I will know what you mean.

And that, if a building is properly designed, one should be able with a little attention, to read *through* that building to the *reason* for that building.

Go on.

Well, that's all right for the logical part of it; but where does the artistic side come in?

No matter about the artistic side of it. Go on with your story.

But—

Never mind the buts.

Well then, I suppose if the law is true of the building as a whole, it must hold true of its parts.

That's right.

Consequently each part must so clearly express its function that the function can be read through the part.

Very good. But you might add that if the work is to be organic the function of the part must have the same *quality* as the function of the whole; and the parts, of themselves and by themselves, must have the quality of the mass; must partake of its identity.

What do you mean by organic?

I will tell you, later on.

Then if I am on the right track, I'm going to try to keep on it. It's rather fun to do your own thinking, isn't it?

Yes, it is: and rather good for the health and the happiness. Keep on, and some day you will get the blood to your brain. If the surge is not too sudden, you may yet become a useful citizen.

I overlook your sneer, because I am interested in what I, myself, am saying. I would observe in passing, however, that you are not any too considerate. But, to go on: If it is true of the parts in a larger sense, then it must be equally true of the details, and in the same sense, isn't it?

In a similar sense, yes.

Why do you say similar?

Because I mean similar. The details are not the same as the parts and the mass; they cannot be. But they can be and should be similar to the parts and to the mass.

Isn't that splitting hairs?

If there were more of such hair-splitting it would be well for our architecture.

Why so? I don't understand.

Because its significance reverts to the *organic quality* which I mentioned to you. There is no limit to the subdivisibility of *organic thinking*.

And what is the difference between logical thinking and organic thinking?

A world of difference. But we haven't come to that yet.

Then, I infer, I can go on and consider my detail as of itself a mass, if I will, and proceed with the regular and systematic subdivision of function with form, as before, and I will always have a similarity, an organic quality—if I can guess what you mean—descending from the mass down to the minutest subdivision of detail. That's interesting, isn't it? The subdivisions and details will descend from the mass like children, grandchildren and great-grandchildren, and yet, they will be, all, of the same family.

That's the first enlivening word I've heard you say.

Well, it's catching, you know. I begin to get an inkling now of what you meant by the "voice, calling, afar in the woods." Perhaps, too, some of the little seeds are coming up and will need watering by and by.

Yes, yes. Very good as far as you go. But I wish to warn you that a man might follow the program you have laid down, to the very last detail of details, and yet have, if that were his make-up, a very dry, a very pedantic, a very prosaic result. He might produce a completely logical result, so-called, and yet an utterly repellent one—a cold, a vacuous negation of living architecture—a veritable pessimism.

How so?

Simply because logic, scholarship, or taste, or all of them combined, cannot make organic architecture. They may make logical, scholarly or "tasty" buildings, and that is all. And such structures are either dry, chilling or futile.

Well then, tell me *now*, in anticipation, what characterizes a real architect?

First of all a poetic imagination; second, a broad sympathy, humane character, common sense and a thoroughly disciplined mind; third, a perfected technique; and, finally, an abundant and gracious gift of expression.

Then you don't value logic.

It has its excellent uses.

But cannot everything be reduced to the syllogism?

So the text books would seem to claim; yet I should not wish to see a rose reduced to syllogism; I fear the result would be mostly syllogism and that poetry would "vanish with the rose." Formal logic cannot successfully deal with the creative process, for the creating function is vital, as its name implies, whereas the syllogism is an abstraction, fascinating as a form of the function, so-called pure reason; yet, when subordinate to inspiration, it has a just and high value. I say there is a logic over and above book-logic, namely, the subconscious energy we call imagination. Nevertheless, formal logic has its purpose and its place.

Then you do prize logic?

I surely do. It is a power of the intellect; but it has its limitations. It must not play the tyrant.

By the way; you were to explain the word organic.

You have a memory—which shows that you are following and, still better, anticipating my argument. I had for the moment overlooked the item. But we will take it up next time, when we may discuss it leisurely.

I think this is great sport.

So do I.

XLII. WHAT IS AN ARCHITECT?

What's on your mind this time?

Pater, this is, for sure, a weary world! I cannot reach the heights of it: I am hung up by the middle. Suspended in the center of a minute vacuum of my own, by a string invisible, the end of which reaches up beyond my ken. Yet do I gravitate by my own weight, feathery tho' that be; and if the string were cut, I flutter, like an autumn leaf, and settle upon the solid earth of another vacuum unreal and intangible as this Infinite of which you speak, illusory and elusive as the democracy of which you speak, unreal and intangible and yet just as commonplace as the land and the people of which you speak—fugitive and furtive and evanescent as the realities of which you speak.

Ah, that which is near at hand is farther off than mountains! Why did you tell me that the near-at-hand might be grasped? The nearer at hand the farther away! It is only illusions that can be grasped and held! Realities escape our every touch; they recede as we advance.

We are creatures of illusion and must remain ever such—for realities, as you have said, are divine; they are of and for the Infinite; they are not for us.

Yet am I not sad, nor cast down, but resolute—I am merely out of focus; for no man can look forward and backward, up and down, right and left, near and far at the same time.

Go on, pater; I have girded up my heart! I am your hardy mariner O.K., but it is a heavy, foggy calm, and dead-reckoning is no joke! No; I will not be a porcelain ship upon a porcelain sea! Let the waves break and roar! Better to drown in turbulent waters than collapse in a tenuous air!

I am a seed deep in the dark ground! Would that I might spout, and my spear shoot into the lambent light and air, and delicately pierce the melody of spring!

Realities, realities! What are realities to the living-dead! What are sights to the eyeless! What are sounds to the earless! What are joys and sorrows to the heartless! What is the Infinite to the mindless! What is man—to man the beast?

Ah, it's all very fine, very fine indeed to be out of focus; especially when you know it. What does it comfort me that most men are out of focus!—for they know naught of the open air, while I—I have had glimpses—I!—only to lose them—except in memory's hold! Verily life has every weather, every water's depth!

Why is it farther to the nearest dewdrop than to the moon? Why is the nearest man you know unreachable as the pole? And yet, and yet, we press a button and a current flows that did not flow before, and there is light—an artificial light to be sure. But what are all our lights but artificial lights?

While you have been talking, I have been thinking, pater. Perhaps my thoughts were tinkling bells—who can say! Time alone can tell, and Time is rudely silent thereupon. Will she consecrate or will she blast—I do not care! For I am stubborn, now, with Fate, and must push on!

To what depths must we dig to find a solid soil! What a ridiculously elaborate scaffolding must we erect! And when our little structure's done and the scaffold down and the tools and the rubbish removed and our darling left to the world, the Stupid says: "Oh, how stupid: I could do that." I do not care; even though to move a people is harder than to move a rock! I suppose when Moses struck the rock and the waters flowed forth, that was another oriental allegory. I don't care whether it was or not, if it has to be explained. Why must we be eternally explaining things! Why don't things explain themselves! Why don't we understand without these everlasting explanations which explain nothing! We either see or don't see, don't we? And that's about the beginning and the end of it, isn't it? We are a dull crew all of us, and I am superlatively dull! When will the scales stay fallen from my eyes! When shall I be born again in strength! What avails it that I think, if my thought is sterile and brings forth not something fruitful into the light! Yet what do I care! Why should I care?

What is an architect, anyway, pater? I mean a real architect? I know what the common breed is. What sort of unusual hocus-pocus is he? From what particular heavenly menagerie is he supposed to have escaped, that he is to roam thus, as you intimate, through the wilderness of our land and day? You implied that he comes as a storm; and I think your whole storm-business was merely an occidental allegory. Allegories are all right if you are talking to an imaginative people; but—stop to think!

That a poet should arise as an exhalation from the spiritual agony and drought of his people, to condense, and return the waters, and after that that there should be rainbows and other beautiful things is fine, but it's too metaphysical. It's taken me three months to get it through my head. I thought, at the time, that you were talking and rhapsodizing about the actual physical storm we saw and felt. How could I know for a certainty that you were at the same time talking about a storm that I did not see and could not feel? But let that go, I want to think about it some more.

The main question in my mind is, what is an architect? Just as another question is: What is American; or, for that matter, what is an apple, a horse, a pine-tree—and, of course, ultimately, what is a building? And, again, more ultimately, what is architecture, what is a man, what are you, what am I, what is God, what is anything, and so on and on, around and around the circle, only to go around and around again, like a moth fluttering around the reality of a candle flame, which after all is only an illusion for the moth—the reality comes when the moth is burned.

Pater, learning this metaphysical business is a good deal like learning to control an aeroplane: the main thing is to keep your balance, not lose confidence, and go ahead. I shall learn the vertiginous game after a little, because I've made up my mind to it, and because I'm beginning to see that there is a deal in it that is useful in the way of aerial observation.

But for the moment let's bar it. Tell me what an architect is in fact, in reality, so to speak. I'm getting my own mind pretty well made up, after what you said on Culture, but I want to hear your view first—just to see if it's right, so to speak—you know. I want to get down to the practicalities.

Now don't look wistful, and tell me that if I want to see what an unreal architect is like to go look long and steadily in a mirror and learn by contrast. I don't like these sarcasms. They hurt now, for I have growing-pains; I am beginning to take myself very seriously, and flippancy scratches. From the duplicity of your heights, where contraries unite, you may treat serious matters with a certain irony and disdain—or am I entirely mistaken! In any event, kindly bear in mind that I am the shorn lamb and that you have shorn me; so temper the wind while I gather new wool—for what is art but wool-gathering after all?

But I digress. What I want to know is, what is an architect? Let's get down to business—or perhaps I might ask: What is an architect *not?* Shall we proceed by elimination or by cumulation, by frontal or by flank attack? And please bear in mind, pater, that I am an architect. Pardon me—don't look at me like that—I hasten to amend—I *think* I am an architect and—

Oh, let up, boy; you tire me to death. Bottle up that effervescence and save it for your next fit of blues.

That's right, daddy. I kiss the hand that chastens. I don't believe that an architect is a plumber, or a bricklayer or a mortar-mixer, or a teamster or a quarry-man, or a woodchopper, or a saw-mill, or a railroad, do you?

Of course not?

Nor is he a tinsmith, a glazier, a drain-layer, a roofer, a stone-cutter, a marble worker, a tile-layer, a jack-carpenter, a cabinet-maker, a wood-finisher, a painter, a derrick hand, a wire cable, or coal, or water, or the earth on which the building rests, or the air in which it grows—is he?

No.

I intend no allegory.

Go on, go on!

I am speaking objectively.

Will you go on!

Nor is he a moulder, a blacksmith, a forge, an anvil, a miner digging in the mines, a blast furnace, a rolling-mill.

Well, what of it?

Why, this: All these men and all these things enter as a genesis into the creation of a building, do they not? And yet they are not architects.

First rate. Go on.

Neither is he a surveyor, a mechanical engineer, an electrical engineer, a civil engineer, is he? Otherwise why are these men so called? Why are they not called architects?

That is well put.

Nor yet is he a builder, else why the name builder?

Very good.

And yet as regards a building the builder has his function, the engineer has his, the blacksmith his, the stone-cutter his, the man with a shovel his, the railroad trainman his, the railroad president his, the steel mill superintendent his, the banker his, the merchant his, the policeman his, and so on and on and on in an ever including and widening *cyclus* which extends ever outward and inward from the center to the borders of our civilization, and from its borders to the center. And why? Because Man has a desire to shelter himself and his products from the elements. Yet, so far, we have no architect. And why? Because none of these people and none of these things is called architect. Yet there is a name architect, therefore there must be a function architect—a real function—a real architect—an architect *solus.*

I have been thinking this out all by myself. You see, I want to isolate the architect and study him, just as biologists isolate a bacillus and study *him.* The bacillus is not the fever, the bacillus is the bacillus. So the architect is not the building, the architect is the architect. The bacillus *causes* the fever by acting on the body corporeal; so the architect *causes the building* by acting on the body social. The simile is not a nice one; in fact it's rather crude; but it gives you an idea of what I'm thinking.

But, on the other hand, the architect is a *product* of the body social, a product of our civilization. This you have shown me clearly. My simile breaks down here in a measure, but let it go—I'm through with it. So we approach him from two sides—as a product and as an agency; so of course I come at once to his true function, namely the double one: *to interpret and to initiate!*

That's very well done. You are beginning to show that you possess a logical and a perspicacious mind, and that you know how to use it.

Thank you. That's the first sincere compliment you've paid me.

It's the first you have earned.

Well, now, if our architect is at once a product and an agency, and if his function is at once to interpret and to initiate, *what is he to interpret and what is he to initiate?* What is it that justifies the name architect, what is his special, exclusive function? What is he expected to do, and what is he, alone, assumed to have the capacity to do, under our scheme and arrangement of civilization?

I hereby wave aside from the inquiry the hybrid-architect: the architect who believes himself an engineer, a carpenter, a merchant, a broker, a manufacturer, a business man or what not—and never stops to inquire if he is or is not an architect. If the merchant, broker, etc., were architects they would be called architects. They are not architects and that is why they are not called architects. Conversely, the architect who deems himself merchant, broker, etc., ceases to be architect and becomes hybrid, just to the extent that he believes it.

Of course, I assume that other men than architects may be and are products and agencies, and interpret and initiate. The dramatist may be such, the merchant such and many others: in fact, in the broadest sense, all are such, in larger or lesser degree, under the terms and conditions of modern civilization. But not one of these is expected to interpret the wants of the people with a view to initiate buildings. *Hence the true function of the architect is to initiate such buildings as shall correspond to the real needs of the people.*

Very good. Have you finished? If—

No, no! Let me talk. I have thought about this a great deal, in my own way. I am coming to the crux of the discussion; it is this: if it be true, as I have declared, that the true function of the architect is to initiate such buildings as shall correspond to the real needs of the people, how shall I infuse such unmistakable integrity of meaning and purpose into the word, *initiate*, the word *correspond*, and the phrase, *real needs of the people*, that mutton-heads and knaves can't use them for their own shameful purposes, by effecting a change of significance in the formula?

My boy, formulas are dangerous things. They are apt to prove the undoing of a genuine art, however helpful they may be, in the beginning, to the individual. The formula of an art remains and becomes more and more dry, rigid and shriveled with time, while the spirit of that art escapes, and vanishes forever. The bright spirit of art must be free. It will not live in a cage of words. Its willing home is in boundless nature, in the heart of the people, in the heart of the poet and in the work of the poet. It cannot live in text-books, in formulas, or in definitions. It must be free, else it departs as the light departs with the setting sun, and the darkness of folly is upon us.

Yes, I feel that, and I am beginning to feel in a very practical way the truth of what you said concerning the trickiness of words. Yet what am I to do—I must make others understand what I mean.

You can never make others understand what you mean. It's sheer folly to think of it. That, my boy, is an illusion—a fetish of the learned.

You understand what you understand, and another understands what he understands. You can't understand him and he can't understand you—and that's a beginning and an end of it. There exists between you and every one of your fellow beings a chasm infinitesimally narrow, yet absolutely uncrossable. The heart cannot cross it, the soul cannot cross it: much less can words cross it. Thus do you, thus does every human being live in the solitude of isolation—whence comes the word *identity*. This isolation is unreachable and unescapable. It is for each one of us a dungeon, or a boundless universe according to the largeness or the littleness of his soul; and around every living thing is there such an infinitesimal yet impassible gulf: around every tree, around every animal, every insect, every bird, every plant. Yet, within the confines of that circling chasm, lies an identity, a soul—unreachable, inscrutable; the ultimate reality; the very presence of the Eternal Spirit—a spirit of such infinite marvel that it brings forth an infinitude of infinitudes of identities—wonderful! wonderful! Spirit of the Universe! The Eternal Sun!

So, my boy, do not trouble yourself as to whether or not others understand your words as you do. Seek rather to understand yourself—regardless of words; and in due time, if so it be written in the great book of destiny, others will perceive in your works more or less of what you, more or less adequately, have thought, felt, lived, loved and understood.

Yes, that's doubtless all true, although I had never thought of it in just that way. Moreover, it's a rather creepy and scary thought—this notion of an invisible, impassible gulf which separates you from everything and everybody, so that you even cannot understand a friend. But still that shouldn't prevent me from attempting to define myself with a reasonable degree of clearness. So again, let me try to be explicit concerning the words *interpret*, and *initiate*, and the phrase, *real needs of the people*, as I understand them. To my own statement that the true function of the architect is to initiate such buildings as shall correspond to the real needs of the people, I now add your statement, that he must cause a building to grow naturally, logically and poetically out of its conditions. Now all of this means, and practically all that you have said to me means, I take it, in a few words, that the real architect is first, last and all the time, not a merchant, broker, manufacturer, business man, or anything of that sort, but *a poet who uses not words but building materials as a medium of expression:* Just in the same sense that a great painter uses pigments as *his* medium of expression; a musician, *tones;* a sculptor, *the marble block;* a literatus, *the written word;* and an orator, *the spoken word*—and, like them, to be truly great, really useful, he must impart to the passive materials a subjective or spiritual human quality which shall make them live for other humans—otherwise he fails utterly and is, in a high sense, a public nuisance instead of a public benefactor. Isn't that so?

It is indeed so.

Well, then, if it is so, and if it is true that this is the core of the matter, what's the use of talking about the so-called practicabilities. It can go without the saying, can't it, that a knowledge of administration, construction, equipment, materials, methods, processes and workmanship are part of his technical equipment whereby he has the efficiency and power to express the poetic thought—just as language and a knowledge of words are the technical equipment of the literatus. It is not, I take it, the words that make the poem, it is the manner in which the words are marshaled, organized and vitalized, that makes a poem a poem. And just so with building materials; they must be organized and vitalized in order that a real building may exist. Therefore to vitalize building materials, to animate them collectively with a thought, a state of feeling, to charge them with a subjective significance and value, to make them a visible part of the genuine social fabric, to infuse into them the true life of the people, to impart to them the best that is in the people, as the eye of the poet, looking below the surface of life, sees the best that is in the people—such is the real function of the architect; for, understood in these terms, the architect is one kind of poet, and his work one form of poetry—using the word in its broad, inclusive, actual sense. And if this view of the function of the architect be the true one, the real one, I can now understand what I did not fully grasp at the time, namely, your views concerning the methods of our architectural schools, your exasperation at the professor, and your contempt for what is currently called scholarship and culture. Truly it is inspiring, when one begins to acquire the faculty of looking at things with the inner or spiritual eye! Truly such an eye illuminates that which it sees, and opens to the inner view, and to the grasp of understanding, the great world of realities. This is, substantially, about as far as I can carry my thesis, with my present incomplete understanding of it. I suppose I have dropped a few stitches in knitting my argument.

No matter about the dropped stitches, for the present. You have done very well. Keep on observing, thinking—in the back of your head, in your spinal marrow, in your blood corpuscles, in your heart, liver, stomach, little finger, or wheresoever or by whatsoever real thinking is done—I don't know—and, slowly, but surely, you will find your thought grow, develop, personify itself and take on the inscrutable quality of identity: just as a plant grows by nutrition, assimilation and organization: and, when your flowering time comes—ah, my lad, when your flowering time comes!—your thought will flower and exhale the perfume I call architecture. You will be a real architect; sound of spirit, head, and clean of heart.

That is very kind. You fill me with hope. But don't you wish to take up my thesis where I left it and carry it on to a full and fine conclusion?

No, that isn't necessary. As I told you, long ago, you must do your own thinking. My task is simply to coach you a little, in calling your attention to certain things, certain conditions, certain powers, that exist in nature, in the world of men in your land, in your people and in yourself, and to point out to you certain things or essences that are eternal. My chiefest joy, and my greatest care, has been and is to protect you, until you are really strong, against illusions, delusions, and that self-secreted poison we call self-deception; and to inspire you with courage, manliness and an abiding sense of personal accountability. In such regard my work has been, is and shall continue to the end a work of love, born of reverence for youth and of fidelity to country and mankind. But I repeat, and should repeat over and over again: all the rest *you* must do. I cannot do your thinking, your living or your growing for you. I cannot define your personality: I will not delimit it. The true work of the architect is to organize, integrate and glorify *utility*. Then and then only is he truly *master-worker*.

Moreover, we still have far to go, through shadowy valleys, over chilling heights, through flowering meadows, before you shall be prepared to reach, by yourself, the threshold of the hidden temple of our art. Indeed, I fear lest as we come in sight of it that temple will recede, like a fearful rainbow: for of all things elusive, the fair spirit of art, whose abode is that temple, is the most unreal in the evanescence of its reality. If it come at all, it comes to us; we cannot go to it. And that it may come to us, that it may desire to come to us, we must ever truly seek it within the boundless power, beauty, and the sumptuous, fertile chastity of Nature. We must seek with fervent minds, with open hearts—in the *plein air* of the spirit.

Amen! I see I have some *job* before me. The architect is now hovering in my maturing imagination, not as a super-man, but as a real man—a philosophic man of the world: as the creating, guiding, sustaining *spirit*: to the end that the finished building may and shall be an ethical *totality*—however large, however small.

44   L. Sullivan, The Autobiography of an Idea* *1922-23*

In 1922, at the suggestion of Charles Whitaker, editor of the *Journal of the American Institute of Architects,* Sullivan began to write his autobiography, an endeavor that renewed his spirits and brought him a measure of happiness in his last years.[†] His energy momentarily returned, he also began preparing a series of large pencil drawings illustrating "A System of Ornament According with a Philosophy of Man's Powers," conceived to accompany the autobiography. He finished the manuscript in 1923 and the drawings soon after, and saw printed copies of both in 1924 shortly before his death; meanwhile, the autobiography had already been serialized in the *Journal of the American Institute of Architects.* The autobiography is a curious

---

* Louis H. Sullivan, *The Autobiography of an Idea* (New York, 1924), pp. 189–91, 219–21, 256–59, 314–15, 320–26, published serially in *Journal of the American Institute of Architects* (June 1922–September 1923); reprinted in book form (New York, 1934, 1949, and 1956).

† Whitaker's active role in the creation of the autobiography is noted in Sherman Paul, *Louis Sullivan: An Architect in American Thought* (Englewood Cliffs, N.J., 1962); see also Narciso Menocal, *Architecture as Nature: The Transcendendalist Idea of Louis Sullivan* (Madison, Wis., 1981).

Figure 55. Louis H. Sullivan, Plate 13 for *A System of Ornament According with a Philosophy of Man's Powers,* signed and dated July 6, 1922 (courtesy, Burnham Library, Art Institute of Chicago).

document. It is written in the third person and has decided foci on some portions of Louis's life and great gaps concerning others. Originally, Sullivan had ended the book with Chapter XIV, "Face to Face," on a positive tone, but at the insistence of Whitaker he added the last chapter, "Retrospect," contrasting his perception of architecture with that of Daniel Burnham which he considered fallacious. With this added chapter, which also concerns the impact of the Columbian Exposition of 1893, the book ends on a decidedly negative note. He provided no insight on his last skyscrapers, his split with Adler, the Carson, Pirie, Scott Store, nor any of the rural midwestern banks of the early twentieth century. He closed the door on his last years of frustration and disappointment, choosing instead to direct attention to his youth and education, his earlier years of promise and achievement.

CHAPTER X. FAREWELL TO BOSTON

Louis made up his mind that he would leave "Tech" [Massachusetts Institute of Technology] at the end of the school year, for he could see no future there. He was progressive, aggressive and impatient. He wished to live in the stream of life. He wished to be impelled by the power of living. He knew what he wanted very well. It behooved him he thought before going to the Beaux Arts, to see what architecture might be like in practice. He thought it might be advisable to spend a year in the office of some architect of standing, that he might see concrete preparations and results; how, in effect, an actual building was brought about. So he said a warm good-bye to Boston, to Wakefield (to his dear South Reading of the past), to all his friends, and made straightway for Philadelphia where he was to find his uncle and his grandpa. On the way he stopped over in New York City for a few days. Richard M. Hunt was the architectural lion there, and the dean of the profession. Louis called upon him in his den, told him his plans and was patted on the back and encouraged as an enterprising youngster. He listened to the mighty man's tale of his life in Paris with Lefuel, and was then turned over to an assistant named Stratton, a recent arrival from the Ecole to whom he repeated the tale of his projects.

Friend Stratton was most amiable in greeting, and gave Louis much time, receiving him in the fraternal spirit of an older student toward a younger. He sketched the life in Paris and the School—and in closing asked Louis to keep in touch with him and be sure to call on him on the way abroad. Thus Louis, proud and inflated, went on his joyous way to face the world. He arrived in Philadelphia in due time, as they say. He had noticed in New York a sharper form of speech, an increase of energetic action over that he had left behind, and also a rougher and more arrogant type of life. Stratton had mentioned that Louis, on his arrival in Philadelphia, should look up the firm of Furness & Hewitt, architects, and try to find a place with them. But this was not Louis's way of doing. Once settled down in the large quiet village, he began to roam the streets, looking quizzically at buildings as he wandered. On the west side of South Broad street a residence, almost completed, caught his eye like a flower by the roadside. He approached, examined it with curious care, without and within. Here was something fresh and fair to him, a human note, as though someone were talking. He inquired as to the architect and was told: Furness & Hewitt. Now, he saw plainly enough that this was not the work of two men but of one, for he had an instinctive sense of physiognomy, and all buildings thus made their direct appeal to him, pleasant or unpleasant.

He made up his mind that next day he would enter the employ of said Furness & Hewitt, they to have no voice in the matter, for his mind was made up. So next day he presented himself to Frank Furness and informed him he had come to enter his employ. . . .

CHAPTER XII. PARIS

After a brief stay at the Hôtel St. Honoré, Louis found permanent quarters on the seventh floor of a rooming hotel, at the southeast corner Rue Monsieur Le Prince and Rue Racine, in the Latin Quarter. Nearby were the "Boule Miche" toward the east, the Odeon, the Luxembourg Palace and its gardens to the southwest. From this lofty perch which he always reached on the run, two steps at a time, the City of Paris spread before him to the north, and on the small balcony, reached by casement doors, he would sometimes sit in the twilight and be caught by the solitary boom of the great bell of Notre Dame.

Early he had discovered that the French of his High School, for excellence in which he had taken first prize in a matter of course way, was not quite the colloquial French he now heard, spoken with exasperating rapidity and elision. As to the bill of fare, the *Menu*, at the first attempt he perspired awhile in anguish, then put his finger on a line at random, and set down the result in a special notebook. He must learn current French in a hurry. He engaged a teacher to come every day at a fixed hour. When on the streets, he walked close to the people ahead, to catch every word; in this way his ear caught up words, locutions, intonations, and emphasis; and soon he began to feel he was on the way, even though he did not understand a tenth of what he heard.

He early visited the American Legation, complied with requirements, received information and advice, was told to buy certain textbooks, and was referred to a certain Monsieur Clopet as the very best tutor in mathematics. At the Legation he made the startling discovery that the Beaux Arts entrance examinations were to begin in six weeks; and furthermore, he had scanned the Program of Admission, and was startled again at the range of subjects he was not up on. Was he downhearted? Not a bit. It was a *certainty* he would pass because he must *pass*. He had come to Paris from far-away Chicago with that sole end in view; so why argue? He knew it meant six weeks of the hardest work he had ever done. He figured on eighteen hours a day. He knew he was in physical condition. He would allot one hour each day to gymnasium work, and keep on simple diet. What stood uppermost in his mind and gave him self-reliance to face any task, was his assurance: Had he not been trained in discipline and self-discipline by Moses Woolson? Had he not been trained and tried by that great teacher in the science and the art of thinking, of alertness, of close attention and quick action, in economy of time, in sharp analysis, in the high values of contemplation?

He lost no time in calling upon Monsieur Clopet. He was greeted in simple gracious words, by a small dark man, who, to Louis's joy, spoke only French. The preliminaries over, Monsieur Clopet asked: "And what are the books you have under your arm?" Louis replied: "Books I was told at the American legation I would need." "Ah, yes, let me see them." He took the books, selected a large work on Descriptive Geometry, and began to turn the pages. "Now observe: Here is a problem with five exceptions or special cases; here a theorem, three special cases; another nine, and so on and on, a procession of exceptions and special cases. I suggest you place the book in the waste basket; we shall not need of it here; *for here our demonstrations shall be so broad as to admit of no exception!"*

At these amazing words Louis stood as one whose body had turned to hot stone, while his brain was raging. Instantly the words had flashed, there arose a vision and a fixed resolve; an instantaneous inquiry and an instant answer. The inquiry: If this can be done in Mathematics, why not in Architecture? The instant answer: It can, and it shall be! *no one has—I will!* It may mean a long struggle; longer and harder than the tramp through the forest of Brown's Tract. It may be years from now, before I find what I seek, but I shall find it, if otherwere and otherwise, with or without guide other than my *flair,* my will and my apprehension. It shall be done! I shall live for that!—no one, no thing, no thousand shall deter me. The world of men, of thoughts, of things, shall be mine. Firmly I believe that if I can but interpret it, that world is filled with evidence. I shall explore that world to seek, to find. I shall weigh that world in a balance. I shall question it, I shall examine and cross-examine, I shall finally interpret—I shall not be withheld, I shall prevail! . . .

CHAPTER XIII. THE GARDEN CITY

On the first day of May, 1880, D. Adler & Co. moved into a fine suite of offices on the top floor of the Borden Block. . . . On the first day of May, 1881, the firm of Adler & Sullivan, Architects, had its name on the entrance door. All of which signifies, after long years of ambitious dreaming and unremitting work, that at the age of 25, Louis H. Sullivan became a full-fledged architect before the world, with a reputation starting on its way, and in partnership with a man he had least expected as such; a man whose reputation was solidly secured in utter honesty, fine intelligence and a fund of that sort of wisdom which attracts and holds. Between the two there existed a fine confidence and the handling of the work was divided and adjusted on a temperamental basis—each to have initiative and final authority in his own field, without a sharp arbitrary line being drawn that might lead to dissension. What was particularly fine, as we consider human nature, was Adler's open frank way of pushing his young partner to the front.

Now Louis felt he had arrived at a point where he had a foothold, where he could make a *beginning* in the open world. Having come into its responsibilities, he would face it boldly. He could now, undisturbed, start on the course of practical experimentation he long had in mind, which was to make an architecture that fitted its functions—a realistic architecture based on well defined utilitarian needs—that all practical demands of utility should be paramount as basis of planning and design; that no architectural dictum, or tradition, or superstition, or habit, should stand in the way. He would brush them all aside, regardless of commentators. For his view, his conviction was this: That the architectural art to be of contemporary immediate value must be *plastic;* all senseless conventional rigidity must be taken out of it; it must intelligently serve—it must not suppress. In this wise the forms under his hand would grow naturally out of the needs and express them frankly, and freshly. This meant in his courageous mind that he would put to the test a formula he had evolved, through long contemplation of living things, namely that *form follows function,* which would mean, in practice, that architecture might again become a living art, if this formula were but adhered to.

The building business was again under full swing, and a series of important mercantile structures came into the office, each one of which he treated experimentally, feeling his way toward a basic process, a grammar of his own. The immediate problem was increased daylight, the maximum of daylight. This led him to use slender piers, tending toward a masonry and iron combination, the beginnings of a vertical system. This method upset all precedent, and led Louis's contemporaries to regard him as an iconoclast, a revolutionary, which was true enough—yet into the work was slowly infiltrated a corresponding system of artistic expression, which appeared in these structures as novel and to some repellent, in its total disregard of accepted notions. But to all objections Louis turned a deaf ear. If a thousand proclaimed him wrong, the thousand could not change his course. As buildings varying in character came under his hand, he extended to them his system of form and function, and as he did so his conviction increased that architectural manipulation, as a homely art or a fine art must be rendered completely plastic to the mind and the hand of the designer; that materials and forms must yield to the mastery of his imagination and his will; through this alone could modern conditions be met and faithfully expressed. This meant the casting aside of all pedantry, of all the artificial teachings of the schools, of the thoughtless acceptance of inane traditions, of puerile habits of uninquiring minds; that all this mess, devoid of a center of gravity of thought, and vacant of sympathy and understanding, must be superseded by a sane philosophy of a living architecture, good for all time, founded on the only possible foundation—Man and his powers. Such philosophy Louis had already developed in broad outline in the course of his many dissatisfactions and contemplations. He wished now to test it out in the broad daylight of action, and to perfect its form and content. This philosophy developed will be set forth in these closing chapters.

It is not to be supposed that Louis arrived directly at results as though by magic. Quite the contrary, he arrived slowly though boldly through the years, by means of incessant thought, self correction, hard work and dogged perseverance. For it was his fascinating task to build up a system of technique, a mastery of technique. And such a system could scarcely be expected to reach its fullness of development, short of maturity, assuming it would reach its fullness then, or could ever reach it; for the world of expression is limitless; the theory so deep in idea, so rich in content, as to preclude any ending of its beneficent, all-inclusive power. And we may here recall Monsieur Clopet, the book of descriptive geometry that went into the waste basket, and the thunderclap admonition: "Our demonstrations shall be such as to admit of no exception."

CHAPTER XV. RETROSPECT

In Chicago the tall office building would seem to have arisen spontaneously, in response to favoring physical conditions, and the economic pressure as then sanctified, combined with the daring of promoters. . . .

The stream of immigration [into the city] was enormous, spreading over vast areas, burrowing in the mines or clinging to the cities. Chicago had passed St. Louis in population and was proud. Its system of building had become known as the "Chicago Construction." It was pushing its structures higher and higher, until the Masonic Temple by John Root had raised its head far into the air, and the word "skyscraper" came into use. Chicago was booming. It had become a powerful magnet. Its people had one dream in common: That their city should become the world's metropolis. There was great enthusiasm and public spirit. So things stood, in the years 1890, 1891 and 1892. John Root had said to Louis: "You take your art too seriously." Burnham had said to Louis: "It is not good policy to go much above the general level of intelligence.". . .

Chicago was ripe and ready [to play host to the Columbian Exposition celebrating the four hundredth anniversary of the discovery of the New World]. It had the required enthusiasm and the will. It won out in a contest between the cities. The prize was now in hand. It was to be the city's crowning glory. A superb site on the lake adjoined the southern section of the city. This site was soon to be transformed and embellished by the magic of American prowess, particularly in its architectural aspects, as to set forth the genius of the land in that great creative art. It was to be a dream city, where one might revel in beauty. It was to be called The White City by the Lake. . . .

A layout was submitted to the Board as a basis for discussion. It was rearranged on two axes at right angles. The buildings were disposed accordingly. By an amicable arrangement each architect was given such building as he preferred, after consultation. The meeting then adjourned.

The story of the building of the Fair is foreign to the purpose of this narrative, which is to deal with its more serious aspects, implications and results. Suffice it that Burnham performed in a masterful way, displaying remarkable executive capacity. He became open-minded, just, magnanimous. He did his great share.

The work completed, the gates thrown open 1 May, 1893, the crowds flowed in from every quarter, continued to flow throughout a fair-weather summer and a serenely beautiful October. Then came the end. The gates were closed.

These crowds were astonished. They beheld what was for them an amazing revelation of the architectural art, of which previously they in comparison had known nothing. To them it was a veritable Apocalypse, a message inspired from on high. Upon it their imagination shaped new ideals. They went away, spreading again over the land, returning to their homes, each one of them carrying in the soul the shadow of the white cloud, each of them permeated by the most subtle and slow-acting of poisons; an imperceptible miasm within the white shadow of a higher culture. A vast multitude, exposed, unprepared, they had not had time nor occasion to become immune to forms of sophistication not their own, to a higher and more dexterously insidious plausibility. Thus they departed joyously, carriers of contagion, unaware that what they had beheld and believed to be truth was to prove, in historic fact, an appalling calamity. For what they saw was not at all what they believed they saw, but an imposition of the spurious upon their eyesight, a naked exhibitionism of charlatanry in the higher feudal and domineering culture, conjoined with expert salesmanship of the materials of decay. Adventitiously, to make the stage setting complete, it happened by way of apparent but unreal contrast that the structure representing the United States Government was of an incredible vulgarity, while the building at the peak of the north axis, stationed there as a symbol of "The Great State of Illinois" matched it as a lewd exhibit of drooling imbecility and political debauchery. The distribution at the northern end of the grounds of many state and foreign headquarters relieved the sense of stark immensity. South of them, and placed on the border of a small lake, stood the Palace of the Arts, the most vitriolic of them all—the most impudently thievish. The landscape work, in its genial distribution of lagoons, wooded islands, lawns, shrubbery and plantings, did much to soften an otherwise mechanical display; while far in the southeast corner, floating in a small lagoon or harbor, were replicas of the three caravels of Columbus, and on an adjacent artificial mound a representation of the Convent of La Rabida. Otherwhere there was no evidence of Columbus and his daring deed, his sufferings, and his melancholy end. No keynote, no dramatic setting forth of that deed which, recently, has aroused some discussion as to whether the discovery of America had proven to be a blessing or a curse to the world of mankind. . . .

From the height of its Columbian Ecstacy, Chicago drooped and subsided with the rest, in a common sickness, the nausea of overstimulation. This in turn passed, toward the end of the decade, and the old game began again with intensified fury, to come to a sudden halt in 1907. There are those who say this panic was artificial and deliberate, that the battle of the saber-toothed tigers and the mastodons was on.

Meanwhile the virus of the World's Fair, after a period of incubation in the architectural profession and in the population at large, especially the influential, began to show unmistakable signs of the nature of the contagion. There came a violent outbreak of the Classic and the Renaissance in the East, which slowly spread westward, contaminating all that it touched, both at its source and outward. The selling campaign of the bogus antique was remarkably well managed through skillful publicity and propaganda, by those who were first to see its commercial possibilities. The market was ripe, made so through the hebetude of the populace, big business men, and eminent educators alike. By the time the market had been saturated, all sense of reality was gone. In its place had come deep-seated illusions, hallucinations, absence of pupillary reaction to light, absence of knee-reaction—symptoms all of progressive cerebral meningitis: The blanketing of the brain. Thus Architecture died in the land of the free and the home of the brave,—in a land declaring its fervid democracy, its inventiveness, its resourcefulness, its unique daring, enterprise and progress. Thus did the virus of a culture, snobbish and alien to the land, perform its work of disintegration; and thus ever works the pallid academic mind, denying the real, exalting the fictitious and the false, incapable of adjusting itself to the flow of living things, to the reality and the pathos of man's follies, to the valiant hope that ever causes him to aspire, and again to aspire; that never lifts a hand in aid because it cannot; that turns its back upon man because that is its tradition; a culture lost in ghostly *mésalliance* with abstractions, when what the world needs is courage, common sense and human sympathy, and a moral standard that is plain, valid and livable.

The damage wrought by the World's Fair will last for half a century from its date, if not longer. It has penetrated deep into the constitution of the American mind, effecting there lesions significant of dementia.

Meanwhile the architectural generation immediately succeeding the Classic and Renaissance merchants, are seeking to secure a special immunity from the inroads of common sense, through a process of vaccination with the lymph of every known European style, period and accident, and to this all-around process, when it breaks out, is to be added the benediction of good taste. Thus we have now the abounding freedom of Eclecticism, the winning smile of taste, but no architecture. For Architecture, be it known, is dead. Let us therefore lightly dance upon its grave, strewing roses as we glide. Indeed let us gather, in procession, in the night, in the rain, and make soulful, fluent, epicene orations to the living dead we neuters eulogize. . . .

45   F. L. Wright, The Art and Craft of the Machine*   *1901, 1930*

At the time Frank Lloyd Wright (1867–1959) prepared this address, he and Sullivan were not speaking. Sullivan had summarily dismissed his assistant in 1893 when he discovered Wright was taking on private work during his off hours (they were reconciled shortly before Wright left for Europe in 1910 and remained close thereafter).[†] Wright shared Sullivan's view concerning the debasement of the profession, and in 1900 he discussed the plight of the architect in a paper read before the annual meeting of the Architectural League of America in Chicago, claiming the architect had sold out, that he had made himself a salesman of prepackaged styles.[‡] An even more important indication of his developing philosophy was Wright's lecture, "The Art and Craft of the Machine," given at a meeting of the Arts and Crafts Society at Hull House, Chicago, the next year. The way out of the dilemma, Wright proposed, was by embracing the machine, exploiting its potential and developing a new architecture on the basis of this new sensitivity. How this might be done he illustrated in designs for small single-family houses published at the same time in popular journals.[§] Wright slightly revised this lecture for delivery before the Western Society of

* Frank Lloyd Wright, "The Art and Craft of the Machine," from *Modern Architecture: Being the Kahn Lectures for 1930* (Princeton, 1930), pp. 7–23.

† See Wright's *Genius and the Mobocracy* (New York, 1949), his biographical tribute to Sullivan.

‡ "The Architect," *Brickbuilder* 9 (June 1900), 124–28.

§ "A Home in a Prairie Town" and "A Small House with 'Lots of Room in It,'" *The Ladies' Home Journal* 18 (February and July 1901), pp. 17, 15. These were two of hundreds of designs *Journal* editor Edward Bok requested of many prominent and rising architects and published in the magazine between 1895 and 1915.

Engineers in 1901, published it in the catalogue of the Chicago Architectural Club exhibition of 1901, and revised it once more for presentation before the Daughters of the American Revolution in Chicago in 1904. He expanded on it once again, returning to a challenge he believed had yet to be taken up, to open the series of four lectures he delivered at Princeton University in 1930.

No one, I hope, has come here tonight for a sociological prescription for the cure of evils peculiar to this machine age. For I come to you as an architect to say my word for the right use upon such new materials as we have, of our great substitute for tools—machines. There is no thrift in any craft until the tools are mastered; nor will there be a worthy social order in America until the elements by which America does its work are mastered by American society. Nor can there be an art worth the man or the name until these elements are grasped and truthfully idealized in whatever we as a people try to make. Although these elemental truths should be commonplace enough by now, as a people we do not understand them nor do we see the way to apply them. We are probably richer in raw materials for our use as workmen, citizens or artists than any other nation—but outside mechanical genius for mere contrivance we are not good workmen, nor, beyond adventitious or propitious respect for property, are we as good citizens as we should be, nor are we artists at all. We are one and all, consciously or unconsciously, mastered by our fascinating automatic "implements," using them as substitutes for tools. To make this assertion clear I offer you evidence I have found in the field of architecture. It is still a field in which the pulse of the age throbs beneath much shabby finery and one broad enough (God knows) to represent the errors and possibilities common to our time-serving time.

Architects in the past have embodied the spirit common to their own life and to the life of the society in which they lived in the most noble of all noble records—buildings. They wrought these valuable records with the primitive tools at their command and whatever these records have to say to us today would be utterly insignificant if not wholly illegible were tools suited to another and different condition stupidly forced to work upon them; blindly compelled to do work to which they were not fitted, work which they could only spoil.

In this age of steel and steam the tools with which civilization's true record will be written are scientific thoughts made operative in iron and bronze and steel and in the plastic processes which characterize this age, all of which we call machines. The electric lamp is in this sense a machine. New materials in the man-machines have made the physical body of this age what it is as distinguished from former ages. They have made our era the machine age—wherein locomotive engines, engines of industry, engines of light or engines of war or steamships take the place works of art took in previous history. Today we have a scientist or an inventor in place of a Shakespeare or a Dante. Captains of industry are modern substitutes, not only for kings and potentates, but, I am afraid, for great artists as well. And yet—man-made environment is the truest, most characteristic of all human records. Let a man build and you have him. You may not have all he is, but certainly he is what you have. Usually you will have his outline. Though the elements may be in him to enable him to grow out of his present self-made characterization, few men are ever belied by self-made environment. Certainly no historical period was ever so misrepresented. Chicago in its ugliness today becomes as true an expression of the *life* lived here as is any center on earth where men come together closely to live it out or fight it out. Man is a selecting principle, gathering his like to him wherever he goes. The intensifying of his existence by close contact, too, flashes out the human record vividly in his background and his surroundings. But somewhere—somehow—in our age, although signs of the times are not wanting, beauty in this expression is forfeited—the record is illegible when not ignoble. We must walk blindfolded through the streets of this, or any great modern American city, to fail to see that all this magnificent resource of machine-power and superior material has brought to us, so far, is degradation. All of the art forms sacred to the art of old are, by us, prostitute.

On every side we see evidence of inglorious quarrel between things as they were and things as they must be and are. This shame a certain merciful ignorance on our part mistakes for glorious achievement. We believe in our greatness when we have tossed up a Pantheon to the god of money in a night or two, like the Illinois Trust Building or the Chicago National Bank. And it is our glory to get together a mammoth aggregation of Roman monuments, sarcophagi and temples for a post office in a year or two. On Michigan Avenue Montgomery Ward presents us with a nondescript Florentine palace with a grand campanile for a "farmer grocery" and it is as common with us as it is elsewhere to find the giant stone Palladian "orders" overhanging plate glass shop fronts. Show windows beneath Gothic office buildings, the office-middle topped by Parthenons, or models of any old sacrificial temple, are a common sight. Every commercial interest in any American town, in fact, is scurrying for respectability by seeking some advertising connection, at least, with the "classic." A commercial renaissance is here; the renaissance of "the ass in the lion's skin." This much, at least, we owe to the late Columbian Fair—that triumph of modern civilization in 1893 will go down in American architectural history, when it is properly recorded, as a mortgage upon posterity that posterity must repudiate not only as usurious but as forged.

In our so-called "skyscrapers" (latest and most famous business-building triumph), good granite or Bedford stone is cut into the fashion of the Italian followers of Phidias and his Greek slaves. Blocks so cut are cunningly arranged about a structure of steel beams and shafts (which structure secretly robs them of any real meaning), in order to make the finished building resemble the architecture depictured by Palladio and Vitruvius—in the schoolbooks. It is quite as feasible to begin putting on this Italian trimming at the cornice, and come on down to the base as it is to work, as the less fortunate Italians were forced to do, from the base upward. Yes, "from the top down" is often the actual method employed. The keystone of a Roman or Gothic arch may now be "set"—that is to say "hung"—and the voussoirs stuck alongside or "hung" on downward to the haunches. Finally this mask, completed, takes on the features of the pure "classic," or any variety of "renaissance" or whatever catches the fancy or fixes the "convictions" of the designer. Most likely, an education in art has "fixed" both. Our Chicago University, "a seat of learning," is just as far removed from truth. If environment is significant and indicative, what does this highly reactionary, extensive and expensive scene-painting by means of hybrid collegiate Gothic signify? Because of Oxford it seems to be generally accepted as "appropriate for scholastic purposes." Yet, why should an American university in a land of democratic ideals in a machine age be characterized by second-hand adaptation of Gothic forms, themselves adapted previously to our own adoption by a feudalistic age with tools to use and conditions to face totally different from anything we can call our own? The public library is again asinine renaissance, bones sticking through the flesh because the interior was planned by a shrewd library board—while an "art architect" (the term is Chicago's, not mine) was "hired" to "put the architecture on it." The "classical" aspect of the sham-front must be preserved at any cost to sense. Nine out of ten public buildings in almost any American city are the same.

On Michigan Avenue, too, we pass another pretentious structure, this time fashioned as inculcated by the Ecole des Beaux Arts after the ideals and methods of a Graeco-Roman, inartistic, grandly brutal civilization, a civilization that borrowed everything but its jurisprudence. Its essential tool was the slave. Here at the top of our culture is the Chicago Art Institute, and very like other art institutes. Between lions—realistic—Kemyss would have them so because Barye did—we come beneath some stone millinery into the grandly useless lobby. Here French's noble statue of the republic confronts us—she too, imperial. The grand introduction over, we go further on to find amid plaster casts of antiquity, earnest students patiently gleaning a half-acre or more of archaeological dry-bones, arming here for industrial conquest, in other words to go out and try to make a living by making some valuable impression upon the machine age in which they live. Their fundamental tool in this business about which they will know just this much less than nothing, is—the machine. In this acre or more not one relic has any vital relation to things as they are for these students, except for the blessed circumstance that they are more or less beautiful things in themselves—bodying forth the beauty of "once upon a time." These students at best are to concoct from a study of the aspect of these blind reverences an extract of antiquity suited to modern needs, meanwhile knowing nothing of modern needs, permitted to care nothing for them, and knowing just as little of the needs of the ancients which made the objects they now study. The tyros are taught in the name of John Ruskin and William Morris to shun and despise the essential tool of their age as a matter commercial and antagonistic to art. So in time they go forth, each armed with his little Academic extract, applying it as a sticking-plaster from without, wherever it can be made to stick, many helplessly knowing in their hearts that it should be a development from within—but how? And this is an education in art in these United States.

Climb now the grand monumental stairway to see the results of this cultural effort—we will call it "education"—hanging over the walls of the exhibition galleries. You will find there the same empty reverences to the past at cost to the present and of doubtful value to the future, unless a curse is valuable. Here you may see fruits of the lust and pride of the patron-collector but how shamefully little to show by way of encouraging patronage by the artist of his own day and generation. This is a temple of the fine arts.

A sacred place! It should be the heart-center, the emotional inspiration of a great national industrial activity, but here we find tradition not as an *inspiring* spirit animating progress. No. Now more in the *past* than ever! No more, now, than an ancient mummy, a dead letter. A "precedent" is a "hang over" to copy, the copy to be copied for machine reproduction, to be shamelessly reproduced until demoralized utterly or unrecognizable.

More unfortunate, however, than all this fiasco, is the fiasco al fresco. The suburban house-parade is more servile stil!. Any popular avenue or suburb will show the polyglot encampment displaying, on the neatly kept little plots, a theatrical desire on the part of fairly respectable people to live in châteaux, manor houses, Venetian palaces, feudal castles, and Queen Anne cottages. Many with sufficient hardihood abide in abortions of the carpenter-architect, our very own General Grant Gothic perhaps, intended to beat all the "lovely periods" at their own game and succeeding. Look within all this typical monotony-in-variety and see there the machine-made copies of handicraft originals; in fact, unless you, the householder, are fortunate indeed, possessed of extraordinary taste and opportunity, all you possess is in some degree a machine-made example of vitiated handicraft, imitation antique furniture made antique by the machine, itself of all abominations the most abominable. Everything must be curved and carved and carved and turned. The whole mass a tortured sprawl supposed artistic. And the floor-coverings? Probably machine-weavings of oriental rug patterns—pattern and texture mechanically perfect; or worse, your walls are papered with paper-imitations of old tapestry, imitation patterns and imitation textures, stamped or printed by the machine; imitations under foot, imitations overhead and imitations all round about you. You are sunk in "imitation." Your much-molded woodwork is stained "antique." Inevitably you have a white-and-gold "reception-room" with a few gilded chairs, an overwrought piano, and withal, about you a general cheap machine-made "profusion" of—copies of copies of original imitations. To you, proud proprietors—do these things thus degraded mean anything aside from vogue and price? Aside from your sense of quantitative ownership, do you perceive in them some fine fitness in form, line and color to the purposes which they serve? Are the chairs to sit in, the tables to use, the couch comfortable, and are all harmoniously related to each other and to your own life? Do many of the furnishings or any of the window-millinery serve any purpose at all of which you can think? Do you enjoy in "things" the least appreciation of truth in beautiful guise? If not, you are a victim of habit, a habit evidence enough of the stagnation of an outgrown art. Here we have the curse of stupidity—a cheap substitute for ancient art and craft which has no vital meaning in your own life or our time. You line the box you live in as a magpie lines its nest. You need not be ashamed to confess your ignorance of the meaning of all this, because not only you, but every one else, is hopelessly ignorant concerning it; it is "impossible." Imitations of imitations, copies of copies, cheap expedients, lack of integrity, some few blind gropings for simplicity to give hope to the picture. That is all.

Why wonder what has become of the grand spirit of art that made, in times past, man's reflection in his environment a godlike thing? *This* is what has become of it! Of all conditions, this one at home is most deplorable, for to the homes of this country we must look for any beginning of the awakening of an artistic conscience which will change this parasitic condition to independent growth. The homes of the people will change before public buildings can possibly change.

Glance now for a moment behind this adventitious scene-painting passing, at home, for art in the nineteenth century. Try to sense the true conditions underlying all, and which you betray and belie in the name of culture. Study with me for a moment the engine which produces this wreckage and builds you, thus cheapened and ridiculous, into an ignoble record.

Here is this thing we call the machine, contrary to the principle of organic growth, but imitating it, working irresistibly the will of man through the medium of men. All of us are drawn helplessly into its mesh as we tread our daily round. And its offices—call them "services"—have become the commonplace background of modern existence; yes, and sad to say, in too many lives the foreground, middle distance and future. At best we ourselves are already become or are becoming some cooperative part in a vast machinery. It is, with us, as though we were controlled by some great crystallizing principle going on in nature all around us and going on, in spite of ourselves, even in our very own *natures*. If you would see how interwoven it is, this thing we call the machine, with the warp and the woof of civilization, if indeed it is not now the very basis of civilization itself, go at nightfall when all is simplified and made suggestive, to the top of our newest skycraper, the Masonic temple. There you may see how in the image of material man, at once his glory and his menace, is this thing we call a city. Beneath you is the monster stretching out into the far distance. High overhead hangs a stagnant pall, its fetid breath reddened with light from myriad eyes endlessly, everywhere blinking. Thousands of acres of cellular tissue outspread, enmeshed by an intricate network of veins and arteries radiating into the gloom. Circulating there with muffled ominous roar is the ceaseless activity to whose necessities it all conforms. This wondrous tissue is knit and knit again and inter-knit with a nervous system, marvelously effective and complete, with delicate filaments for hearing and knowing the pulse of its own organism, acting intelligently upon the ligaments and tendons of motive impulse, and in it all is flowing the impelling electric fluid of man's own life. And the labored breathing, murmur, clangor, and the roar—how the voice of this monstrous force rises to proclaim the marvel of its structure! Near at hand, the ghastly warning boom from the deep throats of vessels heavily seeking inlet to the waterway below, answered by the echoing clangor of the bridge bells. A distant shriek grows nearer, more ominous, as the bells warn the living current from the swinging bridge and a vessel cuts for a moment the flow of the nearer artery. Closing then upon the great vessel's stately passage the double bridge is just in time to receive in a rush of steam the avalanche of blood and metal hurled across it; a streak of light gone roaring into the night on glittering bands of steel; an avalanche encircled in its flight by slender magic lines, clicking faithfully from station to station—its nervous herald, its warning and its protection.

Nearer, in the building ablaze with midnight activity, a spotless paper band is streaming into the marvel of the multiple-press, receiving indelibly the impression of human hopes and fears, throbbing in the pulse of this great activity, as infallibly as the gray-matter of the human brain receives the impression of the senses. The impressions come forth as millions of neatly folded, perfected news-sheets, teeming with vivid appeals to good and evil passions; weaving a web of intercommunication so far-reaching that distance becomes as nothing, the thought of one man in one corner of the earth on one day visible on the next to all men. The doings of all the world are reflected here as in a glass—so marvelously sensitive this simple band streaming endlessly from day to day becomes in the grasp of the multiple-press.

If the pulse of this great activity—automatons working night and day in every line of industry, to the power of which the tremor of the mammoth steel skeleton beneath your feet is but an awe-inspiring response—is thrilling, what of the prolific, silent obedience to man's will underlying it all? If this power must be uprooted that civilization may live, then civilization is already doomed. Remain to contemplate this wonder until the twinkling lights perish in groups, or follow one by one, leaving others to live through the gloom; fires are banked, tumult slowly dies to an echo here and there. Then the darkened pall is gradually lifted and moonlight outlines the shadowy, sullen masses of structure, structure deeply cut here and there by half-luminous channels. Huge patches of shadow in shade and darkness commingle mysteriously in the block-like plan with box-like skylines—contrasting strangely with the broad surface of the lake beside, placid and resplendent with a silver gleam. Remain, I say, to reflect that the texture of the city, this great machine, is the warp upon which will be woven the woof and pattern of the democracy we pray for. Realize that it has been deposited here, particle by particle, in blind obedience to law—law no less organic so far as we are concerned than the laws of the great solar universe. That universe, too, in a sense, is but an obedient machine.

Magnificent power! And it confronts the young architect and his artist comrades now, with no other beauty—a lusty material giant without trace of ideality, absurdly disguised by garments long torn to tatters or contemptuously tossed aside, outgrown. Within our own recollection we have all been horrified at the bitter cost of this ruthless development—appalled to see this great power driven by greed over the innocent and defenseless—we have seen bread snatched from the mouths of sober and industrious men, honorable occupations going to the wall with a riot, a feeble strike, or a stifled moan, outclassed, outdone, outlived by the machine. The workman himself has come to regard this relentless force as his nemesis and combines against machinery in the trades with a wild despair that dashes itself to pieces, while the artist blissfully dreaming in the halls we have just visited or walking blindly abroad in the paths of the past, berates his own people for lack luster senses, rails against industrial conditions that neither afford him his opportunity, nor, he says, can appreciate him as he, panderer to ill-gotten luxury, folding his hands, starves to death. "Innocuous martyr upon the cross of art!" One by one, tens by tens, soon thousands by thousands, handicraftsmen and parasitic artists succumb to the inevitable as one man at a machine does the work of from five to fifty men in the same time, with all the art there is meanwhile prostituting to old methods and misunderstood ideals the far greater new possibilities due to this same machine, and doing this disgracefully in the name of the beautiful!

American society has the essential tool of its own age by the blade, as lacerated hands everywhere testify!

See the magnificent prowess of this unqualified power—strewing our surroundings with the mangled corpses of a happier time. We live amid ghostly relics whose pattern once stood for cultivated luxury and now stands for an ignorant matter of taste. With no regard for first principles of common sense the letter of tradition is recklessly fed into rapacious maws of machines until the reproduction, reproduced *ad nauseam*, may be had for five, ten or ninety-nine cents although the worthy original cost ages of toil and patient culture. This might seem like progress, were it not for the fact that these butchered forms, the life entirely gone out of them, are now harmful parasites, belittling and falsifying any true perception of normal beauty the Creator may have seen fit to implant in us on our own account. Any idea whatever of fitness to purpose or of harmony between form and use is gone from us. It is lacking in these things one and all, because it is so sadly lacking in us. And as for making the best of our own conditions or repudiating the terms on which this vulgar insult to tradition is produced, thereby insuring and rectifying the industrial fabric thus wasted or enslaved by base imitation—the mere idea is abnormal, as I myself have found to my sorrow.

And among the few, the favored chosen few who love art by nature and would devote their energies to it so that it may live and let them live— any training they can seek would still be a protest against the machine as the creator of all this iniquity, when (God knows) it is no more than the creature.

But, I say, usurped by greed and deserted by its natural interpreter, the artist, the machine is only the creature, not the creator of this iniquity! I say the machine has noble possibilities unwillingly forced to this degradation, degraded by the arts themselves. Insofar as the true capacity of the machine is concerned it is itself the crazed victim of artist-impotence. Why will the American artist not see that human thought in our age is stripping off its old form and donning another; why is the artist unable to see that this is his glorious opportunity to create and reap anew?

But let us be practical—let us go now afield for evident instances of machine abuse or abuse by the machine. I will show you typical abuses that should serve to suggest to any mind, capable of thought, that the machine is, to begin with, a marvellous simplifier in no merely negative sense. Come now, with me, and see examples which show that these craft-engines may be the modern emancipator of the creative mind. We may find them to be the regenerator of the creative conscience in our America, as well, so soon as a stultified "culture" will allow them to be so used.

First—as perhaps wood is most available of home-building materials, naturally then the most abused—let us now glance at wood. Elaborate machinery has been invented for no other purpose than to imitate the wood-carving of early handicraft patterns. Result? No good joinery. None salable without some horrible glued-on botchwork meaning nothing, unless it means that "art and craft" (by salesmanship) has fixed in the minds of the masses the elaborate old hand-carved chair as ultimate ideal. The miserable tribute to this perversion yielded by Grand Rapids alone would mar the face of art beyond repair, to say nothing of the weird or fussy joinery of spindles and jig-sawing, beamed, braced and elaborated to outdo in sentimentality the sentiment of some erstwhile overwrought "antique." The beauty of wood lies in its qualities as wood, strange as this may seem. Why does it take so much imagination—just to see that? Treatments that fail to bring out those qualities, foremost, are not *plastic*, therefore no longer appropriate. The inappropriate cannot be beautiful.

The machine at work on wood will itself teach us—and we seem so far to have left it to the machine to do so—that certain simple forms and handling serve to bring out the beauty of wood, and to retain its character, and that certain other forms and handling do not bring out its beauty, but spoil it. All wood-carving is apt to be a forcing of this material likely to destroy the finer possibilities of wood as we may know those possibilities now. In itself wood has beauty of marking, exquisite texture, and delicate nuances of color that carving is likely to destroy. The machines used in woodwork will show that by unlimited power in cutting, shaping, smoothing, and by the tireless repeat, they have emancipated beauties of wood-nature, making possible, without waste, beautiful surface treatments and clean strong forms that veneers of Sheraton or Chippendale only hinted at with dire extravagance. Beauty unknown even to the Middle Ages. These machines have undoubtedly placed within reach of the designer a technique enabling him to realize the true nature of wood in his designs harmoniously with man's sense of beauty, satisfying his material needs with such extraordinary economy as to put this beauty of wood in use within the reach of everyone. But the advantages of the machines are wasted and we suffer from a riot of aesthetic murder and everywhere live with debased handicraft.

Then, at random, let us take, say, the worker in marbles—his gang-saws, planers, pneumatic-chisels and rubbing-beds have made it possible to reduce blocks ten feet long, six feet deep, and two feet thick to sheets or thin slabs an inch in thickness within a few hours, so it is now possible to use a precious material as ordinary wall covering. The slab may be turned and matched at the edges to develop exquisite pattern, emancipating hundreds of superficial feet of characteristic drawing in pure marble colors that formerly wasted in the heart of a great expensive block in the thickness of the wall. Here again a distinctly new architectural use may bring out a beauty of marbles consistent with nature and impossible to handicraft. But what happens? The "artist" persists in taking dishonest advantage of this practice, building up imitations of solid piers with molded caps and bases, cunningly uniting the slabs at the edge until detection is difficult except to the trained eye. His method does not change to develop the beauty of a new technical possibility; no, the "artist" is simply enabled to "fake" more architecture, make more piers and column shafts because he can now make them hollow! His architecture becomes no more worthy in itself than the cheap faker that he himself is, for his classical forms not only falsify the method which used to be and belie the method that is, but they cheat progress of its due. For convincing evidence see any public library or art institute, the Congressional Library at Washington, or the Boston Library.

In the stone-cutting trade the stone-planer has made it possible to cut upon stone any given molded surface, or to ingrain upon that surface any lovely texture the cunning brain may devise, and do it as it never was possible to do it by hand. What is it doing? Giving us as near an imitation of hand tooth-chiselling as possible, imitating moldings specially adapted to wood, making possible the lavish use of miles of meaningless molded string courses, cornices, base courses—the giant power meanwhile sneered at by the "artist" because it fails to render the wavering delicacy of "touch" resulting from the imperfections of hand-work.

No architect, this man! No—or he would excel that "antique" quality by the design of the contour of his sections, making a telling point of the very perfection he dreads, and so sensibly designing, for the prolific dexterity of the machine, work which it can do so well that handwork would seem insufferably crude by comparison. The deadly facility this one machine has given "book architecture" is rivalled only by the facility given to it by galvanized iron itself. And if, incontinently, you will still have tracery in stone, you may arrive at acres of it now consistently with the economy of other features of this still fundamental "trade." You may try to imitate the hand-carving of the ancients in this matter, baffled by the craft and tenderness of the originals, or you may give the pneumatic chisel and power-plane suitable work to do which would mean a changed style, a shift in the spiritual center of the ideal now controlling the use of stone in constructing modern stone buildings.

You will find in studying the group of ancient materials, wood and stone foremost among them, that they have all been rendered fit for *plastic* use by the machine! The machine itself steadily making available for economic use the very quality in these things now needed to satisfy its own art equation. Burned clay—we call it terra cotta—is another conspicuous instance of the advantage of the "process." Modern machines (and a process is a machine) have rendered this material as sensitive to the creative brain as a dry plate is to the lens of the camera. A marvelous simplifier, this material, rightly used. The artist is enabled to clothe the steel structure, now becoming characteristic of this era, with modestly beautiful, plastic robes instead of five or more different kinds of material now aggregated in confused features and parts, "composed" and supposedly picturesque, but really a species of cheap millinery to be mocked and warped by the sun, eventually beaten by wind and rain into a variegated heap of trash. But when these great possibilities of simplicity, the gift of the machine, get to us by way of the architect, we have only a base imitation of the hand-tooled blocks—pilaster-cap and base, voussoirs and carved spandrils of the laborious man-handled stonecrop of an ancient people's architecture!

The modern processes of casting in metal are modern machines too, approaching perfection, capable of perpetuating the imagery of the most vividly poetic mind without hindrance—putting permanence and grace within reach of every one, heretofore forced to sit supine with the Italians at their Belshazzar-feast of "renaissance." Yes, without exaggeration, multitudes of processes, many new, more coming, await sympathetic interpretation, such as the galvano-plastic and its electrical brethren—a prolific horde, now cheap makers imitating "real" bronzes and all manner of metallic antiques, secretly damning all of them in their vitals, if not openly giving them away. And there is electro-glazing, shunned because its straight lines in glasswork are too severely clean and delicate. Straight lines it seems are not so susceptible to the traditional designer's lack of touch. Stream lines and straight lines are to him severely unbeautiful. "Curved is the line of beauty"—says he! As though nature would not know what to do with its own rectilinear!

The familiar lithograph, too, is the prince of an entire province of new reproductive but unproductive processes. Each and every one has its individualities and therefore has possibilities of its own. See what Whistler made and the Germans are making of the lithograph: one note sounded in the gamut of its possibilities. But that note rings true to process as the sheen of the butterfly's wing to that wing. Yet, having fallen into disrepute, the most this particular "machine" did for us, until Whistler picked it up, was to give us the cheap imitative effects of painting, mostly for advertising purposes. This is the use made of machinery in the abuse of materials by men. And still more important than all we have yet discussed here is the new element entering industry in this material we call steel. The structural necessity which once shaped Parthenons, Pantheons, cathedrals, is fast being reduced by the machine to a skeleton of steel or its equivalent, complete in itself without the artist-craftsman's touch. They are now building Gothic cathedrals in California upon a steel skeleton. Is it not easy to see that the myriad ways of satisfying ancient structural necessities known to us through the books as the art of building, vanish, become history? The mainspring of their physical existence now removed, their spiritual center has shifted and nothing remains but the impassive features of a dead face. Such is our "classic" architecture.

For centuries this insensate or insane abuse of great opportunity in the name of culture has made cleanly, strengthy and true simplicity impossible in art or architecture, whereas now we might reach the heights of creative art. Rightly used the very curse machinery puts upon handicraft should emancipate the artist from temptation to petty structural deceit and end this wearisome struggle to make things seem what they are not and can never be. Then the machine itself, eventually, will satisfy the simple terms of its modern art equation as the ball of clay in the sculptor's hand yields to his desire—ending forever this nostalgic masquerade led by a stultified culture in the name of art.

Yes—though he does not know it, the artist is now free to work his rational will with freedom unknown to structural tradition. Units of construction have enlarged, rhythms have been simplified and etherealized, space is more spacious and the sense of it may enter into every building, great or small. The architect is no longer hampered by the stone arch of the Romans or by the stone beam of the Greeks. Why then does he cling to the grammatical phrases of those ancient methods of construction when such phrases are in his modern work empty lies, and himself an inevitable liar as well?

Already, as we stand today, the machine has weakened the artist to the point of destruction and antiquated the craftsman altogether. Earlier forms of art are by abuse all but destroyed. The whole matter has been reduced to mere pose. Instead of joyful creation we have all around about us poisonous tastes—foolish attitudes. With some little of the flame of the old love, and creditable but pitiful enthusiasm, the young artist still keeps on working, making miserable mischief with lofty motives: perhaps, because his heart has not kept in touch or in sympathy with his scientific brother's head, being out of step with the forward marching of his own time.

Now, let us remember in forming this new Arts and Crafts Society at Hull House that every people has done its work, therefore evolved its art as an expression of its own life, using the best tools; and that means the most economic and effective tools or contrivances it knew: the tools most successful in saving valuable human effort. The chattel slave was the essential tool of Greek civilization, therefore of its art. We have discarded this tool and would refuse the return of the art of the Greeks were slavery the terms of its restoration, and slavery, in some form, would be the terms.

But in Grecian art two flowers did find spiritual expression—the acanthus and the honeysuckle. In the art of Egypt—similarly we see the papyrus, the lotus. In Japan the chrysanthemum and many other flowers. The art of the Occident has made no such sympathic interpretation since that time, with due credit given to the English rose and the French fleur-de-lis, and as things are now the West may never make one. But to get from some native plant an expression of its native character in terms of imperishable stone to be fitted perfectly to its place in structure, and without loss of vital significance, is one great phase of great art. It means that Greek or Egyptian found a revelation of the inmost life and character of the lotus and acanthus in terms of lotus or acanthus life. That was what happened when the art of these people had done with the plants they most loved. This imaginative process is known only to the creative artist. Conventionalization, it is called. Really it is the dramatizing of an object—truest "drama." To enlarge upon this simple figure, as an artist, it seems to me that this complex matter of civilization is itself at bottom some such conventionalizing process, or must be so to be successful and endure.

Just as any artist-craftsman, wishing to use a beloved flower for the stone capital of a column-shaft in his building must conventionalize the flower, that is, find the pattern of its life-principle in terms of stone as a material before he can rightly use it as a beautiful factor in his building, so education must take the natural man, to "civilize" him. And this great new power of the dangerous machine we must learn to understand and then learn to use as this valuable, *"conventionalizing"* agent. But in the construction of a society as in the construction of a great building, the elemental conventionalizing process is dangerous, for without the inspiration or inner light of the true artist—the quality of the flower—its very life—is lost, leaving a withered husk in the place of living expression.

Therefore, society in this conventionalizing process or culture, has a task even more dangerous than has the architect in creating his building forms, because instead of having a plant-leaf and a fixed material as ancient architecture had, we have a sentient man with a fluid soul. So without the inner light of a sound philosophy of art (the educator too, must now be artist), the life of the man will be sacrificed and society gain an automaton or a machine-made moron instead of a noble creative citizen!

If education is doomed to fail in this process, utterly—then the man slips back to rudimentary animalism or goes on into decay. Society degenerates or has a mere realistic creature instead of the idealistic creator needed.

The world will have to record more "great dead cities."

To keep the artist-figure of the flower *dramatized for human purposes*—the socialist would bow his neck in altruistic submission to the "harmonious" whole; his conventionalization or dramatization of the human being would be like a poor stone-craftsman's attempt to conventionalize the beloved plant with the living character of leaf and flower left out. The anarchist would pluck the flower as it grows and use it as it is for what it is—with essential reality left out.

The hereditary aristocrat has always justified his existence by his ability, owing to fortunate propinquity, to appropriate the flower to his own uses after the craftsman has given it life and character, and has kept the craftsman too by promising him his flower back if he behaves himself well. The plutocrat does virtually the same thing by means of "interests." But the true democrat will take the human plant as it grows and—in the spirit of using the means at hand to put life into his conventionalization—preserve the individuality of the plant to protect the flower, which is its very life, getting from both a living expression of essential man-character fitted perfectly to a place in society with no loss of vital significance. Fine art is this flower of the man. When education has become creative and art again prophetic of the natural means by which we are to grow—we call it "progress"—we will, by means of the creative artist, possess this monstrous tool of our civilization as it now possesses us.

Grasp and use the power of scientific automatons in this *creative sense* and their terrible forces are not antagonistic to any fine individualistic quality in man. He will find their collective mechanistic forces capable of bringing to the individual a more adequate life, and the outward expression of the inner man as seen in his environment will be genuine revelation of his inner life and higher purpose. Not until then will America be free!

This new American liberty is of the sort that declares man free only when he has found his work and effective means to achieve a life of his own. The means once found, he will find his due place. The man of our country will thus make his own way, and *grow* to the natural place thus due him, promised—yes, promised by our charter, the Declaration of Independence. But this place of his is not to be made over to fit him by reform, nor shall it be brought down to him by concession, but will become his by his own use of the means at hand. He must *himself* build a new world. The day of the individual is not over—instead, it is just about to begin. The machine does not write the doom of liberty, but is waiting at man's hand as a peerless tool, for him to use to put foundations beneath a genuine democracy. Then the machine may conquer human drudgery to some purpose, taking it upon itself to broaden, lengthen, strengthen and deepen the life of the simplest man. What limits do we dare imagine to an art that is organic fruit of an adequate life for the individual! Although this power is now murderous, chained to botchwork and bunglers' ambitions, the creative artist will take it surely into his hand and, in the name of liberty, swiftly undo the deadly mischief it has created.

46   F. L. Wright, Building the New House, and Designing Unity Temple*   *1926-32*

In the wake of the loss of several potentially important commissions and the murders and fire at his home at Taliesin, during the mid-1920s Wright began to examine his life and work, commencing to write *An Autobiography*. Divided into three long "books" and first published in 1932, it is a remarkable account—difficult, rhapsodic, revealing, defensive, and not always dispassionately accurate in detail or date. Still, it is the best record of how Wright viewed his own contributions and of the evolution of his Prairie architecture. Much of the theoretical content of the two passages reprinted here had already been presented by Wright in two essays, "In the Cause of Architecture," published in *Architectural Record* in March 1908 and May 1914.[†]

AN AUTOBIOGRAPHY

Building the New House

The first thing to do in building the new house was to get rid of the attic and therefore of the dormer, get rid of the useless "heights" below it. Next, get rid of the unwholesome basement, entirely, yes absolutely—in any house built on the prairie. Instead of lean, brick chimneys, bristling up everywhere to hint at "Judgment" from steep roofs, I could see necessity for one chimney only. A broad generous one, or at most, two, these kept low-down on gently sloping roofs or perhaps flat roofs. The big fireplace in the house below became now a place for a real fire, and justified the great size of this chimney outside. A real fireplace at that time was extraordinary. There were mantels instead. A "mantel" was a marble frame for a few coals. Or it was a piece of wooden furniture with tile stuck in it around a "grate," the whole set slam up against the wall. An insult to comfort. So the *integral* fireplace became an important part of the building itself in the houses I was allowed to build out there on the prairie.

Comforting to see the fire burning deep in the masonry of the house itself.

Taking a human being for my "scale" I brought the whole house down in height to fit a normal one—*ergo*, 5' 8" tall, say. Believing in no other scale than the human being I broadened the mass out all I possibly could, brought it down into spaciousness. It has been said that were I three inches taller (I am 5' 8½" tall) all my houses would have been quite different in proportion. Perhaps.

---

*Frank Lloyd Wright, *An Autobiography* (New York, 1932), pp. 138–44, 153–64.

† These first two articles in the *Architectural Record*, and the subsequent fourteen which appeared from May 1927 through December 1928, are reprinted in *In the Cause of Architecture: Essays by Frank Lloyd Wright for the Architectural Record, 1908-1952*, ed. F. Gutheim (New York, 1975).

House walls were now to be started at the ground on a cement or stone water table that looked like a low platform under the building, and usually was. But the house walls were stopped at the second-story windowsill level, to let the bedrooms come through above in a continuous window series under the broad eaves of a gently sloping, overhanging roof. For in this new house the wall as an impediment to outside light and air and beauty was beginning to go. The old wall had been a part of the box in which only a limited number of holes were to be punched. It was still this conception of a wall which was with me when I designed the Winslow house. But after that my conception began to change.

My sense of wall was not a side of a box. It was enclosure to afford protection against storm or heat when this was needed. But it was also increasingly to bring the outside world into the house, and let the inside of the house go outside. In this sense I was working toward the elimination of the wall as a wall to reach the function of a screen, as a means of opening up space, which, as control of building materials improved, would finally permit the free use of the whole space without affecting the soundness of structure.

The climate being what it was, violent in extremes of heat and cold, damp and dry, dark and bright, I gave broad protecting roof shelter to the whole, getting back to the original purpose for which the cornice was designed. The underside of the roof projections was flat and light in color to create a glow of reflected light that made upper rooms not dark, but delightful. The overhangs had double value: shelter and preservation for the walls of the house as well as diffusion of reflected light for the upper story, through the "light screens" that took the place of the walls and were the windows.

And at this time I saw a house primarily as liveable interior space under ample shelter. I liked the sense of "shelter" in the look of the building. I still like it.

Then I went after the popular abuses. Eliminated odds and ends in favor of one material and a single surface as a flat plane from grade to eaves. I treated these flat planes usually as simple enclosing screens or else I again made a plain band around the second story above the windowsills turned up over onto the ceiling beneath the eaves. This screen band would be of the same material as the underside of the eaves themselves, or what architects call the "soffitt."

The planes of the building parallel to the ground were all stressed—I liked to "stress" them—to grip the whole to Earth. This parallel plane I called, from the beginning—the plane of the third dimension. The term came naturally enough: really a spiritual interpretation of that dimension.

Sometimes I was able to make the enclosing wall screen below this upper band of the second story—from the second-story windowsill clear down to the ground—a heavy "wainscot" of fine masonry material resting on the cement or stone "platform" laid on the foundation. I liked the luxury of masonry material, when my clients felt they could afford it.

As a matter of form, too, I liked to see the projecting base or water table of masonry set out over the foundation walls themselves, as a substantial "visible" preparation for the building. I managed this by setting the studs of the walls to the inside of the foundation walls instead of to the outside.

All door and window tops were now bought into line with each other with only comfortable head clearance for the average human being.

Eliminating the sufferers from the "attic" enabled the roof to lie low.

The house began to associate with the ground and become natural to its prairie site.

And would the young man in Architecture believe that this was all "new" then? Yes—not only new, but it was all destructive heresy—or ridiculous eccentricity. Stranger still all somewhat so today. But then it was all so *new* that what prospect I had of ever earning a livelihood by making houses was nearly wrecked. At first, "they" called the houses "dress reform" houses, because society was just then excited about that particular "reform." This simplification looked like some kind of "reform" to the provincials.

Oh, they called the new houses all sort of names that cannot be repeated, but "they" never found a better term for the work unless it was "horizontal Gothic," "temperance Architecture" (with a sneer), and so on. I don't know how I escaped the accusation of another "Renaissance-Japanese" or "Bhutanese" from my complimentary academic contemporaries. Eclectics can imagine only eclecticism.

What I have just described was all on the *outside* of the house. But it was there, chiefly because of what had happened *inside*.

Dwellings of that period were cut up, advisedly and completely, with the grim determination that should go with any "cutting" process. The "interiors" consisted of boxes beside boxes or inside boxes, called *rooms*. All boxes were inside a complicated outside boxing. Each domestic "function" was properly box to box.

I could see little sense in this inhibition, this cellular sequestration that implied ancestors familiar with penal institutions, except for the privacy of bedrooms on the upper floor. They were perhaps all right as "sleeping boxes."

So I declared the whole lower floor as one room, cutting off the kitchen as a laboratory, putting the servants' sleeping and living quarters next to the kitchen but semidetached, on the ground floor. Then I screened various portions of the big room for certain domestic purposes, like dining or reading—receiving callers.

There were no plans in existence like these at the time, but my clients were pushed toward these ideas as helpful to a solution of the vexed servant problem. Scores of unnecessary doors disappeared and no end of partition. Both clients and servants liked the new freedom. The house became more free as "space" and more liveable too. Interior spaciousness began to dawn.

Thus an end to the cluttered house. Fewer doors; fewer window holes, though much greater window area; windows and doors lowered to convenient human heights. These changes made, the ceilings of the rooms could be brought down over onto the walls, by way of the horizontal broad bands of plaster on the walls themselves above the windows, colored the same as the room ceilings. This would bring the ceiling surface and color down to the very window tops. The ceilings thus expanded by way of the wall band above the windows gave generous overhead to even the small rooms.

The sense of the whole was broadened, made plastic, too, by this means.

Here entered the important new element of plasticity—as I saw it. And I saw it as indispensable element to the successful use of the machine. The windows would sometimes be wrapped around the building corners as emphasis of plasticity and sense of interior space. I fought for outswinging windows because the casement window associated the house with the out of doors, gave free openings, outward. In other words the so-called "casement" was simple, more human in use and effect, so more natural. If it had not existed I should have invented it. But it was not used at that time in the United States so I lost many clients because I insisted upon it. The client usually wanted the "guillotine" or "double-hung" window in use then. The guillotine was neither simple nor human. It was only expedient. I used it once in the Winslow house and rejected it thereafter forever. Nor at that time did I entirely eliminate the wooden trim. I did make it "plastic," that is to say, light and continuously flowing instead of the prevailing heavy "cut and butt" carpenterwork. No longer did "trim," so called, look like "carpenterwork." The machine could do it all perfectly well as I laid it out, in the search for "quiet." This plastic trim, too, enabled poor workmanship to be concealed. There was need of that trim to conceal much in the way of craftsmanship because machines versus the union had already demoralized the workmen.

The machine resources of the period were so little understood that extensive drawings had to be made merely to show the millman what to leave off. But finally the trim thus became only a single flat narrow, horizontal band running around the room walls at the top of the windows and doors and another one at the floors. Both were connected with narrow vertical thin wood bands that were used to divide the wall surfaces of the whole room smoothly and flatly into color planes folded about the corners—exterior corners or interior corners—and in the trim merely completed the window and door openings in this same plastic sense. When the handling of the interior had thus become wholly plastic instead of structural—a new element, as I have already said, had entered the prairie-house architecture. Strangely enough an element that had not existed in architecture before, if architectural history is to be credited. Not alone in the trim but in numerous ways too tedious to describe in words, this revolutionary sense of the *plastic* whole, began to work more and more intelligently and have fascinating unforeseen consequences. Here was something that began to organize itself. When several houses had been finished, compared with the house of the period there was very little of that house left standing. But that little was left standing up very high indeed. Nearly everyone had endured the house of the period as long as possible, judging by the appreciation of the change. Now all this probably tedious description is intended to indicate in bare outline how thus early there was an ideal of organic simplicity put to work, with historical consequences, in this country.

Let me now put all this in clear outline for you. The main motives and inclinations were—and I enjoyed them all . . . and still enjoy them—

First . . . to reduce the number of necessary parts of the house or the separate room to a minimum, and make all come together as free space—so subdivided that light, air, and vista permeated the whole with a sense of unity.

Second . . . to associate the building as a whole with its site by extension and emphasis of the planes parallel to the ground, but keeping the floors off from the best part of the site thus leaving that better part for use in connection with the use of the house. Extended level planes or long narrow levels were found useful in this connection.

Third . . . to eliminate the rooms as boxes and the house itself as another boxing of the boxes, making all walls enclosing screens; ceilings and floors to flow the enclosing screen as one large enclosure of space, with minor or subordinate subdivisions only. And also to make all proportions more liberally human, eliminate waste space in structure, and make structure more appropriate to material. The whole made more sensible and liveable. Liberal is the best word. Extended straight lines or streamlines were useful in this.

Fourth . . . to get the unwholesome basement up out of the ground, entirely above it as a low pedestal for the living portion of the home, making the foundation itself visible as a low masonry platform on the ground on which the building would stand.

Fifth . . . to harmonize all necessary openings to outside or inside with good human proportions and make them occur naturally, singly, or in series, in the scheme of the whole building. Usually they now appeared as light screens—usually turning the corners—instead of walls, because chiefly the architecture of the house was expressed in the way these openings happened to such walls as were grouped about the rooms anyway. The room was now the essential architectural expression. And there were to be no holes cut in walls anywhere or anyhow as holes are cut in a box, because this was not in keeping with the ideal of "plastic." Cutting holes was violence.

I saw that the insensate, characterless flat surface, cut sheer, had geometric possibilities . . . but it has, also, the limitations of bare geometry. Such negation in itself is sometimes restful and continually useful—as a foil—but not as the side of a box.

Sixth . . . to eliminate combinations of different materials in favor of mono-material so far as possible, and to use no ornament that did not come out of the nature of materials or construction to make the whole building clearer and more expressive as a place to live in and give the conception of the building as appropriate revealing emphasis. Geometrical or straight lines were natural to the machinery at work in the building trades then, so the interiors took on this rectilinear character naturally.

Seventh . . . to so incorporate all heating, lighting, plumbing that these mechanical systems became constituent parts of the building itself. These service features became architectural features. In this attempt the ideal of an organic architecture was at work.

Eighth . . . to incorporate as organic architecture, so far as possible, furnishings, making them all one with the building, designing the equipment in simple terms for machinework. Again straight lines and rectilinear forms. Geometrical.

Ninth ... eliminate the decorator. He was all "appliqué" and all efflorescence, if not all "period." Inorganic.

This was all rational so far as the thought of an organic architecture went. The particular forms this thought took in the feeling of it all could only be personal to myself.

There was nothing whatever at this time to help make them what they were.

But all this seemed to me the most natural thing in the world and grew up out of the circumstances of the moment.

What the ultimate "forms" may be worth in the long run is all they are worth.

Now simplicity—organic simplicity—in this early constructive effort I soon found to be a matter of the sympathy with which such coordination might be effected. Plainness was not necessarily simplicity. That was evident. Crude furniture of the Roycroft-Stickley-Mission style, which came along later, was offensively plain, plain as a barn door—but never simple in any true sense. Nor, I found, were merely machine-made things in themselves necessarily simple. To "think," as the Master used to say, "is to deal in simples." And that means with an eye single to the altogether. This, I believe, is the single secret of simplicity: that we may truly regard nothing at all as simple in itself. I believe that no one thing in itself is ever so, but much achieve simplicity—as an artist should use the term—as a perfectly realized part of some organic whole. Only as a feature or any part becomes harmonious element in the harmonious whole does it arrive at the state of simplicity. Any wild flower is truly simple, but double the same wild flower by cultivation, it ceases to be so. The scheme of the original is no longer clear. Clarity of design and perfect significance both are first essentials of the spontaneous born simplicity of the lilies of the field. "They toil not, neither do they spin." As contrasted with Solomon who "toiled and spun" and who, no doubt had put on himself and had put on his temple properly "composed" everything in the category of good things but the cookstove. Solomon in his day was probably "fundamentalist" in his architecture—that is to say, "by book." He had "tastes" and may have been something of a functioneer.

Designing Unity Temple

Let us take Unity Temple to pieces in the thought of its architect and see how it came to be the Unity Temple you now see.

Had Dr. Johonnot, the Universalist pastor of Unity Church, been Fra Junipero the "style" of Unity Temple would have been predetermined. Had he been Father Latour it would have been Midi-Romanesque. Yes, and perhaps being what he was, he was entitled to the only tradition he knew—that of the little white New England Church, lean spire pointing to heaven —"back East." If sentimentality were sense this might be so.

But the pastor was out of luck. Circumstances brought him to yield himself up "in the cause of architecture." The straight line and the flat plane were to emerge as the cantilever slab.

And to that cause every one who undertakes to read what follows is called upon to yield. It should only be read after studying the plans and perspective of Unity Temple. Constant reference to the plan will be necessary if the matter is to come clear.

Our building committee were all "good men and true." One of them, Charles E. Roberts, a mechanical engineer and inventor, enlightened in creation.

One, enlightened, is leaven enough in any Usonian lump. The struggle . . . it is always a struggle in architecture for the architect where "good men and true" are concerned—began.

First came the philosophy of the building.

Human sensibilities are the strings of the instrument upon which the true artist plays . . . "abstract" . . .? But why not avoid the symbol, as such? The symbol is too literal. It is become a form of literature in the arts.

Let us abolish, in the art and craft of architecture, literature in any "symbolic" form whatsoever. The sense of inner rhythm, deep planted in human sensibility, lives far above other considerations in art.

Then why the steeple of the little white church? Why *point* to heaven?

I told the committee a story. Did they now know the tale of the holy man who, yearning to see God, climbed up and up the highest mountain—up and up on and to and up the highest relic of a tree there was on the mountain too? Ragged and worn, there he lifted up his eager perspiring face to heaven and called on "God." A voice . . . bidding him get down . . . go back!

Would he really see God's face? Then he should go back, go down there in the valley below where his own people were—there only could *he* look upon God's countenance.

Was not that "finger," the church steeple, pointing on high like the man who climbed on high to see *Him?* A misleading symbol perhaps. A perversion of sentiment—sentimentality.

Was not the time come now to be more simple, to have more faith in man on his Earth and less anxiety concerning his Heaven about which he could *know* nothing. Concerning this heaven he had never received any testimony from his own senses.

Why not, then, build a temple, not to GOD in that way— more sentimental than sense—but build a temple to man, appropriate to his uses as a meeting place, in which to study man himself for his God's sake? A modern meeting house and good-time place.

Build a beautiful *Room* proportioned to this purpose. Make it beautiful in this *simple* sense. A *natural* building for natural Man.

The pastor was a "liberal." His liberality was thus challenged, his reason piqued, and the curiosity of all aroused.

What would such a building be like? They said they could imagine no such thing.

"That's what you came to me for," I ventured. "I can imagine it and will help you create it."

Promising the building committee something tangible to look at soon—I sent them away, they not knowing, quite, whether they were foolish, fooled, or fooling with a fool.

That *Room*; it began to be that same night.

Enter the realm of architectural ideas.

The first idea—to keep a noble *Room* in mind, and let the room shape the whole edifice, let the room inside be the architecture outside.

What shape? Well, the answer lay, in what material? There was only one material to choose, as the church funds were $45,000, to "church" 400 people in 1906. Concrete was cheap.

Concrete alone could do it. But even concrete as it was in use at that time meant wood "forms" and some other material than concrete for outside facing. They were in the habit of covering the concrete with brick or stone, plastering and furring the inside of the walls. Plastering the outside would be cheaper than brick or stone but wouldn't stick to concrete in our climate. Why not make the wooden boxes or forms so the concrete could be cast in them as separate blocks and masses, these separate blocks and masses grouped about an interior space in some such way as to preserve this desired sense of the interior space in the appearance of the whole building? And the block-masses be left as themselves with no "facing." That would be cheap and permanent.

Then, how to cover the separate features and concrete masses as well as the sacrosanct space from the extremes of northern weather. What roof?

What had concrete to offer as a cover shelter? The slab—of course. The reinforced slab. Nothing else if the building was to be thoroughbred, meaning built in character out of one material.

Too monumental, all this? Too forthright for my committee I feared. Would a statement so positive as that final slab over the whole seem irreligious to them? Profane in their eyes? Why?

The flat slab was direct. It would be "nobly" simple. The wooden forms or molds in which concrete buildings must at that time be cast were always the chief item of expense, so to repeat the use of a single one as often as possible was desirable, even necessary. Therefore a building all four sides alike looked like the thing. This, in simplest terms, meant a building square in plan. That would make their temple a cube, a noble form.

The slab, too, belonged to the cube by nature. "Credo simplicitas."

That form is most imaginative and "happy" that is most radiant with the "aura" or overtone of superform.

Geometric shapes through human sensibility have thus acquired to some extent human significance as, say, the cube or square, integrity; the circle or sphere, infinity; the straight line, rectitude. If long drawn out . . . repose; the triangle . . . aspiration, etc.

There was no money to spend in working on the concrete mass outside or with it after it was once cast.

Good reason, this, if no other, for getting away from any false facing. Couldn't the surface be qualified in the casting process so this whole matter of veneered "façade" could be omitted with good effect? This was later the cause of much experiment, with what success may be seen.

Then the Temple itself—still in my mind—began to take shape. The site was noisy, by the Lake Street car tracks. Therefore it seemed best to keep the building closed on the three front sides and enter it from a court at the center of the lot.

Unity Temple itself with the thoughts in mind I have just expressed, arrived easily enough, but there was a secular side to Universalist church activities—entertainment—Sunday school, feasts, etc. . . .

To embody these latter with the temple would spoil the simplicity of the room—the noble *Room*—in the service of *Man* for the worship of *God*.

So finally I put the space as "Unity House," a long free space to the rear of the lot, as a separate building to be subdivided by movable screens, on occasion. It thus became a separate building but harmonious with the Temple—the entrance to both to be the connecting link between them. That was that.

To go back to the Temple itself. What kind of "square room"? How effect the cube and best serve the purpose of audience room?

Should the pulpit be put toward the street and let the congregation come in and go out at the rear in the usual disrespectful church fashion so the pastor missed contact with his flock? And the noise of the street cars on Lake Street come in?

No. Why not put the pulpit at the entrance side at the rear of the square Temple entirely cut off from the street and bring the congregation into the room at the sides and on a lower level so those entering would be imperceptible to the audience? This would make the incomers as little a disturbance or challenge to curiosity as possible. This would preserve the quiet and the dignity of the room itself. Out of that thought came the depressed foyer or "cloister" corridor either side leading from the main entrance lobby at the center to the stairs in the near and far corners of the room. Those entering the room in this way could see into the big room but not be seen by those already seated within it.

And when the congregation rose to disperse here was opportunity to move forward toward their pastor and by swinging wide doors open beside the pulpit let the flock pass out by the minister and find themselves directly in the entrance loggia from which they had first come in. They had gone into the depressed entrances at the sides from this same entrance to enter the big room. But it seemed more respectful to let them go out thus toward the pulpit than turn their backs upon their minister to go out as is usual in most churches. This scheme gave the minister's flock to him to greet. Few could escape. The position of the pulpit in relation to the entrance made this reverse movement possible.

So this was done.

The room itself—size determined by comfortable seats with leg room for four hundred people—was built with four interior free-standing posts to carry the overhead structure. These concrete posts were hollow and became free-standing ducts to ensure economic and uniform distribution of heat. The large supporting posts were so set in plan as to form a double tier of alcoves on four sides of this room. Flood these side alcoves with light from above: get a sense of a happy cloudless day into the room. And with this feeling for light the center ceiling between the four great posts became skylight, daylight sifting through between the intersections of concrete beams filtering through amber glass ceiling lights thus the light would, rain or shine, have the warmth of sunlight. Artificial lighting took place there at night as well. This scheme of lighting was integral, gave diffusion and kept the room space clear.

The spacious wardrobes between the depressed foyers either side of the room and under the auditorium itself, were intended to give opportunity to the worshippers to leave their wraps before entering the worshipful room. And this wardrobe would work as well for the entertainments in the long room to the rear because it was just off the main entrance lobby.

The secular hall—Unity House—itself, was tall enough to have galleries at each side of the central space—convertible into classroom space.

A long kitchen connected to each end of the secular space was added to the rear of Unity House for the Temple "feasts."

The pastor's offices and study came of themselves over the entrance lobby the connection between the two buildings. The study thus looked down through swinging windows into the secular hall— while it was just a step behind the pulpit.

All this seemed in proper order. Seemed natural enough.

Now for proportion—for the "concrete" expression of concrete in this natural arrangement—the ideal of an organic whole well in mind.

For observe, so far, what has actually taken place is only reasoned *arrangement*. The "plan" with an eye to an exterior in the realm of ideas but "felt" in imagination.

First came the philosophy of the thing in the little story repeated to the trustees. All artistic creation has its own. The first condition of creation. However, some would smile and say, "the result of it."

Second there was a general purpose of the whole to consider in each part: a matter of reasoned arrangement. This arrangement must be made with a sense of the yet-unborn whole in the mind, to be blocked out as appropriate to concrete masses cast in wooden boxes. Holding all this diversity together in a preconceived direction is really no light matter but is the condition of creation. Imagination conceives here the *Plan* suitable to the material and the purpose—seeing the probable—possible form.

Imagination reigns supreme, when now the *form* the whole will naturally take, must be seen.

And we have arrived at the question of *style*.

But if all this preliminary planning has been well conceived, that question in the main is settled. The matter may be intensified, made eloquent or modified and quieted. It cannot much change. Organic is this matter of style now. The concrete forms of Unity Temple will take the character of all we have so far done, if all we have so far done is harmonious with the principle we are waking to work. The structure will not put forth its forms as the tree puts forth branches and foliage—if we do not stultify it, do not betray it in some way.

We do not choose the style. Style is what this is now and what we *are*. A thrilling moment this in any architect's experience. He is about to see the countenance of something he is invoking. Out of this sense of order and his love of the beauty of life—something is to be born maybe to live long as a

message of hope and joy or a curse to his kind. *His* message he feels. Nonetheless is it "theirs," and rather more. And it is out of love and understanding such as this on the part of an architect that a building is born to bless or
curse those it is built to serve.

Bless them if they will see and understand. Curse them and be cursed
by them if either they or the architect should fail to understand. . . . This is
the faith and the fear in the architect as he makes ready—to draw his design.

In all artists it is the same.

Now comes to brood—to suffer doubt and burn with eagerness. To test
bearings—and prove assumed ground by putting all together to definite
scale on paper. Preferably small scale at first. Then larger. Finally still larger
scale studies of parts.

This pure white sheet of paper! Ready for the logic of the plan.

T-square, triangle, scale—seductive invitation lying upon the spotless
surface.

Temptation!

"Boy! Go tell Black Kelly to make a blaze there in the workroom fire-
place! Ask Brown-Sadie if it's too late to have baked Bermudas for supper!
Then go ask your mother—I shall hear her in here—to play something-
—Bach preferred, or Beethoven if she prefers."

An aid to creative effort, the open fire. What a friend to the laboring
artist, the poetic baked onion. Real encouragement to him is great music.

Yes, and what a poor creature, after all, creation comes singing
through. About like catgut and horsehair in the hands of Sarasate.

Night labor at the drafting board is best for intense creation. It may
continue uninterrupted.

Meantime reflections are passing in the mind—"design is abstraction of
nature, elements in purely geometric terms"—that is what we ought to call
pure design? . . . But—nature, pattern and nature, texture in materials themselves often approach conventionalization, or the abstract, to such a degree
as to be superlative means ready to the designer's hand to qualify, stimulate,
and enrich his own efforts. . . . What texture this concrete mass? Why not its
own gravel? How to bring the gravel clean on the surface?

Here was reality. Yes, the "fine thing" is reality. Always reality?

Realism, the subgeometric, is, however, the abuse of this fine thing.

Keep the straight lines clean and significant, the flat plane expressive
and clean cut. But let texture of material come into them.

Reality is spirit . . . essence brooding just behind aspect!

Seize it! And . . . after all, reality *is* supergeometric, casting a spell or a
"charm" over any geometry, as such, in itself.

Yes, it seems to me, that is what it means to be an artist . . . to seize this
essence brooding just behind aspect. These questionings arising each with its
train of thought by the way, as at work.

It is morning! To bed for a while!

Well, there is Unity Temple at last. Health and soundness in it, though still far to go.

But here we have penciled on the sheet of paper, in the main, the plan, section and elevation as in the drawings illustrated here, all except the exterior of "Unity House," as the room for secular recreation came to be called.

To establish harmony between these buildings of separate function proved difficult, utterly exasperating.

Another series of concentrations—lasting hours at a time for several days. How to keep the noble scale of the temple in the design of the subordinate mass of the secular hall and not falsify the function of that noble mass? The ideal of an organic architecture is severe discipline for the imagination. I came to know that full well. And, always, some minor concordance takes more time, taxes concentration more than all besides. To vex the architect, this minor element now becomes a major problem. How many schemes I have thrown away because some one minor feature would not come true to form!

Thirty-four studies were necessary to arrive at this as it is now seen. Unfortunately they are lost with thousands of others of other buildings. The fruit of similar struggles to coordinate and perfect them all as organic entities—I wish I had kept.

Unity House looks easy enough now, for it is right enough.

But this *"harmony of the whole"* where diverse functions cause diverse masses to occur is no light affair for the architect—nor ever will be if he keeps his ideal high.

Now observe the plans and the elevations, then the model or photograph of the building. See, now, how all that has taken place is showing itself *as it is* for what it is.

A new industrial method for the use of a new material is improved and revealed. Roof slabs—attic walls—screen walls—posts and glass screens enclose, as architecture, a great room.

The sense of the room is not only preserved—*it may be seen as the soul of the design.* Instead of being built into the heart of a block of sculptured building material, out of sight, sacrosanct space is merely screened in . . . it comes through as the living "motif" of the architecture.

The grammar of such style as is seen here is simply and logically determined by the concrete mass and flat layer formation of the slab and box construction of the square room, proportioned according to concrete-nature —or the nature of the concrete. All is assembled about the coveted space, now visibly cherished.

Such architectural forms as there are, each to each as all in all, are cubical in form, to be cast solid in wooden boxes. But *one* motif may be seen, the "inside" becoming "outside." The groups of monoliths in their changing phases, square in character, do not depart from that single *Idea.* Here we have something of the organic integrity in structure out of which issues character as an aura. The consequence is style. A stylish development of the square becoming the cube.

Understanding Unity Temple one may respect it. It serves its purpose well. It was easy to build. Its harmonies are bold and striking, but genuine in melody. The "square," too positive in statement for current *"taste,"* the straight line and the flat plane uncompromising, yes. But here is an entity again to prove that architecture may, if need be, live again as the nature-of-the-thing in terms of building material. Here is one building rooted in such modern conditions of work, materials, and thought, as prevailed at the time it was built. Single-minded in motif. Faithful in form.

Out of this concentration in labor will come many subsequent studies in refinement—correction of correlation, scale tests for integration. Overcoming difficulties in detail, in the effort to keep all clean and simple as a whole, is continued during the whole process of planning and building.

Many studies in detail yet remain to be made—determine what further may be left out to protect the design. These studies seem never to end, and in the sense, no organic building may ever be "finished." The complete goal of the ideal of organic architecture is never reached. Nor need be. What worthwhile ideal is ever reached?

But, we have enough now on paper to make a perspective drawing to go with the plan for the committee of "good men and true" to see. Usually a committee has only the sketch to consider. But it is impossible to present a "sketch" when working in this method. The building as a whole must be all in order before the "sketch," not after it.

Unity Temple is a complete building on paper, already. There is no "sketch" and there never has been one.

Hardest of an architect's trials, to show his work, first time, to anyone not entirely competent, perhaps unsympathetic.

Putting off the evil contact as long as possible—letting all simmer. The simmering process, too, is valuable. There is seldom enough of it.

What hope to carry all through? The human ground for hope is gone over carefully again and again—wakeful nights. Already the architect begins to fear for the fate of his design. If it is to be much changed he prefers to throw it all away and begin all over again.

No—not much hope except in Mr. Roberts. Why not ask him to see the design and explain it to him first? This is done. He is delighted. He *understands!* He is himself an inventor. And every project in architecture needs this one intimate friend in order to proceed. Mr. Roberts suggests a model. The model is soon made.

All right; let the committee come now. They do come—all curious. Soon confounded—taking the "show-me" attitude.

At this moment the creative architect is distinctly at disadvantage as compared with his obsequious brother of the "styles." His brother can show his pattern-book of "styles," speak glibly of St. Mark's at Venice or Capella Palatine, impress the no less craven clients by brave show of erudite authorities—abash them.

But the architect with the ideal of an organic architecture at stake can talk only principle and sense. His only appeal must be made to the independent thought and judgment of his client. The client, too, must know how to think from generals to particulars. How rare it is to go into court where that quality of mind is on the bench! This architect has learned to dread the personal idiosyncrasy—offered him three times out of five—substitute for such intelligence.

But, we try and we use all our resources, we two—the inventor and myself—and win a third member of the committee at the first meeting. Including the pastor, there are now four only left in doubt.

One of the four openly hostile—Mr. Skillin. Dr. Johonnot, the pastor, himself impressed but cautious—very—and tactful. He has a glimpse of a new world.

There is hope, distinctly hope, when he makes four as he soon does and the balance of power is with us.

We need three more, but the architect's work is done now. The four will get the others. The pastor is convinced. He will work! So doubt and fears are finally put to sleep—all but Mr. Skillin's. Mr. Skillin is sure the room will be dark—sure the acoustics will be bad. Finally the commission to go ahead is formally given over his dissent and warnings. Usually there is a Mr. Skillin in Usonia on every building project.

Now, who will build the Temple? After weeks of prospecting, no one can be found who wants to try it. Simple enough—yes—that's the trouble. So simple there is nothing at all to gauge it by. Requires too much imagination and initiative to be safe. The only bids available came in double, or more, our utmost limit. No one really wanted to touch it. Contractors are naturally gamblers, but they usually bet on a sure thing—as they see it.

Now Paul Mueller comes to the rescue, reads the scheme like easy-print. Will build it for only a little over their appropriation—and does it. He takes it easily along for nearly a year but he does it. Doesn't lose much on it in the end. It is exciting to him to rescue ideas, to participate in creation. And together we overcame difficulty after difficulty in the field, where an architect's education is never finished.

This building, however, is finished, to be opened on a Sunday.

I do not want to go. Stay at home.

When the church was opened the phone began to ring. Listened to happy contented voices in congratulation. Finally weary, I take little Francie by the hand to go out into the air with her to get away from it all. Enough.

But just as my hat goes on my head, another ring, a voice, Mr. Skillin's voice—"Take back all I said . . . Light everywhere—all pleased."

"Hear well?"

"Yes, see and hear fine—see it all now."

"Glad."

"Goodbye." At last the doubting member was now sincere in praise and a "good sport" besides.

Francie got tossed in the air. She came down with a squeal of delight.

And that is how it was and is and will be.

Now, even though you are interested in architecture this story is more or less tedious and meaningless to you, as you were fairly warned it would be at the beginning, without close study of the plans and photographs as it is read. I have undertaken here, for once, to indicate the process of building on principle to ensure character and achieve style, as near as I can indicate it by taking Unity Temple to pieces. Perhaps I am not the one to try it.

As for the traditional church as modern building! Religion and art are forms of inner experience—growing richer and deeper as the race grows older. We will never lose either. But I believe religious experience is outgrowing the church—not outgrowing religion but outgrowing the church as an institution. Just as architecture has outgrown the Renaissance and for reasons human, scientific, and similar. I cannot see the ancient institutional form of any church building as anything but sentimental, or survival for burial. The Temple as forum and good-time place—beautiful and inspiring as such—yes. A religious edifice raised in the sense of the old ritual? No. I cannot see it at all as living. It is no longer free.

Of course what is most vitally important in all that is to be explained cannot be said at all. It need not be, I think. Here in this searching process may be seen work, as the boys in the studio would crowd around and participate in it. As you too, perhaps, may see certain wheels go around. Certain hints coming through between the lines may help someone who needs help in comprehending what a building really means.

This brief indication of the problem of building out of the man will not clear up the question as to what is style much either. But a little by way of suggestion, I hope.

Man's struggle to illumine creation, is another tragedy.

47   C. R. Ashbee, Frank Lloyd Wright: A Study and an Appreciation*   *1911*

The work of Wright was warmly received by the avant-garde in Europe, even more than Richardson's or Sullivan's had been before; the selections by Ashbee and Berlage which follow illustrate this well. The chief agent in bringing Wright to the attention of Europe was the publication of a folio of delicate drawings prepared by Wright and his studio assistants (especially Marion Mahoney). *Ausgeführte Bauten und Entwürfe von Frank Lloyd Wright* (Completed Buildings and Designs by Frank Lloyd Wright) was published in 1910 by Ernst Wasmuth, Berlin.[†] This oversized costly production was followed a year later by a less expensive smaller book, *Frank Lloyd Wright Ausgeführte Bauten* (Frank Lloyd Wright: Completed Buildings), illustrated with photographs and a limited number of plans from the preceding folio (some of which are reprinted in the *Concise History*). Wright wished to have an introductory essay for the smaller book, and he asked Charles Robert Ashbee (1863–1942), the English architect active in the Arts and Crafts Movement whom he

*C. R. Ashbee, "Frank Lloyd Wright: A Study and an Appreciation," Introduction to *Ausgeführte Bauten* (Berlin, 1911), pp. 1–7, from *Frank Lloyd Wright: The Early Work* (New York, 1968), pp. 3–10. (Added portions translated by L. M. Roth and Gisela Stehr with the help of Dr. Hermann G. Pundt.)

[†]See H. Allen Brooks, "Frank Lloyd Wright and the Wasmuth Drawings," *Art Bulletin* 48 (June 1966), pp. 193–202.

had come to know, to prepare it. Wright had first met Ashbee during the period 1900–1901, when the Englishman had been sent to the United States to observe and report on related Arts and Crafts activities here. Ashbee visited Oak Park then and again in 1908 during a second trip to the United States. Wright felt confident, that of the leading European architects, Ashbee was best acquainted with his work, and while en route to Germany in 1910 he paused in England to make his request of Ashbee.‡ For many years the smaller *Ausgeführte Bauten* was available only in selected rare book libraries, but a larger English version was at long last published in 1968 including an introduction by Edgar Kaufman. In reprinting Ashbee's original English text, two insertions were retained in German. Both have been translated and inserted here in the positions they had in the original edition of 1911. One was evidently added by a Wasmuth editor, while the other was in Ashbee's style and incorporated a paraphrase from Wright's major essay "In the Cause of Architecture," *Architectural Record* 23 (March 1908), 155–221.

In the modern development of the arts America excels in the art of Architecture, and there are few cities upon the great continent but can show some piece of good building, or an effort in that direction; it is a popular instinct. The rich man strives to mark his wealth in stone, the cities have great libraries, clubs, colleges and schools, the states vie with one another in the splendour of their state-houses. Into spheres in which with us the architect seldom penetrates, he in America leaves his mark; the office and business building has become his province.

The names of many of the leading architects in the last two generations have been well enough known in Europe: Richardson, Hunt, McKim, Mead and White; Cope and Stewardson; Day, Clipston Sturges, Carrere and Hastings, Cass Gilbert, and many others. The buildings of these men will take their place in the sequence of architectural history; the libraries at Boston, and Washington, the Statehouses of Pittsburgh and Providence, the Metropolitan Club in New York, the collegiate buildings in Philadelphia, in Cambridge, in San Francisco.

To us, who look at them with the eyes of the old world, American buildings connote four things in style. They stand first for the English tradition, whether through the "old Colonial" or more recent importation of English forms; the French "Beaux Arts" as we see it in Washington or Fifth Avenue, New York; the purely utilitarian as in that distinctly American Business Product, the "sky scraper"; and they stand lastly for what may be called the buildings of a new spirit, as we see it on the Pacific coast and in the Middle West. It is of these last as expressed by the work of Frank Lloyd Wright that I wish specially to speak, because he first and before all other American architects seems to embody it.

This new spirit has for us in Europe a peculiar charm and piquancy, just because we do not see in it that reflection of European forms to which we have been so long accustomed. Its characteristics are a departure from tradition, a distinctiveness of surrounding, and a consequent character of its own, a delight in new materials, and an honest use of machinery. There are

‡ See Allen Crawford, "Ten Letters from Frank Lloyd Wright to Charles Robert Ashbee," *Architectural History* 13 (1970), pp. 64–76.

features that give to the buildings of the Pacific coast a character quite distinct from the School of Chicago as the conditions are not the same, and I have been in houses on the Arroyo that appeal to me more than Frank Lloyd Wright's; but all the men of the new spirit have these characteristics, and the work of Frank Lloyd Wright has them fundamentally and more markedly than any of his contemporaries. This is not to be wondered at, because it has grown within its own province—the sphere of the Middle West—and is something absolutely new and original. Trained in the office of Louis Sullivan, who first gave rational character to the industrial building of Chicago, Frank Lloyd Wright has carried the new spirit into domestic work and produced a type of building that is absolutely his own. In so doing he has given to the great city of the Prairie something she had never had before, and what is equivalent to a new architecture.

In estimating the achievement for which Wright stands, we have to consider the difficulties he had to face. With no background of tradition, with no forms about him upon which to model a style, surrounded by purely commercial conditions, and in the face of actual and fierce hostility, or the persecutions of "that little knowledge which is a dangerous thing," he carved out a manner of his own and worked out his own principles of design, before the English Arts and Crafts Movement, the German Secession, or the European Art Nouveau had in any way touched America. His Winslow House was designed in 1893, and other of his buildings in which the elements of his style are in formation bear approximately early dates. I sum up the characteristics of his work thus: first, nobility of plan—some of Frank Lloyd Wright's plans have the cleanness and simplicity we see in the planning of Gothic houses, or in the work of Bramante; then a fine proportion, witness the Oak Park houses with their long firm horizontal lines. Next, a feeling for mass and colour, as in the Unity Temple and the Coonley house; a fertility of resource in adapting means to ends; and lastly a determination, amounting sometimes to heroism, to master the machine and use it at all costs, in an endeavour to find the forms and treatment it may render without abuse of tradition. In a suggestive and interesting monograph which he contributed in 1908 to the "Architectural Record" of New York, entitled 'In the cause of Architecture,' Frank Lloyd Wright laid down the principles that inspired his work. From among them I am tempted to extract the following because it is so significant of the work and what it stands for:

"Buildings, like people, must first be sincere, must be true and then withal as gracious and lovable as may be."

"Above all, integrity. The machine is the normal tool of our civilization; give it work that it can do well—nothing is of greater importance. To do this will be to formulate the new industrial ideals we need if Architecture is to be a living Art."

Here we are brought face to face with the problem of our civilization, the solution of which will determine the future of the Arts themselves. It is significant that from Chicago, quite independently of England, of France, of Germany or elsewhere, here is a voice calling, offering a solution.

"An artist's limitations are his best friends. The machine is here to stay. It is the forerunner of the Democracy that is our dearest hope. There is no more important work before the architect now than to use this normal tool of civilization to the best advantage, instead of prostituting it as he has hitherto done in reproducing with murderous ubiquity forms born of other times and other conditions, and which it can only serve to destroy."

There is greatness in this idea, and the future will I think show that, in the case of Frank Lloyd Wright, the man's product has been worthy of the idea that has guided its development and in a measure inspired its creation. Out of it has come a different conception as to what constitutes a modern building.

Greatness demands its price, and this has often to be paid in a certain barrenness and sterility of detail owing to the severity of the limitations, a certain disregard of the intimate and personal things that make a building lovable in the sacrifice of tenderness for integrity. This is not so much the fault of the architect as of the conditions in which he is set to work. The machine is not yet mastered in modern life, or is it possible for any individual, however strong, to accomplish the mastery. This is the community's need, a social need, and it is one which we feel essentially in the Art of America.

Through the United States indeed the traditions of craftsmanship, upon which the arts professedly rest, have been broken down by mechanical power more than with us in Europe, and the American Architects, with all their greater organizing power, their combinations, and their opportunities which are supreme, have not yet devised a way of re-establishing them, of finding their equivalent, of readjusting the balance. It is to the credit of Frank Lloyd Wright that he is the first American architect who has sought to consciously express this fact, to readjust this balance. He is thus a typical product of modern America, and of that aspect of America which is Chicago. He has its strength as well as its weakness, its romance as well as its freakishness and immaturity, its barrenness as well as its sanity, its fertility of resource, and he has perhaps in an exaggerated degree its individualism. I use the word as Murray defines it, of self-centered conduct or feeling as a principle, and mode of life, in which the individual pursues his own ends or follows his own ideas. I do not know why this individualism takes its extremest form in Chicago. Every street, every avenue of that great-souled and generous, but at the same time brutal and remorseless, city tells of this. It tells somehow of the New Englander driven westward and unrestrained, in a commercial world; of the Puritan cut adrift from his gods and from his conventions, striving to make new ones out of himself. "Striving," as Blake the Seer put it, "with systems to deliver individuals from those systems." I see this striving in the work of Frank Lloyd Wright more than in any of his contemporaries.

The result is what has been called the style of the Middle West, and after accounting for him in his relation to Louis Sullivan, that style is more of his making than that of any other man. Destiny permits a man to strive, mocks him in his struggle, and in the end collects some of the fragments—that which was best and most enduring—for the greater work that is to remain. Thus styles are made, and this is so of architecture before all the arts. One may pardon in a strong man a display of individualism that one cannot forgive in a weaker; what is the character in the one becomes pettishness, or mannerism or affectation in the other, but we artists of Europe, while we appreciate and criticise the product, and while we often admire, may be forgiven when we say that in our feeling it sometimes needs to mellow. Yet whatever we may think of this individualism, and however it may win or repel us personally, it expresses for the time being a national condition. For my own part, speaking as an architect, I think this individualism, as seen in Frank Lloyd Wright's work, strong and sound to the core; there is in it a national ideal, but I do not always like it. It gives me at times the same feeling of irritation which Walt Whitman gives me, when, after some supreme passage at which one's whole heart goes out, the poet tumbles over some trifle badly handled, as when, for instance, in that sublimest of his songs, "Come, I will make the continent indisoluble," he ends up with the words "For you, Oh Democracy, MA FEMME!" He forgets that we are of the same flesh and blood, and have a sense of humour; that this trivial note tumbles us from the sublime, into detail that is badly done. I do not mean to insinuate by this example that Frank Lloyd Wright's work has inconsistence of this nature; the analogy cannot of course be pressed, and the deduction applies only to my own personal feeling regarding the sometimes undigested trivialities I find. I hold moreover that his work in architecture, while it merits the comparison, in greatness and unity, with Whitman's work in literature, is quite strong enough to stand a corresponding criticism of its limitations or its faults.

A comparison of the work of Frank Lloyd Wright with modern work in England or Germany would take me too far afield; but a certain kinship is significant and may be referred to in passing. In Germany the names of Olbrich, Hoffman, Moser, Bruno Paul, Mohring suggest themselves. In England those of us who are sometimes called the Arts and Crafts men, Lethaby, Voysey, Lutyens, Ricardo, Wilson, Holden, Blow, Townsend, Baillie Scott. We feel that between us and him there is a kinship. We may differ vitally in manner of expression, in our planning, in our touch, in the way we clothe our work, in our feeling for proportion, but although our problems differ essentially, we are altogether at one in our principles. We guard in common the lamp of truth. We hold equally with Frank Lloyd Wright that structure should be self-explanatory, that iron is there for man's service, only he must learn to use it rightly, and not learn to lie or cheat about it, that the forms of the ancient world, the traditions of the "Beaux Arts," and the old Colonial, even "Greek purism" have their place, but that their place is not necessarily the Prairie. Their place may be Connecticut, or Virginia, may be the Boulevard Montparnasse, or Buckinghamshire, but for the great open spaces of the new world something else is wanted. This land, pierced by the great trunk lines of the Middle West, the new cities of the miners, the cattlebreeders, the canners and the grain exporters, the men of ideas and invention, make a new appeal. The men who have created it, however we may view them, stand for something new, and the time is ripe for a new form to express the life they lead, or toward which they may aspire. And this life is a large life, it has given to the work of Frank Lloyd Wright that unity of idea, that largeness which his plans and drawings reveal. I have seen it, too, in such buildings as the Coonley House near Chicago and the Larkin Building in Buffalo. It is the architect's business to express life, and to ennoble it in the expression. Frank Lloyd Wright has done this; and yet all the honour is not his. To see these buildings, or think through these drawings, brings home to one how much he owes his clients. They have felt the greatness themselves, and have themselves sought to become articulate. No one can study the simple and convincing forms of the Larkin Building in Buffalo without a feeling that bigness in business organization has called forth a corresponding mood in the architect.

[The following section was evidently inserted by a Wasmuth editor.]

With hungry eye we European architects often look to our more fortunate colleagues in the New World because of their excellent site conditions, vast stretches of uninhabited countryside, and towns yet untouched by an artist, awaiting the generous hand of the patron who is willing to invest in their development. What we are envious of above all is the flavor of a "new life." Not restrained by tradition and customs, their life is much more vibrant than here in Europe. Here we are burdened with restraints as soon as we attempt to be creative, whether it is in wood, stone, iron, or concrete. The reasons for this are easily understandable in view of the different life styles of an American patron and a European magnate. The former is so much unrestricted, full of great ideas, but at the same time—it has to be said—his life is so much rougher and more commonplace. Your American customer wants large rooms, wide open spaces of even temperature; he desires exactitude; hurrying seems to be an important element in his life; he lacks a sense of leisure. On the other hand, he has great understanding for the expensive labor of the plumber; and with a child-like abandon he tries to get as much bric a brac in Europe as he can.

How much different are the people of means and wealth in England and Germany. They have limitations. The wealthy bourgeois German feels above him the Emperor's protective yet restraining hand. He probably doesn't even like his Emperor, but the Emperor wears a uniform and is a representative of another dimension. He is like a supreme apparition of another realm, out of reach, glittering in a thousand colors.

In Britain there is the House of Lords with its snares; here it is the landed gentry who greatly influence the construction and decoration of houses. An English gentleman would think he is paying tribute to a very low-ranking and costly passion if he were to pay the bill of an American plumber—which in large buildings in fact could amount to several thousand marks. He would fear the discipline of servants might be shaken and his horse's feelings hurt.

Equally different are the conditions of construction of public buildings. Of the three countries mentioned, England is the most democratic in the sense that Abraham Lincoln used the word. Germany displays the strictest discipline, whereas in America the power of money or the person who owns it undoubtedly rules. Consequently in the construction of our public buildings the decisions are made by committees, made up of shopkeepers who think only in terms of dimes and nickels [literally, "who deal out change"]. That is why we often end up with buildings the sight of which makes us feel melancholic. In America the "boss system" rules, which means—though not always—that the most capable man is promoted to the top. Contrary to this, in Germany public affairs are dominated by an old tradition which is also well manifest in its buildings. From a psychological point of view it seems quite logical that the forces just described have left their mark on the life styles of the three countries. In order to search for similar traits we first have to examine the common grounds.

[Ashbee's text resumes:]

We artists ourselves are too apt to think that we are the discoverers of forms that come new to us. It is not so. We ourselves are but the instruments through which breathes the Over-soul, the Zeitgeist. Those rapid nervous lines, those big masses, this sense of a new proportion, this breaking away from old traditions, this monotony that results from constant mechanical repetition, this longing for individual expression as a refuge from it; we all have this in our work, and it has its psychological reason. Industrial concentration, rapid locomotion, the telephone, the electric light and the lines it demands, mechanical power which has enormously cheapened and as equally permeated certain conditions of labour, the breakdown of the old productive system, the photograph, the telegraph, the development of the press and more particularly the illustrated press, these and many others are the influences that unconsciously move us all, and make us speak, puppets that we are, in ways we do not know, and, what seems so strange to each of us individually, make us speak with a common voice. Thus again, styles are made, and the style of the 20th century can never have real quality if it does not somehow express those influences behind the life of the time.

[The following section, deleted from English edition in 1968, is apparently not by Ashbee.]

I am purposely not going to elaborate in detail on the interior architecture of Lloyd Wright's buildings. This is not where the main emphasis of his work lies; it is not typical for him. In other words, it reflects the struggle to master the machine, and herein lie his limitations.

Often we detect Japanese influence. We can see how he strives to adapt Japanese forms to American conditions, even though the artist himself does not admit to this influence. The influence of the East is no doubt unconscious, but I can see it in most of his architectural drawings and in the way he expresses the picturesque element in his buildings. His buildings are very attractive to me and some illustrations in this booklet give an impression of the extent of his accomplishments in the field of room design and decoration using various kinds of materials such as glass and textiles. He also designed carpets and furniture, and we cannot deny our admiration of them as they logically complement his buildings. However, to us Europeans they do not give as convincing proof of the great personality as do his structures. Nevertheless, in the area of interior architecture, his principles are of an elevated character. They are most clearly expressed in the artist's own words:

> In order to design a building as a totality, in harmony with its environment and its interiors, it is critical that the various elements be subordinated to the underlying purpose of the whole, whatever its nature might be, aesthetic or functional. The structure as a whole has to integrate the elements and it is the architect's task to see that they complement the

building's true nature. Herein lies the principal domain of the modern architect; he has to know how to create a building as a fully integrated work of art, reflecting faithfully the activities and feelings of its inhabitants. Thus his luminous expression of materials and their organization becomes a true manifestation of the artist,

[Ashbee's text concludes:]

So far Frank Lloyd Wright has been given but little opportunity in public building, but in what he has done he has left his mark. No one can look at the Unity Temple in Oak Park, its monumental character, its frank revival of the temple form as best suited to a place of modern worship, its method of construction, solid monolith, cast in concrete, reinforced with steel strands, a construction that will last for hundreds of years after the whole suburb has passed away, without a sense that here is the new spirit, and distinctively American.

On the Romanesque churches of the old world, later generations set the mosaic, the tracery, the refinement and the culture that came with more leisure and sympathy; another century may do the same with the great experiments in architecture that America is putting forth. I have seen buildings of Frank Lloyd Wright's that I would like to touch with the enchanted wand; not to alter their structure in plan or form, or carcass, but to clothe them with a more living and tender detail. I do not know how, and the time is not yet—nor would I like to see Wright do it himself, because I do not believe he could; for thus to clothe them would mean a school of Craftsmanship that would tell of the intimate life of America, and imply a little of that quietude and poetry and scholarship which our English churches and country houses have received from the caressing hands of generations of craftsmen.

Here at all events, witness these pages, the buildings are, and they are worthy of the life.

Morris said to me once, in praise of noble decoration, "we do not want it at all unless at the outset buildings upon which we place it are noble."

In the buildings of Frank Lloyd Wright that postulate is granted.

48 H. P. Berlage, The New American Architecture* *1912*

Dutch architect, Hendrik Petrus Berlage (1856–1934) had a special admiration for and understanding of American architecture among his countrymen. He had studied H. H. Richardson's work in publication, and his own brick masterwork, the Amsterdam Exchange, 1896–1903, bore some similarities to Richardson's Sever Hall, Harvard University, 1882. By 1906 he was drawn more to the work of Sullivan and Wright, and in 1911 he was able to make a long-awaited trip to the United States to examine closely the architecture he already knew so well.† He met Sullivan, though not Wright, who was then in Europe. The lectures he gave during his tour were noted in the professional journals such as *Western Architect*. Shortly after his return, he began addressing his European colleagues about what he had seen; this selection comes from a lecture presented to Swiss architects and engineers in Zurich in March 1912 and published that September with illustrations. His observations subsequently appeared in *Reiseerinnerungen* (Rotterdam, 1913). While Berlage's own architecture thereafter bore the imprint of Sullivan, his younger countrymen were more influenced by the work of Wright which Berlage had set before them. Such Wrightian houses as those by Robert van t'Hoff at Huis der Heide or by Jan Wils in Woerden during the period 1915–17 show clearly the influence Wright had on the origins of Der Stijl movement in the Netherlands.‡ Berlage was widely read, too, in Germany, and Le Corbusier first became familiar with Wright's work through Berlage.

Frank Lloyd Wright is a student of Sullivan's and is an architect of very special importance. I do not know whether Sullivan studied in Paris, but Wright is a student of the Ecole des Beaux Arts.[1] Like Sullivan, Wright has nothing in his design-forms that reminds us of historical styles; his is an absolutely independent architecture. Wright leans on modern European architects more than Sullivan did, and like the modern Europeans, Wright struggles to simplify architectural masses and to treat ornament only as an aside; but his grouping of masses is so original that in the final analysis no European tendency is evident in his work.

Wright's specialty is the design of elegant country houses. He has built many in the vicinity of Chicago. The design of the D. D. Martin House [Buffalo, New York] is typical. The building has only two floors. The ground floor consists of living quarters and a children's playroom. The wall surfaces

---

*H. P. Berlage, "Neurere Amerikanische Architektur," *Schweizerische Bauzeitung* 60 (September 1912), pp. 165–67 (translated by Lily Boecher).

† See Leonard K. Eaton, *American Architecture Comes of Age* (Cambridge, Mass., 1972), pp. 208–32.

‡ These are illustrated in H.-R. Hitchcock, "American Influence Abroad," in *The Rise of an American Architecture*, ed. E. Kaufmann (New York, 1970), pp. 36–37.

[1] Berlage has this backward. It was Sullivan, of course, who had been in Paris briefly.—ED.

of this floor are almost uninterrupted by windows. In impressive contrast the upper floor has continuous rows of small windows; all the remaining rooms are in this upper floor. The ground floor lends itself to an organization in extended horizontal sequence since all the rooms open into each other and are also connected by long corridors. The Americans do not like to separate living areas with doors but prefer occasionally to close the openings with curtains. As a result, the interior affords beautiful views, not only from room to room, but also from the rooms into the halls, toward the staircase, and so on. These effects are heightened because the Americans are adept at decorating their houses with objects of art. Americans are fond of books as well. and often have shoulder-high bookshelves along the walls. Wright also likes flower decorations, and he likes to project out the walls of the ground floor at the height of the windows of the second floor in a way that forms a sort of outside trench in which flowers can be planted. The view from within, out over the flowers, into the garden beyond provides a rare sensation.

The low-pitched roof rests, in an unexpected way, directly on top of the upper floor; many of the rooms on that floor have the roof for a ceiling. This, together with the radically projected eaves, gives the rooms a quiet tone. One can imagine that such a house is extremely attractive. I had the impression of an extraordinary intimacy, and only with great effort could I tear myself away from those rooms. The originality of the rooms can best be described by the word "plastic"—in contrast to European interiors which are flat and two-dimensional. Outwardly as well as inwardly one can recognize an originality in these country houses—an originality that may enable one to talk about a new and native American architecture because there is nothing like it in Europe. Just as the English country house became the model for the European private house, so, no doubt, Wright's country houses will become the models for American private houses. Indeed this is already the case as can be seen in country houses built by many different architects since the beginning of Wright's career.

Some of the details of Wright's designs are particularly charming, for instance: entrances and halls, motifs with which he likes to work and through which he knows how to accomplish decorative effects. Such things are, however, difficult to describe; and since I have to restrict myself, these pictures will have to suffice.

Wright has also built a church, actually a sort of meeting hall, which again reflects the great originality of his art. The interior of the church proper is designed as a square; the Sunday school is housed in another part of the building. Wright has worked here with the same contrasts that he uses in his country houses; he has placed the row of windows high up under the roof of the church; and this placement, together with the solid base of the wall, creates a unified space in the interior. The flat roof is projected out and casts a beautifully decorative shadow. The "plasticity" of this building is imposing in the generosity of its scale, reminiscent of the scale of an Egyptian temple. I have heard that the elders of the church were extreme in their opposition to this building. I can understand this because the elders must have had, as in the case of the Sullivan church, an entirely different image of a Protestant church.[2]

[2] More about this interesting building and the spirit of Wright's architecture is available in a small pamphlet with pictures, plans, and figures: "The New Edifice of Unity Church, Oak

I was told that Wright's masterwork is the office building of the Larkin Company in Buffalo, New York. I went to see it, and I must confess that that is not to say enough. The building consists of only one room because the modern American concept is that an office should not be divided into separate rooms. The head of the office works at the same table with his employees, and from his table his view can reach out into the entire forceful space with its various open floors which, like galleries, surround the central hall. The building is made of brick, and it looks like a warehouse from the outside. The interior hall has excellent light in spite of the masses of brick which surround the exterior corner towers. The effect is similar to that of the Unity Temple where the staircases in the corner towers are lighted from the inside. The galleries in the Larkin Building get their light through windows set in between the massive exterior pillars. The building is conceived in terms of contrasts and with very powerful effect. Whatever concept one may have of an office building, particularly here in Europe, there is no office building here with the monumental power of this American one. The material of the interior (as of the exterior) walls is brick which alternates with the concrete ceilings. The detailing is handled naturally and in accordance with Wright's originality, and again it shows his strong creative genius.

I left convinced that I had seen a great modern work, and I am filled with respect for this master who has been able to create a building which has no equal in Europe. I have tried to give you a brief glimpse of modern American architecture by describing works of the two greatest American architects of our time. Perhaps I have not done justice to others; during my short stay in America many things which might have been worth seeing may have remained unknown to me. Upon the advice of a young colleague of mine who worked in Sullivan's office, I concerned myself primarily with the work of Sullivan and Wright. But in so doing I may say that I have not strayed far from the truth; and my colleague, whose judgment I value highly, is of the same opinion.

Certainly—and I have already had the opportunity of stating this before—Wright has many followers who continue the work in terms of his ideas; and yet these other architects work outside of Wright's direct influence and demonstrate an ability to be independent at the same time that they honor the good principles of the master.

Some of the most interesting recent buildings in America are apartment houses of 10 to 12 or even more floors. The demand for apartments is even greater in America than it is here in Europe. Because domestic help is so expensive in America, people are forced to live as economically and as simply as possible, and they are forced therefore to build comfortably designed apartments, each with its own kitchen. In Europe, and especially in Germany, there are good recent examples by well-known architects of this kind of building. These European buildings are remarkable architecturally; but the conception of the American apartment buildings is at least their equal.

I had occasion to admire the correct principle of the mass effect of

Park, Illinois, Frank Lloyd Wright, Architect." Descriptive and historical matter by Dr. Rodney F. Johonnot, Pastor. Published by the New Unity Church Club, June, 1906.—BERLAGE'S NOTE.

these American buildings. All decorations which could damage this effect are avoided. Great wall surfaces are composed in a well-balanced distribution of pedestal, structure, and cap. The windows are cut in without elaborate frames. The brick, which is the material throughout, is beautiful in its color. These simple elements have to accomplish the whole effect and certainly do so.

In the end, this undecorated structural simplicity has become the reigning principle in America, and not just for apartment buildings in particular, but for modern American architecture in general. Shouldn't it be possible to talk now of a relationship between the efforts there and here in Europe? I came back from America convinced that a new architecture is growing and that this architecture already shows striking results. We Europeans certainly have no reason to regard American architecture as inferior. On the contrary, the designs of the best American architects show an originality and an imagination which promise a great evolution in the future. I hope that with this short description I have succeeded in showing the readers of this magazine that American architecture should be accorded the high estimation which it really deserves.

49 A. D. F. Hamlin, The Battle of the Styles* *1892*

The problem of "style" vexed Sullivan and Wright, as it concerned all perceptive architects of the period. Robert Andrews neatly summed up the problem in 1904: "To get a style by avoiding a style—that is the paradox of American architecture." And Bertram G. Goodhue, who was to combine tradition and progressive idealism with so much promise, confessed in 1905 "it is probable that we shall never again have a distinctive style, but what I hope and believe we shall some day possess is something akin to a style—so flexible that it can be made to meet every practical and constructive need, so beautiful and complete as to harmonize the heretofore discordant notes of Art and Science, and to challenge comparison with the wonders of past ages, yet malleable enough to be moulded at the designer's will."†

An early and well-informed discussion of this issue is by Hamlin. Albert Dwight Foster Hamlin (1855–1926) was born to missionaries in Turkey, studied at

---

*A. D. F. Hamlin, "The Battle of the Styles," *Architectural Record* 1 (January–March and April–June 1892), pp. 265–75, 405–13.

†Robert D. Andrews, "The Future of American Architecture," *Catalogue* Boston Architectural Club Exhibition, Boston, 1904, p. 12; and Bertram G. Goodhue, "The Modern Architectural Problem: Discussed from the Professional Point of View," *Craftsman* 8 (June 1905), pp. 332–33. These are cited in Richard W. Longstreth, "Academic Eclecticism in American Architecture," *Winterthur Portfolio* 17 (Spring 1982), pp. 55–82. See also Walter C. Kidney, *The Architecture of Choice: Eclecticism in America, 1880–1930* (New York, 1974).

Amherst College, and then pursued architectural studies at M.I.T. during 1876–77, finished by three years at the École des Beaux-Arts in Paris, (1878–81).[1] He then worked for about two years in the office of McKim, Mead and White, leaving to become a special assistant to William R. Ware who had left M.I.T. to form a department of architecture at Columbia University (then Columbia College). Hamlin remained there the rest of his life, teaching architecture and architectural history. He published several texts and wrote an extended series on architecture and its critics for the *Architectural Record* (May 1915–December 1927). It appears to have been pure coincidence that accompanying the first portion of Hamlin's essay was a photo essay on Burnham and Root's Rookery, Chicago, and that following the second part was an illustrated article by Dankmar Adler on the Chicago Auditorium.

It is generally admitted that the decorative and architectonic forms in which the conceptions of modern architecture are expressed are the weakest side of its development. They have exposed it to the reproach of insincerity and untruthfulness, of lack of invention and of fundamental inconsistency between its construction and decoration. It has developed no architectural language of its own, but has used the dead languages of extinct styles, copying incessantly where it should have invented. As a result we behold in modern work a bewildering variety of styles, whose employment in most cases seems to have been determined by no more serious consideration than the architect's personal predilection, and the changing fads or fashions of the day. There has been within forty years a veritable revolution in building methods and processes and materials, but these changes seem to have had little influence in developing any truly modern and characteristic system of constructive and decorative forms.

Fergusson, writing of England in 1873, uses these words: "Architecture never was in so false a position in this country since the Reformation as it is at this moment, nor practiced on such entirely mistaken principles." "Whatever the other merits of modern buildings may be, the element of truthfulness is altogether wanting." And of France, where more than anywhere else there is at least the semblance of a modern style, Viollet-le-Duc observes in his "discourses," that "instead of availing ourselves of the immense resources furnished by modern industry . . . to produce a new style of architecture, which shall be the natural expression of our era and our civilization, we straiten and limit our means under an architectural system theorized out of the past and conventionalized by academic usage." Our modern American architecture has been criticised with equal severity by more than one writer of note, yet still around us rise Romanesque and Renaissance designs side by side, and still the battle of the styles continues. While we implore the combatants to listen to reason (*our* reason), they keep right on, Romanesque, Byzantine, Gothic, Cinque Cento and Louis Quinze, all striving for the mastery. The men who create, who feel and handle the forces which the critic and philosopher only see; who know the limitations of circumstance and conditions and struggle therewith, give little heed to the philosopher, to the man who analyzes and can only proceed on general principles and abstrac-

[1] *Dictionary of American Biography* 8:193–94.

tions. Mankind is not always right nor the critics always wrong, but we must guard against the illusions of a false perspective. On the battlefield there seems to be only "confusion worse confounded," but from the mountain-height one may discern a plan of campaign, a system governing the apparent chaos of movements, a final result planned from the beginning and at last triumphantly achieved. Perchance some future age may perceive in the architectural tumult about us germs of a coming cosmos of beauty and strength all invisible to our nearer view, and so judge otherwise than we.

If we divide the general question of styles in modern architecture into several inquiries, their separate consideration may throw some light on the correctness or erroneousness of the common assumptions that modern architecture, in its outward expression, is wholly untruthful, and that the chaos of styles about us is a wholly unmitigated evil. We may put these inquiries into forms like these:

1. Why have we no styles of our own as previous ages have had?
2. Can a historic style be truthfully and logically employed in modern designs, and if so, in what manner?
3. Can several historic styles be concurrently employed without inconsistency?
4. Is there hope of developing a distinct system of architectural forms appropriate to our age and civilization?

I. To answer the first inquiry at length would involve too long and detailed a recapitulation of the course of modern architectural history from the Middle Ages down. We can only notice its most salient facts.

The foundations of modern civilization were laid in the fifteenth century. The revival of classic studies in Italy was only one symptom of the revolution that was taking place in human life and thought. As the Middle Ages represent the negation of individualism under supreme authority—the absorption of the unit in the mass—so the Renaissance, if it meant anything, was the breaking up of the mass and the emergence of the unit. The individual consciousness asserted itself; the right of every man to question, doubt, investigate, acquire for himself. Out of this spirit have grown modern conceptions of liberty, modern Protestantism, science, invention and discovery, popular education, modern democracy, and the industrial and commercial system of our day—in short, the nineteenth century.

Now Gothic art, developing throughout Western Europe as a mighty system, carried out with varying details, but under the pressure of universal principles of development, was only possible under a universal church, and by the absorption of the unit in the mass. As was pointed out in a previous article,[1] the efforts of architects all over Europe were concentrated for over three hundred years upon a single architectural problem, and under the influence of a universal church which ignored the bounds of country and differences of race. When the Renaissance dawned, the architectural system thus developed had culminated and begun a career of decline, marked by the quest for extravagant effects of clever construction and ostentatious decoration. It was wholly unsuited to the tastes and requirements of the new

[1]"The Difficulties of Modern Architecture," *Architectural Record* 1 (October–December 1891), pp. 137–50.

civilization. The new era was worldly in its tastes and aspirations; rising in revolt against the mediæval asceticism, which would suppress beauty and joy as legitimate objects of pursuit, it found in the art and literature of classic times a spirit more akin to its own. The poetry of classic mythology, the splendid material environments of Roman civilization, the Greek worship of beauty, appealed powerfully to the neo-paganism of those times. That they appropriated to their own use every tangible vestige of classic art was the inevitable consequence of this spirit. They had no Ruskin and no Fergusson to tell them they were setting forth on a false career, and to indoctrinate them with a system of æsthetic morals which they could not have comprehended had they listened to its preachment. Indeed, classic art was the only mine open to them to work. They could not build upon the Gothic, so foreign to their tastes and already in its decrepitude. They could not invent a new architecture out of whole cloth; the thing is impossible. They could not revert to Greek forms, of which they were absolutely ignorant. They could not but use the details of Roman art with which they were surrounded, and which they had never discarded, even in the fullest tide of their mediæval art. The new style of the Renaissance was nevertheless not a copying, and however much the men of the time may have imagined they were reproducing Roman architecture (a statement often made, but certainly open to doubt) they were really adapting classic details freely to their own uses, and with a grace and a taste betokening a truly artistic spirit. The path on which they set out was not only the one path alone open to them, it was also the natural and logical path to follow.

The decline of the art, out of which the modern chaos has grown, began when the Roman orders in their entirety, as a completely formulated system, came to be looked upon as the only adequate medium for architectural expression. When the wayward genius of Michael Angelo had furthermore set the example of disregarding the wise limits of scale in their use, the rapidly-degenerating taste of the succeeding period forsook the restraints of logic and common sense, and abandoned itself to the extravagances of the Jesuit and Roccoco styles. A reaction was inevitable; but the architects of the eighteenth century, instead of going back to the parting of the roads—to the architecture of the first half of the sixteenth century—sought perfection in the imitation of the works of antiquity, a radically different thing from the adaptation of their details to modern uses. Such buildings as the façades of St. John Lateran and St. Peter's in Rome, and the Madeleine and Panthéon in Paris, were the result. For a century, more or less, European architecture was occupied with a series of efforts based on the same fundamental blunder—the restoration in modern times of the architecture of a by-gone age. Every designer sought to do as exactly as possible what he supposed an architect of the period he was imitating would have done with the same programme and under the same conditions. The monumental absurdity of imagining a classic Roman architect, or a contemporary of Phidias, or a mediæval master-of-works, as occupied with such a programme under such conditions, never troubled his mind. His aim was accomplished if the details he used could each claim an exact historic precedent, so that (if properly shattered and discolored) they might be mistaken for genuine products of the age they pretended to belong to, no matter how incongruous with the spirit and methods of that age might be the plan and construction of the building.

This absurdity lies at the base of all the "revivals"—the Greek, the Roman and the Gothic—whether in England, France or Germany, and was fatal to them all. The talent, devotion and perseverance of their adherents produced many beautiful works, it is true. They contributed much to the adornment of modern cities; they stimulated historic study and the preservation of ancient monuments, and gave to the profession a new tone of seriousness and scholarliness, but they could not put the breath of life into dead systems.

Moreover their labors were prosecuted in a period of rampant philistinism. The first half of this century was well-nigh dead to the claims of true art. Commerce, politics, war and mechanical invention seemed to have stifled all considerations of loveliness in life and art. Engineering monopolized whatever real progress was being made in building. Metal construction was coming into general use for bridges and for structures with large roofs, such as railroad stations and exhibition buildings, the most characteristic products of the constructive skill of the time. These works were intrusted to engineers; the architects were so preoccupied with their mistaken efforts to resuscitate historic styles that they wholly failed to discover the possibilities of the new material, and scornfully abandoned it to the mathematicians and iron-founders. As a result, it was handled without grace or feeling, and is only in our own day slowly gaining recognition as a possible means to artistic ends.

The same things were largely true of architecture in our own land. The one phase of its history which we can claim as in any sense national was the Colonial style, which was a free adaptation to our own uses, especially to work in wood, of the Queen Anne and Adamsite details which our builders had inherited from England. But it was swamped by the wave of the imported Greek revival, with its mistaken taste. This in its turn gave way to the pseudo-Gothic, which has left so many atrocious mementos of its passage across the continent. The Gothic revival here lacked the inspiration of the monuments which in the Old World were the objects of the architect's ceaseless study. Trained practitioners were few, and technical skill among our artisans, especially in carving and decoration, was deplorably lacking. Still more disastrous was the low estate of public taste and information in art matters, and the general toleration of the most wretched shams. However open to criticism such designs as Trinity, St. George's (Stuyvesant Square), and Grace Church, in New York City, may be in our eyes, they were a veritable oasis in the wilderness of bad Gothic of their day.

Meanwhile the French had been coming nearer to a true reform in architecture than any other people. Starting with the elements of classic design, they had developed out of them a more or less rational and consistent system of treatment, in which they avoided on the one hand the academic stiffness of the Vignolesque school and on the other the extravagances of the Rococo. It had, and still retains, at least the merit of modernness and consistency, and is often used in such a manner as to acquit it of the reproach sometimes brought against it, of artificiality and want of relation to the system of construction employed. The brilliant incursion of the Néo-Grec school of Duc, Duban and Labrouste, in the second third of the century, infused into it a certain grace and freedom which it has never since wholly lost, and it has exerted a powerful influence upon the more recent architecture of Germany, and especially of Austria. The École des Beaux-Arts has done much to unify the style and to give a thorough training to its practitioners and, in spite of the officialism and restraint of free-development alleged against it—certainly with far less justification to-day than when first advanced by Viollet-le-Duc—it has proved the value of its instruction, independently of the special classicism it is supposed to inculcate, by such free and iconoclastic work as that of H. H. Richardson, who was trained in its *ateliers,* and by such buildings in Paris itself as the Trocadero and the metallic structures of the late Exposition. In these last we see at least partially realized the early promise of the Halles Centrales of Baltard. Both in their planning and in their decorative treatment of constructive forms they display remarkable taste and inventiveness, which we are as yet far from equaling in this country, in our treatment of constructive iron-work.

The influence of the French school on American architecture began in the persons of R. M. Hunt and H. H. Richardson, the pioneers of the American colony of architectural students in Paris. This influence was strongly stimulated by the Centennial Exposition of 1876, which started a veritable renaissance in American art. Undoubtedly the school of architecture of the Massachusetts Institute of Technology had done much to prepare the way for this; and it has ever since maintained a high standard of scholarship and efficiency, and in conjunction with the other strong schools which have been established since that date has contributed largely to swell the number of thoroughly educated and enthusiastic men in the ranks of the profession, even in distant Western and Southern regions.

These architects of our land and day come to their work with no traditions but those of the schools or offices where they have been trained; a mantle loosely worn, and flung away on the first occasion. Historical examples fail them as exact precedents for the new and ever-changing problems that meet them. On the other hand, invention "out of whole cloth" is disastrous to good design. The most horrible compositions that disfigure our streets, the most *outré,* barbarous and illogical hotch-potches of mistaken design to be found in our cities, are quite as apt to be the work of intelligent men of fair general education who are nevertheless possessed of the idea that "absolute originality" is the chiefest of architectural virtues, to be attained only by absolutely disregarding all historical precedent, as they are to be the productions of illiterate and philistine builders. The total absence in the historic styles of anything exactly corresponding to the varied types of building which our ever-changing conditions are constantly calling into being, while it has operated to prevent any mechanical copying or wholesale importation of those styles in recent years, has also retarded the convergence of American practice into anything like a national uniformity or type of character, except perhaps in the one domain of domestic architecture. Each designer makes use of the style which he imagines to best befit his special problem, or whose "grammar" he has most thoroughly mastered; as a rule, he uses it freely, adapting and modifying not always with the most perfect logic, but generally according to his lights. For this diversity of practice to crystallize into unity requires time. Mixture and fusion must precede the emergence of the crystal; whether these processes have begun among us is a part of the fourth of our questions; but even if they have, there has not yet been time for their completion. Their culmination is opposed by many forces; the constant change in the problems presented, in their special requirements and in the resources for their solution; the hostility of modern engineering to art; the progressive specialization both in building industries and in the arts of design; the increasing urgency and imperiousness of purely mechanical considerations, and the ever-growing complexity of modern buildings; these things unite to promote the restlessness and variety so conspicuous in American design, and so hostile to the development of a simple, dignified and monumental architecture.

II. Before we turn the pages of history for light on our second question let us stop a moment to define our terms, and so make certain that writer and reader shall proceed on a common understanding. The distinction between *style* in the abstract and *a style* in the concrete is fundamental to our discussion. Without entering into any lengthy illustration like those in the sixth of Viollet-le-Duc's "Discourses" we may express the distinction as that between a quality and a historic fact. *Style* is character, unity of effect proceeding from some dominant quality in the design. *A style*, on the other hand, is a particular manner of designing peculiar to a race, age or person; an "understood way of working" (to use Mr. Schuyler's felicitous phrase), resulting usually in a recognized system of forms and combinations of detail. A given style may possess very little *style;* and, again, there may be excellent style in a work whose particular style it would be hard to designate.

Our second question then resolves itself into this: Can the "understood way of working" of a past age, its peculiar system of architectural forms, be rationally applied to modern purposes? The affirmative answer seems obvious, whenever the style lends itself to such uses. Indeed, there is no alternative but to use the forms of a historic style in modern architecture, unless we resort to invention pure and simple. But all the invention in the world will never produce a new style, and it is a mournful fact that whenever invention has built otherwise than upon the foundation of some already-established system of form, it has only resulted in idiosyncrasies and eccentricities of the worst kind. The great styles of historic architecture have always grown up by gradual and minute accretions, suppressions and modifications of existing forms. We, who have no existing system of form, and can find none in the immediate past as the starting-point for any reform in modern design, can therefore do no otherwise than resort to the remoter past. To forbid this, as some theorists would, upon any fine-spun theory of the "inherent untruth of working in the fashion of an extinct civilization," is a fantastic refinement of an imaginary system of morals. The fallacy in the "revivals" of the last hundred years lay not in the fact that the forms they used belonged to a more or less remote past, but in their irrational use of those forms. Absolute reproduction of the old combinations was essayed, instead of a free adaptation of their elements to each special programme; and thus planning and construction were subordinated to the style instead of controlling it. The Victorian Gothic was nearer to truth and reason than the earlier revivals in its freer adaptation of means to ends. It was a legitimate, a rational effort to develop out of the mediæval architecture of England a flexible and characteristic modern style. It came to grief because it was too artificial, corresponding to no spontaneous movement of popular taste; and because the style on which it was based was intractable to modern uses. It has fared differently with the American revival of the Romanesque for the converse of the above reasons. It *has* "taken" with the people, finding a ready echo in the popular taste; and it is based upon a style which was still undeveloped when it made way for the pointed arch, and therefore had in it the seeds of vitality and the flexibility of a still immature and incomplete system.

So with the Italian Renaissance. As long as it employed only the elements of Roman architecture, it could develop them in its own fashion, adapting them freely to immediate needs; and just so long did it retain its power of growth. The early palaces, the doorways and tombs of Florence, the Palazzo del Consiglio at Verona, the beautiful arcaded court-yards of Tuscany and Lombardy, are all as un-Roman as possible, although their details are entirely based on classic models. That which sterilized Italian architecture was not the mere fact of the adoption, in the sixteenth century, of pilasters and entablatures; for pilasters and entablatures and complete "orders" figure frequently in the finest Cinque Cento design. Nor was it, even, as some have claimed, the purely decorative employment of constructive features. Not only was classic Roman architecture—surely a virile art—characterized by the purely decorative use of the orders which were constructive features in Greek art, but the Greeks themselves, in the age of Phidias, had never abandoned their mutules, triglyphs and guttæ, which were purely decorative survivals from an earlier system of construction. Decorative shafts, balustrades and gables are among the most striking features of fine Gothic work; and, indeed, there has never been a highly-developed phase of art in which the same phenomenon has not been repeated. What caused ossification of Italian architecture was the adoption *en bloc* of the whole Roman system of design treated as a formula, or canon, any departure from which was considered an impropriety. Thus accepted, the style could not be rationalized nor assimilated to the constructive methods or special requirements of the age, and the Roccoco was simply an effort to escape the stiffness and barrenness that ensued. Admirable as are the earlier productions of the Purist school of Palladio and Vignola, they inaugurated a false principle, whose disastrous consequences we can avoid only by heeding their plain warning.

We are in more senses than one the heirs of the ages. The monuments of historic art of all lands and periods we may possess if we will; and travel, description, drawing, printing and photography have placed them all within our reach. Truly unhappy are we if we may not use the inestimable treasures with which modern science and the patient erudition of centuries have enriched us! All other ages have borrowed from their predecessors. Greek ornament may be largely traced back to the Egyptian lotus, as Mr. W. H. Goodyear has demonstrated. Roman art is based on Greek art; the Byzantines borrowed freely from Rome, Venice from Byzantium, and southern France from Venice. The first part of the question we have asked is therefore answered in the affirmative by all the testimony of history; it only remains to inquire what principles should control in the use of a historic style.

One or two inferences seem obvious from the historical facts we have already cited. We should avoid the example of the earlier revivalists, and on no account seek to resuscitate the whole architectural system of another age. Whatever may be the style from which we draw our inspiration, or to which we resort for suggestions of form and composition, the materials it affords must be used with careful discrimination between what is capable of adaptation to our purpose and what is not. This can only be attained by a thorough mastery of the style. If we would know what to use and what to reject, we must first know what we have to draw from. The masterpieces of the art should be studied, not only for their general composition, but for their detail. We should also familiarize ourselves with its lesser monuments, that we may learn the humbler applications of the style. Its history, its planning, its system of construction, its decoration in its general principles and in its details, the very technique of its execution, all these things are pertinent. Only by such thorough study can one penetrate the spirit and find out the animating principles of the style, and to possess one's self completely of these is essential. Half-knowledge, which is sometimes the worst kind of ignorance, is responsible for many of the architectural villainies perpetrated by well-meaning men.

It follows as a natural corollary that if the above be the true way to prepare for the use of a historic style a man cannot well succeed in mastering more than two in a lifetime. Indeed, no.

Having thus learned what we have to select from, a second principle may be laid down: that the style should be subordinated to the scheme of composition best befitting the programme; that is, the style should be a means, not an end. Its application should begin when the scheme of the design has been determined upon, not before. Thus the designer is unhampered by the artificial restraint of a formulated style while preparing his general scheme, and can determine the latter wholly by considerations of fitness, convenience and sound construction. Too often the spectacle is met with of a design whose appropriateness and convenience have been sacrificed to the fancied exigencies of a style whose historic combinations the architect did not dare to modify.

The third inference we would draw from what has gone before, is the necessity as well as the difficulty of modifying and adapting historic details for modern uses. If thorough familiarity with a style is necessary in order to select from the materials it offers, still more is it essential to any real assimilation of those materials. How skillfully and beautifully was this done by the Cinque Centists in Italy! One has only to compare their work with the classic models which inspired it to appreciate their mastery of those models and the purity of their taste. Byzantine architecture is another example of the adaptation and transformation of Roman details; how complete was the transformation and how splendid the result!

And, finally, the only safe pilot between the Scylla of servile imitation on the one hand and the Charybdis of an eccentric originality on the other is a thoroughly disciplined and cultured taste. Culture comes from reading and study, and from contact with what is fine and noble in art and in humanity. Discipline comes from training, self-restraint, constant practice. Perhaps the lesson of self-restraint is the one most needed in these days for our American architects. This lesson the schools of architecture endeavor to teach, while enriching the mind and training the perceptions and reasoning powers of the student. The work they have done is invaluable, and is destined to bear even richer fruit in the future.

Before entering upon our third inquiry it may be well to recapitulate some of the conclusions reached in our first paper. It was there contended, as the reader may remember, that of the two alternatives between which the non-existence of a true modern style places the architect—namely the employment of historic styles or the invention of a new one—the latter has been proved hopeless by the lamentable and grotesque failure of every attempt it has prompted; and that the real question before the architect is as to the way in which historic forms should be employed. The writer endeavored to show what were the true principles underlying the rational use of historic forms, and called attention to the necessity of thoroughly mastering at least one historic style, and to the difficulty, not to say impossibility, of mastering more than two in an ordinary lifetime. It was pointed out that the style selected should be one possessing the seeds of vitality and progress, and consequently one not already developed into final completeness in the past, and that it must be capable of adaptation to our special needs. It must in some degree correspond to the movement and demands of modern taste, which though it may lead and develop, it must not too far outrun. Convenience and logic should not be overridden by the demands of mere historic precedent; the ordering of plan and mass and the general composition should be determined by modern requirements, and the historic style employed to give body and clothing to the structure so contrived, furnishing the details of form and decoration as well as the principles to guide in their combination. And in all these operations the dictates of a cultivated taste are the final law.

III. While the rational application of these principles still leaves open the third query, "Can several distinct styles be concurrently employed without inconsistency," the contentions just rehearsed throw light on the answer. For if historic styles may and must be used in modern work, we must expect to see the forms of different epochs used side by side in our streets until architects be found all of one mind and clients all of one taste; or until the widely varying practice of our time shall converge into the uniformity of a new and vital style, under the pressure of new conditions and a more perfect civilization. So long as one architect finds the sturdy forms of the Romanesque better suited than all others to express his conceptions, while another, with a different cast of mind, prefers the more sumptuous and delicate Renaissance, and a third draws his suggestions of design from the ecclesiastic art of the fourteenth century, this variety will continue; and the question resolves itself therefore into the simple inquiry, "Are these men all pursuing a rational course?" Those who reply in the negative must bear the burden of proof. If but one style must prevail, which shall it be? And no one can answer this. The mere fact of the diversity of modern practice is presumptive evidence against the possibility of final agreement upon any one system of historic forms; and two other important facts stand opposed to any such united action. The first is the extraordinary increase in the number of kinds of buildings erected, and in the variety of requirement in buildings of the same kind in our times, as compared with any former period in history. All the great styles of the past have been developed in one, or at most two or three classes of structure. Classic Greek architecture was an architecture of temples. The forms used for stoas and gymnasia were those which had developed in temple design. The Roman styles were developed primarily in theatres and amphitheatres, their temples being free imitations of Greek models. A second and more magnificent phase of Roman design was worked out in the great Thermae, which were the prototypes of many features of Byzantine art. The latter in its turn was an architecture of churches, while in the Middle Ages three or four centuries successively made their contributions to the elaboration of a single type of building, the Cathedral. In the Renaissance the variety of architectural problems was greater; and yet palaces, town halls and domed churches constitute nine-tenths of the architectural monuments of the centuries from the fifteenth to the eighteenth; and in them we trace the whole evolution and decline of Neo-Roman art in Italy, France, Germany and Spain. No commercial buildings (if we except a few *loggie* in Italy, the Bank at Genoa, the Halle aux Blés in Paris, and one or two other scattered examples); no theatres; no railway stations; no parliament houses nor capitols; no post-offices; no museums;[2] no concert halls; no hotels; no exhibition buildings; no hippodromes; no manufactories; no observatories; no private architecture worth the name, except the palaces of the great lords and merchant princes; none of these multifarious, ever-changing, ever more perplexing problems of our day obtruded themselves into the quiet development of palace-designing.

The second of the two facts referred to is the rapid development in modern times of wholly new principles of construction and of new materials for building, involving changes in architectural practice which soon outrun the slower developments of style and form. The men of historic times never had to deal with the perplexing problem of adapting their customary methods to new and suddenly-appearing materials and to suddenly-revolutionized methods of construction. These difficulties, unknown to them, are so common among us as to pass unnoticed; they are accepted as matters of course. We forget that while it takes decades for a style to crystallize into form, it takes but a year or two, in these days, to revolutionize methods of construction; and the historic style which suits well enough the constructive practice of this year may be wholly incompatible with that of 1893. The architect who uses classic sculptured pediments and Corinthian colonnades upon the legislative palace he is planning, would certainly turn to other resources of design for his railroad station or armory. In other words, there has never yet been developed a system of forms and combinations, an "understood way of building," equally applicable to requirements so various as those of our modern civilization. Whether among the historic styles there be one capable of ultimate development into such diverse adaptations is another question: none has yet received such a Protean development.

Thus, even if architects could unite upon some one style as the basis of their work—an impossible thing in itself—they would find themselves face to face with a problem more difficult than any they have heretofore encoun-

---

[2] It must be remembered that the great Renaissance collections of antique art, like many of the modern museums of painting and sculpture, were housed, not in buildings specially designed for the purpose, but in palaces, villas and garden casinos.

tered: that, namely, of adapting a single basic system of form and composition to narrow "sky-scrapers," as well as to long and low and broad railroad stations; to street façades composed of 25-foot slices and to the huge masses of exhibition buildings; to churches and to theatres; to skating-rinks and prisons; to triumphal arches and to clock towers; to market buildings and to State capitols. The style must be equally adapted to hard and unfeeling granite, to noble and delicate marble, to the sturdy and sober limestones and the coarse-grained sandstones; to brick and terra cotta, to wrought and cast-iron, glass, tile, timber, shingled, slated, concrete and plaster buildings. No style that falls short of such universal adaptability need present its claims for universal adoption. It cannot fill the bill presented by the advocates, if such exist, of uniformity in the use of historic architecture. Until such a style be produced, and its claims at least presumptively established, the "concurrent use of several historic styles in the work of our time" will be inevitable, and therefore consistent with reason and common sense, however undesirable it may seem from an abstract and purely philosophical point of view.

But the concurrent or contemporaneous use of several distinct styles may be practised in several different ways. The mixing up in one design of several styles is one thing; the use of different styles in different works or classes of work by the same architect is another; still another case is presented in the contemporaneous use of different styles by different architects, each retaining some one style as the basis of his work.

The first of these three cases gives us eclecticism in its extreme form. It is inconceivable that two or three different systems of design, developed in different ages and for widely separated purposes, and each associated with a particular system of planning and construction, should be equally appropriate for one and the same problem, and at the same time harmonious with each other. The mixed forms of transitional periods mark the tenacious hold of long-established uniformity of practice struggling against innovation and change. These periods are brilliant and brief; brilliant, because of the sincerity, simplicity and earnestness of purpose and the artistic vitality which characterize them; brief, because such sincere and earnest effort is soon rewarded by emancipation from the old into the free atmosphere of the new. The difference is heaven-wide between this and the deliberate and intentional mixing of incongruous styles. Not conviction, not necessity, but affectation is stamped upon such work, unless, indeed, the mixture be the product of dense ignorance.

Moreover, no man can reasonably hope to completely master more than two really distinct styles in a lifetime; but to combine harmoniously the elements of even two requires a masterful knowledge of both, except when, as in transitional times, it is done naively under the pressure of circumstances. And it may well be doubted whether any man, having mastered two styles, would venture to attempt marrying them. He, far better than the neophyte, comprehends their incompatibility. I do not refer to the occasional introduction of details, hints and suggestions from one style into work mainly based upon another. We may fairly be accused of having studied to very little purpose if after all that archæology and draughtsmanship and photography have done for us in bringing the past within reach, we can find absolutely nothing in one style in the way of suggestion, detail or spirit which may serve us in our use of another. But it must be confessed that to attempt to do this has its dangers, and none but the most experienced men, with the most cultivated taste, can safely venture upon a path where indiscretions and mistakes of taste are so easy and so disastrous.

Again, styles historically diverse may occur in different works by the same hand, and may be justified on the ground just stated, that there has thus far been found no style capable of immediate adaptation to all the variety of purposes and types of building of our day. The classicist may well be excused if he turns to mediæval models in designing churches, and the mediævalist in like manner may find his customary methods inappropriate for a museum of classic sculpture or a State capitol. No one thinks of blaming him if his open-air theatre or *café-restaurant* in a park—structures in their nature trivial, playful and gay—are Moorish with cusped horse-shoe arches and plaster diaper-ornament. But these excursions into other styles than that which is one's own by choice and by long practice should be the exception, dictated by strong conviction of necessity. As time goes on, the work of our men of longest and most thorough experience is generally seen to be increasingly dominated by the style which each has found most congenial; practice and study and experience constantly enlarging the scope of its applications, and subduing to its control a larger variety of the knotty problems of modern design.

And if there may be variety in the use of styles in different works by the same designer, still more must we look for variety in the works of different hands. Indeed, there is a touch of the absurd in the outcry against such mingling of styles. It is hardly rational to demand uniformity in the use of historic styles in this age of rampant eclecticism in all fields of life and taste, of triumphant individualism, when authority sits so lightly on men's interests and lives; in this age of archæology, when the different periods of history are made to live again in our imaginations, and one man is an Ægyptologist, and another a Hellenist, and a third an enthusiast in Roman or mediæval lore; in this age of rapid change and transition, when the garments of custom are outgrown in a day, and new discoveries overturn the established order with every decade. The universal adoption of any one historic style would be perfunctory at least; our architecture would lose all spontaneity, vitality and snap, and become monotonous, stiff and formal. No unity of art can be desirable which is not free and natural, like the unity of a plant or tree, a product of the soil and sun and atmosphere that give life to the vital seed. To such free unity of style, consistent with our modern civilization, we must surely come in time, out of this seeming chaos of transition. But we must await the processes of evolution, which may be encouraged, but cannot be hurried. The marshaling of so many styles side by side in modern work is a necessary outcome of history, and some of us can see even here the "promise and potency" of a coming crystal of twentieth century architecture which shall be worthy of its day.

And, indeed, there is nothing absolutely anomalous in this modern mixture. We find something like it in the mediæval art of Italy, where the Byzantine and Lombard and Roman styles were being practised contemporaneously in the same or in neighboring cities and provinces. In Sicily, Norman work jostles the Arabic and Byzantine in many a town and building, and the Byzantine of Venice was at first an out-and-out importation from abroad into the midst of the then-prevailing local style. The same is true of the German Gothic of certain North Italian monuments; and so careless were the Italians always about consistency of style, that round and pointed arches were used again and again in the same buildings long after the first introduction of Gothic forms into that country.

It may still be objected that this concurrent use of various styles, however unavoidable, is not on that account "without inconsistency." To which the reply is fair, that beyond the consistency of perfect mutual harmony, which no one would claim for these juxtaposed examples of various styles, there is the higher consistency with the spirit of the times and with reason and propriety; and this is what was contemplated in the third query. But before proceeding to the brief consideration of the fourth and last question let me pray the patient reader not to confound the ideal concurrence of styles treated of in the foregoing paragraphs with the wretched actualities of which too many examples are scattered about us. That our streets are full of terrible abortions of architecture in various dress is painfully true; but their abominableness lies in their bad design, not in the diversity of their styles. And, on the other hand, the reasonableness of the variety of practice which we have been discussing is proved by the fact that those of our buildings which by general consent receive the highest praise, exemplify a considerable variety of styles. No one would condemn Trinity Church because it is Gothic; nor assert that the Madison Square Garden would have been better if "done in Romanesque," nor wish the national capitol changed into a Francis I. design; nor the "Ponce de Leon" converted into a Roman palazzo. We all recognize that the excellence of these buildings results in large measure from the right choice of the historic dress in which these architectural conceptions are clothed; that is to say, from the appropriateness of the style of each to the special purpose of the building.

IV. To the final question, "Is there hope of developing a distinct system of architectural forms appropriate to our age and civilization," we can only offer a suggestive, not a prophetic answer. But there are one or two considerations full of significance. The first is the vitality and freedom of the best American work in design. This is becoming more and more generally recognized abroad. In wooden architecture applied to dwellings we have evolved a truly national type, belonging to our civilization and easily recognized under all the variations caused by climate and locality.

In the more monumental branches of our art we have by no means emerged into any broad generality of character. But that very vitality and freedom of spirit which in untrained designs takes the form of a wild aspiration for originality, and perpetrates those eccentricities and vagaries which are a cause of weariness to cultured natures, brings forth rich fruit when subjected to the restraints of thorough training and cultivated taste.

The second consideration to be noticed is the earnest purpose and conscientiousness of the practitioners who give tone and character to the profession. They are the true exponents of our art, and no one can be intimately acquainted with them, follow their discussions, visit their offices, mark their desire for the highest good of their art and their disinterested devotion to its cause, without a strong conviction that however faulty their works may sometimes be, they are not thoughtless, nor careless, nor foolish, nor unreasonable designs, and that with such a spirit animating its leaders, our architecture must advance in both artistic quality and national character; must be better in 1895 than in 1892; must be nearer the goal of unity in spirit and system and appropriateness to its age and environment.

Thirdly, our large buildings furnish striking suggestions of convergence towards something like unity of style. Of a number of the best of these, if the mere details of their decorative treatment were suppressed, it would be hard to say whether they were Renaissance or Romanesque in design. That is to say, our modern commercial architecture and methods of construction have developed a style of composition of high basements, many-storied piers and arches, with attic arcades and heavy cornices, to which the details of either of these prevalent styles may be applied at will. Different in detail and even in general aspect as are, for example, the four great hotels just built or building on Fifth avenue in this city, the Holland House, the Waldorf, and the two at Fifty-ninth street, no one could possibly fail to recognize them all as examples of American architecture of the last decade of the nineteenth century. Does not this point to an ultimately consistent, not to say uniform style, characteristic of modern American civilization? And is it not significant that in this battle of the styles the contestants have practically narrowed down to two—the Romanesque and the various forms of the earlier Renaissance? Perhaps neither may finally become supreme; their elements fused in the heat of architectural competition, and subjected to the irresistible forces of environment and practical needs and a purified taste, may finally emerge indistinguishably combined in the crystal of a new architecture, as perfect, as rational, as noble as any that has gone before. If so, it will be an architecture bound by no stiff canon of formulated rule and precedent, fitted only for one narrow zone of climate and of population, but strong enough, and free and large and flexible enough for all the boundless variety of climate, and habit, and material and surroundings of this great land. Our "architectural aberrations" are the slag and scoriae thrown off in this crystallizing process. Our worthiest performances, whether Romanesque or Renaissance in detail, are strongly American in character, and I cannot help thinking them finger-posts (if I may here change my metaphor) pointing to a still more truly American architecture which in some future time, nearer or more remote, shall be worthy of the age and of the people that gave it existence.

50   L. Kip, The Building of Cities*   *1870*

Following the Civil War, with the emergence of full industrial development and coincident with the arrival of large numbers of European immigrants, Americans seemed to move en masse into the cities. A city might be defined as having a minimum population of 25,000 people, as that number seems to require urban amenities and suggests a certain density of population. U.S. census figures show that in 1870 there were only 52 places of that size or larger, while in 1910 there were 228, and in 1950 there were 506; there was a jump of 338 percent in the number of towns in the forty years after the Civil War and an increase of only 121 percent during the next forty years. The total urban population, using this definition, went from 5,828,346 (1870) to 28,504,450 (1910) and to 63,016,291 (1940); the rate of increase was a striking jump of 389 percent (1870 to 1910) but only 121 percent after that (1910 to 1950). Clearly, the four decades after 1870 were the period in which the modern urban network was created; the years following were marked more by consolidation than by dramatic increases. Indeed, the most active and important part of the national economy during these four critical decades was the building industry. Construction permits reached a peak in the early 1880s that was not exceeded until the mid-1920s with the rapid growth of suburbs.† The rapid growth of cities did not start, of course, exactly at 1870, for the trend was already sufficiently evident to prompt the comment reprinted here. Seven years later, in 1877, the *American Architect* advised its readers: "It falls to Americans as to no other people in the world to take up the responsibility of deliberately laying out their towns."

    As a habit, we of the Western Continent have not always hitherto been accustomed to pride ourselves overmuch upon our cities, or upon the abstract attractions of our city life. Listening to the reiterated and somewhat commonplace fancies and argumentations of poetry, as well as to the more practical representations of health and scenery, we have been rather wont to bestow the greater portion of our admiration and affections upon fields and pastures, and the more open and extended inducements supposed to be held out by country life. It is true that we have submitted to all this with occasional heartburnings and with much secret jealousy of the more favored rival; but none the less have the bucolic persuasions of romance induced us to admit as a sad and incontestable truth, that our cities are mere plaguespots upon the earth, to be tolerated only by reason of the necessities of trade, and never to be looked upon with any emotion of pride or fondness, excepting as we might be occasionally actuated by some insane perversion of taste or weakening of judgment. And it must be confessed that, up to a comparatively recent period, our cities have presented few attractions to the cultivated eye. In the matter of association, the headquarters of a Revolutionary general, perhaps, or some isolated, quaint residence, remarkable only

* Leonard Kip, "The Building of Our Cities," *Hours at Home* 11 (July 1870), pp. 206–12.

† See Manuel Gottlieb, "Estimates of Residential Building, United States, 1840–1939," Technical Paper number 17, National Bureau of Economic Research (New York, 1964).

for being a hundred and fifty years old,—or, in the matter of architecture, a Gothic church or two, or a Doric-columned city hall;—and that was all.

But of late years it seems as though we were beginning to learn a new lesson upon the subject. A more metropolitan taste is evidently controlling us, and we are gradually losing that olden spirit of contempt for city life and scenes, and little by little gaining for them some more genial habit of respect. And though as yet we cannot expect to love our cities for their associations or antiquity, as so often is the case abroad, we find that at least we can appreciate them for their developing faculties of adornment, convenience, and architectural grandeur. In fact, we are beginning slowly to understand what of itself ought rather to have been accepted from the first as an axiom, that uncleanliness, inordinate disproportion of crime, and a dingy absence of beauty, are not of themselves the necessary concomitants of city life, but are rather mere unholy parasites which long neglect has allowed to cluster around it; and that it is possible, with good management, to retain the advantages afforded by large massing of population, and not necessarily to assume its disadvantages also. Learning this, we are now gradually taking the matter to heart, as we look around for some way to practically apply the truth; and we can see a new era steadily approaching. We are losing that shamefacedness with which we were wont to speak disparagingly of the city as brick and mortar, and the hypocrisy with which we affected to gloat over country freedom. So, little by little, the steam of cultivation is beginning to set citywards. Men who have made fortunes and wish to retire upon them are now as prone to seek metropolitan life as formerly they were to build their country villas; nor do they feel compelled any longer to apologize for their peculiar taste. Yearly the current enlarges. Some may lament the fact, and with long columns of figures, undertake to prove that it is the commencement not only of country depletion, but of natural degeneracy and corruption. Still the great fact remains; and in view of it we must accept it cordially and look around to see how to make the most of it,—how the swelling cities should best accommodate themselves to the new condition of things,—how most properly they can be made, by fulfilling all their destiny and exerting all their capacity for improvement, to increase the comfort and happiness of those who seek their shelter,—and how, in equal measure, they can attract new crowds of willing subjects within their borders.

It is fortunate that we are so seldom able to foresee the successive growths from a single house into village, and from village into city. If it were otherwise, it is to be feared that, in our feverish preparation for the coming greatness, we should be led into the unhappy mistake of giving up everything to utilitarianism, and, in the initiatory selection of our ground-plan, sacrificing all genial tastefulness to mere cold outline—creating a broad, tiresome, and most unpleasant expanse of straight streets and rectangular blocks. In many instances in the West, and one or two in the East, is has happened that some prophetic inspiration of future greatness has led to such a mistake; and these cities, so deliberately and with forethought planned, have become masterpieces of dull, severe, correct, and chilling weariness of spirit. To other places a better destiny has been allotted, and they have passed almost unconsciously through all the stages from insignificance to grandeur, until it is only at the end that the inhabitants have awakened from their contented lethargy and discovered that circumstances have conspired to make their places great. Then they have aroused themselves, and with the air of people who fear they are beginning too late, look with dismay at the tangled labyrinth of their streets and lanes; and, to the extent of their means, hurry to carve out a straight, broad avenue here and there, with moody regret that they can do so little to recover from the neglects and errors of the past. But when at last they have done all that is in their power, they have often created a very pleasant city, in which the convenience of a few straightened streets, conspiring with the natural harmony of those that are irredeemably crooked, imparts to the whole plan a charming mingling of utility and taste.

There is indeed no policy so mistaken as that of desiring a city to be made up relentlessly of square blocks and air-line avenues. As a measure of utility itself it is an error; for though we thereby avoid the depreciation in the value of a few sharp angles, we often prevent that natural centralization of wealth and trade which gives extraordinary appreciation to certain choice quarters; and though the transit from one side to the other, following the most direct line of the streets, may be shortened, yet there can be no such thing as crossing such a city diagonally without passing over an unreasonably lengthened route; while as a matter of simple taste such a place may soon become monotonous in an unpleasant degree. Not merely is this likely to be so in respect of single streets, where we can see the broad route of travel marked out before us to the vanishing point, miles beyond, and, gazing forward as upon the undeviating correctness of a country turnpike, miss thereby the pleasant little surprises which might be continually brought before our eyes from behind unlooked-for curves and corners. Looking upon such a city as a whole, it can scarcely fail to be dispiriting with its regularity,—unimpressive, except perhaps for mere size, a quality which very soon ceases to impress,—and intolerable with its dull uniformity, since when the resident can see the whole street rolled out before him as a diorama, he soon ceases to feel any spark of individual taste, but, catching the spirit of others, builds and rebuilds in the same style as every one around him, and so, in having a house, becomes the owner, not of a home, but merely of a certain number of lineal feet measured off from a rule.

We can mark, in a comparison of other cities, the difference of sentiment that a variation in this matter of plan is apt to produce. There are few more beautiful cities in Europe than Turin, with its breadth of street and correctness of architecture. There are many handsome churches and a gallery, a museum and palace; and one might imagine that a stranger could pass a few days there very enjoyably. But there is something so dispiriting in the universal regularity of the streets, that, in spite of enthusiasm for research, the spirits soon become dampened, and the traveller hastens away with his investigations only half completed. But how when he has reached Genoa—so aptly called La Superba? With what joyous contentment he wanders through its winding alleys, finding new surprises at every corner! How lovingly he learns to recognize certain open spaces as old friends, from the mere incident of so often unexpectedly stumbling upon them, when he had supposed that he was far away! What a joyous relaxation he seems to find in the manner of the people themselves,—far different from the prosy, straightened primness of the Turanese! And how reluctantly he leaves old

Genoa at last, preferring to linger on there, if he dared, and forget that Florence and Rome have any claims upon his time!

In like manner, looking at our own side of the water, we can compare two other cities,—Philadelphia and Boston. The one is severely rectangular—the other is a twisted net-work of lanes and alleys, with no more apparent method of arrangement than the frost lines upon a window-pane. In the one place the people are coldly proud of their city, admiring it for its size, counting and recounting its population, and often making their boast of the number of its houses; but all the while seeming to supplement their pride with little real affection. In the other place, there is found mingled with the pride which indulges in much boasting, an undeniable love for the city as for a dear friend. In the eye of the Bostonian it is something which peculiarly belongs to himself, and no alien person can ever hope to fitly share the proprietorship with him. Strangers coming may get lost in the twisted maze, or, almost as bad, may find themselves continually brought back to their starting-point; and the Bostonian, looking on serenely, feels his love for the city increased by the pleasing comparison of his own familiarity with it. He never gets lost. He was born and brought up to the labyrinth, and it has no unexplained puzzle for him. Even at three years of age he could run away from his nurse and wander around the seven-sided block and safely find his way home again. And in his grown-up passing to and fro, he has discovered little quiet short-cuts, where he meets so few people that in time he comes to look upon those secluded passages as a sort of peculiar revelation to himself alone, to be enjoyed by him in exclusive ownership. The inhabitant of the one city glories in it as one might delight in the vastness of his favorite hotel,—the dweller in the other cherishes a love for his city, as one learns to gather to the heart a snug, crookedly made up, rambling little home. And even in the matter of a comparison of homes, we know how much more readily a quaint, twisted-up dwelling, full of dark passages and unexpected staircases, will attract our regard, than will a squarely planned residence of the customary four-story-and-basement pattern.

Perhaps in its presentation of a pleasant combination of well-controlled streets and others left to wander loosely at their will,—of public convenience properly subserved in a few essentials and civic taste otherwise suitably preserved, there is no modern city which can rival Paris. In it we find a kind of formal ground-plan that serves its uses of easy communication, and yet is partially hidden by other features from too glaring obtrusiveness. There is the river running with tolerable directness through the centre of the city, —broad quays on either side,—upon the right a long line of palaces and gardens, and upon the left a row of legislative and scientific buildings. Crossing these at right angles, the splendid Boulevard Sebastopol,—at a reasonable distance around, an encircling boulevard, not too accurately defined, and holding river, quay, and Boulevard Sebastopol as the tire of a wheel will enclose four spokes. Beyond all, another longer boulevard, forming one more enclosing and roughly drawn circle,—and in among these prominent avenues a network of smaller alleys and streets, confusing the senses at every step. Through these we wander at will, finding a new prospect at each turn, and invariably pleasantly losing ourselves. Losing ourselves, that is, with the full knowledge that we cannot be disagreeably led out of the way; for when, after a while, we begin to tire of the ramble, we have only to continue on for a minute or two longer in some particular direction, and lo! there comes a clearer light ahead or at the side, and the houses recede, and we are in one of the broad skeleton boulevards, and can at once leave the twining mass of nerves and find our way home again. This is what has come from letting a city take care of itself for a few centuries, until its characteristics have become fixed, and then supplementing them with such few improvements as modern civilization imperiously demands; and this is perhaps the only manner in which a city can be made thoroughly pleasant to the eye of taste, as well as convenient for carrying on its necessary avocations.

Every city cannot, however, be like Paris. Left in the same approved manner to follow in its upward growth its own impulses and carve out its separate conformation, subject only to subsequent partial correction, it can only become that which circumstances and situation will allow it to be, —better or worse, in proportion as accident develops it for good or bad. Therefore we will leave this topic, as one which will admit of being discussed aesthetically, but in practice can be but little affected by the criticism or supervision of man, and we will turn to other matters wherein direct labor can have its due influence. Nor in this shall we give attention to the common affairs of drainage, and paving, and the like. We all know and acknowledge the necessity of these. From schoolboy times we have been shown how the Romans, when building cities, gave early attention to a grand system of sewerage, and how that, if we do not now copy and even improve upon their ideas, we shall be held recreant to the cause of an advancing civilization. We are daily told that our streets should be better paved and our wharves improved,—our lighting conducted upon more liberal principles,—our public buildings constructed with more economy and taste. These things have become an old story, well conned by every one; and, as such, need not be enlarged upon. What we would now do in noting the building of our cities, would be to throw out a few suggestions, which of right should be considered axioms, but which, like so many principles that, after final settlement, become so glaring in their truth as to excite our wonder at never having noticed them before, in this present day of their slow birth are hardly recognizable as principles at all.

Of these perhaps the most important consists in the fact that we should awaken to the necessity of liberal expenditure in promoting the comfort and elegance of our cities, and freely comprehend that, while no great improvement can be made without the provision of large funds, so our experience of the past shows that few great expenditures for public good have ever been entered into without bringing with them their reward and repayment. We do not mean, of course, that money cannot be too lavishly spent, or public works be inconsiderately constructed. On the contrary, we have abundant examples among us wherein unscrupulous officials have knavishly wasted the people's property to no good purpose, thereby not only adding to the sum of taxation, but also producing well-founded distrust of all future suggestion of city advancement. We simply mean that when, as we have likewise examples to prove, great works are beneficially undertaken and are prosecuted with honorable and painstaking spirit, there can hardly be found an instance where even lavish expenditure in behalf of really magnificent

conceptions has not, in the end, been found to be a source of civic profit,
pleasure, and congratulation.

We remember once reading a pleasant little account of the progress of
Marseilles. The city, having become fired with sudden zeal for improvement, borrowed money and proceeded to open new streets; and at once
those streets began to pay for themselves in increase of valuation. Then,
taking fresh courage, the city borrowed more money and laid out a park;
and with the same satisfactory result. After that a gallery and museum, and
new markets and quays, and what not; and ever with the same agreeable
conclusion as to cost. In fine, no matter how much the city went into debt,
its revenues insisted upon increasing in corresponding ratio, and at the end
of a few years it was vastly richer than when it had started in the race. All
this was several years ago. What Marseilles has since then become,—whether
there has been any success in that attempt of indebtedness to catch up with
capital, we do not know. We all know, however, to what a pitch of magnificence Paris has attained by reason of concerted effort, and how abundantly
the increasing wealth of the Imperial city is sufficing to meet even the immense debt thus created. And we have evidences that the force of its example is infecting other European cities with similar zeal for improvement, so
that in every direction the great capitals are laying out avenues and parks,
and turning insignificant lanes into broad boulevards. Only in America does
the public temper seem to falter and fail to catch the spirit of the times.

It is true that we do a little something, and that once in a while we
congratulate ourselves upon some addition made to our metropolitan health
or convenience or beauty. A street is widened here, or a public park laid out
there,—and so far it is all very well. But the trouble is, that these efforts are
mere disorganized fragments of what should constitute a great, comprehensive design, to be prosecuted with force and energy as a whole; and that,
when we accomplish even the smallest results we feel disposed to praise
ourselves too highly for our enterprise, to be too leisurely occupied over it,
and, at the end, to rest too long before undertaking any additional design.
We would fain lay out a new street, for instance; and after years of civic
wrangling it is done, or, as likely as not, left undone, because some one may
be indirectly going to make something out of it. We decide to put up a
public building;—and other years are wasted in first selecting a site and then
a plan. While, at each step of the way, we calculate the cost so dolefully, that
at last we become horrified at the task we have set ourselves; and the dread
of any further expenditure so surely mingles with our complacency over the
labor finished, that a long period is certain to elapse before we recover sufficient equanimity and courage to press forward again. Since calculations
must be made, is there no way of causing the people to understand that a
calmly digested plan and a liberal expenditure for instant, elaborate, and
wide-spread improvement is the most far-sighted economy that could be
adopted? In the prosecution of comprehensive schemes for new public
works, and for the tasteful elaboration of what has already been achieved,
large sums must be spent, it is true; and yet there can be little doubt that
good and sufficient drainage, well-paved streets, new avenues cut through
and old ones enlarged, markets rebuilt, and stone or iron wharves replacing
rotten wooden ones would, up to a certain point, lead to an increased valua-

tion abundantly sufficient to satisfy the additional burden.

And this brings us to one further and last suggestion. Having our cities laid out and fully built upon, then comes the question of their beautifying and adornment. In some respects this is a topic kindred to the former one, for the chief germ of its complaint is public apathy and indifference, want of knowledge about what should be entered upon, and too elate satisfaction at which has already been done. To many persons the question of civic decoration is a novel one, for it seems to them that when clean, straight streets are laid out and lined with costly buildings, and all such mere matters of comfort, convenience, and easy intercourse attended to, the whole thing is finished. They cannot comprehend that in every city there are waste places which should be made pleasant, and that there must always be, here and there, quiet corners which should be turned into bowers of beauty, and which, by contrast with the angular and more artificial surroundings, will be certain to confer upon the passer-by a pleasure far beyond that which they might otherwise give. While of those who admit the necessity and propriety of such adornment there are very few who understand all its hidden capabilities, and who are not meekly content with the slightest approximation to what should be looked upon as actual necessity.

The whole course of our city ornamentation shows this. In a spasm of reform, we banish from our streets all unsightly wooden awning-posts, and then stand enraptured at our perfection of taste; and while we remain thus entranced and gaping, wealthy telegraph companies, who in any other land would be obliged to purchase their right of way over the roofs, plant, unreproved, along our streets, great ugly trunks of half-grown pine trees, not even turned by the lathe into decent symmetry, and giving the look of actual trees which have gradually lost their bark from frequent blazing by countrymen afraid of losing their way. We resolve upon a railing about some little square, and months are consumed in making the contract, discussing the work, and afterwards chronicling its slow progress. We plant our squares with grass and believe that we have done our best; but if we look abroad we would see in Paris every open space or pleasure-ground, even the borders of the long Champs Elysées, gleaming with all the richest glories of any well-matured private flower-garden. We plant here and there a mere squirt of enormous power and call it a fountain, and it uses so much water that we cannot afford to let it play more than an hour or two each day, while we remain in blissful ignorance that we could take from abroad ideas for artistic bronze or marble groups, which in themselves it would be a pleasure to gaze upon, and which by their economy of water could be allowed to throw up their sparkling jets unceasingly from morning until night. We think that we would like a statue; and we sedulously record the advance in the subscription, the contract with the artist, and the general progress of the casting, until after years of expectation the statue arrives, and, in our exultation, half of the population turns out in mass and loses a day in what is called inaugurating the work. Meanwhile, perhaps that very day in Paris, or Vienna, a splendid statue is quietly put into place, and thereby, without excitement or long-talked-of preliminary, a new attraction is added to the hundreds that have been placed there before. The consequence of all this apathy, easy satisfaction, and want of enlarged, comprehensive system upon our part is, that instead of making our cities beautiful they are almost absolutely without any decoration at all. Here a statue, it may be—there a poorly designed fountain basin; but it is a question whether in all our cities together, from Portland to San Francisco, we could gather together as much worthy, notice-able art as smiles upon us from the single open space, the Place de la Con-corde.

In some respects, indeed, we have improved upon the cities of the last generation. Looking back upon them with a critical eye, we can now see that there was little in them to attract. Even in the best streets we can remember only ill-built jumbles of shabby brick houses, with here and there one carried up to four stories to excite our complacent admiration; rough cobble-stone pavements, and clumsy wooden awning-posts lining the sidewalks. Here and there, indeed, a note-worthy building, but altogether so few that in an hour's time we could exhaust the whole merits of the place. In a material aspect there is a great stride in the present appearance of our cities; and some among us, seeing this, might be disposed to rest awhile, as though the good work were already done. But to the truly metropolitan spirit it is only just begun. Prophetically we can look forward and see the picture as it will be spread out twenty years hence if the proper ideas of enlarged and continu-ing improvement are stimulated. We can see the business portions of our cities almost entirely rebuilt, and with magnificence,—underground rail-ways affording new facilities for intercourse,—beautiful bridges spanning the rivers,—perfectly systematized drainage, paving, and lighting, —wooden wharves replaced by others of stone or iron,—new and elegant halls and markets studding the thoroughfares,—new churches, such as we do not now dream of,—galleries and museums to vie with those of Euro-pe,—and every public square a bower of loveliness, with its wealth of flow-ers, statuary, and fountains. This, in a greater or less degree, is for any city no far-off prospect, to be toiled up to with long-protracted anxiety, and wait-ing, and endurance; it is the natural result, to be freely and coolly taken as a matter of right, if the true, enlarged metropolitan spirit is properly cultivat-ed throughout the country. It is what, perhaps, will some day happen almost of itself; but it can be made to commence at once if the necessity for a liberal principle of action be acknowledged and its practice be fostered.

Then, perhaps, the long-standing jealousy between town and country may die out, never to be renewed; since each will be recognized as holding its separate place, to which the other should not hope to aspire. If the city with its attractions draws strength from the country, it will send back both beauty and intelligence from its overflowing stores of art and education. Having learned so magnificently to glorify itself, it will teach the country to put on new charms, and to banish old deformities, so that in the end the now plain country-house will become a creation of taste, appropriately adapting itself for its needs; and the roads and by-ways no longer made hideous with unsightly rail fences and standing pools, will be flanked with broad green hedges, and learning in actual fact to imitate romance, will blossom with loveliness and smell sweet with bordering roses. To the city will be surren-dered the domain of art and architecture, and to the country that of rural culture;—each giving up for the embellishment of the other whatever it can most appropriately contribute from its own exhaustless treasures. And so at last the two, no longer like bitter rivals, but rather as brother and sister, will go down the path of time united in friendly appreciation, gathering new ideas with which to give increase to our civilization and refinement, and even in their intercourse shedding happiness and pleasant contentment upon each other.

51 W. G. Marshall, The Elevated Railroad* *1881*

As the density of population increased, the need for moving greater numbers faster and easier became paramount; the horse-drawn omnibuses gave way to horse-drawn cars on rails during the 1840s, and the lessened friction improved the ride and allowed for slightly larger carriages, but motorized traction was essential. Where steep grades were difficult to negotiate because metal drive wheels slipped on the rails, subsurface cable systems that could be grasped by clamps extending down from the cars were installed. Such systems also centralized the noisy and smoky steam power plants. Of the many such systems, only that in hilly San Francisco, begun in 1872, still thrives—although it is reduced in size. Streets crowded with carriages, heavy horse-drawn drays, and ever-more rapidly moving horse cars were dangerous; the solution to increasing carrying capacity and safety was to separate the modes of transportation. During the 1870s two companies began to build tracks over New York streets on metal bridge-work (Jasper Cropsey's design for the Gilbert Elevated Railroad station is illustrated in the *Concise History*, figure 142). In 1875 the first Rapid Transit Commission was set up in New York City.[†] The New York system is described here by a visiting English observer. The elevated railroad, even though steam-powered, was widely adopted despite the noise and threat of falling embers and oil. Once Thomas Edison had developed an electrical motor, it was only necessary for his assistant Frank J. Sprague to perfect a practical heavier traction motor, which he installed in street cars in Richmond, Virginia, in 1888.[‡] Once the polluting drive system was thus transformed, underground subways became possible, eventually replacing in turn many of the unsightly elevated railroads.

---

* Walter Gore Marshall, *Through America; or, Nine Months in the United States* (London, 1881), pp. 24–28.

† See Blake McKelvey, *The Urbanization of America 1860–1915* (New Brunswick, N.J., 1963). A classic study of the impact of transit systems on the patterns and rate of urban growth is, Sam B. Warner, *Streetcar Suburbs: The Process of Growth in Boston, 1870–1900* (Cambridge, Mass., 1962).

‡ For electrification and the developments preceding Sprague's, see Carl W. Condit, *The Port of New York: A History of the Rail and Terminal System from the Beginnings to Pennsylvania Station* (Chicago, 1980), pp. 183–88.

And now how to get about New York. There is first the elevated railway. Answering to our "underground" in London, in affording rapid conveyance through the city without interfering with the traffic, it is raised high above the streets instead of being tunnelled under them. The effect of the "elevated"—the "L," as New Yorkers generally call it—is, to my mind, anything but beautiful; but this, perhaps, is only a matter of taste. The tracks are lifted to a height of thirty feet (in some places higher) upon iron pillars, the up line on one side of the street and the down on the other,—in a few of the streets, where there is room enough, there are three tracks built,—and to prevent as far as possible the train from tipping over, the metals are laid on sleepers in a deep furrow or groove cut out of long pieces of timber, which are firmly bolted to the sleepers. Beneath the raised lines is the roadway for horses and carriages, and the lines of rail for the tramway cars, with the pavements beyond. As you sit in a car on the "L" and are being whirled along, you can put your head out of window and salute a friend who is walking on the street pavement below. In some places, where the streets are narrow, the railway is built right over the "sidewalks" (pavements) close up against the walls of the houses. In Pearl-street, for instance, this is especially the case, for just after leaving the Fulton-street station, on your way towards the Bowery, you find you are on a level with the rooms of the third story of the United States Hotel, and able easily to see into them, which is not very pleasant, I should imagine, for the occupants of those rooms.

As might be expected, the elevated railway is immensely patronized. Trains run at frequent intervals on the several lines, from 5:30 in the morning till 12 o'clock at night, and during the crowded hours, namely from 5:30 a.m. to 7:30 a.m., and from 5 p.m. to 7 p.m., they follow each other as fast as can be managed. One company—the Metropolitan, or Sixth Avenue—runs daily 840 trains (420 each way) up and down its line between 5:30 a.m. and 12 p.m.; seventy trains per hour are run during the crowded hours mornings and evenings. The fare during these busy hours is five cents (2½d.), at other times ten cents. . . . the three companies working the elevated railways (the Metropolitan, the Manhattan, and New York companies), having carried their lines far into the upper portion of the city, you can, for the sum of five cents, take a ride of some ten or twelve miles, and without changing cars. The trains are run at a good speed, and there is but little delay at the stations; indeed sometimes the train does not pull up at all, and yet people recklessly jump on and off all the same. . . . The average height of the "L" above the street-level is thirty feet; but in one place it is fifty-seven feet, namely beyond Central Park, on the west side of the island. From end to end it is a veritable railway in the air, for nowhere does the track descend to the level of the street. As a financial enterprise the elevated railway has turned out a success beyond even the expectations of its promoters. "One hundred and seventy-five thousand passengers are carried over the city lines daily," says a gentleman officially connected with one of the "L" roads, "or 12,000 tons of human flesh, averaging each person at 140 lbs." Thirty million dollars have already been expended on the enterprise,—that is up to the end of 1879, the first "L" line having been opened in May, 1878—and 5,000,000 more will be required to finish all the city railways that are in contemplation. "L" roads are at present only in operation in New York City, but these lines are rapidly being extended into the suburbs, and Brooklyn already has one in process of erection, and Philadelphia is to have one too, and even sedate Boston is thinking of providing herself with one, so that it seems as if the popularity of this mode of locomotion is on the increase in the large cities: but dangers are looming ahead which bid fair to stem the tide of prosperity which the promoters of "rapid transit" have been enjoying hitherto, and to render the enterprise in the future costly rather than lucrative. As a natural consequence of the introduction of the elevated railway, property lying contiguous to the overhead lines has considerably depreciated in value. The nineteen hours and more of incessant rumbling day and night from the passing trains; the blocking out of a sufficiency of light from the rooms of houses, close up to which the lines are built; the full, close view passengers on the cars can have into rooms on the second and third floors; the frequent squirtings of oil from the engines, sometimes even finding its way into the private rooms of a dwelling-house, when the windows are left open—all these are objections that have been reasonably urged by unfortunate occupants of houses whose comfort has been so unjustly molested. . . .

52 M. Schuyler, Last Words About the World's Fair* *1894*

The nineteenth century was one of exhibitions; one was held somewhere in the United States or Europe virtually every year between 1851 and 1914. In the United States the exhibition most important in establishing the planning profession was that celebrating the four-hundredth anniversary of Columbus's famous voyage—the World's Columbian Exposition in Chicago, 1893. In fact, this pivotal turning point in American planning is documented in Mel Scott's history, *American City Planning Since 1890* (Berkeley, 1969), which opens with an examination of the Exposition.

Because of political delays and the great scale proposed for the fair, formal organization was delayed until 1890, and although planning commenced in 1891 and construction was started in advance of formal dedication on Columbus Day, 1892, the Exhibition did not open to the public until the spring of 1893 and closed the following October. It was an instant popular success, and despite the onset of a business depression, people came from the corners of the nation to see it. Hamlin Garland dashed off letters, advising his parents to "sell the cookstove if necessary and come. You *must* see this fair"; to Barr Ferree, he wrote that to visit Chicago but not see the fair was like visiting Rome without going to St. Peter's.[†] The importance of the planning and architecture of the fair was assessed by William Dean Howells in

---

*Montgomery Schuyler, "Last Words About the World's Fair," *Architectural Record* 3 (January–March 1894), pp. 291–301.

† These comments and a wealth of information are found in David F. Burg, *Chicago's White City of 1893* (Lexington, Ken., 1976). See, too, Thomas S. Hines, *Burnham of Chicago: Architect and Planner* (New York, 1974), pp. 92–138.

his series, "Letters of an Altrurian Traveller," written as though by a visitor from some far-distant utopia to a friend at home.‡ Chicago he described as "the realized ideal of that largeness, loudness and fastness, which New York has persuaded the Americans is metropolitan." But in building the fair "the capitalists put themselves into the hands of the artists, . . . and for the first time since the great ages, since the beauty of antiquity and the elegance of the renaissance, the arts were reunited. The greatest landscape gardeners, architects, sculptors and painters, gathered at Chicago for a joyous interchange of ideas and criticisms; and the miracle of beauty which they have wrought grew openly in their breadth and under their hands." The ensemble of grounds and buildings was "a design, the effect of a principle, and not the straggling and shapeless accretion of accident." Howells was convinced he saw in the fair buildings "a glimpse of the glorious capitals which will whiten the hills and shores of the east and the borderless plains of the west." The concepts of detailed preliminary planning and artistic collaboration were the essential contributions of the fair, thought Howells, for "an immortal principle, higher than use, higher even than beauty, is expressed in it, and the time will come when they will look back upon it . . . and will cherish it forever in their history, as the earliest achievement of a real civic life."

Montgomery Schuyler likewise stressed the planning of the ensemble, not the fake plaster facades, in his assessment.

I

Whether the cloud-capped towers and the gorgeous palaces of the World's Fair are to dissolve, now that the insubstantial pageant of the Fair itself has faded, and to leave not a rack behind, is a question that is reported to agitate Chicago. There is much to be said, doubtless, on both sides of it. While it is still unsettled seems to be a good time to consider the architecture which it is proposed to preserve for yet awhile longer, in order to determine, so far as may be, what influence the display at Chicago is likely to have upon the development of American architecture, and how far that influence is likely to be good and how far to be bad. That it is likely to be in any degree bad is a proposition that may be startling and seem ungracious, but there is no reason why it should. Certainly to question the unmixed beneficence of its influence is not to pass the least criticism upon the architects, the brilliant success of whose labors for their own temporary and spectacular purpose has been admitted and admired by all the world. The very brilliancy of this success may constitute a danger in the imitation which it induces, if it induce any. Absolutely without influence such a display can hardly be. The promiscuous practitioner of architecture in America, or in any other modern country, is not of an analytical turn of mind. When things please him, he is not apt to inquire into the reasons why they please him, and to act accordingly. He is more apt to reproduce them as he finds them, so far as this is mechanically possible. For this process our time affords facilities unprecedented in history. Photographs are available of everything striking or memorable that has been built in the world, and that survives even in ruins. The "wander-years" of the young architect are not so necessary to him as they used to be. The necessity of travel, as part of a professional apprentice-

‡ William Dean Howells, "Letters of an Altrurian Traveller, II," *Cosmopolitan* 16 (December 1893), pp. 218–32.

ship, had its advantages. On the spot one can see what he cannot see so well in photographs and sometimes cannot see at all, how much of its effect a building may owe to circumstances more or less adventitious to its design—to situation, to scale, to material, to color. The photograph enables him merely to reproduce what he admires, and increases the desirableness that he should admire rightly; that he should admire with discrimination; that he should analyze what he admires far enough to find out what it is that he admires it for, and what it is that may be useful to him in his own work. To teach this is a large part of professional education. An architect who learns this will not be misled by the success of the buildings of the World's Fair into reproducing or imitating them, because he will know too well what are the necessary conditions of their effectiveness, and that these conditions cannot be reproduced except in another World's Fair, and not literally even there. Men bring not back the mastodon, nor we those times. It is, however, the architects who do not know these things with whom we have so largely to reckon, and it is upon such architects that the buildings in Jackson Park are more likely to impose themselves as models for more or less direct imitation in the solution of problems more usual. The results of such an imitation can hardly fail to be pernicious.

Doubtless the influence of the most admired group of buildings ever erected in this country, the public buildings at Washington not excepted, must be great. What it is likely to be has been expressed by Mr. Burnham, the Director of Works of the Columbian Exposition, in some remarks, published in a Chicago newspaper, which crystallize into a lucid and specific form a general hazy expectation, and which may well serve us for a text:

> The influence of the Exposition on architecture will be to inspire a reversion toward the pure ideal of the ancients. We have been in an inventive period, and have had rather contempt for the classics. Men evolved new ideas and imagined they could start a new school without much reference to the past. But action and reaction are equal, and the exterior and obvious result will be that men will strive to do classic architecture. In this effort there will be many failures. It requires long and fine training to design on classic lines. The simpler the expression of true art the more difficult it is to obtain.
>
> The intellectual reflex of the Exposition will be shown in a demand for better architecture, and designers will be obliged to abandon their incoherent originals and study the ancient masters of building. There is shown so much of fine architecture here that people have seen and appreciated this. It will be unavailing hereafter to say that great classic forms are undesirable. The people have the vision before them here, and words cannot efface it.

Doubtless the architecture of the Exposition will inspire a great many classic buildings, which will be better or worse done according to the training of the designers, but it is not likely that any of these will even dimly recall, and quite impossible that they should equal the architectural triumph of the Fair. The influence of the Exposition, so far as it leads to direct imitation, seems to us an unhopeful rather than a hopeful sign, not a promise so much as a threat. Such an imitation will so ignore the conditions that have made the architectural success of the Fair that it is worth while to try to discern and to state these conditions, and that is the purpose of this paper.

In the first place the success is first of all a success of unity, a triumph of *ensemble*. The whole is better than any of its parts and greater than all its parts, and its effect is one and indivisible. We are speaking now of the Court of Honor, which alone it is proposed to preserve, and which forms an architectural whole. The proposal to remove the largest building of the group, that of Manufactures, and to set it up by itself in a permanent form on the lake front in Chicago, though the proposition was not made by an architect, is an excellent illustration how easy it is to mistake the significance of the architecture and the causes of its success. It is a masterpiece of misappreciation. The landscape plan of the Fair, with the great basin, open at one end to the lake and cut midway by canals, may be said to have generated the architecture of the Court of Honor. Any group of educated architects who had assembled to consider the problem presented by the plan must have taken much the same course that was in fact taken. The solution of the problem presented by the plan was in outline given by the plan. That the treatment of the border of this symmetrical basin should be symmetrical, that the confronting buildings should balance each other, these were requirements obviously in the interest of unity and a general unity was obviously the result to be sought and the best result that could be attained. The conditions of this unity were all that it was necessary to stipulate for. Variety enough had been secured by the selection of an individual designer for each of the great buildings, and the danger was that this variety would be excessive, that it would degenerate into a miscellany. Against this danger it was necessary to guard if the buildings should appear as the work of collaborators rather than of competitors, and it was guarded against by two very simple but quite sufficient conditions. One was that there should be a uniform cornice-line of sixty feet, the other that the architecture should be classic. The first requirement, keeping a virtually continuous sky-line all around the Court of Honor, and preventing that line from becoming an irregular serration, was so plainly necessary that it is not necessary to spend any words in justifying it. The second may seem more disputable, but in reality it was almost as much a matter of course as the first. Uniformity in size is no more necessary to unity than uniformity in treatment, and classic architecture was more eligible than any other for many tolerably obvious reasons. There are perhaps no effects attained in the exhibition that could not have been attained in other architecture. The obvious effect of the "magnitude, succession, and uniformity," which the aestheticians describe as the conditions of the "artificial infinite" has been sought and attained in the treatment of the great buildings. . . .

Nevertheless, the choice of classic architecture was almost as distinctly imposed upon the associated architects as the choice of a uniform cornice line. In the first place, the study of classic architecture is a usual, almost an invariable part of the professional training of the architects of our time. It is an indispensable part, wherever that training is administered academically, and most of all at Paris, of which the influence upon our own architecture is manifestly increasing and is at present dominant. Most of the architects of the World's fair are of Parisian training, and those of them who are not have felt the influence of that contemporary school of architecture which is most highly organized and possesses the longest and the most powerful tradition. Presumably, all of them were familiar with the decorative use of "the orders" and knew what a module meant. What most of them had already practiced in academic exercises and studies, they were now for the first time permitted to project into actual execution. Nobody can fail to understand the comment of a distinguished French painter, made, possibly, in a satirical spirit: *"On me dit que les bâtiments à Chicago sont des anciens concours des Beaux Arts."* [1] This is in fact the reflection that several of the buildings are calculated to excite, that their designs are the relics of student-competitions, while at least one such relic is alleged to have been built in Jackson Park.

That would be one good reason for the adoption of a given style—that all the persons concerned knew how to work in it. Another is that the classic forms, although originally developed from the conditions of masonic structure, have long since, and perhaps ever since they became "orders," been losing touch with their origin, until now they have become simply forms, which can be used without a suggestion of any real structure or any particular material. We know them in wood and metal, as well as in stone. They may be used, as they are used in Jackson Park, as a decorative envelope of any construction whatever without exciting in most observers any sense of incongruity, much less any sense of meanness such as is at once aroused by the sight of "carpenter's Gothic." A four-foot column, apparently of marble, may have aroused such a sentiment during the process of construction, when it might have been seen without a base and supported upon little sticks, with its apparent weight thus emphatically denied. Such a sentiment may have been aroused again in the closing days of the Fair, when it was no longer thought necessary to repair defects as fast as they showed themselves, and where the apparent masonry disclosed in places the lath-backing. But when the buildings were ready for the public no such incongruity was forced upon the observer, as it would have been forced upon him if the forms that were fused had been such as are still associated with the structure that gave rise to them. The alternative to the use of classic architecture was the development in a few months of an architecture of plaster, or "staff." For this there are no precedents completely available in the world, while the world is full of precedents for the employment of the orders, and precedents which do not imply that the orders are real and efficient constructions, as indeed they have never been since the Romans began to use columnar architecture as the decoration of an arched construction.

It is not to be supposed for a moment that the architects of the Fair would have attained anything like the success they did attain, if instead of working in a style with which all of them were presumably familiar, they had undertaken the Herculean task of creating a style out of these novel conditions. In fact the architects of the Court of Honor might "point with

[1] "They say the buildings at Chicago are the old student designs of the École." [Unlocated source.] The group of buildings around the Court of Honor was shaped by classical design principles, but the only building actually patterned after an École project was Charles B. Atwood's Fine Arts Building at the north end of the lagoon, drawn from Emile Bénard's *Palais pour l'exposition des Beaux-Arts*, Grand Prix de Rome, 1867.—ED.

pride" to the result of such efforts as were made in that direction by other architects as a sufficient justification for their own course, if such a justification were needed.

The landscape-plan is the key to the pictorial success of the Fair as a whole, and, as we say it generated the architecture of the watercourt by supplying indications which sensitive architects had no choice but to follow. In no point was the skill of Mr. Olmsted and his associate more conspicuous than in the transition from the symmetrical and stately treatment of the basin to the irregular winding of the lagoon. As the basin indicated a bordering of formal and symmetrical architecture so the lagoon indicated and invited a picturesque and irregular architecture. Of the associated architects, those who most conspicuously availed themselves of this invitation were the designers of the Fisheries and of the Transportation building. The success of the former is not disputed nor disputable. The plan was determined by the requirements of the building and worked out very naturally into the central mass, the connecting arcades and the terminal pavilions, of which the form suggested the treatment of Romanesque baptisteries, and may very possibly have determined the style of the building. There was ample scope left for the inventiveness of the designer in the detail conventionalized so happily and successfully from marine motives, and the success of this detail of itself vindicates the author's choice of a style and passes a conclusive criticism upon the choice of classic architecture for his purpose. Not only would his spirited and ingenious detail have been sacrificed, but the general composition of his building could not have been attained by the use of classic forms without doing violence both to the letter and to the spirit of them. But that he was right for his purpose proves all the more that the architects of the Court of Honor were right for theirs. One can imagine, perhaps, that the Court of Honor might have been lined with buildings in the style of the Fisheries building, and yet not have lost the unity it now possesses provided all the buildings had been done by the same designer and he had been unlimited in the time required to meditate his design. But one cannot imagine that an equal effect of unity could have been gained by a number of architects, working under pressure, if they had chosen a free and romantic instead of a formal and classic style.

The Transportation building bears still stronger testimony to the same effect, since, while everybody finds it interesting and suggestive, nobody ventures to say that it is distinctly and, on the whole, successful. It is the most ambitious of all the great buildings, for it is nothing less than an attempt to create a plaster architecture. Even the Fisheries building, free as it is in design, bears no reference in its design to its material. It is not a building of staff but a simulacrum of a building in masonry. In the Transportation building alone has it been undertaken architecturally to treat the material of which all the buildings are composed. To comprehend the ambitiousness of the attempt one has only to bear in mind that there is no such thing as an exterior architecture of plaster in the world. The "half-timbered" constructions of Europe and the adobe of our own continent do not carry us very far. The Saracens, indeed, attained an interior architecture of plaster, and this architecture comprises all the precedents that were available for the architects of the Transportation building. The outsides of those

Saracenic buildings of which the interiors are most admired are not only of masonry, but some of them are little more than dead walls. One cannot fail to respect the courage and sincerity with which the architects of the Transportation building tackled their task, even though he find in the result a justification for the architects who have forborne the attempt. It was here a perfectly legitimate attempt, since the Transportation building does not form part of an architectural group, and a separate and distinctive treatment was not a grievance to the spectator, nor to the architects of any other buildings, though it was rather curiously resented by some of these. That it is a plaster building is entirely evident, as evident in a photograph as in the fact. It cannot be called an "incoherent originality," for its departures from convention are evidently the result of a studious analysis. A plaster wall is especially in need of protection by an ample cornice, and the ample cornice is provided. But the mouldings that are appropriate to masonry are meaningless in plaster, and the wall is a dead expanse, that would be entirely devoid of interest if left alone. Whether it could not profitably have been enlivened in the Saracenic manner by patterns stamped in relief—a treatment especially adapted to the material—is a question that the designers might perhaps profitably have entertained. But at any rate they determined to enliven the expanse only with color, and the color treatment is not successful. The most pretentious and perhaps the most successful feature of it—the famous Golden Doorway—suffers from being an isolated fragment, entirely unrelated to the general scheme, and its admirable detail does not for this reason excite the admiration it deserves. The moulded ornament in this, however, is less successful than the moulded ornament elsewhere in the building, which is charged with an astonishing spirit and inventiveness and which is, moreover, unmistakably moulded ornament, neither imitative of nor imitable by the work of the chisel. There is certainly no better detail than this in the Fair grounds, but it also loses much of the effect to which it is entitled by its surroundings, and especially by its association with the queerest sculpture that is to be seen on the grounds, and that is saying a great deal. The comparative failure of the color-decoration is very pardonable in so difficult and so unprecedented an essay, but it entails the comparative failure of the design of which it is an integral part, quite independently of other defects in that design.

But, perhaps, the strongest proof of the good judgment of the architects of the Court of Honor is that the effect of unity is not disturbed by those buildings that are in themselves the least successful. . . .

There have been critics who insist that, comprehensive as it is, the epithet "classic" is not comprehensive enough to take in all the architecture of the Court of Honor. One of these critics, a Frenchman, found himself unable to reconcile the more fantastic erections with the rest of the architecture of the Court. He referred, it is to be presumed, to the steeples of Machinery Hall, and the belvederes of the building of Electricity, and he failed to perceive the motive of the introduction, which apparently was to give the buildings as much "Americanism" or Columbianism as was compatible with classicism by borrowing suggestions from the Spanish Renaissance in which were erected the earliest of the European buildings of the new continent. The incongruity is obvious enough, for nothing could be less like classic severity than any suspicion of *bizarrerie*, and *bizarrerie* is characteristic of the exuberance of the Spanish builders of the Renaissance. Perhaps it becomes even rather violent in the contrast between the severe colonnades and the fantastic steeples of Machinery Hall, and one may reasonably wish that the steeples had been omitted even at the sacrifice of the Columbianism. If the incongruity be less apparent in the Electricity building, that is perhaps because that edifice had less character to be disturbed or contradicted, and that one cannot so readily designate any particular feature that prevents it from attaining style, either in the academic or in the æsthetic sense of the term. The Mining building is a much franker example of modern American- ism, franker even than the treatment of the Manufactures building, although the classicism of that is visible only in the monumental entrances and pavil- ions. No sensitive beholder, with the greatest willingness in the world to admire, could succeed in admiring the Mining building if it stood alone, and he would have his difficulties with the Electrical building, in spite of such features as the double apse at the north end and the large half-domed en- trance at the south. But the great advantage of adopting a uniform treat- ment, even when the uniformity is so very general as is denoted by the term classic, and even when the term has been so loosely interpreted, as it has been by some of the associated designers in Jackson Park, is that the less successful designs do not hinder an appreciation of the more successful, nor disturb the general sense of unity in an extensive scheme, which is so much more valuable and impressive than the merits of the best of the designs taken singly. Our enjoyment of the Adminstration building or of the Agricul- tural building might be very seriously marred by the juxtaposition of build- ings equally good unrelated in scale or in manner, while it is not marred by the actual surroundings. The scheme, of a group of monumental buildings, does not depend for its effectiveness upon the equal excellence, or even, as we cannot help seeing, upon the positive excellence of all the parts that go to make it up. It is a scheme and it has been carried out not only in the huge buildings of unequal merit that we have been considering, but in all the accessories of a monumental composition. This has been done with notewor- thy skill and discretion in the peristyle and its flanking buildings, and in the terminal station, any one of which, if done without reference to the rest, under the inspiration of what Mr. Burnham calls an "incoherent originality" or even a coherent originality might have gone for to spoil the whole. It has been carried out also in the minor details that are scarcely noticeable in their places, but that would have been painfully noticeable if they had been out of place, in the plazas and the bridges and the promenades that are the accesso- ries of a pompous architectural composition. It has been carried out too in the sculptural adornment, not only of the building but of the grounds, while in the sculpture it is even more evident to the wayfaring man than in the architecture that the effect of the whole does not depend upon the excel- lence of the parts, and that sculpture that will not bear an analytic inspection may contribute, almost as effectively as sculpture that will, to the decoration of a great pleasance and the entertainment of a holiday crowd. The condi- tion upon which the effectiveness of the whole depends is that there shall be a whole, that there shall be a general plan to the execution of which every architect and every sculptor and every decorator concerned shall contribute.

That condition has been fulfilled in the architecture of the Exposition, at least in the architecture of the "Court of Honor," which is what everybody means when he speaks of the architecture of the Exposition, and it is by the fulfillment of this condition that the success of the Fair has been attained. That success is, first of all, a success of unity.

II

Next after unity, as a source and explanation of the unique impression made by the World's Fair buildings, comes magnitude. It may even be questioned whether it should not come first in an endeavor to account for that impression. If it be put second, it is only because unity, from an artistic point of view, is an achievement, while magnitude from that point of view, is merely an advantage. The buildings are impressive by their size, and this impressiveness is enhanced by their number. Mere bigness is the easiest, speaking aesthetically, though practically it may be the most difficult to attain, of all the means to an effect. It constitutes an opportunity, and one's judgment upon the result, as a work of art, depends upon the skill with which the opportunity has been embraced and employed. But bigness tells all the same, and the critical observer can no more emancipate himself from the effect of it than the uncritical, though he is the better able to allow for it. In this country mere bigness counts for more than anywhere else, and in Chicago, the citadel of the superlative degree, it counts for more, perhaps, than it counts for elsewhere in this country. To say of anything that it is the "greatest" thing of its kind in the world is a very favorite form of advertisement in Chicago. One cannot escape hearing it and seeing it there a dozen times a day, nor from noting the concomitant assumption that the biggest is the best. This assumption was very naively made by the enthusiastic citizen whose proposition we have already noted to occupy the Lake Front, which is one of the few features of the city of Chicago and one of the most attractive of them, with a full-sized reproduction of the Manufactures building. If one ask why Manufactures building, the civic patriot has his answer ready: "Because it is the biggest thing on earth," as indeed it is, having not much less than twice the area of the Great Pyramid, the type of erections that are effective by sheer magnitude. The Great Pyramid appeals to the imagination by its antiquity and its mystery as well as to the senses by its magnitude, but it would be impossible to erect anything whatever of the size of the Manufactures building or even of the Great Pyramid that would not forbid apathy in its presence. A pile of barrels so big as that would strike the spectator. It would be a monument of human labor, even though the labor had been misdirected, and the evidence of crude labor, if it be on a large enough scale, is effective as well as the evidence of artistic handicraft, though of course neither in the same kind nor in the same degree. "These huge structures and pyramidal immensities" would make their appeal successfully though they were merely huge and immense brute masses quite innocent of art. The art that is shown in this respect is in the development of the magnitude, the carrying further of an inherent and necessary effect and the leading of the spectator to an appreciation of the magnitude by devices that magnify and intensify the impression it makes. That is to say, the art consists in giving it scale. It is a final censure upon the treatment of a piece of architecture which aims at overpowering the spectator by its size that it does not look its size; as is the current and accepted criticism upon St. Peter's. To quote the æstheticians again, succession and uniformity are as essential as magnitude to the "artifical infinite," and it is necessary to it that there should be a repetition, an interminable repetition of the unit, the incessant application of the module. It is an effect quite independent of the style. . . .

The devices by which these inordinate dimensions are brought home to the comprehension of the spectator are various, but they consist, in most cases, at least of a plinth and a parapet in which the height of a man is recalled, as in an architectural drawing the draughtsman puts in a human figure "to give the scale." While the Fair was in progress the moving crowds supplied the scale, but this was given also by all the architectural appurtenances, the parapets of the bridges and the railings of the wharves, so that the magnitude of the buildings was everywhere forced upon the sense. To give scale is also the chief contribution to the effect of a general survey that is made by the accessory and decorative sculpture of the buildings and of the grounds. In this respect, and without reference to their merits strictly as sculpture, the statuary that surmounts the piers and cupolas of the Agricultural building and that with which the angles of the Administration building bristle are particularly fortunate. On the other hand the figures of the peristyle were unfortunate, being too big and insistent for their architectural function of mere finials.

It would be pleasant to consider in detail the excellencies of the buildings that are most admirable, and the sources of their effectiveness, and to consider, also, the causes of the shortcomings of the less successful buildings. But the success of the architectural group, as a whole, is a success not disturbed by the shortcomings and the consequent success of the associated architects from their own point of view and for their special purpose, is a matter upon which we are all agreed. It is only with the influence of what has been done in Jackson Park upon the architecture of the country that we are now concerned; with the suitableness of it for general reproduction or imitation, and with the results that are likely to follow that process, if pursued in the customary manner of the American architect. The danger is that that designer, failing to analyze the sources of the success of the Fair will miss the point. The most obvious way in which he can miss it is by expecting a reproduction of the success of one of the big buildings by reproducing it in a building of ordinary dimensions. It is necessary, if he is to avoid this, that he should bear in mind how much of the effect of one of the big buildings comes from its very bigness, and would disappear from a reproduction in miniature.

III

There is still another cause for the success of the World's Fair buildings, a cause that contributes more to the effect of them, perhaps, than both the causes we have already set down put together. It is this which at once most completely justifies the architects of the Exposition in the course they have adopted, and goes furthest to render the results of that course ineligible for reproduction or for imitation in the solution of the more ordinary problems of the American architect. The success of the architecture at the World's

Fair is not only a success of unity, and a success of magnitude. It is also and very eminently a success of illusion.

What the World's Fair buildings have first of all to tell us, and what they tell equally to a casual glimpse and to a prolonged survey is that they are examples not of work-a-day building, but of holiday building, that the purpose of their erection is festal and temporary, in a word that the display is a display and a triumph of occasional architecture. As Mr. Burnham well described it, it is a "vision" of beauty that he and his co-workers have presented to us, and the description implies, what our recollections confirm, that it is an illusion that has here been provided for our delight. It was the task of the architects to provide the stagesetting for an unexampled spectacle. They have realized in plaster that gives us the illusion of monumental masonry a painter's dream of Roman architecture. In Turner's fantasias we have its prototype much more nearly than in any actual erection that has ever been seen in the world before. It is the province and privilege of the painter to see visions and of the poet to dream dreams. . . .

The poet's or the painter's spell or the spell of the architect of an "unsubstantial pageant" cannot be wrought upon the spectator who refuses to take the wonder-worker's point of view and instead of yielding himself to the influence of the spectacle insists upon analyzing its parts and exposing its incongruities. There would be a want of sense as well as a want of imagination in pursuing this course and criticising a passing show as a permanent and serious piece of building.

It is the part of the spectator who would derive the utmost pleasure from the spectacle to ignore the little incongruities that he might detect and loyally to assist the scenic artist in his make-believe. Nay, the consciousness of illusion is a part of the pleasure of the illusion. It is not a diminution but an increase of our delight to know that the cloud-capped towers, the gorgeous palaces, and the solemn temples, the images of which scenic art summons before us are in sober reality "the baseless fabric of a vision."

Such a pleasure and such an illusion the architects of Jackson Park have given us. The White City is the most integral, the most extensive, the most illusive piece of scenic architecture that has ever been seen. That is praise enough for its builders, without demanding for them the further praise of having made a useful and important contribution to the development of the architecture of the present, to the preparation of the architecture of the future. This is a praise that is not merely irrelevant to the praise they have won, but incompatible with it. It is essential to the illusion of a fairy city that it should not be an American city of the nineteenth century. It is a seaport on the coast of Bohemia, it is the capital of No Man's Land. It is what you will, so long as you will not take it for an American city of the nineteenth century, nor its architecture for the actual or the possible or even the ideal architecture of such a city. To fall into this confusion was to lose a great part of its charm, that part which consisted in the illusion that the White City was ten thousand miles and a thousand years away from the City of Chicago, and in oblivion of the reality that the two were contiguous and contemporaneous. Those of us who believe that architecture is the correlation of structure and function, that if it is to be real and living and progressive, its forms must be the results of material and construction, sometimes find ourselves reproached with our admiration for these palaces in which this belief is so conspicuously ignored and set at naught. But there is no inconsistency in entertaining at the same time a hearty admiration for the Fair and its builders and the hope of an architecture which in form and detail shall be so widely different from it as superficially to have nothing in common with it. Arcadian architecture is one thing and American architecture is another. The value of unity, the value of magnitude are common to the two, but for the value of illusion in the one there must be substituted in the other, if it is to come to its fruition, the value of reality. We may applaud the skill of the stage-carpenter who gives us a theatric illusion without the slightest impulse to tell the common carpenter of every day to go and do likewise. In the world of dreams, illusion is all that we require. In the world of facts, illusion may be merely sham, and it suffices to say of what is presented for our acceptance that it is "not so." One can imagine what would be the result of an indiscriminate admiration of the buildings of the World's Fair. Nay, we do not need to resort to imagination, for have we not had our classic revival already? The prostylar villa in white pine remains to testify to it not less than the crop of domed state houses that sprang up in reproduction or in imitation of the Capitol at Washington. It is true that these were ill-done, even in the comparison with their immediate prototype, not to speak of their ultimate originals. As Mr. Burnham says, it requires long and fine training to design on classic lines, and this truth is impressed upon us when we come to make comparisons among the buildings even of the Fair itself. But granted the training, would a sensitive person desire to see even the best of these buildings reproduced for the adornment of an American town, apart from the setting that in Jackson Park so enhances the merits of the best and redeems the defects of the worst? What would it be without the unity by which its greatest value is the contribution it makes to the total effect? Even if this could be in part retained by the reproduction of a fragment of the group, how ineffectual it would be on the scale of our ordinary building or even on a scale considerably larger than the ordinary building. Who that has seen the originals would care to have his recollection disturbed, under pretense of having it revived, by a miniature plaza, with a little Administration building at one end, flanked by a little Manufactures building and a little Machinery Hall? Above all, who would care to have the buildings reproduced without the atmosphere of illusion that enveloped them at Jackson Park and vulgarized by being brought into the light of common day? "This same truth is a naked and open daylight that doth not show the masques and mummeries and triumphs of the world half so stately and daintily as candle lights."[2]

It was a common remark among visitors who saw the Fair for the first time that nothing they had read or seen pictured had given them an idea of it, or prepared them for what they saw. The impression thus expressed is the impression we have been trying to analyze, of which the sources seem to be unity, magnitude and illusion, and the greatest of these is illusion. To reproduce or to imitate the buildings deprived of these irreproducible and inimitable advantages, would be an impossible task, and if it were possible it

[2] Bacon, *Essays*, "Of Truth."

would not be desirable. For the art of architecture is not to produce illusions or imitations, but realities, organisms like those of nature. It is in the "naked and open daylight" that our architects must work, and they can only be diverted from their task of production by reproduction. It is not theirs to realize the dreams of painters, but to do such work as future painters may delight to dream of and to draw. If they work for their purposes as well as the classic builders wrought for theirs, then when they, in their turn, have become remote and mythical and classic, their work may become the material of an illusion, "such stuff as dreams are made of." But its very fitness for this purpose will depend upon its remoteness from current needs and current ideas, upon its irrelevancy to what will then be contemporary life.

53   D. H. Burnham and E. H. Bennett, Plan of Chicago* *1909*

Because of his eminently successful administration in planning and building the Columbian Exposition, Daniel Burnham (1846–1912) gained an immediate reputation as a planner. In 1900, when it was proposed that the disjointed development of L'Enfant's Washington plan be restudied and corrected, Burnham was the natural choice for consulting planner. He in turn selected as fellow planners Frederick Law Olmsted, Jr., for the park plan, Charles F. McKim, who did the design for central Washington, and Augustus Saint-Gaudens, who advised on placement of sculpture.[†] Burnham was then engaged, in 1902–03, to work with John M. Carrère and Arnold W. Brunner in developing a scheme for rebuilding the governmental center of Cleveland. In 1903 he was formally appointed to draw up a much more extensive plan for the city of San Francisco. Although his report, written with his planning assistant Edward H. Bennett, was completed in the fall of 1905, it had limited effect when the city had to be rapidly re-established after the earthquake in April 1906.

Burnham was offered a position on a permanent planning commission in San Francisco, an offer he was obliged to decline to devote his time to an even more ambitious project already under way—the sweeping plan for his beloved Chicago. He had hoped of devising a plan for Chicago shortly after the Columbian Exposition, and he began to speak before civic and business organizations to build interest. During the years 1902–06, he worked on portions of his plan for two business organizations, with the result that the two clubs merged to implement Burnham's study. The expanded Commercial Club underwrote all expenses, and Burnham donated his time

* Daniel H. Burnham and Edward H. Bennett, with Charles Moore, *Plan of Chicago*, Chicago, 1909, pp. 1–8.

† See the summary account in John Reps, *The Making of Urban America* (Princeton, 1965), pp. 501–25, and the detailed presentation in his *Monumental Washington: The Planning and Development of the Capital Center* (Princeton, 1967). See too, Hines, *Burnham of Chicago*, pp. 139–157.

and services. During the years 1907–08, he worked continuously on the plan, much of the time in a small rooftop studio he had built atop his firm's Railway Exchange Building (1903–04), with its view of the entire lakeshore from Evanston to the north to the newly founded steel town, Gary, Indiana, to the southeast. The plan was presented to the club in 1909 in an exhibition consisting of huge mounted colored plans and aerial perspectives, and a plan document published in an elegant volume illustrated with color reproductions of the drawings.‡

George E. Hooker, Secretary of the City Club of Chicago, reviewed the plan in *Survey* in 1909, observing it was "most comprehensive and by far the most beautifully presented" of any such plan, as indeed it was.§ Burnham stressed the regional basis of any successful broad planning venture, opening the book with a full-page color aerial view of Chicago as viewed from about two hundred miles in the air; this, he suggested, was the scale on which to plan. Nevertheless the plan document was not a series of charts, tables, or official expert reports, as Hooker pointed out; it was written for the public and lavishly illustrated to make certain Burnham's objectives were easily grasped. Over $80,000 had been spent, Hooker noted, on production and printing of the book. As with the Washington, D.C., plan proposal, Burnham understood that only small fragments of his scheme could be acted upon immediately, but a great comprehensive scheme, clearly presented, would be persuasive for many years. The epigram attributed to him precisely sums up what the plan of Chicago was meant to do:

> Make no little plans; they have no magic to stir men's blood and probably themselves will not be realized. Make big plans; aim high in hope and work, remembering that a noble diagram once recorded will never die, but long after we are gone will be a living thing, asserting itself with evergrowing insistency. Remember that our sons and grandsons are going to do things that would stagger us. Let your watchword be order and your beacon beauty.

Contents.
 Chapter I. Origin of the Plan of Chicago
 Chapter II. City Planning in Ancient and Modern Times
 Chapter III. Chicago, The Metropolis of the Middle West
 Chapter IV. The Chicago Park System
 Chapter V. Transportation
 Chapter VI. Streets Within the City
 Chapter VII. The Heart of Chicago (Michigan Avenue, Financial Quarter, Cultural Center, Civic Center, etc.)
 Chapter VIII. Plan of Chicago
 Appendix. Legal Aspects of the Plan of Chicago by Walter L. Fisher

---

‡ For Burnham's Chicago plan see Hines, *Burnham of Chicago*, pp. 312–45. The *Plan of Chicago*, limited to 1,650 copies in 1909, was republished in an exacting facsimile (New York, 1970). To mark the seventieth anniversary of the plan, the now-fragile drawings were restored and exhibited at the Art Institute of Chicago in 1979; see the catalogue, *The Plan of Chicago: 1909–1979*, ed. J. Zukowsky (Chicago, 1979), with essays by Zukowsky, Sally Chappell, and Robert Bruegmann.

§ George E. Hooker, "A Plan for Chicago," *The Survey* 22 (September 4, 1909), pp. 778–90.

CHAPTER I. ORIGIN OF THE PLAN OF CHICAGO:
THE WORLD'S COLUMBIAN EXPOSITION OF 1893
AND ITS RESULTS: THE SPIRIT OF CHICAGO

The tendency of mankind to congregate in cities is a marked characteristic of modern times. This movement is confined to no one country, but is world-wide. Each year Rome, and the cities of the Orient, as well as Berlin, New York, and Chicago, are adding to their population at an unprecedented rate. Coincident with this urban development there has been a widespread increase in wealth, and also an enlarged participation on the part of the people in the work of government. As a natural result of these causes has come the desire to better the conditions of living. Men are becoming convinced that the formless growth of the city is neither economical nor satisfactory; and that overcrowding and congestion of traffic paralyze the vital functions of the city. The complicated problems which the great city develops are now seen not to be beyond the control of aroused public sentiment; and practical men of affairs are turning their attention to working out the means whereby the city may be made an efficient instrument for providing all its people with the best possible conditions of living.

Chicago, in common with other great cities, realizes that the time has come to bring order out of the chaos incident to rapid growth, and especially to the influx of people of many nationalities without common traditions or habits of life. Among the various instrumentalities designed to accomplish this result, a plan for a well-ordered and convenient city is seen to be indispensable; and to the task of producing such a plan the Commercial Club has devoted its energies for the past three years.

It is not to be expected that any plan devised while as yet few civic problems have received final solution will be perfect in all its details. It is claimed for the plan herein presented, that it is the result of extended and careful study of the needs of Chicago, made by disinterested men of wide experience, amid the very conditions which it is sought to remedy; and that during the years devoted to its preparation the plan has had the benefit of varied and competent criticism. The real test of this plan will be found in its aplication; for, such is the determination of the people to secure more perfect conditions, it is certain that if the plan is really good it will commend itself to the progressive spirit of the times, and sooner or later it will be carried out.

It should be understood, however, that such radical changes as are proposed herein cannot possibly be realized immediately. Indeed, the aim has been to anticipate the needs of the future as well as to provide for the necessities of the present: in short, to direct the development of the city towards an end that must seem ideal, but is practical. Therefore it is quite possible that when particular portions of the plan shall be taken up for execution, wider knowledge, longer experience, or a change in local conditions may suggest a better solution; but, on the other hand, before any departure shall be determined upon, it should be made clear that such a change is justified.

If many elements of the proposed plan shall seem familiar, it should be remembered that the purpose has not been to invent novel problems for solution, but to take up the pressing needs of today, and to find the best methods of meeting those requirements, carrying each particular problem to its ultimate conclusion as a component part of a great entity,—a well-ordered, convenient, and unified city.

This conception of the task is the justification of a comprehensive plan of Chicago. To many who have given little consideration to the subject, a plan seems to call for large expenditures and a consequent increase in taxation. The reverse is the case. It is certain that civic improvement will go on at an accelerated rate; and if those improvements shall be marshaled according to a well-ordered plan great saving must result. Good order and convenience are not expensive; but haphazard and ill-considered projects invariably result in extravagance and wastefulness. A plan insures that whenever any public or semi-public work shall be undertaken, it will fall into its proper and predetermined place in the general scheme, and thus contribute to the unity and dignity of the city.

The plan frankly takes into consideration the fact that the American city, and Chicago preeminently, is a center of industry and traffic. Therefore attention is given to the betterment of commercial facilities; to methods of transportation for persons and for goods; to removing the obstacles which prevent or obstruct circulation; and to the increase of convenience. It is realized, also, that good workmanship requires a large degree of comfort on the part of the workers in their homes and their surroundings, and ample opportunity for that rest and recreation without which all work becomes drudgery. Then, too, the city has a dignity to be maintained; and good order is essential to material advancement. Consequently, the plan provides for impressive groupings of public buildings, and reciprocal relations among such groups. Moreover, consideration is given to the fact that in all probability Chicago, within the lifetime of persons now living, will become a greater city than any existing at the present time; and that therefore the most comprehensive plans of to-day will need to be supplemented in a not remote future. Opportunity for such expansion is provided for.

The origin of the plan of Chicago can be traced directly to the World's Columbian Exposition. The World's Fair of 1893 was the beginning, in our day and in this country, of the orderly arrangement of extensive public grounds and buildings. The result came about quite naturally. Chicago had become a commercial community wherein men were accustomed to get together to plan for the general good. Moreover, those at the head of affairs were, many of them, the same individuals who had taken part in every movement since the city had emerged from the condition of a mere village. They were so accustomed to results even beyond their most sanguine predictions, that it was easy for them to believe that their Fair might surpass all fairs that had preceded it.

Then, too, the men of Chicago, trained in intense commercial activity, had learned the lesson that great success cannot be attained unless the special work in hand shall be entrusted to those best fitted to undertake it. It had become the habit of our business men to select some one to take the responsibility in every important enterprise; and to give to that person earnest, loyal, and steadfast support. Thus the design and arrangement of the buildings of the World's Columbian Exposition, which have never been surpassed, were due primarily to the feeling of loyalty to the city and to its undertakings; and secondly, to the habit of entrusting great works to men trained in the practice of such undertakings.[1]

The results of the World's Fair of 1893 were many and far-reaching. To the people of Chicago the dignity, beauty, and convenience of the transitory city in Jackson Park seemed to call for the improvement of the water front of the city. With this idea in mind, the South Park Commissioners, during the year following the Fair, proposed the improvement of the Lake front from Jackson Park to Grant Park. Following out this suggestion, a plan for a connection between the two parks was drawn to a large scale, and the project was presented at a meeting of the West and South Park Commissioners. Later this design was exhibited at a dinner given by the Commercial Club; and many business men were emphatic in expressing their conviction that the proposed scheme would be of enormous value to Chicago, and that it should be adopted and carried into execution. This was the inception of the project for a park out in the Lake, having a lagoon between it and the shore.

During the next three or four years more careful studies of the Lake front scheme were made, and very large drawings were prepared for a meeting at the Women's Club and the Art Institute, and for a Merchants Club dinner at the Auditorium. The newspapers and magazines, both at home and throughout the country, united in commenting on and commending the undertaking; and during the decade that has elapsed since the plans were first presented, the proposed improvement has never been forgotten, but has ever been looked upon as something sure to be accomplished. This was the beginning of a general plan for the city.

While these projects were in course of preparation, an extensive expansion of the South Parks system was in progress, and a plan was formulated for a metropolitan park system, including an outer belt of parks and parkways. These movements were started with energy in 1903; under the general direction of the South Park Commissioners and the Special Park Commis-

---

[1] A significant illustration of the spirit in which the World's Fair work was conceived is found in one incident. On the appointed day the architects assembled to submit to the general committee sketches of their several buildings. There had been a luncheon, prolonged by animated discussion. The scheme as a whole had begun to take hold of the men. The short winter afternoon was approaching an end, when Richard M. Hunt (then the dean of the architectural profession), suffering from the severe pains of rheumatism, slowly arose to speak of the Administration Building, a sketch of which he fastened to the wall. The New York architect who followed Mr. Hunt had on his building a dome four hundred and fifty feet high. Instantly a murmur ran around the group. The designer turned from the sketch. "I think," he said, with deliberation, "I shall not advocate that dome; and probably I shall modify the building." There was a breath of satisfaction. The next architect had a portico extending out over the terrace. Without waiting for criticism, he said he should draw the portico back to the face of the building. As one by one each man fastened his sketch to the wall, it was as still as death in the room; and those present could feel the great work drawing them as by a magnet; and each was willing to sacrifice his personal ideas to secure the unity of the whole composition. Finally the last drawing was shown; the last explanation had been made. Mr. Saint-Gaudens, who had sat in a corner all day listening, but never speaking and scarcely moving, went over to Mr. Burnham, and taking both his hands exclaimed: "Do you realize that this is the greatest meeting of artists since the fifteenth century?"

sion; and the results of their work have been useful to those who have undertaken the present task.

Early in 1906 the Merchants Club arranged for the preparation of a complete project for the future development of Chicago. In order to facilitate the progress of the work, rooms were built on the roof of the Railway Exchange Building, where the drawings have been prepared and the studies have been made. The Merchants Club and the Commercial Club having been merged in 1907 under the name of the latter organization, the work has continued under the auspices of that association. The committee on the plan has held several hundred meetings; during many weeks meetings have taken place daily; and throughout the entire time no week has passed without one or more such gatherings. By invitation of the Club, the Governor of Illinois, the Mayor of Chicago, and many other public officials have visited the rooms where the work was in progress, and have become familiar with the entire scheme as it was being worked out. The Department of State, through the United States consuls in various European cities, has furnished valuable information relative to civic developments now in progress. Thus the plans have had the benefit of many criticisms and suggestions, made by persons especially conversant with existing conditions. Moreover, visitors interested in the improvement of cities and in park work of all kinds have come from both our own and foreign towns; and from them also much of value and encouragement has been gained.

In presenting this report, the Commercial Club realizes that from time to time supplementary reports will be necessary to emphasize one feature or another which may come prominently before the public for adoption. At the same time, it is confidently believed that this presentation of the entire subject accomplishes the task which has been recognized from the outset, namely:

First, to make the careful study of the physical conditions of Chicago as they now exist;

Second, to discover how those conditions may be improved;

Third, to record such conclusions in the shape of drawings and texts which shall become a guide for the future development of Chicago.

In creating the ideal arrangement, every one who lives here is better accommodated in his business and his social activities. In bringing about better freight and passenger facilities, every merchant and manufacturer is helped. In establishing a complete park and parkway system, the life of the wage-earner and of his family is made healthier and pleasanter; while the greater attractiveness thus produced keeps at home the people of means and taste, and acts as a magnet to draw those who seek to live amid pleasing surroundings. The very beauty that attracts him who has money makes pleasant the life of those among whom he lives, while anchoring him and his wealth to the city. The prosperity aimed at is for all Chicago.

This same spirit which carried out the Exposition in such a manner as to make it a lasting credit to the city is still the soul of Chicago, vital and dominant; and even now, although many new men are at the front, it still controls and is doing a greater work than it was in 1893. It finds the men; it makes the occasion; it attracts the sincere and unselfish; it vitalizes the organization, and impels it to reach heights not believed possible of attainment. This spirit still exists. It is present to-day among us. Indeed, it seems to gather force with the years and the opportunities. It is even now impelling us to larger and better achievements for the public good. It conceals no private purpose, no hidden ends. This spirit—the spirit of Chicago—is our greatest asset. It is not merely civic pride: it is rather the constant, steady determination to bring about the very best conditions of city life for all the people, with full knowledge that what we as a people decide to do in the public interest we can and surely will bring to pass.

54 J. Nolen, City Making* *1909*

By the time Burnham completed and presented the Chicago plan, the planning profession in the United States was well established. Indeed, in 1917 when the American Institute of Architects published *City Planning Progress in the United States,* reviewing the programs underway, a total of 233 were tallied. Journals specifically devoted to the new profession and progressive urban ideals, such as *The American City,* began to appear. There was growing recognition that the time had come, as John Nolen wrote, "when art and skill and foresight should control what hitherto has been left to chance to work out . . . , that there is a real art of city making, and that it behooves this generation to master and apply it." John Nolen (1869–1937) was one of the principal planners and landscape architects of the early part of this century; his wide influence was due not only to his many designs but to his frequent lecturing and many books.† He studied at the University of Pennsylvania but at thirty-four took up his chosen profession, enrolling in the newly established School of Landscape Architecture at Harvard. During his career he and his associates worked on over four hundred projects, among them: the war housing complex of Union Park Gardens, Wilmington, Delaware, 1917; new towns such as Kingsport, Tennessee, and Mariemont, near Cincinnati, Ohio; plans for redevelopment of older cities such as Akron, Ohio, and Madison, Wisconsin; and regional plans for San Diego, California, New York City, and Philadelphia. A consultant to the Department of the Interior, he worked on housing for the PWA and the Resettlement Administration during the Depression. Among his principal books are: *City Planning* (New York, 1916); *New Ideals in the Planning of Cities, Towns and Villages* (New York, 1919); and *New Towns for Old* (Boston, 1927). The article reprinted here, however, dates from the beginning of his career.

*John Nolen, "City Making," *American City* 1 (September 1909), pp. 15–19. (Paper read at a meeting of the American Civic Association.)

†See John L. Hancock, "John Nolen: The Background of a Pioneer Planner," *Journal, American Institute of Planners* 26 (November 1960), pp. 302–12; and his *John Nolen: A Bibliographical Record of Achievement* (Ithaca, N.Y., 1976).

To make Cities—that is what we are here for. For the City is strategic. It makes the towns; the towns make the villages, the villages make the country. He who makes the City makes the world. After all, though men make Cities, it is Cities which make men. Whether our national life is great or mean, whether our social virtues are mature or stunted, whether our sons are moral or vicious, whether religion is possible or impossible, depends upon the City.

HENRY DRUMMOND

General Principles

City Making or City Planning is simply a recognition of the sanitary, economic, and aesthetic laws which should govern the original arrangement and subsequent development of our cities. These laws, however, are not easily understood nor applied. They are themselves complex and each must be adjusted harmoniously to the other, so that health, utility, and beauty may each have proper consideration. Then the conditions to which these laws must be applied are exceedingly varied, each city being different in some respect from every other, parts of the same city different from its other parts, and the same parts often varying in their use and purpose from decade to decade.

Considering that little or nothing has been done in most of our cities and towns to provide intelligently for their plan and growth, it is not surprising that they are monumental examples of what man can do to produce inconvenient, unhealthy, and unlovely surroundings. The most callous are at last awakening. In a dim sort of way, an English leader in city improvement has recently pointed out, many persons understand that the time has come when art and skill and foresight should control what hitherto has been left to chance to work out; that there should be a much more orderly conception of civic action; that there is a real art of city making, and that it behooves this generation to master and apply it.

The interrelation and interdependence of these sanitary, economic, and aesthetic laws is a point not to be longer neglected. Heretofore we have thought that we could follow one regardless of the other, but experience has taught us otherwise. At last we know, for example, that there can be no great and permanent business success without providing convenient and sanitary surroundings; indeed not without surroundings which have the mark of beauty, if by beauty we mean fitness and appropriateness.

Then different cities have different purposes. There are various types —commercial, manufacturing, governmental, educational and artistic, residential, and so on, each type requiring different treatment if it is to serve well its ends. Examples could easily be given of each. These types are not absolutely distinct, but in many cities one element or another predominates or controls and gives a special character to the city. And there are also other circumstances of origin, history, population, or topography that give, or should give, a distinctive quality to cities which are in the same class. Chicago, Pittsburgh, New York; San Francisco, Savannah, Boston; New Orleans, Denver, Washington; do not these names bring at once before the imagination cities that differ radically, each possessing an individuality, a personality, that separates it from every other? What is true of these larger cities is equally, if not more, true of many of the smaller towns and villages.

The Relation of Replanning to Original Plans

There are two important phases of city planning: Cities planned largely in advance of population, and established cities replanned or remodeled to meet new conditions. The former method has obviously great advantages, and many cities established for governmental, industrial, or residential purposes have been so planned. It is a method which needs wider use. Washington is the most notable illustration of this method. The conditions that created it were unique. But we should remember that its large and far-seeing plan must have been for several generations a source of daily inconvenience and discomfort. Dickens' description of it as a city "of spacious avenues that begin in nothing and lead nowhere; streets miles long that want only houses, roads, and inhabitants; public buildings that need but a public to be complete," may show lack of faith and foresight in the novelist, but it describes accurately the appearance of Washington in 1842, a half century after being laid out.

The method of Washington is applicable to the normal city only to a limited degree. After all, it is seldom possible to foresee the future of a city or to plan for it from the very start, and the complex influences which determine the selection of site and the location of streets and buildings must usually be left to work out their natural results. But when a small population has been attracted to a town by natural causes, and there are unmistakable indications that because of situation, climate, the trend of trade and commerce or other forces, an important city is to be established, then it is entirely practicable to intelligently replan the town so as to provide properly for its future. There are scores of cities in this country with a population today of 50,000 people that will have 100,000 in two generations or less, and the same rate of increase may be predicted with equal confidence of cities of greater population. The gravest neglect is right here: the failure to replan and replan, to readjust and readjust, to constantly use art and skill and foresight to remodel existing conditions and to mould and fit for use the new territory about to be invaded.

The people who laid out the first streets in London or Boston provided with considerable common sense for the needs of their time and could scarcely have been expected to foresee the requirements of a large city; their successors long generations afterwards who vetoed Sir Christopher Wren's plan for the improvement of London and the plans for the betterment of Boston after the fire of 1872, displayed a lack of good sense and taste in providing for their own time and even greater lack of foresight and public spirit with regard to the future. Many other illustrations might be given. Oglethorpe, in Savannah, and Penn, in Philadelphia, made plans for their respective cities which have many merits; the succeeding generations in extending those plans into new territory added nothing to their value and left out many features—for instance, a regular system of open spaces and occasional avenues of unusual breadth—that were of very great value.

The emphasis needs to be placed less on the original plan and more on replanning and remodeling. The beautiful cities of Europe, the cities that are constantly taken as illustrations of what modern cities should be, are without exception the result of a picturesque, accidental growth, regulated, it is true, by considerable common sense and respect for art, but improved and again improved by replanning and remodeling to fit changed conditions and new ideals. It is here that we fall short. Throughout the land there are cities with relatively easy opportunities before them to improve their water fronts, to group their public buildings, to widen their streets, to provide in twentieth century fashion for transportation, and to set aside the areas now considered indispensable for public recreation. And yet most of these cities have until recently stood listless, without the manliness and courage to begin the work that must sooner or later be done.

Two Methods: The Formal and the Picturesque

The keen interest at the present time in city improvement has brought into discussion and contrast the formal method and the informal. The formal is best represented in a city like Paris, with its broad, straight avenues, terminated with great public buildings or triumphal arches; its symmetrical, stately effects, and its general grandeur. It is monumental, often impressive, always artificial in the highest degree. It is, however, well adapted for certain purposes and has many merits. The other, the informal treatment, is to be seen in old English and German cities and towns, and in those modern cities and towns which have followed their lead and striven above all for irregularity and picturesqueness.

There can be no question about the charm that Oxford, parts of Hamburg and Nurnberg possess, and the modern city planners are pointing out in the most convincing manner that by this method a fine type of civic beauty can be secured, especially well adapted for residence sections, with less destruction of existing conditions, at much less cost, and without sacrificing the needs of convenience. They hold that city and town plan which have originated naturally, which are based upon necessity, have always a peculiar charm and are more beautiful than the straight streets laid out according to rectilinear principles. They go further; they believe that this irregularity has an influence upon civic virtue and civic spirit. Von Moltke attributed to people living in the rectilinear cities of France a patriotism inferior to that of people living in cities with crooked streets. And another German leader compared regular cities with the structure of the lower animals and the old cities to the forms of richly organized beings permeated with intelligence.

As in Europe, so in this country there are examples of both methods, only here neither has been so well done. Washington is, without question, our best illustration of the formal style, and it can be confidently asserted that even the most advanced German city planner would be satisfied with the informality and irregularity of old Boston. Which method should we favor in our subsequent development? We may answer by asking: Why should we favor either? Are not both good? And have we not need for both? Does not each serve a different purpose and should not the choice of one or the other rest largely upon the physical, social, and financial conditions of each particular case?

Problems Common to All

Although cities differ in their character, there are some problems more or less common to all. Such for instance, as the circulation of traffic, the subdivision of the city into parts to serve various purposes, the provision for the dispatch of public business, the approaches by water and rail, and the needs of recreation.

A more adequate solution of the problems of circulation would alone justify city planning on its practical side. Our cities will remain inconvenient, congested, and ugly until we understand better the place and function of the street—where it should go, how it should be divided, what it should look like, and the need for differentiation between one street and another. Different streets have as different functions as different buildings. Unless they are carefully located and designed to fulfill these various functions there must inevitably be incalculable loss and waste. We have curved streets where they should be straight, straight streets where they should be curved, narrow streets where they should be broad, occasionally broad streets where they should be narrow, and no street connection at all where one is imperatively needed. We have streets too near each other and streets too far apart. Illustrations could readily be given of each of these mistakes in street planning. Then when the location, the grade, the width and the distance from one another are right, the street is undeveloped, lacking those features which are essential to its proper appearance and agreeable use.

The subdivision of our cities and towns into parts, each to serve a peculiar need, is a subject to which we have hardly turned attention. We must consider the value of the "zone" treatment used in European cities, each zone controlled by different regulations. It is a method that we must soon adopt if we are to avoid the waste and folly that characterize our cities at present. Homogeneity of neighborhoods and stability of real estate values are points of importance in this connection.

We are now giving more attention to the subject of public buildings and the advantages of grouping them, even in smaller cities. The arguments for such action are definite and unanswerable. (1) Their arrangement around a square or plaza, or in some well related design, as now being planned for so many American cities, adds immeasurably to the convenient and agreeable conduct of business between one department and another. (2) If artistically planned, and conceived in proper scale and happy harmony, buildings so related contribute more than any other factor to an impression of dignity and appropriate beauty in a city—an impression which has a daily influence upon citizens and strangers alike. There is no comparison between the noble effect which the group plan makes possible as against the location of each building in different parts of the city or even in the same part if on unrelated lots. (3) This grouping of the city's buildings forms a rallying place for the city's life. Here the best impulses may crystallize, inspired by the noble character of the edifice, into devoted action for the public good.

The approaches to a city by water or land are of preëminent importance. No contrast could be greater than the European and American methods of dealing with water fronts. In Europe the importance of the water front for commerce and recreation is wisely recognized, and vast sums have been spent on the construction of docks, piers, promenades, embankments, and parks. One can name places almost at random—Naples, Genoa, Nice, Mentone, Lucerne, Cologne, Hamburg, Paris, London, Liverpool—in all these and innumerable others the water fronts have been improved according to carefully prepared plans and through improvement made a source of prosperity and pleasure scarcely equaled by any other.

In this country it is quite different. Cities fronting on the Atlantic and on the Pacific, on the great rivers that traverse the continent and on the lakes, have not developed in an adequate, businesslike way the opportunities that their situations afford. This contrast has now attracted wide attention, and American cities of all classes, cities situated in different sections of the country, have taken steps to better utilize their water frontages. Witness the plans for Boston, Philadelphia, and Chicago; Buffalo, Cleveland, and Detroit; Harrisburg, Roanoke, and Savannah; Madison, La Crosse, and Milwaukee, in illustration of this movement. The railroad approach is equally important and of even wider application. Several instructive examples might be given of railroad corporations in this country that have had regard for the appearance of things, and have found it profitable.

No phase of civic improvement is more noteworthy than that of the modern conception of the need for recreation. Parks, playgrounds, and open spaces are now classed, and properly so, with the necessities of city life. They provide fresh air and sunshine and the opportunity for exercise which the character of modern cities and modern methods of living have made imperative. At least ten per cent of the city's area should be set aside for recreation and each tract should be skillfully handled so as to make it answer well its purpose. "The strong love of outdoor recreation," said ex-President Cleveland, "is not possessed by every one; yet nature has made it a law that every one is in need mentally and physically, of relaxation in the open air. And in these times of dollar-chasing, many of the most vital necessities of normal life are being neglected.

"In my experience I have found that impressions which a man receives who walks by the brook-side or in the forest or by the seashore, make him a better man and a better citizen. They lift him above the worries of business and teach him of a power greater than human power. It is unquestionably true that nearness to nature has an elevating influence upon the heart and character. Nature is a school of all the hardier virtues. What, for instance, can impart a more effective lesson in patience than a day's fishing for the whimsical black bass? As I have said on a previous occasion, the real worth and genuineness of the human heart are measured best by its readiness to submit to the influence of nature, and to appreciate the goodness of the Supreme Power, who is its creator. This is the central point in my philosophy of life."

Methods of Achievements

How are better results in city planning to be secured? Much can be done by private initiative, by voluntary contributions, as is well illustrated in the work of the Madison, Wisconsin, Park and Pleasure Drive Association. For seventeen years that association has collected small subscriptions and used the total of $300,000 so obtained to add to the attractiveness and convenience of that city so beautifully located on Lakes Monona and Mendota. Another method is that of coöperation between private individuals and public authorities. The Metropolitan Museum of Art in New York, the Museum of Natural History, and the Zoölogical Gardens are examples of the good results possible by this method. But none of these is adequate. The problems are too large. Back of comprehensive city planning there must be complete public authority and the public funds. The really noteworthy results are in places like Kansas City and Harrisburg, where sound and far-seeing plans have been supported by the municipality. Sooner or later we must have permanent city plan commissions like that now working in Hartford, Conn., and proposed for Wisconsin cities, with proper authority to take land, to borrow money, to use expert advice, and to carry out large and wise plans for the benefit of the whole people.

The great need at the present time, the greatest need, I believe, is a more aroused and enlightened public opinion. Therefore nothing is more significant, nothing more useful, than such work as that represented by the National Municipal League and the American Civic Association. Intelligent city planning is one of the means toward a better utilization of our resources, toward an application of the methods of private business to public affairs, toward efficiency, toward a higher individual and higher collective life. If we want such substantial things as health and wealth and joy, if we want the equally indispensable element of beauty in our daily lives, if we want to avoid waste of money and time, we must find ways to avail ourselves more fully of the incalculable advantages of skillful city planning.

VII

DICHOTOMY: TRADITION AND AVANT-GARDE

55   R. A. Cram, The Philosophy of the Gothic Restoration* *1913*

In this address, Ralph Adams Cram (1863–1942) surveyed the development of contemporary architecture, concluding there were seven major divisions—steel frame, secessionist (by which he meant Wright, Sullivan, the Greene brothers, and Maybeck), three types of classic, and two kinds of Gothic. He himself had been instrumental in reestablishing Gothic after the rather inventive and adventurous departures of High Victorian Gothic. Born in New Hampshire and the son of a minister, Cram studied art and nearly entered a career as a journalist (he was an active speaker and writer all his life). In 1889 he formed a partnership with Charles Wentworth, which later was joined by Bertram Goodhue. He quickly developed a mature expression, and his All Saints Church, Ashmont, Massachusetts, built in 1891–94, served along with the work of Henry Vaughan to reestablish correct but freely modulated Gothic for churches. Cram turned to Gothic not because it was a style but because, like A. W. N. Pugin and William Morris, he believed "religion is the essence of human life." Moreover, Gothic architecture, like the medieval society which produced it, combined an optimum of liberty and order. And it was an architecture in which all the arts cooperated; "by itself," Cram wrote, "architecture is nothing; allied with the structural crafts and the artist crafts, it is everything."† Cram is well known for St. Thomas's, New York, 1906-14, the West Point Chapel, 1903-14, the Princeton Graduate School complex, 1911-29, and the continuation of the great Cathedral Church of St. John the Divine, New York, 1915-41. Other excellent examples of his translation of Gothic are the First Unitarian Church, West Newton, Massachusetts, 1905-09, and the Church of the Holy Rosary, Pittsburgh, 1926-31. Yet Cram used Georgian classic for several churches, such as the Second Unitarian, Audubon Circle, Boston, built in 1913–17—despite his attack on Renaissance architecture in this selection. An indefatigable writer and speaker, he collected many of his addresses for publication, as was the case with this lecture. Among his many books are: *English Country Churches* (Boston, 1898); *Church Building* (Boston, 1914); *Impressions of Japanese Architecture and the Allied Arts* (Boston, 1906), written as a result of an unsuccessful trip to Japan in 1898 to win the commission for a projected parliament building which he and Goodhue based on Ashikaga and Fujiwara architecture; *The Ministry of Art* (Boston, 1914); *The Substance of Gothic* (Boston 1917); and his autobiography, *My Life in Architecture* (Boston, 1936).‡ Cram was also chiefly instrumental in persuading Henry Adams to allow the American Institute of Architects

---

*Ralph Adams Cram, "The Philosophy of the Gothic Restoration," in his *The Ministry of Art* (Boston, 1914), pp. 21–63. The first half of this, with slight revisions, Cram published as "Style in American Architecture," *Architectural Record* 34 (September 1913), pp. 232–39; originally it was a paper read before the Contemporary Club of Philadelphia.

†Ralph Adams Cram, *The Significance of Gothic Art* (Boston, 1918), p. 13; R. A. Cram, *The Ministry of Art* (Boston, 1914), pp. 148–52.

‡See the extensive bibliographies in Douglass Shand Tucci, *Ralph Adams Cram: American Medievalist* (Boston, 1975); Robert Muccigrosso, *American Gothic: The Mind and Art of Ralph Adams Cram* (Washington, D.C., 1980).

to reprint the latter's *Mont-Saint-Michel and Chartres* in 1913 for which Cram then wrote an introduction. This was the first public printing of this remarkable work, for Adams had only a small number printed at his own expense in 1904.

I am convinced there is nothing accidental in our stylistic development, or in the universe, for that matter. . . . So, chaotic and illogical as our devious wanderings after the strange gods of style may be, I am disposed to think that even here we may find evidences of design, of a Providence that over-rules all things for good; "an idea," as Chesterton would say, "not without humour."

For chaos is the only word that one can justly apply to the quaint and inconsequent conceits in which we have indulged since that monumental moment in the early nineteenth century when, architecturally, all that had been since the beginning ceased, and that which had never been before, on land or sea, began. A walk up Fifth Avenue in New York, from Madison Square to the Park, with one's eyes open, is an experience of some surprises and equal illumination, and it leaves an indelible impression of that primal chaos that is certainly without form, if it is not wholly void. Here one may see in a scant two miles (scant, but how replete with experiences!) treasure-trove of all peoples and all generations: Roman temples and Parisian shops; Gothic of sorts (and out of sorts) from the "carpenter-Gothic" of 1845, through Victorian of that ilk, to the most modern and competent recasting of ancient forms and restored ideals; Venetian palaces and Louis Seize palaces, and Roman palaces, and more palaces from wherever palaces were ever built; delicate little Georgian ghosts, shrinking in their unpremeditated contact with Babylonian skyscrapers that poise their towering masses of plausible masonry on an unconvincing substructure of plate glass. And it is all contemporary,—the oldest of it dates not back two generations,—while it is all wildly and improbably different.

The experience prompts retrospection, and we turn over the dog-eared leaves of the immediate past; apparently it was the same, only less so, back to the decade between 1820 and 1830, and there we find a reasonably firm foothold. Here at last, at the beginning of the century, we discover actual unanimity, and with some relief we go back century after century, tracing variations, but discovering no precedent for the chaos we have left. From time to time, even to the first Olympiad, we suddenly find ourselves at some brief period where a fight is manifestly going on; but there were never more than two parties to the contest, and this once passed, we have another four or five centuries of peaceful and unified development. Our own Colonial merges without a shock in English Georgian; this, through Inigo Jones, in the Renaissance of the Continent. A generation of warfare lands us in Flamboyant Gothic, and so to real Gothic that stretches back through logical vicissitudes to the twelfth century. Another upheaval, and in a moment we are with the Romanesque that touches Rome itself, and behind Rome lies Greece. No chaos here; definite and lawful development; infinite variety, infinite personality, and a vitality that demands a more illimitable word than "infinite." What happened, then, in 1825; what is happening now; what is going to happen, and why?

We may try for an answer, but first we must lightly run over the well-thumbed leaves again.

We all know what our own Colonial was like; perhaps we do not fully realize how varied it was as between one section and another, but at least we appreciate its simplicity and directness, its honesty, its native refinement and delicacy, its frequent originality. It is not the same as English Georgian; sometimes it is distinctly better; and, however humble or colloquial, it is marked always by extreme good taste. If anything it improved during the almost two centuries of Colonial growth, and when the nineteenth century opened it was still instinct with life. A half-century later where were we? Remember 1850, and all that that date connotes of structural dishonesty, barbarism, and general ugliness! Here is the debatable period; and we may narrow it, for in 1810, in 1820, good work was still being done, while in 1840, yes, in 1830 the sodden savagery diluted with shameless artifice was generally prevalent. To me this decade between 1820 and 1830 is one of the great moments in architectural history, for then the last flicker of instinctive art amongst men died away, and a new period came in. . . . In a word, what happened about 1825 was anomalous; it happened for the first time; and for the first time whatever man tried to do in art was not only wrong, it was absolutely and unescapably bad.

I should like to deal with this matter in detail, but we have no time. In a word, what had happened, it seems to me, was this: The Renaissance had struck a wrong note—and in several things besides architecture; for the first time man self-confidently set to work to invent and popularize a new and perfectly artificial style. I am not concerned here with the question whether it was a good style or not; the point is that it was done with malice afore-thought; it was invented by a cabal of painters, goldsmiths, scenic artists, and literary men, and railroaded through a stunned society that, busied with other matters, took what was offered it, abandoned its old native ways, and later, when time for thought offered, found it was too late to go back. Outside Italy there was as little desire for the new-fangled mode as there was for the doctrinal Reformation outside Germany. In France and England good taste still reigned supreme, and though the dogmatic iconoclasts took good care that the best of the old work should be destroyed and that suspicion should be cast on what—from sheer exhaustion—they allowed to remain; though for one reason and another the new Classic style came in, the good taste of the people still remained operative, and while Italy and Germany were mired in Rococo and Baroque, they continued building lovely things that were good in spite of their artificial style, because their people had not lost their sense or their taste.

It could not last, however: certain essential elements had been lost out of life during the Renaissance and the Reformation; the Revolution—third act in the great melodrama—was a foregone conclusion. It completed the working-out of the foreordained plot, and after it was over and the curtain had been rung down, whatever had been won, good taste had been lost, and remained only the memory of a thing that had been born with man's civilization and had accompanied it until that time.

You cannot sever art from society; you cannot make it grow in unfavourable soil, however zealously you may labour and lecture and subsidize.

It follows from certain spiritual and social conditions, and without these it is a dead twig thrust in sand, and only a divine miracle can make such bloom, as blossomed the staff of St. Joseph of Arimathea at Glastonbury.

Well, Alberti and Palladio and Inigo Jones had dissolved and disappeared in the slim refinements of American Colonial. What followed? For a brief time and in one or two categories of activity the spacious and delusive imitations that Jefferson more or less popularized, the style sometimes known as "Neo-Grec," but more accurately termed—because of its wide use for Protestant meeting-houses in country districts—the "Græco-Baptist" style. You know it?—Front porticoes of well-designed, four-foot Classical columns made of seven-eighths-inch pine stock, neatly nailed together, painted white, and echoing like a drum to the incautious kick of the heel; slab sides covered with clapboards, green blinds to the round-topped windows, and a little bit of a brick chimney sticking up at the stern where once, in happier days, stood the little cote that housed the Sanctus bell.

Then came what is well called "Carpenter-Gothic," marked by the same high indifference to structural integrity, and with even less reliance on precedent for its architectural forms; a perfectly awful farrago of libelous details,—pointed arches, clustered columns, buttresses, parapets, pinnacles,—and all of the ever-present pine lumber painted gray, and usually sanded as a final refinement of verisimilitude. And with these wonderful monuments, check by jowl, Italian villas, very white and much balconied, Swiss chalets and every other imaginable thing that the immortal Batty Langly, or later the admirable Mr. Downing, could invent, with, for evidence of sterling American ingenuity, the "jig-saw-and-batten" refinement of crime. We really could not stand all this, you know, and when the Centennial in Philadelphia finally revealed us as, artistically speaking, the most savage of nations, we began to look about for means of amendment. We were not strikingly successful, as is evidenced by the so-called "Queen Anne" and "Eastlake" products of the morning after the celebration; but the Ruskinian leaven was working, and a group of men did go to work to produce something that at least had some vestiges of thought behind it. There is much of this very strange product now at large; it is generally considered very awful, indeed,—and so it is—but it was the first sincere and enthusiastic work for generations, and demands a word of recognition. Its vivid ugliness is due to the fact that in the space of seventy-five years the last faintest flicker of sense of beauty had vanished from the American citizen; its intensity of purpose bears witness to the sincerity of the men who did it, and I for one would give them praise, not blame.

We are approaching—in our review—another era in the development of our architecture. Let us gather up the many strands in preparation therefor. Here were the "wild and whirling words" of Hunt, Eidlitz, Furness; here is the grave old Gothic of Upjohn's following, Renwick, Congdon, Haight,—admirable, much of it, in little country churches; here is the Ruskinian fold, Cummings, Sturgis, Cabot,—rather Bostonian, you will note; here was the old Classical tradition that had slipped very, very far from the standards of Thornton, Bulfinch, McComb, now flaring luridly in the appalling forms of Mullet's Government buildings, and the Philadelphia City Hall. Let us pursue the subject no further: there were others, but let them be nameless; we have enough to indicate a condition of some complexity and a certain lack of conviction, or even racial unity. Then the Event occurred, and its name was H. H. Richardson. The first great genius in American architecture, he rolled like an æsthetic Juggernaut over the prostrate bodies of his peers and the public, and in ten years we did have substantial unity. We were like the village fireman who didn't care what colour they painted the old tub, so long as they painted her red: we didn't care what our architecture was so long as it was Romanesque. For another ten years we had a love-feast of cavernous arches, quarry-faced ashlar, cyclopean voussoirs and seaweed decorations; village schools, railway stations, cottages,—all, all were of the sacrosanct style of certain rather barbarous peoples in the south of France at the close of the Dark Ages.

And in another ten years Richardson was dead, and his style, which had followed the course of empire to the prairies, and the alkali lands, and the lands beyond the Sierras; and a few years ago I found some of if in Japan! It was splendid, and it was compelling, as its discoverer handled it, but it was alien, artificial, and impossible, equally with the bad things it displaced. But it *did* displace them, and Richardson will be remembered, not as the discoverer of a new style, but as the man who made architecture a living art once more.

Eighteen hundred and ninety, and we start again. Two tendencies are clear and explicit. A new and revivified Classic with McKim as its protagonist, and a new Gothic. The first splits up at once into three lines of development: pure Classic, Beaux Arts, and Colonial, each vital, brilliant, and beautiful in varying degrees. The second was, and remains, more or less one, a taking-over of the late Gothic of England and prolonging it into new fields, sometimes into new beauties. So matters run on for another ten years. At the end of that time the pure Classic has won new laurels for its clean and scholarly beauty; the Beaux Arts following has abandoned much of its banality of French bad taste and has become better than the best contemporary work in France; the neo-Colonial has developed into a living thing of exquisite charm, while the Gothic advance has been no less than that of its Classical rival—or should I say, bedfellow?

And now two new elements enter; steel-frame construction on the one hand, on the other, the secessionist. The steel frame is the *enfant terrible* of architecture, but like so many of the same genus it may grow up to be a serious-minded citizen and a good father. It isn't that now; it is a menace, not only to architecture, but to society, but it is young and it is having its fling. If we can make it realize that it is a new force, not a substitute, we shall do well. When it contents itself in its own proper sphere, and the municipality says kindly but firmly, "Thus far and no farther,"—the "thus far" being about one hundred and twenty-five feet above street level, as in my own wise town of Boston,—then it may be a good servant. Like all good servants it makes the worst possible master; and it claims as its chiefest virtue that it enables us to reproduce the Baths of Caracalla, vaults and all, at half the price, or build a second Chartres Cathedral with no danger from thrusting arches, and with flying buttresses that may be content beautifully to exist, since they will have no other work to do, then it is time to call a halt. The foundation of good architecture is structural integrity, and it does not matter if a building is as beautiful as the Pennsylvania Station in New York; if its columns merely hide the working steel within, if its vast vaults are plaster on steel frame and expanded metal, then it is not architecture, it is scene-painting, and it takes its place with that other scene-painting of the late Renaissance to which we mistakenly apply the name of architecture.

The secessionist—one might sometimes call him Post-Impressionist, Cubist, even—is the latest element to be introduced, and in some ways he is the most interesting. Unlike his *confrères* in Germany, Spain, and Scandinavia, he shows himself little except in minor domestic work—for at heart we *are* a conservative race, whatever individuals may be,—but here he is stimulating. His habitat seems to be Chicago and the Pacific Coast; his governing conviction a strongly developed enmity to archæological forms of any kind. Some of the little houses of the Middle West are striking, quite novel, and inordinately clever; some of the Far Western work, particularly around Pasadena, is exquisite,—no less. Personally I don't believe it is possible wholly to sever one's self from the past and its forms of expression, and it certainly would be undesirable; on the other hand, however, the astute archæology of some of our best modern work, whether Classical or Gothic, is stupefying and leads nowhere. Out of the interplay of these two much of value may arise.

And there you are: three kinds of Classic, two kinds of Gothic, skeleton-frame, and secessionist, all are operative to-day; each with its strong following, each, one admits, consummately clever and improving every day; for there is no architectural retrogression in America; there is steady and startling advance, not only in facility for handling and developing styles, but in that far more important matter, recognition of the fact that styles matter far less than style. From a purely professional standpoint the most encouraging thing is that breadth of culture, that philosophical insight into the essence of things, that liberality of judgment that mark so many of the profession to-day. Gone are the old days of the "Battle of the Styles"; the swords are beaten into pruning-hooks, and these are being used very efficiently in clearing away the thicket of superstitions and prejudices that for so long choked the struggling flower of sound artistic development. The Goth and the Pagan can now meet safely in street or drawing-room without danger of acute disorder; even the structural engineer and the artist preserve the peace (in public); for all have found out that architecture is much bigger than its forms, that the fundamental laws are the same for all good styles, and that the things that count are structural integrity, good taste, restraint, vision, and significance. No one now would claim with the clangour of trumpets that the day of victory was about to dawn for the Beaux Arts, Gothic, or steel-frame styles, or for any other, for that matter; each is contributing something to the mysterious alembic we are brewing, and all we hope is that out of it may come the Philosopher's Stone, that, touching base metal, shall turn it into refined gold—which, by the way, is the proper function of architecture and of all the arts.

Chaos then confronts us, in that there is no single architectural following, but legion; and in that fact lies the honour of our art, for neither is society one, or even at one with itself. Architecture is nothing unless it is intimately expressive, and if utterly different things clamour for voicing, different also must be their architectural manifestation. You cannot build a Roman Catholic or Episcopal church in the Beaux Arts vernacular (it has been done, but it is extremely silly); because the Church is the eternal and fundamentally immutable thing in a world of change and novelty and experiment, and it has to express this quality through the connotation of the forms it developed through a thousand years to voice the fulness of its genius that was developing simultaneously. Neither can you use the steel frame or reënforced concrete to the same ends, though this very sordid wickedness has also been perpetrated, I have grounds for believing. On the other hand, think of using the consummate art of Chartres Cathedral for a railway terminal, or the Ste. Chapelle for a stock exchange, or Haddon Hall for an Atlantic City hotel, or the Ducal Palace in Venice for a department store, or the Erechtheion for a fire-engine house. The case has merely to be stated to be given leave to withdraw, and with it goes for the first time the talk we once heard of an "American Style." Styles come from unity of impulse; styles come from a just and universal estimate of comparative values; styles come where there is the all-enveloping influence and the vivid stimulus of a clear and explicit and compelling religious faith; and these occur, not at the moment of wild confusion when one epoch of five centuries is yielding to another, but after the change in dynasty has been effected, and the new era has begun its ascending course. The only premeditated architecture I know, the only style that was deliberately devised and worked out according to preconceived ideas,—the style of the Renaissance,—was yet not half so artificial as it looks (and as some of us would like to think), for in a sense it was inevitable, granting the postulates of the humanists and the flimsy dogmas of the materialists of the fifteenth century. It did not develop insensibly and instinctively like Hellenic and Byzantine and Gothic and Chinese Buddhist art,—the really great arts in history,—but once the great parabola of mediæval civilization curved downward to its end, once Constantinople fell, something of the sort was not to be escaped.

Now I do not feel that we shall be content with an art of the scope of that of the Renaissance; I do not feel that we shall be content with a new epoch of civilization on Renaissance lines. . . .

Reduced to its simplest terms, our architecture is seen to have had two epochs; the first the attempted conservation of a definite style which, whatever its genesis, had become an essential part of our racial character, and its complete disappearance exactly at the time when the serious and conservative nature of the people of the United States gave place, with almost equal suddenness, to a new quality born partly of political independence, partly of new and stimulating natural conditions, partly of the back-wash from Continental revolution, and above all of the swift working-out, at last, of powers latent in the Renaissance-Reformation itself. Second, the confused activities of many men of many minds, who had cut loose from tradition become moribund, and who were in the position of the puppy sent by express, whose destination could not be determined because, as the expressman said, he "had eat his tag." Communal interests, the sense of solidarity inherited from the Middle Ages (which gives us the true pattern of the only possible socialism) persisting in strange new forms even through the Renaissance epoch itself, had yielded to a crescent individualism, and architecture, like a good art, followed close to heel.

This is really all there is to our architectural history between James-town and Plymouth Rock at one end, and syndicalism and the Panama Ex-position at the other, and I have used many words in saying what might have been expressed in a sentence. The old solidarity in life which expressed itself for four thousand years in a succession of quite distinct, but always sequent, styles died out at last, and the new individualism of pigeonhole society and personal followings came in. What lies before us? More pigeon-holes, more personal followings, more individualism, with anarchy at the end? I do not think so, but rather exactly the reverse. Architecture, I insist, is always expressive; sometimes it reveals metaphysical and biological truth, when in itself there is no truth whatever.

. . . Can we, from what we are doing to-day, predict anything of the future? Not of our future style; that will be what our society makes it; but of society itself? For my own part, I think we can. To me all that we are doing in architecture indicates the accuracy of the deduction we draw from myri-ad other manifestations, that we are at the end of an epoch of materialism, rationalism, and intellectualism, and at the beginning of a wonderful new epoch, when once more we achieve a just estimate of comparative values; when material achievement becomes the slave again, and no longer the slave-driver; when spiritual intuition drives mere intellect back into its prop-er and very circumscribed sphere; and when religion, at the same time dog-matic, sacramental, and mystic, becomes, in the ancient and sounding phrase, "One, Holy, Catholic, and Apostolic," and assumes again its rightful place as the supreme element in life and thought, the golden chain on which are strung, and by which are bound together, the varied jewels of action.

Everywhere, and at the very moment when our material activity and our material triumphs seem to threaten the high stars, appear the evidences that this wonderful thing is coming to pass, and architecture adds its modi-cum of proof. What else does it mean, that on every hand men now demand in art better things than ever before and get them, from an ever increasing number of men, whether they are Pagans, Goths, or Vandals? What is the meaning of the return to Gothic, not only in form, but "in spirit and in truth"? Is it that we are pleased with its forms and wearied of others? Not at all. It is simply this, that the Renaissance-Reformation-Revolution having run its course, and its epoch having reached its appointed term, we go back, deliberately, or instinctively,—back, as life goes back, as history goes back, to restore something of the antecedent epoch, to win again something we had lost, to return to the fork in the roads, to gain again the old lamps we credulously bartered for new. Men laugh (or did; I think they have given it over of late) at what they call the reactionary nature and the affectation of the Gothic restoration of the moment, and they would be right if it meant what they think it means. Its significance is higher than their estimate, high-er than the conscious impulses of those who are furthering the work, for back of it all lies the fact that what we need to-day in our society, in the State, in the Church, is precisely what we abandoned when, as one man, we arose to the cry of the leaders and abettors of the Renaissance. We lost much, but we gained much; now the time has come for us to conserve all that we gained of good, slough off the rest, and then gather up once more the priceless heritage of mediævalism, so long disregarded.

And that is what the Gothic restoration means, a returning to other days—not for the retrieving of pleasant but forgotten forms, but for the recovery of those impulses in life which made these forms inevitable. Do you think the Pugins in England in the early part of the nineteenth century chose to build Gothic churches because they liked the forms better than those of the current Classic then in its last estate? Not at all, or at all events, not primarily; but rather because they passionately loved the old Catholic religion that voiced itself in these same churches they took as their models. And the same is true of those of us who build Gothic churches to-day: instinctively we revolt from the strange religion that, under Medici and Borgia, built the Rococo abominations of Italy, and equally from that other religion that found adequate self-expression in the barren meeting-houses of Puritan England and America; and when again we try to restore to our colleges, as at Princeton and the University of Pennsylvania and Chicago and Bryn Mawr, something of the wonderful dynamic architecture of Oxford and Cambridge and Eton and Winchester, we do it far less because we like the style better than that—or rather those—of Columbia and Harvard and Yale, than because we are impelled to our course by an instinctive mental affiliation with the impulses behind the older art and with the cultural and educational principles for which they stand.

I want to emphasize this point very fully: the Gothic restoration is neither a fad nor a case of stylistic predilections. Of course, we like it better than any of the others to which we have any shadow of right, and we think it better art than anything the Renaissance ever produced; but back of this is either a clear conviction or a dim instinct (one is as good as the other as an incentive) that the power that expressed itself through Gothic forms was a saner and more wholesome and altogether nobler thing than that which expressed itself through the art of the Renaissance and all that has succeeded it. In other words, the world is coming to realize something of the significances of art, and its import as human language, not spoken,—for the audible tongue has its own function of expressing mental concepts,—but conveying its message symbolically, and to the imagination, the intuition—if you like, to the soul.

. . . To some of us it [the word "Gothic"] is like an oriflamme, a standard set up by the king for the rallying of loyalty: the fiery cross of Constantine with its prophetic legend, "By this sign conquer!" Whether we know it or not,—and some of us act by instinct rather than conviction,—we are fighting the battles of a new civilization, which, like all true civilization, is also the old. And it is for this very reason that, unlike our forebears of the beginnings of the crusade, we cannot urge our Gothic as either a universal style, fitted for all conceivable purposes, or as a final thing which consists in the restoration and perpetuation of a mode of art sufficiently determined in the Middle Ages, as Greek, for example, was determined in the Hellenic epoch. Let me say a word on these two points.

The argument—one might almost say the passionate prayer—for a "National Style" is based on an insufficient apprehension of the premises. A national style implies unity of civilization, such, for instance, as happened in the fourth century B.C., the fourth century A.D. in the Eastern Empire, or the thirteenth century throughout Christian Europe: such a condition does not exist to-day—is as far from existence as then it was near. This twentieth century is like a salad dressing: composed of two opposite ingredients which, nevertheless, assembled in unstable equilibrium, produce a most interesting and even useful condiment. On the one hand, we have all the amazing precedents of the last four centuries, from materialism, intellectualism, atheism, and democracy to "big business," syndicalism, and "Votes for Women"; on the other, we have an inheritance from alien and far-distant times: the Home (as distinguished from the uptown flat), the School (when it has not surrendered to manual, vocational, and business training), and the Church, in its ancient aspect, untouched by rationalism, the social club idea, and emotional insanity. There are infinite ramifications of each branch, but the branches are distinct, and like a trunk grafted with apples and roses (I believe this may be done), the flowers are different, and the fruit. Now, as I have said before (and as my hour prolongs itself more strenuously maintain), art is expressive, the highest voicing of the highest things, and if it has two opposites to make manifest it must be true to each and express them in different ways. I do not know what may be the exact and perfect architectural expressions of Wall Street, yellow journalism, commercial colleges, the Structural Steel Union, Christian Science, and equal suffrage: I dare say they are, or may be made, as beautiful as Hellenic or Byzantine or Buddhist architecture; but I am reasonably sure they are not like any of these, and I am firmly persuaded that they cannot be Gothic in any form. On the other hand, as I think I have said before, I am equally sure that a Christian home, a conscientious and high-minded university, and the Catholic Faith are not to be put forward in the sight of men clothed in the Rococo raiment of a Medici-Borgia masquerade or the quaint habiliments of the École des Beaux-Arts.

"Every man to his taste," and to each category of human activity its own stylistic expression, for each has its own and nothing is gained by a confusion of categories. Because, we will say, the art of Imperial Rome best expresses the spirit and the function of a metropolitan railway station, it does not follow that it must also be used for the library of a great university; because the soul of the École des Beaux-Arts as made manifest through the apartment houses of the Boulevard Raspail, must also inspire the material form of the town house of a "Captain of Industry," it need not inevitably perform the same function in the case of a cathedral; because Gothic of some sort or other best reveals the lineage, the impulse, and the law of an Episcopal parish church, we are not compelled to postulate it for a stock exchange or a department store. In fact, the very reverse is true in all these instances, and those who are most zealous in urging the cause of Gothic for church and school and home are also most jealous of its employment elsewhere; for they know that only those elements in modern civilization which still retain something of the spirit that informed their immediate forebears in the Middle Ages have any right to the forms that spirit created for its own self-expression.

And now, just a word as to these forms themselves, lest you should think, as others have, that the Gothic restoration aims not only at universal sovereignty, but that it is content as well with the restoration as such, aiming to bring back in all its integrity both a dead civilization and its forms. Such an idea would be far from the facts; it is true that at present those that are engaged in the Gothic restoration seldom diverge very far from historical methods and forms. Perhaps the late J. D. Sedding, and George Scott, architect for Liverpool Cathedral, and Leonard Stokes, sometime president of the Royal Institute, diverge farther in this direction; but even they venture but a little way into untrodden paths, while the great majority of practitioners, such as the late George Bodley in England, and Vaughan in America, adhere very closely, indeed, to what has been, adapting it rather than transforming it. This is not because there is anything sacrosanct in these forms and methods, it is not because, as individuals, the men I have named lack either inspiration or power of invention; it is simply because, in the first place, they know that man must not only destroy but restore before he can rebuild, and, in the second place, because they lack the great push behind them of a popular uprising, the incentive of a universal demand, which alone can make individualism creative rather than destructive, dynamic rather than anarchical. This is a fact that is frequently forgotten in categories of activity other than those purely æsthetic, and if in economics, politics, and philosophy men would realize its truth, we should less often be threatened by plausible reforms that are actually deformatory in their character. However this may be, it is certainly so in architecture, and, therefore, we are content at present to restore; for we know that by so doing not only do we regain a body of laws, precedents, and forms that are the only foundation for the superstructure of which we dream, but also because through these very qualities we may, in a measure, establish and make operative again, by analogy and suggestion, those stimuli that in time may react on society itself, transforming it into a new estate, when man will enter into the new spiritual life which will demand a creative and revealing art, such as that of the Middle Ages, and in accordance with law this demand will guarantee the supply.

For art of all sorts is not only expressive, it is also creative: if it is in one sense the flower of a civilization, it is in another the fruit, and in its burgeoning lies also the promise of a new life after the winter of the declining curve is past and the new line begins its ascending course. Bad art—for there is such, though it is a contradiction in terms—works powerfully for bad living and bad thinking, while, on the other hand, good art is in its very nature regenerative and beneficent. It cannot save the age of which it is the flower from inevitable decay, but, even as the treasures of classical civilization were preserved in the monasteries of the Dark Ages until better days, so does it lie fallow for generations only to rise again into the light for the inception of a new civilization.

This, then, is the significance of the contemporary Gothic restoration, and we who believe in it, who give it our most earnest support, do so less as artists than as missionaries, confident that if we can bring it back, even at first on the old lines, we shall have been working in the service of humanity.

Shall we rest there? Shall we restore a style, and a way of life, and a mode of thought? Shall we re-create an amorphous mediævalism and live listlessly in that fool's paradise? On the contrary. When a man finds himself confronting a narrow stream, with no bridge in sight, does he leap convulsively on the very brink and then project himself into space? If he does he is very apt to fail of his immediate object, which is to get across. No; he retraces his steps, gains his running start, and clears the obstacle at a bound. This is what we architects are doing when we fall back on the great past for our inspiration; this is what, specifically, the Gothicists are particularly doing. We are getting our running start, we are retracing our steps to the great Christian Middle Ages, not that there we may remain, but that we may achieve an adequate point of departure; what follows must take care of itself.

And, by your leave, in following this course we are not alone, we have life with us; for at last life also is going backward, back to gather up the golden apples lost in the wild race for prizes of another sort, back for its running start, that it may clear the crevasse that startlingly has opened before it. Beyond this chasm lies a new field, and a fair field, and it is ours if we will. The night has darkened, but lightened toward dawn; there is silver on the edges of the hills and promise of a new day, not only for architects, but for every man.

56   Chicago *Tribune* Building
Competition.   *Program and Jury Report* 1925*

The most celebrated design competition in the United States in the early part of this century was that for the Chicago *Tribune*, the "*Tribune* Tower." Because of the $100,000 offered in prize money, a large number of entrants submitted proposals— over 280 entries in all, the majority from the United States but others from Canada, England, Scotland, France, Belgium, Holland, Germany, Austria, Italy, Norway, Hungary, Australia, and the two from Finland highly praised by the jury.[†] Perhaps, too, there were so many entries because of the avowed purpose "to erect the most beautiful and distinctive office building in the world." Seldom if ever had architects been given so free a hand. The jury opted in favor of the more conservative, if consummately detailed, Gothic tower submitted by John Mead Howells and Raymond Hood, loosely patterned after the "Tower of Butter" of Notre Dame in Rouen, France, 1485. The second-place design by Eliel Saarinen, however, ultimately exerted more influence on subsequent high-rise building design, as much so as if it had been built. In one of his last publications, Louis Sullivan emphatically pronounced it far superior to the winning Gothic design.[‡]

---

* *The International Competition for a New Administration Building for the Chicago Tribune MCMXXII Containing All the Designs* . . . (Chicago, 1925), pp. 17–18, 37–47.

† The original publication of drawings has been reprinted in facsimile (New York, 1980).

‡ See Louis H. Sullivan, "The Chicago Tribune Competition," *Architectural Record* 53 (February 1923), pp. 151–57.

PROGRAM OF THE COMPETITION

The Chicago Tribune proposes to erect an office building upon its North Michigan Avenue property for the housing of its executive and business departments, the project to include enlarged quarters for the steadily expanding departments now operating in the Plant Building. The new structure will be erected directly in front of the Plant with a frontage of 100 feet along Michigan Boulevard, and will become the headquarters of this great city newspaper. In addition to ample facilities for present operations, the building will be adaptable to the future expansion of all departments.

To erect the most beautiful and distinctive office building in the world is the desire of The Tribune, and in order to obtain the design for such an edifice, this competition has been instituted. In opening the competition, The Chicago Tribune is following a well-recognized method of procedure and is being guided by the recommendations and usage of the American Institute of Architects as outlined in the Standard Form of Competition Program.

The Competition will be of international scope, qualified Architects of established reputation in all parts of the world being eligible, and not more than ten (10) Architects or firms of Architects of repute in the United States will be specially invited to submit designs. The names of the specially invited competitors will be announced simultaneously with the publication of the Program of the Competition. Architects wishing to submit designs under the general invitation shall file their applications and credentials mentioned hereinafter, on or before October 1, 1922. At that time the full list of Competitors will be available. Each of the specially invited Architects will be compensated to the extent of $2,000, but no compensation other than the opportunity to win one of the prizes shall be available to the Competitors who participate under the general invitation.

The ten best designs selected from those submitted in response to the general invitation shall be given equal consideration with the designs of the specially invited Competitors. Final judgment upon the twenty or less designs will then be made by the Jury of Award, whereupon cash prizes will be awarded as follows:

For the winning design, an award of	$50,000
For the design placed second	20,000
For the design placed third	10,000

It is understood that the winner of the Competition if properly qualified shall be engaged by the Owner as Architect for the building, and that the above-mentioned $50,000 awarded for the winning design shall be included as a part of his fee. Should the award result in the selection of a Competitor who in the opinion of the Owner is not properly equipped to execute this commission, the Owner shall pay the cash prize of $50,000 to the said Competitor for the winning design and require him to associate with a qualified Architect of the Owner's selection as hereinafter set forth, and in the event the name of the winning Competitor shall appear upon all plans as "Associate Architect."

After the award the Owner reserves the right to reduce the building size and to make such changes in the "Conditions and Requirements of the Building" (Part IV) as it may consider advisable. However it is understood that these changes are to be made from the drawings submitted in competition without expense to the Owner by the Competitor or Architect selected by the Owner for the execution of the commission, but any expense involved through changes required after proceeding with working drawings and specifications, shall be borne by the Owner. The Architect appointed for the execution of the project shall have the full and usual authority of Architect of the Work during the construction of the building, under and in accordance with the terms of the schedule of charges and the principles of professional practice of the American Institute of Architects. He will be required to enter into a contract of agreement with said Owner in the terms hereinafter stated.

[There follows a list of particulars and conditions: describing the site, indicating that *Tribune* publishers Robert R. McCormick and Joseph M. Patterson had authority to select the winning architect, citing Howard L. Cheney as the author of the building program, listing the jury members (architect Alfred Granger, Colonel Robert R. McCormick, Captain Joseph M. Patterson, Edward S. Beck, and Holmes Onderdonk), requiring a written report from the jury, retaining publication rights of the submitted designs for the *Tribune*, requiring all submissions to remain anonymous but identified by a sealed envelope, listing the mandatory drawings, prescribing the exact method of presentation, and granting all rights of design and supervision of construction to the winning architect.]

REPORT OF THE JURY OF AWARD

The competition for a monumental building conducted by The Chicago Tribune under the auspices of the American Institute of Architects has been something unique in the history of American architecture.

It is the first time that any corporation, civic, commercial or political (and The Tribune as a great newspaper represents all three types) has recognized the importance of a commercial building as a force for beauty and inspiration in the daily life of the average American citizen.

The program for the competition was first prepared by the owners of The Tribune and then submitted to the Committee on Competitions of the A.I.A. at the fifty-fifth annual convention of the Institute, and after some modifications had been made, was unanimously approved by the Committee on Competitions and announced to the profession by President Kendall as the last official act of his administration, at the banquet given to the convention held in the famous Palace of Fine Arts of the World's Columbian Exposition on June 9, 1922.

It seemed most fitting that the announcement of what The Tribune proposes to do for the improvement of American commercial architecture should be made under the dome of the beautiful building which the American Institute of Architects is trying to preserve for the inspiration of future generations because The Tribune has been foremost in abetting the A.I.A. in this most laudable purpose.

The Tribune specially invited ten architects of established reputation to

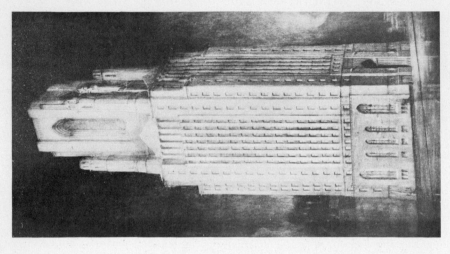

Figure 57. Holabird & Roche, third prize winning entry, Tribune Tower competition, Plate 20 from *International Competition . . .*

Figure 56. Howells & Hood, winning entry, Tribune Tower competition, 1922, Plate 1 from *International Competition for a New Administration Building for the Chicago Tribune . . .*, Chicago, 1925.

submit designs for their proposed Administration Building and at the same time extended a general invitation to the architects of the world to enter the competition.

The prizes offered were so large and the requirements of the competition so simple (in the way of drawings asked for) and the conditions regulating the final judgment so absolutely fair that it was hoped many architects would feel inspired to enter. That hope has been realized with notable results. Of the 189 designs submitted, 54 were from foreign countries, 135 from architects from all over the United States.

The Jury has spent many hours in careful study of plans, elevations, sections and perspective drawings before attempting to arrive at any decision. Greatest care has been taken to literally follow the mandatory conditions of the program, and because of non-compliance with these conditions, a number of drawings were necessarily eliminated from the competition, among those being design No. 60, submitted by one of the architects specially invited.

After daily examination of the drawings by the Jury of Award, individually and collectively, a first ballot was taken among the jury on November 13th, the results of which were—

First prize	design No. 69
Second prize	design No. 90
Third prize	design No. 104

On November 21st the Advisory Committee, consisting of representatives from the Chicago City Council, the Chicago City Plan Commission and the North Central Association, submitted to the Jury of Award the following report of their study of the drawings:

Dear Sirs:

The Advisory Committee, after a careful and exhaustive investigation of the 167 beautiful designs submitted you in connection with the Architectural Competition for an Administration Building for The Chicago Tribune, beg to make the following report of our findings:

The designs we have selected are numbered thus:

47	104	151
78	18	83
90	72	23
69	111	141

We have made these selections without knowing the identity of any of the competitors, and the numbers were selected without preference, and we regret that many meritorious designs could not be considered because the Architect did not comply with the mandatory requirements contained in the program.

The Committee further reports that many of the plans submitted expressed the highest ideal in architectural design and the Committee believes that the selection of any one of the numbers herewith presented would be a credit to Chicago, Michigan Avenue and The Tribune.

We wish to express our appreciation to The Tribune for the opportunity of having a part in this great undertaking.

Yours very truly,

(signed) B. M. Winston
Chairman

Figure 58. (*left*) Bertram Grosvenor Goodhue, honorable mention design in Tribune Tower competition, Plate 97 from *International Competition* . . .

Figure 59. Adolf Loos, entry in Tribune Tower competition, Plate 106 from *International Competition* . . . Although this seems to contradict Loos's avowed elimination of ornament, the entry portico is similar to that in Loos's Goldman & Salatsch Building, Vienna, 1910, while the gigantic Doric column alludes to late work for Stanford White and especially the huge Doric column of the Perry Memorial, Put-in-Bay, Lake Erie, 1911–15, by Freedlander & Seymour.

As the date for the reception of drawings from foreign competitors had been placed one month later than for American drawings because of difficulties in transportation, no final decision could be arrived at before December 1st.

On November 27th a second secret ballot of the jury was taken. Between these two ballots fifty foreign designs had been received, but the result of the second ballot was exactly the same as the first, namely 69, 90 and 104 for 1st, 2d and 3d places, respectively.

On the morning of November 29th, a consignment from Finland was received, which, when opened disclosed two designs of such astonishing merit that the Jury had been in almost constant session from November 29th until the morning of December 1st.

The final decision, arrived after exhaustive study of the three designs chosen on the first and second ballots and design No. 187, one of the designs in the Finnish consignment was:

First prize	No. 69
Second prize	No. 187
Third prize	No. 90

The Jury was absolutely of one mind in the awarding of the 1st and 2d prizes.

For the 3d prize there was a difference of opinion, four voting for No. 90, and one, the Chairman of the Jury, for No. 104.

In view of the fact that the majority vote for No. 90 as third prize winner was so overwhelming the minority voter at once withdrew his vote and moved that the decision of the award be made unanimous.

Of the designs submitted and complying in every way with the mandatory conditions of the program, 25 are of such unusual merit that the Jury feels that any one of these would fulfill The Tribune's desire to erect the most beautiful office building in the world. That out of these 25 designs, 3 should have stood out from the first as having such surpassing merit, that they held first place with the Jury until the arrival of the design from Finland on practically the last day of the competition is indicative of the fairness of the final decision.

Had not design No. 187 been of such unusual beauty and shown such a remarkable understanding of the requirements of an American office building as to compel its being awarded second place on its self-evident merit the final and first ballots of the Jury would have remained the same.

In the Architectural profession this competition has, for six months, been of paramount interest and its influence upon the American mind towards the profession of Architecture will last for generations.

The program of the competition repeatedly states that the main desire on the part of The Tribune is to create a building of surpassing beauty. Never before has the "quality of beauty" been recognized as of commercial value by an American business corporation, and yet all the greatest architecture of the past has been based upon beauty as its fundamental essential. To the trained architect the quality of beauty in plan and in the design as expressing the plan has always been the goal to be striven for. Let us hope that the results of The Tribune Competition may impress this essential upon the mind of American business so emphatically that the whole aspect of our

American cities may be permanently influenced thereby.

One gratifying result of this world competition has been to establish the superiority of American design. Only one foreign design stands out as possessing surpassing merit, and this truly wonderful design did not come from France, Italy or England, the recognized centers of European culture, but from the little northern nation of Finland.

The two Finnish designs express a unity of composition, a grasping of the problem as a whole, which was not achieved by any of the other foreign competitors nor by any of the American ones, but this unity of composition and truthful expression of the plan have been qualities which have brought about the unanimous decision of the Jury.

When the winning design is executed we feel that the judgment of the Jury will be more than justified and The Tribune amply compensated for what it has done to elevate Commercial Architecture into the realm of the Fine Arts and create for its own administrative headquarters the most beautiful office building in the world to date, a fitting monument to the pioneer newspaper of the great middle west.

Respectfully submitted,

Alfred Granger
Chairman of
Jury of Award

The Automobile—Its Province and Problems   *1924*

In the years just before and after the First World War, European visionaries such as Paul Scheerbart called for a reformation of society through architecture—in his case an architecture entirely of colored glass; if other utopians favored different means, their goals were identical with Scheerbart's.* This idealism was not to be transported to the United States until the arrival of émigrés such as Mies van der Rohe, but in the United States an even more sweeping social transformation was being wrought by the impact of industrial mass production, not of structural steel and plate glass, but of private automobiles. The gasoline-fueled internal combustion engine had been developed in France in 1860 and then used to power small vehicles by Daimler and Benz in Germany; in the United States George B. Seldon filed patent papers for an "improved road engine" in 1879 but then built nothing; eventually (by 1895), practical but expensive automobiles were produced by Ransom E. Olds and the Duryea brothers. The next year, Henry Ford built his

---

*See Kenneth Frampton, *Modern Architecture: A Critical History* (New York, 1980), chapter 13; Scheerbart's essay, "*Glasarchitektur*," is translated in part in Ulrich Conrads, *Programs and Manifestoes on 20th Century Architecture* (Cambridge, Mass.), pp. 32–38.

first machine, but his output was overshadowed by the scores upon scores of producers who were hand building cars. Even the large companies which soon emerged, such as Buick and Cadillac, emphasized the diversity of their products. The Ford Motor Company, organized in 1903, however, began to focus on a single model. Progressing through a series of modifications named by going through the alphabet, Ford settled in 1908 on the Model T. Not only were Ford's cars inexpensive, made affordable through financing to wage earners and farmers, but, because of precision mass production on the moving assembly line, they performed as well as or better than hand-built expensive cars.[†]

The result, after fifteen years of production, is demonstrated by the special issue of the *Annals of the American Academy of Political and Social Science* (November 1924), from which the following two selections are taken. Fifty-three articles covered a broad range of issues, including the automobile industry as an industry, the growth of the trucking industry, driving as a leisure activity, the accompanying growth of roadside camps and concern for the purity of drinking water, the appearance of the mobile library van, the use of automobiles in transporting school children, the impact of the automobile on the urban church and rural church, the growing use of billboard advertising, highway design and financing, traffic violations, the impact of the automobile on urban planning, and (a continuing problem) the development of the foreign oil policy of the United States. In a foreword, editor Clyde L. King observed: "the automobile is revolutionizing American life and American industry. The gas-driven machine has brought an era as distinct and creative as that brought by steam." He pointed out that of the eighteen million cars and trucks then existing, fifteen million were in use in the United States. He continued:

> Not a phase of American life, not even her humor, has been untouched by the automobile. The home, the school, the church; recreation, production, distribution; agriculture, advertising, plant location; legislation, highway safety, the court; city planning, public expenditures, international problems—all have felt the driving power of the automobile and the motor truck.

[†] See James J. Flink, *America Adopts the Automobile, 1895–1910* (Cambridge, Mass., 1970), and his *The Car Culture* (Cambridge, Mass., 1975); James B. Rae, *The American Automobile, A Brief History* (Chicago, 1965).

57 J. F. Harbeson, The Automobile and the "Home" of the Future*

We are still apt to think of home as an individual house—detached, as the realtors say, or at least semi-detached—with its own yard and garden, at any rate with a space for children to play in; having a dining room on the first floor as well as a living room, pantry and kitchen; and above stairs a spare room and a store room as well as the bedrooms of the family, these latter still ample in size.

Modern Living Destroys the Home

However, if we make a survey of housing today, we find this picture represents but a small proportion of this element and that proportion is decreasing each year. Housing is tending to change in several ways, the extreme being the efficiency apartment, "all front and no back." This usually contains a living room, which becomes at other times dining room or bedroom by means of various ingenious folding devices, there being in addition to this room of all purposes only a small and compact bath and a likewise small and compact kitchenette, or possibly only a closet space in which are placed a gas stove, refrigerator and sink with ingenious racks and drawers for supplies and utensils. This type of home houses a small percentage of the population as yet, but is one which is growing yearly.

In between these two extremes are various types of housing, ranging up the line of compactness and so-called efficiency, but becoming more materialistic and less sentimental as they grow more compact and efficient.

This progressive change in housing has of course been caused by like changing conditions of the life of present-day civilization. As a people we were originally simple in our tastes and demands, perhaps because we did not know of anything else. We are become luxury-loving, pleasure-seeking, less placid and more nervous. Luxuries and pleasures cost money. Large rooms and detached houses cost money—more of course than before—because the workmen who build them are paid higher wages than formerly, they, too, demanding their share of the luxuries and comforts, and therefore the money that makes these possible. As a people we are choosing the smaller rooms, the pleasures and excitements, and the expensive comforts. We are spending money on a number of things our grandfathers did not have: a bath to each bedroom—this is certainly the tendency; a heat of more than 70 degrees throughout the winter; running hot water, day or night, and in quantity; excitement at meals—music; and our pleasures have become expensive: theatre tickets now costing what would have been within the memory of man a week's wages of a laborer. Even our attempts at physical well-being cost money, it being essential that we wear the proper sports attire, and these always of the latest model.

*John F. Harbeson, "The Automobile and the 'Home' of the Future," *American Academy of Political and Social Science Annals*, 116 (November 1924), 58–60. John F. Harbeson taught in the School of Fine Arts, University of Pennsylvania.

In addition to the demands of modern life already mentioned is the automobile, which is sometimes a convenience, sometimes a means of recreation, but in either case has a considerable effect on present day living. It is an expense, as are the other luxuries of modern life, and somewhere in the budget of the motorist must be found an average of $500 yearly for running charges, taking no account of depreciation. In reducing the proportion of one's earnings which can be spent for so many square feet of home, the automobile has therefore been an additional cause.

The automobile has also had another effect on modern housing. As cities have become crowded there has of course been a tendency to spread. Within the past this has been stopped by the limits which one could ordinarily walk to and from the nearest means of transportation. This has meant that suburbs have grown in a thin line along the railroads and in clusters around the ends of such electric railway lines as went beyond the city limits. The growth of the automobile industry and the enormous production, which has so lessened the first cost of these machines as to tempt a large proportion of the population to invest in them, have caused an ever-increasing number of suburbs to be built, of which the principal means of communication with the towns about which they cluster, and from which they largely derive their means of support, is the automobile.

Along with its use as a means of transportation is of course the everpresent pleasure of being skipper of one's own ship and spending one's time in the fresh air. It is natural, therefore, that we are gradually drifting to the general opinion that ample rooms are of small importance, as we spend so much time out of them. When we realize that this process is hastened by other economic factors such as the diminution in the supply of efficient house servants, which causes those that are available to be increasingly expensive, and which likewise causes the servantless multitudes to eat the majority of their meals in restaurants or other public hostelries, we see that the change in the composition of the home is one that has come to stay.

At present there is in almost all of these suburban houses a garage, built either in the basement or at the back of the property. It is a question whether this is a tendency we can consider as permanent. With the still greater increase in the use of the automobile and the increasing modern tendency to do away with all replacement and buy a new machine rather than repair the old—therefore causing us to take much less trouble about keeping the old in good condition—it is quite probable that a neighborhood garage will take the place of these individual store spaces, it being more convenient in many ways and less expensive, considering the service rendered. . . .

58 J. Ihlder, The Automobile and Community Planning*

The automobile found us in our customary frame of mind, resentful of an innovation which interfered with established habits. From the day when the drivers of horses cursed an occasional devil wagon to the present, when crowds of pedestrians, many of them car owners themselves, denounce the delays and hazards at busy crossings, our attitude has been negative. Probably if we had realized back in 1900 just how drastic are the changes which the automobile is forcing upon us we would have organized a crusade against it. For our lack of imagination, instead of being the handicap we usually consider it, is probably one of the chief factors in our progress; it gives us the courage or the indifference of ignorance.

But we have now reached a point where we can no longer progress backwards, seeking means of keeping things as nearly as possible as they were in the days of our fathers. Suppression has become the dream of a fanatic. We find it difficult to remember even back to the time when it was not good form to go to church in an automobile—the very thought suggests all manner of irrelevancies—and when our feelings were outraged by the sight of an automobile at a funeral. And now regulation is proving a broken reed. So we have got to turn about and face a future in which adequate provision will be made for automobiles. This involves a revision of our practice in city building.

Dreams in City Building and Results

For centuries our cities have been closely built. An occasional Utopian dreamed of green and spacious cities, an even more occasional one sought to create them. William Penn had a vision of city dwellings set among green gardens and orchards. Yet before the Liberty Bell rang out its message his city had become red with its solid rows of brick houses. Washington and L'Enfant had the vision when they planned the Federal City and sought to safeguard it by making wide, tree-lined avenues. Today, behind the building lines of private property the federal city is almost as overcrowded with buildings as is Philadelphia, and proposals to cut down street trees and widen roadways are constantly being advanced.

This tendency to over-build has its root in the human desires for a minimum of effort, for conveniences, for companionship. When Benjamin Franklin first walked into Philadelphia, every step counted. Even in his later days when he could drive, distance was a matter to take into serious account. But the dream persisted. The mass of men had caught the vision of the Utopians and desired more spacious cities. Because of that dream they welcomed rapid transit—horse cars, elevated railroads, trolleys, subways—believing that each of these would make the dream come true. On the strength of the dream they made a radical change in their manner of life. More and

*John Ihlder, "The Automobile and Community Planning," *American Academy of Political and Social Science Annals*, 116 (November 1924), pp. 199–205. John Ihlder was manager of the Civic Development Department, U.S. Chamber of Commerce.

more those who could afford it deserted the dwelling above the store or beside the printing office and set up their homes at a distance made accessible by the new means of transit. So our cities spread out.

But each of these means of transit had its counter effect. As it made the suburbs more accessible from the center of town, so it made the center of town more accessible from suburbs and what had once been distant communities. Consequently more and more people came in to the center to do their shopping, to attend the theaters, to consult their lawyers. And to serve these buyers, patrons, clients, more people were employed in the center of town, people whose hours of work or scale of pay made it inconvenient for them to live at a distance from their places of employment. So we had, as on the lower East Side of New York, constantly more numerous, more rapid, more expensive and more *crowded* means of transit provided in order that the workers of Manhattan might live in the green fields of the Bronx and Flatbush—fields and green when the means of transit were first provided, but quite different now—while at the same time the population of the thronging East Side increased steadily and rapidly. The dream did not come true.

Then city planning in its modern phase began. It had run true to form in its development. It looked backward for its inspiration. It saw Old World civic centers that put our haphazard locating of public buildings to shame. It saw broad boulevards which added to the dignity of cities. So we started out to beautify. We again began to dream and in some places this dream is coming true. Cleveland is about to realize its dream after some two decades of effort and fighting. Denver has realized its dream. So has Des Moines. In other cities there is progress and promise.

With achievement our dream became more magnificent. From civic centers and a few great boulevards we advanced to visions of park systems with connecting parkways. We drew plans which included not only the whole city, but much of the surrounding country. And again some of our dreams are coming true. Chicago, in the generation since the World's Fair, has educated its electorate to support the magnificent city plan that is now gradually taking form. Cleveland and other progressive cities are expanding their vision and giving it form.

Increasing Congestion and Efforts to Avert

But so far we followed traditional lines. Except where parks or water or steep hills interfered, our cities grew solidly, the more open suburban developments swallowed by advancing rows of buildings. And behind these rows came skyscrapers, most numerous in the center of town but sporadically shooting up in other sections.

It was the skyscrapers that finally aroused us and forced us to realize that ancient and medieval and even modern Old World examples, though supplemented by rapid transit, do not give us all we need, that we must do some thinking for ourselves. Old time habits of concentrating nearly all the business life of the community were producing conditions that mean constant loss. High buildings crowded closely together darken each other's windows, cut off each other's air, turn streets into sunless canyons inadequate to carry the traffic demanded by the abutting population. Rapid transit instead of solving the problem has intensified it. Now comes the automobile.

The first obvious effects of the automobile's arrival are in our streets. These streets are crowded to a degree of which their dedicators could not conceive. Their death and casualty lists exceed those of battle fields. But— much more important from the point of view of securing action—their inadequacy hampers us in our daily life. We are continually annoyed and handicapped by the steady procession of cars that holds us chafing on the curb, or we are prevented from leaving our car where we wish to alight because someone else has already parked there. Our first and natural impulse is to widen the streets. Every day in every city there is discussion of the pros and cons of street widening, either by setting back the abutting buildings, or, as a less expensive compromise, narrowing the sidewalks and so securing more space for roadway.

Evidently such remedies as these, taken up piece-meal, are mere temporary palliatives. Any practicable increase of street or road width is immediately filled with more automobiles and the *status quo ante* is restored. So we have reluctantly begun to realize that we must be more thoroughgoing in our search for a remedy, must even examine anew some of our most firmly established practices in city building. This brings us face to face with what seems to be the fact, that the automobile differs from our former methods of rapid transit in that it demands a good deal of space for itself. Instead of enabling us to crowd more people into a given area, it is forcing us to diminish the density of population. The alternatives seem to be, either fewer people per square foot or fewer automobiles. Assuming what again appears to be the fact, that we shall elect to have *more* automobiles, the problem is squarely before us.

Following our natural bent as an ingenious people who delight in complicated and expensive contrivances for getting things that nature is ready to give us for nothing—such as light and air which we first build out and then force in—supplemented by our tendency to the spectacular, some of our cities are proposing to double-deck their streets or to dig automobile subways. Of course the recent experience of Pittsburgh with its suffocating tunnel is not to be taken as a warning against such projects if they are really necessary. This merely demonstrated that there are technical problems still to be solved, problems relating to the automobile as well as to the tunnel; for the automobile should not give off deadly gasses whether it is in a tunnel or on the open street. The real argument against these proposals is that when they have been carried to triumphant completion, we shall be in the same situation that we are now, with an added tax burden.

A dim realization of the futility of such proposals is making us begin to ask some questions. For example, what is the most efficient width of roadway in terms of number of traffic lanes? Most of us, accustomed to rather narrow streets packed to capacity, now believe that widening will give relief and that "adequate" widening will give "adequate" relief. But some who have lived beside very wide streets with very wide roadways know from experience that they are not only very expensive, increasingly hazardous to pedestrians—for whom isles of safety must be made, so narrowing the effective roadway by a series of bottle-necks—increasingly difficult to police for traffic regulation; but that they are also comparatively inefficient for traffic flow because they tempt drivers to pursue a devious and traffic checking course. If it were not for considerations such as these we might, despite its cost, widen our streets until by the consequent diminution of building sites we had achieved that which we must finally achieve, though it is to be hoped by less costly means, a proper ratio between the carrying capacity of the street and the traffic needs of the people who occupy the abutting buildings.

But this method of winning through attrition is too costly. Before the war could be fought to a conclusion on this basis it is probable that many battlegrounds near the centers of our cities would be deserted by a large part of their population who would move to other and better planned areas. Essentially similar to the proposal for widening streets and thereby diminishing abutting building sites, is the proposal to cut new streets through built-up areas. The principal effect is the same, more street area, less building area. But again this is so expensive that there seems little likelihood of its being carried through on an adequate scale. Its advantage is that instead of making roadways inefficently wide, it can make them of the proper width.

So we incline to turn to zoning as offering the most promising way out of our dilemma. If a given bulk of building of a given character—industrial plant, retail store, theatre, apartment house, one-family dwelling—originates a given amount of traffic of given character—heavy trucks, delivery cars, street cars and busses, taxis, private passenger cars, pedestrians—on the abutting street, we have a basis for computing the ratio which should be established between the building bulk and street width or roadway width. If a given roadway width is most efficient for traffic flow we have another factor which can be taken into account. Then we can decide whether to widen the street, to open a new street or to regulate the character and the bulk of abutting buildings. The last seems likely to prove the least expensive and the most effective.

But this, of course, takes account only of the first obvious effect of the automobile's arrival. The picture we have had before our mind's eye so far has been a busy business district with nearly continuous lincs of moving cars. Except for those of us who live or work in the centers of a very few of the largest cities this picture is supplemented by one of even more continuous rows of parked automobiles. In the very few exceptional cities the parked car has almost disappeared downtown where the streets wear a comparatively deserted look to the visitor from a bustling town up state or out west. The revulsion against much too much has thrown them all out, with what effect upon the business of the downtown area is only just beginning to be indicated by stories of firms which have moved to sites where automobile customers can still get at them. This moving of business firms because of traffic congestion is one we must study with some care. Because certain chain stores were located on corners where traffic counts showed the greatest number of pedestrians passing, many of us jumped to the conclusion that these were the most valuable locations for business, or at any rate for retail business. Now because certain stores are moving from the center of town many of us are getting ready to jump to the conclusion that all businesses depend on an automobile trade. This jumping habit saves mental effort, but it does not lead to good city planning.

The Parked Car

The parked car, however, again raises the question of space and of a ratio. First, shall parking space be provided by the city, (a) on its streets, (b) on other public property, and, if so, shall it be provided free or for a fee? Present practice is to provide it free and on the street until the situation becomes intolerable, then to seek other public spaces and perhaps to charge a fee. But except where streets are very wide or where considerable unbuilt-upon areas remain within easy reach of the city center, these expedients promise no adequate relief. New space invites more cars. So we return to the ratio. A given bulk of building of a given character draws to it cars the number and character of which can be fairly definitely determined. Shall the city provide parking space for these cars or shall the building itself make such provision? Shall we widen the street and so diminish the building site, or shall we provide on the building site storage space adequate to meet the needs of its occupants? Indications are that the latter will prove our ultimate policy and that in those sections of the city where populous and expensive buildings cannot be remodeled, either near-by accommodations will be found for the cars of tenants or those sections will find themselves in a losing competition with sections more fortunately situated. In either case density of population will be diminished for the car will displace a human, and the capacity of streets to carry traffic, of private land to shelter both cars and their owners, will tend to set a limit upon land occupancy.

So in new areas, more slowly in old areas as existing buildings are displaced by modern structures, we shall tend to establish an equilibrium between building and street so far as regular occupants of the building are concerned. But additional to the regular occupants are many casuals who visit the building or the district only occasionally. Experience should show how many of these may be expected in an area of a given character. Accuracy of estimate increases with the size of the unit. We can forecast fairly definitely the death rate of a city, but we cannot foretell the death rate among six specified individuals. The casuals visiting a certain office building or retail store may vary considerably from year to year with changes of tenancy, but the casuals visiting a number of office buildings or patronizing a number of stores are more likely to remain nearly constant. It will be a business asset to the district if parking space is provided for them, and such provision may be considered a proper public function, because it affects the general well-being instead of redounding to the continued profit of easily ascertained individuals. Whether this public parking space should be on the street—provided it does not interfere with traffic flow—or on less expensive locations is a question that each community must answer for itself. Were it not that accessible locations off the street are likely to be built up unless secured immediately, the question might be left until moving traffic pushes the parked car off the street. Because of that likelihood the city planner must indicate public parking spaces now.

What Is Happening to Our Streets

While the downtown or business areas we have been discussing constitute the most urgent part of the problem, it is not the only one that has engaged our attention. Almost equally interesting is the arterial highway by which the working population of the city centers speeds to its homes, or along which moves the traffic between separate business districts. These arterial highways are already in existence. Some of them were created for their arterial purpose in accordance with old time city plans, some are merely streets differing from others only in that they afford a more nearly direct through route than do neighboring streets. For them a new definition of an old word has been evolved. They are styled boulevards and traffic on them has right-of-way over traffic on cross streets. Had the city planners and city builders of a decade or more ago clearly foreseen the time when their arteries would be dedicated to automobiles at express speed they might have saved us some expense by avoiding grade crossings. For the elimination of grade crossings, not yet complete along the railway lines, will before long appear as an item of importance in street and highway building.

Another change made by the automobile in once accepted city plans is that a considerable proportion of these through routes or arteries avoid the city center, diverting traffic away from, not toward the business streets. Unless they are successful in this the calculations of those who are figuring ratios between bulk and character of building and street width will be complicated by the necessity of making provision for through traffic which has no purpose in invading the downtown area. We still get an occasional traffic report which rejoices in a showing that prohibition of downtown parking has permitted through traffic to move more smoothly. The parked car had a purpose where it was, the through car came that way to everyone's annoyance merely because no equally good alternative route had been provided.

Away from the center or the centers, branching off from the arteries, are the neighborhood roads, leading to the homes of the community. Here again we face the questions of space and of ratio. One of our newest dreams in city building, made more practicable by the distance-shortening automobile, is that our communities shall no longer be expanding solid masses of brick and stone and paving material. In order to make our vision clearer we have begun to talk planning, not in terms of a city but in terms of a metropolitan area. In that area we picture a considerable number of communities, each more or less self-sufficient, grouped about a metropolitan center which was the old time city. These communities are separated from the center and from each other by broad belts of open land, not parks merely but farms, orchards, truck gardens, woods. With well-paved arterial highways, or perhaps even narrow strips of built-up land crossing them, as old London Bridge with its flanking rows of shops crossed the River Thames, these open spaces mean to the automobilist only five minutes more in the open air. But that is still largely of the future; for while industries and commerce are now establishing the satellite communities we have not yet found a means of preventing them and the parent city from constantly extending their edges over the open area between until they merge as have those of Philadelphia with Kensington, Nicetown, Tacony. So, home neighborhoods for the majority of large-city dwellers still mean rows of houses or apartment buildings connected with their work places by other rows of buildings. In such neighborhoods the ratio must be applied. Especially in apartment house districts has it become necessary to decide for or against street widening and to seek storage space similar to that provided downtown.

Classifying Traffic

To the dweller in these crowded home neighborhoods has become increasingly important the question of segregation or classification of traffic. It is bad enough to have the curb before his house constantly occupied by the cars of strangers, but it is even worse to have his peace disturbed, his house shaken, by heavy lumbering trucks and to have his special assessments increased by bills for repaving the streets those trucks have broken up. Zoning classifies buildings by use, creates districts of distinctive character. City or community planning is called upon to supplement this by providing thoroughfares of like distinction. To build all streets strong enough to carry heavy trucks is extravagance. To pave and repave streets ruined by uses for which they were not designed is folly. To classify traffic and provide for the needs of each class is an economy upon which we are about to enter.

And this again will make for spaciousness in our cities. The cost of a house lot is not so much in the land as in the improvements. A light roadway, the medium priced roadway for which the engineers are now seeking, reduces the cost of the lot. Zoning, which not only determines for a long period the character of a neighborhood but sets a fairly definite limit to its population by determining the height and percentage of lot occupancy of its buildings, makes possible other economies. The size of sewers and water mains as well as the type of paving may be decided upon with some assurance. So space will not mean as it has, an undue burden of cost necessitated by an unprophesiable future.

The speed and flexibility of the automobile—for its owner is not bound to given routes or to a time schedule—makes possible not only greater spaciousness but better planning of new home neighborhoods. The great arterial highways which lead from center to center, the rapid transit lines gradually converted from local to through express routes with lower peaks and higher valleys in their daily schedules, will become boundaries far within which will be placed the schools and recreation places. Children will no longer cross lines of heavy traffic as part of their routine.

The human desires for a minimum of effort, for conveniences, for companionship, are as strong and compelling today as they were in Franklin's day, but the automobile apparently has put them within our reach without our crowding. It is doing more, it is compelling us to cease crowding if we would take full advantage of what it offers. Apparently its arrival will introduce a new era in community planning, or to speak more accurately since we have long *planned* spacious communities, a new era in community building.

59 F. L. Wright, Broadacre City: A New Community Plan* *1935*

Of American architects, the one who most fully recognized the possibilities of the private automobile and attempted to design a city based around it was Frank Lloyd Wright.[†] He had never been entirely sanguine about the American city as he found it, although he designed several projects for high-density urban housing during the period 1895–1915. After returning from Europe in 1911, he considered building a townhouse of his own on Chicago's near north side. His later apartment tower designs for Saint Mark's-in-the-Bowery, New York, and for Chicago, both in 1929–30, and the huge glass National Life Insurance Company project of 1924 were urban in scale, character, and density, but none were built. As these projects failed to materialize, Wright began to examine the basis of the city, arguing that it was too dense and ultimately unhealthy.[‡] A new image of a completely decentralized "city" began to take shape, a nonurban city with houses scattered across the landscape; the individual homes, with about one acre of land for each, would be connected to the decentralized amenities by the automobile. These were lean years for Wright, because those clients who had not turned their backs on him because of the upheavals in his personal life found their ability to build diminished after the Crash of 1929. In 1932 Wright began to gather about him students who paid to live and study at his rebuilt Wisconsin home-studio, and shortly this Taliesin Fellowship of students was put to work constructing a twelve-by-twelve-foot model of this ideal community spread out across the land—"Broad-acre City." Work continued almost round the clock from January through March 1935 in preparation for showing the model at the Industrial Arts Exposition in Rockefeller Center, New York, in April. The article by Wright reprinted here announced the opening of the exhibit. The model was modified slightly and exhibited again in 1940 at the Musuem of Modern Art. In addition to this description of the plan, Wright published in 1943 a fragment, *Book Six, Broadacre City* (Spring Green, Wisc.), intended as a supplement to the *Autobiography*, and in the most recent edition of *An Autobiography* (New York, 1977), this has been incorporated in the body of the text.[§]

Given the simple exercise of several inherently just rights of man, the freedom to decentralize, to redistribute and to correlate the properties of the life of man on earth to his birthright—the ground itself—and Broadacre City becomes reality.

*Frank Lloyd Wright, "Broadacre City: A New Community Plan," *Architectural Record* 77 (April 1935), pp. 243–54.

[†] The planners who best understood both the potential and the threat of the automobile were Clarence Stein and Henry Wright; Stein's collection of essays describing his principal designs, *Toward New Towns for America* (Liverpool, 1951) is still in print.

[‡] Frank Lloyd Wright, *The Disappearing City* (New York, 1932).

[§] See too George R. Collins, "Broadacre City: Wright's Utopia Reconsidered," in *Four Great Makers of Modern Architecture* (New York, 1963), pp. 55–75.

As I see Architecture, the best architect is he who will devise forms nearest organic as features of human growth by way of changes natural to that growth. Civilization is itself inevitably a form but not, if democracy is sanity, is it necessarily the fixation called "academic." All regimentation is a form of death which may sometimes serve life but more often imposes upon it. In Broadacres all is symmetrical but it is seldom obviously and never academically so.

Whatever forms issue are capable of normal growth without destruction of such pattern as they may have. Nor is there much obvious repetition in the new city. Where regiment and row serve the general harmony of arrangement both are present, but generally both are absent except where planting and cultivation are naturally a process or walls afford a desired seclusion. Rhythm is the substitute for such repetitions everywhere. Wherever repetition (standardization) enters, it has been modified by inner rhythms either by art or by nature as it must, to be of any lasting human value.

The three major inventions already at work building Broadacres, whether the powers that over-built the old cities otherwise like it or not are:

(1) The motor car: general mobilization of the human being.

(2) Radio, telephone and telegraph: electrical intercommunication becoming complete.

(3) Standardized machine-shop production: machine invention plus scientific discovery.

The price of the major three to America has been the exploitation we see everywhere around us in waste and in ugly scaffolding that may now be thrown away. The price has not been so great if by way of popular government we are able to exercise the use of three inherent rights of any man:

(1) His social right to a direct medium of exchange in place of gold as a commodity: some form of social credit.

(2) His social right to his place on the ground as he has had it in the sun and air: land to be held only by use and improvements.

(3) His social right to the ideas by which and for which he lives: public ownership of invention and scientific discoveries that concern the life of the people.

The only assumption made by Broadacres as ideal is that these three rights will be the citizen's so soon as the folly of endeavoring to cheat him of their democratic values becomes apparent to those who hold (feudal survivors or survivals), as it is becoming apparent to the thinking people who are held blindly abject or subject against their will.

The landlord is no happier than the tenant. The speculator can no longer win much at a game about played out. The present success-ideal placing, as it does, premiums upon the wolf, the fox and the rat in human affairs and above all, upon the parasite, is growing more evident every day as a falsity just as injurious to the "successful" as to the victims of such success.

Well—sociologically, Broadacres is release from all that fatal "success" which is after all, only excess. So I have called it a new freedom for living in America. It has thrown the scaffolding aside. It sets up a new ideal of success.

In Broadacres, by elimination of cities and towns the present curse of petty and minor officialdom, government, has been reduced to one minor government for each county. The waste motion, the back and forth haul, that today makes so much idle business is gone. Distribution becomes automatic and direct; taking place mostly in the region of origin. Methods of distribution of everything are simple and direct. From the maker to the consumer by the most direct route.

Coal (one third the tonnage of the haul of our railways) is eliminated by burning it at the mines and transferring that power, making it easier to take over the great railroad rights of way; to take off the cumbersome rolling stock and put the right of way into general service as the great arterial on which truck traffic is concentrated on lower side lanes, many lanes of speed traffic above and monorail speed trains at the center, continuously running. Because traffic may take off or take on at any given point, these arterials are traffic not dated but fluescent. And the great arterial as well as all the highways become great architecture, automatically affording within their structure all necessary storage facilities of raw materials, the elimination of all unsightly piles of raw material.

In the hands of the state, but by way of the county, is all redistribution of land—a minimum of one acre going to the childless family and more to the larger family as effected by the state. The agent of the state in all matters of land allotment or improvement, or in matters affecting the harmony of the whole, is the architect. All building is subject to his sense of the whole as organic architecture. Here architecture as landscape takes on the character of architecture by way of the simple process of cultivation.

All public utilities are concentrated in the hands of the state and county government as are matters of administration, patrol, fire, post, banking, license and record, making politics a vital matter to every one in the new city instead of the old case where hopeless indifference makes "politics" a grafter's profession.

In the buildings for Broadacres no distinction exists between much and little, more and less. Quality is in all, for all, alike. The thought entering into the first or last estate is of the best. What differs is only individuality and extent. There is nothing poor or mean in Broadacres.

Nor does Broadacres issue any dictum or see any finality in the matter either of pattern or style.

Organic character is style. Such style has myriad forms inherently good. Growth is possible to Broadacres as a fundamental form: not as mere accident of change but as integral pattern unfolding from within.

Here now may be seen the elemental units of our social structure: The correlated farm, the factory—its smoke and gases eliminated by burning coal at places of origin, the decentralized school, the various conditions of residence, the home offices, safe traffic, simplified government. All common interests take place in a simple coordination wherein all are employed: *little* farms, *little* homes for industry, *little* factories, *little* schools, a *little* university going to the people mostly by way of their interest in the ground, *little* laboratories on their own ground for professional men. And the farm itself, notwithstanding its animals, becomes the most attractive unit of the city. The husbandry of animals at last is in decent association with them and with all else as well. True farm relief.

To build Broadacres as conceived would automatically end unemployment and all its evils forever. There would never be labor enough nor could under-consumption ever ensue. Whatever a man did would be done—obviously and directly—mostly by himself in his own interest under the most valuable inspiration and direction: under training, certainly, if necessary. Economic independence would be near, a subsistence certain; life varied and interesting.

Every kind of builder would be likely to have a jealous eye to the harmony of the whole within broad limits fixed by the county architect, an architect chosen by the county itself. Each county would thus naturally develop an individuality of its own. Architecture—in the broad sense—would thrive.

In an organic architecture the ground itself predetermines all features; the climate modifies them; available means limit them; function shapes them.

Form and function are one in Broadacres. But Broadacres is no finality. The model shows four square miles of a typical countryside developed on the acre as unit according to conditions in the temperate zone and accommodating some 1,400 families. It would swing north or swing south in type as conditions, climate and topography of the region changed.

In the model the emphasis has been placed upon diversity in unity, recognizing the necessity of cultivation as a need for formality in most of the planting. By a simple government subsidy certain specific acres or groups of acre units are, in every generation, planted to useful trees, meantime beautiful, giving privacy and various rural divisions. There are no rows of trees alongside the roads to shut out the view. Rows where they occur are perpendicular to the road or the trees are planted in groups. Useful trees like white pine, walnut, birch, beech, fir, would come to maturity as well as fruit and nut trees and they would come as a profitable crop meantime giving character, privacy and comfort to the whole city. The general park is a flowered meadow beside the stream and is bordered with ranks of trees, tiers gradually rising in height above the flowers at the ground level. A music-garden is sequestered from noise at one end. Much is made of general sports and festivals by way of the stadium, zoo, aquarium, arboretum and the arts.

The traffic problem has been given special attention, as the more mobilization is made a comfort and a facility the sooner will Broadacres arrive. Every Broadacre citizen has his own car. Multiple-lane highways make travel safe and enjoyable. There are no grade crossings nor left turns on grade. The road system and construction is such that no signals nor any lamp-posts need be seen. No ditches are alongside the roads. No curbs either. An inlaid purfling over which the car cannot come without damage to itself takes its place to protect the pedestrian.

In the affair of air transport Broadacres rejects the present airplane and substitutes the self-contained mechanical unit that is sure to come: an aerator capable of rising straight up and by reversible rotors able to travel in any given direction under radio control at a maximum speed of, say, 200 miles an hour, and able to descend safely into the hexacomb from which it arose or anywhere else. By a doorstep if desired.

The only fixed transport trains kept on the arterial are the long-distance monorail cars traveling at a speed (already established in Germany) of 220 miles per hour. All other traffic is by motor car on the twelve lane levels or the triple truck lanes on the lower levels which have on both sides the advantage of delivery direct to warehousing or from warehouses to consumer. Local trucks may get to warehouse-storage on lower levels under the main arterial itself. A local truck road parallels the swifter lanes.

Houses in the new city are varied: make much of fireproof synthetic materials, factory-fabricated units adapted to free assembly and varied arrangement, but do not neglect the older nature-materials wherever they are desired and available. Householders' utilities are nearly all planned in prefabricated utility stacks or units, simplifying construction and reducing building costs to a certainty. There is the professional's house with its laboratory, the minimum house with its workshop, the medium house ditto, the larger house and the house of machine-age-luxury. We might speak of them as a one-car house, a two-car house, and three-car house and a five-car house. Glass is extensively used as are roofless rooms. The roof is used often as a trellis or a garden. But where glass is extensively used it is usually for domestic purposes in the shadow of protecting overhangs.

Copper for roofs is indicated generally on the model as a permanent cover capable of being worked in many appropriate ways and giving a general harmonious color effect to the whole.

Electricity, oil and gas are the only popular fuels. Each land allotment has a pit near the public lighting fixture where access to the three and to water and sewer may be had without tearing up the pavements.

The school problem is solved by segregating a group of low buildings in the interior spaces of the city where the children can go without crossing traffic. The school building group includes galleries for loan collections from the museum, a concert and lecture hall, small gardens for the children in small groups and well-lighted cubicles for individual outdoor study; there is a small zoo, large pools and green playgrounds.

This group is at the very center of the model and contains at its center the higher school adapted to the segregation of the students into small groups.

This tract of four miles square, by way of such liberal general allotment determined by acreage and type of ground, including apartment buildings and hotel facilities, provides for about 1,400 families at, say, an average of five or more persons to the family.

To reiterate: the basis of the whole is general decentralization as an applied principle and architectural reintegration of all units into one fabric; free use of the ground held only by use and improvements; public utilities and government itself owned by the people of Broadacre City; privacy on one's own ground for all and a fair means of subsistence for all by way of their own work on their own ground or in their own laboratory or in common offices serving the life of the whole.

There are too many details involved in the model of Broadacres to permit complete explanation. Study of the model itself is necessary study. Most details are explained by way of collateral models of the various types of construction shown: highway construction, left turns, crossovers, underpasses and various houses and public buildings.

Any one studying the model should bear in mind the thesis upon which the design has been built by the Taliesin Fellowship, built carefully not as a finality in any sense but as an interpretation of the changes inevitable to our growth as a people and a nation.

Individuality established on such terms must thrive. Unwholesome life would get no encouragement and the ghastly heritage left by overcrowding in overdone ultra-capitalistic centers would be likely to disappear in three or four generations. The old success ideals having no chance at all, new ones more natural to the best in man would be given a fresh opportunity to develop naturally.

60   H.-R. Hitchcock and P. Johnson, The International Style* *1932*

The genesis of this small book, which christened the architecture of the twentieth century, is told by Hitchcock himself in a foreword prepared for the reprinting of 1966. In 1931 the fledgling Museum of Modern Art, only two years old and primarily a museum of painting, determined to hold its premier architectural exhibition; director Alfred H. Barr, Jr., asked Philip Johnson and Henry-Russell Hitchcock to prepare the show, in conjunction with which they also wrote *The International Style: Architecture Since 1922*, to be published concurrently with the exhibition in 1932.† Hitchcock, born in 1903, was twenty-eight when work on the project started, and Johnson, born in 1906, was but twenty-five. Both had been educated at Harvard, Hitchcock reading in art history and Johnson in classics. In 1930, following a tour of Europe in which he studied contemporary architecture and met Mies van der Rohe, Johnson had been appointed head of the architecture section of the museum; the year before, Hitchcock had published *Modern Architecture: Romanticism and Reintegration* (New York), establishing his position as a critic and historian of the new architecture of Europe.‡ As Barr points out in the introduction to *The International*

*Henry-Russell Hitchcock and Philip Johnson, *The International Style: Architecture Since 1922* (New York, 1932), pp. 11–39.

†Hitchcock asserts that it was Barr who coined the term "International Style," having been inspired by Gropius's *Internationale Architektur* (Munich, 1925). See his *Architecture: Nineteenth and Twentieth Centuries* 3rd ed. (Baltimore, 1968), p. 468, note 1.

‡Johnson's early architectural criticism, 1931–33, is reprinted in *Philip Johnson: Writings* (New York, 1979). See, too, Hitchcock's autobiographical "Modern Architecture—A Memoir," *Journal, Society of Architectural Historians* 27 (December 1968), pp. 227–33, which ends with the writing of *The International Style*.

Style, the new idiom, so unlike work up to that point in the United States (except for that by a very few émigrés) begged definition; this the young authors set out to do, emphasizing formal and aesthetic properties and giving little attention to purely technical or sociological matters—since they were attempting to outline the distinguishing morphology of this new expression, then just a decade old. A significant portion of the book consisted of plans and photographs of a selection of buildings from across Europe. In the chapters which follow those reprinted here, the authors sketched out the major features of international modernism: architecture as the enclosing of volumes rather than the shaping of masses (facilitated by the use of metal or reinforced concrete frames); the corollary emphasis on thin, stretched wall-membranes of glass or stucco; minimized textures; regularity of cubic form (also encouraged by frame construction); the avoidance of applied decoration; a dimming of the distinction between "high art architecture" and "mere building" (as Ruskin contrasted these terms); free plans in which volumes could be enclosed and isolated or open and continuous; and plans more closely determined by utilitarian functional uses.

PREFACE

Mr. Hitchcock and Mr. Johnson have studied contemporary architecture with something of the scholarly care and critical exactness customarily expended upon Classical or Mediæval periods. This book presents their conclusions, which seem to me of extraordinary, perhaps epoch-making, importance. For they have proven beyond any reasonable doubt, I believe, that there exists today a modern style as original, as consistent, as logical, and as widely distributed as any in the past. The authors have called it the International Style.

To many this assertion of a new style will seem arbitrary and dogmatic. For it has become almost customary among the more serious American and English writers on modern architecture to conclude their essays by remarking that we are in a "period of gestation," that we have not yet "arrived at a consistent style." Such a conclusion is plausible enough to one who drives down Fifth Avenue, walks through the annual circus of the Architectural League, or reads the somewhat superficial books and articles published in the United States.

This uncertainty of direction is clearly demonstrated by two recent magazine articles, one on European and one on American architecture. The first, called *New Building for the New Age*, is illustrated by photographs of six buildings supposedly representative of "what is happening in architecture on the continent of Europe." They include Saarinen's pre-War Railway Station at Helsingfors; the bizarre Expressionist Einstein Tower (1920) at Potsdam and a ponderous department store, both by Mendelsohn; Tengbom's Concert Hall at Stockholm with its portico of tall decagonal columns surmounted by Corinthian capitals; a school by Dudok, one of the more advanced members of the conservative Amsterdam group; and a theatrical Danish church façade derived from Hanseatic Gothic prototypes. Could we have added the Romanesquoid Stuttgart Railway Station, a cubistic house from the rue Mallet-Stevens, a concrete church by the brothers Perret, and the neo-Barocco-Romanesque Town Hall of Stockholm, we would have nearly a complete list of the modern European buildings most familiar to the

American public and, we are forced to believe, most admired by the large majority of American architects.

Poets in Steel, a characteristic essay on modern American architecture, is as one might expect primarily concerned with skyscrapers, although one of Mr. Cram's churches is illustrated and Frank Lloyd Wright is mentioned only to be dismissed as a mere theorist. But skyscrapers are accepted as "one of the most magnificent developments of our times"—Romanesque, Mayan, Assyrian, Renaissance, Aztec, Gothic, and especially Modernistic—everything from the stainless steel gargoyles of the Chrysler Building to the fantastic mooring mast atop the Empire State. No wonder that some of us who have been appalled by this chaos turn with the utmost interest and expectancy to the International Style.

It should be made clear that the æsthetic qualities of the Style are the principal concern of the authors of this book. Mr. Hitchcock has written elsewhere on its history and has published studies of several leading modern architects.[1] He and Mr. Johnson have also made little attempt to present here the technical or sociological aspects of the style except in so far as they are related to problems of design. They admit, of course, the extreme importance of these factors, which are often stressed in the criticism of modern architecture to the practical exclusion of problems of design.

The distinguishing æsthetic principles of the International Style as laid down by the authors are three: emphasis upon volume—space enclosed by thin planes or surfaces as opposed to the suggestion of mass and solidity; regularity as opposed to symmetry or other kinds of obvious balance; and, lastly, dependence upon the intrinsic elegance of materials, technical perfection, and fine proportions, as opposed to applied ornament.

The section on functionalism should be, I feel, of especial interest to American architects and critics. Functionalism as a dominant principle reached its high water mark among the important modern European architects several years ago. As was to be expected, several American architects have only recently begun to take up the utility-and-nothing-more theory of design with ascetic zeal. They fail to realize that in spite of his slogan, the house as a *machine à habiter*, Le Corbusier is even more concerned with style than with convenient planning or plumbing, and that the most luxurious of modern German architects, Miës van der Rohe, has for over a year been the head of the Bauhaus school, having supplanted Hannes Meyer, a fanatical functionalist. "Post-functionalism" has even been suggested as a name for the new Style, at once more precise and genetically descriptive than "International."

American skyscraper architects with cynical good humor have been willing to label their capricious façade ornament "functional"—"one function of the building is to please the client." We are asked to take seriously the architectural taste of real estate speculators, renting agents, and mortgage brokers! It is not surprising that the modern critic should feel more sympathy with the sound academic achievements of conservative contemporaries than with these modernistic impresarios. One can never forget the naive megalomania expressed in the remark of one of our best known "mas-

[1] *Frank Lloyd Wright*, Paris, 1928; *Modern Architecture: Romanticism and Reintegration* (New York, 1929); *J. J. P. Oud* (Paris, 1931). Mr. Johnson has in preparation a monograph on Mies van der Rohe.

ters of the skyscraper." "What! You wouldn't include so-and-so among your important architects? Why, he's built over two hundred million dollars' worth!" (Poor Ictinus with his couple of temples! Poor Peruzzi with his handful of palaces!)

It is, then, from the commercially successful modernistic architects that we may expect the strongest opposition to the Style. For even more than the great styles of the past it requires restraint and discipline, the will to perfect as well as to invent. And this is contrary to the American cult of individualism, whether genuinely romantic, as in the case of Frank Lloyd Wright, or merely the result of the advertising value of a 1932 model. American nationalists will also oppose the Style as another European invasion. But Oud and Gropius are proud to consider Frank Lloyd Wright among their artistic ancestors, even though their emulation of his work belongs definitely to the past.

Nevertheless, the International Style has already gained signal victories in America as is proven by a glance at the illustration of the skyscraper by Howe and Lescaze. George Howe was formerly a well-established traditional architect in Philadelphia. And a comparison in sequence of Raymond Hood's four famous skyscrapers tells its own story: the Tribune Tower, Chicago, followed by the Radiator Building (1924), New York, both of them luxuriantly wigged and bearded with applied Gothic; then the spectacular verticalism of the Daily News Building (1930), and finally the McGraw-Hill building (1931), which is more in the Style than any other New York skyscraper. A superficial but more general influence of the Style may be seen in the rapid change from vertical to horizontal emphasis in much recent metropolitan building.

In Europe, too, one may recall how during recent years Peter Behrens, the dean of German architects, and Mendelsohn, once the most conspicuous of the Expressionists, have both gone over to the International Style. Even in Stockholm—that shrine for our architectural schools—Asplund, the designer of the neo-classic Town Library, astonished the world by his mastery of "post-functionalist" design in the building of the Stockholm Exposition two years ago.

A preface should doubtless direct the attention of the reader to the text. And as in this book the text itself is intended as an introduction to the illustrations, one need scarcely speak at length about them. The authors have spent nearly two years in assembling the photographic and documentary material from which the illustrations were chosen. They form a carefully selected anthology of the Style as it has developed in Germany, Holland and France, and spread throughout the world, extending from Finland to Italy, from England to Russia, and beyond to Japan and the United States.

Alfred H. Barr, Jr.

I. INTRODUCTION: THE IDEA OF STYLE

The light and airy systems of construction of the Gothic cathedrals, the freedom and slenderness of their supporting skeleton, afford, as it were, a presage of a style that began to develop in the nineteenth century, that of metallic architecture.

With the use of metal, and of concrete reinforced by metal bars, modern builders could equal the most daring feats of Gothic architects without endangering the solidity of the structure. In the conflict that obtains between the two elements of construction, solidity and open space, everything seems to show that the principle of free spaces will prevail, that the palaces and houses of the future will be flooded with air and light. Thus the formula popularized by Gothic architecture has a great future before it. Following on the revival of Græco-Roman architecture which prevailed from the sixteenth century to our own day, we shall see, with the full application of different materials, a yet more enduring rebirth of the Gothic style.

Salomon Reinach, *Apollo, 1904*

Since the middle of the eighteenth century there have been recurrent attempts to achieve and to impose a controlling style in architecture such as existed in the earlier epochs of the past. The two chief of these attempts were the Classical Revival and the Mediæval Revival. Out of the compromises between these two opposing schools and the difficulties of reconciling either sort of revivalism with the new needs and the new methods of construction of the day grew the stylistic confusion of the last hundred years.

The nineteenth century failed to create a style of architecture because it was unable to achieve a general discipline of structure and of design in the terms of the day. The revived "styles" were but a decorative garment to architecture, not the interior principles according to which it lived and grew. On the whole the development of engineering in building went on regardless of the Classical or Mediæval architectural forms which were borrowed from the past. Thus the chaos of eclecticism served to give the very idea of style a bad name in the estimation of the first modern architects of the end of the nineteenth and the beginning of the twentieth century.

In the nineteenth century there was always not one style, but "styles," and the idea of "styles" implied a choice. The individualistic revolt of the first modern architects destroyed the prestige of the "styles," but it did not remove the implication that there was a possibility of choice between one æsthetic conception of design and another. In their reaction against revivalism these men sought rather to explore a great variety of free possibilities. The result, on the whole, added to the confusion of continuing eclecticism, although the new work possessed a general vitality which the later revivalists had quite lost. The revolt from stylistic discipline to extreme individualism at the beginning of the twentieth century was justified as the surest issue from an impasse of imitation and sterility. The individualists decried submission to fixed æsthetic principles as the imposition of a dead hand upon the living material of architecture, holding up the failure of the revivals as a proof that the very idea of style was an unhealthy delusion.

Today the strict issue of reviving the styles of the distant past is no longer one of serious consequence. But the peculiar traditions of imitation and modification of the styles of the past, which eclecticism inherited from the earlier Classical and Mediæval Revivals, have not been easily forgotten. The influence of the past still most to be feared is that of the nineteenth century with its cheapening of the very idea of style. Modern architecture has nothing but the healthiest lessons to learn from the art of the further past, if that art be studied scientifically and not in a spirit of imitation. Now that it is possible to emulate the great styles of the past in their essence without imitating their surface, the problem of establishing one dominant style, which the nineteenth century set itself in terms of alternative revivals, is coming to a solution.

The idea of style, which began to degenerate when the revivals destroyed the disciplines of the Baroque, has become real and fertile again. Today a single new style has come into existence. The æsthetic conceptions on which its disciplines are based derive from the experimentation of the individualists. They and not the revivalists were the immediate masters of those who have created the new style. This contemporary style, which exists throughout the world, is unified and inclusive, not fragmentary and contradictory like so much of the production of the first generation of modern architects. In the last decade it has produced sufficient monuments of distinction to display its validity and its vitality. It may fairly be compared in significance with the styles of the past. In the handling of the problems of structure it is related to the Gothic, in the handling of the problems of design it is more akin to the Classical. In the preëminence given to the handling of function it is distinguished from both.

The unconscious and halting architectural developments of the nineteenth century, the confused and contradictory experimentation of the beginning of the twentieth, have been succeeded by a directed evolution. There is now a single body of discipline, fixed enough to integrate contemporary style as a reality and yet elastic enough to permit individual interpretation and to encourage general growth.

The idea of style as the frame of potential growth, rather than as a fixed and crushing mould, has developed with the recognition of underlying principles such as archæologists discern in the great styles of the past. The principles are few and broad. They are not mere formulas of proportion such as distinguish the Doric from the Ionic order; they are fundamental, like the organic verticality of the Gothic or the rhythmical symmetry of the Baroque. There is, first, a new conception of architecture as volume rather than as mass. Secondly, regularity rather than axial symmetry serves the chief means of ordering design. These two principles, with a third proscribing arbitrary applied decoration, mark the productions of the international style. This new style is not international in the sense that the production of one country is just like that of another. Nor is it so rigid that the work of various leaders is not clearly distinguishable. The international style has become evident and definable only gradually as different innovators throughout the world have successfully carried out parallel experiments.

In stating the general principles of the contemporary style, in analysing their derivation from structure and their modification by function, the appearance of a certain dogmatism can hardly be avoided. In opposition to those who claim that a new style of architecture is impossible or undesirable, it is necessary to stress the coherence of the results obtained within the range of possibilities thus far explored. For the international style already exists in the present; it is not merely something the future may hold in store. Architecture is always a set of actual monuments, not a vague corpus of theory.

II. HISTORY

The style of the twelfth and thirteenth century was the last before our own day to be created on the basis of a new type of construction. The break away from the High Gothic in the later Middle Ages was an æsthetic break without significant structural development. The Renaissance was a surface change of style generally coupled with actual regression in terms of structure. The Baroque and *a fortiori* the Romantic Age concerned themselves all but exclusively with problems of design. When a century ago new structural developments in the use of metal made their appearance they remained outside the art of architecture. The Crystal Palace at the London Exposition of 1851, Paxton's magnificent iron and glass construction, has far more in common with the architecture of our day than with that of its own. Ferroconcrete, to which the contemporary style owes so much, was invented in 1849. Yet it was at least fifty years before it first began to play a considerable part in architectural construction.

Metal had begun to be used incidentally in architecture before the end of the eighteenth century. Thenceforth it achieved a place of increasing importance, even in buildings of the most traditional design. Finally in the eighties it made possible the first skyscrapers. But on the whole the "arcades," the train sheds, the conservatories and the exhibition halls, of which the London Crystal Palace was the earliest and the finest, were adjuncts to, or substitutes for, conventional masonry buildings.

Behind the conventional story of nineteenth century revivals and eclecticism there are two further histories of architecture. One deals with the science of building alone. It traces the development of new engineering methods of construction and the gradual replacement of traditional masonry structure by successive innovations. The other history deals with the development of the art of architectural design regardless of specific imitations. Design was freed here and there from the control of the past. Some architects even sought novel forms and many aimed at a more direct expression of the new methods of construction. A new art of proportioning plane surfaces, a free study of silhouette, even a frank use of metal appear in the work of most of the leading nineteenth century architects. Soane in England, Schinkel and his followers in Germany, and Labrouste in France, were among these early precursors of modern architecture.

Within the Classical Revival there developed a new sense of design, purer and more rational than that of the Renaissance or the Baroque, yet not restricted merely to the purity and rationalism of the Greeks. Within the Mediæval Revival there grew up a body of doctrine, based on the practice of the builders of the Middle Ages, which foreshadowed the theories of our own day. There is not much to change today in the passage that has been quoted from Salomon Reinach's *Apollo*. As late as 1904 it was possible to conceive of modern architecture chiefly as a sort of renaissance of the Gothic. Yet it should be stressed that the relation of the modern style to the Gothic is ideological rather than visual, a matter of principle rather than a matter of practice. In design, indeed, the leading modern architects aim at Greek serenity rather than Gothic aspiration.

In writing on modern architecture some few years ago it was possible to accept that the individualists of the end of the nineteenth century and the beginning of the twentieth, who first broke consciously with the nominal discipline of the revivals, established tentatively a *New Tradition.* It appeared then as a sort of style in which the greatest common denominator of the various revivals was preserved and fused with the new science of building. Today it seems more accurate to describe the work of the older generation of architects as half-modern. Each architect broke in his own way with the immediate past, each sought in his own direction the positive elements which have been combined in the last decade. But there was no real stylistic integration until after the War.

The industrial achitecture of Peter Behrens in Germany in the years before the War was already extremely simplified and regular. The effect of volume began to replace the traditional effect of mass. Otto Wagner, a decade earlier in Vienna, cultivated qualities of lightness and developed the plane surfaces of his architecture for their own sake. The Belgian Van de Velde experimented with continuity of surface, making much use of curves. Berlage at Amsterdam based his compositions on geometry and handled both old and new materials with unusual straightforwardness. In the constructions of Perret in France the use of ferroconcrete led to a visible articulation of the supporting skeleton with the walls treated as mere screens between the posts. Thus in the different countries of Europe before the War the conceptions of the international style had come independently into existence. It remained for the younger generation to combine and crystallize the various æsthetic and technical results of the experimentation of their elders.

But it was in America that the promise of a new style appeared first and, up to the War, advanced most rapidly. Richardson in the seventies and eighties often went as far as did the next generation on the Continent in simplification of design and in direct expression of structure. Following him, Root and Sullivan deduced from steel skyscraper construction principles which have been modified but not essentially changed by later generations. Their work of the eighties and nineties in Chicago is still too little known. We have in America only a few commercial buildings of 1900 to compare with the radical steel and glass department stores of Europe; but these few are more notable than all the skyscrapers of the following twenty-five years.

In the first decades of the new century Frank Lloyd Wright continued brilliantly the work of the Chicago school in other fields of architecture. He introduced many innovations, particularly in domestic building, quite as important a those of the Art Nouveau and Jugendstil in France and Germany. His open planning broke the mould of the traditional house, to which Europe clung down to the War. He also was the first to conceive of architectural design in terms of planes existing freely in three dimensions rather than in terms of enclosed blocks. Wagner, Behrens and Perret lightened the solid massiveness of traditional architecture; Wright dynamited it.

While much of the innovation in Europe merely consisted in expressing more frankly new methods of construction within a framework of design still essentially Classical or Mediæval, Wright from the beginning was radical in his æsthetic experimentation. One may regret the lack of continuity in his development and his unwillingness to absorb the innovations of his contemporaries and his juniors in Europe. But one cannot deny that among the architects of the older generation Wright made more contributions than any other. His consciously novel ornament may appear to lack even the vitality of the semi-traditional ornament of the first quarter of the century in Europe. Perret was, perhaps, a more important innovator in construction; Van de Velde showed a greater consistency and a purer taste in his æsthetic experiments. But Wright preserved better the balance between the mere expression of structure and the achievement of positive form.

There is, however, a definite breach between Wright and the younger architects who created the contemporary style after the War. Ever since the days when he was Sullivan's disciple, Wright has remained an individualist. A rebel by temperament, he has refused even the disciplines of his own theories. Instead of developing some one of the manners which he has initiated, he has begun again and again with a different material or a different problem and arrived at a quite new manner. The new manner often enough contradicts some of the essential qualities of his previous work, qualities which European followers have emulated with distinction and used as the basis of further advance. In his refusal of the shackles of a fixed style he has created the illusion of infinite possible styles, like the mathematicians who have invented non-Euclidean geometries. His eternally young spirit rebels against the new style as vigorously as he rebelled against the "styles" of the nineteenth century.

Wright belongs to the international style no more than Behrens or Perret or Van de Velde. Some of these men have been ready to learn from their juniors. They have submitted in part to the disciplines of the international style. But their work is still marked by traces of the individualistic manners they achieved in their prime. Without their work the style could hardly have come into being. Yet their individualism and their relation to the past, for all its tenuousness, makes of them not so much the creators of a new style as the last representatives of Romanticism. They are more akin to the men of a hundred years ago than to the generation which has come to the fore since the War.

The continued existence of Romantic individualism is not a question of architecture alone. There is a dichotomy of the spirit more profound than any mere style can ever resolve. The case against individualism in architecture lies in the fact that Wright has been almost alone in America in achieving a distinguished architecture; while in Europe, and indeed in other parts of the world as well, an increasingly large group of architects work successfully within the disciplines of the new style.

There is a basic cleavage between the international style and the half-modern architecture of the beginning of the present century. We must not forget the debt that Le Corbusier, Gropius, Mies van der Rohe, Oud and the rest owe to the older men with whom they studied. We must not forget such exceptional monuments of the nineteenth century as the Crystal Palace. We must not dismiss as lacking historical significance the fine sense of proportion and the vigorous purity of the Classical Revival, or the splendid theories and the stupid practice of the Gothic Revival. Even the absurdities of Romantic artificial ruins and the linear and naturalistic ornament of 1900 have a place in the pedigree of the contemporary style. But the new style after ten years of existence and growth may now be studied for itself without continual reference to the immediate past.

There are certain times when a new period truly begins despite all the preparation that may be traced behind the event. Such a time came immediately after the War, when the international style came into being in France, in Holland, and in Germany. Indeed, if we follow the projects of the War years made by the Austrian Loos and the Italian Sant' Elia, it may appear that the new style was preparing on an even broader front. While the innovations of the half-moderns were individual and independent to the point of divergence, the innovations of their juniors were parallel and complementary, already informed by the coherent spirit of a style in the making.

It is particularly in the early work of three men, Walter Gropius in Germany, Oud in Holland, and Le Corbusier in France, that the various steps in the inception of the new style must be sought. These three with Mies van der Rohe in Germany remain the great leaders of modern architecture.

Gropius' factory at Alfeld, built just before the War, came nearer to an integration of the new style than any other edifice built before 1922. In industrial architecture the tradition of the styles of the past was not repressive, as many factories of the nineteenth century well illustrate. The need for using modern construction throughout and for serving function directly was peculiarly evident. Hence it was easier for Gropius to advance in this field beyond his master, Behrens, than it would have been in any other. The walls of the Alfeld factory are screens of glass with spandrels of metal at the floor levels. The crowning band of brickwork does not project beyond these screens. The purely mechanical elements are frankly handled and give interest to design fundamentally so regular as to approach monotony. There is no applied ornamental decoration except the lettering. The organization of the parts of the complex structure is ordered by logic and consistency rather than by axial symmetry.

Yet there are traces still of the conceptions of traditional architecture. The glass screens are treated like projecting bays between the visible supports. These supports are sheathed with brick so that they appear like the last fragments of the solid masonry wall of the past. The entrance is symmetrical and heavy. For all its simplicity it is treated with a decorative emphasis. Gropius was not destined to achieve again so fine and so coherent a production in the contemporary style before the Bauhaus in 1926. There he profited from the intervening æsthetic experimentation of the Dutch Neoplasticists. The Bauhaus is something more than a mere development from the technical triumph of the Alfeld factory.

During the years of the War, Oud in Holland came into contact with the group of Dutch cubist painters led by Mondriaan and Van Doesburg, who called themselves Neoplasticists. Their positive influence on his work at first was negligible. Oud remained for a time still a disciple of Berlage, whose half-modern manner he had previously followed rather closely. He profited also by his study of the innovations of Wright, whose work was already better known in Europe than in America. Then he sought consciously to achieve a Neoplasticist architecture and, from 1917 on, the influence of Berlage and Wright began to diminish. At the same time he found in concrete an adequate material for the expression of new conceptions of form.

Oud's projects were increasingly simple, vigorous and geometrical. On the analogy of abstract painting he came to realize the æsthetic potentialities of planes in three dimensions with which Wright had already experimented. He reacted sharply against the picturesqueness of the other followers of Berlage and sought with almost Greek fervor to arrive at a scheme of proportions ever purer and more regular.

In his first housing projects carried out for the city of Rotterdam in 1918 and 1919 he did not advance as far as in his unexecuted projects. But at Oud-Mathenesse in 1921–22, although he was required to build the whole village in traditional materials and to continue the use of conventional roofs, the new style promised in his projects came into being. The avoidance of picturesqueness, the severe horizontality of the composition, the perfect simplicity and consistency which he achieved in executing a very complex project, all announced the conscious creation of a body of æsthetic disciplines.

Oud-Mathenesse exceeded Gropius' Alfeld factory in significance if not in impressiveness. Gropius made his innovations primarily in technics, Oud in design. He undoubtedly owed the initial impetus to the Neoplasticists, but his personal manner had freed itself from dependence on painting. The models Van Doesburg made of houses in the early twenties, in collaboration with other Neoplasticists, with their abstract play of volumes and bright colors, had their own direct influence in Germany.

But the man who first made the world aware that a new style was being born was Le Corbusier. As late as 1916, well after his technical and sociological theorizing had begun, his conceptions of design were still strongly marked by the Classical symmetry of his master Perret. His plans, however, were even more open than those of Wright. In his housing projects of the next few years he passed rapidly beyond his master Perret and beyond Behrens and Loos, with whom he had also come in contact. His *Citrohan* house model of 1921 was the thorough expression of a conception of architecture as radical technically as Gropius' factory and as novel æsthetically as Oud's village. The enormous window area and the terraces made possible by the use of ferroconcrete, together with the asymmetry of the composition, undoubtedly produced a design more thoroughly infused with a new spirit, more completely freed from the conventions of the past than any thus far projected.

The influence of Le Corbusier was the greater, the appearance of a new style the more remarked, because of the vehement propaganda which he contributed to the magazine *L'Esprit Nouveau*, 1920–1925. Since then, moreover, he has written a series of books effectively propagandizing his technical and æsthetic theories. In this way his name has become almost synonymous with the new architecture and it has been praised or condemned very largely in his person. But he was not, as we have seen, the only innovator nor was the style as it came generally into being after 1922 peculiarly his. He crystallized; he dramatized; but he was not alone in creating.

When in 1922 he built at Vaucresson his first house in the new style, he failed to equal the purity of design and the boldness of construction of the *Citrohan* project. But the houses that immediately followed this, one for the painter Ozenfant, and another for his parents outside Vevey, passed further beyond the transitional stage than anything that Oud or Gropius were to build for several more years. Ozenfant's sort of cubism, called Purism, had perhaps inspired Le Corbusier in his search for sources of formal inspiration for a new architecture. But on the whole Le Corbusier in these early years turned for precedent rather to steamships than to painting. Some of his early houses, such as that for the sculptor Miestchaninoff at Boulogne-sur-Seine, were definitely naval in feeling. But this marine phase was soon over like Oud's strictly Neoplasticist phase, or the Expressionist period in the work of the young architects of Germany. Various external influences helped to free architecture from the last remnants of a lingering traditionalism. The new style displayed its force in the rapidity with which it transmuted them beyond recognition.

Mies van der Rohe advanced toward the new style less rapidly at first than Gropius. Before the War he had simplified, clarified, and lightened the domestic style of Behrens to a point that suggests conscious inspiration from Schinkel and Persius. After the War in two projects for skyscrapers entirely of metal and glass he carried technical innovation even further than Gropius, further indeed than anyone has yet gone in practice. These buildings would have been pure volume, glazed cages supported from within, on a scale such as not even Paxton in the nineteenth century would have dreamed possible. However, in their form, with plans based on clustered circles or sharp angles, they were extravagantly Romantic and strongly marked by the contemporary wave of Expressionism in Germany.

It was in Mies' projects of 1922 that his true significance as an æsthetic innovator first appeared. In a design for a country house he broke with the conception of the wall as a continuous plane surrounding the plan and built up his composition of sections of intersecting planes. Thus he achieved, still with the use of supporting walls, a greater openness even than Le Corbusier with his ferroconcrete skeleton construction. Mies' sense of proportions remained as serene as before the War and even more pure. This project and the constructions of Oud and Le Corbusier in this year emphasize that it is just a decade ago that the new style came into existence.

The four leaders of modern architecture are Le Corbusier, Oud, Gropius and Mies van der Rohe. But others as well as they, Rietveld in Holland, Lurçat in France, even Mendelsohn in Germany, for all his lingering dalliance with Expressionism, took parallel steps of nearly equal importance in the years just after the War. The style did not spring from a single source but came into being generally. The writing of Oud and Gropius, and to a greater degree that of Le Corbusier, with the frequent publication of their projects of these years, carried the principles of the new style abroad. These projects have indeed become more famous than many executed buildings.

From the first there were also critics, who were not architects, to serve as publicists. Everyone who was interested in the creation of a modern architecture had to come to terms with the nascent style. The principles of the style that appeared already plainly by 1922 in the projects and the executed buildings of the leaders, still control today an ever increasing group of architects throughout the world.

III. FUNCTIONALISM

In part the principles of the international style were from the first voiced in the manifestoes which were the order of the day. In part they have remained unconscious, so that even now it is far simpler to sense them than to explain them or to state them categorically. Many who appear to follow them, indeed, refuse to admit their validity. Some modern critics and groups of architects both in Europe and in America deny that the æsthetic element in architecture is important, or even that it exists. All æsthetic principles of style are to them meaningless and unreal. This new conception, that building is science and not art, developed as an exaggeration of the idea of functionalism.

In its most generally accepted form the idea of functionalism is sufficiently elastic. It derives its sanctions from both Greek and Gothic architecture, for in the temple as well as in the cathedral the æsthetic expression is based on structure and function. In all the original styles of the past the æsthetic is related to, even dependent on, the technical. The supporters of both the Classical Revival and the Mediæval Revival in the nineteenth century were ready to defend much of their practice by functionalist arguments. The so-called rationalism of architects like Schinkel and Labrouste was a type of functionalism. It is vigorously advocated, moreover, in the archæological criticism of Viollet-le-Duc and the ethical criticism of Pugin and Ruskin. Morris and his disciples brought this sort of functionalist theory down to our own day.

The doctrine of the contemporary anti-æsthetic functionalists is much more stringent. Its basis is economic rather than ethical or archæological. Leading European critics, particularly Siegfried Giedion, claim with some justice that architecture has such immense practical problems to deal with in the modern world that æsthetic questions must take a secondary place in architectural criticism. Architects like Hannes Meyer go further. They claim that interest in proportions or in problems of design for their own sake is still an unfortunate remnant of nineteenth century ideology. For these men it is an absurdity to talk about the modern style in terms of æsthetics at all. If a building provides adequately, completely, and without compromise for its purpose, it is to them a good building, regardless of its appearance. Modern construction receives from them a straightforward expression; they use standardized parts whenever possible and they avoid ornament or unnecessary detail. Any elaboration of design, any unnecessary use of specially made parts, any applied decoration would add to the cost of the building. It is, however, nearly impossible to organize and execute a complicated building without making some choices not wholly determined by technics and economics. One may therefore refuse to admit that intentionally functionalist building is quite without a potential æsthetic element. Consciously or unconsciously the architect must make free choices before his design is completed. In these choices the European functionalists follow, rather than go against, the principles of the general contemporary style. Whether they admit it or not is beside the point.

In America also there are both architects and critics who consider architecture not an art, as it has been in the past, but merely a subordinate technic of industrial civilization. Æsthetic criticism of building appears to them nearly as meaningless as æsthetic criticism of road building. Their attitude has been to some extent a beneficial one in its effect on American building, even from the æsthetic point of view. Most European critics feel rightly that American engineers have always been far more successful with their technics than American architects with their æsthetics.

But to the American functionalists, unfortunately, design is a commodity like ornament. If the client insists, they still try to provide it in addition to the more tangible commodities which they believe rightly should come first. But they find one sort of design little better than another and are usually as ready to provide zigzag trimmings as rhythmical fenestration. For ornament can be added after the work is done and comes into no direct relation with the handling of function and structure. American modernism in design is usually as superficial as the revivalism which preceded it. Most American architects would regret the loss of applied ornament and imitative design. Such things serve to obscure the essential emptiness of skyscraper composition.

The European functionalists are primarily builders, and architects only unconsciously. This has its advantages even for architecture as an art. Critics should be articulate about problems of design; but architects whose training is more technical than intellectual, can afford to be unconscious of the æsthetic effects they produce. So, it may be assumed, were many of the great builders of the past. Since the works of the European functionalists usually fall within the limits of the international style, they may be claimed among its representatives. Naturally these doctrinaires achieve works of æsthetic distinction less often than some others who practice the art of architecture as assiduously as they pursue the science of building.

The American functionalists claim to be builders first. They are surely seldom architects in the fullest sense of the word. They are ready, as the European functionalists are not, to deface their building with bad architectural design if the client demands it. Nor can they claim for their skyscrapers and apartment houses the broad sociological justification that exists for the workers' housing, the schools and hospitals of Europe. On the whole, American factories, where the client expects no money to be spent on design, are better buildings and at least negatively purer in design than those constructions in which the architect is forced by circumstances to be more than an engineer. Technical developments, moreover, are rapidly forcing almost all commercial and industrial building into the mould of the international style.

It is not necessary to accept the contentions of the functionalists that there is no new style or even to consider their own work still another kind of architecture. While the older generation has continued faithful to individualism, a set of general æsthetic principles has come into use. While the functionalists continue to deny that the æsthetic element in architecture is important, more and more buildings are produced in which these principles are wisely and effectively followed without sacrifice of functional virtues.

VIII

PURE FUNCTION, PURE FORM

61   Mies van der Rohe, Inaugural Address* *1938*

It has not been uncommon for some architects to have exerted particular influence even though they wrote very little—McKim, Mead and White and Mies van der Rohe are good examples. Accordingly the few public statements such architects made acquire special importance. Ludwig Mies (1886–1969)—he later added his mother's surname—was born in Aachen (Aix-la-Chapelle) and learned stone masonry from his father. When he was fifteen he entered an architect's office in Berlin, having already attended trade school and worked as a draftsman for architects near his home; soon after, however, he apprenticed himself to Bruno Paul, the leading German furniture and cabinet designer. After two years, in 1907, he executed his first independent architectural commission, but during the years 1908–11 he worked for Peter Behrens, rising to a position of supervisory responsibility in Behrens's office. Through Behrens, Mies was introduced to the neoclassic precision of Karl Friedrich Schinkel, as well as to the Deutscher Werkbund and other progressive elements in Berlin architectural circles. After the First World War he designed a number of projects, most notably two glass skyscrapers and a concrete office building, all 1919–22, and produced the magazine *G* (derived from *Gestaltung,* "configuration" or "creative force"). Some of his earliest epigrammatic statements concerning the new architecture appeared in *G*: "Architecture is the will of the age conceived in spatial terms," "the maximum effect with the minimum expenditure of means," "buildings consisting of skin and bones." From exposure to Behrens's extensive work for the AEG (German General Electric Company), Mies formed his own view of the role of industry in architecture; in *G* he wrote in 1924: "I see in industrialization the central problem of building in our time. If we succeed in carrying out this industrialization, the social, economic, technical, and also artistic problems will be readily solved." †
He also was active in the *Novembergruppe* founded to propagandize modern art.

Gradually, in the post-war years, Mies developed a limited practice and became extremely active in the Deutscher Werkbund (he was responsible for planning and supervising the Weissenhof Siedlung in Stuttgart, in 1927). The apogee of these early years was reached in the pavilion Mies designed for the German exhibition at the International Exposition at Barcelona, 1929, and in the Tugendhat house, Brno, Czechoslovakia, 1930, based on it. Some projects and buildings followed, but when the National Socialists came to power, their program of regional and typological associationalism in architecture conflicted with the universal functionalist idiom advocated by Mies. He took charge of the Bauhaus after Gropius fled, but political pressure forced the school to close in 1933. Mies managed to subsist until Philip Johnson, a staunch supporter since 1930, obtained for him a domestic project for the Stanley B. Resors in Jackson Hole, Wyoming, in 1937, a project which prompted

---

*Ludwig Mies van der Rohe, "Inaugural Address as Director of Architecture at Armour Institute of Technology," 1938, reprinted from Philip Johnson, *Mies van der Rohe*, 3rd ed. (New York, 1978), pp. 196–200.

†These are reprinted in Ulrich Conrads, ed., *Programs and Manifestoes on Twentieth Century Architecture*, trans. M. Bullock (Cambridge, Mass., 1970); and Philip Johnson, *Mies van der Rohe*, 3rd ed. (New York, 1978).

Mies to leave Germany for the United States. Meanwhile, he was suggested by architect John A. Holabird as a candidate for director of architecture of the Armour Institute, Chicago (later the Illinois Institute of Technology). He received this appointment, resulting in one of the longest of his rare public or printed statements, his inaugural address, delivered at a dinner at Chicago's Palmer House at which Mies asked Frank Lloyd Wright to introduce him. The draft of the speech had occupied Mies for months. In it he reiterated themes he had broached more than a decade earlier, echoing Sullivan: "We shall examine one by one every function of a building and use it as a basis for form," ending by quoting St. Augustine, "Beauty is the splendor of Truth."

All education must begin with the practical side of life.

Real education, however, must transcend this to mould the personality.

The first aim should be to equip the student with the knowledge and skill for practical life.

The second aim should be to develop his personality and enable him to make the right use of this knowledge and skill.

Thus true education is concerned not only with practical goals but also with values.

By our practical aims we are bound to the specific structure of our epoch. Our values, on the other hand, are rooted in the spiritual nature of men.

Our practical aims measure only our material progress. The values we profess reveal the level of our culture.

Different as practical aims and values are, they are nevertheless closely connected.

For to what else should our values be related if not to our aims in life?

Human existence is predicated on the two spheres together. Our aims assure us of our material life, our values make possible our spiritual life.

If this is true of all human activity where even the slightest question of value is involved, how especially is it true of the sphere of architecture.

In its simplest form architecture is rooted in entirely functional considerations, but it can reach up through all degrees of value to the highest sphere of spiritual existence into the realm of pure art.

In organizing an architectural education system we must recognize this situation if we are to succeed in our efforts. We must fit the system to this reality. Any teaching of architecture must explain these relations and interrelations.

We must make clear, step by step, what things are possible, necessary and significant.

If teaching has any purpose, it is to implant true insight and responsibility.

Education must lead us from irresponsible opinion to true responsible judgment.

It must lead us from chance and arbitrariness to rational clarity and intellectual order.

Therefore let us guide our students over the road of discipline from materials, through function, to creative work. Let us lead them into the healthy world of primitive building methods, where there was meaning in every stroke of an axe, expression in every bite of a chisel.

Where can we find greater structural clarity than in the wooden buildings of old? Where else can we find such unity of material, construction and form?

Here the wisdom of whole generations is stored.

What feeling for material and what power of expression there is in these buildings!

What warmth and beauty they have! They seem to be echoes of old songs.

And buildings of stone as well: what natural feeling they express!

What a clear understanding of the material! How surely it is joined!

What sense they had of where stone could and could not be used!

Where do we find such wealth of structure? Where more natural and healthy beauty?

How easily they laid beamed ceilings on those old stone walls and with what sensitive feeling they cut doorways through them!

What better examples could there be for young architects? Where else could they learn such simple and true crafts than from these unknown masters?

We can also learn from brick.

How sensible is this small handy shape, so useful for every purpose! What logic is in its bonding, pattern, and texture!

What richness in the simplest wall surface! But what discipline this material imposes!

Thus each material has its specific characteristics which we must understand if we want to use it.

This is no less true of steel and concrete. We must remember that everything depends on how we use a material, not on the material itself.

Also new materials are not necessarily superior. Each material is only what we make it.

We must be as familiar with the functions of our buildings as with our materials. We must analyze them and clarify them. We must learn, for example, what distinguishes a building to live in from other kinds of building.

We must learn what a building can be, what it should be, and also what it must not be.

We shall examine one by one every function of a building and use it as a basis for form.

Just as we acquainted ourselves with materials and just as we must understand functions, we must become familiar with the psychological and spiritual factors of our day.

No cultural activity is possible otherwise; for we are dependent on the spirit of our time.

Therefore we must understand the motives and forces of our time and analyze their structure from three points of view: the material, the functional, and the spiritual.

We must make clear in what respects our epoch differs from others and in what respects it is similar.

At this point the problem of technology of construction arises.

We shall be concerned with genuine problems—problems related to the value and purpose of our technology.

We shall show that technology not only promises greatness and power, but also involves dangers; that good and evil apply to it as to all human actions; that it is our task to make the right decision.

Every decision leads to a special kind of order.

Therefore we must make clear what principles of order are possible and clarify them.

Let us recognize that the mechanistic principle of order overemphasizes the materialistic and functionalistic factors in life, since it fails to satisfy our feeling that means must be subsidiary to ends and our desire for dignity and value.

The idealistic principle of order, however, with its over-emphasis on the ideal and the formal, satisfies neither our interest in simple reality nor our practical sense.

So we shall emphasize the organic principle of order as a means of achieving the successful relationship of the parts to each other and to the whole.

And here we shall take our stand.

The long path from material through function to creative work has only a single goal: to create order out of the desperate confusion of our time.

We must have order, allocating to each thing its proper place and giving to each thing its due according to nature.

We would do this so perfectly that the world of our creations will blossom from within.

We want no more; we can do no more.

Nothing can express the aim and meaning of our work better than the profound words of St. Augustine: "Beauty is the splendor of Truth."

62   Mies van der Rohe, Address to the Illinois Institute of Technology* *1950*

A second extended statement, similarly a crystallization of epigrammatic propositions, was presented at I.I.T. In this, perhaps as a result of the experience of teaching at I.I.T. or seeing realized, at last, buildings only dreamed of in Weimar Germany, Mies praised technology, seeming to diminish the spiritual content in architecture that he had stressed in 1938. "Whenever technology reaches its real fulfillment," he now proposed, "it transcends into architecture." In Mies's hands it did, but for his many imitators, beguiled by his arduously restudied simplicity, technology by itself did not necessarily transcend.

*Reprinted from Philip Johnson, *Mies van der Rohe*, 3rd ed. (New York, 1978), pp. 203–204.

Technology is rooted in the past.
It dominates the present and tends into the future.
It is a real historical movement—
one of the great movements which shape and
represent their epoch.
It can be compared only with the Classic
discovery of man as a person,
the Roman will to power,
and the religious movement of the Middle Ages.
Technology is far more than a method,
it is a world in itself.
As a method it is superior in almost every respect.
But only where it is left to itself as in
gigantic structures of engineering, there
technology reveals its true nature.
There it is evident that it is not only a useful means,
that it is something, something in itself,
something that has a meaning and a powerful form—
so powerful in fact, that it is not easy to name it.
Is that still technology or is it architecture?
And that may be the reason why some people
are convinced that architecture will be outmoded
and replaced by technology.
Such a conviction is not based on clear thinking.
The opposite happens.
Wherever technology reaches its real fulfillment,
it transcends into architecture.
It is true that architecture depends on facts,
but its real field of activity is in the realm
of significance.
I hope you will understand that architecture
has nothing to do with the inventions of forms.
It is not a playground for children, young or old.
Architecture is the real battleground of the spirit.
Architecture wrote the history of the epochs
and gave them their names.
Architecture depends on its time.
It is the crystallization of its inner structure,
the slow unfolding of its form.
That is the reason why technology and architecture
are so closely related.
Our real hope is that they grow together,
that someday the one be the expression of
the other.
Only then will we have an architecture worthy
of its name:
Architecture as a true symbol of our time.

63 L. Mumford, Crystal Lantern* 1954

Among those who best understood and extrapolated Mies's doctrine was Skidmore, Owings & Merrill, as this firm amply demonstrated in its Manufacturers Hanover Bank branch on Fifth Avenue, New York, 1953–54, the work discussed in this essay by Mumford in *The New Yorker*. Lewis Mumford, born in 1895 in Flushing, Long Island, New York, has been one of the most informed and wide-ranging critics of modern culture since the mid-1920s. He has also been the recipient of numerous awards and fellowships, and has held teaching and research posts at leading universities, yet he earned no academic degree. Following high school, during the years 1912–17, he studied, sometimes simultaneously, at the City College of New York and Columbia University, followed by a year at the New School for Social Research. During an illness which forced him to forgo formal academic studies, he began corresponding with the Scotch social philosopher and planner, Patrick Geddes, who Mumford readily acknowledges exerted a strong influence on him. Mumford then set about studying New York City, reading voraciously and exploring its neighborhoods on foot. He began contributing articles to *Forum* and *The New Republic* and produced a series of books in the 1920s which demonstrated his broad interests: *The Story of Utopias* (1922); *Sticks and Stones*, on American architecture (1924); *The Golden Day*, on American culture (1926); and *Herman Melville* (1929). During the 1930s he published *The Brown Decades* (1931), in which he redirected attention to H. H. Richardson and Olmsted; *Technics and Civilization* (1934); and *The Culture of Cities* (1938), which provided the basis for what is perhaps his magnum opus, *The City in History* (1961). From 1931 to 1963 he wrote architectural criticism in the column "The Sky Line" in *The New Yorker*, where this essay first appeared.†

The Manufacturers Trust Company's new Fifth Avenue office, at the southwest corner of Forty-third Street, revives the dream of building a whole city of glass that haunted the Victorian imagination. Most of the big cities of Europe perpetuated that dream to the extent of building at least one glass-covered shopping arcade; George Pullman, in projecting his ill-fated town of Pullman, Illinois, built a great glass-covered market and community hall; even Ebenezer Howard, most practical of idealists, conceived an enormous under-glass shopping avenue as one of the spectacular features of his proposed Garden City near London; and the dream of sparkling crystalline cities, all glass and metal, figured in more than one of H. G. Wells's many utopias. But only in our time has this dream begun to come nearer to general realization, and among the architects who have done most to put the idea to

---

*Lewis Mumford, "Crystal Lantern," *The New Yorker* 30 (November 13, 1954), pp. 197–204, reprinted by Mumford in *From the Ground Up* (New York, 1956).

†Mumford comments on his writing in *My Works and Days: A Personal Chronicle* (New York, 1979), in the foreword to an anthology: Lewis Mumford, *Architecture as a Home for Man: Essays for Architectural Record* (New York, 1975), and in *Sketches From Life: The Autobiography of Lewis Mumford* (New York, 1982).

practical use—Philip Johnson in his own house, in New Canaan; Mies van der Rohe in the Lake Shore Drive Apartments, in Chicago; Frank Lloyd Wright in the S. C. Johnson & Son's Laboratory, in Racine, Wisconsin—none has done more (in New York, anyway) than the firm of Skidmore, Owings & Merrill. In the Manufacturers Trust, they have followed up their Lever House with a quite different mode of design, and in the course of executing it they have pointed up many of the possibilities of glass, both structurally and aesthetically.

While Lever House is, at most times of the day and the night, a dark-green, almost opaque building, in which the glass sheath seems stretched taut, like a film, over the frame it conceals, this new bank is a paradoxical combination of transparence and solidity—crystalline, yes, but not in the slightest frail or film-like, for, if anything, it is both rugged and monumental. Lacking any vestige of classic Greek or Roman form, or anything to remind one of the conventional banking temple except its low, four-square form, it nevertheless expresses the classic qualities of dignity, serenity, and order. To the observer approaching it along Fifth Avenue, this structure, with its heavy vertical aluminum ribs and its massive glass wall panels, conveys the feeling that it is there to stay. The over-all treatment of the façade actually says aloud what the engineer's calculations had indicated—that these glass walls could withstand a wind of up to a hundred miles an hour, a velocity that, because of its sheltered position, the building would never be subjected to.

The notion of designing a bank with an all-glass façade was first broached, I believe, in these columns in the nineteen-thirties, the theory being that exposure to public view was a much greater protection against assault and robbery than any number of stately Corinthian columns and bronze grille cages. As a matter of fact, the classic column, once the pat symbol of conservatism and financial solvency, did not, as a symbol, survive the awful financial revelations of the great depression, yet it was a long time after that before banks began to free themselves of this antique image. The move toward modern design in banks first manifested itself only in the interiors; the cold, chilly, railroad-station atmosphere was gradually warmed up with "homey" touches of the sticky kind associated with Georgian revivalism, and later with equally dubious attempts at mural painting in the genteel tradition of the eighteen-nineties. During the past ten years, though, many banks—there is a whole nest of them around Rockefeller Center—have adopted modern decoration of the sort one might expect to find in a fancy club. But nowhere have both interior and exterior been conceived more effectively as a whole, or treated in a more forthright manner, at once businesslike and elegant, than in this new structure. The great merit of the Manufacturers Trust's new quarters is that, being all of one piece, every part tells the same story, and to perfection. This is true of the little things as well as of the big ones; thus, the clock on the second floor, ignoring the foolish modern convention that requires blank dials and small, stubby hands that don't indicate more than a vague approximation of the time of day, actually tells the hour with pointed precision. Admittedly, part of the building's success is due to the very special advantages of its site, which I will more fully touch on later, but the fact that the architects made use of these advantages is no little part of their achievement.

Viewed from outside, this building is essentially a glass lantern, and, like a lantern, it is even more striking by dark than by daylight. The main shell contains four floors, counting the street-level one, and it is topped by a fifth floor, a penthouse that is set back to provide a terrace, which, like the Fifth Avenue frontage, is planted with trees, thus suggesting the natural landscape so many of us leave behind when we must do business in the Plutonian underworld of megalopolis. This landscaping makes the building an urban equivalent of Poe's "Domain of Arnheim." Indeed, the bank is as prodigal in the luxuriance of its vegetation as in the luxury of its working equipment, for the extensive greenery, planned and installed by Clarke & Rapuano, landscape architects, requires the services of a gardener two full days a week. The glass walls of this building—there are no windows—are set between tall, vertical ribs of aluminum that rise from a scuffle base of black granite. These walls are interrupted only by three emphatic spandrels of dark-gray glass that girdle the upper floors, while the second story, a mezzanine, is fringed by a thinner band of leafy plants, which offer a contrasting touch of green. The crystalline quality of the structure is further brought out by sheathing the ceilings in opaque plastic panels, ribbed like a washboard, behind which cold-cathode lamps evenly diffuse a pale-yellow light throughout every floor. The only screen of any kind against sunlight is provided by spun-glass curtains of neutral color and texture, which are probably more useful for insulation than for visual protection. The glass panels are really curtains themselves, for although they are firmly fixed in place, their crushing weight is actually suspended from the roof, which, like the floors, is cantilevered out from the columns that support the entire building. The suspending of these walls eliminates the need for heavy, clumsy supporting beams, and thus adds to the feeling of lightness in the structure. This is but one of the many costly technical feats that make this whole audacious enclosure of space seem so simple and so effortless. Another trick is using only eight of these columns, all of them freestanding and all of them set well back from the outer walls of glass, to support the building. This device, which opens up the interior space by eliminating the once mandatory row upon row of supporting columns, is one of the positive contributions of modern engineering to the luminous, lantern-like effect of this building.

To the passing spectator, there are two features that become striking only when he nears the building. One is the great horizontal banks of foliage in the huge boxes that serve as pedestals for the pair of rapidly moving escalators that rise from the main floor to the mezzanine on the Fifth Avenue side. The other is the vast round entrance, also on the Avenue side, to the vaults of the bank, with its massive door of shiny metal—the most impressive possible symbol of security. This thirty-ton door holds the eyes of a constant crowd on the sidewalk, as once upon a time the white-capped chef making hot cakes held people in front of Childs. (Customers with business in the safe-deposit vaults enter them through a series of less ostentatious but well-guarded portals from a small side door at the western end of the Forty-third Street façade.) By raising the most dramatic physical object in a bank from the cellar to the ground floor, the architects have made the most of a natural advertisement. This is what one might call inherent symbolism; it contrasts sharply with the more traditional kind, as old as Assyria—a symbolism that might be represented by two ferocious granite lions. This use of the bank's vaults as an expressive and visible feature was truly an inspiration.

The main entrance to the bank is on the Forty-third Street side, near the corner, and it is clearly indicated by a vertical slab of black granite in the middle of it and a horizontal siding of the same stone, with the bank's name, above it. There are two even more modest legends, in stainless-steel letters, at eye level on the glass of the Fifth Avenue façade. Remembering how one of Louis Sullivan's little banks in Iowa was bedeviled by no less than seven signs, all frantically proclaiming the name of the bank, one is grateful to the Manufacturers Trust for believing that this is enough; after all, the building has already become self-identifying.

At last we are ready to enter the building. On the ground floor, the main æsthetic ingredients of the whole composition are on display—the ceiling of corrugated plastic exuding that even yellow light; the pale terrazzo floor; the open tellers' counters, minus the old grilles and cages, forming an ell against the back walls; i.e., the south and west ones. The first of these walls, which also serves as an outer wall of the bank vault, is of black granite up to the mezzanine, and then white, light-green, and blue plaster on successive floors; the other is of sky-blue plaster up as far as the mezzanine, and then gray marble. (The walls of the fifth, or penthouse, floor are all of glass.) Since the escalators go no higher than the mezzanine, there is a bank of elevators, with handsome red-lacquered doors, in this wall. The bases of the tellers' counters are of ebony wood set between vertical ribs of stainless steel. The tops of the counters are done in a beautiful, creamy Italian marble, with a light-tan figure weaving through it. The ebony of the counters is repeated in the long, bowed table in the directors' room on the top floor, and the marble of the counters is used again for the floor of the president's room, and as a wall panel on the fifth floor. This flow of materials and colors from one floor to another, now for one purpose, now for another, contributes powerfully to the unity of the building, while the basic palette used by the design consultant, Eleanor Le Maire, is sufficiently comprehensive—white, light yellow, tan, brown, blue, and black are her principal colors—to be capable of endless variations and combinations. Radically contrasting colors are introduced only in the powder room, on the fifth floor—where all sorts of lipstick pinks and reds dominate—and in the employees' lounge, in the basement, where, doubtless in an attempt to be gay and to put banking associations aside, the color scheme is somewhat distracting, if not incongruous. Apart from this lapse, and the fact that the sky blue of various wall spaces is not merely cold but is at odds with the indigo blue in some of the textiles and leathers, Miss Le Maire's decoration seems in admirable accord with the spirit of the whole structure, including its directness—one might also say its masculinity.

Æsthetically, the topmost floor and the main banking floor are almost without reproach. The first of these is the final word in quiet luxury, though it utilizes no materials or motifs that are not already at work on the other floors. The most notable part of its decoration is the perilously artful arrangement of potted tropical plants (such as philodendrons) whose waxen perfection rouses a suspicion of complete artificiality, and the series of modern prints, paintings, and sculptures that bring into this highly rationalized interior some of the more subjective emotional elements that are usually absent from the surface operations of a banker's mind, and certainly absent from the kind of art that banks have in general patronized. But the second floor, dedicated to the senior officers of this branch of the bank, and to the Trust and Foreign Departments, is the crown of the architects' and decorator's æsthetic achievement. The noble height of this story, the tallest of the five, emphasizes its almost unbroken space, and the cold pallor of the white walls and the white marble-sheathed columns is softened by a splatter of vermilion chairs, in a reception area near the escalators, and the brilliance of a huge golden screen that is placed near the west end of this floor to separate the counter in front of it from the elevators behind. This screen is a feature that I gravely doubted when I saw the preliminary illustrations, but the truth is that it lifts the whole composition to a higher plane. It is a mass of loosely assembled and variously twisted oblong steel plaques, plated with bronze and gold and welded together, and it has just enough minor variations in texture and color, plus an occasional break into abstract shapes, to make it stand out from the glossy mechanical refinement of the rest of the structure. The screen is the work of Harry Bertoia, the Pennsylvania sculptor. Though it is purely abstract, making no effort at symbolic significance, it humanizes these quarters even more effectively than the living plants, mainly because it suggests something frail, incomplete, yet unexpected and defiant of rational statement, and thus lovable, a note that is not audible in most of the representative architectural expressions of our time. On this ground, one might also defend the tangled hair-net of wire that floats in the air above the escalators as they end, on the second floor, and that was meant to cast a complicated shadow on the south wall, but, frankly, this creation does not seem worthy of the sculptor and craftsmen who executed the screen. And the shadow has evaporated in the diffused glare of the overhead lights, since the spotlights that were to produce it were too strong for the tellers' eyes. (This problem, however, is being given further study.)

All in all, then, the Manufacturers Trust Building is perhaps as complete a fusion of rational thinking and humane imagination as we are capable of producing today. If you reject it, you reject many of the notable excellences of our age. As a symbol of the modern world, this structure is almost an ideal expression. The interpenetration of inner space and outer space, the fact that the principal functions of the building are as visible from the outside as those of a supermarket, that the same freedom of space and light has been provided in every part of the structure, thus giving the executive officers, the staff, the clients the same architectural background—this surely reflects the economic, the social, and the æsthetic principles of the modern business world at their best. This architecture is a formal expression of the culture that has explored the innermost recesses of the atom, that knows that visible boundaries and solid objects are only figments of the intellect, that looks with the aid of X-rays and radioactive isotopes at the innerness of any sort of object, from armor plate to human bodies. That architects and sculptors should seek to express this world of transparent forms and dynamic processes, that they should actually revel in this exposure is natural, since it is the eternal business of the artist to express in new forms what would otherwise remain at the commonplace levels of daily perception.

But there is a catch to this method of symbolic interpretation that some of our best architects have too often overlooked. Achieving effective symbolic expression frequently demands a surrender of practical convenience to expressiveness, a sacrifice acceptable only for religious ends. An all-glass building, fully exposed to sunlight, is a hotbox in our climate, and then the penalty one usually must pay for symbolism is to cower a large part of the time behind a Venetian blind, which robs the form of its æsthetic significance. Happily for the architects of this bank, its location and its purpose greatly reduced the practical objections to an all-glass structure. Because it is surrounded by taller buildings, there is no need for screens or blinds or green heat-ray-resistant glass. In addition, the architects, instead of treating all the functions of the bank as public ones, because of a theoretic commitment to the open plan, have provided a series of snug rooms, with doors, on the third floor to insure privacy where privacy is desirable. In other words, the functional requirements of this building coincide remarkably well with the symbolic or expressive functions, and the result is a bold, straightforward design, consistent in every detail wit'out being arbitrary or formalistic. But let novices take warning! An attempt to imitate this design under different physical conditions might easily result in lamentable sacrifices of pleasure and comfort.

And this brings me to the last factor that insured the excellence of this structure: no expense was spared in its conception and execution. By making this building just large enough for its own uses, instead of pushing it up to a height of ten or fifteen stories to provide pigeonholes for other tenants, the bank not only refrained from adding to the congested population of Fifth Avenue but enabled the architects to conceive a completely articulated and unified structure. Some of the best features of its design would have been forfeited if it had been necessary to build the usual steel skeleton with the usual number of columns. Again, the system of ceiling and cove lighting chosen was an expensive installation, but it may be that because of its unity, efficiency, and pleasantness it will turn out much cheaper in the long run. In other words, the richness and perfection of the interior are due largely to the fact that there was no penny-pinching about first costs. Perhaps the bank's president, Mr. H. C. Flanigan, took to heart the lesson of this bank's only architectural rival, the handsome P.S.F.S. Building, in Philadelphia, done by Howe & Lescaze in 1932. For there the costly materials and meticulous craftsmanship have, in the course of a quarter century, paid off in utility, low upkeep costs, and undatable beauty. What matters, really, is not first costs but final costs. Possibly the cheapest quarters in the world, as regards *total* cost, and the most profitable in the long run, are the group of buildings—originally residences—that frame the Place Vendôme in Paris. They are still spacious and sound enough to be serviceable (and bring high rents as offices) after two and a half centuries. By thinking in such long-range terms, more New York enterprises might produce buildings and even whole districts of comparable excellence.

64   The Housing Act of 1949*

The deep slump in the American housing industry after World War Two, coupled with deteriorating housing conditions in the urban core, prompted Congress to enact on July 15 what was labeled the Housing Act of 1949. The groundwork had been established in an earlier act of 1937, in which it was "declared to be the policy of the United States to promote the general welfare of the Nation by employing its funds and credit . . . to assist the several States . . . to alleviate present and recurring unemployment and to remedy the unsafe and unsanitary housing conditions and the acute shortage of decent, safe, and sanitary dwellings for families of low income, in rural or urban communities, that are injurious to the health, safety, and morals of the citizens of the Nation." † This represented a radical change in attitude, for the federal government had formally intervened in the housing market only with great reluctance in 1917–18. After the Housing Act of 1949, such support was to be on-going, thus providing the basis of the urban renewal of the 1950s and 1960s. Together with the highway act of 1958, this contributed to a near-lethal combination where the life of the cities was concerned. The early public housing of the 1930s, built with "standardized dimensions and methods of assembly," was characterized by Lewis Mumford from the start as the slums of the future; and as well-intended as the housing acts of 1937 and 1949 were, the results in the long run have proven to be as deleterious as Mumford predicted. The well-known case study is the Pruitt-Igoe housing complex of St. Louis, which was built in 1952–55 after designs by Minoru Yamasaki, and dynamited in part by the city at 3:32 P.M. on July 15, 1972.

HOUSING ACT OF 1949

An Act

To establish a national housing objective and the policy to be followed in the attainment thereof, to provide Federal aid to assist slum-clearance projects and low-rent public housing projects initiated by local agencies, to provide for financial assistance by the Secretary of Agriculture for farm housing, and for other purposes.

Be it enacted by the Senate and House of Representatives of the United States of America in Congress assembled, That this Act may be cited as the "Housing Act of 1949."

DECLARATION OF NATIONAL HOUSING POLICY

Sec. 2. The Congress hereby declares that the general welfare and security of the Nation and the health and living standards of its people require housing production and related community development sufficient to remedy the serious housing shortage, the elimination of substandard and other inadequate housing through the clearance of slums and blighted areas, and the realization as soon as feasible of the goal of a decent home and a suitable living environment for every American family, thus contributing to the de-

---

* *Housing Act of 1949,* Public Law 171, July 15, 1949, *Statutes at Large* 63 (1949), pp. 413–14.

  † *United States Housing Law of 1937,* Public Law 412, September 1, 1937, *Statutes At Large* 50 (1937).

velopment and redevelopment of communities and to the advancement of the growth, wealth, and security of the Nation. The Congress further declares that such production is necessary to enable the housing industry to make its full contribution toward an economy of maximum employment, production, and purchasing power. The policy to be followed in attaining the national housing objective hereby established shall be: (1) private enterprise shall be encouraged to serve as large a part of the total need as it can; (2) governmental assistance shall be utilized where feasible to enable private enterprise to serve more of the total need; (3) appropriate local public bodies shall be encouraged and assisted to undertake positive programs of encouraging and assisting the development of well-planned, integrated residential neighborhoods, the development and redevelopment of communities, and the production, at lower costs, of housing of sound standards of design, construction, livability, and size for adequate family life; (4) governmental assistance to eliminate substandard and other inadequate housing through the clearance of slums and blighted areas, to facilitate community development and redevelopment, and to provide adequate housing for urban and rural nonfarm families with incomes so low that they are not being decently housed in new or existing housing shall be extended to those localities which estimate their own needs and demonstrate that these needs are not being met through reliance solely upon private enterprise, and without such aid; and (5) governmental assistance for decent, safe, and sanitary farm dwellings and related facilities shall be extended where the farm owner demonstrates that he lacks sufficient resources to provide such housing on his own account and is unable to secure necessary credit for such housing from other sources on terms and conditions which he could reasonably be expected to fulfill. The Housing and Home Finance Agency and its constituent agencies, and any other departments or agencies of the Federal Government having powers, functions, or duties with respect to housing, shall exercise their powers, functions, and duties under this or any other law, consistently with the national housing policy declared by this Act and in such manner as will facilitate sustained progress in attaining the national housing objective hereby established; and in such manner as will encourage and assist (1) the production of housing of sound standards of design, construction, livability, and size for adequate family life; (2) the reduction of the costs of housing without sacrifice of such sound standards; (3) the use of new designs, materials, techniques, and methods in residential construction, the use of standardized dimensions and methods of assembly of home-building materials and equipment, and the increase of efficiency in residential construction and maintenance; (4) the development of well-planned, integrated, residential neighborhoods and the development and redevelopment of communities; and (5) the stabilization of the housing industry at a high annual volume of residential construction.

65   The Federal Highway Act of 1958*

The urgency of moving troops and matériel during the Second World War pointed up the inadequacy of the American highway system. A comprehensive new road system was needed, comparable to the German autobahns begun in the 1930s and extended to 1,300 miles by 1942. Accordingly, in 1944, a federal aid highway act was passed. In 1956, Congress began to augment both this and the original federal law of 1916, that had been devised to aid road construction. The Federal-Aid Highway Act of 1956 set up a national system of interstate highways, and a fully revised highway code was enacted in 1958.† In all, 41,000 miles of multi-lane highways were to be built by 1969 at a projected cost of $24.8 billion, this cost to be divided in a ratio of 90 to 10 with the individual states. As construction progressed during the 1960s, estimates of the eventual cost rose to $37 billion. The addition of 2,000 miles and the inflation of construction expenses boosted the final cost, in 1974 when building came to a halt, to approximately $76 billion. The chief purpose had been to connect all cities of more than 50,000 people and to handle as much as a fifth of the nation's traffic; however, with ninety percent of the cost borne by the federal government, it proved almost impossible to resist cutting broad new thoroughfares through whole sections of the urban core deemed "deteriorated." Often these thruways were flanked by low-income housing towers also federally subsidized; an example is the Dan Ryan Expressway, Chicago, built in 1957–62, alongside of which rose the Robert R. Taylor Homes complex, designed by Shaw, Metz and Associates for the Chicago Housing Authority and built in 1959–63—this and other such examples show the numbing result of the application of the federal housing and highway acts with consummate insensitivity and deadly efficiency.

FEDERAL-AID HIGHWAY ACT OF 1958

An Act to revise, codify, and enact in law, title 23 of the United States Code, entitled "Highways."

Title 23—Highways

CHAPTER 1. FEDERAL-AID HIGHWAYS

Sec. 101. *Declaration of policy.*—(b) It is hereby declared to be in the national interest to accelerate the construction of the Federal-aid highway systems, including the National System of Interstate and Defense Highways, since many of such highways, or portions thereof, are in fact inadequate to meet the needs of local and interstate commerce, for the national and civil defense.

Federal-Aid Highway Act of 1958, Public Law 85-767, August 27, 1958, *Statutes at Large* 72 (1958), p. 885 ff.

†*Federal-Aid Highway Act of 1956*, Public Law 627, June 29, 1956, *Statutes at Large* 70 (1956), p. 374 ff; this was augmented by Public Law 85-381, April 16, 1958, *Statutes at Large* 72 (1958), p. 89 ff.

It is hereby declared that the prompt and early completion of the National System of Interstate and Defense Highways, so named because of its primary importance to the national defense and hereafter referred to as the "Interstate System," is essential to the national interest and is one of the most important objectives of this Act. It is the intent of Congress that the Interstate System be completed as nearly as practicable over the period of availability of the thirteen years' appropriations authorized for the purpose of expediting its construction, reconstruction, or improvement, inclusive of necessary tunnels and bridges, through the fiscal year ending June 30, 1969, under section 108(b) of the Federal-Aid Highway Act of 1956 (70 Stat. 374), and that the entire System in all States be brought to simultaneous completion. Insofar as possible in consonance with this objective, existing highways located on an interstate route shall be used to the extent that such use is practicable, suitable, and feasible, it being the intent that local needs, to the extent practicable, suitable, and feasible, shall be given equal consideration with the needs of interstate commerce. . . .

Sec. 103. *Federal-aid systems.*—(a) For the purposes of this title, the three Federal-aid systems, the primary and secondary systems, and the Interstate System, are continued pursuant to the provisions of this section.

(b) The Federal-aid primary system shall consist of an adequate system of connected main highways, selected or designated by each State through its State highway department, subject to the approval of the Secretary as provided by subsection (e) of this section. This system shall not exceed 7 per centum of the total highway mileage of such State, exclusive of mileage within national forests, Indian, or other Federal reservations and within urban areas, as shown by the records of the State highway department on November 9, 1921. Whenever provision has been made by any State for the completion and maintenance of 90 per centum of its Federal-aid primary system, as originally designated, said State through its State highway department by and with the approval of the Secretary is authorized to increase the mileage of its Federal-aid primary system by additional mileage equal to not more than 1 per centum of the total mileage of said State as shown by the records on November 9, 1921. Thereafter, it may make like 1 per centum increases in the mileage of its Federal-aid primary system whenever provision has been made for the completion and maintenance of 90 per centum of the entire system, including the additional mileage previously authorized. This system may be located both in rural and urban areas. The mileage limitations in this paragraph shall not apply to the District of Columbia, Hawaii, Alaska, or Puerto Rico.

(c) The Federal-aid secondary system shall be selected by the State highway departments and the appropriate local road officials in cooperation with each other, subject to approval by the Secretary as provided in subsection (e) of this section. In making such selections, farm-to-market roads, rural mail routes, public school bus routes, local rural roads, county roads, township roads, and roads of the county road class may be included, so long as they are not on the Federal-aid primary system or the Interstate System. This system shall be confined to rural areas, except (1) that in any State having a population density of more than two hundred per square mile as shown by the latest available Federal census, the system may include mileage in urban areas as well as rural, and (2) that the system may be extended into urban areas subject to the conditions that any such extension passes through the urban area or connects with another Federal-aid system within the urban area, and that Federal participation in projects on such extensions is limited to urban funds.

(d) The Interstate System shall be designated within the United States, including the District of Columbia, and it shall not exceed forty-one thousand miles in total extent. It shall be so located as to connect by routes, as direct as practicable, the principal metropolitan areas, cities, and industrial centers, to serve the national defense and, to the greatest extent possible, to connect at suitable border points with routes of continental importance in the Dominion of Canada and the Republic of Mexico. The routes of this system, to the greatest extent possible, shall be selected by joint action of the State highway departments of each State and the adjoining States, subject to the approval by the Secretary as provided in subsection (e) of this section. All highways or routes included in the Interstate System are finally approved, if not already coincident with the primary system, shall be added to said system without regard to the mileage limitation set forth in subsection (b) of this section. This system may be located both in rural and urban areas. . . .

66   L. Mumford, The Highway and the City* *1958*

Lewis Mumford responded to the passage of the highway acts almost before the ink was dry. He was aware from their inception what the ultimate impact would be, for he saw that the American was sacrificing "his life as a whole to the motor car." Increasingly, Mumford stressed the primacy of human community over man's machines, and he foresaw that priority being inverted by the federally subsidized obsession with the automobile. Unlike Wright, whom he otherwise praised, Mumford favored the complexity and concentration of the urban core and derided the dispersal and decentralization of Broadacre City now actually being realized. When he collected his essays for later anthologies, Mumford customarily modified passé references, sometimes deleting or adding passages to heighten the original theme. When this essay was prepared for the concluding selection of the anthology also entitled *The Highway and the City*, Mumford added this closing exhortation: "The first lesson we have to learn is that a city exists, not for the constant passage of motor cars, but for the care and culture of men."

*Lewis Mumford, "The Highway and the City," *Architectural Record* 123 (April 1958), pp. 179–86, reprinted in *The Highway and the City* (New York, 1963) and in *Architecture as a Home for Man* (New York, 1975).

The God on Wheels

When the American people, through their Congress, voted last year for a twenty-six-billion-dollar highway program, the most charitable thing to assume about this action is that they hadn't the faintest notion of what they were doing. Within the next fifteen years they will doubtless find out; but by that time it will be too late to correct all the damage to our cities and our countryside, to say nothing of the efficient organization of industry and transportation, that this ill-conceived and absurdly unbalanced program will have wrought. Yet if someone had foretold these consequences before this vast sum of money was pushed through Congress, under the specious guise of a national defense measure, it is doubtful whether our countrymen would have listened long enough to understand; or would even have been able to change their minds if they did understand. For the current American way of life is founded not just on motor transportation but on the religion of the motor car, and the sacrifices that people are prepared to make for this religion stand outside the realm of rational criticism. Perhaps the only thing that could bring Americans to their senses would be a clear demonstration of the fact that their highway program will, eventually, wipe out the very area of freedom that the private motor car promised to retain for them.

Our Motorized Mistress

As long as motor cars were few in number, he who had one was a king: he could go where he pleased and halt where he pleased; and this machine itself appeared as a compensatory device for enlarging an ego which had been shrunken by our very success in mechanization. That sense of freedom and power remains a fact today only in low-density areas, in the open country; the popularity of this method of escape has ruined the promise it once held forth. In using the car to flee from the metropolis the motorist finds that he has merely transferred congestion to the highway; and when he reaches his destination, in a distant suburb, he finds that the countryside he sought has disappeared: beyond him, thanks to the motorway, lies only another suburb, just as dull as his own. To have a minimum amount of communication and sociability in this spread out life, his wife becomes a taxi-driver by daily occupation, and the amount of money it costs to keep this whole system running leaves him with shamefully overtaxed schools, inadequate police, poorly staffed hospitals, overcrowded recreation areas, ill-supported libraries.

In short, the American has sacrificed his life as a whole to the motor car, like someone who, demented with passion, wrecks his home in order to lavish his income on a capricious mistress who promises delights he can only occasionally enjoy.

Delusions of Progress

For most Americans, progress means accepting what is new because it is new, and discarding what is old because it is old. This may be good for a rapid turnover in business, but it is bad for continuity and stability in life. Progress, in an organic sense, should be cumulative, and though a certain amount of rubbish-clearing is always necessary, we lose part of the gain offered by a new invention if we automatically discard all the still valuable inventions that preceded it. In transportation, unfortunately, the old-fashioned linear notion of progress prevails. Now that motor cars are becoming universal, many people take for granted that pedestrian movement will disappear and that the railroad system will in time be abandoned; in fact, many of the proponents of highway building talk as if that day were already here, or if not, they have every intention of making it dawn quickly. The result is that we have actually crippled the motor car, by placing on this single means of transportation the burden for every kind of travel. Neither our cars nor our highways can take such a load. This overconcentration, moreover, is rapidly destroying our cities, without leaving anything half as good in their place.

What's Transportation For?

This is a question that highway engineers apparently never ask themselves: probably because they take for granted the belief that transportation exists for the purpose of providing suitable outlets for the motor car industry. To increase the number of cars, to enable motorists to go longer distances, to more places, at higher speeds has become an end in itself. Does this over-employment of the motor car not consume ever larger quantities of gas, oil, concrete, rubber, and steel, and so provide the very groundwork for an expanding economy? Certainly, but none of these make up the essential purpose of transportation, which is to bring people or goods to places where they are needed, and to concentrate the greatest variety of goods and people within a limited area, in order to widen the possibility of choice without making it necessary to travel. A good transportation system minimizes unnecessary transportation; and in any event, it offers a change of speed and mode to fit a diversity of human purposes.

Diffusion and concentration are the two poles of transportation: the first demands a closely articulated network of roads—ranging from a footpath to a six-lane expressway and a transcontinental railroad system. The second demands a city. Our major highway systems are conceived, in the interests of speed, as linear organizations, that is to say as arteries. That conception would be a sound one, provided the major arteries were not over-developed to the exclusion of all the minor elements of transportation. Highway planners have yet to realize that these arteries must not be thrust into the delicate tissue of our cities; the blood they circulate must rather enter through an elaborate network of minor blood vessels and capillaries. As early as 1929 Benton MacKaye worked out the rationale of sound highway development, in his conception of the Townless Highway; and this had as its corollary the Highwayless Town. In the quarter century since, all the elements of MacKaye's conception have been carried out, except the last—certainly not the least.

The Highway as a Work of Art

In many ways, our highways are not merely masterpieces of engineering, but consummate works of art: a few of them, like the Taconic State Parkway in New York, stand on a par with our highest creations in other fields. Not every highway, it is true, runs through country that offers such superb opportunities to an imaginative highway builder as this does; but then not every engineer rises to his opportunities as the planners of this highway did, routing the well-separated roads along the ridgeways, following the contours, and thus, by this single stratagem, both avoiding towns and villages and opening up great views across country, enhanced by a lavish planting of flowering bushes along the borders. If this standard of comeliness and beauty were kept generally in view, highway engineers would not so often lapse into the brutal assaults against the landscape and against urban order that they actually give way to when they aim solely at speed and volume of traffic, and bulldoze and blast their way across country to shorten their route by a few miles without making the total journey any less depressing.

Perhaps our age will be known to the future historian as the age of the bulldozer and the exterminator; and in many parts of the country the building of a highway has about the same result upon vegetation and human structures as the passage of a tornado or the blast of an atom bomb. Nowhere is this bulldozing habit of mind so disastrous as in the approach to the city. Since the engineer regards his own work as more important than the other human functions it serves, he does not hesitate to lay waste to woods, streams, parks and human neighborhoods in order to carry his roads straight to their supposed destination.

The Need for a Transportation System

The fatal mistake we have been making is to sacrifice every other form of transportation to the private motor car—and to offer as the only long-distance alternative the airplane. But the fact is that each type of transportation has its special use; and a good transportation policy must seek to improve each type and make the most of it. This cannot be achieved by aiming at high speed or continuous flow alone. If you wish casual opportunities for meeting your neighbors, and for profiting by chance contacts with acquaintances and colleagues, a stroll at two miles an hour in a relatively concentrated area, free from vehicles, will alone meet your need. But if you wish to rush a surgeon to a patient a thousand miles away, the fastest motorway is too slow. And again, if you wish to be sure to keep a lecture engagement in winter, railroad transportation offers surer speed and better insurance against being held up than the airplane. There is no one ideal mode or speed: human purpose should govern the choice of the means of transportation. That is why we need a better transportation *system*, not just more highways. The projectors of our national highway program plainly had little interest in transportation. In their fanatical zeal to expand our highways, the very allocation of funds indicates that they are ready to liquidate all other forms of land and water transportation.

The Traffic Pyramids

In order to overcome the fatal stagnation of traffic in and around our cities, our highway engineers have come up with a remedy that actually expands the evil it is meant to overcome. They create new expressways to serve cities that are already overcrowded within, thus tempting people who had been using public transportation to reach the urban centers to use these new private facilities. Almost before the first day's tolls on these expressways have been counted, the new roads themselves are overcrowded. So a clamor arises to create other similar arteries and to provide more parking garages in the center of our metropolises; and the generous provision of these facilities expands the cycle of congestion, without any promise of relief until that terminal point when all the business and industry that originally gave rise to the congestion move out of the city, to escape strangulation, leaving a waste of expressways and garages behind them. This is pyramid building with a vengeance: a tomb of concrete roads and ramps covering the dead corpse of a city.

But before our cities reach this terminal point, they will suffer, as they now do, from a continued erosion of their social facilities: an erosion that might have been avoided if engineers had understood MacKaye's point that a motorway, properly planned, is another form of railroad for private use. Unfortunately, highway engineers, if one is to judge by their usual performance, lack both historic insight and social memory: accordingly, they have been repeating, with the audacity of confident ignorance, all the mistakes in urban planning committed by their predecessors who designed our railroads. The wide swathes of land devoted to cloverleaves and expressways, to parking lots and parking garages, in the very heart of the city, butcher up precious urban space in exactly the same way that freight yards and marshalling yards did when the railroads dumped their passengers and freight inside the city. These new arteries choke off the natural routes of circulation and limit the use of abutting properties, while at the points where they disgorge their traffic, they create inevitable clots of congestion, which effectively cancel out such speed as they achieve in approaching these bottlenecks.

Today the highway engineers have no excuse for invading the city with their regional and transcontinental trunk systems: the change from the major artery to the local artery can now be achieved without breaking the bulk of goods or replacing the vehicle: that is precisely the advantage of the motor car. Arterial roads, ideally speaking, should engirdle the metropolitan area and define where its greenbelt begins; and since American cities are still too impoverished and too improvident to acquire greenbelts, they should be planned to go through the zone where relatively high-density building gives way to low-density building. On this perimeter, through traffic will by-pass the city, while cars that are headed for the center will drop off at the point closest to their destination. Since I don't know a city whose highways have been planned on this basis, let me give as an exact parallel the new semi-circular railroad line, with its suburban stations, that by-passes Amsterdam. That is good railroad planning, and it would be good highway planning, too, as the Dutch architect H. Th. Wijdeveld long ago pointed out. It is on relatively cheap land, on the edge of the city, that we should be building parking areas and garages: with free parking privileges, to tempt the commuter to leave his car and finish his daily journey on the public transportation system. The public officials who have been planning our highway system on just the opposite principle are likewise planning to make the central areas of our cities unworkable and uninhabitable. Route 128 in Boston is a belated effort to provide such a circular feeder highway; but its purpose is cancelled by current plans for arterial roads gouging into the center of the city.

Down and Up with the Elevated

Just as highway engineers know too little about city planning to correct the mistakes made in introducing the early railroad systems into our cities, so too, they have curiously forgotten our experience with the elevated railroad—and unfortunately most municipal authorities have been equally forgetful. In the middle of the nineteenth century the elevated seemed the most facile and up-to-date method of introducing a new kind of rapid transportation system into the city; and in America, New York led the way in creating four such lines on Manhattan Island alone. The noise of the trains and the overshadowing of the structure lowered the value of the abutting properties even for commercial purposes; and the supporting columns constituted a dangerous obstacle to surface transportation. So unsatisfactory was elevated transportation even in cities like Berlin, where the structures were, in contrast to New York, Philadelphia, and Chicago, rather handsome works of engineering, that by popular consent subway building replaced elevated railroad building in all big cities, even though no one could pretend that riding in a tunnel was nearly as pleasant to the rider as was travel in the open air. The destruction of the old elevated railroads in New York was, ironically, hailed as a triumph of progress precisely at the moment that a new series of elevated highways were being built, to repeat on a more colossal scale the same errors.

Highway Robbery

Like the railroad, again, the motorway has repeatedly taken possession of the most valuable recreation space the city possesses, not merely by thieving land once dedicated to park uses, but by cutting off easy access to the waterfront parks, and lowering their value for refreshment and repose by introducing the roar of traffic and the bad odor of exhausts, though both noise and carbon monoxide are inimical to health. Witness the shocking spoilage of the Charles River basin parks in Boston, the arterial blocking off of the Lake Front in Chicago (after the removal of the original usurpers, the railroads), the barbarous sacrifice of large areas of Fairmount Park in Philadelphia, the proposed defacement of the San Francisco waterfront. One may match all these social crimes with a hundred other examples of barefaced highway robbery in every other metropolitan area. Even when the people who submit to these annexations and spoliations are dimly aware of what they are losing, they submit without more than a murmur of protest. What they do not understand is that they are trading a permanent good for a very temporary advantage, since until we subordinate highway expansion to the more permanent requirements of regional planning, the flood of motor traffic will clog new channels. What they further fail to realize is that the vast sums of money that go into such enterprises drain necessary public monies from other functions of the city, and make it socially if not financially bankrupt.

The Cart Before the Horse

Neither the highway engineer nor the urban planner can, beyond a certain point, plan his facilities to accommodate an expanding population. On the overall problem of population pressure, regional and national policies must be developed for throwing open, within our country, new regions of settlement, if this pressure, which appeared so suddenly, does not in fact abate just as unexpectedly and just as suddenly. But there can be no sound planning anywhere until we understand the necessity for erecting norms, or ideal limits, for density of population. Most of our congested metropolises need a lower density of population, with more parks and open spaces, if they are to be attractive enough physically to retain even a portion of their population for day-and-night living; but most of our suburban and exurban communities must replan large areas at perhaps double their present densities in order to have the social, educational, recreational, and industrial facilities they need closer at hand. Both suburb and metropolis need a regional form of government, working in private organizations as well as public forms, to reapportion their resources and facilities, so as to benefit the whole area.

To say this is to say that both metropolitan congestion and suburban scattering are obsolete. This means that good planning must work to produce a radically new pattern for urban growth. On this matter, public policy in the United States is both contradictory and self-defeating. Instead of lowering central area densities, most urban renewal schemes, not least those aimed at housing the groups that must be subsidized, either maintain old levels of congestion, or create higher levels than existed in the slums they replaced. But the Home Loan agencies, on the other hand, have been subsidizing the wasteful, ill-planned, single-family house, on cheap land, ever remoter from the center of our cities; a policy that has done as much to promote the suburban drift as the ubiquitous motor car. In order to cement these errors in the most solid way possible, our highway policy maximizes congestion at the center and expands the area of suburban dispersion—what one might call the metropolitan "fall-out." The three public agencies concerned have no official connections with each other: but the total result of their efforts proves, once again, that chaos does not have to be planned.

Tiny Tims on Wheels

Motor car manufacturers look forward confidently to the time when every family will have two, if not three, cars. I would not deny them that hope, though I remember that it was first voiced in 1929, just before the fatal crash of our economic system, too enamored of high profits even to save itself by temporarily lowering prices. But if they don't want the motor car to paralyze urban life, they must abandon their fantastic commitment to the indecently tumescent chariots they have been putting on the market. For long-distance travel, the big car of course has many advantages; but for town use, let us insist upon a car that fits the city's needs: it is absurd to make over the city to fit the swollen imaginations of Detroit. The Isetta and the Gogomobil have already pointed the way; but what we need is an even smaller vehicle, powered by electricity, delivered by a powerful storage cell, yet to be invented. Maneuverability and parkability are the prime urban virtues in cars; and the simplest way to achieve this is by designing smaller cars. These virtues are lacking in all but one of our current American models. But why should our cities be destroyed just so that Detroit's follies should remain unchallenged and unchanged?

The Place of the Pedestrian

If we want to make the most of our New Highway program, we must keep most of the proposed expressways in abeyance until we have done two other things. We must re-plan the inner city for pedestrian circulation, and we must rebuild and extend our public forms of mass transportation. In our entrancement with the motor car, we have forgotten how much more efficient and how much more flexible the footwalker is. Before there was any public transportation in London, something like 50,000 people an hour used to pass over London Bridge on their way to work: a single artery. Mass public transportation can bring from forty to sixty thousand people per hour, along a single route, whereas our best expressways, using far more space, cannot move more than four to six thousand cars, and even if the average occupancy were more than one and a half passengers, as at present, this is obviously the most costly and inefficient means of handling the peak hours of traffic. As for the pedestrian, one could move a hundred thousand people, by the existing streets, from, say, downtown Boston to the Common, in something like half an hour, and find plenty of room for them to stand. But how many weary hours would it take to move them in cars over these same streets? And what would one do with the cars after they had reached the Common? Or where, for that matter, could one assemble these cars in the first place? For open spaces, long distances and low densities, the car is now essential; for urban space, short distances and high densities, the pedestrian.

Every urban transportation plan should, accordingly, put the pedestrian at the center of all its proposals, if only to facilitate wheeled traffic. But to bring the pedestrian back into the picture, one must treat him with the respect and honor we now accord only to the automobile: we should provide him with pleasant walks, insulated from traffic, to take him to his destination, once he enters a business precinct or residential quarter. Every city should heed the example of Rotterdam in creating the Lijnbaan, or of Coventry in creating its new shopping area. It is nonsense to say that this cannot be done in America, because no one wants to walk. Where walking is exciting and visually stimulating, whether it is in a Detroit shopping center or along Fifth Avenue, Americans are perfectly ready to walk. The legs will come into their own again, as the ideal means of neighborhood transportation, once some provision is made for their exercise, as Philadelphia is now doing, both in its Independence Hall area, and in Penn Center. But if we are to make walking attractive, we must not only provide trees and wide pavements and benches, beds of flowers and outdoor cafes, as they do in Rotterdam: we must also scrap the monotonous uniformities of American zoning practice, which turns vast areas, too spread out for pedestrian movement, into single-district zones, for commerce, industry, or residential purposes. (As a result, only the mixed zones are architecturally interesting today despite their disorder.)

Why should anyone have to take a car and drive a couple of miles to get a package of cigarettes or a loaf of bread, as one must often do in a suburb? Why, on the other hand, should a growing minority of people not be able again to walk to work, by living in the interior of the city, or, for that matter, be able to walk home from the theater or the concert hall? Where urban facilities are compact, walking still delights the American: does he not travel many thousands of miles just to enjoy this privilege in the historic urban cores of Europe? And do not people now travel for miles, of an evening, from the outskirts of Pittsburgh, just for the pleasure of a stroll in Mellon Square? Nothing would do more to give life back to our blighted urban cores than to re-instate the pedestrian, in malls and pleasances designed to make circulation a delight. And what an opportunity for architecture!

The Case for Mass Transportation

While federal funds and subsidies pour without stint into highway improvements, the two most important modes of transportation for cities—the railroad for long distances and mass transportation, and subway for shorter journeys—are permitted to languish and even to disappear. This is very much like what has happened to our postal system. While the time needed to deliver a letter across the continent has been reduced, the time needed for local delivery has been multiplied. What used to take two hours now sometimes takes two days. As a whole our postal system has been degraded to a level that would have been regarded as intolerable even thirty years ago. In both cases, an efficient system has been sacrificed to a new industry, motor cars, telephones, airplanes; whereas, if the integrity of the system itself had been respected, each of these new inventions could have added enormously to the efficiency of the existing network.

If we could overcome the irrational drives that are now at work, promoting shortsighted decisions, the rational case for re-building the mass transportation system in our cities would be overwhelming. The current objection to mass transportation comes chiefly from the fact that it has been allowed to decay: this lapse itself reflects the general blight of the central areas. In order to maintain profits, or in many cases to reduce deficits, rates have been raised, services have decreased, and equipment has become obsolete, without being replaced and improved. Yet mass transportation, with far less acreage in roadbeds and rights of way, can deliver at least ten times more people per hour than the private motor car. This means that if such means were allowed to lapse in our metropolitan centers—as the inter-urban electric trolley system, that beautiful and efficient network, was allowed to disappear in the nineteen twenties—we should require probably five to ten times the existing number of arterial highways to bring the present number of commuters into the city, and at least ten times the existing parking space to accommodate them.

This reduces a one-dimensional transportation system, by motor car alone, to a calamitous absurdity, as far as urban development goes, even if the number of vehicles and the population count were not increasing year by year. Now it happens that the population of the core of our big cities has remained stable in recent years: in many cases, the decline which set in as early as 1910 in New York seems to have ceased. This means that it is now possible to set an upper limit for the daily inflow of workers, and to work out a permanent mass transportation system that will get them in and out again as pleasantly and efficiently as possible. In time, if urban renewal projects become sufficient in number to permit the design of a system of minor urban throughways, at ground level, that will by-pass the neighborhood, even circulation by motor car may play a valuable part in the total scheme—provided, of course, that minuscule size town cars take the place of the long-tailed dinosaurs that now lumber about our metropolitan swamps.

But the notion that the private motor car can be substituted for mass transportation should be put forward only by those who desire to see the city itself disappear, and with it the complex, many-sided civilization that the city makes possible.

Brakes and Accelerations

There is no purely engineering solution to the problems of transportation in our age: nothing like a stable solution is possible without giving due weight to all the necessary elements in transportation—private motor cars, railroads, airplanes and helicopters, mass transportation services by trolley and bus, even ferryboats, and finally, not least, the pedestrian. To achieve the necessary over-all pattern, not merely must there be effective city and regional planning, before new routes or services are planned; we also need eventually—and the sooner the better—an adequate system of federated metropolitan government. Until these necessary tools of control have been created, most of our planning will be empirical and blundering; and the more we do, on our present premises, the most disastrous will be the results. What is needed is more thinking on the lines that Robert Mitchell, Edmund Bacon, and Wilfred Owens have been following, and less action, until this thinking has been embodied in a new conception of the needs and possibilities of contemporary urban life. We cannot have an efficient form for our transportation system until we can envisage a better permanent structure for our cities.

67   L. Mumford, The Disappearance of Pennsylvania Station* *1958*

In his *Sticks and Stones* (New York, 1924), the first study of American architecture considered as a whole, Mumford directed severe criticism at the architecture of Daniel Burnham and Charles Follen McKim, which represented what he then termed "the Imperial Facade." He begrudgingly allowed that "the finest element in the Pennsylvania station is the train hall where the architect has dealt sincerely with his steel element and has not permitted himself to a cast a fond, retrospective eye upon the Roman baths." He outlined "a criterion which will enable us to sum up the architecture of the imperial age, and deal justly with these railroad stations and stadiums, these sewers and circuses. . . . Our imperial architecture is an architecture of compensation: it provides grandiloquent stones for people who have been deprived of bread and sunlight and all that keeps man from becoming vile. Behind the monumental facades of our metropolises trudges a landless proletariat, doomed to the servile routine of the factory system."

*Lewis Mumford, "The Disappearance of Pennsylvania Station," *The New Yorker* 34 (June 7, 1958), pp. 106–11 and also in the *Journal, American Institute of Architects* 30 (October 1958), pp. 40–43; and reprinted in *The Highway and the City* (New York, 1963).

However, a third of a century spent *using* Pennsylvania Station gradually redirected Mumford's opinion by almost 180 degrees, for he came to see that in fact the great soaring covered spaces, even if they were inspired by Roman baths, were "not only imposing but soothing and reassuring, as if a load were taken off one's chest." In this essay he pointed out the crystal clarity of McKim's plan, which gave circulation "the effortless inevitability of a gravity-flow system." Indeed, perhaps it was Mumford's basic aversion to academic classicism that allowed him to see so well how Pennsylvania Station worked, for his perceptions were not conditioned by stylistic bias. His analysis, of the station, short though it is, remains one of the best.[†] With customary prescience, Mumford saw that the callous misuse and pointless modernization of the station foreshadowed its eventual demolition—it was, in fact, destroyed five years after this article appeared.

For perhaps two years, I have watched, with silent misgiving, the reorganization of the interior of Pennsylvania Station. As the extent of the demolition grew, my bewilderment grew with it. I hardly believe that any rational purpose could justify the devastation that was being worked, and as the bottoms of the row of great stone columns that run from north to south across the station were chipped away and covered with a light-hued plastic, my bewilderment became incredulity. So I waited, hoping that some brilliant stroke of planning, beyond any notions I could form from the unfinished work, would turn the phantasmagoria my eyes beheld into a benign dream. But now that the scheme had taken shape, it is plain that I waited in vain. As things are going, I fully expect that Jules Guerin's begrimed mural maps, which adorn the walls above the concourse and which were once, not unjustly, described as one of the few examples of successful mural art in the country, will give way to colossal color transparencies or winking whiskey ads. The only consolation is that nothing more that can be done to the station will do any further harm to it. As in nuclear war, after complete destruction has been achieved, one cannot increase the damage by doubling the destructive forces.

The Pennsylvania Station, now half a century old, was the collaborative product of Alexander Johnston Cassatt, the Pennsylvania Railroad's president, and Charles Follen McKim, of McKim, Mead & White, who got the commission in 1902 and finished the job in 1910, after four years of building. The purpose Mr. Cassatt had in mind was to provide a magnificent, monumental structure that would serve the railroad well and embellish the city. "Certain preliminary matters had to be settled with President Cassatt before McKim could begin to think of the design," Charles Moore, McKim's biographer, notes. "The company had a notion of utilizing the very valuable air space above the station by building a hotel. Mr. McKim argued that the great Pennsylvania Railroad owed the metropolis a thoroughly and distinctly

[†] Although McKim himself never prepared a finished statement of his design intentions in Pennsylvania Station, his assistant, William Symmes Richardson, who actually built the station, published two descriptive analyses of the station: "The Architectural Motif of the Pennsylvania Station," in *A History of the Construction Engineering . . . of the Pennsylvania Railroad Company's New York Terminal and Approaches*, ed., William Couper (New York, 1912), pp. 77–78; and "The Terminal—The Gate of the City," *Scribner's* 52 (October 1912), pp. 401–16.

monumental gateway." And professional and civic pride won out over cu-
pidity. But, unfortunately, the spirit of adventure had gone out of American
architecture. Except for Louis Sullivan, Frank Lloyd Wright, and a handful
of their followers, no one any longer had the courage or the imagination to
create new forms native to our own culture and the century. So the station
was cast in the classic form of the Roman baths of Caracalla; indeed, McKim
had intuitively prepared himself for this commission, in 1901, by assembling
a gang of workmen in those very baths, so that he could study the esthetic
effect of the huge scale of the structure on the crowds passing under its
arches. The punctuating beat of the rows of vast classic columns, without
and within, of Pennsylvania Station turned out to be the dying note of the
classic revival that had begun in 1893 with the Chicago World's Fair. But
though the classic forms were symbolically dead and functionally meretri-
cious, McKim's handling of the main elements of the design for the station
was superb. The basic practical problem, created by the fact that the railway
tracks, in order to pass under the East and Hudson Rivers on their way out
of town, were far below ground, has, it is true, never been properly solved.
Above the track level is a second level, along which one makes one's way
from the trains to the subway lines on Seventh and Eighth Avenues; above
this is a third level, containing the concourse and the ticket offices, and
flanked by the taxicab ramps. Even this level is well below ground, and it is
reached from east, west, north, and south by broad stairways from the streets
surrounding the station. The ambiguity of the many exits from the trains,
some leading to the second level and some to the third, is baffling to anyone
attempting to meet a person arriving on a train, and creates a certain degree
of confusion for the traveller seeking a taxi or a subway. Even worse, the
inadequacy of the escalator system handicaps the passenger with heavy baggage much more today than it did in those fabled days when porters were
numerous and did not become invisible when a train arrived. In these respects, the Thirtieth Street Station in Philadelphia and the Union Station in
Washington, even with their two levels of railway tracks are more satisfactory, despite the fact that the system of widely space doubled exits in the
Philadelphia station makes meeting an incoming passenger difficult without
prearrangement.

But, apart from these vexatious lapses, the general plan of Pennsylvania
Station had a noble simplicity that helped it to work well. A broad, unobstructed corridor, running from east to west, was the visible expression of the
station's axis, from Seventh Avenue clear through to Eighth Avenue. McKim
made good use of his eight-acre site, which covered two entire blocks, by
providing a sunken entrance, at the concourse level, for vehicles on both the
north and the south sides of the station—far more adequate than the accommodations at Grand Central. If one approached the station by car, one had
to walk but a short distance to the ticket windows and the trains. The ticket
offices, the big waiting rooms, and the ample concourse, capable of embracing the largest holiday crowds, were at right angles to the axis and flanked
the broad corridor. McKim, wishing to keep the axis and corridor clear, even
placed the information booth in a northern corner, in a niche formed by the
men's waiting room and some of the ticket booths, but wiser heads soon
moved this important facility to the center of the ticket hall, so that passen-

gers could approach it from the four points of the compass.

McKim's plan had a crystal clarity that gave the circulation the effortless inevitability of a gravity-flow system, with pools of open space to slow down or rest in when one left the main currents. Movement is the essence of transportation, and movement is what McKim's plan magnificently provided for. Amplifying this spaciousness were the great columns and high ceilings of both the main entrance corridor (leading west from Seventh Avenue and lined with shops and restaurants) and the ticket hall, waiting rooms, and concourse—the scale gigantic, the effect not only imposing but soothing and reassuring, as if a load were taken off one's chest. In this terminal, meant to encompass crowds, there was no sense of crowding; the ticket hall was as long as the nave of St. Peter's. The shopworn tags of McKim's classic decoration receded from consciousness, and what remained was a beautiful ordering of space, whose proportions veiled the appropriate decorative pomp and nullified the occasional irritations of the ascent from or descent to the trains. Even the fifty-year accumulation of grime on the travertine walls of the interior has not robbed this building of its essential grandeur, which now suggests the musty subterranean passages in the contemporary remains of a Roman bath. There is never too much of that grand Roman quality in a modern city. It comes from a princely sense of magnificence, a willingness to spend munificiently on a purely esthetic pleasure, instead of squeezing out the last penny of dividends. American railroad stations as late as twenty-five years ago compared favorably with those of England and the Continent, because of their interior serenity and dignity as well as the fact that they were then altogether free of advertisements—a point the European traveller often remarked on with surprise, as a pleasing contradiction in the land of the almighty dollar.

No one now entering Pennsylvania Station for the first time could, without clairvoyance, imagine how good it used to be, in comparison to the almost indescribable botch that has been made of it. To take the most favorable view of the new era, let us enter the main approach, from Seventh Avenue—the only element left that faintly resembles the original design. But the spaciousness of the corridor, with its long view, has been diminished by a series of centrally placed advertisements—a large aluminum-framed glass box for posters; then that standard fixture of today's railroad station, a rubber-tired confection from Detroit suggesting to the guileless traveller the superior claims of private motor transportation; then another poster box, holding an illuminated color photograph of a steak dinner. These nagging intrusions are only a modest beginning; in time, the top of this great, barrel vaulted corridor will probably, like the concourse, be punctuated with transparencies and flying signs.

Happily, these obstacles serve an esthetic function; they soften the shock that one encounters at the head of the stairs to the main floor. There one discovers that almost the whole interior arrangement has been swept away. The broad east-west corridor has vanished, and in its place a huge plastic crescent canopy, brittle, fragile, and luminous, opens out, fanlike, across one's view—a canopy slanting upward at an awkward angle and suspended in midair by wires from the sturdy-looking stone columns of the original design: in all, a masterpiece of architectural and visual incongruity. This vast arched canopy drenches the space below it with diffused fluorescent light, illuminating a semicircle of ticket counters and, behind them, clerks at ranks of desks. The semicircle completely blocks the main channel of circulation to the concourse; moreover, it conceals the bottom half of the great window that once marked the western end of the station's axis. The counters of the ticket office are laid out in saw-tooth indentations—open and without grillwork, like the ones in the newer banks—and a closed-circuit television set beside each counter presents the intending traveller with a visual summary of the accommodations available for the next week or so on whatever train he has in mind. This saw-toothed arrangement and the abandonment of the framed booth are the only elements in the design for which the most charitable observer can say a good word: let the reader linger over this moment of praise. The rest of this new office is a symposium of errors. To provide enough space in the rear for the booking clerks, once housed in the innards of the station, the designer wiped out both waiting rooms, for which a wholly inadequate substitute has been provided by a few benches on the concourse. To reach these, and the trains, one must walk all the way around the ticket counters. And the large central information booth has disappeared, to be replaced by a tiny counter tucked away north of the stairs from the Seventh Avenue entrance in such a fashion that people making inquiry at it obstruct one exit to the subways. "Meet me at the information booth" is now, at any busy hour, a useless suggestion. "Meet me at Travelers Aid" would be more to the point. To conceal the information booth so neatly and to block so effectively an exit is a feat that only emphasizes the quality of this renovation—its exquisite precision in matching bad esthetics to a bad plan.

And there are other places in Pennsylvania Station where this carefree treatment has been equally successful. There are separate counters for buyers of coach, parlor-car, and sleeping-car tickets, but since the counters are identified only by numbered orange, green, blue, or red signboards, one must consult an index board beforehand. The use of colors is an excellent means of identification for all but the color-blind. Unfortunately, though, the numerals, which are white, do not show up clearly against the light green, and they virtually dissolve into the dull orange; only the red and blue backgrounds have a decent visibility. (Bold numerals, like the ones used in the central Rome railroad station, would remove the need for color identification.) No one can claim that this feeble, reticent color scheme represents an unwillingness to introduce a strong discordant note, for of such notes there is a jarring plenitude—the greenery-yallery walls next to the train hall, the stark white and black of the telephone booths, the effulgent stainless steel of the new shops and booths that have been erected on the main floor; in short, a West Forty-second Street garishness and tawdriness characterize the whole reconstruction. With this over-all design to establish the level of taste, the fevered illuminations of the soft-drink machines are fitting embellishments of the general chaos.

But these are minor matters; the great treason to McKim's original design, and the overpowering blunder, is the conception of these misplaced ticket counters, with their background of ticket clerks busily acting their parts under television's myriad eyes. If treated rationally and straightforwardly, the change-over to open counters with television equipment and doubled space for ticket selling could have been accomplished without destroying a single important feature of the whole station. But rational considerations of fitness, function, and form, with a view to the ultimate human decencies, seem as unimportant in the reconstruction of Pennsylvania Station as they do to some of our designers of motorcars. One suspects that the subversion of McKim's masterly plan was due simply to the desire to make the whole design an immense advertising display, and, in fact, this design now centers on the suspended canopy, which not merely provides a ceiling of light for the office space below but juts out many feet beyond the counters, as if it had the function it might serve in the open air—of offering shelter against rain. The purpose of such a design, psychologically speaking, is possibly to convince the railroad user either that the Pennsylvania Railroad has gone modern and that the old station can be as pinched for space, as generally commonplace, as a bus terminal, or else that it can be as aerodynamic in form as an airport terminal. The effort to shorten the time needed to make reservations is a laudable one, though it may be doubted whether electronic feathers will do much to improve a system whose worst bottleneck is not communications but wholesale advance bookings by business corporations (often far in excess of their needs), which create the difficulty of allotting too few spaces to too many. But let us nevertheless assume that the new installation provides handsome gains in efficiency. These gains must be weighed against serious losses of efficiency at other points. There is no reason, for instance, that the booking clerks should occupy the space once given over to waiting rooms. As a result of this pointless dramatization of the process of ticket selling, the waiting passengers are now squeezed onto a few benches, many of them a constant obstacle to passenger circulation.

What on earth were the railroad men in charge really attempting to achieve? And why is the result such a disaster? Did the people who once announced that they were planning to convert the station property into a great skyscraper market and Fun Fair decide, finding themselves temporarily thwarted in that scheme, to turn their energies to destroying the station from the inside, in order to provide a better justification for their plans? Or did the management see pictures of the new Rome station and decide that it would be nice to have a station equally up-to-date, and even more flashily so? But they forgot that though the Rome booking hall is in effect a canopy, it is a free-standing structure poised dynamically on its own base, serving not as a piece of phony stage decoration but as a shelter for its activities. To transport the idea of a canopy into Pennsylvania Station, whose overwhelming quality, esthetically, depends upon its free command of space, was to nullify not merely its rational plan but its height, its dignity, and its tranquil beauty. If the planners had cut the height of the main level in two by inserting another floor above it, they could not have debased the original design more effectively than they have by introducing that mask of light, suspended by wires. This glaring device was not necessitated by the television system of communication. The special merit of such a system is that the headquarters of the operation can be miles away from the place where the information registers. To disrupt the whole flow of traffic through the station so as to put the system on display is a miscarriage of the display motive.

Behind this design, one must assume, was the notion that has made automobile manufacturers add airplane fins to their earth-bound products. This shows a loss of faith in their trade, on the part of railroad men, that may hasten the demise of the railways. If they had sufficient pride in their own method of transportation, they would emphasize the things that make it different from air or motor transportation—its freedom from tension and danger, the fact that planes stack up interminably over airports in poor weather, the fact that a motor expressway, according to surveys, can handle only four thousand people an hour, while a railroad line can handle forty thousand people an hour. This capacity for coping quickly with crowds that would clog the best highway facilities for hours is the special achievement of the railroad. What the railroad does superbly the motor expressway does badly, and planes, even though they travel at supersonic speed, cannot do at all. This was boldly dramatized by McKim in the great vomitoria he designed to handle the crowds in Pennsylvania Station. Everything that clutters up a railroad terminal either physically or visually must accordingly be rated as bad design, and, ultimately, because of its retarding effect on convenience and comfort, as bad publicity, too.

Some of the engineering ingenuity that was spent in devising the vast electronic jukebox of Pennsylvania Station might well have gone into repairing the crucial error in McKim's design—the failure to carry the system of circulation into its final stage; that is, an adequate method of passing immediately to and from the trains. As it is, a beautiful trip out of town can be soured in a few minutes by the poverty of mechanical means for changing levels and for transporting hand baggage. Moving platforms, escalators, lightweight two-wheeled luggage trucks, like the carts at a supermarket; identification signs for baggage lockers, so that one might recognize at a distance where one left one's bags, just by looking at the color of one's key; a well-identified enclosure for meeting—such highly desirable improvements as these are untouched by the present innovations.

The lack of improvements in these essential matters is a symptom of the bureaucratic fossilization in railroading, and that backwardness cannot be overcome by jazzing up the ticket service. If the Pennsylvania Railroad had given thought to these inefficiencies and discomforts and inconveniences, it would have treated the improvement of the ticket services with the same sharp eye on the business of railroading, and with the same readiness to keep the original design quietly up-to-date, without sacrificing the qualities in it that are timeless. Such a thorough renovation might be even more expensive than the present disarrangement, but it would pay off by improving every aspect of the service, instead of simply faking a loudly "modern" setting in the hope that the passenger will forget the many ancient coaches and Pullman cars, with their shabby upholstery, that are still in service.

But no sort of renovation of Pennsylvania Station makes sense until the railroad is ready to commission the one operation that would really cause it to look fresh and bright without benefit of fluorescent lighting—a complete cleansing of its soiled interior. The plaster has begun to crack and peel in the Seventh Avenue corridor; the mural maps are almost invisible; and, as if to accentuate the dirt, the thrifty management has merely scoured the columns and walls to a height of ten feet, making the worst of a bad job. As for the vast blaze of light from the low ceiling in the renovated portions, its chief effect at night is to make the train hall look as though it were under an air-raid blackout. If it was sad that Alexander Cassatt should have died in 1906, without seeing his great station erected, it was a mercy that he did not live until 1958, to witness its bungling destruction. It would take even mightier powers than these old railroad titans wielded to undo this damage.

68   J. Jacobs, The Death and Life of Great American Cities* *1961*

In his later writing, most especially in *The City in History* (New York, 1961), Mumford argued that the city, the nurturing source of civilization, was being eviscerated and dehumanized through misdirected "modernization," exemplified in the treatment of Pennsylvania Station. Joining Mumford in what was seen around 1960 as a Quixotic attack on International Modernism and concomitant urban renewal was Jane Jacobs. Born in 1916 in Scranton, Pennsylvania, she pursued a career in journalism there and in New York, writing in particular about its working districts; like Mumford she came to understand the inner workings of the city by exploring its streets, not by earning an academic degree. In 1944 she married architect Robert Hyde Jacobs, and for a time they resided in Greenwich Village, New York, an experience which shaped her view of the social vitality of the urban street. From 1952 to 1963 she was associate and then senior editor of *Architectural Forum*, contributing "Downtown Is for People," to *The Exploding Metropolis* by the editors of *Fortune* (New York, 1958). In this she asserted that the renewal projects then on the drawing boards across the country "will not revitalize downtown; they will deaden it. For they work at cross-purposes to the city. They banish the street." To Jacobs the city was not an accretion of buildings but a network of intricately connected organisms. Diversity and complexity she saw as the key to urban vitality, opening *Death and Life of Great American Cities* with a quote from Oliver Wendell Holmes, Jr.: "The chief worth of civilization is just that it makes the means of living more complex; that it calls for great and combined intellectual efforts, instead of simple, uncoordinated ones." The proposals she outlined in this book grew out of her study of the building projects she had been assigned to cover for *Fortune*. Her second major book, *The Economy of Cities* (New York, 1969), explored how cities prosper and how they can fuel their own regeneration.

*Jane B. Jacobs, *The Death and Life of Great American Cities* (New York, 1961), pp. 3–16.

Introduction

This book is an attack on current city planing and rebuilding. It is also, and mostly, an attempt to introduce new principles of city planning and rebuilding, different and even opposite from those now taught in everything from schools of architecture and planning to the Sunday supplements and women's magazines. My attack is not based on quibbles about rebuilding methods or hairsplitting about fashions in design. It is an attack, rather, on the principles and aims that have shaped modern, orthodox city planning and rebuilding.

In setting forth different principles, I shall mainly be writing about common, ordinary things: for instance, what kinds of city streets are safe and what kinds are not; why some city parks are marvelous and others are vice traps and death traps; why some slums stay slums and other slums regenerate themselves even against financial and official opposition; what makes downtowns shift their centers; what, if anything, is a city neighborhood, and what jobs, if any, neighborhoods in great cities do. In short, I shall be writing about how cities work in real life, because this is the only way to learn what principles of planning and what practices in rebuilding can promote social and economic vitality in cities, and what practices and principles will deaden these attributes.

There is a wistful myth that if only we had enough money to spend—the figure is usually put at a hundred billion dollars—we could wipe out all our slums in ten years, reverse decay in the great, dull, gray belts that were yesterday's and day-before-yesterday's suburbs, anchor the wandering middle class and its wandering tax money, and perhaps even solve the traffic problem.

But look what we have built with the first several billions: Low-income projects that become worse centers of delinquency, vandalism and general social hopelessness than the slums they were supposed to replace. Middle-income housing projects which are truly marvels of dullness and regimentation, sealed against any buoyancy or vitality of city life. Luxury housing projects that mitigate their inanity, or try to, with a vapid vulgarity. Cultural centers that are unable to support a good bookstore. Civic centers that are avoided by everyone but bums, who have fewer choices of loitering place than others. Commercial centers that are lackluster imitations of standardized suburban chain-store shopping. Promenades that go from no place to nowhere and have no promenaders. Expressways that eviscerate great cities. This is not the rebuilding of cities. This is the sacking of cities.

Under the surface, these accomplishments prove even poorer than their poor pretenses. They seldom aid the city areas around them, as in theory they are supposed to. These amputated areas typically develop galloping gangrene. To house people in this planned fashion, price tags are fastened on the population, and each sorted-out chunk of price-tagged populace lives in growing suspicion and tension against the surrounding city. When two or more such hostile islands are juxtaposed the result is called "a balanced neighborhood." Monopolistic shopping centers and monumental cultural centers cloak, under the public relations hoohaw, the subtraction of commerce, and of culture too, from the intimate and casual life of cities.

That such wonders may be accomplished, people who get marked with the planners' hex signs are pushed about, expropriated, and uprooted much as if they were the subjects of a conquering power. Thousands upon thousands of small businesses are destroyed, and their proprietors ruined, with hardly a gesture at compensation. Whole communities are torn apart and sown to the winds, with a reaping of cynicism, resentment and despair that must be heard and seen to be believed. A group of clergymen in Chicago, appalled at the fruits of planned city rebuilding there, asked,

> Could Job have been thinking of Chicago when he wrote:
> Here are men that alter their neighbor's landmark . . . shoulder the poor aside, conspire to oppress the friendless.
> Reap they the field that is none of theirs, strip they the vineyard wrongfully seized from its owner . . .
> A cry goes up from the city streets, where wounded men lie groaning . . .

If so, he was thinking of New York, Philadelphia, Boston, Washington, St. Louis, San Francisco and a number of other places. The economic rationale of current city rebuilding is a hoax. The economics of city rebuilding do not rest soundly on reasoned investment of public tax subsidies, as urban renewal theory proclaims, but also on vast, involuntary subsidies wrung out of helpless site victims. And the increased tax returns from such sites, accruing to the cities as a result of this "investment," are a mirage, a pitiful gesture against the ever increasing sums of public money needed to combat disintegration and instability that flow from the cruelly shaken-up city. The means to planned city rebuilding are as deplorable as the ends.

Meantime, all the art and science of city planning are helpless to stem decay—and the spiritlessness that precedes decay—in ever more massive swatches of cities. Nor can this decay be laid, reassuringly, to lack of opportunity to apply the arts of planning. It seems to matter little whether they are applied or not. Consider the Morningside Heights area in New York City. According to planning theory it should not be in trouble at all, for it enjoys a great abundance of parkland, campus, playground and other open spaces. It has plenty of grass. It occupies high and pleasant ground with magnificent river views. It is a famous educational center with splendid institutions—Columbia University, Union Theological Seminary, the Julliard School of Music, and half a dozen others of eminent respectability. It is the beneficiary of good hospitals and churches. It has no industries. Its streets are zoned in the main against "incompatible uses" intruding into the preserves for solidly constructed, roomy, middle-and upper-class apartments. Yet by the early 1950's Morningside Heights was becoming a slum so swiftly, the surly kind of slum in which people fear to walk the streets, that the situation posed a crisis for the institutions. They and the planning arms of the city government got together, applied more planning theory, wiped out the most run-down part of the area and built in its stead a middle-income cooperative project complete with shopping center, and a public housing project, all interspersed with air, light, sunshine and landscaping. This was hailed as a great demonstration in city saving.

After that, Morningside Heights went downhill even faster.

Nor is this an unfair or irrelevant example. In city after city, precisely the wrong areas, in the light of planning theory, are decaying. Less noticed, but equally significant, in city after city the wrong areas, in the light of planning theory, are refusing to decay.

Cities are an immense laboratory of trial and error, failure and success, in city building and city design. This is the laboratory in which city planning should have been learning and forming and testing its theories. Instead the practitioners and teachers of this discipline (if such it can be called) have ignored the study of success and failure in real life, have been incurious about the reasons for unexpected success, and are guided instead by principles derived from the behavior and appearance of towns, suburbs, tuberculosis sanatoria, fairs, and imaginary dream cities—from anything but cities themselves.

If it appears that the rebuilt portions of cities and the endless new developments spreading beyond the cities are reducing city and countryside alike to a monotonous, unnourishing gruel, this is not strange. It all comes, first-, second-, third- or fourth-hand, out of the same intellectual dish of mush, a mush in which the qualities, necessities, advantages and behavior of great cities have been utterly confused with the qualities, necessities, advantages and behavior of other and more inert types of settlements.

There is nothing economically or socially inevitable about either the decay of old cities or the fresh-minted decadence of the new unurban urbanization. On the contrary, no other aspect of our economy and society has been more purposefully manipulated for a full quarter of a century to achieve precisely what we are getting. Extraordinary governmental financial incentives have been required to achieve this degree of monotony, sterility and vulgarity. Decades of preaching, writing, and exhorting by experts have gone into convincing us and our legislators that mush like this must be good for us, as long as it comes bedded with grass.

Automobiles are often conveniently tagged as the villains responsible for the ills of cities and the disappointments and futilities of city planning. But the destructive effects of automobiles are much less a cause than a symptom of our incompetence at city building. Of course planners, including the highwaymen with fabulous sums of money and enormous powers at their disposal, are at a loss to make automobiles and cities compatible with one another. They do not know what to do with automobiles in cities because they do not know how to plan for workable and vital cities anyhow—with or without automobiles.

The simple needs of automobiles are more easily understood and satisfied than the complex needs of cities, and a growing number of planners and designers have come to believe that if they can only solve the problems of traffic, they will thereby have solved the major problem of cities. Cities have much more intricate economic and social concerns than automobile traffic. How can you know what to try with traffic until you know how the city itself works, and what else it needs to do with its streets? You can't.

It may be that we have become so feckless as a people that we no longer care how things do work, but only what kind of quick, easy outer impression they give. If so, there is little hope for our cities or probably for much else in our society. But I do not think this is so.

Specifically, in the case of planning for cities, it is clear that a large number of good and earnest people do care deeply about building and renewing. Despite some corruption, and considerable greed for the other man's vineyard, the intentions going into the messes we make are, on the whole, exemplary. Planners, architects of city design, and those they have led along with them in their beliefs are not consciously disdainful of the importance of knowing how things work. On the contrary, they have gone to great pains to learn what the saints and sages of modern orthodox planning have said about how cities *ought* to work and what *ought* to be good for people and businesses in them. They take this with such devotion that when contradictory reality intrudes, threatening to shatter their dearly won learning, they must shrug reality aside.

Consider, for example, the orthodox planning reaction to a district called the North End in Boston. This is an old, low-rent area merging into the heavy industry of the waterfront, and it is officially considered Boston's worst slum and civic shame. It embodies attributes which all enlightened people know are evil because so many wise men have said they are evil. Not only is the North End bumped right up against industry, but worse still it has all kinds of working places and commerce mingled in the greatest complexity with its residences. It has the highest concentration of dwelling units, on the land that is used for dwelling units, of any part of Boston, and indeed one of the highest concentrations to be found in any American city. It has little parkland. Children play in the streets. Instead of super-blocks, or even decently large blocks, it has very small blocks; in planning parlance it is "badly cut up with wasteful streets." Its buildings are old. Everything conceivable is presumably wrong with the North End. In orthodox planning terms, it is a three-dimensional textbook of "megalopolis" in the last stages of depravity. The North End is thus a recurring assignment for M.I.T. and Harvard planning and architectural students, who now and again pursue, under the guidance of their teachers, the paper exercise of converting it into super-blocks and park promenades, wiping away its nonconforming uses, transforming it to an ideal of order and gentility so simple it could be engraved on the head of a pin.

Twenty years ago, when I first happened to see the North End, its buildings—town houses of different kinds and sizes converted to flats, and four- or five-story tenements built to house the flood of immigrants first from Ireland, then from Eastern Europe and finally from Sicily—were badly overcrowded, and the general effect was of a district taking a terrible physical beating and certainly desperately poor.

When I saw the North End again in 1959, I was amazed at the change. Dozens and dozens of buildings had been rehabilitated. Instead of mattresses against the windows there were Venetian blinds and glimpses of fresh paint. Many of the small, converted houses now had only one or two families in them instead of the old crowded three or four. Some of the families in the tenements (as I learned later, visiting inside) had uncrowded themselves by throwing two older apartments together, and had equipped these with bathrooms, new kitchens and the like. I looked down a narrow alley, thinking to find at least here the old, squalid North End, but no: more neatly repointed brickwork, new blinds, and a burst of music as a door opened. Indeed, this was the only city district I had ever seen—or have seen to this day—in which the sides of buildings around parking lots had not been left raw and amputated, but repaired and painted as neatly as if they were intended to be seen. Mingled all among the buildings for living were an incredible number of splendid food stores, as well as such enterprises as upholstery making, metal working, carpentry, food processing. The streets were alive with children playing, people shopping, people strolling, people talking. Had it not been a cold January day, there would surely have been people sitting.

The general street atmosphere of buoyancy, friendliness and good health was so infectious that I began asking directions of people just for the fun of getting in on some talk. I had seen a lot of Boston in the past couple of days, most of it sorely distressing, and this struck me, with relief, as the healthiest place in the city. But I could not imagine where the money had come from for the rehabilitation, because it is almost impossible today to get any appreciable mortgage money in districts of American cities that are not either high-rent, or else imitations of suburbs. To find out, I went into a bar and restaurant (where an animated conversation about fishing was in progress) and called a Boston planner I know.

"Why in the world are you down in the North End?" he said. "Money? Why, no money or work has gone into the North End. Nothing's going on down there. Eventually, yes, but not yet. That's a slum!"

"It doesn't seem like a slum to me," I said.

"Why, that's the worst slum in the city. It has two hundred and seventy-five dwellings units to the net acre! I hate to admit we have anything like that in Boston, but it's a fact."

"Do you have any other figures on it?" I asked.

"Yes, funny thing. It has among the lowest delinquency, disease and infant mortality rates in the city. It also has the lowest ratio of rent to income in the city. Boy, are those people getting bargains. Let's see . . . the child population is just about average for the city, on the nose. The death rate is low, 8.8 per thousand, against the average city rate of 11.2. The TB death rate is very low, less than 1 per ten thousand, can't understand it, it's lower even than Brookline's. In the old days the North End used to be the city's worst spot for tuberculosis, but all that has changed. Well, they must be strong people. Of course it's a terrible slum."

"You should have more slums like this," I said. "Don't tell me there are plans to wipe this out. You ought to be down here learning as much as you can from it."

"I know how you feel," he said. "I often go down there myself just to walk down the streets and feel that wonderful, cheerful street life. Say, what you ought to do, you ought to come back and go down in the summer if you think it's fun now. You'd be crazy about it in the summer. But of course we have to rebuild it eventually. We've got to get those people off the streets."

Here was a curious thing. My friend's instincts told him the North End was a good place, and his social statistics confirmed it. But everything he had learned as a physical planner about what is good for people and good for city neighborhoods, everything that made him an expert, told him the North End had to be a bad place.

The leading Boston savings banker, "a man 'way up there in the power structure," to whom my friend referred me for my inquiry about the money, confirmed what I learned, in the meantime, from people in the North End. The money had not come through the grace of the great American banking system, which now knows enough about planning to know a slum as well as the planners do. "No sense in lending money into the North End," the banker said. "It's a slum! It's still getting some immigrants! Furthermore, back in the Depression, it had a very large number of foreclosures; bad record." (I had heard about this too, in the meantime, and how families had worked and pooled their resources to buy back some of those foreclosed buildings.)

The largest mortgage loans that had been fed into this district of some 15,000 people in the quarter-century since the Great Depression were for $3,000, the banker told me, "and very, very few of those." There had been some others for $1,000 and for $2,000. The rehabilitation work had been almost entirely financed by business and housing earnings within the district, plowed back in, and by skilled work bartered among residents and relatives of residents.

By this time I knew that this inability to borrow for improvement was a galling worry to North Enders, and that furthermore some North Enders were worried because it seemed impossible to get new building in the area except at the price of seeing themselves and their community wiped out in the fashion of the students' dreams of a city of Eden, a fate which they knew was not academic because it had already smashed completely a socially similar—although physically more spacious—nearby district called the West End. They were worried because they were aware also that patch and fix with nothing else could not do forever. "Any chance of loans for new construction in the North End?" I asked the banker.

"No, absolutely not!" he said, sounding impatient at my denseness. "That's a slum!"

Bankers, like planners, have theories about cities on which they act. They have gotten their theories from the same intellectual sources as the planners. Bankers and government administrative officials who guarantee mortgages do not invent planning theories nor, surprisingly, even economic doctrine about cities. They are enlightened nowadays, and they pick up their ideas from idealists, a generation late. Since theoretical city planning has embraced no major new ideas for considerably more than a generation, theoretical planners, financers and bureaucrats are all just about even today.

And to put it bluntly, they are all in the same stage of elaborately learned superstition as medical science was early in the last century, when physicians put their faith in bloodletting, to draw out the evil humors which were believed to cause disease. With bloodletting, it took years of learning to know precisely which veins, by what rituals, were to be opened for what symptoms. A superstructure of technical complication was erected in such deadpan detail that the literature still sounds almost plausible. However, because people, even when they are thoroughly enmeshed in descriptions of reality which are at variance with reality, are still seldom devoid of the powers of observation and independent thought, the science of bloodletting, over most of its long sway, appears usually to have been tempered with a certain amount of common sense. Or it was tempered until it reached its highest peaks of technique in, of all places, the young United States. Blood-letting went wild here. It had an enormously influential proponent in Dr. Benjamin Rush, still revered as the greatest statesman-physician of our revolutionary and federal periods, and a genius of medical administration. Dr. Rush Got Things Done. Among the things he got done, some of them good and useful, were to develop, practice, teach and spread the custom of blood-letting in cases where prudence or mercy had heretofore restrained its use. He and his students drained the blood of very young children, of consumptives, of the greatly aged, of almost anyone unfortunate enough to be sick in his realms of influence. His extreme practices aroused the alarm and horror of European bloodletting physicians. And yet as late as 1851, a committee appointed by the State Legislature of New York solemnly defended the thoroughgoing use of bloodletting. It scathingly ridiculed and censured a physician, William Turner, who had the temerity to write a pamphlet criticizing Dr. Rush's doctrines and calling "the practice of taking blood in diseases contrary to common sense, to general experience, to enlightened reason and the manifest laws of the divine Providence." Sick people needed fortifying, not draining, said Dr. Turner, and he was squelched.

Medical analogies, applied to social organisms, are apt to be farfetched, and there is no point in mistaking mammalian chemistry for what occurs in a city. But analogies as to what goes on in the brains of earnest and learned men, dealing with complex phenomena they do not understand at all and trying to make do with a pseudoscience, do have point. As in the pseudoscience of bloodletting, just so in the pseudoscience of city rebuilding and planning, years of learning and a plethora of subtle and complicated dogma have arisen on a foundation of nonsense. The tools of technique have steadily been perfected. Naturally, in time, forceful and able men, admired administrators, having swallowed the initial fallacies and having been provisioned with tools and with public confidence, go on logically to the greatest destructive excesses, which prudence or mercy might previously have forbade. Bloodletting could heal only by accident or insofar as it broke the rules, until the time when it was abandoned in favor of the hard, complex business of assembling, using and testing, bit by bit, true descriptions of reality drawn not from how it ought to be, but from how it is. The pseudoscience of city planning and its companion, the art of city design, have not yet broken with the specious comfort of wishes, familiar superstitions, oversimplifications, and symbols, and have not yet embarked upon the adventure of probing the real world.

So in this book we shall start, if only in a small way, adventuring in the real world, ourselves. The way to get at what goes on in the seemingly mysterious and perverse behavior of cities is, I think, to look closely, and with as little previous expectation as is possible, at the most ordinary scenes and events, and attempt to see what they mean and whether any threads of principle emerge among them. This is what I try to do in the first part of this book.

One principle emerges so ubiquitously, and in so many and such complex different forms, that I turn my attention to its nature in the second part of this book, a part which becomes the heart of my argument. This ubiquitous principle is the need of cities for a most intricate and close-grained

diversity of uses that give each other constant mutual support, both economically and socially. The components of this diversity can differ enormously,
but they must supplement each other in certain concrete ways.

I think that unsuccessful city areas are areas which lack this kind of intricate mutual support, and that the science of city planning and the art of
city design, in real life for real cities, must become the science and art of
catalyzing and nourishing these close-grained working relationships. I think,
from the evidence I can find, that there are four primary conditions required for generating useful great city diversity, and that by deliberately
inducing these four conditions, planning can induce city vitality (something
that the plans of planners alone, and the designs of designers alone, can
never achieve). While Part I is principally about the social behavior of people in cities, and is necessary for understanding what follows, Part II is principally about the economic behavior of cities and is the most important part
of this book.

Cities are fantastically dynamic places, and this is strikingly true of
their successful parts, which offer a fertile ground for the plans of thousands
of people. In the third part of this book, I examine some aspects of decay
and regeneration, in the light of how cities are used, and how they and their
people behave, in real life.

The last part of the book suggests changes in housing, traffic, design,
planning and administrative practices, and discusses, finally, the *kind* of
problem which cities pose—a problem in handling organized complexity.

The look of things and the way they work are inextricably bound together, and in no place more so than cities. But people who are interested
only in how a city "ought" to look and uninterested in how it works will be
disappointed by this book. It is futile to plan a city's appearance, or speculate
on how to endow it with a pleasing appearance of order, without knowing
what sort of innate, functioning order it has. To seek for the look of things as
a primary purpose or as the main drama is apt to make nothing but trouble.

In New York's East Harlem there is a housing project with a conspicuous rectangular lawn which became an object of hatred to the project tenants. A social worker frequently at the project was astonished by how often
the subject of the lawn came up, usually gratuitously as far as she could see,
and how much the tenants despised it and urged that it be done away with.
When she asked why, the usual answer was, "What good is it?" or "Who
wants it?" Finally one day a tenant more articulate than the others made
this pronouncement: "Nobody cared what we wanted when they built this
place. They threw our houses down and pushed us here and pushed our
friends somewhere else. We don't have a place around here to get a cup of
coffee or a newspaper even, or borrow fifty cents. Nobody cared what we
need. But the big men come and look at that grass and say, 'Isn't it wonderful! Now the poor have everything!' "

This tenant was saying what moralists have said for thousands of years:
Handsome is as handsome does. All that glitters is not gold.

She was saying more: There is a quality even meaner than outright
ugliness or disorder, and this meaner quality is the dishonest mask of pretended order achieved by ignoring or suppressing the real order that is struggling to exist and to be served.

In trying to explain the underlying order of cities, I use a preponderance of examples from New York because that is where I live. But most of the basic ideas in this book come from things I first noticed or was told in other cities. For example, my first inkling about the powerful effects of certain kinds of functional mixtures in the city came from Pittsburgh, my first speculations about street safety from Philadelphia and Baltimore, my first notions about the meanderings of downtown from Boston, my first notions to the unmaking of slums from Chicago. Most of the material for these musings was at my own front door, but perhaps it is easiest to see things first where you don't take them for granted. The basic idea, to try to begin understanding the intricate social and economic order under the seeming disorder of cities, was not my idea at all, but that of William Kirk, head worker of Union Settlement in East Harlem, New York, who, by showing me East Harlem, showed me a way of seeing other neighborhoods, and downtowns too. In every case, I have tried to test out what I saw or heard in one city or neighborhood against others, to find how relevant each city's or each place's lessons might be outside its own special case.

I have concentrated on great cities, and on their inner areas, because this is the problem that has been most consistently evaded in planning theory. I think this may also have somewhat wider usefulness as time passes, because many of the parts of today's cities in the worst, and apparently most baffling, trouble were suburbs or dignified, quiet residential areas not too long ago; eventually many of today's brand-new suburbs or semisuburbs are going to be engulfed in cities and will succeed or fail in that condition depending on whether they can adapt to functioning successfully as city districts. Also, to be frank, I like dense cities best and care about them most.

But I hope no reader will try to transfer my observations into guides as to what goes on in towns, or little cities, or in suburbs which still are suburban. Towns, suburbs and even little cities are totally different organisms from great cities. We are in enough trouble already from trying to understand big cities in terms of the behavior, and the imagined behavior, of towns. To try to understand towns in terms of big cities will only compound confusion.

I hope any reader of this book will constantly and skeptically test what I say against his own knowledge of cities and their behavior. If I have been inaccurate in observations or mistaken in inferences and conclusions, I hope these faults will be quickly corrected. The point is, we need desperately to learn and to apply as much knowledge that is true and useful about cities as fast as possible. . . .

69 L. Mumford, Monumentality, Symbolism, and Style* *1949*

The intent of International Modernism at root had been to develop rational analyses of utilitarian building functions, similarly to develop rational structural systems, and to bring the two together in perfectly realized environmental envelopes. Since such investigations were quantifiable and admitted no variables of location or ethnicity, it was theoretically possible to propose, as did Le Corbusier in 1930, "one single building for all nations and climates."† With piquant irony, immediately after World War II, many of those who a decade and a half before had most vigorously championed the new expression-free architecture now began to write about monumentality and meaning in architecture, beginning with Sigfried Giedion who spoke on the "need for a new monumentality" before the Royal Institute of British Architects in September, 1946. So pronounced was the interest this generated that the *Architectural Review* devoted its issue of September, 1948, to the subject, requesting critics and architects such as Henry-Russell Hitchcock, Giedion, Gropius, Lucio Costa, and others to discuss what monumentality meant to them. The symposium concluded with this essay by Lewis Mumford, which documents the shift in view which informed all his later writing. The criterion now was not whether architecture satisfied immediate utilitarian needs but whether it also sustained the spirit and gladdened the eye, whether it enlarged the capacity for aesthetic enjoyment.

The Expressive Function

Recently, Dr. Sigfried Giedion has given a new turn to architectural criticism by suggesting that there is a need for the monumental in modern architecture. 'Monumentality' is a dangerous concept to use; for it has by now many unfortunate connotations, of empty grandeur, of pretentious display, of over-forced impressiveness; so that there is almost as much danger in reviving the term as in forgetting the important function of architecture to which Dr. Giedion has thereby called our attention. The qualities that Dr. Giedion would like to reinstate are, if I understand him rightly, manifold: they might be treated under the heads of symbolism, of visible hierarchic order, of æsthetic expressiveness, of civic dignity. Unfortunately, these terms are almost as full of insidious meanings as monumentalism, and are as capable of being misunderstood. Perhaps the best way to restate Giedion's thesis would be to say that it is not enough for a modern building to be something and do something; it must also say something. What is this, however, but a return 'commodity, firmness, and delight' with the emphasis, once more, on delight? Is it not, in effect, a restatement of Ruskin's belief that architecture begins where building leaves off; though not with Ruskin's reduction of ar-

*Lewis Mumford, "Monumentality, Symbolism, and Style," *Architectural Review* 105 (April 1949), pp. 173–80.

†Le Corbusier, *Précision sur un état présent de l'architecture et de l'urbanisme* (Paris, 1930), p. 64.

chitecture proper to the effects produced through the use of painting and sculpture? This new interest in the expressive element seems to me healthy; it means, or it should mean, that modern architects have mastered their grammar and vocabulary and are ready for speech. Awaiting that day, Dr. Walter Curt Behrendt called his book, not Modern Architecture, but Modern Building.

Modern Architecture and the 'International Style'

Once we admit that a building should not merely facilitate function but disclose human intention, we open up the grand problem of style: the expression of an informing idea and purpose. Contrary to Mr. Thomas Creighton's position in *Progressive Architecture*, the modern architect, in abandoning his long tedious flirtations with historic styles associated with different cultures than his own, has not earned the right to disregard style entirely: rather he has made it possible to make more fundamental choices in form, choices between ponderosity and lightness, between magnificence and humility, between complexity and simplicity: choices which are ultimately not pragmatic and technical, but æsthetic, ethical, personal. It was not until modern forms were accepted as the common underlying foundation that such choices could be rationally made.

Before one can talk intelligently about the problem of style today one must first define what one means by 'modern' in architecture. As usual, in dealing with historic processes, there are two schools, those that emphasize the element of continuity, and those that emphasize discontinuity. In his first book on modern architecture Mr. Henry-Russell Hitchcock gave these schools the names of 'New Traditionalists' and 'New Pioneers': a happy differentiation, all the happier, it seems to me, because the New Traditionalists, in their further development—witness Fritz Schumacher and the Perrets and the elder Moser—moved closer to the New Pioneers, and because the Pioneers, on approaching maturity, promptly reached back for certain elements they had dropped in their first one-sided absorption in expressing technical processes: van der Rohe's traditional use of fine materials in the Barcelona Pavilion was an early departure in this direction. In *Modern Architecture*, his first essay, Hitchcock even allowed for the fact that the New Pioneers would not be forever identifiable through the starkness and nakedness of their forms: he pointed to the possibility of the same kind of maturation that other primitive styles had gone through, with the development of the ornamental and the symbolic. Such change might take place rapidly or slowly; it might be extraneous and effortful, or organic and intrinsic; but surely no definition of the modern can be framed that would not include, as part of the very concept of modernity, the possibility of further change. The unforgivable error, from the standpoint of either philosophy or historic scholarship, would be to identify the modern with one phase or one moment of the modern movement, as if 'art stopped short at the cultivated court of the Empress Josephine,' in W. S. Gilbert's properly mocking words.

There are two ways, then, in which one may consider modern architecture. The sound way, it seems to me, is to associate it with the increasing use of new materials, of new technical processes, of new forms of construction, along with an æsthetic infused with the conceptions of time, space, energy, life and personality that have been developing since the sixteenth century. Viewed in this way, modern architecture has been long in process; and it has left over the landscape of the Western world a succession of significant buildings and monuments, sometimes faintly adumbrated, sometimes almost completely realized, in terms of their immediate intentions, like Paxton's Crystal Palace or Root's Monadnock Building, to mention only the work of earlier generations. Modern architecture is, accordingly, an inclusive name for an effort which has a single trunk, but many different branches— branches that sometimes flourished and then withered, like L'Art Nouveau. In this movement, it is the technical basis that has been most firmly established: but the final process of expressing human purpose, of interpreting in new terms our fresh conceptions of life and personality, has been late in its development, more tentative, more self-contradictory, in its achievements, ranging there from Frank Lloyd Wright to van der Rohe, from Baillie Scott and Mackintosh to Aalto and Mendelsohn.

But there is another way of defining modern architecture: that of restricting the term to that segment of the modern movement which was affected by the Cubist theories of painting and by the mechanocentric attitude that Le Corbusier sought to translate into æsthetic terms in the early twenties. This narrow canon of modernity gives an arbitrary starting-point for the movement and produces a new kind of academicism, in which a very limited system of architectural forms takes the place of the classic five orders. This restrictive definition of modern architecture was popularized by the Museum of Modern Art show of 1932 in New York; and it is still maintained by Alfred Barr: see his address at the Museum's symposium in February 1948 on *What Is Happening to Modern Architecture*. The criteria of the International Style, as Hitchcock and Johnson set them forth in the Museum catalogue, were three: emphasis on volume rather than on mass, regularity rather than axial symmetry, and proscription of arbitrary decoration. These canons of style were vague enough to seem innocent; but in application they carried with them certain other very positive æsthetic preferences, which a glance at the buildings selected under the canon immediately disclosed. Positively, the International Style favoured two-dimensional façades, cantilevered walls, flat roofs, smooth surfaces, compositions as elementary as a Mondrian painting: negatively, it not merely proscribed 'arbitrary decoration' but favoured black and white, opposed colour, disliked contrasts in texture, recoiled from three-dimensional composition, as revealed in overhangs, setbacks, and interpenetrations of mass and volume.

As an emblem of revolt, the International Style was exciting: but as architectural achievements the purest of its buildings had the misfortune, too often, to be æsthetically dull, precisely in proportion to their programmatic correctness. Fortunately for the modern movement, vigorous personalities, like Breuer, Aalto, Sert, never kept to the letter of the law. Nevertheless, the law itself did something less than justice to the vitality of the movement as a whole: for the fashionable criteria had the effect of pushing to one side many excellent architects, like Wright, Mendelsohn, Dudok, whilst various inferior designers, whose work fitted into the limitations of the 1932 formula, were thrust into positions of eminence their work did not entitle them to. 'Wright' said the Museum of Modern Art catalogue in 1932, 'belongs to the

International Style no more than Behrens or Perret or Van de Velde.' I should hesitate to resurrect those words, at this late date, were it not for the fact that they disclose the limitations, not of modern architecture, but of the concept of the International Style.

Plainly, one can make this criticism without in the least rejecting the creative contributions that Le Corbusier, Gropius, van der Rohe, Neutra, and their immediate followers and colleagues, actually made. From the standpoint of an organic architecture, adequately tapping all the positive forces in our society, the modern was enriched by the conscious attempt to formulate, more rigorously and more artfully than the nineteenth century engineers, the technical bases of modern expression: the scientific, the mechanocentric, the objective, the non-humanistic. Any valid formulation of the modern must include the so-called International Style in its exploratory, experimental efforts to establish the limits of mechanism, functionally and æsthetically: not least æsthetically. But modern life cannot stop at that point. Having invented, for example, the neat, compact, shipshape 'laboratory kitchen' we are now in the process of reconverting the kitchen, where means are available, once more into a humanly conceived living room, because we have discovered that other functions must be served in a kitchen besides those of organic chemistry. Similarly, we may no longer identify a modern composition by the fact that the outer wall is post-free, or its first floor rises free of the ground, like those neolithic Swiss lake dwellings Le Corbusier's unconscious ancestral memories have, perhaps, revived: similarly to avoid the use of columns or pitched roofs, merely to prove one is modern, is too simple a means of self-identification. It is just its freedom from the dry International Style formula that has perhaps called down such abuse on 'bay region cottage architecture.' In loyalty to their original premises, the advocates of the International Style have deliberately rejected every manifestation of the modern but their own. Here time has brought about a sweet revenge; for by now their formula is old-fashioned: indeed dated.

The Influence of Painting

What influence should painting have on the development of modern architecture? Perhaps some of the most acrimonious differences that have developed in recent years can be traced back to the way in which this question is answered. Obviously, the Cubists, the Suprematists, and the Purists had a direct influence upon the brilliant young Dutchmen and Frenchmen who were developing modern architecture during the twenties: indeed, the International Style, as it came to be defined, owed more to the painter than it did to the engineer: to some extent one may say that the control of the machine liberated the architects of this school from the canons of architecture and enabled them to superimpose on their compositions the canons of painting. In this respect, the Cubists and Suprematists, with their geometrical figures, had the same effect upon construction as the advocates of the Wavy Line had, a generation before, upon ornament—though many of the Art Nouveau buildings were often far more audacious as technical achievements. My own answer to this vexed question is that the direct effect of painting upon buildings is a bad one, to the extent that it tempts the architect to treat his building as if it were a composition uninfluenced—as architecture on the contrary must be—by the passage of the spectator towards it, around it, and through it. Living in the same environment of ideas, the modern architect will necessarily draw from the same sources as the modern painter, even as he draws from the same sources as the scientist and the philosopher, who attempt to interpret the emergent forces of his age. So one should expect to find an underlying kinship between architecture and painting and sculpture; each will tend to express the same ideas and feelings, in forms that will be deeply, rather than superficially, related. But the imitation of painting by architecture is a backward step. The relation between sculpture and building, on the other hand, is a closer one; and there are modern sculptors like Naum Gabo, a man of original genius, whose work is much closer to architecture than that of many architects. Yet here, too, the development of the two arts should be parallel; and the interaction should be mainly a spiritual one, for the architect should not and cannot limit himself to the problems that the sculptor faces; since buildings must be used in a quite different sense from the way in which sculpture is used. This standard of judgment works both ways: not merely should a building not seek to imitate a painting; but one should never judge the success of a building, even aesthetically, merely by looking at a photograph of it. Though the eye embraces both painting and architecture, the two arts are, from my standpoint, almost as far apart as dance and music. Does this negative judgment also apply to the modern architect's use of Arp's irregular curved surfaces for all kinds of flat surfaces, instead of more orderly geometric figures? I am afraid it does; except as a momentary gesture of freedom. Such forms come properly under the ban on 'arbitrary ornament': for here the International Style fashion has plainly defied its own canons.

The Importance of Style

On this interpretation the epithet 'International Style' was ill-chosen. For, in the Western world at least, every genuine style has been international in its development: Romanesque, Gothic, Renaissance, Baroque, even the pseudo-styles of neo-classic and neo-gothic have been the expression of our whole civilization. This universalism is precisely what distinguishes style—the forms by which men express their purposes, values, and ends—from the little local and temporal eddies of fashion. But limiting the modern to the current fashios of Paris and Berlin failed to do justice to the deep-seated internationalism of the contemporary movement, belittling the contributions of the British at the beginning of the present century, and forgetting the work that had been done in California at the same time: work not unaffected by contact with the Japanese and the Chinese, to say nothing of the Polynesians and the Hindus. (If one examines the bungalow Robert Louis Stevenson built for himself in Samoa, for example, one will discover how much merely living in the tropics did to alter the traditional relation of window and wall, and the very words 'bungalow,' 'verandah,' 'lanai,' suggest a new relationship between the house and its green surroundings.) If modern architecture is truly indigenous to our culture, one should expect to find it springing up independently in various areas, gathering into the main stream various regional experiments; and that is what has actually been happening, now with Chicago dominating, now with Brussels or Paris, now with San Francisco or

Rio de Janeiro. In such a movement, the regional will bear the universal stamp and the universal, fully embraced, will incorporate and further the regional. Where the canon of the 'International Style' has been strictly followed there is a certain æsthetic uniformity in all its examples. But for an inclusive kind of modernism what one should seek is not uniformity but unity: the working out of fresh adaptations and forms, with all the wealth of expression that life and personality provide.

This interplay of the universal and the regional is what the pseudo-International Style denies: often with absurd results, as in the transplantation of façades of glass, that visual tag of modernism, to cities like Moscow, where the climate invites extra protective devices for the winter, and to regions like North Africa where the great architectural problem is protection against the sun, rather than fullest exposure. In the current conception of the International Style one discovers, not internationalism, but the covert imperialism of the great world Megalopolises, claiming to dominate the culture of their time, and rejecting all forms of art except those which have been created by the few to whom it has given the stamp of approval. Once these severe criticisms have been made, however, I would join with the exponents of the International Style in an emphasis of the conscious international intention which should pervade all architecture today: warning against any idiom so local, so exclusive, so indigenous that it denies, rather than affirms, the common elements upon which our whole civilization rests. Hence the Russian return to the ponderous forms of classicism, the typical architecture of autocracy and bureaucracy, is not merely æsthetically reactionary: it is a denial of that common world which men of good will in all countries seek to build; and its official adoption in the thirties warned all sensitive observers in advance of the turn toward isolationism and imperialism that Russian policy was taking.

The Problem of Symbolism

Architecture grows to self-consciousness and mature expression out of the elemental processes of building, mainly by concern over symbolism. However constant the mechanical functions of a building may remain—so that the form of a court of justice could be taken over by the Christian Church, because both buildings were designed to hold a crowd—the needs of language differ from generation to generation, as each fresh experience of life gives us something new to communicate, or as new evaluations change the relationship of one social institution to another. There are many points of difference between verbal expression and plastic expression; but the need to assimilate and record new experience is common to both. All this is plain in the transformation of historic forms: no internal technical development in building will explain the abandonment of the audacious verticality and sculptural exuberance of medieval building for the more elementary technical forms of Renaissance building, with their horizontal lines, their repeating patterns, their standardized ornament; nor will any purely æsthetic reaction explain the positive hatred with which, by the end of the eighteenth century, especially in France, all Gothic building was viewed by 'progressive' minds. What is superficially a change of form turns out to be something far deeper: a change of meaning. Ornament and decoration sometimes record changes of feeling, sentiments, and attitudes faster than construction. But construction itself is the main language of expression, and is at the service of many different human purposes, other than those satisfied by building proper. The height of a spire meant religious aspiration in the thirteenth century: in the form of a skyscraper, it means publicity and self-advertisement in the twentieth century: yet in more than one medieval church, from Lübeck to Florence, the height and scale of the Church also represented the conscious self-assertion of the bourgeoisie over the clergy: so there is a significant connecting link between the two.

Now we live in an age that has not merely abandoned a great many historic symbols but has likewise made an effort to deflate the symbol itself, by denying the values which it represents. Or rather, our age has deflated every form of symbolism except that which it employs so constantly and so unconsciously that it fails to recognize it as symbolism and treats it as reality itself. Because we have dethroned symbolism, we are now left, momentarily, with but a single symbol of almost universal validity: that of the machine. We should understand certain aspects of modern architecture during the last generation a little better if we realized that many modern architects were trying to pour into this restricted mode of symbolism all the feelings and sentiments that had hitherto flowed freely into love and religion and politics. Much of what was masked as functionalism was in fact fetishism: an attempt, if I may use Henry Adams's well-worn figure, to make the Dynamo serve for the Virgin. Those who had devaluated the personality compensated for this error by over-valuing the machine. In an otherwise meaningless world of sensations and forces the machine alone represented the purposes of life.

Because a large part of our world has been created through physical science, with the aid of mechanical invention, no honest construction in our own time can avoid expressing this immense debt. From Rennie and Paxton and Roebling onward, the most significant structures have usually been those which most fully explored the new media of expression. Unfortunately, the theoretic exposition of the machine, as the exclusive source of modern form, was not expressed with any boldness until Le Corbusier published his famous tract, *Towards a New Architecture;* and the architects who adopted Le Corbusier's line glorified the machine age, with conscious exaggeration, not in 1820, when its limitations had still to be revealed, but in 1920, when the weaknesses of the mechanical ideology had been in fact fully disclosed. Most of these architects concealed what they were actually doing even from themselves by fancying that they had sloughed off symbolism altogether: they were thinking in terms of efficiency, economy, Sachlichkeit, objectivity, physical science. Consciously or unconsciously, they gave to their buildings the stamp of the factory, as their predecessors had given to their buildings that of the Church, or those in the Baroque period that of the Palace. As fact and symbol, the machine took the measure of man.

What we are beginning to witness today is a reaction against this one-sided symbolism and this distorted picture of modern civilization. We can no longer treat the machine as an exclusive architectural symbol at a moment when the whole ideology of the machine is in process of dissolution, for culture is passing now from an ideology of the machine to an ideology of the organism, and the person: from Newton and Descartes to Geddes and Whitehead. We know that the mechanical world is not the real world, but only an aspect of the real world, deliberately abstracted by man for the purpose of expanding his physical power and multiplying the energies he commands. We know, too, that in this over-concentration upon power, many important elements were left out of account—especially those needed for the development of life and personality. *As an integral part of modern culture, the machine will remain as long as modern culture remains:* let me italicize that statement. But as a dominant element, wholly subduing life to the demands of mechanization, reducing the personality and the group to a mechanical unit, performing its limited function in a greater mechanism, concentrating on quantity and denying quality and purpose, the machine is an enemy of human development, rather than an agent. The problem of quantity, the problem of automatism, and the problem of limitless power, which our very success in perfecting machines has raised, cannot be solved in terms of the machine. We must erect a new hierarchy of function, in which the mechanical will give place to the biological, the biological to the social, the social to the personal. For this new order, the machine can no longer serve as symbol: indeed, the emphasis on the impersonal, the anti-organic, the non-humanistic, the 'objective,' must now be counteracted by a temporary over-preoccupation, perhaps, with the organic, the subjective, the personal. On these terms, Frank Lloyd Wright, in 1900, was far in advance of Le Corbusier in 1920; indeed, in a sense, L'Art Nouveau was, despite its ill-conceived ornament, often closer to the human and the organic than the architects of Cubism. To say this is not to desert functionalism in architecture, but to relate it once more to every human function.

Do We Want Architecture at All?

At intervals for the last century or more, people have been predicting the death of painting and sculpture; and without doubt engineering and photography and the motion pictures, the new popular arts, have come to perform many of the functions that these more singular and personal arts, when they were at the service of the reigning ideology, once performed. But rationalists, a hundred years ago, were also confident that religion would, within a measurable time, dissolve: yet the most dogmatic, authoritarian, and anti-rational forms of it have actually gathered strength, rather than lost it, during this period: so that one must assume that Benjamin Kidd, who predicted the revival of religion in the nineties, was a better sociologist than those who opposed him. But how is it with architecture? If the focus of architectural interest shifted wholly from expression to mechanical content, there would come a time when engineering, through the sheer complication and expense of its constantly proliferating devices, would supplant architecture and nullify all efforts at visual expression. With air conditioning and a host of other mechanical instruments, building might return once more to the environment from which it started—the cave: in which the exterior, if visible at all, would become a blank shell, which revealed nothing of what went on within it, and made no effort to organize exterior and interior into a unified whole. At that point we should be driven to ask a critical question: Do we or do we not want architecture? If we do, it may be necessary to retrace some of our steps and seek a new point of departure. For if we want architecture, we must ask for a margin of freedom, a margin above the necessary, the calculable, the economic. It is in that margin for free choice and free decision that architecture moves and breathes and produces a visible effect, designed to impress the human spirit.

The canon of economy remains basic in modern form, then, not as an end in itself, but in order to provide just that extra margin of wealth, energy, and vitality through which the human imagination may more freely express itself. With reason, the architect will continue to make his structure light, spare, elegant, severe; in a large part of his work, he will avoid any superfluity, any structural or spatial over-emphasis, any ornamental elaboration, any departure from standardization and modular forms; and an escape from such forms must be looked upon with distrust, if not with downright disfavour. Yet all this restriction is for the sake of freedom: the freedom, say, to provide an open corridor with a view on a garden, rather than a shorter corridor, with rooms on both sides, as economy might dictate: the freedom to enlarge an entrance for the sake of 'effect' or to employ rich materials and to refine the craftsmanship of visible details: the freedom to provide an approach and a setting that will heighten the visual interest of the spectator, to give him a special sense of the building's purposes and activities by the very means employed in its organization. When human purposes, rather than mechanical requirements, prevail, style becomes the very mirror of personality. But one must not, like Benedetto Croce and Geoffrey Scott, seek to separate the æsthetic moment from the practical, the ethical, and the meaningful attributes of the same activity. A practical miscalculation, like the use of material that weathers badly in a few years' time, or an ethical and political error, like the human overloading of the land in an otherwise admirable apartment house design may, from the present standpoint, undermine the æsthetic result. A humanistic canon of architecture will provide, accordingly, for all the dimensions of the human personality, arranged in the order of their value and significance, and united into an organic, interrelated whole. Translated into practical domestic terms, this means that an architect may deliberately forgo adding an extra bathroom in order to increase the dimensions of the living room or to panel it in a more attractive species of plywood.

The Varieties of Functionalism

The phrase, Form Follows Function, has a long and honourable history. The underlying perception belongs to the biologist Lamarck; a recognition of the fact that all structures in organic nature are purposive, and that all purposive activities become, as it were, formalized: ingrained in structure. The American sculptor, Horatio Greenough, an intellectual man who had doubtless absorbed Lamarckianism, as Emerson had, long before Darwin became fashionable, translated this perception into architecture, with a clarity that still remains admirable. A generation or so later, Louis Sullivan reiterated the same truth in his *Kindergarten Chats*, perhaps rediscovering it for himself, perhaps unconsciously repeating Greenough; and he elaborated the various corollaries that follow its acceptance: namely, that new purposes and new functions demand new forms, that old forms are not adequate for the expression or fulfilment of new functions, that functionless form denotes atrophy, purposelessness, inertia—and so forth. Since modern man has invented a host of new functions, through his command over nature, and since democratic society embodies purposes not accepted by a theocratic or feudal order, this new criterion of form drew a new series of guiding lines for the architect: no one who rejects this fundamental discovery can be a modern architect; and forms that are deliberately defiant of function, even if applied in a superficially modern building, are weak forms, no matter how powerful the first æsthetic impression. But if Lamarck's doctrine is thoroughly sound as a foundation, it does not apply, in its purely physiological form, to the whole of architecture, any more than it applies to the whole of organic nature. The beautiful, Emerson remarked, rests on the foundations of the necessary: Emerson did not make the error of saying that the necessary and the beautiful were one. Darwin himself observed that the sexual functions seemed often to promote excrescences or change of plumage in birds of a purely decorative nature: useful only because, on a human parallel, they seemed to attract the interest of the opposite sex. In short, there are subjective interests derived from spectator and user, that must be taken account of in any sound architectural canon. A building may be functionally adequate from the standpoint of engineering and yet be a failure from that of physiology or psychology. Take the ideal of a constant, equable, unvarying environment which most engineers and even many architects regard as desirable for building interiors. This ideal may well prove to be in opposition to the biological need for small variations and readjustments as one of the very conditions of life. So with every other aspect of architecture: there is not a single function to be satisfied, but a whole interrelated series. In his public buildings, Richardson deliberately slighted the equipment and finish of his interiors in order to have all the means he needed to produce, on the exteriors, an impressive monumental effect, believing that the impression the building made on the passing citizen was a more important function than the immediate gratification it might give to the actual users of the structure.

Now, while the ideal of architecture is surely to give a maximum satisfaction to all functions, there is a tendency, in our age, to regard the mechanical functions as naturally dominant ones: even to view with suspicion any deliberate attempt to produce visual animation or excitement at any sacrifice of either comfort or mechanical perfection. But as modern architecture matures, it must become multi-functional, giving increasing weight to biological, psychological, social, and personal criteria. There is nothing new in this suggestion. Did not the formulators of the 'International Style' deliberately reject functionalism? Le Corbusier's cartesian sense of order rests for example on an æsthetic foundation: he would even select the tenants for his skyscraper village in Marseilles on the basis of their æsthetic response to his architecture, rather than their human need. This æsthetic is, alas, a very limited one; but in so far as it shifts the focus of design to the human purpose or idea, it makes possible the kind of freedom that good architects have always exercised. In this respect the path of modern architectural development is that of all organic development: from the mechanical and the conditioned, the realm of physical necessity, to the vital and the free, the realm of personal choice.

Extroversion and Introversion

On one dogma almost all believers in modern architecture are agreed: namely on the open plan, particularly in dwelling houses, as the very essence of modern expression: free-flowing space, rooms divided by hardly even a visual partition, have become the patent of modern building. Look at a book of modern plans and you will find that only in the water-closet is anything like complete privacy and isolation permitted: even the bedrooms, in many new houses, present walls of glass that give out on an equally open garden. As a movement toward freedom, as an effort to achieve flexibility, this overemphasis on openness, coming as it did from the Middle West, first of all, that land of extroverts, must have our sympathetic assent. But there is nothing final in this achievement; for the open plan is the symbol of an entirely public and outward-turning life: there must come a time when modern architecture will recognize equally the deep human need for the cell: the room with the locked door, secure against all intrusion, giving out, not on open space, but on a garden or walled yard equally inviolate to unwanted visitors. With respect to the needs of the human personality, a good part of modern architecture is lopsided: it provides no means for withdrawal, for solitary meditation or prayer, for the sense of solidity, of security, even of continuity, represented, say, by a wall two feet thick. One would think that nothing ever was, could be or should be performed in private.

Now I am all for open planning and removable partitions: of the latter, for both wall and interior, we have yet to make the fullest use: indeed there has been a singular lack of mechanical ingenuity here, despite the example of the Japanese. But in the very effort to achieve this openness and flexibility, the architect must not forget that there are moments of life that call for darkness and retirement, for recesses and nooks and hide-aways: those moments in life should not be represented, grimly, only in the form of air-raid shelters. Hence, while accepting gladly the current innovations of the extrovert, I would, looking toward the future, provide the corrective contradiction: More light: yes, but some darkness. More openness: yet some enclosures. More volume: but some mass. More flexibility: yet some rigidity. As the modern movement matures, an organic architecture will do justice to the introvert no less than to the extrovert, to the subjective no less than to the objective, to the dark, primitive, unconscious forces as well as to the cold illuminations of science and reason: in short, it will take into account the functions and purposes of the whole man, and not try to whittle him down to the size and shape that will fit some less-than-man-size formula.

What Is Monumentalism?

The other name for monumentalism is impressiveness: the effect produced upon spectator or user by the scale and setting of a building, by its height and reach and splendour, by the dramatic emphasis of its functions and purposes through the means available to the architect: mass, volume, texture, colour, painting and sculpture, gardens, water-courses, and the disposition of the buildings that form the background. It is by its social intention and not by its abstract form that the monument reveals itself; hence the Eiffel Tower is a monument and the chimney of a power plant, even when it is made over into an overbearing classic form, is not. The æsthetic monumentality of Wright's Larkin Building in Buffalo was betrayed by its own limited uses and by the drab neighborhood in which it was set; but one might look far to find a more effective monument—peace to the International Stylists!—than Dudok's Town Hall at Hilversum, to whose impressiveness the architect brought every possible visual aid. In essence, the monument is a declaration of love and admiration attached to the higher purposes men hold in common. An age that has deflated its values and lost sight of its purposes will not, accordingly, produce convincing monuments. Dignity, wealth, power, freedom, go with the conception of monumentality; and its opposites are meanness, poverty, impotence, standardization. Pride and luxury, it is true, often produce bad monuments; but poverty and humility, if left to themselves, would never produce any monuments at all. Most ages, to make the monument possible, have (in Ruskin's terms) lighted the lamp of sacrifice, giving to the temple or the buildings of state, not their surplus, but their very life-blood, that which should have gone into the bare decencies of life for the common man. This fact is responsible for democracy's distrustfulness, its grudging attitude, toward the monument. But, though often painful in the giving, these sacrifices were not without their reward even to the giver, whether that gift was voluntary, as often in the building of the Cathedrals, or exacted by physical force, as in the taxes that made possible the pomp and grandeur of great courts. Denying the claims of the flesh and the prosperity of the household, buildings of permanent value, enriching the eye, sustaining the spirit, not for a few passing days, but for generations and centuries, actually came forth.

To remind oneself of these conditions is almost to explain why we have lost, to such a large degree, the capacity to produce monuments in our time. If surplus wealth were sufficient to produce monuments, we might produce them today as easily as we produce much more costly things like cyclotrons and atomic piles. Never before, surely, has so much physical power and physical wealth been available. But for all this, we spend money for monuments with a bad conscience, when we spend at all. This bad conscience is the product of middle-class convictions and middle-class standards, of course: the poor, precisely because their lot is so constrained, have never lost the sense of life which produces the monument; consider how they will spend on a wedding, and even more on a funeral, the money that might have been 'better' spent—but who shall define and justify this better?—for their children's food or clothes or education. To raise all living standards to a decent level, at least to the 'minimum of existence,' is the aim of modern man: not to elevate and sanctify one side of life at the expense of every other aspect. Plainly, there is reason for this choice: too easily did the upper classes in other periods justify the poverty of the poor and the deprivations of the needy, in order to make possible the grand, the superfluous, the beautiful. But as we approach a high general level of comfort today, the danger is rather just the opposite; that we forget the function of sacrifice: which means ultimately the arrangement of the good life, not in the order that produces merely physical survival, but in the order that conduces to continued spiritual development. If we were better prepared to accept sacrifice, there might be less immediate danger to mankind from the cyclotrons and atomic piles, to whose existence we dedicate every available penny. We spend lavishly on mechanical means: we scrimp on the ultimate human ends. That is why modern monuments are far to seek.

Last year's discussion of monumentalism in *The Architectural Review* suffered a little from a general lack of concrete reference to any monuments later than fifty or seventy-five years ago; and my present thoughts are in the same danger: so let me point to a relatively recent example of monumentality that well illustrates my point; though it does not refer to the kind of structure that is ordinarily termed a monument. I refer to the great semicircular retaining wall that set off Frankfort-Römerstadt from the allotment gardens that spread in serried order below. Since I saw Römerstadt in 1932 and never revisited it, I may have an exaggerated impression of its original brilliance, and of the sense of spacious order contributed to the design itself by this monumental feature. Nevertheless I must record my conviction that it remains one of the high points in the architectural expression of our time, not by the excellence of its individual buildings, but by the ordered relation of the whole: it shows what modern man might do with his freedom once he controlled the forces at work in his society sufficiently to touch every part of it, field and road, house and garden, highway and public building. The only modern architectural work that has given this same impression to me, in similar fullness, and for similar reasons, is the dam, the powerhouse, the road system and the park around the Norris Dam in Tennessee—though I must exclude the town pattern and the houses beyond. Why were these examples of true monumentality; and in what did their impressive effect specially lie?

The first thing to note is the very fact of impressiveness: the retaining wall boldly separates the community itself, on the upper level, from the orderly arrangement of small garden plots and tool sheds below. With a slight loss of land, the retaining wall might have been omitted entirely: by merely grading the land down and planting it with appropriate vines and bushes, the soil itself would have been held back. In the layout of such a suburb it would, again, have been simpler to have united the allotment garden with spaces continuous to the dwelling house, as in the open English plan; but the architects of this project used the very opportunity that came with the low-lying land of the Nidda to separate these two elements: thereby creating, in the gardens and open land behind the houses, a sense of spaciousness and 'aristocratic' ease. As with almost all examples of true monumentality one must pay, in some way, for the æsthetic effect produced: in this case, by a walk to the allotment gardens and by the provision of special tool sheds on the garden plots: sheds which, erected at the beginning, of uniform material and design, add to the sense of order and give scale to the broad sweep of land in the foreground. But note: these arrangements cannot be justified on the score of economy: quite the contrary. The retaining wall itself was far more costly than any grading of the land would have been. Such a monumental treatment of the landscape and city implies a greater amount of wealth, a greater amount of leisure, indeed perhaps a greater capacity for æsthetic enjoyment than the actual inhabitants of Römerstadt possibly ever possessed.

Such planning cannot be justified in terms of immediate needs: hence later housing developments in Frankfort, seeking to meet the requirements of *das Existenzminum,* became more sparing of any form of visual freedom and luxury, more rigorous, more *sachlich*—and more barren of any stirring human reference. But in the long run the treatment provided at Frankfort-Römerstadt would sustain the spirit, by gladdening the eye, while more economical planning would leave the spirit unmoved or actually depressed; and in that case the original cost and effort, seemingly so much in excess of what the day's needs would justify, might turn out to be exceedingly small; as is the case with the great monuments that have existed from three hundred to three thousand years. On this matter, William Bulter Yeats's words, to the Dublin philanthropist who wanted to make sure that the common people would enjoy art before he gave any more bequests, should be remembered and heeded. Monumental architecture is to be justified, not in terms of present necessity and popular demand, but in terms of future liberation: to create a 'nest for eagles.'

70   M. Nowicki, Composition in Modern Architecture* *1949*

Born of Polish parents in Chita, near the Siberian border of China, Matthew Nowicki (1910–1950) was graduated from the architectural school of the Warsaw Polytechnic and soon won a series of prizes in architectural competitions that enabled him to travel to France, Italy, Greece, Egypt, and Brazil.[†] During the German occupation of Poland he taught and continued to study in Warsaw, and after its liberation he was chief of the planners who undertook the reconstruction of the city. In 1947 he toured the United States as a member of the United Nations site-finding committee, subsequently serving on the Board of Design Consultants, which developed the design for the United Nations complex. He was then appointed professor of architecture at the reorganized school of design at North Carolina State College, Raleigh. In association with a local architect, William Henley Deitrick, he designed a series of buildings, starting with the State Fair and Exposition Building constructed in 1954–55 (Figure 60). At this point, however, in collaboration with Albert Mayer, Nowicki took on the task of planning the new capital of East Punjab at Chandigarh, and in the summer of 1950 he went to India to survey the site and sketch out preliminary plans. It was on the return trip from Cairo in August that his airplane went down and Nowicki's promising career was so tragically cut short.

As this article demonstrates, even before International Modernism had established itself firmly among architects in the United States, Nowicki was calling for an

---

* Matthew Nowicki, "Composition in Modern Architecture," *Magazine of Art* 42 (March 1949), pp. 108–11.

[†] An extensive treatment of Nowicki's life and work is found in a series of articles by Lewis Mumford, "The Life, the Teaching, and the Architecture of Matthew Nowicki," in *Architectural Record,* 1954.

Figure 60. Matthew Nowicki and William Henley Deitrick, with engineers Severud, Elstad & Krueger, J. S. Dorton Arena (formerly State Fair and Exposition Building), Raleigh, N.C., 1950–53 (photo: courtesy North Carolina State Fair). The chief structural members are two intersecting reinforced concrete parabolic arches, lifted 22° above the horizontal on steel columns, and between which the roof is suspended on cables.

architecture that would "provide human comfort in the *visual* and *psychological* as well as in the strictly physical sense of the word" (italics added). To speak of "style" and conscious artistic "design" in modern architecture was radical in 1949; even more, to use the word so strongly associated with the École des Beaux-Arts—"composition."

Much has been said and written about the "style" of the building movement of our time, but the problem of composition in architecture has, for the most part, been treated with reluctance or avoided altogether. If form is to be reduced to the automatic consequence of function, then a distrust of the problems of composition insofar as they are the problems of form is justified. Or again, where composition has become synonymous with academicism, its problems may be treated with suspicion by those who wish to stress the differences of our architecture from that of preceding periods.

Frank Lloyd Wright went one step further than his contemporaries when he said: "'Form follows function' is but a statement of fact. When we say, 'Form and function are one,' only then do we take mere fact into the realm of creative thought." In other words, dependence of form on function would be replaced by interdependence of form and function. And if we accept the mutual dependence of form and function, then the problems of form in modern architecture might well be studied as are the problems of function.

Judging modern architecture on the merits of its form, Henry-Russell Hitchcock and Philip C. Johnson baptized it the "international style." Style in art and architecture means a number of striking similarities of form among works of a certain period that distinguishes them from those of other times, and, although we may not like the word "style," it would be difficult to pretend that we do not notice those similarities in our day.

Humanism may well be considered the main principle of the new movement, even though functionalism was its official title. Man and his way of life became the main source of inspiration to a modern architect. Forgotten in the esthetic speculations of the nineteenth century, man, in the basic sense of individual and social character, again became the object of creative attention. Man presented two aspects. The first was the unchanging quality of the human individual: the size of his body, the length of his step and the speed of his walk—the same throughout ages—determine the unchanging factors of scale in architecture; his basic emotions, though changing in form of expression, are as old as the race itself. The second aspect deals with the constant change in human life and the differences that exist not only between generations but between men of different decades. Now this change is rapid and conspicuous, and it demands constant changes in architectural forms.

In direct application to architecture, these rapid changes of environment and technology are seen in the new materials available. The use of iron, steel and reinforced concrete is one source of the greatest revolution that has stirred architecture since the gothic period.

It is no accident that the new principles are already clearly expressed in Paxton's Crystal Palace of 1851. Skeleton construction, with its wide spanned-column layout and the cantilever, permitted a free treatment of plan to express the diversified functions of life. It also allowed for the interpenetration of free space and enclosed form which became one of the main features of the new style. In short, we may say that functionalism could not have developed its present shape if it had not been for the possibilities offered by construction.

Functionalism separated the traditional concept of a bearing wall into a structural element of column and a dividing element of screen, which now could be subjected to their own laws of composition. Construction and partition in a modern plan seem to symbolize the factors of stability and change in architecture. In a certain sense the first acquires an expression of classical discipline while the second becomes an element of romantic freedom. The eternal conflict of classicism and romanticism takes place here and can best be observed in the importance that some architects attach to the discipline of construction, while others subordinate construction to the organic expression of life.

Skeleton construction, despite its achievements, is probably still at the beginning of its possibilities. The use of new structural materials like aluminum, of new concepts of organization like prefabrication and of metal standardized forms for reinforced concrete will bring rich new shapes. Ceilings by Freyssinet in France and Wright's mushroom columns of the Johnson Wax factory in this country may well be considered the precursors of a future wave that will bring unpredicted solutions in form. How this may affect the esthetics of architecture, hitherto based for the most part on a rectangular discipline, still remains to be seen.

Humanism, functionalism and construction have been found to be the backbone of modern form. Esthetic judgment of the new shapes could not take place through the conventional method of comparison, since most of it was without direct precedent in architectural tradition. Therefore this judgment has to be based on the merits of the philosophy responsible for the form and the directness with which this philosophy was expressed in three dimensions.

"Less is more." This statement of Mies van der Rohe expresses one of the principles adopted by our period. Order and elimination seem to be the roots of the simplicity sought for by composition in contemporary architecture. But the latter, in contrast to the architecture of earlier periods, attempts to create an order of freedom instead of one of rigid subordination to a single dominating element. In illustration of these concepts, one might compare the static composition of St. Peter's in Rome (which with a slight stretch of imagination may resemble an outline of a mummy) with the balanced freedom of Le Corbusier's plan.

Though the old academic principle of bilateral symmetry has been replaced in modern composition by a free balance of parts, modern architecture does not reject the use of an abstract, geometrical discipline in plan or façade. Compositions on a large scale seem to demand a certain type of geometrical order that cannot be explained by simple interpretation of function. An important psychological factor of satisfaction and comfort lies in knowing what to expect from the whole by what one has experienced in the parts already seen. Regularity between certain elements of composition can aid in creating that unity which may be established only through a sensation of order.

Diversity is achieved by contrast within an ordered unity. Again a humanized explanation of this abstract approach is simple. Architecture should provide human comfort in the visual and psychological as well as in the strictly physical sense of the word, and understanding is part of psychological comfort. Established relations among the elements of a façade, for instance, though based on a geometrical principle, create an impression of order that is easy to understand and appreciate.

Order is the creation of an intellectual approach and unity based on order always has a classical flavor. Diversity is the expression of creative temperament, imagination and emotion and therefore is a factor of what we may call romanticism. Again the two forces exist side by side, one incomplete without the other, and we may conclude that the search for a balance between them is the objective of composition in modern architecture.

The possibilities offered by the new construction and by the free plan allow the inside of the building to be opened to the penetration of outside space. In modern composition mass is replaced by the conception of volume.

The traditional wall pierced with windows and doors almost belongs to a past period: the transparent or opaque screen, fitted between floor and ceiling, is taking its place. A structural brick wall used today in small architectural problems is often employed with the same feeling of screen principle. The predominant construction of a given period influences the shapes adopted by one less typical for the same time, and thus contemporary brick architecture follows the esthetics characteristic for the column and screen principle.

Relations between notes in music, colors in painting and elements of space in architecture bring pleasure if they satisfy man's instinct of proportion.

There is probably no way to establish rules of good proportion as there is no way to establish rules of beauty, but every period in architecture seems to develop a predilection for certain proportions. In ancient Egypt the element of cult introduced the sacred triangle. Humanism in Greece was based on proportions governing relations among parts of the human body, and the golden section was the result. The abstract simplicity of a square appealed to architects of other times: both the gothic cathedrals and the arches of triumph of the last renaissance are examples of architecture subordinated to this discipline.

Based as it was on the purity of functionalism and the principle of expressing on the exterior a plan evolved from the inside, the modern period could not govern its form by any preconceived geometric rule. It therefore claims that the choice of proportions is a personal and emotional, rather than an intellectual one. Nevertheless it is interesting to note new attempts to introduce into architectural composition factors more stable than individual temperament. "Modulor" of Le Corbusier, a measure to control relations of elements, is the best example of this approach and is evolved from the proportions of the human body.

Since previous techniques had resulted for the most part in a vertical accent, it was some time before modern construction, with its wide spans and the new cantilever, was able to introduce a sympathy for a strong horizontal expression. But now a liking for a wide horizontal shape, related to the rest of the composition through a module, seems to be the principal characteristic of proportion in contemporary architecture.

As every period has its own feeling for proportion, so it has for scale. By scale in composition, we understand the size of an element of this composition—in other words, the size of a unit by the repetition or other use of which the composition is formed. In this way the scale of a building is partly independent of its size. In fact, some of the structures of Palladio in Vicenza, for example, though only some fifty feet high, have a much greater scale than a New York skyscraper fifty stories high, a fact accounted for by the tremendous difference in the size of the respective elements of composition. Just as proportion establishes relations among divisions of space, so scale establishes relations between man and space, so that, properly used, scale can become one of the factors of humanism in architecture.

Humanism, as we have stated, is basic in modern architecture, and man's comfort applies to his psychological relations to space as well as to his physical convenience within it. A great contrast between the size of man and the size of a basic element of composition may provoke many emotions but not a feeling of comfort and well-being, and modern architecture, with its insistence on small scale, is only too conscious of this.

In terms of functionalism, a larger interior must be expressed as frankly as a small one, and a unit planned for crowds should have a different scale from one planned for an individual, so that the scale of modern architecture must allow for a certain flexibility. This raises the controversial problem of monumentality which was, by its opponents, usually linked to the Greek or Roman column, a decorative dome covering a pompous interior, the inconvenience of outside stairs, etc. Monumentality does not in fact depend on any form but is a problem of scale. The humanistic ideal of individual freedom and comfort adopted by our architecture and expressed in its sympathy to the small-scale treatment should influence also the resolution of the monumental problem, just as the large scale of the baroque influenced every small programme of the period. This would seem to eliminate monumentality from modern architecture; but monumentality, in the sense of a contrast between architecture of exceptional importance and the size of an individual, has its true and eternal qualities of which man should not be deprived. Within the realm of its favorite scale, modern architecture should no doubt distinguish a variety of treatments that will be appropriate to the expression of its diversified contents.

Subordinated to order, proportion and scale are the problems of detail and ornament. The detail of today seems to be a direct issue of mass production and standardization. Its uniformity is probably more pronounced than in any other time when it usually was more of an individual problem in esthetics.

In the present use of detail, one must not forget that modern architecture began by a complete elimination of it. Its reappearance, which has been coming gradually, is due both to technical and esthetic reasons. A detail expresses, if only symbolically, the richness and refinement of form, and in its maturity every movement in architecture should express these qualities by the use of detail.

Detail often develops into an ornament that poses a problem of its own today. Modern architecture, committed to the spirit of purity and of freedom, seems to look longingly in its search for the richness of form at the forbidden fruit of ornament. An architect of today hesitates to design an ornament but welcomes into his composition fresco, mosaics, tiles, brick or stone, treating them all as decorative textures, free and independent of architectural rhythm. The concept of a free plan seems to have as a corresponding element the concept of a free ornament.

Architecture may be considered a science, a profession, a craft, a hobby, a way of life and many other things, but it is also an art. All art has its roots in nature and in life, but we realize by now that its purpose is not accurate representation but discovery of underlying truth.

"Exactitude is not truth"—this sentence of Matisse's is beyond any misunderstanding. Exactitude is not the truth in architecture any more than in any other art. Truth in composition is not the exact disclosure of the inside functions of the building on its exterior, nor is it the frank expression of its construction. Both functionalism and construction must be ordered by the truth of unity and the diversity within it; in other words by the basic laws of the universe, the expression of which man calls beauty.

Not until this fact is established in the minds of our architects will there be a reason to study contemporary composition. But it would seem that our period is now ready for this study and ready to submit objects for its criticism—modern buildings rising out of the experience of our times.

71   M. Nowicki, Function and Form*   *1951*

In this essay, published after his death, Nowicki pursued his argument further, maintaining that it was clear "that in the overwhelming majority of modern design form follows *form* and not *function*." That truth in art arose not from exactitude, he had already observed, but now he asserted that not only does art distort to approach truth, but *"in this distortion lies the essence of art"* (his italics).

I suspect that I will no longer provoke you as much as I should by opening these remarks on the origins and trends of modern architecture with a statement that sometime ago our design became a style. No matter how ingeniously we dodge the unpleasant issue, it comes at us with full force in thousands of creations of the contemporary designer. A style, with all the restrictions, disciplines, limitations and blessings that we usually associate with the term. A style in the similarities between designs differing basically in the purpose of their use and destination, subordinating to its demands a refrigerator or a motor car, a factory or a museum. A style which perhaps follows sales, quoting Edgar Kaufmann, just as form followed function in the words of Greenough and the Renaissance architecture followed its antique models in the work of Palladio. A style as pronounced, as defined, more limited perhaps, and as legitimate for our times as the style of Renaissance had been in its days.

In the growing maturity and self-consciousness of our century, we cannot avoid the recognition of this fact, and we have to realize what it stands for. We can no longer avoid this term "style" simply because it brings to our minds unpleasant memories. We cannot keep on pretending that we solve our problems without a precedent in form.

We have to realize that in the overwhelming majority of modern design form follows *form* and not *function*. And even when a form results from a functional analysis, this analysis follows a pattern that leads to a discovery of the same function, whether in a factory or a museum. Approached in a certain way an answer to every architectural problem is a flexible space with no reason why one flexible space should be different

* Matthew Nowicki, "Origins and Trends in Modern Architecture," *Magazine of Art* 44 (November 1951), pp. 273–79.

from another, and many practical reasons why they should be alike.

In saying all this, I am not an advocate of a diversity in design for its own sake. Such a diversity is just confirming the rule of regimentation that always is the result of a style. The more one attempts to escape one's period, the more part of it one becomes. The constructive diversity that provides strength to an expanding and virile civilization comes through a creative sensitivity to the eternally changing circumstance where "every opportunity stands alone."

This sensitivity is the main source of something for which I have no better word than freshness. Freshness is a physical part of youth, and youth disappears with time. This is the law of life true equally in the case of an individual or a civilization. Freshness can be preserved if the source of it depends not on the physical state of being young, but on the consciousness of its origin. Some individuals preserve this creative freshness in their maturity. Those are the great artists. Some civilizations preserve this freshness for ages and then become great cultures. For although maturity aims at perfection and the stride for perfection must end with an unchanging standard of classical excellence, the consciousness of the source of freshness can provide a magnified scope to this stride. The magnitude of this scope is the measure of ambitions and strength of a civilization, and the prophecy of its future achievements.

Thinking in terms of the contemporary, or should I say modern, period of design, we realize by now that it has passed its early youth. The experiments with form, of the new space concept, the playfulness with the machine to live in, the machine to look at or the machine to touch, in architecture, painting and sculpture are more remote from us than the time alone would indicate. There was a freshness in those youthful days of the aesthetic revolution, a physical freshness of a beginning. There was a diversity in those days of forms that grew without a direct precedent in form.

I speak of architecture because it incorporates the full field of design. In its changes we can discover those that affected the interior design, the industrial design, problems of organized landscape and others, with or without a separate name. And, it is these changes of the architectural concept that I propose to analyze with the aim of establishing our present position in their chain. From the analysis of these changes I will not develop any law of analogy, nor will I make predictions on what will be the coming change. I propose to define our present position because this is our strategic point of departure for the investigation of the full field of opportunity that lies within our period. To define our present stage, I shall try to trace it to its origins.

It seems to me that the beginning of modern architecture has its roots in the domestic structure of the late Renaissance. It was then that the problem of human comfort was rediscovered. Functionalism in terms of the importance of good living was introduced along with a number of technical gadgets of which the stove in Fontainebleau was probably a vanguard. Architecture descended from its pedestal of heroism and rapidly started to grow human and even bourgeois. In France after the death of Louis XIV, the despotic "Roi soleil" the private residence "building boom" produced a plan in which areas of different use were defined and located with regard to one another. The plan of this new type differed from its predecessor where a sequence of rectangular, round, oval and otherwise shaped interiors had a changing use, and one ate, slept or entertained in any one of them, according to a passing or a more permanent fancy. This change was not the beginning of functionalism, as architecture always had to satisfy a function, but the beginning of its modern interpretation. Resigning from heroism, architecture diminished its scale becoming cut to the size of an ordinary man. A good illustration of this change is the comparison between the Palace of Versailles and the Petit Trianon.

In the change of the predominant scale and the introduction of the problems of comfort, we can find the beginning of our architecture. These changes, essential as they were, could not alone produce the new form. Other factors were to complete the picture of the final change. One of them was expressed in 1825 by the German architect, Schinkel, after his visit to the industrialized Manchester in his famous question, "Why not a new style." The eternal desire of change was responsible for violent shifts of attitude to form through the 19th century. To illustrate this violence and its extremes, I would like to quote two striking and not very well known examples. In the early years of the century, a French archeologist proposed a system of destroying the Gothic cathedrals, considered in the days of the Empire as edifices of barbarism. Cutting a groove at the base of the limestone columns, then surrounding them with piles of wood and setting fire to them was suggested. The archeologist was convinced that under this treatment the unsavory structure would crumble "in less than ten minutes" relieving civilization of its shameful presence.

A few decades later Ruskin, paving the way for the Pre-Raphaelite movement, wrote in his "Modern Painters" that no public funds should be spent to purchase paintings later than Raphael, as the spirit of art was confined to the medieval period and replaced later by a superficial technology of a craft. Out of these shifts of sympathies came the consciousness that some basic change in the eclectic sequence is indispensable. This was the psychological background to what we call the "modern" form. And although we shudder at the word style, Schinkel's search for its new expression contributed to the birth of modern architecture, perhaps as much as any other factor. No new form of architecture could have been created without a new structure, and the psychological receptiveness had to wait for its fulfillment until the structural possibilities ripened.

The middle of the last century with Paxton's Crystal Palace—its modular re-erection on a new site, its space concept of openness, created a new era. The following use of cast iron then ferroconcrete and steel created the spine of the new frame structure from those days on dominant in modern building. Independence of the partitioning wall from the frame created the free plan and, thus, all elements of the new architecture were present at the beginning of our century.

What would have been the characteristics of modern architecture should it follow the direction of those early days? Its form influenced strongly by the expression of the structure would have been intricate and detailed. The logical development of the skeleton would accentuate the delicate ribs dividing areas of the building into supporting and supported members. The resulting form would perhaps acquire the lightness and openness of lacework filled with translucent or opaque screen. In its final stage the screen would probably be replaced with a secondary skeleton filling the lacework with more lacework.

This is the way the Gothic skeleton developed with its stained glass window and this was the road explored by Paxton, Labrouste, Eiffel and their contemporaries. Modern architecture instead chose a road different in every respect from these expectations. To understand this change of destiny we have to make a digression. Architecture with its social, economic and technical complexities never was in the lead of aesthetic changes. As a rule it followed other media of art. The changes of taste in the XIX century, mentioned before, affected architecture very profoundly but they resulted from factors remote to the problems of building or design.

The great change introduced by the Renaissance can be quoted here as a striking example of the same problem. At the rebirth of the classical idiom the medieval Gothic structure reached the climax of its growth. The future life and growth of this structure was interrupted by an aesthetic wave unrelated to the technics of architecture. No structural competition to the Gothic building was offered by the new style. The building methods of the Renaissance were crude when compared to the advanced standard of the medieval mason. The change in architecture followed the changing aesthetic of the period and the responsibility and credit for this change should rest with its men of letters. In this way Petrarch and Dante fathered the architecture of the Renaissance.

A somewhat similar thing happened to modern architecture. This time the change of taste was inspired by the painters and not by the men of letters. The broad and open manner of Cezanne, the architectonic painting of synthetic Cubism introduced a new taste for the purity and simplicity of form. The development of the structural skeleton mentioned before could not be molded into the new aesthetic. The problems of structure and materials became secondary in a period preoccupied with the aesthetics of form. One has the impression that for an architect of the early twenties construction was the necessary evil. Architecture became "idealized" and "dematerialized." Colorful planes meeting at the corners of the cube emphasized the lack of material thickness. Structural detail was eliminated conforming to the demands of purity and the idealized structure reacted badly to time and weather. A column in this architecture became simply a cylinder surrounded by planes, a vertical among horizontals. The contrast of this juxtaposition had to be achieved to the satisfaction of the intellect so that no shape was created without a function which it should express and serve. But to create the shape a function was created or conveniently over-emphasized. Here my thoughts wander to those two massive cylinders dividing the steps of Le Corbusier's Salvation Army Paris building. Although emphasized more than any other structural element of the building they function as ventilation shafts and maybe even now, if technically obsolete, might have lost their functional meaning preserving the compositional importance. This architecture of the "international style" romantically disposed to the over-impressive technology developed a notion which I shall call *functional exactitude*. The truth of architecture was considered as the exact expression of every function. When a building became technically obsolete and therefore no longer ideally serving those changing functions it was to be removed and replaced by a more efficient one.

The concept of functional exactitude found a source of decorative qualities in the inventive interpretation of human life and movement. One might say that this architecture became the decoration of function. The period of functional exactitude looked for its inspiration towards the physical function. The psychological one was not considered in its philosophy. The concept of controlled environment resulted and the main purpose of architecture was to control *physical* environment to the *physical* satisfaction of the user. Let us see what happened later.

The recent changes in modern architecture are perhaps as basic as those separating the nineteen twenties from their predecessors. True that we share our vocabulary with this period of yesterday but the same words have for us a different and often a basically opposite meaning. We also speak of functionalism but then it meant the exactitude and now it means the flexibility. Those are two opposite concepts. In our thoughts priority often is given to the psychological and not the physical human function. The concept of a short lived structure removed with the rapid change of technology is replaced by a notion of architecture that will be our contribution to the life of future generations. Le Corbusier introduces a measure on which this contribution can be composed, the "modulor" with its mystery of the golden section. This measure of good proportion is most significant for the change of values. No longer the measure of functional space, no longer the measure of time, but a measure of beauty. Whatever the validity of such a measure may be it is interesting to notice that in the sequence of "time, space and architecture" the emphasis is shifting towards the last word in terms of the mystery of its art. The free plan is replaced by the modular plan. Again these are two opposite notions. A module is the most rigid discipline to which a plan can be subjected. A modular plan in reality is the opposite of a free plan. We are no longer preoccupied with the proximities of related functions but with the nature of space that leads from one function to another. It is no longer "how quickly to get there" but "how to get there," that matters most in our plans. It seems that from a quantitative period we have jumped into a qualitative one.

These changes are not always conscious nor pronounced to the degree pointed out in my remarks. It is an irresistible temptation to express those changes in the most striking manner. But, in order to be objective one has to realize that a dividing line between periods can never be geometrically defined. This division can better be compared to a wide ribbon which separates and joins at the same time like a gray belt between fields of black and white.

With respect to the main channels of human creation namely the invention and the discovery, one might say that our present period is also different from the yesterday. The discovery of formal symbol of the unchanging laws of the universe seems to replace the invention of the form without a precedent. The eternal story of gravitation is again consciously contemplated. We are aware that the form of the discovery has to change but the object of it remains the same; over and over discovered in many ways.

Along with these elements of philosophy we also react in a different way to the techniques of our craft. Architecture discovered its own medium of creation and the difference between this medium and the others. Picasso writing recently about his "blue period" of 1912 and several later years said that he discovered late the difference between sculpture and painting. Maturity brings a "sense of medium" and mature architecture in the same way discovered the difference between painting and the art of organizing accessible space. As a result we rely in our expression on the potentialities of materials and structures almost picking up the trend of the XIX century. This interest in structure and material may discover within the building medium decorative qualities of ornament much too involved for the purist of yesterday. The symbolic meaning of a support became rediscovered and a steel column is used frankly as a symbol of structure even when it is not part of the structure itself. The period of functional exactitude expressed its mysterious longings for ornament in the decoration of function.

This period of functional flexibility expresses them in the decoration of structure. Art tends not only to discover the truth but to exaggerate and finally to distort it. *And, maybe in this distortion lies the essence of art.*

I have described our stage of the modern design as a style. Will this style repeat the sad story of other styles becoming an addition to the repertoire of a future eclecticism? The life and the decline of cultures follows an organic pattern which seems to be inevitable. But span of life of a culture and its rebirth into another rests in the hands of the people responsible for its creation. Where is the future of modern design?

It seems to me that it depends on the constant effort of approaching every problem with the consciousness that there is no single way of solving it. "Art una—species mille." This battle cry of the Renaissance should be repeated again and again. Art may be one but there are a thousand species. We must face the dangers of the crystallizing style not negating its existence but trying to enrich its scope by opening new roads for investigation and future refinements.

"Form follows function" may no longer satisfy ambitions aroused when form becomes judged for its universal values, but sensitivity to the minute exigencies of life remains the source of creative invention leading through the elimination of "exactitudes" to the more important and more general truth which equals beauty.

72 E. Saarinen, The Trans World Airlines Terminal* *1959*

How Nowicki might have more fully realized his nascent expressionism can only be conjectured, but the work of Eero Saarinen (1910–1961), whose life was cut short by brain cancer, offered some suggestion. Saarinen shared Nowicki's view of architecture as a vessel of feeling; he wrote in 1957: "A church must have the expression of a church. An airport should be an expression related to flight. It should make one feel the excitement of arrival and departure and the pleasures and adventures of travel."† To do this he relied on bold forms, and one to which he turned repeatedly was the arch; he had used a huge parabolic arch for his winning entry in the Jefferson Westward Expansion Memorial, St. Louis, designed in 1947–48, and a smaller, lower concrete arch to carry a suspended roof in his Ingalls Hockey Rink for Yale University, built in 1956–58. Saarinen desired an equally evocative form for the TWA Terminal, Idlewild (now Kennedy) Airport, New York, built in 1956–62; in his drive to make certain that in all its parts it was "one thing," he made unparalleled use of large detailed study models. When finished, the cantilevered concrete shells appeared to some to resemble a bird in flight, to which Saarinen responded, "The fact that to some people it looked like a bird in flight was really coincidental. That was the last thing we ever thought about. Now, that doesn't mean that one doesn't have the right to see it that way or to explain it to laymen in those terms, especially because laymen are usually more literally than visually inclined."‡

The challenge of the Trans World Airlines terminal was twofold. One, to create, within the complex of terminals that makes up Idlewild, a building for TWA which would be distinctive and memorable. Its particular site—directly opposite Idlewild's main entrance road and at the apex of the curve in the far end of the terminal complex—gave us the opportunity of designing a building which could relate to the surrounding buildings in mass, but still assert itself as a dramatic accent.

Two, to design a building in which the architecture itself would express the drama and specialness and excitement of travel. Thus, we wanted the architecture to reveal the terminal, not as a static, enclosed place, but as a place of movement and of transition.

Therefore, we arrived at this structure, which consists essentially of four interacting barrel vaults of slightly different shapes, supported on four Y-shaped columns. Together, these vaults make a vast concrete shell, fifty feet high and 315 feet long, which makes a huge umbrella over all the passenger areas. The shapes of these vaults were deliberately chosen in order to emphasize an upward-soaring quality of line, rather than the downward gravitational one common to many domed structures. We wanted to coun-

* From Aline Saarinen, ed., *Eero Saarinen on His Work* (New Haven, 1962), p. 60.

† Eero Saarinen, "Function, Structure and Beauty," *Architectural Association Journal* 73 (July–August 1957), p. 49.

‡ A. Saarinen, *Eero Saarinen on His Work*, p. 60.

teract the earthbound feeling and the heaviness that prevails too much in the M.I.T. auditorium. We wanted an uplift. For the same reason, the structural shapes of the columns were dramatized to stress their upward-curving sweep. The bands of skylights, which separate and articulate the four vaults, increase the sense of airiness and lightness.

In studying the problem in model after model, both exterior and interior, we realized that having determined on this basic form for the vaulting, we had committed ourselves to a family of forms and must carry the same integral character throughout the entire building. All the curvatures, all the spaces and elements, down to the shapes of signs, information boards, railings, and counters, would have to have one consistent character. As the passenger walked through the sequence of the building, we wanted him to be in a total environment where each part was the consequence of another and all belonged to the same form-world. It is our strong belief that only through such a consistency and such a consequential development can a building make its fullest impact and expression.

73 L. I. Kahn, Order Is* *1955*

Just as Saarinen devised new architectural languages in response to specific programs and sites, so did Louis Isadore Kahn (1901–1974) create a new but at the same time archaizing architecture which declared human use and constructive process. Moreover, he developed a poetic written language to describe the way in which these buildings became what they wanted to be. It is a poetry of childlike simplicity and multiple meanings, exemplified by the blank verse of "Order Is," written while Kahn taught design at Yale (and at roughly the same time he designed the Yale University Art Gallery addition, built in 1951–53).

The evolution of Kahn's thinking began with his Beaux-Arts training in architecture at the University of Pennsylvania, Philadelphia, where his family had immigrated from Estonia. Under such teachers as Paul P. Cret, Kahn perceived architecture as seriated spaces defined by structural masses. After graduation, during the mid-1920s, he worked in Cret's office but also met George Howe and Oscar Stonorov and was introduced to the writing of Le Corbusier and to the Modern Movement. Yet when he toured Europe in 1928 and 1929, it was Paestum, Siena, and San Gimignano that he visited and sketched.[†]

The depression hit Kahn particularly hard; often on relief himself, he worked

* Louis I. Kahn, "Order Is," *Perspecta* 3 (1955), p. 59.

† Kahn's early writing documents the evolution of his thought. See "Value and Aim in Sketching," *T-Square Club Journal* 1 (May 1931), pp. 4, 18–21; "Monumentality," *New Architecture and City Planning, A Symposium,* ed. Paul Zucker (New York, 1944), pp. 577–88; "On the Responsibility of the Architect," *Perspecta* 2 (1953), pp. 45–57. Complete bibliographies are found in Vincent Scully, *Louis I. Kahn* (New York, 1962); and Heinz Ronner, Sharad Jhaveri, and Alessandro Vasella, *Louis I. Kahn, Complete Works, 1935–1974* (Boulder, Colo., 1977).

for other architects, such as Alfred Kastner, on housing projects, learning to appreciate anew the architect's social responsibility advocated by Gropius. He also read
voraciously, especially Le Corbusier, so much so he recalled, "I came to live in a
beautiful city called Le Corbusier." In 1941 Kahn joined with George Howe and
then Oscar Stonorov, and in the abstracted masonry elements of their Carver Court
housing, Coatesville, Pennsylvania, built in 1941–43, there appeared a hint of Kahn's
later work.

In 1947 Kahn was invited to Yale first as visiting critic and then chief critic in
architectural design (he remained until 1957 when he returned to Philadelphia to
teach at the University of Pennsylvania). Larger buildings now began to come to
him, and from 1950 to 1951 he was resident architect at the American Academy in
Rome, where once again he drew fresh inspiration from antiquity—Karnak, Athens,
Praeneste, and Tivoli.‡ While at Yale he habitually dropped in on art history lectures, particularly those on San Gimignano, Hadrian's villa, or the work of Brunelleschi. So in his work and in the classroom he explored structural purism and economy
of means, while simultaneously he studied space and mass in the architecture of the
past. These disparate inquiries then began to come together in his writings published
in *Perspecta* and in the bold structure and strong internal masses of his Yale Art
Gallery addition. Kahn's maturation as an architect had taken longer than for most,
but it had been a particularly rich process of cross-fertilization, such as was to make
Kahn the most important American and international architect of his generation.

Order is
Design *is form-making in order*
Form emerges out of a system of construction
Growth is a construction
In **order** *is creative force*
In **design** *is the means—where   with what   when   with how much*
The nature of space reflects what it wants to be
        Is the auditorium a Stradivarius
                or is it an ear
        Is the auditorium a creative instrument
                keyed to Bach or Bartok
                played by the conductor
        or is it a convention hall
In the nature of space is the spirit and the will to exist a certain way
        Design *must closely follow that will*
        Therefore a stripe painted horse is not a zebra.
        Before a railroad station is a building
        it wants to be a street
        it grows out of the needs of street
                out of the order of movement
        A meeting of contours englazed.
Thru the nature—why
Thru the **order**—*what*

‡ Kahn's sketches were exhibited in 1978 and 1979; see *The Travel Sketches of Louis I.
Kahn* (Philadelphia, 1978), with introduction by Vincent Scully, and catalogue by Scully and
William Holman.

Thru **design**—*how*
A Form emerges from the structural elements inherent in
   the form.
                  A dome is not conceived when questions arise
                  how to build it.
                  Nervi grows an arch
                  Fuller grows a dome
Mozart's compositions are designs
                        They are exercises of **order**—*intuitive*
                        Design *encourages more designs*
                        Designs derive their imagery from
                        order
                        Imagery is the memory—the Form
                        Style is an adopted order
The same **order** *created the elephant and created man*
                        They are different designs
                        Begun from different aspirations
                        Shaped from different circumstances
Order does not imply Beauty
                  The same order created the dwarf and Adonis
Design *is not making Beauty*
                  Beauty emerges from selection
                              affinities
                              integration
                              love
Art is a form making life in order—psychic
Order is intangible
                  It is a level of creative consciousness
                  forever becoming higher in level
                        The higher the order the more diversity in **design**
Order supports integration
From what the space wants to be the unfamiliar may be revealed
to the architect.
From order he will derive creative force and power of self criticism
to give form to this unfamiliar.
Beauty will evolve

74   L. I. Kahn, Form and Design, and Other Writings* 1957–62

Kahn constructed his theory not so much by crafting finished statements but by a process of successive reiteration and refinement, returning to a theme again and again in lectures to students and in publication, so that the same ideas appear in various forms. For example, the discussion of "Form and Design," prepared by Kahn for the Voice of America *Forum Lectures* in 1960, first appeared in *Architectural Design* (31 [April 1961], pages 145–54), is reprinted in modified form in *The Notebooks and Drawings of Louis I. Kahn* (edited by R. S. Wurman and E. Feldman [Cambridge, Massachusetts, 1973]), and was published in V. Scully, *Louis I. Kahn* (New York, 1962), which version is given here. The sections perforce deleted concern the early studies for the First Unitarian Church of Rochester, the Richards Medical Center, and the Salk Institute. Included here are the adaptation of Kahn's booklet, "A City Tower . . . ," published by the Universal Atlas Cement Company in 1957, and passages from Kahn's notebooks as reprinted in the Wurman and Feldman anthology.

FORM AND DESIGN

A young architect came to ask a question. "I dream of spaces full of wonder. Spaces that rise and envelop flowingly without beginning, without end, of a jointless material white and gold." "When I place the first line on paper to capture the dream, the dream becomes less."

This is a good question. I once learned that a good question is greater than the most brilliant answer.

This is a question of the unmeasurable and the measurable. Nature, physical nature, is measurable.

Feeling and dream has no measure, has no language, and everyone's dream is singular.

Everything that is made however obeys the laws of nature. The man is always greater than his works because he can never fully express his aspirations. For to express oneself in music or architecture is by the measurable means of composition or design. The first line on paper is already a measure of what cannot be expressed fully. The first line on paper is less.

"Then," said the young architect, "what should be the discipline, what should be the ritual that brings one closer to the psyche. For in this aura of no material and no language, I feel man truly is."

Turn to Feeling and away from Thought. In Feeling is the Psyche. Thought is Feeling and presence of Order. Order, the maker of all existence, has No Existence Will. I choose the word Order instead of knowledge because personal knowledge is too little to express Thought abstractly. This Will is in the Psyche.

*From Vincent Scully, *Louis I. Kahn* (New York, 1962), pp. 114–21; and Richard S. Wurman and E. Feldman, ed., *The Notebooks and Drawings of Louis I. Kahn*, 2nd. ed. (Cambridge, Mass., 1972), passim.

All that we desire to create has its beginning in feeling alone. This is true for the scientist. It is true for the artist. But I warned that to remain in Feeling away from Thought means to make nothing.

Said the young architect: "To live and make nothing is intolerable. The dream has in it already the *will to be* and the desire to express this *will*. Thought is inseparable from Feeling. In what way then can Thought enter creation so that this psychic will can be more closely expressed? This is my next question."

When personal feeling transcends into Religion (not a religion but the essence religion) and Thought leads to Philosophy, the mind opens to realizations. Realization of what may be the *existence will* of, let us say, particular architectural spaces. Realization is the merging of Thought and Feeling at the closest rapport of the mind with the Psyche, the source of *what a thing wants to be*.

It is the beginning of Form. Form encompasses a harmony of systems, a sense of Order and that which characterizes one existence from another. Form has no shape or dimension. For example, in the differentiation of a spoon from spoon, spoon characterizes a form having two inseparable parts, the handle and the bowl. A spoon implies a specific design made of silver or wood, big or little, shallow or deep. Form is "what." Design is "how." Form is impersonal. Design belongs to the designer. Design is a circumstantial act, how much money there is available, the site, the client, the extent of knowledge. Form has nothing to do with circumstantial conditions. In architecture, it characterizes a harmony of spaces good for a certain activity of man.

Reflect then on what characterizes abstractly House, a house, home. House is the abstract characteristic of spaces good to live in. House is the form, in the mind of wonder it should be there without shape or dimension. A house is a conditional interpretation of these spaces. This is design. In my opinion the greatness of the architect depends on his powers of realization of that which is House, rather than his design of *a* house which is a circumstantial act. Home is the house and the occupants. Home becomes different with each occupant.

The client for whom a house is designed states the areas he needs. The architect creates spaces out of those required areas. It may also be said that this house created for the particular family must have the character of being good for another. The design in this way reflects its trueness to Form.

I think of school as an environment of spaces where it is good to learn. Schools began with a man under a tree who did not know he was a teacher discussing his realization with a few who did not know they were students. The students reflected on what was exchanged and how good it was to be in the presence of this man. They aspired that their sons also listen to such a man. Soon spaces were erected and the first schools became. The establishment of school was inevitable because it was part of the desires of man. Our vast systems of education, now vested in Institutions, stem from these little schools but the spirit of their beginning is now forgotten. The rooms required by our institutions of learning are stereotype and uninspiring. The Institute's required uniform classrooms, the locker-lined corridors and other so-called functional areas and devices, are certainly arranged in neat packages by the architect who follows closely the areas and budgetary limits as required by the school authorities. The schools are good to look at but are shallow in architecture because they do not reflect the spirit of the man under the tree. The entire system of schools that followed from the beginning would not have been possible if the beginning were not in harmony with the nature of man. It can also be said that the existence will of school was there even before the circumstances of the man under a tree.

That is why it is good for the mind to go back to the beginning because the beginning of any established activity of man is its most wonderful moment. For in it lies all its spirit and resourcefulness, from which we must constantly draw our inspirations of present needs. We can make our institutions great by giving them our sense of this inspiration in the architecture we offer them.

Reflect then on the meaning of school, *a* school, institution. The institution is the authority from whom we get their requirements of areas. A School or a specific design is what the institution expects of us. But School, the spirit school, the essence of the existence will, is what the architect should convey in his design. And I say he must, even if the design does not correspond to the budget. Thus the architect is distinguished from the mere designer. In school as a realm of spaces where it is good to learn, the lobby measured by the institute as so many square feet per student would become a generous Pantheon-like space where it is good to enter. The corridors would be transferred into classrooms belonging to the students themselves by making them much wider and provided with alcoves overlooking the gardens. They would become the places where boy meets girl, where the student discusses the work of the professor with his fellow-student. By allowing classroom time to these spaces instead of passage time from class to class, it would become a meeting connection and not merely a corridor, which means a place of possibilities in self-learning. It becomes the classroom belonging to the students. The classrooms should evoke their use by their space variety and not follow the usual soldier-like dimensional similarity, because one of the most wonderful spirits of this man under the tree is his recognition of the singularity of every man. A teacher or a student is not the same when he is with a few in an intimate room with a fireplace as in a large high room with many others. And must the cafeteria be in the basement, even though its use in time is little? Is not the relaxing moment of the meal also a part of learning? . . .

The realization of what particularizes the domain of spaces good for school would lead an institution of learning to challenge the architect to awareness of what School *wants to be* which is the same as saying what is the form, School. . . .

I want to talk about the difference between form and design, about realization, about the measurable and the unmeasurable aspects of our work and about the limits of our work.

Giotto was a great painter because he painted the skies black for the daytime and he painted birds that couldn't fly and dogs that couldn't run and he made men bigger than doorways because he was a painter. A painter has this prerogative. He doesn't have to answer to the problems of gravity, nor to the images as we know them in real life. As a painter he expresses a reaction to nature and he teaches us through his eyes and his reactions to the nature of man. A sculptor is one who modifies space with the objects expressive again of his reactions to nature. He does not create space. He modifies space. An architect creates space.

Architecture has limits.

When we touch the invisible walls of its limits then we know more about what is contained in them. A painter can paint square wheels on a cannon to express the futility of war. A sculptor can carve the same square wheels. But an architect must use round wheels. Though painting and sculpture play a beautiful role in the realm of architecture as architecture plays a beautiful role in the realms of painting and sculpture, one does not have the same discipline as the other.

One may say that architecture is the thoughtful making of spaces. It is, note, the filling of areas prescribed by the client. It is the creating of spaces that evoke a feeling of appropriate use.

To the musician a sheet of music is seeing from what he hears. A plan of a building should read like a harmony of spaces in light.

Even a space intended to be dark should have just enough light from some mysterious opening to tell us how dark it really is. Each space must be defined by its structure and the character of its natural light. Of course I am not speaking about minor areas which serve the major spaces. An architectural space must reveal the evidence of its making by the space itself. It cannot be a space when carved out of a greater structure meant for a greater space because the choice of a structure is synonymous with the light and which gives image to that space. Artificial light is a single tiny static moment in light and is the light of night and never can equal the nuances of mood created by the time of day and the wonder of the seasons.

A great building, in my opinion, must begin with the unmeasurable, must go through measurable means when it is being designed and in the end must be unmeasurable. The design, the making of things is a measurable act. In fact at that point, you are like physical nature itself because in physical nature everything is measurable, even that which is yet unmeasured, like the most distant stars which we can assume will be eventually measured.

But what is unmeasurable is the psychic spirit. The psyche is expressed by feeling and also thought and I believe will always be unmeasurable. I sense that the psychic Existence Will calls on nature to make what it wants to be. I think a rose wants to be a rose. Existence Will, *man*, becomes existence, through nature's law and evolution. The results are always less than the spirit of existence.

In the same way a building has to start in the unmeasurable aura and go through the measurable to be accomplished. It is the only way you can build, the only way you can get it into being is through the measurable. You must follow the laws but in the end when the building becomes part of living it evokes unmeasurable qualities. The design involving quantities of brick, method of construction, engineering is over and the spirit of its existence takes over.

Take the beautiful tower made of bronze that was erected in New York.[1] It is a bronze lady, incomparable in beauty, but you know she has corsets for fifteen stories because the wind bracing is not seen. That which makes it an object against the wind which can be beautifully expressed, just like nature expresses the difference between the moss and the reed. The base

[1] Seagram Building, New York, built in 1954–58, by Mies van der Rohe with Philip Johnson.—ED.

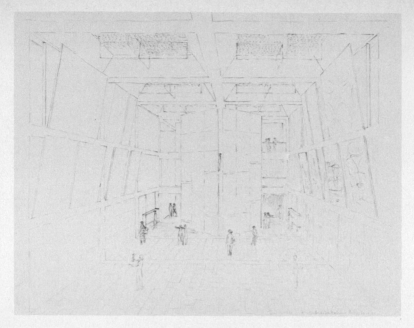

Figure 61. Louis I. Kahn, sketch of main exhibition court in Yale Center for British Art (Mellon Center), New Haven, Conn., penultimate design of 1971 (photo: courtesy of the Louis I. Kahn collection, University of Pennsylvania and the Pennsylvania Historic and Museum Commission). The diamond-shaped staircase was subsequently transformed into a massive cylinder. Of this room Kahn wrote: "The idea of intimacy between book, painting, drawing—this is in the roomlike quality of the collections. The rooms are made with concrete columns and slabs. The slabs contain the air returns, so the galleries are clear of gadgetry. The air risers, however, are exposed. They become a sort of Franklin Stove sitting in a space. The interior is wood; the windows have shutters you can close and hang paintings on. The exterior avoids heavy construction between the columns and is made of mat-finish stainless steel—like pewter."

of this building should be wider than the top, and the columns which are on top dancing like fairies, and the columns below growing like mad, don't have the same dimensions because they are not the same thing. This story if told from realization of form would make a tower more expressive of the forces. Even if it begins in its first attempts in design to be ugly it would be led to beauty by the statement of form. . . .

The institutions of cities can be made greater by the power of their architectural spaces. The meeting house in the village green has given way to the city hall which is no more the meeting place. But I sense an existence will for the arcaded city place where the fountains play, where again boy meets girl, where the city could entertain and put up our distinguished visitors, where the many societies which uphold our democratic ideals can meet in clusters of auditoria in the city place.

The motor car has completely upset the form of the city. I feel that the time has come to make the distinction between the Viaduct architecture of the car and the architecture of man's activities. The tendencies of designers to combine the two architectures in a simple design has confused the direction of planning and technology. The Viaduct architecture enters the city from outlying areas. At this point it must become more carefully made and even at great expense more strategically placed with respect to the centre.

The Viaduct architecture includes the street which in the centre of the city wants to be a building, a building with rooms below for city piping services to avoid interruption to traffic when services need repair.

The Viaduct architecture would encompass an entirely new concept of street movement which distinguished the stop and go staccato movement of the bus from the "go" movement of the car. The area framing expressways are like rivers. These rivers need harbours. The interim streets are like canals which need docks. The harbours are the gigantic gateways expressing the *architecture of stopping.* The terminals of the Viaduct architecture, they are garages in the core, hotels and department stores around the periphery and shopping centers on the street floor.

The strategic positioning around the city centre would present a logical image of protection against the destruction of the city by the motor car. In a sense the problem of the car and city is war, and the planning for the new growth of cities is not a complacent act, but an act of emergency....

Reflect on the Pantheon which is recognized as one of the greatest of buildings. Its greatness has many facets. It is the realization of a conviction that a building could be dedicated to all religions and that this ritual free space can be given expression. It presents a belief of a great man which led to its design as a non directional domed space. If architecture may be expressed as a world within a world, then this building expresses it well, even refining it, by placing the oculus, the only window, in the center of the dome. This building had no precedents; its motivation was clear and full of belief. The force of its "wanting to be" inspired a design equal to its desires in form.

Today, building needs an atmosphere of belief for the architect to work in. Belief can come from recognizing that new institutions want to emerge and be given expression in space. New beliefs come with new institutions that need to be expressed as new spaces and new relationships. The architectural realizations sensitive to the institutions' particular form would set a new precedent, a new beginning. I do not believe that beauty can be deliberately created. Beauty evolves out of a will to be that may have its first expression in the archaic. Compare Paestum with the Parthenon. Archaic Paestum is the beginning. It is the time when the walls parted and the columns became and when music entered architecture. Paestum inspired the Parthenon. The Parthenon is considered more beautiful, but Paestum is still more beautiful to me. It presents a beginning within which is contained all the wonder that may follow in its wake. The columns as a rhythm of enclosure and opening and the feeling of entering through them to the spaces they envelop is an architectural spirit, a religion which still prevails in our architecture today.

A space can never reach its place in architecture without natural light. Artificial light is the light of night expressed in positioned chandeliers not to be compared with the unpredictable play of natural light. The places of entrance, the galleries that radiate from them, the intimate entrances to the spaces of the institution form an independent architecture of connection.

This architecture is of equal importance to the major spaces though these spaces are designed only for movement and must therefore be designed to be bathed in natural light. This Architecture of Connection cannot appear in the program of areas—it is what the architect offers the client in his search for architectural balance and direction. The client asks for areas, the architect must give him spaces; the client has in mind corridors, the architect finds reasons for galleries; the client gives the architect a budget, the architect must think in terms of economy; the client speaks of a lobby, the architect brings to it the dignity of a place of entrance. Architecture deals with spaces, the thoughtful and meaningful making of spaces. The architectural space is one where the structure is apparent in the space itself. A long span is a great effort that should not be dissipated by division within. The art of architecture has wonderful examples of spaces within spaces, but without deception. A wall dividing a domed space would negate the entire spirit of the dome.

The structure is a design in light. The vault, the dome, the arch, the column are structures related to the character of light. Natural light gives mood to space by the nuances of light in the time of the day and the seasons of the year as it enters and modifies the space.

In Gothic times, architects built in solid stones. Now we can build with hollow stones. The spaces defined by the members of a structure are as important as the members. These spaces range in scale from the voids of an insulation panel, voids for air, lighting and heat to circulate, to spaces big enough to walk through or live in. The desire to express voids positively in the design of a structure is evidenced by the growing interest and work in the development of space frames. The forms being experimented with come from a closer knowledge of nature and the outgrowth of a constant search for order. Design habits leading to the concealment of structure have no place in this implied order. Such habits retard the development of an art. I believe that in architecture, as in all art, the artist instinctively keeps marks which reveal how a thing is done. . . . Structures should be devised which can harbor the mechanical needs of rooms and spaces. Ceilings with structure furred in tend to erase scale. If we were to train ourselves to draw as we build, from the bottom up, when we do, stopping our pencil to make a mark at the joints of pouring or erecting, ornament would grow out of our love for the expression of method. It follows that it would become intolerable to hide the source of lighting and unwanted ducts, conduits and pipe lines by pasting acoustical material over structure. The sense of structure of the building and how the spaces are served would be lost. The desire to express how it is done would filter through the entire society of building, to architect, engineer, builder and craftsman.

I do not like ducts; I do not like pipes. I hate them really thoroughly, but because I hate them so thoroughly, I feel they have to be given their place. If I just hated them and took no care, I think they would invade the building and completely destroy it. I want to correct any notion you may have that I am in love with that kind of thing.

75   P. Johnson, The Seven Crutches
of Modern Architecture*   *1954*

After leaving the Museum of Modern Art in 1936, Philip Johnson took up professional studies in architecture under Gropius at Harvard, building for himself an austere
glass-walled house on Ash Street in Cambridge in 1942 and completing his degree in
1943. Having commenced to practice, in 1946 he was appointed director of the
department of architecture and design of the Museum of Modern Art, and it was in
conjunction with an exhibition there that he published in 1947 his monograph on
Mies van der Rohe. Upon seeing his mentor's project for the Farnsworth house, Johnson began work on a similar glass house for himself in New Canaan, Connecticut,
expanding on the theme he had essayed on Ash Street. The residences he designed
from 1946 to 1956 and the addition to the Museum were clearly inspired in their
formal purity and industrial precision by Mies. In 1954 the two joined to execute
Mies's Seagram Building, when New York licensing laws threatened to prevent Mies
from building in that state. Johnson seemed very much Mies's protégé, and felt it no
slur to be called "Mies van der Johnson."

Yet increasingly, after 1954, Johnson moved away from Miesian asceticism
toward a pluralism based on broadly interpreted function, toward expressionism and,
at the same time, toward classical formalism, as was manifest in his Blaffer Trust
"Roofless Church," in New Harmony, Indiana, and the Amon Carter Museum, Fort
Worth. What had seemed cleansing discipline in 1932, two decades later began to
inhibit. With jocular self-deprecation, Johnson poked fun at the rule he himself had
been instrumental in codifying, isolating "seven crutches" of modern design (thus
inverting Ruskin's precepts), and laughingly admitting to breaking the rules. This
informal talk was presented December 7, 1954, to students at the Harvard School of
Architectural Design, where the influence of Gropius was still strong. If Johnson's
remarks were considered rather heretical there, they were quickly published by Yale
architectural students.[†]

Art has nothing to do with intellectual pursuit—it shouldn't be in a
university at all. Art should be practised in gutters—pardon me, in attics.

You can't learn architecture any more than you can learn a sense of
music or of painting. You shouldn't talk about art, you should do it.

If I seem to go into words it's because there's no other way to commu-

---

*Philip C. Johnson, "The Seven Crutches of Modern Architecture," *Perspecta* 3 (1955),
pp. 40–44, originally published under the title "Remarks from an informal talk to students of
Architectural Design at Harvard, December 1954"; reprinted in J. Jacobus, *Philip Johnson*
(New York, 1961), pp. 113–18; and *Philip Johnson: Writings* (New York, 1979), pp. 136–40.

†In *Philip Johnson: Writings* (New York, 1979), p. 136, Robert A. M. Stern writes that
upon reading this, when he began his studies at Yale, he became a convert: "Here was a
document that appeared to say it all. With a couple of class-mates, I hopped in a car on a
Saturday afternoon, drove to New Canaan, and signed up for that continuing Glass House
seminar in architecture which . . . [was] a primary influence on a whole younger generation of
architects trained in New Haven."

nicate. We have to descend to the world around us if we are to battle it. We have to use words to put the "word" people back where they belong.

So I'm going to attack the seven crutches of architecture. Some of us rejoice in the crutches and pretend that we're walking and that poor other people with two feet are slightly handicapped. But we all use them at times, and especially in the schools where you have to use language. It's only natural to use language when you're teaching, because how are teachers to mark you? "Bad entrance" or "Bathrooms not backed up" or "Stairway too narrow" or "Where's head room?," "Chimney won't draw," "Kitchen too far from dining room." It is so much easier for the faculty to set up a set of rules that you can be marked against. They can't say "That's ugly." For you can answer that for you it is good-looking, *de gustibus non est disputandum.* Schools therefore are especially prone to using these crutches. I would certainly use them if I were teaching, because I couldn't criticize extra-aesthetic props any better than any other teacher.

The most important crutch in recent times is not valid now: the Crutch of History. In the old days you could always rely on books. You could say, "What do you mean you don't like my tower? There it is in Wren." Or, "They did that on the Subtreasury Building—why can't I do it?" History doesn't bother us very much now.

But the next one is still with us today although, here again, the Crutch of Pretty Drawing is pretty well gone. There are those of us—I am one— who have made sort of a cult of the pretty plan. It's a wonderful crutch because you can give yourself the illusion that you are creating architecture while you're making pretty drawings. Fundamentally, architecture is something you build and put together, and people walk in and they like it. But that's too hard. Pretty pictures are easier.

The next one, the third one, is the Crutch of Utility, of Usefulness. This is where I was brought up, and I've used it myself; it was an old Harvard habit. They say a building is good architecture if it works. Of course, this is poppycock. All buildings work. This building (referring to Hunt Hall) works perfectly—if I talk loud enough. The Parthenon probably worked perfectly well for the ceremonies that they used it for. In other words, merely that a building works is not sufficient. You expect that it works. You expect a kitchen hot water faucet to run hot water these days. You expect any architect, a graduate of Harvard or not, to be able to put the kitchen in the right place. But when it's used as a crutch it impedes. It lulls you into thinking that that is architecture. The rules that we've all been brought up on "The coat closet should be near the front door in a house," "Cross-ventilation is a necessity,"—these rules are not very important for architecture. That we should have a front door to come in and a back door to carry the garbage out— pretty good, but in my house I noticed to my horror the other day that I carried the garbage out the front door. If the business of getting the house to run well takes precedence over your artistic invention the result won't be architecture at all; merely an assemblage of useful parts. You will recognize it next time you're doing a building: you'll be so satisfied when you get the banks of elevators to come out at the right floor you'll think your skyscraper is finished. I know. I'm just working on one.

That's not as bad, though as the next one: the Crutch of Comfort.

That's a habit that we come by, the same as utility. We are all descended from John Stuart Mill in our thinking. After all, what is architecture for but the comforts of the people that live there? But when that is made into a crutch for doing architecture, environmental control starts to replace architecture. Pretty soon you'll be doing controlled environmental houses which aren't hard to do except that you may have a window on the west and you can't control the sun. There isn't an overhang in the world, there isn't a sun chart in Harvard University that will help. Because, of course, the sun is absolutely everywhere. You know what they mean by controlled environment—it is the study of "microclimatology," which is the science that tells you how to recreate a climate so that you will be comfortable. But are you? The fireplace, for example, is out of place in the controlled environment of a house. It heats up and throws off thermostats. But I like the beauty of a fireplace so I keep my thermostat way down to 60, and then I light a big roaring fire so I can move back and forth. Now that's not controlled environment. I control the environment. It's a lot more fun.

Some people say that chairs are good-looking that are comfortable. Are they? I think that comfort is a function of whether you think the chair is good-looking or not. Just test it yourself. (Except I know you won't be honest with me.) I have had Mies van der Rohe chairs now for twenty-five years in my home wherever I go. They're not very comfortable chairs, but, if people like the looks of them they say "Aren't these beautiful chairs," which indeed they are. Then they'll sit in them and say, "My, aren't they comfortable." If, however, they're the kind of people who think curving steel legs are an ugly way to hold up a chair they'll say "My, what uncomfortable chairs."

The Crutch of Cheapness. That is one that you haven't run into as students because no one's told you to cut $10,000 off the budget because you haven't built anything. But that'll be your first lesson. The cheapness boys will say "Anybody can build an expensive house. Ah, but see, my house only cost $25,000." Anybody that can build a $25,000 house has indeed reason to be proud, but is he talking about architecture or his economic ability? Is it the crutch you're talking about, or is it architecture? That economic motive, for instance, goes in New York so far that the real estate minded people consider it un-American to build a Lever House with no rentals on the ground floor. They find that it's an architectural sin not to fill the envelope.

Then there's another very bad crutch that you will get much later in your career. Please, please watch out for this one: the Crutch of Serving the Client. You can escape all criticism if you can say, "Well, the client wanted it that way." Mr. Hood, one of our really great architects, talked exactly that way. He would put a Gothic door on a skyscraper and say "Why shouldn't I? The client wanted a Gothic door on the modern skyscraper, and I put it on. Because what is my business? Am I not here to please my client?" As one of the boys asked me during the dinner before the lecture, where do you draw the the the line? When do the client's demands permit you to shoot him, and when do you give in gracefully? It's got to be clear, back in your own mind, that serving the client is one thing and the art of architecture another.

Perhaps the most trouble of all is the Crutch of Structure. That gets awfully near home because, of course, I use it all the time myself. I'm going to go on using it. You have to use something. Like Bucky Fuller, who's going around from school to school—it's like a hurricane, you can't miss it if it's coming: he talks, you know, for five or six hours, and he ends up that all architecture is nonsense, and you have to build something like discontinuous domes. The arguments are beautiful. I have nothing against discontinuous domes, but for goodness sakes, let's not call it architecture. Have you ever seen Bucky trying to put a door into one of his domed buildings? He's never succeeded, and wisely, when he does them, he doesn't put any covering on them, so they are magnificient pieces of pure sculpture. Sculpture alone cannot result in architecture because architecture has problems that Bucky Fuller has not faced, like how do you get in and out. Structure is a very dangerous thing to cling to. You can be led to believe that clear structure clearly expressed will end up being architecture by itself. You say "I don't have to design any more. All I have to do is make a clean structural order." I have believed this off and on myself. It's a very nice crutch, you see, because, after all, you can't mess up a building too badly if the bays are all equal and all the windows the same size.

Now why should we at this stage be that crutch conscious? Why should we not step right up to it and face it? The act of creation. The act of creation, like birth and death, you have to face by yourself. There aren't any rules; there is no one to tell you whether your one choice out of, say, six billion for the proportion of a window is going to be right. No one can go with you into that room where you make the final decision. You can't escape it anyhow; why fight it? Why not realize that architecture is the sum of inescapable artistic decisions that you have to make. If you're strong you can make them.

I like the thought that what we are to do on this earth is to embellish it for its greater beauty, so that oncoming generations can look back to the shapes we leave here and get the same thrill that I get in looking back at theirs—at the Parthenon, at Chartres Cathedral. That is the duty—I doubt if I get around to it in my generation—the difficulties are too many, but you can. You can if you're strong enough not to bother with the crutches, and face the fact that to create something is a direct experience.

I like Corbusier's definition of architecture. He expressed it the way I wish I could have: *"L'architecture, c'est le jeux, savant, correct et magnifique, des formes sous la lumière"*—"Architecture is the play of forms under the light, the play of forms correct, wise, magnificent." The play of forms under the light. And, my friends, that's all it is. You can embellish architecture by putting toilets in. But there was great architecture long before the toilet was invented. I like Nietzsche's definition—that much-misunderstood European—he said, "In architectural works, man's pride, man's triumph over gravitation, man's will to power assume visible form. Architecture is a veritable oratory of power made by form."

Now my position in all this is obviously not as solipsistic, not as directly intuitional as all that sounds. To get back to earth, what do we do next? If we don't hang on to any of these crutches. I'm a traditionalist. I believe in history. I mean by tradition the carrying out, in freedom, the development of a certain basic approach to architecture which we find upon beginning our work here. I do not believe in perpetual revolution in architecture. I do not strive for originality. As Mies once told me, "Philip, it is much better to be good than to be original." I believe that. We have very fortunately the work of our spiritual fathers to build on. We hate them, of course, as all spiritual sons hate all spiritual fathers, but we can't ignore them, nor can we deny their greatness. The men, of course, that I refer to: Walter Gropius, Le Corbusier and Mies van der Rohe. Frank Lloyd Wright I should include— the greatest architect of the nineteenth century. Isn't it wonderful to have behind us the tradition, the work that those men have done? Can you imagine being alive at a more wonderful time? Never in history was the tradition so clearly demarked, never were the great men so great, never could we learn so much from them and go our own way, without feeling constricted by any style, and knowing that what we do is going to be the architecture of the future, and not be afraid that we wander into some little bypath, like today's romanticists where nothing can possibly evolve. In that sense I am a traditionalist.

76 P. Johnson, Letter to Jurgen Joedicke* *1961*

In this comment prompted by reading Joedicke's *History of Modern Architecture* (New York 1959), Johnson expressed ideas that were to have increasing currency fifteen and twenty years later. He speaks here of the Modern Movement winding up its days, of the only absolute being the absence of hard and fast rules, and of the rise of a new eclecticism, yet he seems uncomfortable with eclecticism as a philosophy of design. How ironic that in his American Telephone and Telegraph Building, New York, designed in 1978, Johnson should have been accused by some as being too reliant on historical models!

LETTER TO DR. JURGEN JOEDICKE

I am very much impressed by your summation of modern international architecture in 1961. Your sense of organization and characterization in a field as fluid as ours is clear and consistent. . . .

Two points I should like to bring out. First, I wish you had the time to study American architecture more at first hand. The architects best known to European colleagues and journalists are the ones you especially discuss. To us Schindler might be singled out instead of Neutra—Kahn instead of Breuer and so forth. Also in talks perhaps we could make clear the differences between Stone, Yamasaki and myself.

May I say parenthetically, you are very fair with me. Borromini should

*From John Jacobus, *Philip Johnson* (New York, 1962), pp. 120–22; reprinted in *Philip Johnson: Writings* (New York, 1979), pp. 124–26.

not be mentioned in connection with my work. The New Harmony shrine is pure form—ugly or beautiful—but pure form.

There is, as you realize, however, a basic cleavage in our points of view. You criticize from a standpoint (*Standpunkt*). You take a stand (*Stellung nehmen*), on a moral basis of the Modern Movement. You understand the modern movement as deriving "Form" from the proper program (*Aufgabe*) and from structural simplicity and honesty. You take especial stand against using structure shapes as mere applied decoration. You would agree with Goethe: "*Der Pilaster ist eine Lüge.*"[1]

In line with this, you naturally would see the danger of a new Eclecticism in our new approach to history.

Is there not, however, another position we could take? Namely, that the entire modern movement—looked at as an intellectual movement dating from Ruskin and Viollet-le-Duc, going through the Werkbund, Bauhaus, Le Corbusier to World War II—may be winding up its days.

There is only one absolute today and that is change. There are no rules, surely no certainties in any of the arts. There is only the feeling of a wonderful freedom, of endless possibilities to investigate, of endless past years of historically great buildings to enjoy.

I cannot worry about a new eclecticism. Even Richardson who considered himself an eclectic was not one. A good architect will always do original work. A bad one would do bad "modern" work as well as bad work (that is imitative) with historical forms.

Structural honesty seems to me one of the bugaboos that we should free ourselves from very quickly. The Greeks with their marble columns imitating wood, and covering up the wood roofs inside! The Gothic designers with their wooden roofs above to protect their delicate vaulting. And Michelangelo, the greatest architect in history, with his Mannerist column!

No, our day no longer has need of moral crutches of late 19th century vintage. If Viollet-le-Duc was what the young Frank Lloyd Wright was nurtured on, Geoffrey Scott and Russell Hitchcock were my Bibles.

I am old enough to have enjoyed the International Style immensely and worked in it with the greatest pleasure. I still believe Le Corbusier and Mies to be the greatest living architects. But now the age is changing so fast. Old values are swept away by new with dizzying but thrilling speed. Long live Change!

The danger you see of a sterile academic eclecticism is no danger. The danger is the opposite, the sterility of your Academy of the Modern Movement.

---

[1] "The pilaster is a lie."—Ed.

77 V. Scully, The Shingle Style* 1955

The appearance of Rudolf Wittkower's *Architectural Principles in the Age of Humanism* (London, 1949) sparked renewed discourse among architects and helped shape the "New Brutalist" work of the Smithsons. In a similar way, Vincent Scully's book *The Shingle Style* brought to light the free but abstract discipline of American domestic architecture of the 1880s; the book enjoyed the approbation of fellow historians and was read by architects, while, in the classroom, Scully directly influenced a generation of younger architects including Robert A. M. Stern. By 1965 these younger architects were finding in the shingle style inspiration for a revitalized American domestic architecture.

Scully was born in New Haven in 1920 and was admitted to Yale on a full scholarship in 1936; he read literary criticism but, toward the end of his undergraduate years, he found in a course in art history the solid objectivity he missed in literary criticism. During the war he was in the Marine Corps; on returning to Yale in 1946 to pursue a doctorate, he turned to art history. He decided to write on the kind of domestic architecture around New Haven with which he was so familiar, and out of this emerged his dissertation and *The Shingle Style*. At the same time he collaborated with Antoinette F. Downing, writing the second half of *The Architectural Heritage of Newport, Rhode Island* (Cambridge, Massachusetts, 1952). He had begun to teach survey courses in art history at Yale in 1948, and his coverage of the Greek temples impelled him to undertake examining them *in situ*, resulting in his *The Earth, the Temple, and the Gods* (New Haven, 1962). In this book he argued that the temples could be fully understood only by taking account of their relationship to forms in the landscape sacred in myth. While traversing the American southwest, Scully observed that the pueblos manifested a similar connection with that landscape, and in *Pueblo: Mountain, Village, Dance* (New York, 1975), he insisted that without understanding the ceremonial dance and the sacredness of the landscape, one could not understand the architecture. Unlike the temple, however, the pueblo is one with the earth. "The American Indian world is a place where no conception whatever of any difference between men and nature can exist," he wrote, "but only an ineradicable instinct that all living things are one."

Scully's historical analyses repeatedly have presented new critical perceptions—the emergence of democracy as a driving force, in *Modern Architecture* (New York, 1960), or the debts in Wright's work to meso-American Architecture, in *Frank Lloyd Wright* (New York, 1960). If his admonition that American architects learn from the pueblos a new reverence for nature's realities, especially the force in the sun, has only begun to influence design, his appreciation of Beaux-Arts historicist design in *American Architecture and Urbanism* (New York, 1969) had a more marked effect in influencing critical and professional perceptions during the 1970s.†

* Vincent J. Scully, Jr., *The Shingle Style: Architectural Theory and Design from Richardson to the Origins of Wright* (New Haven, 1955), pp. 71, 81–88, 155–61, 163–64. Reissued as *The Shingle Style and the Stick Style* (New Haven, 1971), with preface, V. J. Scully, Jr., "Romantic Rationalism and the Expression of Structure in Wood: Downing, Wheeler, Gardner and the 'Stick Style,' 1840–1876," reprinted from *Art Bulletin* 35 (June 1953), pp. 121–42.

† This awakening to such positive aspects of Beaux-Arts design as the hierarchical ordering of spaces appeared in Scully's *Louis I. Kahn* (New York, 1962), still the best introduction to that architect's work.

In that study he also stressed not only the social accountability of the architect, but his historical responsibility as well, for, he wrote, architecture is "a continuing dialogue between the generations which creates an environment developing across time." With customary modesty, Scully has been able to observe and comment on his influence on recent domestic work in *The Shingle Style Today, or, the Historian's Revenge* (New York, 1974), a publication based on a lecture given at Columbia University the previous year. In this he illustrated the work of the younger architects who were drawing upon the domestic architecture of the 1880s that he had been instrumental in making the subject of serious art historical study.

5. FORMATION OF THE SHINGLE STYLE

The architects of the generation of the late 1870's faced certain possibilities and problems in the design of new domestic buildings: how to develop most fully the spatial possibilities of the living hall, the large areas of glass, and the veranda; how to expand the use of shingles so that their possibilities for continuity could most completely express the continuities now possible in interior space; how to transpose into creative forms—as was being done in theory—the influences of colonial and Queen Anne; and most of all how to discipline the picturesque without falling into the trap of academicism. The various experiments and solutions along these and related lines will be the subject of this and the following chapters. . . .

One house by the firm of McKim, Mead, and Bigelow during this period should . . . be discussed. This is the Mrs. A. C. Alden House, Fort Hill, Lloyd's Neck, Long Island (1879–80).[1] Above a stone foundation this house is sheathed with clapboards on its first story and shingles on its second (Figure 62). The house is simple and quiet, despite its small-paned windows, the touches of plaster decoration in the gables, the one or two small Palladian pediments over windows, and the screen of turned posts at the entrance. The plan is also simple and well organized. At the level of the entrance a moderate hall opens fully onto a long and extended piazza by the water. A library to the left has a parlor behind it. Up a few steps to the right the dining room gives off the staircase hall, and beyond that stretches a long, thin service wing. The mass is extended horizontally in a serene way, anchored by the unobtrusive staircase tower and the easy gable of the main wing. The turrets of the chateaux of the Loire—probably White's, although technically he was not yet part of the firm—are pulled into an over-all unity through an axial scheme, probably by McKim. Moreover, one feels in the Alden House a crisp and clean expression of the light wooden frame. The Alden House is one of the simplest and most coherent of any of the country houses built in America in the period before 1880. With all its variety, it still has sweep and order.

[1] *American Architect*, 6, Aug. 30, 1879. Already noted: McKim's two Taylor Houses at Elberon of 1877 and 1878. Other pertinent buildings finished in 1880 by McKim, Mead, and White include the Elberon Hotel and Cottages, and the Fahnestock, Garland, and Wood Houses, all at Elberon, N.J., and the Brokaw House, Long Branch, L.I. One of the Elberon houses was a simple, low-gabled rectangle, surrounded by porches, somewhat like the Moses Taylor House but with plain wooden detailing rather than pilasters. See Charles Moore, *The Life and Times of Charles Follen McKim*, Boston, 1929, appendix 3, for a list of his work.

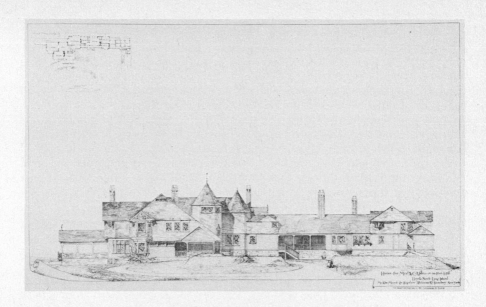

Figure 62. McKim, Mead & Bigelow, A. C. Alden house, "Fort Hill," Lloyd's Neck, Long Island, N.Y., 1879–80, from *American Architect and Building News* 6 (August 30, 1879).

Figure 63. William Ralph Emerson, C. J. Morrill house, Bar Harbor, Me., 1879, from *American Architect and Building News* 5 (March 22, 1879).

One architect in the late 70's probably contributed more to the development of the new architecture—except in some aspects of planning—than any designer discussed so far. William Ralph Emerson, of Boston, not only combined in his own work many of the new characteristics already noted in the work of other architects but also developed from these a type of synthesis beyond which Richardson's own synthesis of the early 80's had only to advance one short step. Emerson began to practice in the early 70's, publishing late stick style and early Queen Anne domestic projects by the middle 70's.[2] Among his early works is the barn which he remodeled and enlarged as a workshop for William Morris Hunt in 1877: "The Hulk," Magnolia, Massachusetts.[3] A simple structure with a projecting roof over a second-story porch, a stick-work balcony, and a general air of studied casualness, "The Hulk" was at least an indication of Emerson's sensitivity to simple materials and his ability to handle small problems lightly and with a sense of scale. One may well shudder at the thought of such a project in the hands of the painter-client's heavy-handed brother, Richard Morris Hunt.[4]

Yet a house of 1878 by Emerson at Milton, Massachusetts, was much less sensitively handled. One wonders whether the original barn from which "The Hulk" was made was not responsible for its final delicacy.[5] The Milton house of this year was a harsh box, undistinguished in plan and overloaded with heavy projecting gables, using both shingles and half-timber and supported by particularly unsuccessful examples of the ubiquitous turned post.

[2] Emerson created at least one extremely sensitive masterpiece in the midcentury stick style, namely the Forbes House at Milton, Mass., published in the *New York Architectural Sketch Book*, 3, 1876. William Ralph Emerson was born in Illinois in 1833; his family moved to Boston when he was young, and he studied architecture with Jonathan Preston (Boston Theater). He was a promoter of both the Boston Architectural Society and the Boston Art Club (*Herringshaw's National Library of American Biography*, 2, Chicago, 1909). Emerson died in 1918.

[3] *Am. Arch.*, 3, Feb. 23, 1878. The *Architect* (p. 66) says of this building: "The Hulk," so called from its fancied resemblance to an old stranded ship, with its ropes for lifting the gangway stairs, its davits for raising the doors of the carriage-house, and the employment of whole ribs and vertebrae for braces, railings, and ornamental features, was built by adding an old barn and carpenter's shop together at Mr. Hunt's suggestion, and affords accommodation for horses, carriages, sleeping-quarters, and a large painting-room.

[4] It is characteristic of Richard Morris Hunt that, generally, while others were building cottages, he was building palazzi. His 1872 remodeling of the Wetmore House in Newport, originally built in 1852, is an excellent example of Hunt's taste for the grand. See Downing and Scully, pp. 139, 147. Hunt's eclecticism during this period is also to be observed in his Vanderbilt House, New York, 1879. This is important as being one of the first of the many François Premier city mansions which formed the urban and less original counterpart to the suburban shingle style of the early 80's. An excellent example is McKim, Mead, and White's Whittier House on the water side of Beacon Street, Boston, 1882–83. See Henry-Russell Hitchcock, *The Architecture of H. H. Richardson and His Times*, New York, 1936, pl. 123. (The building of a house which sounds almost like the Whittier House and which was also on the water side of Beacon was described with considerable architectural sensitivity by William Dean Howells, *The Rise of Silas Lapham*, Boston, 1886.)

[5] *Am. Arch.*, 4, Nov. 9, 1878.

The gables and the partial shingle work were perhaps added to an older structure, like the strange shingled canopy and porch added to the Dr. Francis House at Brookline at this same period.[6]

At any rate it is pleasant to turn from these houses to the one at Mount Desert which Emerson built "for a Boston gentleman" in 1879.[7] This house has perhaps the most distinguished plan to be produced in 1879 (Figure 63). It is conceived as an envelope for varied human movement in space. Its boundaries swell and contract around pools and rivers of spatial rest or direction. One enters under a projection of the second story and emerges into a large hall. To the right opens a parlor and to the left, through a narrow door under the staircase, is the dining room. Directly facing the entrance, four steps rise to a large living hall from which a great bay of continuous fenestration overlooks the sea. From this hall it is possible to look down into the parlor through an arched opening protected by a rail, or to move out through a door to a covered octagonal pavilion which echoes the shape of the window bay of the hall. From the hall, partially two storied, the stairs continue to the second floor. The variety of levels and closed and open spaces is handled easily and without strain. Light is manipulated here as by a painter—dark in the quiet dining room, flooded with sun in the open hall, diffused and mingled in the partially sheltered parlor. The enclosing skins of wall are shingled on both the first and second stories, giving that continuity of surface which had apparently been striven for since 1872 but which was fully attained here for the first time.

This is the first house in the whole development to be completely shingled. The windows are set in the shingled surface with precise wooden trim, expressing thin frame structure. The corner windows of the parlor are noteworthy in this respect, and the slight projection of the wall above them increases the sense of surface continuity retained by the windows and expressive of the volume within. A few eclectic details still appear in the house, and it has a remotely English look. The chimneys are a Queen Anne type, there is some half-timber work in the gables, and the arched window of the parlor with a seat in front of it is definitely a Shavian touch. The clapboarding under the windows of the hall bay, an attempt to express the different level of that area, is perhaps not very successful. Nevertheless, the shingled surface of the house as a whole is richly expressive of its interior volumes, as for example over the rear porch, where the movement in space down the stairs from the hall and toward the pavilion is echoed in the flow of wall into roof above it. In sum, this house by Emerson at Mount Desert, 1879, may be said to be the first fully developed monument of the new shingle style.

Emerson's production at this period was still uneven, and his T. R. Glover House at Milton, also 1879, marks a retreat from the advanced point

[6] *Am. Arch.*, 5, Feb. 8, 1879.

[7] *Ibid.*, p. 93. [Scully, 1970: My note here that this house had probably been destroyed in the fire of 1947 was incorrect. The welcome short monograph on Emerson by Cynthia Zaitzevsky and Myron Miller (cf. *The Architecture of William Ralph Emerson, 1833–1917;* an exhibition presented by the Fogg Art Museum in collaboration with the Carpenter Center for the Visual Arts, Harvard University, Cambridge, 1969, pp. 8–9, 41, fig. 1, pls. 8–10) shows it to be the C. J. Morrill House and still extant.]

reached in the Mount Desert House.[8] The plan of the Glover House is considerably less interesting. The hall is awkward and tight in shape; there are
too many rooms in plan, and the kitchen is an excessive distance from the
dining room, as in an English house. On the exterior Emerson reverts to a
clapboard first story, with shingles above, and he continues the use of heavy
clapboarding under the parlor bay window. The covered portion of the piazza surrounding three sides of the house is supported on bulbous turned posts,
and much half-timbering is used in some of the gables. Although all this
represents a kind of reversion, the mountainous sweep of the shingled roof,
adjusting itself from gable to gable and then gliding down like a deeply
sheltering wing over the piazza, must be considered an important and advanced feature of the house. Through its continuous adjustment all the subsidiary masses are pulled together into one plastic and richly surfaced mass,
various but coherent, indicative of plastic volumes within, and expressive of
shelter. This development of the plastic continuity of roof and wall was peculiarly Emerson's own. Where it is most successful—as in that portion of
the Glover House where the wall above the piazza slopes down into the
piazza roof, which has itself flowed irregularly from the highest gable—the
roof seems to take over the walls, so that the volume of space within is
molded totally from ridge to ground by the continuous and three-dimensional movement of its thin shell. . . .[9]

Two drawings by Emerson in 1880 are interesting because they show
the sketch technique he developed as a means of catching very quickly that
flow of painterly surfaces toward which he was tending in his designs.[10]
These sketches, one for a stable and lodge, the other for a country house, are
made up of fast, coarse pencil lines like brush strokes, creating not an architectonic effect of precise outlines and structural solidity but rather an impression of the mass as revealed in light. The outlines blur, and solid form
tends to dissolve in the patches of light on the shingled surface. This technique was eventually to develop into a burlesque in the Beaux-Arts *esquisse-
esquisse*, where the whole architecture dissolved into a mass impression and
stayed there. In Emerson's hands it was a real tool toward the creation of his
shingled masses.[11]

[8] *Am. Arch.*, 6, Aug. 2, 1879.

[9] Emerson's earlier, stick style Forbes House at Milton should be noted in this respect.
There also he had shown concern for a deeply pitching roof, extended in order to increase a
sense of shelter. It differs from the T. R. Glover roof in being of a single plane from gable to
porch.

[10] *Am. Arch.*, 8, Aug. 21, 1880; Oct. 9, 1880.

[11] The difference between Emerson's rendering as a painterly tool and the Beaux-Arts
esquisse-esquisse can perhaps be made clearer by referring to Ch. 3, p. 52, above, where the
Beaux-Arts projet in general is discussed. That Emerson's approach, and that of shingle style
architects in general, was basically a pictorial one is seen quite clearly in a statement made to
me in personal conversation in August, 1948, by Mr. Von Beren of New Haven. . . . He stated
concerning his design method in houses of this type: "I'd get the picture and then work on the
plan." It should be noted also that Wright felt sometimes that his first master, Silsbee, a shingle
style architect, "was just making pictures." Frank Lloyd Wright, *An Autobiography* (New
York, 1943), p. 71. That Wright admired Silsbee's sketch technique, however, is shown in his

Pictorial vision, as already indicated, was implicit in the whole shift to shingles and in the new sense of space and light. As such, Emerson's technique relates to that of Stanford White, as in the latter's interior perspective of the Watts Sherman hall. . . . It relates also to Richardson's own sketch technique at this period, as seen in his drawing of 1880 for the Crane Memorial Library at Quincy, Massachussetts.[12] Richardson's drawing, however, is at once firmer and more delicate. Less concerned with surface variation, although indicating it warmly enough with a few touches, he never loses the sense—however sketchy the drawing—of the precision of the outlines, the solidity of the mass. His drawing was always specifically architectural. To say further that White's and Emerson's vision of forms dissolving in light may be related to the technique of the French Impressionist painters, maturing through these same years, does not seem too far-fetched.[13] Certainly a sense of the dissolution of precise outlines into splinters of light forms a common bond between the shingle style, its sketch technique, and Impressionist painting. . . .

Perhaps less interesting is the house at Beverly Farms of the same period.[14] Unlike the earlier Mount Desert House, it is not completely shingled but uses a brick first story. Similarly, its plan is less coherent and fluid, with too many rooms, too many spaces (as in much of Emerson's work), and here a rather awkward if deeply sheltering hall. Still, it is a fairly good plan, with some flow between hall, parlor, and dining room, and with that variety of light which Emerson occasionally handled so well. Set deep back in the hall is a dark inglenook with fireplace. Near it rise the stairs, lighted at the landing. Across the back of the house a large piazza opens toward the sea, and on the other side the service wing shoots off at a diagonal. The route between dining room and kitchen is again circuitous. A Palladian window appears in one of the gables, and the detail of the entrance and the staircase window has a definitely Georgian look. There is no half-timbering, and the mass of the house stretches out, easy and horizontal, coherent and assured.

How original and specifically American this house was—even though perhaps less advanced than some of Emerson's earlier work—may be demonstrated by comparing it to a house at Sunninghill, England, by Richard Norman Shaw, republished from *Building News* by the *American Architect* in September, 1880.[15] The Shaw house uses purely decorative and rather heavy half-timbering on the gables of the entrance side and on the whole of the second story of the garden front. The mass is more broken up than in the American house, and each gable asserts itself as a picturesque element. The American house is lighter. The skin of its upper stories is expressed as shingle

---

comment (p. 91) concerning Silsbee's drawing: "Silsbee's way was magnificent, his strokes were like standing corn in the field waving in the breeze."

[12] Hitchcock, *Richardson*, fig. 75.

[13] The same necessity to acquire a technique wherein the momentary effects of light might be re-created quickly worked in both.

[14] *Am. Arch. 9*, June 25, 1881.—ED.

[15] *Am. Arch., 8*, Sept. 25, 1880. 2 pls., entrance and garden views.

sheathing upon a light wood frame. In comparison with the American house, Sunninghill seems assertively Old English, doggedly quaint. If it exerts a more dramatic impact than the American house—a power peculiarly Shavian—it is also more self-conscious. Altogether, when seen with the Emerson house it looks very English, a fact which emphasizes how far the American work had traveled by 1880 from its original Queen Anne inspirations. The plans especially are different in important ways. In the English plan each room is a separate entity, an inviolable cube of space closed off by a narrow door, while in Emerson's house the plan is open and the veranda is an extension of it. If the route to the kitchen in the Emerson house is more circuitous than in most American planning, the English route by comparison is a marathon, even though it is more direct in Sunninghill than in many of Shaw's houses. All these contrasts are even more striking when one looks at Emerson's Mount Desert House of 1879 (Figure 63).

In sum, the American house had now undergone a variety of changes adapting it to American conditions, functional requirements, and materials, which separate it, as an original style, from Norman Shaw's Queen Anne. The openness and flow of its space are American. So are the sheltering void of the piazza, the lightly scaled woodwork, and the rough shingles. By 1880 the American domestic development was clearly, for the time being, at least, on its own. It had assimilated its influences and according to the necessities of its own nature passed beyond them. American architects by 1880 had nothing more to learn from Norman Shaw.[16] Although some of them continued to build Tudor mansions complete with half-timber, the original development continued to grow in its own right. One must recognize, therefore, a mode of building, approaching maturity around 1880, which was specifically American. That it should be called American has nothing to do with chauvinistic enthusiasms or with that piety of place which has corroded some historical studies, especially of the colonial.[17] The term signifies a sensitive adjustment of materials, techniques, and sense of space to specific and newly evaluated conditions of American living. The insistent suburban evocation of a lost agrarian simplicity remained a constant factor, directly related to the simplified life of the shore or the country suburb. In this development the role of the simplest and least pretentious buildings cannot be overestimated. It is natural that some of the most significant aspects of the new architecture should be found in the smallest cottages. . . .

9. CONCLUSION: FRANK LLOYD WRIGHT

Between 1840 and 1875 the architects and theorists of the stick style of the midcentury had laid a broad philosophical and technical platform for

[16] See Fred Symonds Eaton, "Design for a Country House," *Am. Arch.*, 8, Dec. 31, 1880. This was obviously inspired by Sunninghill and is an excellent example of the kind of Tudor manor-house eclecticism which persisted but which the new domestic architecture of the early 80's definitely was *not*.

[17] Perhaps appropriately, the eclectic critics of the early 20th century combined a cultural dependence upon European academicism with this same chauvinism. See, particularly, Dow, *American Renaissance*, as an example of this.

future architectural growth. They had based it upon a feeling for the land, endowed it with the expression of wooden frame techniques, and thereby translated not only the picturesque but also the ethical principles of the Gothic revival into peculiarly practical American terms. Into this had come, in the 1870's, a new sense of space and surface continuity, first developed in America by Richardson and later widely disseminated after an assimilation of influences from the American colonial and the English Queen Anne. By the early 80's a free shingle style had developed: it moved more and more toward cohesion and order in design. It sought for basic forms, for the essential elements of architectural expression. Yet the poignant evocation of past ages was integral in Queen Anne and, especially for Americans, in colonial enthusiasms. From it arose the danger of unoriginal antiquarianism. This, reinforced by a newly growing academic attitude toward design, had produced by 1885 the H. A. C. Taylor House, the first and possibly the best of a long line of Palladian, colonial, and eclectic monuments.

It will not be possible here to discuss the events which took place after 1885 in American domestic architecture. Such might properly be the subject of another volume. Certain lines of future development should, however, be indicated. First of all, in the decades after 1885, the colonial revival became more specifically antiquarian, academic, and unoriginal.[18] Second, allied to this and reinforcing its eclectic academicism, came a preoccupation by the late 80's with public monumentality and great size, even in suburban architecture. This preoccupation would seem to have arisen from the more class-conscious pretensions of the end of the century, and it was destructive to the more democratic orientation of the earlier suburbs.[19] Whatever qualities the architecture so inspired may have possessed,[20] it still struck what was eventually a deathblow to the shingle style. Like the whole domestic development in wood, the shingle style was basically antimonumental in materials, techniques, and point of view. In low cost and great quantity its intent was democratic. Third, by the 90's the growing power of the schools, based primarily upon the "projet" philosophy and the eclectically classicizing forms of the late 19th-century École des Beaux-Arts, militated toward an eclectic, unoriginal, and pretentious kind of design.[21] Coupled with this trend was the

---

[18] An excellent indication of this trend is the fact that in Feb., 1886, the *American Architect* began a series of measured drawings of "Old Colonial Work," consisting mostly of details of moldings, etc., all archaeological in intention rather than re-creative or picturesque. *Am. Arch.*, *19*, Feb. 6, 1886. These were drawn by Frank E. Wallis and were eventually collected and published by William Rotch Ware, who, it will be remembered, had been the first editor of the *American Architect*. William Rotch Ware, *The Georgian Period*, New York, 1898.

[19] Richard Morris Hunt's "Ochre Court," Newport, 1888–91, is an excellent example of this. See Downing and Scully, pp. 159–60; pls. 216, 217. It is at once "archaeological French Late Gothic" and tremendous in size. Compared with the Bell House or even the Goelet House of the early 80's, it may be felt to have left "reality" behind. Even more striking is Hunt's "Breakers," Newport, 1892–95. *Ibid.*, pp. 147–8, 160–1; pls. 196, 218–22. Also, H.-R. Hitchcock, *Rhode Island Architecture*, Providence, 1939.

[20] Some contemporary critics feel that it had a good deal of quality. For a statement of this position see Christopher Tunnard, *The City of Man*, New York, 1953, *passim*.

[21] The schools may really be said to have come into their own in 1895, by which time

continued growth of the large architectural office, where deep thought became of necessity ever more subservient to the day-by-day expediencies of business practice. The loss of a sense of basic needs, real tradition, and cultural daring which these factors entailed may be regarded as bringing about the partial collapse of the native development in American domestic architecture. Yet it did not by any means subdue it entirely. The shingle style, for instance, continued for some time much as it had developed by 1885. Many excellent houses were built not only in the late 80's but also in the 90's and the early 20th century.[22] However, cut off as they became from what were the main architectural movements of the time, these houses eventually became more and more self-consciously countrified, "rustic," exemplifying a slow disintegration of earlier vitality. Unlike the houses of the early 80's, they no longer carried the important aspects of new growth.

To the last phase of an earlier cottage style belong the houses built by Greene and Greene in California in the late 90's and early 20th century, as well as the streets upon streets of "California Bungalows" which copied them in Pasadena and elsewhere.[23]. . .

In a sense the ultimate development of the last and "crafty" phase of the cottage style around 1910 was to be found in the "Craftsman Homes" and furniture of the early 20th century, propaganda for which was carried on most extensively by Gustav Stickley.[24]

McKim, Burnham, and others had succeeded in establishing the American Academy in Rome. See Moore, *McKim*, pp. 128–81. Also important in this, later was the financial assistance of J. P. Morgan. *Ibid.*, pp. 171–81.

[22] A characteristic of this later development was that for some time architects who worked in the most rigidly academic style in public buildings and town houses were capable of building freer shingled houses in the country, where, in a sense, they could relax. Among many, one example is a house at Lake George, New York, by Guy Lowell of Boston, who built Georgian mansions in Cambridge and Boston. For the Lake George House see the Boston *Architectural Review*, 11 (1904), 46–8.

[23] The California bungalow type of the 1900's is a builder's adaptation of Greene and Greene's work to smaller residences, disseminated by a variety of small "bungalow books" in the early 20th century. Examples of such work can be seen at 389 and 390 North Parkway and 460 Ellsworth Avenue, New Haven, Connecticut. The best of the bungalow books is Henry L. Wilson's *The Bungalow Book, a short sketch of the evolution of the bungalow from its primitive crudeness to its present state of artistic beauty and cosy convenience*, 4th ed. Los Angeles, 1908. These books and the thousands of cottages built from their designs represented the last gasp of the shingle-style tradition of open planning and sensitivity to materials as a general vernacular. On the West Coast this tradition was finally destroyed by the California mission style, an eclectic pastiche after Spanish Colonial prototypes which came to prominence with the San Diego Exposition of 1914. This coincided with the San Francisco Exposition of the same year. These expositions completed the movement toward popular eclecticism which the Chicago World's Fair of 1893 began. The architect most influential in Spanish colonial work on the West Coast and to whom the major responsibility for the destruction of the more creative tradition must be assigned was Bertram Goodhue, *beau idéal* of 20th-century Beaux-Arts eclecticism.

[24] Gustav Stickley, *Craftsman Homes*, New York, 1909. Also, *idem, More Craftsman Homes*, New York, 1912. These must be taken as evidence of a preoccupation with dying handicrafts which was probably as architecturally escapist and unrealistic as was the too great

The seeds of future growth apparently lay neither in the eclectic reaction against the free domestic style of the 80's nor in the more and more unrealistic attempt to prolong it without renewed disciplines and restudied objectives. Instead, the main power of growth which lay within the developments in 19th-century American domestic architecture would seem to have entered into the work of Frank Lloyd Wright, and secondarily into that of other members of the Second Chicago School.[25] Indeed, one of the important aspects of the development which has been traced is that it makes Wright's work more explicable, not only by fitting Wright into his historical sequence but also by heightening visual awareness of the factors which entered into the formation of his design. Again, it will by no means be possible to discuss Wright's early work in detail. Certain aspects of it have already been pointed out in passing. It should now be necessary only to indicate how the different threads of the earlier development united in his design. . . .

Wright's introduction to domestic building came in 1887 in the office of an architect who was at that time a practitioner of the free shingle style, namely Joseph Lyman Silsbee, who had come to Chicago from Syracuse in 1885.[26] From him Wright got a sense of picturesque shingled design at the moment when it was beginning to move toward a certain order. Drawings by Wright of houses designed by Silsbee appeared in the *Inland Architect* in 1888.[27] After leaving Silsbee and joining the firm of Adler and Sullivan, Wright built his own house at Oak Park in 1889. A shingled structure, set upon a terrace, and with a gabled roof, it relates visually to McKim, Mead, and White's Low House of 1887, to Stephens' gabled houses, and most of all to the houses which Bruce Price built at Tuxedo Park, 1885–86. These of course were published in Sheldon, which was available to Wright.[28] Moreover, Wright's house—with its terrace, its strong gable, and its window arrangement—is a very close adaptation of Price's W. Chandler Cottage, also at Tuxedo Park and of 1885–86. This was published in the periodical *Build-*

---

lack of concern with basic techniques to be found in the Beaux-Arts schools of the period. Stickley owes a certain debt to Greene and Greene and published photographs of their work. See *Craftsman Homes*, pp. 104, 106–8.

[25] Hugh Garden, George Maher, Mary Mahoney, Walter Burley Griffin, Purcell and Elmslie, Theodore von Holst, and others. The work of this group was published in *Inland Architect and Builder*, Chicago, to 1908, and after that date in *Western Architect*. It tends to fall apart and lose direction by the time of the first World War.

[26] Silsbee was of an old Salem, Mass., family. Through his wife he was allied with several Rhode Island families and visited there often, both before and after he moved to Chicago in 1885. His work was never very distinguished, but he may be considered as the architect who brought the mature shingle style to Chicago. See Wright, *Autobiography*, pp. 67–74. Hitchcock, *In the Nature of Materials*, pp. 3–6; pls. 1, 2.

[27] These were the J. L. Cochrane House, published in *Inland Architect and Builder, II*, No. 3 (1888), and Row houses for William Waller, *ibid.*, No. 6. *Inland Architect* began publication in Feb., 1883.

[28] George William Sheldon, *Artistic Country Seats: types of recent American villas and cottage architecture, with instances of country club-houses*, 2 vols., New York, 1886–87.—ED.

ing in 1886 and was therefore also available to Wright.[29] Wright, at the beginning of his career, was thus seeking direct inspiration from the masters of the developed shingle style, and especially from Bruce Price. He seems to have seized especially upon the essential forms toward which Price and the others had developed, beginning as here, with the decisive and archetypal gable. Hence the articulated and interwoven spaces of Wright's house continue the spatial order of the cottages of the early 80's. Wright also further assimilates Japanese influences.[30] Wright's tie with the shingle style is thus well established and need not be dwelt upon in any greater detail. . . .

Thus, if Wright absorbed the free shingle style of the early 80's in most of its elements, he also assimilated the design discipline of its classic moment and developed it more powerfully than did any of the architects who saw discipline only in the academic rules of the schools.[31]

The freedom of the shingle style and the discipline of a truly classic moment are consequently both present in Wright's design. Finally—and the fact is of interest in relation to the continuing dislike for Wright's work which exists among eclectically "colonial" architects—those qualities which architects valued in the early days of the colonial revival in the 70's are important factors in Wright's houses: the great fireplaces, the low ceilings, the sense at once of shelter and of horizontally extended space.[32] One may say, therefore, that Wright absorbed not only the developed shingle style and the academic reaction against it but also the formal principles of the colonial revival at its most creative. . . .

Not all of Wright's work can be explained by the domestic architectural tradition of the later 19th century, nor can it be understood solely through a discussion of his uses of it. Nevertheless, the tradition fused in him, and through him it formed one of the bases for the modern architecture of the 20th century.[33] One must conclude that in Wright's work the creative tradi-

[29] A plan and two perspectives were published, one of the latter being of the side elevation used by Wright for his façade. *Building, A Journal of Architecture*, 5, September 18, 1886. . .'. Price's "delineator" was Fred Wright, a peculiar coincidence. The Chandler House was later published in 1900 (*Architecture, I*, May, 1900).

[30] Hitchcock, *In the Nature of Materials*, pls. 11–13. It will be recalled that a similar continuity of spatial flow, achieved by the use of the Japanese continuous soffit, had already been achieved by McKim, Mead, and White as early as 1881, in the Newcomb House, Elberon, New Jersey. See also White's dining room in Kingscote, 1880–81; the interiors of the Tilton House, 1881–82; and the Bell House, 1882–83.

[31] Wright's relationship to the academic design of the early 90's is best discussed in H.-R. Hitchcock, "Frank Lloyd Wright and the 'Academic Tradition' of the Early Eighteen-Nineties," *Journal of the Warburg and Courtauld Institutes* 7 (January–June 1944), pp. 46–63.

[32] As discussed in Chs. 2, 3, and 4, above. Of his deep fireplaces Wright (*Autobiography*, p. 141) has this to say: "So the *integral* fireplace became an important part of the building itself in the houses I was allowed to build out there on the prairie. . . . It comforted me to see the fire burning deep in the solid masonry of the house itself. A feeling that came to stay." The low ceilings were also a feature of Japanese architecture, as discussed by Morse in 1886, p. 108.

[33] Wright's influence, through the Wasmuth publications of 1910 and 1911, was apparently direct and formative upon the Dutch De Stijl group and Gropius in the 'teens and through them upon the Bauhaus and Mies van der Rohe in the 20's. . . . Later, in the 20's and

tions of the 19th century still live and have given rise to the new.

Wright's career forces us to return a double answer to the critical question concerning what happened to American invention in domestic architecture during the later 80's. On the one hand it subsided in the East, eventually marking an important cultural break, a temporary exhaustion of experiment. On the other hand Wright picked up and continued the tradition of invention and sustained the architectural program of the single family house as its vehicle. But more than this, he seems to have accomplished the extraordinary feat of constantly redirecting the inheritance of his tradition into new disciplines and fresh sources of inspiration.

The history of the shingle style, therefore, reveals certain characteristics of rupture, discontinuity, and reaction at a significant moment in American culture. It also asserts continuity and the ability to sustain experiment as well. Most of all, the shingle style itself—in its earnest mixture of motives, its quickly fired vitality, and its impatient search for the roots of experience in a newly industrialized world—seems a most poignantly 19th-century and American phenomenon. It can serve as a useful memory for us all.

78   R. Venturi, Complexity and Contradiction in Architecture* *1966*

Perhaps the most influential treatise among younger architects was this by Robert Venturi, a summation of reflections on the provocative ambiguities of mannerist, baroque, and rococo architecture which had been occupying his thoughts for a decade or more; Vincent Scully even proposed in his introduction that it was "the most important writing on the making of architecture since Le Corbusier's *Vers une architecture* of 1923." Although general dissatisfaction with codified International Modernism had been growing since Johnson identified the "Seven Crutches of Modern Architecture" in 1954, Venturi's study now presented a body of historical examples illustrating a theory of design refuting virtually every canon of the Modern Movement. He sketched out why baroque and rococo forms so delight and why, conversely, Aristotelian purism so palls.

Born in 1925 in Philadelphia—where he has practiced since 1958—Venturi received his bachelor's and master of fine arts degrees from Princeton University; it

---

early 30's, Wright in turn was influenced by the European architects. Elsewhere I have briefly attempted to point out this double relationship. See "Frank Lloyd Wright vs. the International Style," *Art News*, 53 (March, 1954), 32 ff. For the objections of several critics to this thesis, and my reply, see *op. cit.* (September, 1954), pp. 48–9.

*Robert Venturi, *Complexity and Contradiction in Architecture* (New York, 1966), with an introduction by Vincent Scully, pp. 18–27, 30–31, 37–39, 46–52, 89–91, 94–95, 96–97, 98–103. (Venturi's presentation is highly visual but the wealth of illustrations he reproduced cannot be included here.)

was while at Princeton that he was exposed to the Beaux-Arts humanism of Jean Labatut.[†] The idea of shaping the "complex whole" began to form itself as a result of Venturi's historical studies, represented in "The Campidoglio: A Case Study," in which he observed: "we see in perceptual wholes," requiring the architect to deal with complex aggregates of conflicting functions and parts.[‡] He pursued these researches further as a fellow at the American Academy in Rome, during 1954–56. Venturi was a designer with Eero Saarinen in 1950–52, and with Louis I. Kahn during 1956–57, entering into partnership with Cope and Lippincott the next year. Meanwhile he was teaching design at the University of Pennsylvania and in 1965 accepted the position of Charlotte Shepard Davenport Professor at Yale, a visiting professorship he held until 1969. In 1960 the partnership had become Venturi and Short, changing to Venturi, Rauch and Scott Brown in 1964; three years later Venturi married his collaborator, Denise Lakofski Scott Brown.

Preface

This book is both an attempt at architectural criticism and an apologia—an explanation, indirectly, of my work. Because I am a practicing architect, my ideas on architecture are inevitably a by-product of the criticism which accompanies working, and which is, as T. S. Eliot has said, of "capital importance . . . in the work of creation itself. Probably, indeed, the larger part of the labour of sifting, combining, constructing, expunging, correcting, testing: this frightful toil is as much critical as creative. I maintain even that the criticism employed by a trained and skilled writer on his own work is the most vital, the highest kind of criticism. . . ."[1] I write, then, as an architect who employs criticism rather than a critic who choose architecture and this book represents a particular set of emphases, a way of seeing architecture, which I find valid.

In the same essay Eliot discusses analysis and comparison as tools of literary criticism. These critical methods are valid for architecture too: architecture is open to analysis like any other aspect of experience, and is made more vivid by comparisons. Analysis includes the breaking up of architecture into elements, a technique I frequently use even though it is the opposite of the integration which is the final goal of art. However paradoxical it appears, and despite the suspicions of many Modern architects, such disintegration is a process present in all creation, and it is essential to understanding. Self-consciousness is necessarily a part of creation and criticism. Architects today are too educated to be either primitive or totally spontaneous, and architecture is too complex to be approached with carefully maintained ignorance.

As an architect I try to be guided not by habit but by a conscious sense

[†] Gustave-Jacques-Jean Labatut, a student of Victor Laloux, won Premier Second Grand Prix at the École in 1926, in 1928 emigrated to the United States, and began teaching at Princeton.

[‡] *Architectural Review* 113 (May 1953), pp. 33–34.

[1] T. S. Eliot: *Selected Essays, 1917–1932*, Harcourt, Brace and Co., New York, 1932; p. 18.

of the past—by precedent, thoughtfully considered. The historical comparisons chosen are part of a continuous tradition relevant to my concerns. When Eliot writes about tradition, his comments are equally relevant to architecture, notwithstanding the more obvious changes in architectural methods due to technological innovations. "In English writing," Eliot says, "we seldom speak of tradition. . . . Seldom, perhaps, does the word appear except in a phrase of censure. If otherwise, it is vaguely approbative, with the implication, as to a work approved, of some pleasing archeological reconstruction. . . . Yet if the only form of tradition, of handing down, consisted in following the ways of the immediate generation before us in a blind or timid adherence to its successes, 'tradition' should be positively discouraged. . . . Tradition is a matter of much wider significance. It cannot be inherited, and if you want it you must obtain it by great labour. It involves, in the first place, the historical sense, which we may call nearly indispensable to anyone who would continue to be a poet beyond his twenty-fifth year; and the historical sense involves perception, not only of the pastness of the past, but of its presence; the historical sense compels a man to write not merely with his own generation in his bones, but with a feeling that the whole of the literature of Europe . . . has a simultaneous existence and composes a simultaneous order. This historical sense, which is a sense of the timeless as well as of the temporal and of the timeless and temporal together, is what makes a writer traditional, and it is at the same time what makes a writer most acutely conscious of his place in time, of his own contemporaneity. . . . No poet, no artist of any kind, has his complete meaning alone."[2] I agree with Eliot and reject the obsession of Modern architects who, to quote Aldo van Eyck, "have been harping continually on what is different in our time to such an extent that they have lost touch with what is not different, with what is essentially the same."[3]

The examples chosen reflect my partiality for certain eras: Mannerist, Baroque, and Rococo especially. As Henry-Russell Hitchcock says, "there always exists a real need to re-examine the work of the past. There is, presumably, almost always a generic interest in architectural history among architects; but the aspects, or periods, of history that seem at any given time to merit the closest attention certainly vary with changing sensibilities."[4] As an artist I frankly write about what I like in architecture: complexity and contradiction. From what we find we like—what we are easily attracted to—we can learn much of what we really are. Louis Kahn has referred to "what a thing wants to be," but implicit in this statement is its opposite: what the architect wants the thing to be. In the tension and balance between these two lie many of the architect's decisions.

The comparisons include some buildings which are neither beautiful nor great, and they have been lifted abstractly from their historical context because I rely less on the idea of style than on the inherent characteristics of specific buildings. Writing as an architect rather than as a scholar, my his-

[2] *Ibid.*; pp. 3–4.

[3] Aldo van Eyck: in *Architectural Design* 12, vol. XXXII, December 1962; p. 560.

[4] Henry-Russell Hitchcock: in *Perspecta 6, The Yale Architectural Journal*, New Haven, 1960; p. 2.

torical view is that described by Hitchcock: "Once, of course, almost all investigation of the architecture of the past was in aid of its nominal reconstitution—an instrument of revivalism. That is no longer true, and there is little reason to fear that it will, in our time, become so again. Both the architects and the historian-critics of the early twentieth century, when they were not merely seeking in the past fresh ammunition for current polemical warfare, taught us to see all architecture, as it were, abstractly, false though such a limited vision probably is to the complex sensibilities that produced most of the great architecture of the past. When we re-examine—or discover—this or that aspect of earlier building production today, it is with no idea of repeating its forms, but rather in the expectation of feeding more amply new sensibilities that are wholly the product of the present. To the pure historian this may seem regrettable, as introducing highly subjective elements into what he believes ought to be objective studies. Yet the pure historian, more often that not, will eventually find himself moving in directions that have been already determined by more sensitive weathervanes."[5]

I make no special attempt to relate architecture to other things. I have not tried to "improve the connections between science and technology on the one hand, and the humanities and the social sciences on the other . . . and make of architecture a more human social art."[6] I try to talk about architecture rather than around it. Sir John Summerson has referred to the architects' obsession with "the importance, not of architecture, but of the *relation* of architecture to other things."[7] He has pointed out that in this century architects have substituted the "mischievous analogy" for the eclectic imitation of the nineteenth century, and have been staking a claim for architecture rather than producing architecture.[8] The result has been diagrammatic planning. The architect's ever diminishing power and his growing ineffectualness in shaping the whole environment can perhaps be reversed, ironically, by narrowing his concerns and concentrating on his own job. Perhaps then relationships and power will take care of themselves. I accept what seem to me architecture's inherent limitations, and attempt to concentrate on the difficult particulars within it rather than the easier abstractions about it ". . . because the arts belong (as the ancients said) to the practical and not the speculative intelligence, there is no surrogate for being on the job."[9]

This book deals with the present, and with the past in relation to the present. It does not attempt to be visionary except insofar as the future is inherent in the reality of the present. It is only indirectly polemical. Everything is said in the context of current architecture and consequently certain targets are attacked—in general, the limitations of orthodox Modern architecture and city planning, in particular, the platitudinous architects who in-

[5] *Ibid.*; p. 3.

[6] Robert L. Geddes: in *The Philadelphia Evening Bulletin.* February 2, 1965; p. 40.

[7] Sir John Summerson: *Heavenly Mansions*, W. W. Norton and Co., Inc., New York, 1963; p. 197.

[8] *Ibid.*; p. 200.

[9] David Jones: *Epoch and Artist*, Chilmark Press, Inc., New York, 1959; p. 12.

voke integrity, technology, or electronic programming as ends in architecture, the popularizers who paint "fairy stories over our chaotic reality"[10] and suppress those complexities and contradictions inherent in art and experience. Nevertheless, this book is an analysis of what seems to me true for architecture now, rather than a diatribe against what seems false.

1. Nonstraightforward Architecture: A Gentle Manifesto

I like complexity and contradiction in architecture. I do not like the incoherence or arbitrariness of incompetent architecture nor the precious intricacies of picturesqueness or expressionism. Instead, I speak of a complex and contradictory architecture based on the richness and ambiguity of modern experience, including that experience which is inherent in art. Everywhere, except in architecture, complexity and contradiction have been acknowledged, from Godel's proof of ultimate inconsistency in mathematics to T. S. Eliot's analysis of "difficult" poetry and Joseph Albers' definition of the paradoxical quality of painting.

But architecture is necessarily complex and contradictory in its very inclusion of the traditional Vitruvian elements of commodity, firmness, and delight. And today the wants of program, structure, mechanical equipment, and expression, even in single buildings in simple contexts, are diverse and conflicting in ways previously unimaginable. The increasing dimension and scale of architecture in urban and regional planning add to the difficulties. I welcome the problems and exploit the uncertainties. By embracing contradiction as well as complexity, I am for vitality as well as validity.

Architects can no longer afford to be intimidated by the puritanically moral language of orthodox Modern architecture. I like elements which are hybrid rather than "pure," compromising rather than "clean," distorted rather than "straightforward," ambiguous rather than "articulated," perverse as well as impersonal, boring as well as "interesting," conventional rather than "designed," accommodating rather than excluding, redundant rather than simple, vestigial as well as innovating, inconsistent and equivocal rather than direct and clear. I am for messy vitality over obvious unity. I include the non sequitur and proclaim the duality.

I am for richness of meaning rather than clarity of meaning; for the implicit function as well as the explicit function. I prefer "both-and" to "either-or," black and white, and sometimes gray, to black or white. A valid architecture evokes many levels of meaning and combinations of focus: its space and its elements become readable and workable in several ways at once.

But an architecture of complexity and contradiction has a special obligation toward the whole: its truth must be in its totality or its implications of totality. It must embody the difficult unity of inclusion rather than the easy unity of exclusion. More is not less.

[10] Kenzo Tange: in *Documents of Modern Architecture*, Jurgen Joedicke, ed., Universe Books, Inc., New York, 1961; p. 170.

2. Complexity and Contradiction vs. Simplification or Picturesqueness

Orthodox Modern architects have tended to recognize complexity insufficiently or inconsistently. In their attempt to break with tradition and start all over again, they idealized the primitive and elementary at the expense of the diverse and the sophisticated. As participants in a revolutionary movement, they acclaimed the newness of modern functions, ignoring their complications. In their role as reformers, they puritanically advocated the separation and exclusion of elements, rather than the inclusion of various requirements and their juxtapositions. As a forerunner of the Modern movement, Frank Lloyd Wright, who grew up with the motto "Truth against the World," wrote: "Visions of simplicity so broad and far-reaching would open to me and such building harmonies appear that . . . would change and deepen the thinking and culture of the modern world. So I believed,"[11] And Le Corbusier, co-founder of Purism, spoke of the "great primary forms" which, he proclaimed, were "distinct . . . and without ambiguity."[12] Modern architects with few exceptions eschewed ambiguity.

But now our position is different: "At the same time that the problems increase in quantity, complexity, and difficulty they also change faster than before,"[13] and require an attitude more like that described by August Heckscher: "The movement from a view of life as essentially simple and orderly to a view of life as complex and ironic is what every individual passes through in becoming mature. But certain epochs encourage this development; in them the paradoxical or dramatic outlook colors the whole intellectual scene. . . . Amid simplicity and order rationalism is born, but rationalism proves inadequate in any period of upheaval. Then equilibrium must be created out of opposites. Such inner peace as men gain must represent a tension among contradictions and uncertainties. . . . A feeling for paradox allows seemingly dissimilar things to exist side by side, their very incongruity suggesting a kind of truth."[14]

Rationalizations for simplification are still current, however, though subtler than the early arguments. They are expansions of Mies van der Rohe's magnificent paradox, "less is more." Paul Rudolph has clearly stated the implication of Mies' point of view: "All problems can never be solved. . . . Indeed it is a characteristic of the twentieth century that architects are highly selective in determining which problems they want to solve. Mies, for instance, makes wonderful buildings only because he ignores many aspects

[11]Frank Lloyd Wright: in *An American Architecture*, Edgar Kaufmann, ed., Horizon Press, New York, 1955; p. 207.

[12]Le Corbusier: *Towards a New Architecture*, The Architectural Press, London, 1927; p. 31.

[13]Christopher Alexander: *Notes on the Synthesis of Form*, Harvard University Press, Cambridge, 1964; p. 4.

[14]August Heckscher: *The Public Happiness*, Atheneum Publishers, New York, 1962; p. 102.

of a building. If he solved more problems, his buildings would be far less potent."[15]

The doctrine "less is more" bemoans complexity and justifies exclusion for expressive purposes. It does, indeed, permit the architect to be "highly selective in determining which problems [he wants] to solve." But if the architect must be "committed to his particular way of seeing the universe," such a commitment surely means that the architect determines how problems should be solved, not that he can determine which of the problems he will solve. He can exclude important considerations only at the risk of separating architecture from the experience of life and the needs of society. If some problems prove insoluble, he can express this: in an inclusive rather than an exclusive kind of architecture there is room for the fragment, for contradiction, for improvisation, and for the tensions these produce. Mies' exquisite pavilions have had valuable implications for architecture, but their selectiveness of content and language is their limitation as well as their strength.

I question the relevance of analogies between pavilions and houses, especially analogies between Japanese pavilions and recent domestic architecture. They ignore the real complexity and contradiction inherent in the domestic program—the spatial and technological possibilities as well as the need for variety in visual experience. Forced simplicity results in oversimplification. In the Wiley House, for instance, in contrast to his glass house, Philip Johnson attempted to go beyond the simplicities of the elegant pavilion. He explicitly separated and articulated the enclosed "private functions" of living on a ground floor pedestal, thus separating them from the open social functions in the modular pavilion above. But even here the building becomes a diagram of an oversimplified program for living—an abstract theory of either-or. Where simplicity cannot work, simpleness results. Blatant simplification means bland architecture. Less is a bore.

The recognition of complexity in architecture does not negate what Louis Kahn has called "the desire for simplicity." But aesthetic simplicity which is a satisfaction to the mind derives, when valid and profound, from inner complexity. The Doric temple's simplicity to the eye is achieved through the famous subtleties and precision of its distorted geometry and the contradictions and tensions inherent in its order. The Doric temple could achieve apparent simplicity through real complexity. When complexity disappeared, as in the late temples, blandness replaced simplicity.

Nor does complexity deny the valid simplification which is part of the process of analysis, and even a method of achieving complex architecture itself. "We oversimplify a given event when we characterize it from the standpoint of a given interest."[16] But this kind of simplification is a method in the analytical process of achieving a complex art. It should not be mistaken for a goal.

[15] Paul Rudolph: in *Perspecta 7, The Yale Architectural Journal*, New Haven, 1961; p. 51.

[16] Kenneth Burke: *Permanence and Change*, Hermes Publications, Los Altos, 1954; p. 107.

An architecture of complexity and contradiction, however, does not mean picturesqueness or subjective expressionism. A false complexity has recently countered the false simplicity of an earlier Modern architecture. It promotes an architecture of symmetrical picturesqueness—which Minoru Yamasaki calls "serene"—but it represents a new formalism as unconnected with experience as the former cult of simplicity. Its intricate forms do not reflect genuinely complex programs, and its intricate ornament, though dependent on industrial techniques for execution, is dryly reminiscent of forms originally created by handicraft techniques. Gothic tracery and Rococo rocaille were not only expressively valid in relation to the whole, but came from a valid showing-off of hand skills and expressed a vitality derived from the immediacy and individuality of the method. This kind of complexity through exuberance, perhaps impossible today, is the antithesis of "serene" architecture, despite the superficial resemblance between them. But if exuberance is not characteristic of our art, it is tension, rather than "serenity" that would appear to be so. . . .

The desire for a complex architecture, with its attendant contradictions, is not only a reaction to the banality or prettiness of current architecture. It is an attitude common in the Mannerist periods: the sixteenth century in Italy or the Hellenistic period in Classical art, and is also a continuous strain seen in such diverse architects as Michelangelo, Palladio, Borromini, Vanbrugh, Hawksmoor, Soane, Ledoux, Butterfield, some architects of the Shingle Style, Furness, Sullivan, Lutyens, and recently, Le Corbusier, Aalto, Kahn, and others.

Today this attitude is again relevant to both the medium of architecture and the program in architecture.

First, the medium of architecture must be re-examined if the increased scope of our architecture as well as the complexity of its goals is to be expressed. Simplified or superficially complex forms will not work. Instead, the variety inherent in the ambiguity of visual perception must once more be acknowledged and exploited.

Second, the growing complexities of our functional problems must be acknowledged. I refer, of course, to those programs, unique in our time, which are complex because of their scope, such as research laboratories, hospitals, and particularly the enormous projects at the scale of city and regional planning. But even the house, simple in scope, is complex in purpose if the ambiguities of contemporary experience are expressed. This contrast between the means and the goals of a program is significant. Although the means involved in the program of a rocket to get to the moon, for instance, are almost infinitely complex, the goal is simple and contains few contradictions; although the means involved in the program and structure of buildings are far simpler and less sophisticated technologically than almost any engineering project, the purpose is more complex and often inherently ambiguous. . . .

4. Contradictory Levels: The Phenomenon of "Both-And" in Architecture

Contradictory levels of meaning and use in architecture involve the paradoxical contrast implied by the conjunctive "yet." They may be more or less ambiguous. Le Corbusier's Shodan House is closed yet open—a cube, precisely closed by its corners, yet randomly opened on its surfaces; his Villa Savoye is simple outside yet complex inside. The Tudor plan of Barrington Court is symmetrical yet asymmetrical. Guarini's Church of the Immaculate Conception in Turin is a duality in plan and yet a unity; Sir Edwin Lutyens' entrance gallery at Middleton Park is directional space, yet it terminates at a blank wall; Vignola's façade for the pavilion at Bomarzo contains a portal, yet it is a blank portico. Kahn's buildings contain crude concrete yet polished granite; an urban street is directional as a route yet static as a place. This series of conjunctive "yets" describes an architecture of contradiction at varying levels of program and structure. None of these ordered contradictions represents a search for beauty, but neither as paradoxes, are they caprice.

Cleanth Brooks refers to Donne's art as "having it both ways" but, he says, "most of us in this latter day, cannot. We are disciplined in the tradition either-or, and lack the mental agility—to say nothing of the maturity of attitude—which would allow us to indulge in the finer distinctions and the more subtle reservations permitted by the tradition of both-and." [17] The tradition "either-or" has characterized orthodox modern architecture: a sun screen is probably nothing else; a support is seldom an enclosure; a wall is not violated by window penetrations but is totally interrupted by glass; program functions are exaggeratedly articulated into wings or segregated separate pavilions. Even "flowing space" has implied being outside when inside, and inside when outside, rather than both at the same time. Such manifestations of articulation and clarity are foreign to an architecture of complexity and contradiction, which tends to include "both-and" rather than exclude "either-or."

If the source of the both-and phenomenon is contradiction, its basis is hierarchy, which yields several levels of meanings among elements with varying values. It can include elements that are both good and awkward, big and little, closed and open, continuous and articulated, round and square, structural and spatial. An architecture which includes varying levels of meaning breeds ambiguity and tension.

Most of the examples will be difficult to "read," but abstruse architecture is valid when it reflects the complexities and contradictions of content and meaning. Simultaneous perception of a multiplicity of levels involves struggles and hesitations for the observer, and makes his perception more vivid.

Examples which are both good and bad at the same time will perhaps in one way explain Kahn's enigmatic remark: "architecture must have bad spaces as well as good spaces." Apparent irrationality of a part will be justified by the resultant rationality of the whole, or characteristics of a part will be compromised for the sake of the whole. The decisions for such valid compromises are one of the chief tasks of the architect. . . .

The tower of Christ Church, Spitalfields, is a manifestation of both-and at the scale of the city. Hawksmoor's tower is both a wall and a tower.

[17] Cleanth Brooks: *The Well Wrought Urn*, Harcourt, Brace and World, Inc., New York, 1947; p. 81.

Toward the bottom the vista is terminated by the extension of its walls into kinds of buttresses perpendicular to the approaching street. They are seen from only one direction. The top evolves into a spire, which is seen from all sides, spatially and symbolically dominating the skyline of the parish. In the Bruges Town Hall the scale of the building relates to the immediate square, while the violently disproportionate scale of the tower above relates to the whole town. For similar reasons the big sign sits on top of the Philadelphia Savings Fund Society building, and yet it is invisible from below. The Arc de Triomphe also has contrasting functions. Seen diagonally from the radial approaches other than the Champs Elysées, it is a sculptural termination. Seen perpendicularly from the axis of the Champs Elysées, it is spatially and symbolically both a termination and a portal. Later I shall analyze some organized contradictions between front and back. But here I shall mention the Karlskirche in Vienna, whose exterior contains elements both of the basilica in its façade and of the central-type church in its body. A convex form in the back was required by the interior program; the urban space required a larger scale and a straight façade in front. The disunity that exists from the point of view of the building itself is contradicted when the building is seen in relation to the scale and the space of the neighborhood.

The double meanings inherent in the phenomenon both-and can involve metamorphosis as well as contradiction. I have described how the omni-directional spire of the tower of Christ Church, Spitalfields, evolves into a directional pavilion at its base, but a perceptual rather than a formal kind of change in meaning is possible. In equivocal relationships one contradictory meaning usually dominates another, but in complex compositions the relationship is not always constant. This is especially true as the observer moves through or around a building, and by extension through a city: at one moment one meaning can be perceived as dominant; at another moment a different meaning seems paramount. In St. George, Bloomsbury, for instance, the contradictory axes inside become alternatingly dominant or recessive as the observer moves within them, so that the same space changes meaning. Here is another dimension of "space, time and architecture" which involves the multiple focus.

5. Contradictory Levels Continued: The Double-Functioning Element

The "double-functioning"[18] element and "both-and" are related, but there is a distinction: the double-functioning element pertains more to the particulars of use and structure, while both-and refers more to the relation of the part to the whole. Both-and emphasizes double meanings over double-functions. But before I talk about the double-functioning element, I want to mention the multifunctioning building. By this term I mean the building which is complex in program and form, yet strong as a whole—the complex unity of Le Corbusier's La Tourette or the Palace of Justice at Chandigarh in contrast to the multiplicities and articulations of his Palace of the Soviets project or the Armée du Salut in Paris. The latter approach separates func-

[18] Wylie Sypher: *Four Stages of Renaissance Style*, Doubleday and Co., Inc., Garden City, 1955; p. 124.

tions into interlocking wings or connected pavilions. It has been typical of orthodox Modern architecture. The incisive separations of the pavilions in Mies' design for the urban Illinois Institute of Technology can be understood as an extreme development of it.

Mies' and Johnson's Seagram Building excludes functions other than offices (except on the ground floor in back), and by using a similar wall pattern camouflages the fact that at the top there is a different kind of space for mechanical equipment. Yamasaki's project for The World Trade Center in New York even more exaggeratedly simplifies the form of an enormous complex. The typical office skyscrapers of the '20s differentiate, rather than camouflage, their mechanical equipment space at the top through architecturally ornamental forms. While Lever House includes differently-functioning spaces at the bottom, it exaggeratedly separates them by a spatial shadow joint. In contrast, one exceptional Modern building, the P.S.F.S., gives positive expression to the variety and complexity of its program. It integrates a shop on the first floor and a big bank on the second with offices above and special rooms at the top. These varieties of functions and scales (including the enormous advertising sign at the top) work within a compact whole. Its curving façade, which contrasts with the rectangularity of the rest of the building, is not just a cliché of the '30s, because it has an urban function. At the lower pedestrian level it directs space around the corner.

The multifunctioning building in its extreme form becomes the Ponte Vecchio or Chenonceaux or the Futurist projects of Sant' Elia. Each contains within the whole contrasting scales of movement besides complex functions. Le Corbusier's Algerian project, which is an apartment house and a highway, and Wright's late projects for Pittsburgh Point and Baghdad, correspond to Kahn's viaduct architecture and Fumihiko Maki's "collective form." All of these have complex and contradictory hierarchies of scale and movement, structure, and space within a whole. These buildings are buildings and bridges at once. At a larger scale: a dam is also a bridge, the loop in Chicago is a boundary as well as a circulation system, and Kahn's street "wants to be a building."

There are justifications for the multifunctioning room as well as the multifunctioning building. A room can have many functions at the same time or at different times. Kahn prefers the gallery because it is directional and nondirectional, a corridor and room at once. And he recognizes the changing complexities of specific functions by differentiating rooms in a general way through a hierarchy of size and quality, calling them servant and major spaces, directional and nondirectional spaces, and other designations more generic than specific.

6. Accommodation and the Limitations of Order: The Conventional Element

In short, that contradictions must be accepted.[19]

A valid order accommodates the circumstantial contradictions of a complex reality. It accommodates as well as imposes. It thereby admits "control *and*

[19] David Jones, *op. cit.*

spontaneity," "correctness *and* ease"—improvisation within the whole. It tolerates qualifications and compromise. There are no fixed laws in architecture, but not everything will work in a building or a city. The architect must decide, and these subtle evaluations are among his principal functions. He must determine what must be made to work and what it is possible to compromise with, what will give in, and where and how. He does not ignore or exclude inconsistencies of program and structure within the order.

I have emphasized that aspect of complexity and contradiction which grows out of the medium more than the program of the building. Now I shall emphasize the complexity and contradiction that develops from the program and reflects the inherent complexities and contradictions of living. It is obvious that in actual practice the two must be interrelated. Contradictions can represent the exceptional inconsistency that modifies the otherwise consistent order, or they can represent inconsistencies throughout the order as a whole. In the first case, the relationship between inconsistency and order accommodates circumstantial exceptions to the order, or it juxtaposes particular with general elements of order. Here you build an order up and then break it down, but break it from strength rather than from weakness. I have described this relationship as "contradiction accommodated." The relationship of inconsistency within the whole I consider a manifestation of "the difficult whole," which is discussed in the last chapter.

Mies refers to a need to "create order out of the desperate confusion of our time." But Kahn has said "by order I do not mean orderliness." Should we not resist bemoaning confusion? Should we not look for meaning in the complexities and contradictions of our times and acknowledge the limitations of systems? These, I think, are the two justifications for breaking order: the recognition of variety and confusion inside and outside, in program and environment, indeed, at all levels of experience; and the ultimate limitation of all orders composed by man. When circumstances defy order, order should bend or break: anomalies and uncertainties give validity to architecture.

Meaning can be enhanced by breaking the order; the exception points up the rule. A building with no "imperfect" part can have no perfect part, because contrast supports meaning. An artful discord gives vitality to architecture. You can allow for contingencies all over, but they cannot prevail all over. If order without expediency breeds formalism, expediency without order, of course, means chaos. Order must exist before it can be broken. No artist can belittle the role of order as a way of seeing a whole relevant to its own characteristics and context. "There is no work of art, without a system" is Le Corbusier's dictum. . . .

I have been referring to one level of order in architecture—that individual order that is related to the specific building it is part of. But there is convention in architecture, and convention can be another manifestation of an exaggeratedly strong order more general in scope. An architect should use convention and make it vivid. I mean he should use convention unconventionally. By convention I mean both the elements and methods of building. Conventional elements are those which are common in their manufacture, form, and use. I do not refer to the sophisticated products of industrial design, which are usually beautiful, but to the vast accumulation of standard, anonymously designed products connected with architecture and construction, and also to commercial display elements which are positively banal or vulgar in themselves and are seldom associated with architecture.

The main justification for honky-tonk elements in architectural order is their very existence. They are what we have. Architects can bemoan or try to ignore them or even try to abolish them, but they will not go away. Or they will not go away for a long time, because architects do not have the power to replace them (nor do they know what to replace them with), and because these commonplace elements accommodate existing needs for variety and communication. The old clichés involving both banality and mess will still be the context of our new architecture, and our new architecture significantly will be the context for them. I am taking the limited view, I admit, but the limited view, which architects have tended to belittle, is as important as the visionary view, which they have tended to glorify but have not brought about. The short-term plan, which expediently combines the old and the new, must accompany the long-term plan. Architecture is evolutionary as well as revolutionary. As an art it will acknowledge what is and what ought to be, the immediate and the speculative.

Historians have shown how architects in the mid-nineteenth century tended to ignore or reject developments in technology when related to structure and methods as unconnected with architecture and unworthy of it; they substituted in turn Gothic Revivalism, Academic revivalism or the Handicraft Movement. Are we today proclaiming advanced technology, while excluding the immediate, vital if vulgar elements which are common to our architecture and landscape? The architect should accept the methods and the elements he already has. He often fails when he attempts per se the search for form hopefully new, and the research for techniques hopefully advanced. Technical innovations require investments in time and skills and money beyond the architect's reach, at least in our kind of society. The trouble with nineteenth century architects was not so much that they left innovation to the engineers as that they ignored the technical revolution developed by others. Present-day architects, in their visionary compulsion to invent new techniques, have neglected their obligation to be experts in existing conventions. The architect, of course, is responsible for the how as well as the what in his building, but his innovating role is primarily in the what; his experimentation is limited more to his organization of the whole than to technique in the parts. The architect selects as much as creates.

These are pragmatic reasons for using convention in architecture, but there are expressive justifications as well. The architect's main work is the organization of a unique whole through conventional parts and the judicious introduction of new parts when the old won't do. Gestalt psychology maintains that context contributes meaning to a part and change in context causes change in meaning. The architect thereby, through the organization of parts, creates meaningful contexts for them within the whole. Through unconventional organization of conventional parts he is able to create new meanings within the whole. If he uses convention unconventionally, if he organizes familiar things in an unfamiliar way, he is changing their contexts, and he can use even the cliché to gain a fresh effect. Familiar things seen in an unfamiliar context become perceptually new as well as old.

Modern architects have exploited the conventional element only in limited ways. If they have not totally rejected it as obsolete or banal, they have embraced it as symbolic of progressive industrial order. But they have seldom used the common element with a unique context in an uncommon way. Wright, for instance, almost always employed unique elements and unique forms, which represented his personal and innovating approach to architecture. Minor elements, like hardware by Schlage or plumbing fixtures by Kohler of Kohler, which even Wright was unable to avoid using, read as unfortunate compromises within the particular order of his buildings, which is otherwise consistent. . . .

Bernard Maybeck is the unique architect in recent times to employ contradictory combinations of vernacular industrial elements and eclectic stylistic elements (for example, industrial sash and Gothic tracery) in the same building. Using convention unconventionally is otherwise almost unknown in our recent architecture. . . .

The value of such contradictory meanings has been acknowledged in both evolutionary and revolutionary architecture—from the collages of fragments of post-Roman architecture, the so-called Spolium architecture in which column capitals are used as bases, for instance, to the Renaissance style itself, where the old Classical Roman vocabulary was employed in new combinations. And James Ackerman has described Michelangelo as "rarely adopting a motif [in his architecture] without giving it a new form or a new meaning. Yet he invariably retained essential features from ancient models in order to force the observer to recollect the source while enjoying the innovations."[20]

Ironic convention is relevant both for the individual building and the townscape. It recognizes the real condition of our architecture and its status in our culture. Industry promotes expensive industrial and electronic research but not architectural experiments, and the Federal government diverts subsidies toward air transportation, communication, and the vast enterprises of war or, as they call it, national security, rather than toward the forces for the direct enhancement of life. The practicing architect must admit this. In simple terms, the budgets, techniques, and programs for his buildings must relate more to 1866 than 1966. Architects should accept their modest role rather than disguise it and risk what might be called an electronic expressionism, which might parallel the industrial expressionism of early Modern architecture. The architect who would accept his role as combiner of significant old clichés—valid banalities—in new contexts as his condition within a society that directs its best efforts, its big money, and its elegant technologies elsewhere, can ironically express in this indirect way a true concern for society's inverted scale of values.

I have alluded to the reasons why honky-tonk elements in our architecture and townscape are here to stay, especially in the important short-term view, and why such a fate should be acceptable. Pop Art has demonstrated that these commonplace elements are often the main source of the occasional variety and vitality of our cities, and that it is not their banality or vulgarity

---

[20] James S. Ackerman: *The Architecture of Michelangelo*, A. Zwemmer, Ltd., London, 1961; p. 139.

as elements which make for the banality or vulgarity of the whole scene, but rather their contextual relationships of space and scale.

Another significant implication from Pop Art involves method in city planning. Architects and planners who peevishly denounce the conventional townscape for its vulgarity or banality promote elaborate methods for abolishing or disguising honky-tonk elements in the existing landscape, or, for excluding them from the vocabulary of their new townscapes. But they largely fail either to enhance or to provide a substitute for the existing scene because they attempt the impossible. By attempting too much they flaunt their impotence and risk their continuing influence as supposed experts. Cannot the architect and planner, by slight adjustments to the conventional elements of the townscape, existing or proposed, promote significant effects? By modifying or adding conventional elements to still other conventional elements they can, by a twist of context, gain a maximum of effect through a minimum of means. They can make us see the same things in a different way.

Finally, standardization, like convention, *can* be another manifestation of the strong order. But unlike convention it has been accepted in Modern architecture as an enriching product of our technology, yet dreaded for its potential domination and brutality. But is it not standardization that is without circumstantial accommodation and without a creative use of context that is to be feared more than standardization itself? The ideas of order and circumstance, convention and context—of employing standardization in an unstandard way—apply to our continuing problem of standardization versus variety. Giedion has written of Aalto's unique "combination of standardization with irrationality so that standardization is no longer master but servant."[21] I prefer to think of Aalto's art as contradictory rather than irrational —an artful recognition of the circumstantial and the contextual and of the inevitable limits of the order of standardization. . . .

10. The Obligation Toward the Difficult Whole

. . . Toledo [Ohio] was very beautiful.[22]

An architecture of complexity and accommodation does not forsake the whole. In fact, I have referred to a special obligation toward the whole because the whole is difficult to achieve. And I have emphasized the goal of unity rather than of simplification in an art "whose . . . truth [is] in its totality."[23] It is the difficult unity through inclusion rather than the easy unity through exclusion. Gestalt psychology considers a perceptual whole the result of, and yet more than, the sum of its parts. The whole is dependent on the position, number, and inherent characteristics of the parts. A complex system in Herbert A. Simon's definition includes "a large number of parts that interact in a non-

[21] Sigfried Giedion: *Space, Time and Architecture*, Harvard University Press, Cambridge, 1963; p. 565.

[22] Gertrude Stein: *Gertrude Stein's America*, Gilbert A. Harrison, ed., Robert B. Luce, Inc., Washington, D.C., 1965.

[23] Heckscher, *op. cit.*; 287.

simple way."[24] The difficult whole in an architecture of complexity and contradiction includes multiplicity and diversity of elements in relationships that are inconsistent or among the weaker kinds perceptually.

Concerning the positions of the parts, for instance, such an architecture encourages complex and contrapuntal rhythms over simple and single ones. The "difficult whole" can include a diversity of directions as well. Concerning the number of parts in a whole, the two extremes—a single part and a multiplicity of parts—read as wholes most easily: the single part is itself a unity; and extreme multiplicity reads like a unity through a tendency of the parts to change scale, and to be perceived as an overall pattern or texture. The next easiest whole is the trinity: three is the commonest number of compositional parts making a monumental unity in architecture.

But an architecture of complexity and contradiction also embraces the "difficult" numbers of parts—the duality, and the medium degrees of multiplicity. If the program or structure dictates a combination of two elements within any of the varying scales of a building, this is an architecture which exploits the duality, and more or less resolves dualities into a whole. Our recent architecture has suppressed dualities. The loose composition of the whole used in the "binuclear plan" employed by some architects right after the Second World War, was only a partial exception to this rule. But our tendency to distort the program and to subvert the composition in order to disguise the quality is refuted by a tradition of accepted dualities, more or less resolved, at all scales of building and planning—from Gothic portals and Renaissance windows to the Mannerist façades of the sixteenth century and Wren's complex of pavilions at Greenwich Hospital . . . .

Sullivan's Farmers' and Merchants' Union Bank in Columbus, Wisconsin, is exceptional in our recent architecture. The difficult duality is prominent. The plan reflects the bisected inside space which accommodates the public and the clerks on different sides of the counter running perpendicular to the façade. On the outside the door and the window at grade reflect this duality: they are themselves bisected by the shafts above. But the shafts, in turn, divide the lintel into a unity of three with a dominant central panel. The arch above the lintel tends to reinforce duality because it springs from the center of a panel below, yet by its oneness and its dominant size it also resolves the duality made by the window and the door. The façade is composed of the play of diverse numbers of parts—single elements as well as those divided into two or three are almost equally prominent—but the façade as a whole makes a unity.

Gestalt psychology also shows that the nature of the parts, as well as their number and position, influences a perceptual whole and it also has made a further distinction: the degree of wholeness can vary. Parts can be more or less whole in themselves, or, to put it in another way, in greater or lesser degree they can be fragments of a greater whole. Properties of the part can be more or less articulated; properties of the whole can be more or less accented. In the complex compositions, a special obligation toward the

---

[24] Herbert A. Simon: in *Proceedings of the American Philosophical Society,* vol. 106, no. 6, December 12, 1962; p. 468.

whole encourages the fragmentary part or, as Trystan Edwards calls it, the term, "inflection." [25]

Inflection in architecture is the way in which the whole is implied by exploiting the nature of the individual parts, rather than their position or number. By inflecting toward something outside themselves, the parts contain their own linkage: inflected parts are more integral with the whole than are *un*inflected parts. Inflection is a means of distinguishing diverse parts while implying continuity. It involves the art of the fragment. The valid fragment is economical because it implies richness and meaning beyond itself. Inflection can also be used to achieve suspense, an element possible in large sequential complexes. The inflected element can be called a partial-functioning element in contrast to the double-functioning element. In terms of perception it is dependent on something outside itself, and in whose direction it inflects. It is a directional form corresponding to directional space . . . .

At the scale of the town, inflection can come from the position of elements which are in themselves uninflected. In the Piazza del Popolo the domes of the twin churches confirm each building as a separate whole, but their single towers, symmetrical themselves, become inflective because of their asymmetrical positions on each church. In the context of the piazza each building is a fragment of a greater whole and a part of a gateway to the Corso. At the smaller scale of Palladio's Villa Zeno the asymmetrical positions of the symmetrical arched openings cause the end pavilions to inflect toward the center, thus enforcing the symmetry of the whole composition. This kind of inflection of asymmetrical ornament within a symmetrical whole is a dominant motif in Rococo architecture. For example, on the side altars at Birnau, and on the characteristic pairs of sconces, or andirons, doors, or other elements, the inflection of the rocaille is part of an asymmetry within a larger symmetry that exaggerates the unity yet creates a tension in the whole. . . .

Inflection accommodates the difficult whole of a duality as well as the easier complex whole. It is a way of resolving a duality. . . .

Modern architecture tends to reject inflection at all levels of scale. In the Tugendhat House no inflecting capital compromises the purity of the column's form, although the sheer forces in the supported roof plane must thus be ignored. Walls are inflected neither by bases nor cornices nor by structural reinforcements, such as quoins, at corners. Mies' pavilions are as independent as Greek temples: Wright's wings are interdependent but interlocked rather than independent and inflected. However, Wright, in accommodating his rural buildings to their particular sites, has recognized inflection at the scale of the whole building. For example, Fallingwater is incomplete without its context—it is a fragment of its natural setting which forms the greater whole. Away from its setting it would have no meaning. . . .

On the other hand, an architecture of complexity and contradiction can acknowledge an expressive *dis*continuity, which belies a certain structur-

[25] Arthur Trystan Edwards: *Architectural Style*, Faber and Gwyer, London, 1926; ch. III.

al continuity. In the choir screen in the cathedral at Modena, where one uninflected element precariously supports another in its visual expression, or in the abrupt abutments of the uninflected wings of All Saints Church, Margaret Street, a formal discontinuity is implied where there is a structural continuity. Soane's Gate at Langley Park is made up of three architectural elements totally uninflected and independent; besides the dominance of the middle element, it is the sculptural elements which are inflected and which give unity to the three parts. . . .

The dominant binder is another manifestation of the hierarchical relationships of parts. It manifests itself in the consistent pattern (the thematic kind of order) as well as by being the dominant element. This is not a difficult whole to achieve. In the context of an architecture of contradition it can be a doubtful panacea, like the fallen snow which unifies a chaotic landscape. At a scale of the town in the Medieval period it is the wall or castle which is the dominant element. In the Baroque it is the axis of the street against which minor diversities play. (In Paris the rigid axis is confirmed by cornice heights, while in Rome the axis tends to zigzag and is punctuated by connecting piazzas with obelisks.) The axial binder in Baroque planning sometimes reflects a program devised by an autocracy, which could easily exclude elements that today must be considered. Arterial circulation can be a dominant device in contemporary urban planning. In fact, in the program the consistent binder is most often represented by circulation, and in construction the consistent binder is usually the major order of structure. It is an important device of Kahn's viaduct architecture and Tange's collective forms for Tokyo. The dominant binder is an expediency in renovations. James Ackerman has referred to Michelangelo's predilection for "symmetrical juxtaposition of diagonal accents in plan and elevation" in his design for St. Peter's, which was essentially a renovation of earlier construction. "By using diagonal wall-masses to fuse together the arms of the cross, Michelangelo was able to give St. Peter's a unity that earlier designs lacked.[26]

But a more ambiguously hierarchical relationship of uninflected parts creates a more difficult perceptual whole. Such a whole is composed of equal combinations of parts. While the idea of equal combinations is related to the phenomenon both-and, and many examples apply to both ideas, both-and refers more specifically to contradiction in architecture, while equal combinations refer more to unity. With equal combinations the whole does not depend on inflection, or the easier relationships of the dominant binder or motival consistency. For example, in the Porta Pia the number of each kind of element in the composition of the door and the wall is almost equal—no one element dominates. The varieties of shapes (rectangular, square, triangular, segmental, and round) being almost equal, the predominance of any one shape is also precluded, and the equal varieties of directions (vertical, horizontal, diagonal, and curving) have the same effect. There is similarly an equal diversity in the size of the elements. The equal combinations of parts achieve a whole through superimposition and symmetry rather than through dominance and hierarchy.

[26] Ackerman, *op. cit.;* p. 138.

The window above Sullivan's portal in the Merchants' National Bank in Grinnell, Iowa, is almost identical to the Porta Pia in its juxtaposition of an equal number of round, square and diamond-shaped frames of equal size. The diverse combinations of number analyzed in his Columbia Bank façade (groups of elements involving one, two, and three parts) have almost equal value in the composition. However, there the unity is based upon the relation of horizontal layers rather than on superimposition. The Auditorium exploits the complexity of directions and rhythms that such a program can yield. The simple semicircles of the wall ornament, structure, and segmental ceiling coves counteract, in plan and section, the complex curves of the proscenium arches, rows of seats, balcony slopes, boxes, and column brackets. These, in turn, play against the rectangular relationship of ceilings, walls, and columns.

This sense of the equivocal in much of Sullivan's work (at least where the program is more complex than that of a skyscraper) points up another contrast between him and Wright. Wright would seldom express the contradiction inherent in equal combinations. Instead, he resolved all sizes and shapes into a motival order—a single predominant order of circles or rectangles or diagonals. The Vigo Schmidt House project is a consistent pattern of triangles, the Ralph Jester House of circles, and the Paul Hanna House of hexagons . . . .

Inherent in an architecture of opposites is the inclusive whole. The unity of the interior of the Imatra church or the complex at Wolfsburg is achieved not through suppression or exclusion but through the dramatic inclusion of contradictory or circumstantial parts. Aalto's architecture acknowledges the difficult and subtle conditions of program, while "serene" architecture, on the other hand, works simplifications.

However, the obligation toward the whole in an architecture of complexity and contradiction does not preclude the building which is unresolved. Poets and playwrights acknowledge dilemmas without solutions. The validity of the questions and vividness of the meaning are what make their works art more than philosophy. A goal of poetry can be unity of expression over resolution of content. Contemporary sculpture is often fragmentary, and today we appreciate Michelangelo's unfinished Pietàs more than his early work, because their content is suggested, their expression more immediate, and their forms are completed beyond themselves. A building can also be more or less incomplete in the expression of its program and its form.

The Gothic cathedral, like Beauvais, for instance, of which only the enormous choir was built, is frequently unfinished in relation to its program, yet is is complete in the effect of its form because of the motival consistency of its many parts. The complex program which is a process, continually changing and growing in time yet at each stage at some level related to a whole, should be recognized as essential at the scale of city planning. The incomplete program is valid for a complex single building as well.

Each of the fragmental twin churches on the Piazza del Popolo, however, is complete at the level of program but incomplete in the expression of form. The uniquely asymmetrically placed tower, as we have seen, inflects each building toward a greater whole outside itself. The very complex building, which in its open form is incomplete, in itself relates to Maki's "group form;" it is the antithesis of the "perfect single building"[27] or the closed pavilion. As a fragment of a greater whole in a greater context this kind of building relates again to the scope of city planning as a means of increasing the unity of the complex whole. An architecture that can simultaneously recognize contradictory levels should be able to admit the paradox of the whole fragment: the building which is a whole at one level and a fragment of a greater whole at another level.

In *God's Own Junkyard* Peter Blake has compared the chaos of commercial Main Street with the orderliness of the University of Virginia. Besides the irrelevancy of the comparison, is not Main Street almost all right? Indeed, is not the commercial strip of a Route 66 almost all right? As I have said, our question is: what slight twist of context will make them all right? Perhaps more signs more contained. Illustrations in *God's Own Junkyard* of Times Square and roadtown are compared with illustrations of New England villages and arcadian countrysides. But the pictures in this book that are supposed to be bad are often good. The seemingly chaotic juxtapositions of honky-tonk elements express an intriguing kind of vitality and validity, and they produce an unexpected approach to unity as well.

It is true that an ironic interpretation such as this results partly from the change in scale of the subject matter in photographic form and the change in context within the frames of the photographs. But in some of these compositions there is an inherent sense of unity not far from the surface. It is not the obvious or easy unity derived from the dominant binder or the motival order of simpler, less contradictory compositions, but that derived from a complex and illusive order of the difficult whole. It is the taut composition which contains contrapuntal relationships, equal combinations, inflected fragments, and acknowledged dualities. It is the unity which "maintains, but only just maintains, a control over the clashing elements which compose it. Chaos is very near; its nearness, but its avoidance, gives . . . force."[28] In the validly complex building or cityscape, the eye does not want to be too easily or too quickly satisfied in its search for unity within a whole.

Some of the vivid lessons of Pop Art, involving contradictions of scale and context, should have awakened architects from prim dreams of pure order, which, unfortunately, are imposed in the easy Gestalt unities of the urban renewal projects of establishment Modern architecture and yet, fortunately are really impossible to achieve at any great scope. And it is perhaps from the everyday landscape, vulgar and disdained, that we can draw the complex and contradictory order that is valid and vital for our architecture as an urbanistic whole.

---

[27] Fumihiko Maki: *Investigations in Collective Form*, Special Publication No. 2, Washington University, St. Louis, 1964; p. 5

[28] Heckscher, *op. cit.*; p. 289.

79 R. Venturi, Learning from Las Vegas* *1972*

To Venturi the best and most vital expression of the "difficult whole," in which conflicting pressures and needs are accommodated, is the commercial strip. He, Denise Scott Brown, and Steven Izenour had already begun to examine the strip of Las Vegas in this light, publishing a sketch of their preliminary conclusions in 1968.[†] That autumn the three took architectural students from Yale to Las Vegas to pursue field research, and the results of this investigation appeared as *Learning from Las Vegas* in 1972, a work described by the authors in a preface to the second edition as "a treatise on symbolism in architecture," and reinforced by the addition of a new subtitle: *The Forgotten Symbolism of Architectural Form*. The excerpts given here are from the second edition which should be consulted, too, for an extensive bibliography of writings by or about the authors, jointly and individually.

A SIGNIFICANCE FOR A&P PARKING LOTS, OR LEARNING FROM LAS VEGAS

Substance for a writer consists not merely of those realities he thinks he discovers; it consists even more of those realities which have been made available to him by the literature and idioms of his own day and by the images that still have vitality in the literature of the past. Stylistically, a writer can express his feeling about this substance either by imitation, if it sits well with him, or by parody, if it doesn't.[1]

Learning from the existing landscape is a way of being revolutionary for an architect. Not the obvious way, which is to tear down Paris and begin again, as Le Corbusier suggested in the 1920s, but another, more tolerant way; that is, to question how we look at things.

The commercial strip, the Las Vegas Strip in particular—the example par excellence—challenges the architect to take a positive, non-chip-on-the-shoulder view. Architects are out of the habit of looking nonjudgmentally at the environment, because orthodox Modern architecture is progressive, if not revolutionary, utopian, and puristic; it is dissatisfied with *existing* conditions. Modern architecture has been anything but permissive: Architects have preferred to change the existing environment rather than enhance what is there.

But to gain insight from the commonplace is nothing new: Fine art often follows folk art. Romantic architects of the eighteenth century discovered an existing and conventional rustic architecture. Early Modern archi-

---

*Robert Venturi, Denise Scott Brown, and Steven Izenour, *Learning from Las Vegas*, 2nd ed. (Cambridge, Mass., 1977), pp. 3, 6–8, 52–53, 87, 90, 104–07, 114–15, 134–37, 161–63.

[†] Robert Venturi and Denise Scott Brown, "A Significance for A & P Parking Lots, or Learning from Las Vegas," *Architectural Forum* 128 (March 1968), pp. 36–43, 89–91.

[1] Richard Poirier, "T. S. Eliot and the Literature of Waste," *The New Republic* (May 20, 1967), p. 21.

tects appropriated an existing and conventional industrial vocabulary without much adaptation. Le Corbusier loved grain elevators and steamships; the Bauhaus looked like a factory; Mies refined the details of American steel factories for concrete buildings. Modern architects work through analogy, symbol, and image—although they have gone to lengths to disclaim almost all determinants of their forms except structural necessity and the program —and they derive insights, analogies, and stimulation from unexpected images. There is a perversity in the learning process: We look backward at history and tradition to go forward; we can also look downward to go upward. And withholding judgment may be used as a tool to make later judgment more sensitive. This is a way of learning from everything.

Commercial Values and Commercial Methods

Las Vegas is analyzed here only as a phenomenon of architectural communication. Just as an analysis of the structure of a Gothic cathedral need not include a debate on the morality of medieval religion, so Las Vegas's values are not questioned here. The morality of commercial advertising, gambling interests, and the competitive instinct is not at issue here, although, indeed, we believe it should be in the architect's broader, *synthetic* tasks of which an analysis such as this is but one aspect. The analysis of a drive-in church in this context would match that of a drive-in restaurant, because this is a study of method, not content. Analysis of one of the architectural variables in isolation from the others is a respectable scientific and humanistic activity, so long as all are resynthesized in design. Analysis of existing American urbanism is a socially desirable activity to the extent that it teaches us architects to be more understanding and less authoritarian in the plans we make for both inner-city renewal and new development. In addition, there is no reason why the methods of commercial persuasion and the skyline of signs analyzed here should not serve the purpose of civic and cultural enhancement. But this is not entirely up to the architect.

Billboards Are Almost All Right

Architects who can accept the lessons of primitive vernacular architecture, so easy to take in an exhibit like "Architecture without Architects," and of industrial, vernacular architecture, so easy to adapt to an electronic and space vernacular as elaborate neo-Brutalist or neo-Constructivist megastructures, do not easily acknowledge the validity of the commercial vernacular. For the artist, creating the new may mean choosing the old or the existing. Pop artists have relearned this. Our acknowledgment of existing, commercial architecture at the scale of the highway is within this tradition.

Modern architecture has not so much excluded the commercial vernacular as it has tried to take it over by inventing and enforcing a vernacular of its own, improved and universal. It has rejected the combination of fine art and crude art. The Italian landscape has always harmonized the vulgar and the Vitruvian: the *contorni* around the *duomo*, the *portiere's* laundry across the *padrone's portone*, *Supercortemaggiore* against the Romanesque apse. Naked children have never played in *our* fountains, and I. M. Pei will never be happy on Route 66.

Architecture as Space

Architects have been bewitched by a single element of the Italian landscape: the piazza. Its traditional, pedestrian-scaled, and intricately enclosed space is easier to like than the spatial sprawl of Route 66 and Los Angeles. Architects have been brought up on Space, and enclosed space is the easiest to handle. During the last 40 years, theorists of Modern architecture (Wright and Le Corbusier sometimes excepted) have focused on space as the essential ingredient that separates architecture from painting, sculpture, and literature. Their definitions glory in the uniqueness of the medium; although sculpture and painting may sometimes be allowed spatial characteristics, sculptural or pictorial architecture is unacceptable—because Space is sacred.

Purist architecture was partly a reaction against nineteenth-century eclecticism. Gothic churches, Renaissance banks, and Jacobean manors were frankly picturesque. The mixing of styles meant the mixing of media. Dressed in historical styles, buildings evoked explicit associations and romantic allusions to the past to convey literary, ecclesiastical, national, or programmatic symbolism. Definitions of architecture as space and form at the service of program and structure were not enough. The overlapping of disciplines may have diluted the architecture, but it enriched the meaning.

Modern architects abandoned a tradition of iconology in which painting, sculpture, and graphics were combined with architecture. The delicate hieroglyphics on a bold pylon, the archetypal inscriptions of a Roman architrave, the mosaic processions in Sant'Apollinare, the ubiquitous tattoos over a Giotto Chapel, the enshrined hierarchies around a Gothic portal, even the illusionistic frescoes in a Venetian villa, all contain messages beyond their ornamental contribution to architectural space. The integration of the arts in Modern architecture has always been called a good thing. But one did not paint *on* Mies. Painted panels were floated independently of the structure by means of shadow joints; sculpture was in or near but seldom on the building. Objects of art were used to reinforce architectural space at the expense of their own content. The Kolbe in the Barcelona Pavilion was a foil to the directed spaces: The message was mainly architectural. The diminutive signs in most Modern buildings contained only the most necessary messages, like LADIES, minor accents begrudgingly applied.

Architecture as Symbol

Critics and historians, who documented the "decline of popular symbols" in art, supported orthodox Modern architects, who shunned symbolism of form as an expression or reinforcement of content: meaning was to be communicated, not through allusion to previously known forms, but through the inherent, physiognomic characteristics of form. The creation of architectural form was to be a logical process, free from images of past experience, determined solely by program and structure, with an occasional assist, as Alan Colquhoun has suggested,[2] from intuition.

[2] Alan Colquhoun, "Typology and Design Method," *Arena*, Journal of the Architectural Association (June 1967), pp. 11–14. [For the collected writings of this English architect, a frequent teacher at Princeton University, see Alan Colquhoun, *Essays in Architectural Criticism* (Cambridge, Mass., 1981).—ED.]

But some recent critics have questioned the possible level of content to be derived from abstract forms. Others have demonstrated that the functionalists, despite their protestations, derived a formal vocabulary of their own, mainly from current art movements and the industrial vernacular; and latter-day followers such as the Archigram group have turned, while similarly protesting, to Pop Art and the space industry. However, most critics have slighted a continuing iconology in popular commercial art, the persuasive heraldry that pervades our environment from the advertising pages of *The New Yorker* to the superbillboards of Houston. And their theory of the "debasement" of symbolic architecture in nineteenth-century eclecticism has blinded them to the value of the representational architecture along highways. Those who acknowledge this roadside eclecticism denigrate it, because it flaunts the cliché of a decade ago as well as the style of a century ago. But why not? Time travels fast today.

The Miami Beach Modern motel on a bleak stretch of highway in southern Delaware reminds jaded drivers of the welcome luxury of a tropical resort, persuading them, perhaps, to forgo the gracious plantation across the Virginia border called Motel Monticello. The real hotel in Miami alludes to the international stylishness of a Brazilian resort, which, in turn, derives from the International Style of middle Corbu. This evolution from the high source through the middle source to the low source took only 30 years. Today, the middle source, the neo-Eclectic architecture of the 1940s and the 1950s, is less interesting than its commercial adaptations. Roadside copies of Ed Stone are more interesting than the real Ed Stone. . . .

Inclusion and the Difficult Order

Henri Bergson called disorder an order we cannot see. The emerging order of the Strip is a complex order. It is not the easy, rigid order of the urban renewal project or the fashionable "total design" of the megastructure. It is, on the contrary, a manifestation of an opposite direction in architectural theory: Broadacre City—a travesty of Broadacre City, perhaps, but a kind of vindication of Frank Lloyd Wright's predictions for the American landscape. The commercial strip within the urban sprawl is, of course, Broadacre City with a difference. Broadacre City's easy, motival order identified and unified its vast spaces and separate buildings at the scale of the omnipotent automobile. Each building, without doubt, was to be designed by the Master or by his Taliesin Fellowship, with no room for honky-tonk improvisations. An easy control would be exercised over similar elements within the universal, Usonian vocabulary to the exclusion, certainly, of commercial vulgarities. But the order of the Strip *includes;* it includes at all levels, from the mixture of seemingly incongruous land uses to the mixture of seemingly incongruous advertising media plus a system of neo-Organic or neo-Wrightian restaurant motifs in Walnut Formica. It is not an order dominated by the expert and made easy for the eye. The moving eye in the moving body must work to pick out and interpret a variety of changing, juxtaposed orders, like the shifting configurations of a Victor Vasarely painting. It is the unity that "maintains, but only just maintains, a control over the clashing elements which compose it. Chaos is very near; its nearness, but its avoidance, gives . . . force."[3]

Image of Las Vegas: Inclusion and Allusion in Architecture

Tom Wolfe used Pop prose to suggest powerful images of Las Vegas. Hotel brochures and tourist handouts suggest others. J. B. Jackson, Robert Riley, Edward Ruscha, John Kouwenhoven, Reyner Banham, and William Wilson have elaborated on related images. For the architect or urban designer, comparisons of Las Vegas with others of the world's "pleasure zones"—with Marienbad, the Alhambra, Xanadu, and Disneyland, for instance—suggest that essential to the imagery of pleasure-zone architecture are lightness, the quality of being an oasis in a perhaps hostile context, heightened symbolism, and the ability to engulf the visitor in a new role: for three days one may imagine oneself a centurion at Caesars Palace, a ranger at the Frontier, or a jetsetter at the Riviera rather than a salesperson from Des Moines, Iowa, or an architect from Haddonfield, New Jersey.

However, there are didactic images more important than the images of recreation for us to take home to New Jersey and Iowa: one is the Avis with the Venus; another, Jack Benny under a classical pediment with Shell Oil beside him, or the gasoline station beside the multimillion-dollar casino. These show the vitality that may be achieved by an architecture of inclusion or, by contrast, the deadness that results from too great a preoccupation with tastefulness and total design. The Strip shows the value of symbolism and allusion in an architecture of vast space and speed and proves that people, even architects, have fun with architecture that reminds them of something else, perhaps of harems or the Wild West in Las Vegas, perhaps of the nation's New England forebears in New Jersey. Allusion and comment, on the past or present or on our great commonplaces or old clichés, and inclusion of the everyday in the environment, sacred and profane—these are what are lacking in present-day Modern architecture. We can learn about them from Las Vegas as have other artists from their own profane and stylistic sources.

SOME DEFINITIONS USING THE COMPARATIVE METHOD

> Not innovating willfulness but reverence for the archetype.
>
> Herman Melville

> Incessant new beginnings lead to sterility.
>
> Wallace Stevens

> I like boring things.
>
> Andy Warhol

To make the case for a new but old direction in architecture, we shall use some perhaps indiscreet comparisons to show what we are for and what

---

[3] August Heckscher, *The Public Happiness* (New York: Atheneum Publishers, 1962), p. 289.

we are against and ultimately to justify our own architecture. When architects talk or write, they philosophize almost solely to justify their own work, and this apologia will be no different. Our argument depends on comparisons, because it is simple to the point of banality. It needs contrast to point it up. We shall use, somewhat undiplomatically, some of the works of leading architects today as contrast and context.

We shall emphasize image—image over process or form—in asserting that architecture depends in its perception and creation on past experience and emotional association and that these symbolic and representational elements may often be contradictory to the form, structure, and program with which they combine in the same building. We shall survey this contradiction in its two main manifestations:

1. Where the architectural systems of space, structure, and program are submerged and distorted by an overall symbolic form. This kind of building-becoming-sculpture we call the *duck* in honor of the duck-shaped drive-in, "The Long Island Duckling," illustrated in *God's Own Junkyard* by Peter Blake.[4]

2. Where systems of space and structure are directly at the service of program, and ornament is applied independently of them. This we call the *decorated shed*.

The duck is the special building that *is* a symbol; the decorated shed is the conventional shelter that *applies* symbols. We maintain that both kinds of architecture are valid—Chartres is a duck (although it is a decorated shed as well), and the Palazzo Farnese is a decorated shed—but we think that the duck is seldom relevant today, although it pervades Modern architecture.

We shall describe how we come by the automobile-oriented commercial architecture of urban sprawl as our source for a civic and residential architecture of meaning, viable now, as the turn-of-the-century industrial vocabulary was viable for a Modern architecture of space and industrial technology 40 years ago. We shall show how the iconography, rather than the space and piazzas of historical architecture, forms the background for the study of association and symbolism in commercial art and strip architecture.

Finally we shall argue for the symbolism of the ugly and ordinary in architecture and for the particular significance of the decorated shed with a rhetorical front and conventional behind: for architecture as shelter with symbols on it.

HISTORICAL AND OTHER PRECEDENTS: TOWARDS AN OLD ARCHITECTURE

Historical Symbolism and Modern Architecture

The forms of Modern architecture have been created by architects and analyzed by critics largely in terms of their perceptual qualities and at the ex-

---

[4]Peter Blake, *God's Own Junkyard: The Planned Deterioration of America's Landscape* (New York: Holt, Rinehart and Winston, 1964), p. 101. See also Denise Scott Brown and Robert Venturi, "On Ducks and Decoration," *Architecture Canada* (October 1968).

pense of their symbolic meanings derived from association. To the extent that the Moderns recognize the systems of symbols that pervade our environment, they tend to refer to the debasement of our symbols. Although largely forgotten by Modern architects, the historical precedent for symbolism in architecture exists, and the complexities of iconography have continued to be a major part of the discipline of art history. Early Modern architects scorned recollection in architecture. They rejected eclecticism and style as elements of architecture as well as any historicism that minimized the revolutionary over the evolutionary character of their almost exclusively technology-based architecture. A second generation of Modern architects acknowledged only the "constituent facts" of history, as extracted by Sigfried Giedion,[5] who abstracted the historical building and its piazza as pure form and space in light. These architects' preoccupation with space as *the* architectural quality caused them to read the buildings as forms, the piazzas as space, and the graphics and sculpture as color, texture, and scale. The ensemble became an abstract expression in architecture in the decade of abstract expressionism in painting. The iconographic forms and trappings of medieval and Renaissance architecture were reduced to polychromatic texture at the service of space; the symbolic complexities and contradictions of Mannerist architecture were appreciated for their formal complexities and contradictions; Neoclassical architecture was liked, not for its Romantic use of association, but for its formal simplicity. Architects liked the *backs* of nineteenth century railroad stations—literally the sheds—and tolerated the fronts as irrelevant, if amusing, aberrations of historical eclecticism. The symbol systems developed by the commercial artists of Madison Avenue, which constitute the symbolic ambience of urban sprawl, they did not acknowledge.

In the 1950s and 1960s, these "Abstract Expressionists" of Modern architecture acknowledged one dimension of the hill town-piazza complex: its "pedestrian scale" and the "urban life" engendered by its architecture. This view of medieval urbanism encouraged the megastructural (or megasculptural?) fantasies—in this context hill towns with technological trimmings——and reinforced the antiautomobile bias of the Modern architect. But the competition of signs and symbols in the medieval city at various levels of perception and meaning in both building and piazza was lost on the space-oriented architect. Perhaps the symbols, besides being foreign in content, were at a scale and a degree of complexity too subtle for today's bruised sensibilities and impatient pace. This explains, perhaps, the ironic fact that the return to iconography for some of us architects of that generation was via the sensibilities of the Pop artists of the early 1960s and via the duck and the decorated shed on Route 66: from Rome to Las Vegas, but also back again from Las Vegas to Rome.

The Cathedral as Duck and Shed

In iconographic terms, the cathedral is a decorated shed *and* a duck. The Late Byzantine Metropole Cathedral in Athens is absurd as a piece of architecture. It is "out of scale": Its small size does not correspond to its complex

---

[5] Sigfried Giedion, *Space, Time and Architecture* (Cambridge, Mass.: Harvard University Press, 1944), Part I.

form—that is, if form must be determined primarily by structure—because the space that the square room encloses could be spanned without the interior supports and the complex roof configuration of dome, drum, and vaults. However, it is not absurd as a duck—as a domed Greek cross, evolved structurally from large buildings in greater cities, but developed symbolically here to mean cathedral. And this duck is itself decorated with an appliqué collage of *objets trouvés*—bas-reliefs in masonry—more or less explicitly symbolic in content.

Amiens Cathedral is a billboard with a building behind it. Gothic cathedrals have been considered weak in that they did not achieve an "organic unity" between front and side. But this disjunction is a natural reflection of an inherent contradiction in a complex building that, toward the cathedral square, is a relatively two-dimensional screen for propaganda and, in back, is a masonry systems building. This is the reflection of a contradiction between image and function that the decorated shed often accommodates. (The shed behind is also a duck because its shape is that of a cross.)

The façades of the great cathedrals of the Ile de France are two-dimensional planes at the scale of the whole; they were to evolve at the top corners into towers to connect with the surrounding countryside. But in detail these facades are buildings in themselves, simulating an architecture of space in the strongly three-dimensional relief of their sculpture. The niches for statues—as Sir John Summerson has pointed out—are yet another level of architecture within architecture. But the impact of the facade comes from the immensely complex meaning derived from the symbolism and explicit associations of the aedicules and their statues and from their relative positions and sizes in the hierarchic order of the kingdom of heaven on the facades. In this orchestration of messages, connotation as practiced by Modern architects is scarcely important. The shape of the facade, in fact, disguises the silhouette of nave and aisles behind, and the doors and the rose windows are the barest reflections of the architectural complex inside.

Symbolic Evolution in Las Vegas

Just as the architectural evolution of a typical Gothic cathedral may be traced over the decades through stylistic and symbolic changes, a similar evolution—rare in contemporary architecture—may also be followed in the commercial architecture of Las Vegas. However, in Las Vegas, this evolution is compressed into years rather than decades, reflecting the quicker tempo of our times, if not the less eternal message of commercial rather than religious propaganda. Evolution in Las Vegas is consistently toward more and bigger symbolism. The Golden Nugget casino on Fremont Street was an orthodox decorated shed with big signs in the 1950s—essentially Main Street commercial, ugly and ordinary. However, by the 1960s it was all sign; there was hardly any building visible. The quality of the "electrographics" was made more strident to match the crasser scale and more distracting context of the new decade and to keep up with the competition next door. The freestanding signs on the Strip, like the towers at San Gimignano, get bigger as well. They grow either through sequential replacements, as at the Flamingo, the Desert Inn, and the Tropicana, or through enlargement as with the Caesars Palace sign, where a freestanding, pedimented temple facade was extended laterally by one column with a statue on top—a feat never attempted, a problem never solved in the whole evolution of Classical architecture.

The Renaissance and the Decorated Shed

The iconography of Renaissance architecture is less overtly propagandistic than is that of medieval or Strip architecture, although its ornament, literally based on the Roman, Classical vocabulary, was to be an instrument for the rebirth of classical civilization. However, since most of this ornament depicts structure—it is ornament symbolic of structure—it is less independent of the shed it is attached to than ornament on medieval and Strip architecture. The image of the structure and space reinforces rather than contradicts the substance of the structure and space. Pilasters represent modular sinews on the surface of the wall; quoins represent reinforcement at the ends of the wall; vertical moldings, protection at the edges of the wall; rustication, support at the bottom of the wall; drip cornices, protection from rain on the wall; horizontal moldings, the progressive stages in the depth of the wall; and a combination of many of these ornaments at the edge of a door symbolizes the importance of the door in the face of the wall. Although some of these elements are functional as well—for instance, the drips are, but the pilasters are not—all are explicitly symbolic, associating the glories of Rome with the refinements of building.

But Renaissance inconography is not all structural. The *stemma* above the door is a sign. The Baroque facades of Francesco Borromini, for instance, are rich with symbolism in bas-relief—religious, dynastic, and other. It is significant that Giedion, in his brilliant analysis of the facade of San Carlo alle Quattro Fontane, described the contrapuntal layerings, undulating rhythms, and subtle scales of the forms and surfaces as abstract elements in a composition in relation to the outside space of the street but without reference to the complex layering of symbolic meanings they contain.

The Italian palace is the decorated shed *par excellence*. For two centuries, from Florence to Rome, the plan of rooms *en suite* around a rectangular, arcaded *cortile* with an entrance penetration in the middle of a facade and a three-story elevation with occasional mezzanines was a constant base for a series of stylistic and compositional variations. The architectural scaffolding was the same for the Strozzi Palace with its three stories of diminishing rustication, for the Rucellai with its quasi-frame of three-ordered pilasters, for the Farnese with its quoined corners complementing the focus of the ornamental central bay and its resultant horizontal hierarchy, and for the Odescalchi with its monumental giant order imposing the image of one dominant story on three. The basis for the significant evaluation of the development of Italian civic architecture from the mid-fifteenth to the mid-seventeenth century lies in the decoration of a shed. Similar ornament adorns subsequent palazzi, commercial and *senza cortili*. The Carson Pirie Scott department store supports at the ground floor a cast-iron cladding of biological patterns in low relief with intricate scale appropriate for sustaining the customers' interest at eye level, while abruptly opposing, in the formal vocabulary above it, the ugly and ordinary symbolism of a conventional loft. The conventional shed of a high-rise Howard Johnson motel is more Ville Radieuse slab than palazzo, but the explicit symbolism of its virtually pedimented doorway, a rigid frame in heraldic orange enamel, matches the Classical pediment with feudal crest over the entrance of a patrician palazzo, if we grant the change in scale and the jump in context from urban piazza to Pop sprawl.

Nineteenth-Century Eclecticism

The stylistic eclecticism of the nineteenth century was essentially a symbolism of function, although sometimes a symbolism of nationalism—Henri IV Renaissance in France, Tudor in England, for example. But quite consistently styles correspond to building types. Banks were Classical basilicas to suggest civic responsibility and tradition; commercial buildings looked like burghers' houses; universities copied Gothic rather than Classical colleges at Oxford and Cambridge to make symbols of "embattled learning," as George Howe put it, "tending the torch of humanism through the dark ages of economic determinism,"[6] and a choice between Perpendicular and Decorated for midcentury English churches reflected theological differences between the Oxford and Cambridge Movements. The hamburger-shaped hamburger stand is a current, more literal, attempt to express function via association but for commercial persuasion rather than theological refinement.

Donald Drew Egbert,[7] in an analysis of midcentury submissions for the Prix de Rome at the École des Beaux-Arts—home of the bad guys—called functionalism via association a symbolic manifestation of functionalism that preceded the substantive functionalism that was a basis for the Modern movement: Image preceded substance. Egbert also discussed the balance in the new nineteenth-century building types between expression of function via physiognomy and expression of function via style. For instance, the railroad station was recognizable by its cast-iron shed and big clock. These physiognomic symbols contrasted with the explicit heraldic signing of the Renaissance-eclectic waiting and station spaces up front. Sigfried Giedion called this artful contrast within the same building a gross contradiction—a nineteenth-century "split in feeling"—because he saw architecture as technology and space, excluding the element of symbolic meaning.

Modern Ornament

Modern architects began to make the back the front, symbolizing the configurations of the shed to create a vocabulary for their architecture but denying in theory what they were doing in practice. They said one thing and did another. Less may have been more, but the I-section on Mies van der Rohe's fire-resistant columns, for instance, is as complexly ornamental as the applied pilaster on the Renaissance pier or the incised shaft in the Gothic pier. (In fact, less was more work.) Acknowledged or not, Modern ornament has seldom been symbolic of anything nonarchitectural since the Bauhaus vanquished Art Deco and the decorative arts. More specifically, its content is consistently spatial and technological. Like the Renaissance vocabulary of

[6] George Howe, "Some Experiences and Observations of an Elderly Architect," *Perspecta 2, The Yale Architectural Journal*, New Haven (1954), p. 4.

[7] Donald Drew Egbert, "Lectures in Modern Architecture" (unpublished), Princeton University, c. 1945.

the Classical orders, Mies's structural ornament, although specifically contradictory to the structure it adorns, reinforces the architectural content of the building as a whole. If the Classical orders symbolized "rebirth of the Golden Age of Rome," modern I-beams represent "honest expression of modern technology as space"—or something like that. Note, however, it was "modern" technology of the Industrial Revolution that was symbolized by Mies, and this technology, not current electronic technology, is still the source for Modern architectural symbolism today.

Firmness + Commodity ≠ Delight: Modern Architecture and the Industrial Vernacular

Vitruvius wrote, via Sir Henry Wootton, that architecture was Firmness and Commodity and Delight. Gropius (or perhaps only his followers) implied, via the bio-technical determinism just described, that Firmness and Commodity equal Delight: that structure plus program rather simply result in form; that beauty is a by-product; and that—to tamper with the equation in another way—the process of making architecture becomes the image of architecture. Louis Kahn in the 1950s said that the architect should be surprised by the appearance of his design.

Presumed in these equations is that process and image are never contradictory and that Delight is a result of the clarity and harmony of these simple relationships, untinged, of course, by the beauty of symbolism and ornament or by the associations of preconceived form: Architecture is frozen process.

The historians of the Modern movement concentrated on the innovative engineering structures of the nineteenth and early twentieth centuries as prototypes for Modern architecture, but it is significant that the bridges of Maillart are not architecture, and the hangars of Freysinnet are hardly architecture. As engineering solutions, their programs are simple and without the inherent contradictions of architectural programs. To traverse a ravine directly, safely, and cheaply or to protect a big space from the rain without intervening supports is all that is required of these structures. The unavoidable symbolic content of even such simple, utilitarian constructions and the unavoidable use of what Colquhoun calls typologies were ignored by the theorists of the Modern movement. The not infrequent ornamentation of these forms was excused as a deviant architectural hangover, characteristic of the times. But the ornamentation of utilitarian superstructures is typical of all times. The defensive walls of the medieval city were topped with elaborately varied crenelations and studded with rhetorically ornamented gates. The applied decorations of the classic structures of the Industrial Revolution (we see them as more classic than innovative) are another manifestation of the decorated shed—for example, the elaborated gusset plates of the frame bridges, or the modified Corinthian capitals of the fluted cast-iron columns in loft buildings, or the eclectically stylish entrances and fanciful parapets of their fronts.

The decoration of the shed in nineteenth-century industrial achitecture was often ignored by architects and theorists of the Modern movement through selective viewing of buildings or through contrived cropping of photographs. Even today as architects stress the complexity of these buildings (for instance, the complex massing and clerestoried roof lines of the mills of the English industrial Midlands) rather than their simplicity, their not infrequent ornament is still discounted.

Mies van der Rohe looked at only the backs of Albert Kahn's factories in the Midwest and developed his minimal vocabulary of steel I-sections framing industrial sash. The fronts of Kahn's sheds almost always contained administrative offices and, being early twentieth-century creations, were graciously Art Deco rather than historical eclectic. The plastic massing up front, characteristic of this style, grandly contradicted the skeletal behind.

Industrial Iconography

More important than Mies's forgetting the decoration was his copying the shed, that is, his deriving associations from the body of the building rather than from its facade. The architecture of the Modern movement, during its early decades and through a number of its masters, developed a vocabulary of forms based on a variety of industrial models whose conventions and proportions were no less explicit than the Classical orders of the Renaissance. What Mies did with linear industrial buildings in the 1940s, Le Corbusier had done with plastic grain elevators in the 1920s, and Gropius had done with the Bauhaus in the 1930s, imitating his own earlier factory, the Fagus-werk, of 1911. Their factorylike buildings were more than "influenced" by the industrial vernacular structures of the then recent past, in the sense that historians have described influences among artists and movements. Their buildings were explicitly adapted from these sources, and largely for their symbolic content, because industrial structures *represented*, for European architects, the brave new world of science and technology. The architects of the early Modern movement, in discarding the admittedly obsolete symbolism of historical eclecticism, substituted that of the industrial vernacular. To put it another way, as Romantics still, they achieved a new sensibility through evoking the remote in place—that is, the contemporary industrial quarter on the other side of the tracks, which they transferred to the civic areas of the city—rather than evoking, as did the earlier Romantics, the remote in time through the replication of stylistic ornament of the past. That is, the Moderns employed a design method based on typological models and developed an architectural iconography based on their interpretation of the progressive technology of the Industrial Revolution.

Colquhoun refers to the "iconic power" attributed by "those in the field of design who were—and are—preaching pure technology and so-called objective design method . . . to the creations of technology, which they worship to a degree inconceivable in a scientist.[8] He also writes of "the power of all artifacts to become icons . . . whether or not they were specifically created for this purpose," and he cites nineteenth-century steamships and locomotives as examples of objects "made ostensibly with utilitarian purposes in mind" which "quickly become gestalt entities . . . imbued with aesthetic unity" and symbolic quality. These objects, along with the factories and grain elevators, became explicit typological models that, despite what architects said to the contrary, significantly influenced the method of Modern architectural design and served as sources for its symbolic meanings.

[8] Colquhoun, "Typology and Design Method," pp. 11–14.

Industrial Styling and the Cubist Model

Later critics referred to a "machine aesthetic," and others have accepted the term, but Le Corbusier among the Modern masters was unique in elaborately describing industrial prototypes for his architecture in *Vers une Architecture*. However, even he claimed the steamship and the grain elevator for their forms rather than their associations, for their simple geometry rather than their industrial image. It is significant, on the other hand, that the buildings of Le Corbusier, illustrated in his book, physically resemble the steamships and the grain elevators but not the Parthenon or the furniture in Santa Maria in Cosmedin or Michelangelo's details for Saint Peter's, which are also illustrated for their simple geometric forms. The industrial prototypes became literal models for Modern architecture, while the historical-architectural prototypes were merely analogs selected for certain of their characteristics. To put it another way, the industrial buildings were symbolically correct; the historical buildings were not.

For the abstract geometrical formalism of Le Corbusier's architecture at this time, Cubism was the model. It was the second model, in part countering that of the nautical-industrial images, and it accounted for the hovering, stuccoed planes that enveloped the industrial sash and spiral stairs in the Villa Savoye. Although historians describe the relation between painting and architecture of this period as a harmonious diffusion of the *Zeitgeist*, it was more an adaptation of the language of painting to that of architecture. The systems of pure, simple forms, sometimes transparent, that penetrate flowing space were explicitly associated with Cubism and fitted Le Corbusier's famous definition, of that time, of architecture as "the skillful, accurate and magnificent play of masses seen in light."

Symbolism Unadmitted

A contradiction between what was said and what was done was typical of early Modern architecture: Walter Gropius decried the term "International Style" but created an architectural style and spread a vocabulary of industrial forms that were quite removed from industrial processes. Adolf Loos condemned ornament yet applied beautiful patterns in his own designs and would have erected the most magnificent, if ironic, symbol in the history of skyscrapers if he had won the *Chicago Tribune* competition. The later work of Le Corbusier started a continuing tradition of unacknowledged symbolism, whose indigenous-vernacular forms, in varying manifestations, are still with us.

But it is the contradiction—or at least the lack of correspondence—between image and substance that confirms the role of symbolism and association in orthodox Modern architecture. As we have said, the symbolism of Modern architecture is usually technological and functional, but when these functional elements work symbolically, they usually do not work functionally, for example, Mies's symbolically exposed but substantively encased steel frame and Rudolph's *béton brut* in concrete block or his "mechanical" shafts used for an apartment house rather than a research lab. Some latter-day Modern architectural contradictions are the use of flowing space for private functions, glass walls for western exposures, industrial clerestories for suburban high schools, exposed ducts that collect dust and conduct sound, mass-produced systems for underdeveloped countries, and the impressions of wooden formwork in the concrete of high-labor-cost economies.

We catalog here the failures of these functional elements to function as structure, program, mechanical equipment, lighting, or industrial process, not to criticize them (although on functional grounds they would be criticized), but to demonstrate their symbolism. Nor are we interested in criticizing the functional-technological content of early Modern architectural symbolism. What we criticize is the symbolic content of current Modern architecture and the architect's refusal to acknowledge symbolism.

Modern architects have substituted one set of symbols (Cubist-industrial-process) for another (Romantic-historical-eclecticism) but without being aware of it. This has made for confusing and ironic contradictions that are still with us. The diversity of styles (not to mention the syntactical correctness and suave precision) of the architecture of the 1960s might challenge the versatility of a Victorian eclectic of the 1860s. . . .

High-Design Architecture

Finally, learning from popular culture does not remove the architect from his or her status in high culture. But it may alter high culture to make it more sympathetic to current needs and issues. Because high culture and its cultists (last year's variety) are powerful in urban renewal and other establishment circles, we feel that people's architecture as the people want it (and not as some architect decides Man needs it) does not stand much chance against urban renewal until it hangs in the academy and therefore is acceptable to the decision makers. Helping this to happen is a not-reprehensible part of the role of the high-design architect; it provides, together with moral subversion through irony and use of a joke to get to seriousness, the weapons of artists of nonauthoritarian temperament in social situations that do not agree with them. The architect becomes a jester.

Irony may be the tool with which to confront and combine divergent values in architecture for a pluralist society and to accommodate the differences in values that arise between architects and clients. Social classes rarely come together, but if they can make temporary alliances in the designing and building of multivalued community architecture, a sense of paradox and some irony and wit will be needed on all sides.

Understanding the content of Pop's messages and the way that it is projected does not mean that one need agree with, approve of, or reproduce that content. If the commercial persuasions that flash on the strip are materialistic manipulation and vapid subcommunication,[9] which cleverly appeal to our deeper drives but send them only superficial messages, it does not follow that we architects who learn from their techniques must reproduce the content or the superficiality of their messages. (But we are indebted to them for helping us to recognize that Modern architecture too has a content and a vapid one at that.) Just as Lichtenstein has borrowed the techniques and images of the comics to convey satire, sorrow, and irony rather than violent high adventure, so may the architect's high reader suggest sorrow, irony,

[9] Thomas Maldonado, *La speranza progettuale, ambiente e società*, Chapter 15, Nuovo Politecnico 35 (Turin: Einaudi, 1970).

love, the human condition, happiness, or merely the purpose within, rather than the necessity to buy soap or the possibility of an orgy. On the other hand, the interpretation and evaluation of symbolic content in architecture is an ambiguous process. The didactic symbolism of Chartres may represent to some the subleties of medieval theology and to others the depths of medieval superstition or manipulation. Manipulation is not the monopoly of crass commercialism. And manipulation works both ways: Commercial interests and the billboard lobby manipulate, but so do cultural lobbies and design review boards, when they use their intimidating prestige to promote antisign legislation and beautification.

Summary

The progressive, technological, vernacular, process-oriented, superficially socially concerned, heroic and original content of Modern architecture has been discussed before by critics and historians. Our point is that this content did not flow inevitably from the solving of functional problems but arose from Modern architects' unexplicated iconographic preferences and was manifest through a language—several languages—of form, and that formal languages and associational systems are inevitable and good, becoming tyrannies only when we are unconscious of them. Our other point is that the content of the unacknowledged symbolism of current Modern architecture is silly. We have been designing dead ducks.

We do not know if the time will come for serious architectural oceanographic urbanism, for example, as opposed to the present offshore posturing of the world futurist architectural visionaries. We suspect that one day it may, though hardly in the forms now envisioned. As practicing architects in the here and now, we do not have much interest in such predictions. We do know, however, that the chief resources of our society go into things with little architectural potential: war, electronic communication, outer space, and, to a much lesser extent, social services. As we have said, this is not the time and ours is not the environment for heroic communication via pure architecture.

When Modern architects righteously abandoned ornament on buildings, they unconsciously designed buildings that *were* ornament. In promoting Space and Articulation over symbolism and ornament, they distorted the whole building into a duck. They substituted for the innocent and inexpensive practice of applied decoration on a conventional shed the rather cynical and expensive distortion of program and structure to promote a duck; minimegastructures are mostly ducks. It is now time to reevaluate the once-horrifying statement of John Ruskin that architecture is the decoration of construction, but we should append the warnings of Pugin: It is all right to decorate construction but never construct decoration.

EPILOGUE:

WHERE ARE WE AT?

80   A. L. Huxtable, The Art of Expediency* *1968*

The announcement of impending demolition of Pennsylvania Station in 1963 quickly awoke many to the fact that American cities were losing their priceless architectural heritage, not just in New York where the loss was more dramatically visible, but everywhere. A quality of environment was disappearing, for the old buildings, even if they had columns and pediments, crockets and finials (and some even said *because* they had them) were far better than the speculative buildings that rose in their places. What surprised many were the champions who began to speak in defense of these threatened landmarks—such figures as Arthur Drexler, Lewis Mumford, Philip Johnson, and *New York Times* architectural critic, Ada Louise Huxtable.

Ada Louise Landman Huxtable, a native of New York and graduate of Hunter College, had worked under Johnson at the Museum of Modern Art as assistant curator, in the years 1946–50, pursuing during the following decade a career as freelance writer on architectural subjects, with articles in *Progressive Architecture* and *Art in America*. In 1963 she became architectural critic for the *New York Times*, and her sharp denunciations of scaleless, exploitative, speculative commercial building, which she asserted was killing American urban vitality, earned her a medal from the American Institute of Architects in 1969 and the first Pulitzer prize for distinguished criticism in 1970. She praised good modern design, but she also came to value good "traditional" work as well, so epitomized by Pennsylvania Station. Among her books were *Pier Luigi Nervi* (New York, 1960), and *Classic New York: Georgian Gentility to Greek Elegance* (Garden City, New York, 1964), the first of a projected series. Her most important books have been anthologies of her criticism: *Will They Ever Finish Bruckner Boulevard?* (New York, 1970), and *Kicked a Building Lately?* (New York, 1976).

There used to be a newspaper game called "What's wrong with this picture?" It was a cartoon in which there were a number of things wrong, from doors without handles and upside-down windows to pictures with mismatched halves hidden in the wallpaper. It was a world of cockeyed domesticity, antimacassared and cozily askew. The game was to find and list all the errors, or deviations from the norm.

What's wrong with the pictures on page 637? The ruins of Penn Station in the Secaucus Meadows and a new subway entrance in its replacement building are not quite so simple. To begin with, what they show is the norm, in a world far from cozy and quite askew. They pose disturbing questions and touch problems that go to the core of a culture in which destruction and regeneration, art and nihilism, are becoming indistinguishable. But they say a great deal about how things are, and why, in the world that man is building for himself today.

The picture of what remains of Penn Station in its burial ground in the

*Ada Louise Huxtable, "The Art of Expediency," *New York Times*, May 26, 1968, reprinted in A. L. Huxtable, *Will They Ever Finish Bruckner Boulevard?* (New York, 1970), pp. 143–47.

Figure 64. Wreckage of Pennsylvania Station dumped in the Secaucus Meadows, N.J., (photo: Edward Hausner, courtesy New York Times Pictures).

Figure 65. Subway entrance in the new Pennsylvania Station, New York, N.Y., 1964–66 (photo: William E. Sauro, courtesy New York Times Pictures).

Secaucus Meadows shows a fragment of a classical figure and shards of columns in a setting of macabre surrealist *vérité*.[1] The subway entrance is part of the vast Madison Square Garden–Penn Station complex.

Superficially, the message is terribly clear. Tossed into the Secaucus graveyard are about twenty-five centuries of classical culture and the standards of style, elegance and grandeur that it gave to the dreams and constructions of Western man. That turns the Jersey wasteland into a pretty classy dump.

As for the subway entrance, you could say, in abstract, clinical design terms, that there is nothing very much wrong with it at all: clean tilework, acceptable good graphics, a direct, non-flashy solution to a routine functional problem. And yet—it is a singularly grim picture. It speaks volumes on alienation through architecture. Kafka or Sartre never said it better. That single human figure, equally isolated in a crowd, proceeds through the chill, bleak anonymity of the twentieth-century transit catacombs (ancient catacombs softened even death with frescoes) in a setting of impersonal, ordinary sterility that could just as well be a clean, functional gas chamber. The human spirit and human environment have reached absolute zero.

The easiest indictment to make is that this is a failure of modern architecture. That we have exchanged caryatids and columns for a mess of functional pottage and that Secaucus is the final resting place of our culture.

It would be simple, and false. It is the nostalgic argument of those who believe that re-creating the appearance of the past will bring back the reality of the past or the values of the past. Nothing could be farther from the truth. It is the kind of reasoning that makes well-intentioned people think it is a good idea, for example, to build Benjamin Latrobe's unrealized eighteenth-century theater for Richmond now, because all the drawings still exist.

At the least, that is begging the twentieth century; at the worst, it is the denial and corruption of creativity in our own time. No number of archeological constructions or caryatids can put that world back together again. There is something terribly pathetic in the self-delusory belief that it can be done.

Today's architecture is the highest dramatic revelation of changes in technology, structure, style and need in a revolutionary age. It is one of the genuine revolutions in our revolution-high times. Its monuments are superb; its potential develops constantly.

What that subway picture represents is simply the esthetics of economics. The results are, as much as possible, vandal proof, dirt proof, extravagance proof and delight proof—a kind of penitentiary style. The esthetics of economics characterize not only our common commercial construction but also the institutions and public buildings that were once meant to symbolize the shaky nobility of man. The economic standard is as accepted today as the four orders were in Rome.

Take, for example, the old and new Jersey City courthouses built side by side as if to deliberately make the point. The old courthouse—a solid, turn-of-the-century Beaux-Arts monument of marble, murals and soaring rotunda space—has been in and out of the news in its battle for existence. Its

---

[1] Since then, the classical fragments have been pulverized and buried as "fill," and the "prepared" site offered for commercial development. No trace remains.

replacement, the new courthouse, says nothing about the majesty of the law (the passion for breaking it right now simply underlines its importance) and a great deal about the society that built it. It says that society is mean and cheap and that it considers excellence a gratuitous commodity.

But the real point is that it is a dead match to Jersey City. This is the kind of city that the esthetics of economics makes; a tawdry, formless limbo of hamburger joints, discount stores, parking lots, matchbox houses, cheap office buildings, automobile salesrooms, jarring signs and disruptive highway spaghetti. It is the environment of expediency.

Today we have politics that preach destruction and art that acts out destruction; perhaps this is the architecture of destruction. As we said about something else, society gets the cities it deserves. The courthouse only underlines the process.

Curiously, it is not the Establishment or the older generation that sees old buildings in contemporary urban terms. It is the young people, the architects and city-oriented intellectuals who have rejected the Utopian idea of an artificially imposed new order of the last professional generation and who believe in change, complexity, contrast and a multi-dimensional urban scene. They are not antiquarians. But they are the ones who lead visitors to Victorian monuments, early Chicago skyscrapers, cast-iron buildings in New York, old Texas houses. These are the young professionals who are testing architecture in the shifting values of a world in crisis.

"Values" is a word they avoid, but the commitment to values is there. They are not the values handed down by society or the past. They are often the denial of values as conventionally understood. Realists and futurists, the present generation finds some of its values even in the environment of expediency. Art and life always coexist.

If the wreckage of the nineteenth century is in the Secaucus Meadows, and the failure of the twentieth century is in the landscape of alienation, the promise of the art of building is very much alive. It is not in the individual structure as traditionally designed, but in the relationships of people, land and buildings for life and use—it is in the esthetic and human ferment that is currently called architecture.

81 A. L. Huxtable, Rediscovering the Beaux-Arts* *1975*

Younger scholars had been at work investigating Beaux-Arts and "traditional" architects during the late 1960s, and this editor had participated in the republication of the large *Monograph of the Work of McKim, Mead & White, 1879–1915* (New York, 1973). A rising interest in architectural drawings as works of art in their own right was demonstrated by the exhibition of H. H. Richardson's drawings, 1974, organized by James F. O'Gorman, who also wrote the carefully annotated catalogue. But the enterprise which captured both professional and public attention was the exhibition of École des Beaux-Arts *projet* drawings at the Museum of Modern Art in late 1975, organized by Arthur Drexler. It was as if oil and water had miraculously been made to mix, for the Museum and Drexler had long been the most ardent champions of antihistoricist modernism. So long stored away in Paris as to have been forgotten except to a handful, the huge colored renderings were infrequently published and then only in small murky black and white reproductions. Now presented at their full scale and brilliance, the expansive drawings made it clear that a high standard of draftsmanship had been abandoned; but even more, the accompanying researches of Chafee, Van Zanten, and Levine elucidated a coherent body of theory beneath the drawing.† Of the many notices of the exhibition, this one by Ada Louise Huxtable summarized well its intrinsic importance and what it said concerning the profession in 1975.

The Museum of Modern Art's major fall exhibition, "The Architecture of the Ecole des Beaux-Arts," is clearly meant as an object lesson to architects (particularly to young ones) and a question raiser for everyone. These questions are serious and heretical ones about the doctrine and dogma of modern architecture—the movement that the museum was sublimely instrumental in establishing. They are part of a broader questioning of the whole modern movement reflected in a rising interest in the work of the rejected Academy, the establishment mainstream in all of the arts against which the modernists rebelled.

The Modern's show is, therefore, an extremely significant polemical and art historical event. It follows the Metropolitan's eye-opening and ground-breaking display of nineteenth-century academic French painting last spring, which proclaimed the Academy's return to respectability in pow-

---

*Ada Louise Huxtable, "Rediscovering the Beaux-Arts," *The New York Review*, November 27, 1975, reprinted in A. L. Huxtable, *Kicked a Building Lately?* (New York, 1976), pp. 58–66.

†Unfortunately the exhibition did not travel. The historical background was presented in detail in the handsome book which followed the exhibition: Arthur Drexler, ed., *The Architecture of the École des Beaux-Arts* (New York, 1977); the chapters by Richard Chafee, David Van Zanten, and Neil Levine dealt with early institutional history, mid-nineteenth-century theory, and the contribution of Henri Labrouste. See, too, the study by D. D. Egbert noted on p. 324.

erful, tastemaking art circles, and its assumption of the position of a kind of reverse avant-garde. That show was also a brilliant act of scholarship.

All this is equally true of the Beaux-Arts show. As everyone who follows events of the art world probably knows by now, this is a whopping, more-than-200-item presentation of architectural drawings produced by the students of the Ecole des Beaux-Arts in Paris from the late eighteenth to the early twentieth century, representing the kind of building (and training) that was specifically rejected (and despised) by the leaders of the modernist revolution.

The concept of the exhibition, the painstaking selection of material from forgotten and neglected archives, the application of rigorous research and a knowing eye, must be credited to Arthur Drexler, the director of the museum's Department of Architecture and Design; his achievement is an impressive one. His collaborators in organizing the exhibition and preparing its catalogue, which will be augmented by an important, profusely illustrated book of detailed and murky scholarship later this year, are David Van Zanten, Neil Levine, and Richard Chafee.

There is considerable shock effect for the viewer entering these galleries, so long sacrosanct to the modernists' cause, now filled with huge, precisely and exquisitely rendered classical and eclectic facades of monumental, palatial, and arguably unnecessary casinos, cathedrals, conservatories, water circuses, royal residences, and reconstructions of Greek and Roman antiquities. It is even more of a shock to realize that these frequently superb, if occasionally wildly overreaching, exercises in grandeur were largely the work of students in their late teens and early twenties, responding to a discipline of the hand and mind absolutely unknown today.

While each student progressed individually, his development was rigidly controlled by the *concours* given at every stage of advancement, and by the expertise with which he executed his competition entries. (The Beaux-Arts system, with its indentured ateliers copied from France, dominated architectural education in the United States from the 1860s to the 1930s, until the advent of Gropius and the Bauhaus. It led to the establishment, in emulation of the Prix de Rome and the French Academy, of the American Academy in Rome—a gentlemen's club for creative and scholarly research that is only now facing extinction.) The basic solution to an architectural problem had to be set down in a twelve-hour *esquisse* and then adhered to in the *projet rendu,* which took three to six months to execute. The architects were relentlessly separated from the boys right at the start by the ability to devise a solution immediately, and then to execute it with the highest degree of skill—a painstaking, perfectionist rendering of plan, section, and elevation in a style and technique formularized over two centuries.

The drawings, just as drawings, in ink and colored wash, are magnificent. They are at once grand and delicate, detailed and abstract. In their finished precision, they parallel the Academy in painting, but the similarity stops with the care of execution. The detail was there not to satisfy a nineteenth-century taste and sentiment for verisimilitude but because these were professional architectural renderings upon which the next step, the production of measured working drawings for construction, would be based—if they had not been student projects. Literal, perspective renderings were disdained as less-than-accurate, unprofessional illustrations of the architect's intent, and although they were pushed by Viollet-le-Duc during his aborted Ecole reforms, they never caught on. This careful drawing, therefore, does not approach the polished or licked surface ("*le fini*") of Academy painting,[1] in part because the work was never meant for the public, which judged by realism and finish, but for the professional architectural juries that evaluated them in the endless Ecole competitions. In fact, this is probably the first time that the public has seen these drawings at all, at least in a coordinated display.

A point that Drexler doesn't mind making with the show is that few architecture students can draw today, any more than they can spell or write; there is no requirement for this level of skill. Model-making has become a substitute for draftsmanship. It also frequently substitutes for thinking, and even for design, because it so drastically cuts down the range of conceptualization that can be achieved with the far more flexible pencil in hand. Drexler frankly hopes that this fact will not go unnoticed.

What he hopes most of all is that people will be startled and even seriously upset by the show, which does not—in the museum's customary fashion—present its historicism as proto-modern, but as countermodern. Because Drexler is hellbent on counterrevolution. "History," he says, "is written by the victors, and what they leave out is the losers." In fact, what the architectural modernists attempted to do was to bring history to a halt. Not only was the past rejected out of hand, but the present was to have nothing to do with it. Unlike modern painting, in which a sense of continuity with the past can be traced, however tortuously, from, say, Courbet and the impressionists to cubism, architecture attempted to make the break absolute. The Bauhaus and its successors succeeded in jettisoning history—the Futurists had only hoped to destroy museums and their contents. They were aided by the fact that the industrial and technological revolution made the materials of their art, unlike paint and canvas, totally new; so by abandoning masonry for steel and concrete and a new structural-aesthetic potential, a new vocabulary of forms was made legitimately possible. In one very real sense, this made history and its lessons irrelevant, although they were lessons that the early, Beaux-Arts-trained modernists were never able to forget.

A new absolute was invented—timelessness—and its justifications were ruthlessly edited. For the orderly progression of civilization a false kind of scientistic myth of art-as-technology was substituted, married to the quasi-religious morality of the machine aesthetic. And to make that aesthetic more complex, a new kind of relationship was established with painting. In spite of vows of structural functionalism, both new and old materials were used in building to create a romanticized resemblance to the flat, painterly, geometric abstractions of cubism. Although modernist painting and architecture shared the rejection of the Academy and both contributed to the distortion of the past, only architecture abolished it. But history did not pack up and go away; it stayed, all too solidly, in the cities, and the new buildings violated

[1] See the interesting discussion of *le fini* in nineteenth-century French Academy painting by Charles Rosen and Henri Zerner in their essay "*L'antichambre du Louvre ou l'idéologie du fini*" in the French journal *Critique*, November 1974.

their historic context with an unprecedented vengeance.

And so the exhibition is first of all a revisionist reconsideration of history. But Drexler brusquely rejects any idea of it as an incentive to revivalism. He does not, however, reject the idea of eclecticism as a next step in architecture, although he claims no clairvoyance about the forms it will take.

It is therefore possible to enjoy the display just as a treasury of nineteenth-century styles and standards—revelations of a now unreal world. The drawings are all competition-winners, from the lesser *concours* to the coveted Prix de Rome. The consistent theme is the now discarded classical tradition, the underpinning of the French Academy. But the examples cover everything from late-eighteenth- and early-nineteenth-century romantic classicism to the exotic revivals of the later nineteenth century and the final, consummated, official Beaux-Arts style.

Official meant more than establishment. This is all official architecture in a sense we no longer comprehend—it was not just that it was concerned with public buildings, which was how the Beaux-Arts defined architecture, but that it was state architecture, taught, commissioned, and controlled by a central government authority. The Ecole was a state school, an outgrowth and affiliate of the Academy established by the monarchy in the seventeenth century. The Academy dominated teaching and practice. Its graduates went on to do all official, state-sponsored construction and private construction simply followed along. Ecole graduates automatically received the prominent or prestigious commissions, and were eventually elected to the Academy, a position from which they continued to dictate style and practice to the Ecole.

The exhibition selection begins with the eighteenth-century work of Peyre and Vaudoyer, who influenced so much of the Ecole's teachings, and goes through a galaxy of nineteenth-century ornate and eclectic modes. The arcades of Louis-Ambroise Dubut's Granary of 1797, stretching to near-infinity, recall the almost surreal serenity of Boullée and Ledoux (Dubut was a pupil of Ledoux), and they prefigure Durand's prototypical classical solutions for France's civil engineers. Charles Percier, later one of the chief architects for Napoleon and the Empire, is present with a student project for a colonnaded Menagerie of a Sovereign in 1783. Louis Duc's Colosseum studies (1829), Marie-Antoine Delannoy's Restoration of Tiber Island (1832), and Edouard Loviot's Parthenon Restoration (1881) contributed significantly to the nineteenth-century's lust for classical (not to say imperial) antiquities. François-Louis Boulanger's Library of 1834 could be the work of an ancestor of Louis Kahn (and is, in a sense, since Kahn and other early modernists were Beaux-Arts products) in its "served and servant spaces" and love of courts and walls.

By the end of the nineteenth century, as projects grew ever larger and more elaborate, Louis-Hippolyte Boileau's Casino of 1897 offered a pastry-fantasy in a facile, painterly rendering of a world *perdu*. An 1891 railroad station by Henri-Thomas-Edouard Eustache is so supercolossal in scale that it had to be framed on the museum wall, or it could not have been brought into the building. Tony Garnier's Central State Bank of 1899 symbolizes and synthesizes what had by then become known, internationally, as the Beaux-Arts way of building: the axiomatic French classical manner for the imposing free-standing public monument composed in a calculated, progressive hierarchy of functions, movement, and spaces—composition, *marche*, and *parti*.

A single gallery is devoted to two of the most important, realized structures of leading Beaux-Arts architects—Henri Labrouste's Bibliothèque Sainte-Geneviève of 1845–1850 and Charles Garnier's Paris Opera of 1861–1874, each a textbook study of successful nineteenth-century design. Modernists have been able to admire the library for its handsome and progressive metal framing; the Opera, in spite of the brilliant social and ceremonial planning that it displays, has baffled them with its sensuous decorative excess. Two other galleries contain photographs of executed Beaux-Arts buildings in France and the United States. And as a complement to the exhibition, the Architectural League has prepared a guide to Beaux-Arts buildings in New York, available at the museum.

In the final analysis, however, the chief purpose of this show is to serve as the big gun of the re-examination of the modern movement that is currently under way in episodic fits and starts. The aim obviously goes far beyond historical or esthetic exposition. Its calculated objective is to provoke a far-reaching critique of all contemporary architecture. There has already been much criticism and debate about this subject of course, but most of it tends to be either smugly academic or chicly exotic and arcane in its cultural and historical references. The architect-debaters themselves are given to such gestures as adding naughty paste-on moldings to their safely modernist facades. Most of this has been a tempest in an eyedropper, based on self-indulgent *épater la bourgeoisie* esthetics. The one real contribution has been the heretically perceptive work of Robert and Denise Scott Brown Venturi, with its emphasis on the aspects of complexity and contradiction in architecture, and of inclusivity rather than exclusivity in the environment.

But as important as such a contribution may be, it is still a fragmentary response to a large philosophical problem. In addition to polemical discussion, there is a burgeoning interest in the phenomena of the near past and the modern movement's near-misses. Books are proliferating on Art Moderne and Deco and the Skyscraper Style and such early figures as George Howe, who, with William Lescaze, designed the seminal Philadelphia Savings Fund Society Building. There is bound to be a resurgence of critical analysis of work by almost forgotten or downgraded names, among them Ely Jacques Kahn, Barry Byrne, and Irving Pond. The transitional buildings of Bertram Goodhue and James Gamble Rogers, who have always made the modernists profoundly uneasy, are in for inevitable re-evaluation.

The focus will shift, not always clearly. It is also likely that this esthetic revival will further obscure the essential contributions of men like Clarence Stein to social planning. The cardinal virtues of the modern movement—clarity, simplicity, and logic, qualities extremely rare in art and life—are going to be compromised and downgraded. They are fragile, easily compromised values at best, the first casualties of confusion, pretension, and perverted creativity. These rational responses are the essence of good and great architecture of all periods and styles, as necessary to the Beaux-Arts as to the Bauhaus. Bad architecture is by nature unclear and irrational (not to be confused with the delights of complexity and contradiction). But elaborate bad architecture, the worst kind of all, is what the wrong kind of theory can produce.

Not the least of the probing will be institutional—the role of the Museum of Modern Art then and now. Indeed the relation of the Beaux-Arts administration in Paris to state and economic power could usefully be examined and compared to the situation in architectural patronage today. There will be a lot of belated bandwagon-jumping. But we have reached a point in history where a kind of flawed perspective is beginning to emerge. And the mirror of hindsight combines revelation and narcissism to a seductive degree.

One lesson always looming implicitly in the Beaux-Arts exhibition is that less has indeed become less. Its primary protest is against the relentless stripping down that has characterized the modernist esthetic. By demonstrating what the modern movement denied, it forces the thinking viewer to reconsider what Drexler calls the "platitudes of functionalism," or the modern doctrine of functionalism as a "euphemism for utility." It is also a euphemism for economy and a rationalization for cheapness when building costs are rising relentlessly—a factor Drexler might consider more seriously. (The non-thinking viewer, as always, will like being told what to think by the Museum of Modern Art. But that brings up another subject—whether trends are found or made by our powerful institutions.)

Drexler's point is that utility, or the narrow adherence to use and functional structure as the primary source of the building art, has had an unexpected and undesired result: the impoverishment of architectural design. So many of the expressive and stylistic possibilities of art have been rejected by the modernist practitioner either as superfluous hedonism or as a dangerous kind of playfulness that is not essential to survival—a rationale and rejection that are the routine, predictable, joyless accompaniment of all revolutionary doctrine. Not just decoration but sensuosity and symbolism are casualties. In architecture the suppressed (and unsuppressable) instinct for pleasure and experiment has reemerged as a distorted kind of "play" with form—the stretching and torturing of structure into perverse works of object-sculpture with equally perverse structural and functional rationales—the Venturis' "ducks." Today's architect has built himself into a corner.

At the same time that the Museum is pointing out these failures, it is perpetuating one of the most serious fallacies of the modern movement—the exclusive ideal of the isolated monumental building carried over from the Beaux-Arts by the modernists, a concept that proved impervious to revolution or modification. This institution, dedicated to the life and art of our time, is insisting that nothing of importance has changed except style—that only the monument is still architecture. And it is saying this in the face of a radical change in environmental perceptions that has profoundly altered the art of architecture in our day.

Still, the examination of the Beaux-Arts has an almost eerie relevance right now. By the end of the nineteenth century the work of the Academy reached the point where it was increasingly dedicated to forced and fantastic formal invention, while fundamentally adhering to the monumental conventions of the Beaux-Arts style. Modern architecture has reached that same point (it is also today's Academy) of strained invention within what appear increasingly to be the crippling restrictions of functionalism. The problem here is not with functionalism per se, but the doctrinaire and almost mindless paralysis to which it has been reduced. Today there is also the jarring effect of such architecture on the receiving environment to be considered as well as its place in the history of cities, which are the remarkable survivors of continuing, temporal catastrophes. The barriers to dealing understandingly with the academic past are still great, however; in painting there is the overload of unacceptable sentiment and emphasis on surface, and in architecture the hurdle of a puritan ethic of structure and design.

These questions of art and function, meaning and invention, of creativity and sterility, of commission and omission, are being asked in all of the arts today. But the situation is perhaps unique in architecture. If what is being debated, to a large extent, are the limitations of reduction, or the validity of minimalism, it is above all architecture that has made the philosophy and practice of reduction into a moral imperative rather than an esthetic exploration. Modern architecture since the Bauhaus has based its claims not just on purity of form but on purity of art and soul and societal mission. Only now are we seeing the death of the architect as a self-conceived superman, or kind of god, in a world that scarcely wants him.

Perhaps he was more of a god when he built palaces and pantheons, but both princely and social roles have turned out to be exercises in futility. The end came to the Beaux-Arts in small things: the design of an elevator, an electric chandelier, a utility pole. They had to be conceived of as a sedan chair, an electrified candelabrum, a torchère or baldachino with wires. The intrinsic failure was the inability to visualize the needs of a newly industrialized society, to come to terms with the kind of construction it would require. This the Beaux-Arts never even grasped. It could not recognize the real substance and challenges of the twentieth century. Modernism is clearly entering another age of problematic transition. Are the answers eluding us now?

82   R. A. M. Stern, The Doubles of Post-Modernism* *1980*

"Where are we at?," the question posed by Philip Johnson in 1960 in response to Reyner Banham's wry analysis of *Theory and Design in the First Machine Age* (London, 1960), is even more pertinent now more than a score of years later.† As there have always been, so there are now multiple elements making up the architectural profession—the rear-guard, the "middle-guard," and the avant-grade. In this instance there are two factions to the avant-grade—the neo-purists who advocate

---

*Robert A. M. Stern, "The Doubles of Post-Modernism," *The Harvard Architecture Review* 1 (1980), pp. 75–87.

†Philip Johnson, "Where are we at?," *Architectural Review* 127 (September 1960), pp. 173–75.

non-referential form, and the Eclectic traditionalists of "Post-Modernism" who have achieved particular prominence since 1975. Creative eclecticism, as first defined by Carroll L. V. Meeks, is enjoying a decided resurgence.‡ And chief among its spokemen is architect Robert A. M. Stern.

Born in New York City in 1939, Stern earned his bachelor's degree at Columbia, completing a Master of Architecture at Yale University in 1965. During the following year he was a designer in Richard Meier's office and in 1969 formed a partnership with John S. Hagmann (his firm is now known as Robert A. M. Stern Architects). Like his mentors, Kahn and Venturi, Stern divides his time between the drafting table and the class room; he is associate professor of architecture at Columbia and has had visiting appointments at the Rhode Island School of Design and the University of Pennsylvania, among other schools. His writing has spanned a broad range, beginning with a summary of current trends in *New Directions in American Architecture* (New York, 1969, revised 1977). His *George Howe: Toward a Modern American Architecture* (New Haven, 1975), was a major reassessment of this important designer and educator who grappled with the issue of a modern idiom. He also contributed to *The Architect's Eye: American Architectural Drawings from 1799–1978* (New York, 1979), written with Deborah Nevins, and he prepared the commentary notes for *Philip Johnson: Writings* (New York, 1979). A frequent contributor to architectural journals, his "Stomping at the Savoye," 1973, was part of a group of five articles in response to *Five Architects* (New York, 1972), which had become the principal statement of the neo-purist "White" architects.§ In the essay reprinted here, Stern constructs a rigorously buttressed argument for historicist allusion in architecture as the interrupted continuation of a humanism in architecture extending back over six centuries. This essay may well become the corresponding exegesis of Post-Modern theory.

. . . cubism and superrealism [surrealism], far from being the dawn of a style, are the end of a period of self-consciousness, inbreeding and exhaustion. One thing seems clear to me: that no new style will grow out of a preoccupation with art for its own sake. It can only arise from a new interest in subject matter. We need a new myth in which the symbols are inherently pictorial.[1]

What has been called Modern architecture for the past 50 years is in disarray: though such leading architects as Paul Rudolph, I. M. Pei, and Kevin Roche continue to produce major new work, the forms as well as the theories on which that work is based are systematically being questioned by

‡ See the presentation of Creative Eclecticism in C. L. V. Meeks, *The Railroad Station* (New Haven, 1955), pp. 1–25; and his "Creative Eclecticism," *Journal, Society of Architectural Historians* 11 (1953), pp. 15–18.

§ R. A. M. Stern, "Stomping at the Savoye," *Architectural Forum* 138 (May 1973), pp. 46–48.

[1] Kenneth Clark, "Boredom Blamed," *Art Digest*, Vol X (November 15, 1943) 3. I am indebted to Peter Eisenman, Kenneth Frampton and Vincent Scully for reading and commenting on portions of this manuscript in a much earlier stage of its development; Suzanne Stephens has read it more recently. What is written here is much the better for their advice. Nonetheless, I am sure they will be relieved to learn, I take full responsibility for the final product.

a growing number of younger architects who perceive the waning of modernism and who are questioning the prevailing philosophic basis for architecture and its form language. This questioning sensibility has come to be described, alternately and rather imprecisely, as "Post-Modern" or "Post-Modernist."[2]

Charles Jencks' book, *The Language of Post-Modern Architecture*, is the first to explore the new mood and to begin to erect a scaffolding of theory for post-modernism.[3] Jencks suggests that the term "Post-Modern" is at best "negative and evasive." Nonetheless it does enjoy some precedent in architecture.[4]

The terms "modernism" and "post-modernism" have been used in other disciplines besides architecture, including political history and literary and art criticism. In each of these disciplines, they suggest two different conditions resulting in related sets of what I would describe as "doubles"—the doubles of modernism and of post-modernism. Both grow out of the same two distinct but interrelated sensibilities or conditions, and both fall within the Modern—that is Western Humanist/Post-Renaissance—period.

These conditions affect both modernism and post-modernism. Borrowing the term from Frank Kermode, I would label the first of these conditions "schismatic." The schismatic condition argues for a clean break with Western Humanism. I would label the second condition "traditional," borrowing the term from Stephen Spender. It argues for a recognition of the continuity of the Western Humanist tradition. Traditional modernism can be "conceived of as a return, at once spontaneous, willed to eternal values long forgotten or buried but which a reborn or renewed historical memory makes

---

[2] Portions of this text are based on material introduced by me on previous occasions: See "Postscript at the Edge of Modernism," in my *New Directions in American Architecture*, 2nd edition, revised (New York: Braziller, 1977) 117–136; "Five Houses," G. A. *Houses*, 1 (1976) 36–41; *Architectural Design*, 47, #4 (May 1977); "Something Borrowed, Something New," *Horizon*, 20, #4 (December 1977) 50–57.

[3] Charles Jencks, *The Language of Post-Modern Architecture* (London: Academy Editions, 1977); see also, Jencks, "Post-Modern History," *Architectural Design*, 48, #1 (January 1978) 11–62.

[4] The term seems to have been initiated by Joseph Hudnut in his essay "The post-modern house," *Architectural Record*, 97 (May 1945) 70–75, which was reprinted as Chapter 9 in Hudnut's *Architecture and the Spirit of Man* (Cambridge, MA: Harvard, 1949) 109–119.

Its earliest influential use was in Arnold J. Toynbee's, *A Study in History*, 8 (New York: Oxford, 1954–59) 338.

Peter Eisenman and I discussed the term and its probable definition at considerable length in the summer of 1975. I first "went public" with a definition for the term in relationship to architecture in 1976, using it to characterize a shift in mood represented by an event—the Beaux-Arts exhibition at the Museum of Modern Art—and a shifting of alliances among the architects who constituted the "White" and "Gray" groups of the mid-1970s. See my "Possibly, the Beaux-Arts Exhibit means something after all (with apology to Clement Greenberg, Rosalind Kraus and the month of October)," a paper delivered at the "Oppositions Forum," Institute for Architecture and Urban Studies, 22 January 1976, and published in William Ellis, editor, "Forum of the Beaux-Arts Exhibition," *Oppositions* 8 (Spring 1977) 169–171; see also my "Gray Architecture as Post-Modernism or Up and Down from Orthodoxy" (Gray Architecture: *Quelques Variations Post-Modernistes autour de L'Orthodoxie*), *L'Architecture d'Aujourd'hui*, 186 (Aout/Septembre 1976) 83.

once again present"; schismatic modernism can be seen as a sensibility in which "the new and the modern [are] seen in terms of a birth rather than a rebirth, not a restoration but . . . a construction of the present and future not on the foundations of the past but on the ruins of time."[5]

The two modernisms can be distinguished by their attitudes toward the past: "traditional" modernism, typified by the writings of Proust or Eliot or the paintings of Picasso, views the past as a source of order; "schismatic" modernism, typified by the work of Duchamp or Mondrian, views the past as a burden. Although the two kinds of modernism are distinct, they are linked by an apocalyptic view of the future and by a recognition of Western Humanism as an on-going condition.

It is important to reiterate that the Modern period as a whole encompasses a continuing tradition of humanistic thought and action though some of its stylistic movements—for example Dada and Surrealism—regard humanism as a yoke.

Like the two modernisms, the two post-modernisms can be distinguished by their attitudes toward the past. While the schismatic Post-Modern condition posits a break with both modernism and the Modern period itself, the traditional Post-Modern condition proposes to free new production from the rigid constraints of modernism, especially from its most radical and nihilistic aspects (as exemplified by Dada and Surrealism) while simultaneously reintegrating itself with other strains of Western Humanism, especially those which characterize its last pre-modernist phase, that of the Romanticism which flourished between 1750 and 1850.[6] Thus, schismatic post-modernism is a sensibility that considers itself not only beyond modernism but also outside the Modern period, one which seeks to establish the mode of thought and artistic production that is as free from the 500-year tradition of Western Humanism as that mode was, in its turn, free from the previous Gothic era of religious scholasticism. Traditional post-modernism, on the other hand, is one that seeks to reintegrate or subsume modernism within the broad category of the Modern period as a whole.

In post-modernism, the distinctions between traditional and schismatic conditions are useful in illuminating the distinctions between the work of John Gardner and William Gass in literature or of Peter Eisenman and Michael Graves in architecture. Though the term "Post-Modern" appears to be used to describe sensibilities and theories that share as common ground a reaction to the modernism which has dominated much of the cultural activity of the past 125 years, the traditional and schismatic conditions serve to distinguish between distinct sensibilities within the Post-Modern devolution; these distinctions have at their core the question of the relationship between new work and the tradition of humanism which characterized the Modern period itself.

Thus the doubles of the Post-Modern: two distinct but interrelated

[5] Renato Poggioli, *The Theory of the Avant Garde* (Cambridge, MA: Harvard, 1968) translated by Gerald Fitzgerald, 217; see also, Daniel Bell, *The Cultural Contradictions of Capitalism* (New York: Basic Books, 1976) 34; Frank Kermode, *Continuities* (London: Routledge & Kegan Paul, 1968) 8.

[6] See Stephen Spender, *The Struggle of the Modern* (Berkeley: University of California, 1963) passim.

Post-Modern sensibilities: a schismatic condition that argues for a *clean break* with the 400 year old tradition of Western Humanism and a "traditional" condition that argues for a return to, or a recognition of, the *continuity* of the cultural tradition of Western Humanism of which it holds modernism to be a part.

> Somebody should write the history of the word "modern." The OED isn't very helpful, though most of the senses the word now has have been in the air since the 16th century, and are actually older than Shakespeare's way of using it to mean "commonplace". . . . The New is to be judged by the criterion of novelty, the Modern implies or at any rate permits a serious relationship with the past, a relationship that requires criticism and indeed radical reimagining.[7]

In order to clarify what is meant by the term "Modern" in the phrase "Post-Modern," it is necessary to establish clear definitions for the related terms "Modern" and "modernism." Such a seemingly pedantic exercise is necessary because the distinctions between the older terms have become blurred by daily use, and they have become ineffective for discourse.

What can be called the "Modern period" begins in the 15th century with the birth of Humanism. The renaissance of classicism in architecture is the first of the Modern stylistic phases: the Baroque and the Rococo are subsequent Modern styles. The International Style of ca. 1920–60 is also a Modern style, often thought to be *the* Modern Style in which the meaning of the word "Modern" is transformed and limited so as to represent only those values more properly described as "modernist," a term which describes the urge to produce new artistic work that eschews all known form-language and, ideally, all grammar, in favor of a new self-referential (i.e., in architecture, functionally and technologically determined) language of form whose principal cultural responsibility is toward its moment in time. Modernism sees art as a manifestation of the *zeitgeist;* it strives to reflect the moment of its conception. Modernism, in the most oversimplified terms, represents a moralistic application of a superior value to that which is not only new but also independent of all previous production.

Modernism views the present as a state of continuing crisis; it sees history only as a record of experiences, a body of myth, but not as objective truth, and it is apocalyptic in its relationship to the future. A person who believes in the sensibility of "modernism" is a "modernist" as well as a "Modern," the latter term being the more general one and simply referring to someone who has lived in the "Modern" period and has contended with or at least recognized the issue of "modernity" but who has not necessarily adopted a modernist stance.[8]

Modernism is not a style in and of itself in the sense that the Renaissance and Baroque were styles with unifying principles. It can be regarded as a succession of attempts to redefine the syntax and the grammar of artistic

---

[7] Kermode, *op. cit.*, 27–28.

[8] See Kermode, *op. cit.*, 8, 13; Kermode observes that "the fact that defining the modern is a task that now imposes itself on many distinguished scholars may be a sign that the modern period is over," p 28. See also, Bell, *op. cit.*, 40–52.

composition (the poems of Mallarmé, the stream of consciousness of Joyce and Woolf; the buildings of Mies van der Rohe and Le Corbusier). As a result, and rather perversely, to the extent that it has deliberately been made difficult and inaccessible, artistic production has also shown itself to be modernist. In some cases, there has been an effort to go beyond issues of syntax and grammar and to seek to establish new form languages which, because they are not culturally based (that is, familiar), are by necessity personal or self-referential.[9]

Modernism does not accept the appearance of things as they are in nature and in the man-made world; it seeks always to take them apart in order to discover their hidden and presumably essential character. Modernism seeks to close and ultimately to eliminate the distance between the object perceived and the person perceiving the object. It seeks to do this in two ways: by insisting that all experience and thereby all art exists in the present—Giedion's phrase was the "eternal present"—and by insisting that each work of art and each act of artistic production is a personal act.[10] This presentism and the self-referential aspect of artistic production are fundamental to any examination of the nature of modernism in relationship to the issue of an on-going culture which we call the Western Humanist tradition.

It has been argued that modernism can never be part of any tradition, that it is a thing apart, a parallel tradition to Western Humanism. This issue of modernism as a sensibility apart from the Modern has resulted in that plethora of modernist styles or isms which has made the history of the literature and art of the last 125 years seem so confusing and troubled.

While the term "Modern" as in the phrase "the Modern period," is a term of historical description (like "the Middle Ages"), it is also a term of sensibility and style. It can be used as the term Baroque is used—with and without a capital "B." One can exhibit a baroque or a modern turn of mind while acting outside the Baroque or Modern period.

As a term describing a style, the use of the word "modern" opens up a veritable Pandora's box of confusion: for example, "L'Art Nouveau," for a while known as "Le Style Moderne," is a style in the Modern period and, more specifically, it was a "modernist" style in that it sought to stand free of the *historical continuum*. At the same time, insofar as it is the "fine art" manifestation of the bohemianism of the *fin de siecle* it also represents a sensibility.

Another meaning for "modern" is up-to-date or "contemporary." The term contemporary cannot be used to describe a stylistic sensibility because

[9] See Clement Greenberg, "Modernist Painting" in Gregory Battcock, editor, *The New Art* (New York: Dutton, 1973, revised edition) 100–110.

William Jordy, "The Symbolic Essence of Modern European Architecture of the Twenties and its Continuing Influence," *JSAH*, XXII, #3 (October 1973) 117.

[10] David Watkin writes that "an art historical belief in the all dominating *Zeitgeist*, combined with a historicist emphasis on progress and the necessary superiority of novelty, has come dangerously close to undermining, on the one hand, our appreciation of the genius of the individual and, on the other, the importance of artistic tradition," *Morality and Architecture* (London: Oxford, 1977) 115. See also, John Alford, "Modern Architecture and the Symbolism of the Creative Process," *College Art Journal*, XIV, #2 (1955) 102–33; see also, Bell, *op. cit.*, 13, 20, 46–52.

it signifies merely the absence of any strongly defined period features. Thus, actually all current production is modern: in fact, "the great claim of modernism was that it at last was free of style—finally and forever open to direct experience"[11] is rendered preposterous by the history of the Modern Movement.

As Susan Sontag has observed, this "notion of a style-less transparent art is one of the most tenacious fantasies of modern culture. Artists and critics pretend to believe that it is no more possible to get the artifice out of art than it is for a person to lose his personality. Yet the aspiration lingers—a permanent dissent from Modern art with its dizzying velocity of style *changes*."[12] Harry Levin articulates what I believe to be a fundamental characteristic of the modernist era: "Now we are all contemporaries; about that we have no option, so long as we stay alive. But we may choose whether or not we wish to be modern"[13] (by which I think Levin means modernist).

Thus, one must be wary of the use of the term "modern" in architecture, as in most of the arts and in literature. It is not really a description of a style but, as Irving Howe has observed, a term of critical placement and judgment.[14]

Contemporary historians and critics of Modern architecture, perhaps even more than their counterparts in literature and the fine arts, seem to confuse the broad historical definition of the Modern period with related but distinct ideas pertaining to modernism and to use the terms interchangeably. While this issue of historiography critically affects the seeming confusion of the current situation, it is too long and too complex to be dealt with effectively in this essay. Suffice it to say that until the impact of Hegelian and Marxist thought came to dominate the developing discipline of art and architectural history in Germany in the second half of the nineteenth century, historians undertook to define modern architectural history in broad terms and to regard the Renaissance as the first of a sequence of Modern styles. Even as late as 1929, Henry-Russell Hitchcock in his *Modern Architecture: Romanticism and Reintegration*, embraced a chronologically broad and relatively inclusive definition of Modern architecture. Nonetheless, perhaps under the impact of his subsequent collaboration with the more polemical Philip Johnson on the book *The International Style*, and perhaps as a result of his subsequent contact with European modernist historians such as Giedion and Pevsner, Hitchcock has since drawn back from his earlier and more inclusive position.

In *Modern Architecture*, Hitchcock traces the origins of the Modern

[11] David Antin, "Modernism and Post-Modernism: Approaching the Present in American Poetry," *Boundary* 2.

[12] Susan Sontag, *Against Interpretation* (New York: Delta, 1966) 17.

[13] Harry Levin, "What Was Modernism," in Levin, *Refractions: Essays in Comparative Literature* (New York: Oxford, 1966) 271–295; see also, Robert Martin Adams, "What Was Modernism?" *Hudson Review* XXXI, #1 (Spring 1978) 19–23. Adams' title and themes are deliberately based on those raised by Harry Levin in his earlier essay of the same title; see also, Malcolm Bradbury and James McFarlane, *Modernism 1880–1930* (Harmondsworth: Penguin, 1976).

[14] Irving Howe, *Decline of the New* (New York: Harcourt, Brace, 1970) 3.

period to the breakup of the Gothic style, regarding each phase since that time not as an "independent style" like the Greek or the Egyptian, but rather as a subsidiary manner of one Modern style. Yet, even in *Modern Architecture,* Hitchcock was already under the sway not only of the emerging polemic of the International Style but also of the historical determinism which pervades so much German art historical writing of the period. In *Modern Architecture* Hitchcock claimed that a fundamental characteristic of the Modern style is a "preference for formal experimentation," as if Egyptian and Greek architects in Antiquity were never interested in trying anything new.[15] In his later books, by inference, and explicitly in an essay "Modern Architecture—A Memoir," Hitchcock has altered his original position, claiming that had he followed his initial plan to cover

> . . . the whole range of time from the Late Gothic to the present it would have been more or less analogous to the books of the nineteenth century architectural historians such as James Ferguson (who) . . . dealing with the "modern styles" . . . interpreted "modern" in the old sense as the third portion of the relevant past: "Modern times," that is, the period from the Renaissance onward, in distinction to "antiquity" and the "Middle Ages."

Hitchcock goes on to observe that

> . . . what is, at any given point, accepted more broadly as "modern architecture" can have no fixed beginning—various historians and critics have set its start all the way from the early fifteenth century to the early twentieth. Nor, even more obviously, can it have a fixed ending. What is still properly considered modern architecture began, according to my present view, in the 1880s, not way back in 1750, nor yet in 1900 or in 1920; it will be over when we or the next generation have another name for it.[16]

Thus Hitchcock brings us to a fundamental issue of the moment: although at first glance it seems difficult to sustain as the broadest definition of Modern architecture all the production of the Post-Medieval period, upon further reflection such a definition seems more workable than those later attempts to link the historical definition of the Modern period in architecture too closely with specific economic, political, or cultural events that have occurred since the middle of the 18th century—that is, with the Industrial Revolution, and the political revolutions in the United States and France—or with prior positions taken on behalf of any particular manifestation of current or contemporary production that might seem more "advanced," "innovative" or "progressive." Such a broad view opens up the definition of Mod-

[15] Henry-Russell Hitchcock, *Modern Architecture: Romanticism and Reintegration* (New York: Payson and Clarke, 1929).

[16] Henry-Russell Hitchcock, "Modern Architecture—A Memoir," *JSAH*, 27, #4 (December 1968) 227–33; the broad view was taken by Montgomery Schuyler, for example, who stated that "modern architecture, like modern literature, had its origin in the revival of learning. The Italian Renaissance in architecture was inextricably connected with the awakening of the human spirit which was the beginning of modern civilization." "Modern Architecture," *Architectural Record* IV (July–September 1894).

ern architecture, enabling it to be understood not as a unified style but rather as a humanistic pursuit involving a continuous interweaving of diverse and often contradictory formal tendencies assembled, discovered, sometimes even invented through various processes including eclecticism, modernism, and technological as well as functional determinism. Such a view would hold out 1750 as an important marker in time, as it would also note the decisive shifts that took place in the period 1870–1890 (emergence of a dominant modernism) and again around 1960–70 (emergence of a dominant post-modernism). But this view, as I hope to demonstrate later, would not see decisive reasons why any of these phases should mark the conclusion of the Modern period's larger themes, or their replacement by themes not already present in the formative stages of the Modern period.

It is not Hitchcock, but Giedion, Pevsner and J. M. Richards who have exerted the greatest influence on the profession's and the public's view of what Modern Architecture was and should have been during the past 40 years: much of the confusion about the character and chronology of the Modern period in architecture can be attributed to their tendency to present the history of the architecture of the past 200 years as a series of morality tales involving heroic struggles between pragmatic materialism and high ideals, "good guys" and "bad guys," "progressives" and "transitory" facts. Whole careers and aesthetic movements have been cut off from the so-called "main stream" of historical flow: Giedion's *Space, Time and Architecture* and Pevsner's *Pioneers of the Modern Movement* have been the most influential in the architectural profession and therefore the most troublesome. In these works, as Hitchcock has observed, much of the architecture of the nineteenth century has been treated "as constituent premonitions of [the] 'modern architecture'" of the 1920s and 30s and not as legitimate artistic production in its own right.[17]

Outside the architectural profession, most educated people now in their 40s and 50s were exposed to this point of view in introductory courses in college, sometimes in the original text of Giedion and Pevsner, but more often in such popularizing work as Richards' *Introduction to Modern Architecture* in which

> the words "Modern Architecture" are used here to mean something more particular than contemporary architecture. They are used to mean the new kind of architecture that is growing up with this century as this century's own contribution to the art of architecture; the work of those people, whose number is happily increasing, who understand that architecture is a social art related to the life of the people it serves, not an academic exercise in applied ornament. The question that immediately arises, whether there is in fact enough difference between people's lives as they are lived in previous centuries to justify a truly "modern" architecture being very different from that of the past—and indeed whether "modern" architecture is quite as revolutionary as it is supposed to be.

For whatever reason, modern architecture has been passing through

[17] Hitchcock, "Modern Architecture—A Memoir," passim; Robert Venturi and Denise Scott Brown first used the good-guy, bad-guy analogy in their "Learning from Lutyens or the Case of the Shifting Zeitgeist," *RIBA Journal*, 76 (August 1969) 353–54.

a sort of "puritan" phase, in which the negative virtues of simplicity and efficiency have been allowed to dominate, and since 1939 a concentration on the essentials has also been necessitated in most countries by the over-riding need to build cheaply.[18]

The revisionist architectural history of the 1950s and 60s, which owes a considerable debt to the example of Hitchcock's comprehensive *Architecture: Nineteenth and Twentieth Centuries,* sought to develop a broader characterization of the Modern period which would include the stylistic revivalism of the late 18th and 19th centuries as well as the self-referential modernism of the 20th. But despite Hitchcock's influence, the determinist view of history typified by Giedion's *Space, Time and Architecture* seems to have prevented the revisionists, in their search for a broader view, from considering events earlier than the mid-eighteenth century. Thus, even the very important re-definition of Modern architecture which Scully offered in 1954 and refined in 1961, though the first to free the stylistic analysis of architectural production from the futurist polemic of the Modernist Movement of the 1920s, is not free from political determinism and is not, in the final analysis, sufficiently broad in its historical scope. Acknowledging a debt to Frank Lloyd Wright, Scully offered a definition of Modern architecture as the "architecture of democracy," an "image of ourselves" emerging "precisely at the beginning of industrialism and mass democracy [where] we find it, in terms of fragmentation, mass scale, and new, unfocused continuity."[19] In this sense Scully, seeking to reconcile the views of such early twentieth century historians as Fiske Kimball with those of Giedion and Pevsner, brings us to the threshold of our current perception of the distinctions between the Modern tradition and modernism.[20] As a result it is now possible to see the Modern Movement as an episode in the broad history of Modern architecture itself.

Similarly, one can see modernism not as a style but as a strategy, one of a number of *isms* which have emerged in the Modern era to help the artist express his attitudes toward the present in relation to his sense of the past and/or the future: in architecture "eclecticism," "associationalism," and "technological determinism" are other attitudes which interact with modernism to help organize a theory upon which to base work. Thus, though modernism has had its period of hegemony, resulting in a univalent style whose abstraction rendered it difficult and uncommunicative from the first, it should not be seen as a style in and of itself. The International Style was the great modernist style, and modernism itself remains a Modern sensibil-

[18] J. M. Richards, *Introduction to Modern Architecture* (Harmondsworth: Penguin, 1960) 9, 13; see Watkin, *op. cit,* passim; also Peter Collins, *Changing Ideals in Modern Architecture* (London: Faber and Faber, 1965) passim.

[19] Vincent J. Scully, "Modern Architecture: Toward a Redefinition of Style," *College Art Journal* VII, #2 (Winter, 1958) 140–59; see also Scully's *Modern Architecture* (New York: Braziller) passim.

[20] Fiske Kimball and George H. Edgell, *A History of Architecture* (New York: Harper, 1918); Chapter XII, "Modern Architecture," was written by Kimball; see also, James D. Kornwolf, M. H. *Baillie Scott and the Arts and Crafts Tradition* (Baltimore: Johns Hopkins, 1972) XXLV.

ity. Yet there are those who would argue that it is a sensibility parallel to Western humanism and thereby outside it, that is not at all part of the tradition that began with the Renaissance, and it is this issue which constitutes the crux of the current debate.

The idea of a Post-Modern age was introduced by Arnold Toynbee in his *A Study of History*,[21] and has been developed by a number of historians, most notably Geoffrey Barraclough.[22] The post-Modern Age as discussed by Toynbee and Barraclough is one in which there is increasing recognition that co-existence is the *modus vivendi* of the pluralist condition of our time. This pluralism in turn forces a close examination of the validity of the proposition that the distinction between a single standard and competing standards sets the contemporary of the Post-Modern period apart from the Modern period as a whole. If, as Toynbee and Barraclough argue, the Modern period began at the end of the 15th century, when Western European culture began to exert its hegemony over vast land areas and cultures not its own (and Western European man found himself having to deal not only with the pluralist politics of European nationalism in its formative stages but also with the pluralism brought about by encounters with the "native" populations of the "New World"), then it perhaps can be argued that the Post-Modern or contemporary phase they describe is really just another stage in Modern history, a "global" or "Post-Industrial" Age following a "National" or "Industrial" Age, an era of "relativism" that at once accepts the inherent diversity of the present while seeking order and meaning through a connection with the past, especially with the Romantic era.

Post-modernism should not be seen as a reaction against modernism; it seeks to develop modernism's themes by attempting to examine them in relationship to the wider framework of the Modern period as a whole.

The divided nature of modernism complicates our understanding of the Post-Modern devolution. At the beginning of this essay, I defined two kinds of Post-Modern sensibilities which can now be seen as related to modernism: a traditional one and a schismatic one. But the complex nature of modernism itself, with its two distinct conditions or types united by an apocalyptic view of history—not to mention the claims that are sometimes made for modernism as a sensibility completely independent of Western Humanism—complicates the situation with regard to post-modernism. As a result, it can be argued that there are not one but two sets of Post-Modern doubles: that there are *two types of traditional post-modernism* and *two types of schismatic post-modernism*.

The first type of traditional post-modernism—and the one which I would argue is the more viable of the two—argues for a break with modernism (where modernism is itself seen as a *break with* Western Humanism) and a reintegration with a view of Western Humanism which includes modernism among its many and sometimes conflicting conditions. The second

[21] Toynbee, *op. cit;* see also, Toynbee, *The Present Day Experiment in Western Civilization* (London: Oxford, 1962) 26–37.

[22] Geoffrey Barraclough, *An Introduction to Contemporary History* (New York: Basic Books, 1965).

type sees itself as a continuation of modernism (in which modernism is itself seen as a successor *sensibility* and *style* to the Baroque and Rococo, a sensibility and style that is contradictorily and inexplicably, in its present-ism, a contradiction of the very notion of style.

This second type of traditional post-modernism is somewhat dubious: at the very least it fails to account for the stylistic complexity of the Romantic era, and it leads us to a question of whether such a post-modernism is really different from modernism itself. For if traditional modernism is a condition in which all art is seen as being in the present, though not breaking with the values and symbols of Western Humanism, then where can this second type of post-modernism stand in time? Is there a place beyond the present?

The first type of schismatic post-modernism—and the one which I would argue is the more viable of the two—is the one which argues for a *continuity with* modernism (in which modernism is itself seen as a *break with* Western Humanism). This kind of schismatic post-modernism, like the second type of traditional post-modernism, is a continuing modernism, but the use of the prefix "post" has meaning because it permits the designation of a condition which is distinct from modernism because it breaks with the Western Humanist tradition. Schismatic post-modernism of this type marks the full flowering of a sensibility which has its origins in modernism's aspiration toward a clean break with the Western Humanist tradition.

The second type of schismatic post-modernism is itself seen as a *continuing* tradition. This is the so-called "post-modern breakthrough to post-modernity,"[23] in which a totally new state of consciousness is achieved that insists on the obsolescence of modernism as well as the entire Western Humanist tradition. Attractive though such an image seems to those who view the current situation as unnecessarily confusing, it is difficult to make clear just exactly how this new condition will emerge. As Richard E. Palmer has written:

> Post-modernity raises the question of a transition and transformation so radical as to change the fundamental view of language, history, truth, time and matter—so radical that "understanding" becomes a quite different process. It raises the possibility, in other words, of a "new hermenuetics."
>
> The hermeneutical problem of bridging the gap between modern and post-modern sets-of-mind goes in both directions: the problem of understanding a post-modern way of thinking when the assumptions and furniture of our thinking are themselves given by modernity, and the problem of a person who, having achieved a post-modern, post-spatialized, post-perspectual, or holistic framework, must then communicate it to someone who has not reached it.[24]

[23] Gerald Graff, "The Myth of the Postmodernist Breakthrough," *Tri Quarterly* #26 (Winter, 1973) 383–417; see also, Bell, *op. cit.*

[24] Richard E. Palmer, "Postmodernity and Hermeneutics," *Boundary* 22 (Winter 1977) 363–393. This is the strain of post-modernity that Daniel Bell disapprovingly characterizes as "the psychological spearhead for an onslaught on the values and not rational patterns of 'ordinary' behavior, in the name of liberation, eroticism, freedom of impulse and the good life . . . it means that a crisis of middle class values is at hand." *Op. cit.*, 52; see also, p. 79. On p. 104 Bell

Thus, though there are four conditions of post-modernism, it would seem that in the case of two, questions of considerable complexity remain unanswered at the present moment, thereby limiting the effectiveness of these conditions for artistic production if not for discourse. The difficulties raised by the second type of traditional post-modernism—that is, the notion of a continuing modernism—simultaneously claiming a position within Humanism and apart from history, seem hopelessly contradictory. It seems to be a condition which, despite the Post-Modern label that might be applied to it, is no more or no less than that of the traditional modernism of Marcel Proust, of the James Joyce of *Ulysses*, of Picasso, and of Le Corbusier.

The difficulties of the second type of schismatic post-modernism—the post-modernist breakthrough—have already been discussed. It takes as its point of departure the work of such writers as James Joyce but, as yet, it has not found a truly convincing voice. Such critics at William Spanos and Ihab Hassan are attempting to articulate the nature of the post-modernist breakthrough.[25] Because this type of schismatic post-modernism is only schismatic, it doubles back on itself and reaches a dead end.

Thus it becomes clear that the second type of schismatic post-modernism is not just a shift of emphasis within modernism; its relationship to modernism is not comparable to that which post-impressionism had to impressionism; schismatic post-modernism is radical in the extreme. In an essay on "Joyce, Beckett and the Post-modern Imagination," Ihab Hassan observes that though "one might be inclined to conclude that modernism is simply the earlier movement . . . and that post-modernism is the later movement, which began to dominate Western literature after World War II," one must finally see that "however jagged or ironic modernism allowed itself to be it retained its faith in art, in the imaginative act, even at the end of cultural dissolution . . . Post-Modernism on the other hand, is essentially *subversive* in form and *anarchic* in its cultural spirit. It dramatizes its lack of faith in art even as it produces new works of art intended to hasten *both* cultural and artistic dissolution."[26]

The two conditions of the Post-Modern that are at this moment important, and the ones I should like to consider in some detail in the remaining

---

writes that in the 1960s a "powerful current of post-modern developed which carried the logic of modernism to its furthest reaches. In the theoretical writings of Norman O. Brown and Michel Foucault, in the novels of William Burroughs, Jean Genet and, up to a point, Norman Mailer, and in the porno-pop culture that is now all about us, one sees a logical culmination of modernist intentions. They are, as Diana Trilling put it, 'the adventures beyond consciousness.'"

"Traditional modernism, no matter how daring, played out its impulses in the imagination, within the constraints of art . . . Post-modernism," Bell continues on page 52, describing that of the breakthrough variety, "overflows the vessels of art. It tears down boundaries and insists that *acting out* rather than making distinctions, is the way to gain knowledge."

[25] William Spanos, "The Detective and the Boundary: Some Notes on the Post-Modern Literary Imagination," *Boundary 2*, 1 (Fall 1972) 147–68.

[26] Ihab Hassan, "Joyce, Beckett, and the postmodern imagination," *Tri Quarterly*, XXXIV (Fall 1975) 179–200; see also, Hassan, *Paracriticisms, Seven Speculations of the Times* (Urbana, Illinois: University of Illinois, 1975) 55–56.

pages of this essay, are: 1) the schismatic post-modernism that argues for a clean break with Western Humanism and a continuity with modernism and 2) the traditional post-modernism that argues for a break with modernism and a reintegration with the broader condition of Western Humanism, especially with the Romantic tradition. These seem the only possible categories because they are the only ones that contain in them the "double" sensibilities of continuity and change which are necessary to sustain generative cycles of creation.

The emergence of the Post-Modern sensibility can be seen as a logical result of the opposition between the Romantic and Modernist sensibilities, the former reveling in diversity, the latter struggling to find a universal cultural voice. Post-modernism is not revolutionary in either the political or artistic sense; in fact, it reinforces the effect of the technocratic and bureaucratic society in which we live—traditional post-modernism by accepting conditions and trying to modify them, schismatic post-modernism by proposing a condition *outside* Western Humanism, thereby permitting Western Humanist culture to proceed uninterrupted though not necessarily unaffected.

Post-modernism, though a reaction to modernism, is not a revolutionary movement seeking to overthrow modernism. Modernism cannot be ignored. We cannot pretend that it never existed and that we can return to a pre-modernist condition (such is the folly of such neo-traditionalist architects as John Barrington Bayley or the theorist Conrad Jameson). Post-modernism is especially affected by that aspect of modernism which derived from romanticism itself, particularly the romantic belief in the religious aspect of art. Most importantly, the Post-Modern condition arises out of the need to account for, and to continue to function under, the drastically altered circumstances which emerged from the political and cultural events of the 1920s and 1940s and which continue to condition action in this last third of our century. Thus it must be seen that post-modernism is a Modern sensibility that includes modernism by virtue of its reaction to it; it is the manifestation of what Irving Howe describes as "the radical breakdown of the modernist impulse," which came as a result of the experience of the Holocaust, of World War II, of the use of the atomic bomb. At its root lies existentialism, an attitude toward history and the idea of time which has extended beyond our thought processes to the very mode of our consciousness.

Schismatic post-modernism can be seen as an outgrowth of the anti-intellectualism of the modernism of the 1920s and 30s. In philosophy and literature it is represented by such writers as Norman Brown, Herbert Marcuse, Marshall McLuhan, Donald Barthelme, Samuel Beckett, and William S. Burroughs. In architecture, Peter Eisenman is its leading advocate. It rejects the Western Humanist tradition and, in the realm of aesthetics, it rejects Aristotelian composition. Though very much related to modernism, schismatic post-modernism is nonetheless a distinct sensibility. And it adopts the post-modernist label to differentiate itself from the modernist tradition.

Schismatic post-modernism separates itself from traditionalist post-modernism by suggesting that it is not simply the crises of mid-century life that have irreparably changed the relationship of men to each other and to their ideas, but that these events have rendered untenable that relationship between men, objects, nature, and the sense of the ideal (the deity) which has been accepted since the Renaissance. Schismatic post-modernism sees the relationship between men and objects as a competitive one, and God as dead or, at least, removed from the fray.

It is in this context that Eisenman's position can best be understood. His proposal to make architecture autonomous is anti-historical and anti-symbolic; his endeavors to produce an architecture that is autonomous and self-referential—that is hermetically sealed from all concerns except the process of its own fabrication and fabulation—make his works virtually impenetrable. Eisenman's houses become symbolic of their own process of conception, but that process is so cut off from contemporary culture, history, and pragmatism that in the end, the effectiveness of the symbolic gesture ceases to be symbolic of anything outside itself; the building runs the danger of becoming merely an object which can, at best, make its appeal on a sensuous and hedonistic level. Although it struggles to free itself from all cultural references, by its very physicality it cannot but remind the viewer of some object previously seen or experienced.

Despite his belief in an autonomous architecture, Eisenman's ideology is culturally based. It draws extensively from the linguistic theories of Noam Chomsky and from the work of such literary critics as Roland Barthes and William Gass, who has himself written about one of Eisenman's buildings, House VI.[27] In basing his argument for an autonomous architecture on theories developed in relation to others in parallel but not necessarily related artistic disciplines—and in making comparisons with discoveries in the sciences, especially mathematics and physics, Eisenman seems caught up in a contradiction not unlike the one which characterized the justifications devised for modernist architecture by historians and polemicists such as Giedion, who sought to justify architectural modernism by connecting it with Einsteinian physics.[28] Schismatic post-modernism architecture, as represented by Eisenman (and I can think of no other architect who might be included with him in this category) buoys itself up with analogies to literary and linguistic theory.[29] But where modernism's connection to physics was *ex post facto*, schismatic post-modernism's connections have been established the other way around. As a result there seems to be in Eisenman's work what John Gardner has observed in the work of such schismatic post-modernists as John Cage and William Gass: a sense of "art which is all thought . . . art too obviously constructed to fit a theory."[30]

To sum up: Eisenman's work, in its dazzling extremism, brings into focus the fundamental dilemma of schismatic post-modernism which, to paraphrase Kermode, is based on an inherent contradiction that can be seen in modernism itself: can one reconcile a cult of self-referential form-making

[27] William Gass, "House VI," *Progressive Architecture*, 58, #6 (June 1977) 57–67.

[28] Sigfried Giedion, *Space, Time and Architecture* (Cambridge, MA: Harvard, 1941) passim.

[29] Mario Gandelsonas, "On Reading Architecture," *Progressive Architecture*, 53, #3 (March 1972) 68–88.

[30] John Gardner, *On Moral Fiction* (New York: Basic Books, 1978–79).

with a denial of the existence of form itself? Schismatic post-modernism leaves us little choice: with all of previous culture removed in theory, at least, we are left with an aesthetic of unparalleled abstraction and hermeticism and without, as yet, even a hope for the emergence of an atavistic mythology to help crack the code. Eisenman leaves us terribly alone, naked.

John Gardner has written that the problem with the idea of art as pure language—which it seems to me is the basic concept of Eisenman's position as it is basic to Cage's and Gass'—is "that it shows . . . a lack of concern" on the artist's part for "people who care about events and ideas and thus, necessarily, about the clear and efficient statements of both." "Linguistic opacity," a phrase of Gardner's, suggests that the need to communicate is not a primary function of art. One might ask what can this seeming "search for opacity" do for us? What are we to make of these "linguistic sculptures" which at best make, as Gardner writes, "only the affirmation sandcastles make, that it is pleasant to make things or look at things made, better to be alive than dead"?[31]

It may well be that the extreme position which Eisenman represents in architecture, Cage in music, and Gass in literature, marks an end part in a cycle, and that a viable post-modernism must be one that opens up possibilities for new production rather than describes a situation that can be seen as ultimately futile and nihilistic.

Irving Howe has argued that although there is in modernist literature a "major impulse" to express "a choking nausea before the idea of culture . . ." there is also "another in which the writer takes upon himself the enormous ambition not to reinvent the terms of reality."[32] It is this "realistic," "accepting" aspect of modernism that is carried over in the second, traditional or "inclusive" post-modernist reactions.

Howe regards Saul Bellow, William Styron, and Bernard Malamud as "traditional" Post-Modern writers, in the sense that in their books, the action of individuals takes place in relationship to specific cultural conditions. Robert Gillespie, writing about the younger American novelists of the 1960s, states that the work of a considerable group, among them Wendell Berry, Scott Momaday, Larry McMurtry, Wright Morris and the Ken Kesey of *Sometimes a Great Notion* share a traditional post-modernist point of view. These writers accept

> responsibility for the world's conditions, and therefore of authority in managing it. Consciousness for them is less a curse than it is an act of conscience. They are eager to locate themselves in "a place on earth" (the title of one of Berry's novels) and to merge their lives with that place. From such felt relation comes sustenance . . . so a region has its own mythology which may offer the only sustaining relation between the past and the future.[33]

[31] *Ibid*, 69, 71.

[32] Howe, *op cit.*, 5.

[33] Robert Gillespie, "Beyond the Wasteland: The American Novel in the Nineteen Sixties," *Boundary 2*, III, #2 (Windsor, 1975) 473–81.

Traditional post-modernism is simultaneously inside contemporary society and critically detached from it; it uses art to comment on everyday life; it is at once "satiric" and accepting in its view of culture; in this sense it seeks to make telling interpretations of everyday life. Such a post-modernism begins to "restore that state of balance between unchecked fabulation and objective social realism" necessary to prevent artistic production from degenerating into trivial self-indulgence.[34]

In painting and in architecture, traditional post-modernism relies increasingly on representational as opposed to abstract or conceptual modes. Rackstraw Downes equates traditional post-modernism with a revived realism in painting. Critical of what he describes as modernism's "pictorial narcissism—it became a painting capable only of admiring its own nature," Downes' argument against modernist abstraction and in favor of pre-modernist representation hinges on his criticism of modernism's exclusivist principle of selectivity:

> While Old Master painting had allowed emphasis of the different aspects of form, its nature was holistic and embracing, whereas Modernist styles were partial. As were their means, so was their grasp on reality. Expressionism, Dada and Surrealism were associated styles which dealt respectively with emotions, ideas and fantasies. Hedonistic Impressionism, Cubism—a still life style—and Purism which dealt in Utopian absolutes, concentrated on particular properties of form. Modernism, then, constituted a rapid succession of specialized styles, each one supplying some deficiency of the rest, what they gained in intensity and concentration they lost in comprehensiveness and range.
>
> Modernism was . . . to excel in uncompromisingly personal triumphs and, likewise, fail to produce a syntax sufficiently limber and resourceful to be widely shared and passed along. In fact, that was one of its rules, that no manner should develop into an available language; because if it did so it would become transparent and the Modernist purpose would be lost.[35]

Downes notes that while the modernist looks to the examples of the past in a search "for lessons which it would not have known it could reach," the post-modernist looks back on history "in a spirit of empathy for its ostensible purposes." Nonetheless, traditional post-modernism does not advocate stylistic revival, though it does support the concept of emulation. Traditional post-modernism looks back to history to see how things were done and to remind itself that many good ways of doing things which were cast aside for ideological reasons can be usefully rediscovered. Thus, for example, inclusive post-modernism can employ recognizable imagery in an abstract way—it

[34] Gerald Graff, "Babbitt at the Abyss: The Social Context of Postmodern American Fiction," *Tri Quarterly* #33 (Spring 1976) 307–337.

[35] Rackstraw Downes, "Post-Modernist Painting," *Tracks* (Fall 1976) 70–73; see also, Hilton Kramer, "The Return of Realism," *New York Times*, 12 (March 1978), Section 2, 1, 25; see also, Robert Berlind, "Artist's Choice: Figurative Art," *Arts* LI, #7 (March 1977) 23; see also, Bell, *op cit.*, 104; Peter Collins argues that the idea of "precedent" offers a way beyond the blockage of the art historical concept of "style;" see *Architectural Judgement* (Montreal: McGill-Queens University, 1971) 28–32.

can be at once pre-modernist and modernist.[36]

Traditional post-modernism opens up artistic production to a public role which modernism, by virtue of its self-referential formal strategies, had denied itself. In painting, as William Rubin has observed, "one characteristic of the modern period *seems* to be ending. That is the tradition of the private picture—that is, for the small circle of collectors and friends of artists, who sympathize with vanguard art."[37] In this sense, the current interest in photography should be seen as a last-gasp modernist stance.

Architecture, of course, is by definition a public art. Yet in its modernist phase, it often spoke the private language of painting—one need only recall the arguments advanced in Henry-Russell Hitchcock's book *Painting Toward Architecture*.[38] More importantly, as Suzannah Lessard points out:

> between the abstract beauty of technological principles and the underpinning of intricate solutions to innumerable minute problems, there is a kind of middle ground which was overlooked in the exuberant rush to modernity. Between man's desire to expand his ego and the needs of man as ant—I can think of no better way to express the dual preoccupation of the age of technology—the question of what human life would be in the new world floated unasked, unnoticed.[39]

It is this aspect of social and cultural responsibility—not in the narrowly simplistic sense of architectural do-goodism but in a broader and more profound sense of a genuine and unsentimental humanism—that characterized traditional post-modernism's distinction from the abstract, self-referential schismatic post-modernism which we have already discussed.

Traditional post-modernism rejects the anti-historical biases of modernism; influences from history are no longer seen as constraints on either personal growth or artistic excellence. History, no longer viewed as the dead hand of the past, now seems at the very least a standard of excellence in a continuing struggle to deal effectively with the present. Modernism looked toward the future as an escape from the past; traditional post-modernism struggles with the legacy of that attitude, a world filled with objects whose principal artistic impetus often came from a belief that in order to be "Modern" they must look and function as little as possible like anything that had been seen in the world before. The traditional post-modernist struggle then, is not to free itself from the past, but to relax what has been characterized as

[36] Traditional post-modernism should not be confused with the neo-traditionalism of Henry Hope Reed, John Barrington Bayley, Conrad Jameson. For Bayley and Reed, see Henry Hope Reed, *The Garden City* (New York: Doubleday, 1959) passim.

[37] Rubin is quoted by Douglas Davis' "Post-Modern for Stories Real and Imagined/ Toward a Theory," in his *Art Culture—Essays on the Postmodern* (New York: Harper & Row, 1977). See also the "Post-Modernist Dilemma," a dialogue between Davis and Suzi Gablik, *Village Voice*, March 24, April 3 and April 10, 1978.

[38] Henry-Russell Hitchcock, *Painting Toward Architecture* (New York: Duell, Sloan and Pearce, 1948) passim.

[39] Suzannah Lessard, "The Towers of Light," *The New Yorker*, 54 (July 10, 1978) 32–36, 41–44, 49, 52, 58.

"the stubborn grip of the values created by the rebellion against the past."[40]

Traditional post-modernism rejects what Charles Moore has described as the "obsessive normalization of the recent past, where we have drawn our expressive elegance out of poverty . . . (and) our process out of crisis."[41] It argues that it is proper and sufficient to struggle with the problems of the present viewed in relation to the values continuing from the past while leaving the future to those who will inherit it.

Traditional post-modernism recognizes that the public has lost confidence in architects (though it still believes in the symbolic power of architecture). Modernist architecture offered very little in the way of joy or visual pleasure, its conceptutal basis was limited and disconcertingly materialistic. By once again recognizing the common assumptions a culture inherits from its past, traditional post-modernism is not only an announcement that Modern architecture has emerged from its puritan revolution, its catharsis at last behind it, but it is also an avowal of self-confidence in contemporary architecture's ability and willingness to re-establish itself on a basis which cannot only deal with the past but also match it, value for value, building for building.

Traditional post-modernism seeks to look backward in order to go forward. It should not be regarded as a jettisoning of Modern architecture itself, but as an attempt to pick up the threads of theory and style which were cut by the pioneers of the Modern Movement, especially the concerns for architectural history and for visually comprehensible relationships between old and new buildings. In its inclusiveness, traditional post-modernism does not propose an independent style; it is a sensibility dependent on forms and strategies drawn from the modernist and the pre-modernist work that preceded it, though it declares the obsolescence of both. It is *a* Modern style but not *the* Modern style. In its recognition of the transience and multiplicity of styles within the historical epoch we call Modern, it rejects the emphasis on unity of expression that was so central to modernism itself. Traditional post-modernism recognizes both the discursive and expressive meaning of formal language. It recognizes the language of form as communicating sign as well as infra-referential symbol: that is to say, it deals with both physical and associational experience, with the work of art as an act of "presentation" and "representation." It rejects the idea of a single style in favor of a view that acknowledges the existence of many styles (and the likely emergence of even more) each with its own meanings, sometimes permanently established, but more often shifting in relation to other events in the culture.

In architecture, Robert Venturi and Charles Moore can be seen as the

[40] Lessard, *op. cit.*; James D. Kornwolf makes the interesting observation that "Le Corbusier's generation was misguided not to recognize that the nineteenth century's struggle with the past was also its struggle, and that a new understanding of the past, not a denial of it, was what was needed." *op. cit.*, 513.

Peter Collins observes that "the idea of an 'International Style' was a product of the Renaissance. In fact, the so-called 'battle of the styles' might be more reasonably and meaningfully interpreted as an attempt to refute the concept of an 'International Style,' rather than as a conflict between 'Gothicists' and 'Classicists.' This was certainly the essence of the position taken by Viollet-le-Duc and Ferguson." *op. cit.*, 171–72.

[41] Charles Moore, "Foreword," in Sam Davis, editor, *The Form of Housing* (New York: Van Nostrand Reinhold, 1977), 6.

leading advocates among an older generation of traditional post-modernists; Michael Graves and myself, among others, from the point of view of age, though not from one of ideology, occupy a middle ground (that is we are young enough to have been students of Venturi and Moore), and an even younger generation, including Stuart Cohen, Thomas Gordon Smith and the Arquitectonica group, is beginning to make its positions felt as well.

Venturi and Moore are in many ways transitional figures: their theoretical positions are more "advanced" in the movement toward a position which includes modernist and pre-modernist values than is their built work, which as often as not tends to be abstract and non-representational (Venturi's Oberlin Museum and his Hartford Stage; Moore's own house in Los Angeles) as it is representative of ideas that are contextually based (Venturi's three Brant houses, and his Benjamin Franklin house "restoration"; Moore's Burns House and his Piazza d'Italia). This is not surprising since their education was modernist, and until recently theirs has been a virtually solitary struggle to integrate its ideals with the wider body of architectural culture.

The work of the other traditional post-modernists who have been cited can be characterized by a struggle to use traditional languages without falling into the presumed trap of revivalism. The heritage of modernism remains a problem for all: its impulse to "make it new," as Ezra Pound put it 70 years ago, conflicts with the sensibility to make it legible and make it appropriate; the preoccupation with traditional languages is often at the expense of the languages of modernism, which, no matter how abstract, have come to mean certain things in the culture at large and the recognition of stylistic diversity can be viewed as *laissez faire* permissiveness. Thus, in some traditional post-modernist work the grammar of architectural composition has not been explored with the same care as have the individual elements or the overall meanings; in other words some traditional post-modernist work has become "picturesque."

Everywhere there are signs of an emerging cultural resynthesis: Richard Gilam sees a "new naturalism" in the drama; John Gardner pleads for a "moral fiction" based on a belief in an art dedicated to the "preservation of the word of gods and men;" Daniel Bell states that the "problem then is whether culture can regain coherence, a coherence of substance and experience not only of form." Signs of the shift in sensibility in art and architecture abound. All this seems clear enough, and I hope that what I have written has shed some light on the nature of these shifts. If what I have written has any value, it is as a reminder that all which glitters in a new or different way is not necessarily golden, that the ranks of the avant garde may not any longer be the exclusive defenders of the holy grail of insight: that a shift in sensibility need have very little if anything to do with progress. The fact of the matter is that the reaction to modernism is not only a note of "no confidence" in its ideology but also a recognition that its forms are exhausted. As Gardner observes:

> When modes of art change, the change need not imply philosophical progress; it usually means only that the hunter has exhausted one part of the woods and has moved to a new part, or to a part exhausted earlier, to which the prey have doubled back.

Aesthetic styles—patterns for communicating feeling and thought—

become dull with use, like carving knives, and since dullness is the chief enemy of art, each generation must find new ways of slicing the fat off reality.[42]

The fundamental nature of this shift to post-modernism has to do with the reawakening of artists in every field to the public responsibilities of art. Once again art is being regarded as an act of communication as opposed to one of production or revelation (of the artist's ego and/or of his intentions for the building or his process of design). Though art is based on personal invention it requires public acceptance to achieve real value—to communicate meaning. An artist may choose to speak a private language, but a viewer must be willing and able to "read" the work, whether it be a book, a painting, or a building, for the work to have any kind of public life at all. To the extent that contemporary artists care about the public life of art, they are post-modernists (modernist artists make things for only themselves and/or for the gods); to the extent that an artist believes in the communicative role of form but is not willing to accept that such a role necessarily carries with it cultural meanings, that are not inherent to the form, his is a schismatic post-modernism.

Modernism in architecture was premised on a dialectic between things as they are and things as they ought to be; post-modernism seeks a resolution between—or at least a recognition of—things as they were and as they are. Modernism imagined architecture to be the product of purely rational and scientific process; post-modernism sees it as a resolution of social and technological processes with cultural concerns.

Post-modernism seeks to regain the public role that modernism denied architecture. The Post-Modern struggle is the struggle for cultural coherence, a coherence that is not falsely monolithic, as was attempted in the International Style in architecture or National Socialism in the politics of the 1920s and 30s, but one whose coherence is based on the heterogeneous substance and nature of modern society: post-modernism takes as its basis things as they are, *and* things as they were. Architecture is no longer an image of the world as architects wish it to be or as it will be, but as it is.

[42] Gardner, *op. cit.*

Index